PSYCHOLOGY FOR TEACHING

PSYCHOLOGY FOR TEACHING eighth edition

A bear ~~always usually sometimes rarely never always faces the front will not commit himself just now~~ faces the future

GUY R. LEFRANÇOIS
University of Alberta

Wadsworth Publishing Company
Belmont, California
A Division of Wadsworth, Inc.

Sponsoring Editor: Kristine Clerkin
Editorial Assistant: Kate Peltier
Production Editor: Angela Mann
Managing Designer: Carolyn Deacy
Print Buyer: Karen Hunt
Art Editor: Donna Kalal
Permissions Editor: Jeanne Bosschart
Copy Editor: Polly Kummel
Designer: Jeanne Calabrese Design
Photo Researcher: Stephen Forsling and Bobbie Broyer
Cartoonists: Tony Hall and Jeff Littlejohn
Technical Illustrator: Teresa Roberts
Compositor: TSI Graphics
Cover Illustration: Jim Dryden/The Schuna Group

Printed in the United States of America
 2 3 4 5 6 7 8 9 10 — 98 97 96 95 94
Library of Congress Cataloging-in-Publication Data
Lefrançois, Guy R.
    Psychology for teaching : a bear always, usually, sometimes, rarely, never, always faces the front, will not commit himself just now, faces the future / Guy R. Lefrançois. — 8th ed.
        p. cm.
    Words in subtitle: "always, usually . . . now" shown typographically lined out on t.p.
    Includes bibliographical references (p.) and indexes.
    ISBN 0-534-20550-X
    1. Educational psychology. 2. Teaching – Psychological aspects. 3. Learning, Psychology of. I. Title.
    LB1051.L568 1994
    370. 15–dc20   93-13461

p. 3: Culver Pictures, Inc.; *p. 4:* © Elizabeth Crews; *p. 15:* © Elizabeth Crews; *p. 23:* © 1986 James Cuebas/Impact Visuals; *p. 24:* © Elizabeth Crews/The Image Works; *p. 35:* The "Bizarro" cartoon by Dan Piraro is reprinted by permission of Chronicle Features, San Francisco, California; *p. 50:* © 1992 Nita Winter Photography; *p. 52:* Idea and art by Joey Waldon/ © Maine Line Company; *p. 81:* © Jean Guamy/Magnum Photos, Inc.; *p. 82:* © Cary Wolinsky/Stock Boston; *p. 118:* © Elizabeth Crews; *p. 124:* Rousseau, Henri. *The Dream.* 1910. Oil on canvas, 6'8 $\frac{1}{2}$" x 9'9 $\frac{1}{2}$". The Museum of Modern Art, New York. Gift of Nelson A. Rockefeller.; *p. 141:* © Sidney Harris; *p. 146:* © Elizabeth Crews; *p. 151:* © Elizabeth Crews/Stock Boston; *p. 176:* © Michael Siluk/The Image Works; *p. 185:* © Sidney Harris; *p. 187:* © Jean-Claude Lejeune/Stock Boston; *p. 192:* © Sidney Harris; *p. 205:* © Evan Johnson/Jeroboam, Inc.; *p. 206:* © Bob Daemmrich/The Image Works; *p. 217:* © Elizabeth Crews; *p. 238:* © Cornell Capa/Magnum Photos, Inc.; *p. 263:* © Elizabeth Crews/Stock Boston; *p. 264:* Jean-Claude Lejeune/Stock Boston; *p. 266:* © Bob Kramer/Stock Boston; *p. 268:* Nina Leen, *Life* Magazine, © Time, Inc.; *p. 290:* © Elizabeth Crews; *p. 309:* © Elizabeth Crews; *p. 322:* © Elizabeth Crews; *p. 325:* © Elizabeth Crews; *p. 348:* © Elizabeth Crews; *p. 388:* © 1989 Nita Winter Photography

For my first teacher, my father,

who taught me to love books and learning,

and

For my mother,

who taught me to love people and life.

BRIEF CONTENTS

CONTENTS

PREFACE

This is a basic text in educational psychology. Its goal is to make you a better teacher. It tries to do this in two ways: by presenting the most important and the most useful research and theory in educational psychology clearly, accurately, and in an engaging way; and by challenging you to examine your beliefs about teaching, learning, and learners.

ABOUT THE EIGHTH EDITION

Like its predecessors, this edition continues to emphasize teaching and learning. Content is selected and presented always with an eye to instructional implications and actual classroom applications. This edition provides more classroom illustrations than earlier editions, many of them in the form of thought-provoking samples of classroom interaction set aside as boxed mini-cases.

Succeeding Bears have continued to discard material that is primarily historical, and most of the earlier references to rats, pigeons, chimpanzees, and other nonhuman creatures have been deleted—save, of course, for wild cows, which are not easily dealt with.

Other changes in this edition of the Bear include new or expanded coverage of important concerns, such as performance-based approaches to assessment, individual education plans, cooperative learning, learning/thinking strategies, giftedness, classroom management, virtual reality and multimedia technologies in education, and the multicultural context of schooling. There is renewed emphasis on the role of intrinsic motivation, mastery orientations, and cognitive emphases in educational psychology and more attention to the need to have students become autonomous learners. In addition, information is thoroughly updated throughout.

There are several organizational changes in this edition. The text is now one chapter shorter, which should make it more suitable for a one-semester course. Material from the deleted chapter (5), which included topics such as teaching thinking, effective thinking, and instructional objectives, has been moved to chapters that include related theory and research. In addition, the text has been restructured to conform to the more usual teaching sequence, which presents development before learning.

This edition continues to resist the temptation to reduce the craft of teaching to a handful of instructions. You will find few lists of do's and don'ts in this text. Like its predecessors, Bear VIII believes that the best teaching decisions are based on sound psychological principles applied with enthusiasm and imagination and tempered with a love of children and of teaching—not on the application of prescriptions copied like recipes from instruction booklets. Teaching and children are too complex for simple recipes.

Considerable effort has been devoted to keeping this text relatively short, as well as motivating, informative, and practical. I hope that as a result Bear VIII is more teachable, more interesting, and more useful than it was when younger.

ABOUT THE BEAR AND WILD COWS

In this book, there are occasional references to a bear and to wild cows. Lest their purpose seem overly mysterious to you—and their inclusion frustrating—let me explain.

In the first edition, subtitled *A bear always faces the front*, the bear was largely whimsy—but not entirely purposeless whimsy. A bear strutting through the pages of a serious textbook was a bit of a jolt. It broke the tedium of uninterrupted academic content; it sometimes made readers smile—or even laugh. And it didn't detract from the serious "nuts and bolts" of the chapters. So the bear continued in all later revisions. Subsequent editions went from a bear *always* facing the front to a bear who *usually, sometimes, rarely, never,* and finally, once more, *always* faced that direction. By the seventh edition, grizzled, battle-scarred, and considerably wiser, the bear would no longer commit himself.

Over the years, the bear has become something more than whimsy, something more than a break: He has become a metaphor. A metaphor is not, of course, a real thing. It's an invention. The bear metaphor was invented as much by readers of earlier editions as by me. Some of these readers have decided that the bear is a metaphor for a teacher, or perhaps for teaching. Others reached different conclusions. All are correct; inventions are never flatly wrong.

The bear, this wonderful metaphoric bear, continues in this, the eighth edition. This is a bear who has sniffed the winds of change, who has witnessed some extraordinary social and political events. Sadly, he is also witness to the cumulative effects of disastrous ecological changes. Bear VIII has seen the invasion of wild cows. But, emboldened by a new resolve, he has become an environmental crusader. Now, in the eighth edition, the bear looks to the future.

As is explained in the glossary, the bear and the wild cows may be seen as metaphors for two great universals: good and evil. (Few things are entirely good, nor are many entirely evil.)

At another level, the bear and the wild cows—which appear only occasionally in chapter introductions but seldom anywhere else in the text—may be viewed as no more than a piece of whimsy, a tidbit of absurdity, a tiny mockery.

You may choose to completely ignore the bear and wild cows (which need be of no consequence to your performance on exams, to your eventual competence as a teacher, or to your happiness) or you might make them into your own metaphors.[*]

---

[*]PPC[†]: Can you tell us a little more about wild cows?

Author: Not much, but there is a little more in the glossary under the entry **wild cow**. There is also more about the bear in the epilogue on page 388 and in the glossary under **bear**.

[†]A PPC is a prepublication critic—one of a number of educational psychologists who read the manuscript before publication. Some of these reviewers' comments are footnoted in the text.

Thank you to

- the people whose ideas are acknowledged in these pages (and to those whose ideas sneaked in unrecognized)
- Richard L. Greenberg, editor for the first Bears
- Roger Peterson, Bob Podstepny, Marshall Aronson, Joan Garbutt, and Stephanie Surfus, editors for the middle Bears
- Suzanna Brabant, editor for the most recent Bears
- Tony Hall and Jeff Littlejohn, cartoonists
- Angela Mann, production editor
- Polly Kummel, copy editor
- Carolyn Deacy, designer
- Reviewers of the first seven editions
- Reviewers of this edition: Pauline Applefield, University of North Carolina at Wilmington; Gordon Greenwood, University of Florida; Kathryn W. Linden, Purdue University; Sharon McNeely, Northeastern Illinois University; William L. Merrill, Central Michigan University; Wayne A. Nelson, Southern Illinois University at Edwardsville
- Marie, Laurier, Claire, and Rémi, who make it all worth a great deal more than my while.

PSYCHOLOGY FOR TEACHING

part one | THE BEGINNING

Begin at the beginning, the King said, gravely,
and go on till you come to the end: then stop.
Lewis Carroll, *Alice in Wonderland*

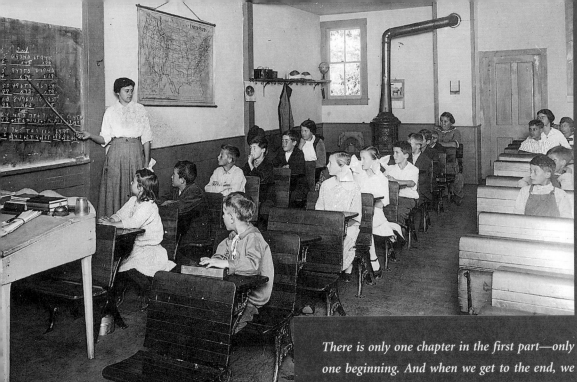

Chapter 1
Psychology and Teaching

There is only one chapter in the first part—only one beginning. And when we get to the end, we will stop.

The beginning says what educational psychology is, looks at teaching as a career, and presents an overview of each of the remaining twelve chapters. These chapters are organized into parts according to their major emphases. The second part looks at human development, at how children change through the school years. The third part examines explanations of learning and thinking, looks at individual differences in social, intellectual, and physical development and functioning, and presents a humanistic view of teaching. And the last part looks at topics important to the teaching/learning process: motivation, classroom management, individualized instruction, and assessment.

And somewhere the subtitle of this book becomes more significant.

Chapter 1 | PSYCHOLOGY AND TEACHING

PREVIEW There is a preview at the beginning of each chapter in this text. Previews organize and summarize important concepts and increase the meaningfulness of material to be learned—sometimes by stimulating recall of important material discussed previously, sometimes by providing new information, and sometimes by clarifying relationships. This first chapter is a preview of the remainder of the text. Among other things, it points out some important reasons for taking this course other than the fact that it might be compulsory.

Excerpt from Learn 'em Well

I don't know for a fact that my father actually wanted me to be a teacher. But I do know that as my taste for misbehavior blossomed, he despaired that I could ever become anything of value. I suspect that my mother, too, almost gave up hope during those times.

But I was not always disordered, undisciplined, and confused. There was a time, early in my childhood, when I was as exemplary a child as one could reasonably wish for. It was then, I think, that my father thought I might be a teacher. And that was maybe why he gave me my first formal opportunity to instruct when I was just a skinny seven-year-old.

It all began with John George, a Cree boy who attended the rural school where my dad taught. When John George first came to school, he was a withdrawn boy who spoke no English or French and whose habits were not always the same as ours.

On his first day at school, in the middle of the morning, John George felt the call of nature, got out of his desk, and ran to the far corner of the schoolyard. There, to our great amusement as we watched through the windows, he squatted and attended to that call.

My father, a resourceful and very capable teacher, rushed to the corner of the yard and tried to explain to John George, using very interesting body language, that the little building in the other corner was equipped to handle problems like the one the boy had just solved. But there are some signs that are not universally understood by frightened six-year-old boys whose pants have settled around their ankles.

Later that day, my dad made me a teacher. "Show him where it is and what it's for," he said.

I did. And now that I think of it, it might have been at that moment, too, that I noticed a bear strolling across the pasture just beyond the schoolyard. He was walking on a cow path.

WHY STUDY EDUCATIONAL PSYCHOLOGY?

Unfortunately, "showing them" is not all there is to teaching, my successful assignment with John George notwithstanding. And although this text, *Psychology for Teaching*, might not have been very useful to me that day, it would have come in very handy some years later when I tried teaching other, less natural things to people whose need to learn was not quite so insistent. You see, contrary to what I had hoped, teaching skills turned out not to be hereditary; we can't count on our genes to endow us with teaching ability or with what is called the "craft knowledge" of teaching—the knowledge that expert teachers seem to have (Grimmett & Mackinnon, 1992). Fortunately, however, we now have a large body of information that can help novice teachers become more expert, and that can contribute dramatically to the effectiveness of teachers and of schools. This textbook is your introduction to that information. Its goal is to make you a better teacher. As its title indicates, it presents a psychology for teaching.

Teaching Decisions and Beliefs

Teaching is a complex sequence of ongoing actions. It may involve as many as a thousand or more teacher-student interactions in a single day. Each of these interactions requires a decision: what to do, what to say, how to react, where to go next.

Much of what the teacher is required to do in the classroom is immediate: There is often little time for careful reflection. Hence, many of the teacher's actions are based on habit and on preestablished beliefs. In fact, everything a teacher does in the classroom reflects personal beliefs. This does not mean, of course, that all of a teacher's behaviors are carefully planned and deliberate. When teacher's responses have to be immediate, as is often the case, there is little time to plan and deliberate. But even our most impulsive and habitual actions reveal our underlying convictions and implicit theories—in other words, our beliefs. It is for this reason, suggests Richardson (1990), that getting teachers to change is a difficult undertaking. We do not easily discard old beliefs and adopt new ones.

What Are Beliefs? Beliefs are personal convictions. Unlike knowledge, which tends to be impersonal and impartial, beliefs often have strong emotional components. Thus, beliefs are reflected in attitudes, prejudices, judgments, and opinions.

Experiences, both personal and secondhand, are closely involved in the development of our beliefs. Pajares (1992) notes that beliefs are often formed early in life and may be maintained even in the face of strong contradiction. Such beliefs act as a sort of filter through which people view the world and interpret information.

Beliefs result not only from personal experiences but also from information we acquire through education and from other sources. For example, what we believe about the effects of smoking may result more from what we have read or heard than from what we have experienced. Similarly, what we believe about human nature, or about human learning, may be based partly on our own experiences and partly on what we have learned from more formal educational experiences.

How Beliefs Affect Decisions. Beliefs are what guide our thinking and our actions, says Pajares (1992). All teachers have beliefs about their work, their students, how learning occurs, the subjects they teach. A teacher who believes students learn best by memorizing assigns memory work; one who is convinced students remember only what they understand takes more pains to explain and clarify. A teacher who believes students cheat when given the opportunity supervises her examinations closely; one who thinks students are basically honest prepares her lessons while students write their tests.

One example is Mr. Busenius (see the case on page 7) who believes, among other things, that

Mr. Busenius teaches a sixth-grade language class. The class is generally well behaved; most students appear interested and attentive—except Helena, who in Mr. Busenius's not-too-polite words "is one #!!*# of a nightmare." Today, he has asked students to write two paragraphs describing the most interesting thing that happened to them over the weekend. Helena does not seem especially anxious to write about her weekend. Instead, she finds a brush and begins to brush her hair.

But before she has completed her third stroke, Mr. Busenius has quietly reached her desk, taken the brush from her, and jabbed his calloused index finger twice, quite emphatically, on the blank sheet of paper on Helena's desk.

She bends to her task. "Last weekend," she writes, "Tommy and I, I don't know if I should write this, but I will, what we did is . . ."

---

1. Offenders must be made to stop immediately before misbehavior spreads.

2. It is better to reprimand silently and at close range without disrupting ongoing classroom activities.

Mr. Busenius might have selected other options. For example, he might simply have ignored Helena—if he *believed* that her behavior was designed to get attention and that she therefore would be less likely to repeat it if he ignored her. Or he might have used some form of punishment, such as detention, *believing* that Helena would subsequently behave so as to avoid punishment. Alternatively, he might have gone over to Roberta and praised her remarkable paragraphs just loudly enough to draw Helena's attention, *believing* that this might encourage Helena to build her own remarkable paragraphs. Also, he might have taken the time to explain how important it is to learn to express oneself in the **belief**[*] that this might motivate Helena to greater efforts; he might have explained to Helena how her hair brushing was distracting and upsetting the others, *believing* that her need for social approval would convince her to put her brush away.

Which of these behaviors is best? Is it always best? Which of these beliefs is most accurate and most useful?

This text is designed to help you answer these questions.

[*]Boldfaced terms are defined in the glossary.

This Text and Your Beliefs

It's clear that beliefs that are inaccurate or prejudicial may lead to teaching behaviors that are inappropriate and ineffective. Accordingly, one important aim of this text is to encourage you to examine your beliefs—especially those that have to do with learners and with teaching—and to discard or alter them if necessary. It attempts to do this in two related ways. The first is by providing you with important information about learners of different ages and about the processes involved in learning, organizing, remembering, thinking, solving problems, and being creative. The second is by describing and illustrating practical strategies for facilitating the teaching/learning process.

Among the most useful of your beliefs as a teacher are those that have to do with how students change, how they learn, what motivates, reinforces, and punishes them, and what is interesting and important to them. These topics fall within the realm of **psychology**. Hence this *psychology for teaching*.

PSYCHOLOGY

Psychology is the study of human **behavior** and experience. These are fascinating but highly complex subjects. As a result, although all psychologists are concerned with behavior in one way or another, many specialties and divisions have arisen within the field, each concentrating on specific aspects of the human experience. For example, developmental psychologists look at how behavior changes with the passage of time, clinical psychologists deal with behavioral and emotional problems, and educational psychologists are interested in the scientific study of behavior in educational settings. These are only three of the divisions in psychology; Table 1.1 labels and describes several others and provides a clearer picture of psychology's scope.

SCIENCE

The psychologist does not study or attempt to understand behavior simply by thinking about the various factors that might be involved in behaving. Rather, psychology as a **science** involves the application of scientific procedures and approaches in an attempt to understand human behavior.

Science is as much an attitude as a collection of methods. As an attitude, science insists on precision, consistency, and replicability. The methods resulting from this attitude consist of rules intended to eliminate subjectivity, bias, and the influence of random factors—in short, rules designed to maximize the extent to which we can have confidence in the conclusions of science. For most of the past century (psychology is approximately one hundred years old), the attitudes and the methods that have governed the psychologist's search for greater understanding of humans and their behavior have emphasized precision, replicability, and objectivity above all else.

Unfortunately for the psychologist, human behavior is not as predictable as events in the physical world. Using the same attitudes and scientific methods as the psychologist, the chemist and the physicist have been able to discover replicable and precise laws that govern the behaviors of molecules and planets. But the psychologist has been hard-pressed to discover a single precise **law** governing the behavior of humans (more about laws shortly).

The problem for the psychologist goes beyond the observation that the behavior of humans is influenced by a tremendous variety of forces, some of which we don't understand at all well (yet). Many aspects of human behavior cannot be measured in the way that the speed, direction, and mass of a planet or molecule can be measured. Nor are changes in human behavior as precise and predictable as changes in the behavior of physical matter.

However, these observations should not lead you to conclude that we know little about human behavior. Nor are they meant to encourage pessimism (although a very slight skepticism might not be entirely inappropriate). Rather, what these observations emphasize is the complexity of human thought and behavior and consequently the real difficulties of reducing these events to simple laws and principles.

Facts and Theories

Science, as we have seen, is a collection of methods and attitudes that relate directly to the ways in which we discover and accumulate facts. In this context, however, the word **fact** is perhaps too strong; it implies a degree of certainty and accuracy that is not always possible in psychology or education. In these areas, our facts are simply observations of events, behaviors, or relationships. The important point is that science insists that these observations be made under controlled conditions so that anyone can make the same observations—that is, so that they can be replicated.

Facts (or observations), by themselves, would be of limited value to educators and psychologists if they were not organized, summarized, and simplified. That's where **theory** comes in. In a simple sense, a theory is a collection of related statements, the principal function of which is to summarize and explain observations. For example, when I observe that Roland Littlefork repeatedly refuses to join us for our annual fishing excursion,

TABLE 1.1 What Psychologists Do

SUBFIELD*	MAJOR CONCERNS AND ACTIVITIES
Clinical	Diagnosing and treating illnesses and disturbances, frequently in a hospital or clinical setting
Counseling and guidance	Evaluating and counseling clients' behavioral, emotional, and other problems not serious enough to require hospital or clinical treatment; also, assisting with important decisions (career, marriage, and so on)
Developmental	Studying changes that define growth, maturation, and learning from birth to death; applying findings in education programs
Educational	Researching learning, thinking, remembering, instructing, and related topics in educational settings; developing and applying learning programs for students
Industrial and personnel	Applying psychology in business and industry; developing and administering tests to evaluate aptitudes; conducting workshops and programs dealing with motivation, management, interpersonal relations, and related areas
Personality	Identifying and describing important, stable characteristics of individuals; developing classification schemes for personality characteristics as well as methods for identifying and assessing these characteristics
School	Identifying individual aptitudes and skills among learners in a school setting; developing and administering tests pertinent to school-related abilities
Experimental, comparative, and physiological	Exploring psychology as an experimental science; conducting research on comparisons among species; investigating physiological functioning as it relates to psychological functioning.
Psychometrics	Testing and measuring psychological characteristics and making sense of resulting measures; developing tests and measurement devices
Social	Doing research and consulting on the relationship between individuals and groups.

*Not all psychologists fall neatly into one of these categories. Many would consider themselves as belonging to several areas, both by the nature of their interests and by their activities. Others would hesitate to be classified in any of these subfields.

our regular poker games, our Christmas celebration, or our Halloween masquerade, I might develop a theory about his behavior. "I have a theory about Roland," I might say, and everybody would understand what I meant. "He doesn't like social gatherings," I might continue. That, in a nutshell, would be my theory. It summarizes and

explains my observations admirably. It is a statement that might be described as a naïve theory or, as Grippin and Peters (1984) put it, an implicit theory. Naïve or implicit theories differ from more formal theories in one important respect: Naïve theories express personal convictions that need only be believed but not scientifically proved; formal theories must be tested. It isn't sufficient simply to assume that a psychological theory accounts for all the important observations and relationships; this must be demonstrably true.

There are many theories in psychology; not all are equally good. Some, for instance, do not reflect the facts very well. Let's say, for example, that Roland Littlefork plays poker regularly with George's group and that he also accepts other social invitations. If this were the case, my theory about Roland's behavior would not fit all the facts.

That it reflect all important facts is only one of the requirements of a good theory. R. M. Thomas (1992) suggests a number of others: A theory is good if it (1) accurately reflects observations, (2) is expressed clearly, (3) is useful for predicting as well as explaining, (4) is applicable in a practical sense, (5) is consistent rather than self-contradictory, and (6) is not based on numerous assumptions (unproven beliefs). A good theory should also be thought provoking and should provide satisfying explanations, says R. M. Thomas (1992).

Of these criteria, one of the most important for the educator is that of predicting. The most useful theories are those that serve to explain observations and to predict events. My naïve theory about Roland Littlefork, for example, allows me to predict that he will refuse all social invitations, no matter who issues them. As we saw, however, in this case the prediction is inaccurate because the theory does not account for certain important facts. Presumably, a theory that fits the facts better would lead to more accurate predictions.

A theory, then, is a statement or, more often, a collection of related statements, the main function of which is to summarize, simplify, organize, and explain observations and to permit predictions about events relating to this set of observations. Some of these statements may be described as laws, others as principles, and many as beliefs.

Laws, Principles, and Beliefs

Laws are statements that generally are accurate beyond question. Physics, chemistry, astronomy, and other natural sciences have discovered numerous important laws ($E = mc^2$, for example). As we saw earlier, however, the regularity and unwavering predictability that characterize laws rarely characterize human behavior.

Principles are statements that are probable rather than certain. Unlike laws, they are always open to a degree of doubt, to a certain level of improbability. Accordingly, most psychological statements about human behavior and experience take the form of principles rather than laws.

As we saw, beliefs are more private and personal than either principles or laws. Beliefs are our individual convictions, our personal attempts to explain observations. Beliefs are often based on personal experience but can also be based on the same sorts of scientific observations that give rise to more formal theories. One of the most important goals of *Psychology for Teaching* is to provide you with a more valid basis for forming and examining important personal beliefs. After all, our beliefs are the basis of our behaviors (Pajares, 1992).

Models

One additional term is relevant here: **model**. A model is like a pattern or a blueprint; it's a representation of the way things are or of the way they can or should be. Models can be very specific and concrete, say Reese and Overton (1970), and are often included in or derived from theories. For example, there are models of atomic structures, models of the universe, and teaching models.

Models can also be very general. For example, they can represent all our beliefs and assumptions about human nature. In this sense, each of us has implicit models that govern our view of the world and that guide our perceptions and our behavior.

Two general models underlie much of what psychologists think and believe about human beings. On the one hand, the mechanistic model reflects the belief that it is useful to think of humans as being much like machines—predictable and highly responsive to environmental influences. On the other hand, the organismic model holds that it is more useful to view humans as dynamic, active, exploring organisms that are more responsive to internal forces than to external stimulation.

In a very real sense, psychological models are metaphors. They don't say "Humans are this or that" so much as "Humans behave as though they were like this or like that." Accordingly, models, like theories, cannot be judged in terms of their accuracy so much as in terms of their usefulness. A theory—or a model—is not right or wrong, say Wellman and Gelman (1992); it is simply more or less useful.

TEACHING AS PROBLEM SOLVING

In its simplest sense, to teach is to impart skills, knowledge, attitudes, and values. It involves bringing about, or at least facilitating, changes in learners. Teaching can be accomplished by telling and persuading, by showing and demonstrating, by guiding and directing the learner's efforts, or by a combination of these actions. It might involve only the teacher's own resources, knowledge, and skills, or it might rely on professionally prepared materials (films or computer software, for example), resource people, or the combination of talents, skills, and information learners already have.

Some researchers suggest that it is useful to view teaching as an exercise in problem solving (for example, Leinhardt & Greeno, 1986; Burns & Anderson, 1987). According to this model, teaching involves the ongoing solution of a series of problems. Some problems, such as those relating to specific course or lesson objectives, are clear and obvious. For example, if one goal of a lesson in mathematics is for students eventually to learn division, one problem that requires solution is that of arranging for student experiences that lead to the competency in question. Other related problems are not so obvious. These have to do with managing the classroom environment, monitoring ongoing activities, evaluating and assessing the interest and understanding of individual students, and so on.

Craft Knowledge

It seems that expert teachers develop sequences of routines and strategies that they can apply almost unconsciously as they teach. As a result, much of what they do in the classroom is, in a sense, on automatic pilot (Kagan, 1988). They are sensitive to the possibility of restlessness and inattention even before these occur. They become skilled in recognizing potential problems and in applying unobtrusive solutions. Automatically—and without breaking the continuity of their ongoing activity—they bring into play new patterns of interaction that serve to shift focus, that draw students back into the flow of activity and rechannel their attention.

A general term for the many skills involved in teaching is *craft knowledge*. Craft knowledge is a sort of practical wisdom, say Sykes and Bird (1992), that cannot always be verbalized completely clearly but that can be learned through practice or perhaps by studying and analyzing cases that illustrate teaching problems and principles.

Craft knowledge includes general information about teaching as well as specific information about teaching particular subjects and lessons to students with identifiable characteristics. It can also include "fragmentary, superstitious, and often inaccurate opinions," says Leinhardt (1990, p. 18). That is, craft knowledge can be based on inaccurate and inappropriate beliefs.

Knowledge of the craft of teaching is often evident in the patterns and routines that are such an important part of the classroom. These routines involve two different sets of activities: those relating to classroom management and discipline and those having to do specifically with instructing—with giving students information and establishing learning habits. Accordingly, acquiring these patterns and routines—that is, learning the *craft* of teaching—requires a wealth of information about both learners and the process of learning. The purpose of this text is to provide you with that information.

But there is more to being an expert teacher than you can learn from one textbook—or even a dozen texts. Not only do you need information about learners and learning, about human development, and about motivation and interests but you need to synthesize this information—to understand it, to integrate it with your values, your goals, your personality, and your preferences. Teachers have their own styles of teaching. No teacher-training program can—or should—make us all alike.

Teaching has often been described as both an art and a science. In fact, some writers argue that expert teaching is a far more artistic activity than we might think. Eisner (1982) suggests that every successful teaching performance can be analyzed both in terms of the science involved in instruction and classroom management and in terms of the art involved in creating the environment—the context—in which learning occurs.

Although a textbook such as this one is forced to deal with the science rather than with the art, it is worth keeping in mind that we should not resort to art only when science fails; rather, art can and should be an integral part of all classroom activity. Poetry and enchantment can have a place in even the most apparently mundane lesson in an ordinary classroom on a Tuesday. That is one of the things that makes teaching so exciting.

TEACHING AS EMPOWERING STUDENTS

From the teacher's point of view, then, teaching can be seen as a problem-solving activity—that is, an activity that involves the ongoing solution of problems relating to communication, instruction, motivation, classroom management, evaluation, and so on.

Another way of looking at teaching is to view it in terms of its objectives rather than its processes. The teacher must be concerned with the details of lesson organization and with the hundreds of routines and procedures that contribute to classroom management and effective learning—as well as with the goals of the instructional process. What is it that schools ought to accomplish? What are the important objectives of education?

The answers to these questions are fundamental to the teaching/learning process. They determine not only the content of the school curriculum but also the goals of the instructional process. Educational goals can be general (for example, to develop good citizens) or specific (to teach children to add two-digit numbers). For our purposes, a useful way of looking at educational objectives is to view them in the broadest, most general of all terms: The goal of education is to empower students.

Literally, **empower** means to give power to—in short, to enable. At the most obvious level, education empowers students by enabling them to do things they could not do otherwise. Reading, writing, and arithmetic empower us as surely as do sight, hearing, and our other senses, for while our senses enable us to perceive the world, the "three Rs" empower us to deal with it at a quite complex and sophisticated level. Without all sorts of school-related knowledge, we would be hard-pressed to function easily and effectively. We need to know a great deal if we are to use our banking machines, understand our instruction manuals, determine how much we owe our governments, read our newspapers, and on and on.

Specific skills like reading and writing are only one of the sources of empowerment schools bestow. In addition, schools foster in students the personal power that comes with social competence and the accompanying feelings of personal confidence, of being a unique and worthwhile individual. It is perhaps a cliché, but no less true for it, that schools must do more than teach subjects; it is far more important that they teach individual students.

Schools provide empowerment through the information they impart, through the feelings of confidence and personal power they foster, and through the learning strategies they develop in students. It is becoming increasingly clear, and increasingly true, that because so much information exists in our advanced technological societies, it is impossible for students to learn more than a fraction of it. And, given the rate at which information changes or becomes obsolete, it would probably be unwise to try. As a result, it is perhaps more important to learn how to learn and how to solve problems—to learn what Mulcahy, Peat, Andrews, Darko-Yeboah, and Marfo (1990) label **learning/thinking strategies**—than it is to learn only specific items of information. These strategies are the tools of knowing. In fact, argue Husén and Tuijnman (1991), formal schooling actually increases people's intelligence as measured by standardized tests. That's because the sorts of strategies we learn in school are what we use to think, to analyze, and to monitor and evaluate our intellectual activities. We apply them to all sorts of situations throughout our lives. Accordingly, such strategies are a tremendous source of personal power—of empowerment.

We are a clever species, Nickerson (1986) muses. So smart are we that as a result of our "technological wizardry" we have reached a point at which we can destroy everything around us and ourselves as well. In fact, not only do we have this power but we are in imminent danger of using it, perhaps without even wanting to. If we are to save ourselves, Nickerson cautions, we must rely not on instinct—as might another animal—but on intelligence. Hence, our ultimate survival depends on how well we can think. That, of course, is another important reason for teaching students how to learn and how to think: to encourage them to be worthwhile human beings whose concerns extend beyond the self to include the well-being of all others.

But we are in danger of moving ahead of ourselves. This chapter is simply an introduction. Later we will speak again of learning/thinking strategies, as well as of morality and ethics and of the personal power of warriors, saints, and others.

A TEACHING MODEL

To simplify without unduly distorting reality, we analyze the teaching process in terms of three stages, each characterized by different demands on the teacher: before teaching, during teaching, and after teaching (see Figure 1.1). And contrary to what we might immediately assume, the teaching stage is no more important than what occurs before or after. What we say about each of these stages, here and elsewhere in this text, is closer to the science of teaching than it is to the art of teaching, which does not make the art any less important.

Before Teaching

In order to be an effective, perhaps even exemplary, teacher, you must make a number of critical decisions before even walking into your classroom and actually engaging in the business of teaching. First, you must decide on both the long-range and short-term goals of the instructional process. To determine these goals, you must answer such questions as what you expect and intend specific learning outcomes will be. How do these tie in with the broad goals of the educational process in this subject? this grade? this school? this city or county? How do these goals fit in with your values and beliefs? How important are they?

Once you have determined your instructional goals, you must select a teaching strategy to attain these goals, and you must invent, make, or at least collect materials that are useful for teaching. What is required here is not only knowledge

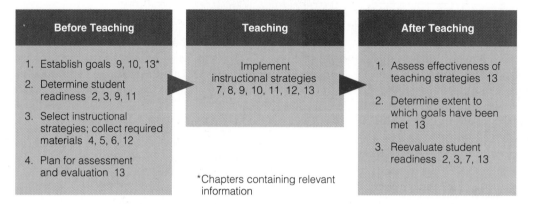

The Instructional Process

Before Teaching	Teaching	After Teaching
1. Establish goals 9, 10, 13*	Implement instructional strategies 7, 8, 9, 10, 11, 12, 13	1. Assess effectiveness of teaching strategies 13
2. Determine student readiness 2, 3, 9, 11		2. Determine extent to which goals have been met 13
3. Select instructional strategies; collect required materials 4, 5, 6, 12		3. Reevaluate student readiness 2, 3, 7, 13
4. Plan for assessment and evaluation 13	*Chapters containing relevant information	

FIGURE 1.1 A three-stage model of the teaching process.

of the strategies themselves but also of the skills required to implement them effectively. And, perhaps most important, you must be aware of the extent to which students are ready for this specific teaching/learning experience. Students' readiness involves a variety of factors, including essential prerequisite knowledge and skills, as well as appropriate motivation. Clearly, students who are eager to learn are most likely to profit from instruction; just as clearly, students who have already mastered prerequisite knowledge and skills are more likely to attain advanced instructional objectives. These facts highlight the importance of knowledge about how students learn and about how humans develop and what motivates them.

Our analysis of the teaching process thus far indicates that the preteaching phase involves three steps: setting appropriate goals, determining student readiness, and selecting appropriate instructional strategies. A fourth critical step is planning for assessment: How will you determine the extent to which instructional goals have been met? By what procedures will you evaluate the instructional process itself, as well as changes that might occur among learners? How will the results of your evaluation procedures influence subsequent teaching decisions?

Teaching

The instructional process—commonly called "teaching"—involves implementing strategies designed to lead learners to attain certain goals. In general, these strategies involve communication, leadership, motivation, and control (discipline or management).

Following an extensive review of research on effective teaching, MacKay (1982) identifies twenty-eight behaviors that most often characterize the teaching strategies of highly effective teachers. MacKay describes these as "suggested" or "recommended" behaviors rather than as the firm conclusions of scientific research. The behaviors are related to four aspects of the teaching process: classroom management and discipline; instructional organization, sequence, and presentation; verbal interaction (communication); and interpersonal interaction. The twenty-eight behaviors are summarized in the box entitled "Recommended Behaviors for Effective Teaching." They are well worth thinking about.

It is worth noting that, in a year-long study involving seventy-two teachers of third- and sixth-grade mathematics and language arts, researchers found a positive relationship between

Psychology answers important questions about how people learn, what motivates them, and what instructional procedures are most effective for which students, and for which teachers.

student achievement and each of these twenty-eight strategies, except for statements 1, 4, 7, 9, 11, 13, and 14. However, these seven recommended behaviors have been found to relate positively to effective teaching in other studies, notably Evertson, Anderson, and Brophy (1978) and Brophy and Evertson (1974).

After Teaching

The third phase of the teaching process involves assessing the outcomes of instruction in relation to the goals that you set in the preteaching phase. This process of evaluation reveals the effectiveness of your teaching; it might also say a great deal about the appropriateness of your instructional goals, the readiness of your students, the appropriateness of your teaching strategies, and even the relevance and appropriateness of your evaluation procedures.

PSYCHOLOGY AND TEACHING

Psychology's contribution to teaching, viewed within the context of this simple model (preteaching, teaching, and postteaching activities), is clear. It provides us with answers to such important questions as how do people learn? How can we use what we know about learning and motivation to increase the effectiveness of our instructional procedures? What do we know about people that might be of value to teachers who face student misbehavior or wish to avoid being faced with such behavior? How can we motivate learners? and a thousand other related questions.

recommended behaviors for effective teaching

1. Teachers should use a system of rules to deal with personal and procedural matters.

2. Teachers should prevent misbehaviors from continuing.

3. Teachers should direct disciplinary action accurately.

4. Teachers should move around the room a lot (monitoring seat work).

5. Teachers should handle disruptive situations in a low-key manner (nonverbal messages, proximity, eye contact).

6. Teachers should ensure that assignments are interesting and worthwhile, especially when children work independently.

7. Teachers should use a system of rules that allows students to carry out learning tasks with a minimum of direction.

8. Teachers should optimize academic learning time. Students should be actively involved and productively engaged in learning tasks.

9. Teachers should use a standard signal to get students' attention.

10. Teachers should not begin speaking to the group until all students are paying attention.

11. Teachers should use a variety of instructional techniques, adapting instruction to meet learning needs.

12. Teachers should use a system of spot-checking assignments.

13. Teachers should relate mathematics (or other) games and independent activities to the concepts being taught.

14. Teachers should use techniques that provide for the gradual transition from concrete to more abstract activities.

15. Teachers should use an appropriate mixture of high- and low-order questions.

16. Teachers should be aware of what is going on in the classroom.

17. Teachers should be able to attend to more than one issue at a time.

18. Teachers should smooth the flow of the lesson or provide a smooth transition from one activity to another.

19. Teachers' behavior should maintain the pace of the lesson.

20. Teachers should be clear in presentations to the class.

21. Teachers should be able to motivate children.

22. Teachers should provide evidence of caring, accepting, and valuing the children.

23. Teachers should respond accurately to both obvious and subtle meanings, feelings, and experiences of the children.

24. Teachers should direct questions to many different students.

25. Teachers should use techniques such as rephrasing, giving clues, or asking a new question to help students give improved responses when their answers are incorrect or only partially correct.

26. Teachers should use praise to reward outstanding work as well as to encourage students who are not always able to do outstanding work.

27. Teachers should use mild criticism on occasion to communicate expectations to more able students.

28. Teachers should accept and integrate student-initiated interaction such as questions, comments, or other contributions.

Source: Adapted from research on effective teaching by A. MacKay, "Project Quest: Teaching Strategies and Pupil Achievement." Occasional Paper Series, Centre for Research in Teaching, Faculty of Education, University of Alberta, Edmonton, Alberta, 1982, pp. 42–44.

By answering these questions, psychology can make a tremendous contribution to teaching. In fact, when teachers are asked what kind of assistance they require in order to become more effective, the needs they express typically reflect these questions. For example, after surveying 247 randomly selected elementary school teachers (22 male and 225 female), Moore and Hanley (1982) identified thirteen specific tasks with which teachers felt they could use help (see Table 1.2). The need mentioned most often was assistance in helping students become better learners, particularly with respect to acquiring basic skills. Other needs that these teachers expressed had to do with discipline, motivating learners, identifying and developing readiness for learning, and helping students establish realistic goals. Each of these needs falls within the scope of educational psychology.

Educational psychology may be defined as the study of human behavior in educational settings. As Wittrock (1992) emphasizes, it involves both the application of existing psychological knowledge to educational theory and practice and the development of new knowledge and procedures. Accordingly, educational psychology deals with learning processes, human development and motivation, social learning, human personality (especially characteristics such as intelligence and creativity), discipline and other aspects of classroom management, measuring and evaluating student development and learning, and other related questions. These broad topics, divided into four major units (thirteen chapters), are the substance of this text.

TABLE 1.2 Thirteen Tasks with Which Teachers Want Help
(ranked from most important to least important)

1. Developing effective learners and a mastery of the basic skills
2. Guiding children to set up and achieve realistic goals
3. Locating materials and in-service support for more effective teaching
4. Establishing and maintaining discipline
5. Identifying and understanding readiness factors that affect learning
6. Motivating children to learn
7. Designing assessment devices and interpreting the resulting data
8. Supporting teaching and technological methods and materials
9. Understanding interpersonal factors that influence a child's educational goals
10. Developing a greater understanding of human behavior
11. Updating in curriculum content areas and methodologies
12. Improving multipurpose classroom grouping techniques
13. Obtaining administrative assistance with instructional planning

Source: K. D. Moore and P. E. Hanley, "An Identification of Elementary Teacher Needs," *American Educational Research Journal*, 1982, pp. 19, 140. Copyright 1982, American Educational Research Association, Washington, D.C.

I HOPE THIS ATTENTION-GRABBING STRATEGY WORKS.......

TEACHING AS A CAREER

My father was a teacher for forty-one years. Not all of those years were easy. For some of the first years he didn't always get paid, and when he did, it was never very much. And many years he had enormous classes—as many as fifty students in an isolated, one-room school, spanning the first through the eighth grades. Nor were the teaching tasks always simple and straightforward; often his beginning students didn't even know English— only French or Cree.

But my father truly loved what he did. He knew how important teaching is, and he was proud to be a teacher. Maybe it was partly because of this that he taught as well as he did. In the end, and in spite of the fact that it was situated in an economically depressed area, his one-room

school produced several dozen university graduates, including at least two who earned doctorates and several who obtained master's degrees.

Teaching is important. It's stimulating and exciting, and it can be highly rewarding. But it isn't overwhelmingly lucrative. Nor is it exceedingly easy.

Teaching in schools like those discussed in the case on page 19 is often challenging and difficult. There are obvious problems associated with teaching students who represent such a vast range of motivation, abilities, time, and energy. In addition, dramatic increases in the amount of information available to today's teachers (and students), coupled with increasingly complex tools for handling information (computers, for example), have made teaching more complex rather than more simple (Downes, 1991). In short, teaching today brings with it a variety of sources of stress: pressures to be more effective and accountable for the outcomes of the teaching/learning process; drug-related school problems, including threats of violence; responsibilities associated with large enrollments; and demands resulting from mainstreaming (a policy whereby exceptional children—those who are gifted or talented or disadvantaged—are placed in regular classrooms rather than being segregated). Furthermore, teaching positions are sometimes difficult to obtain (although at other times there are teacher shortages and positions are abundant).

A relatively large proportion of beginning teachers either do not obtain starting positions or abandon their careers after a few years. Twelve years after they first started teaching, half of all young male teachers have left the teaching profession (Murnane, Singer, & Willett, 1988); about a quarter of these male teachers later resume teaching. Not surprisingly, given that many interrupt their careers for childbearing and -rearing, half of all beginning female teachers are no longer teaching within six years. However, almost one-third of these female teachers subsequently return to teaching. Thus, although many beginning teachers abandon or switch their careers, the majority

Reporter Marina Jimenez spent a week in a local high school as an undercover student (Jimenez, 1992). At 2,300 students, the school is the largest in western Canada, serving people from a tremendous range of backgrounds and offering a huge variety of programs. Some students are primarily in academic programs, taking such core courses as English, social studies, and the sciences. Others study skin and nail care, learn to drive cars, or earn full course credits for grilling hamburgers in the school cafeteria. Of the students who graduated from the school last year, 34 percent earned diplomas or certificates that did not qualify them for admission to university. Many work twenty-five or more hours a week in shops, garages, or fast-food outlets. Some of these still manage to do well in academic programs. Others come to school primarily for its social opportunities. Many of these students go to bars and clubs, not only on weekends but during the week, and often don't get home until 3 or 4 in the morning. Attendance is low in many classes. Not surprisingly, some students sleep through their classes. Seventy-two students in this school live on their own, many because of serious problems at home.

There is racial tension in this school, Jimenez reports. Last year there were racially motivated brawls. And this year a police officer is assigned to the school on a permanent basis.

make lifelong careers out of teaching. Many—perhaps most—love what they do.

But many nevertheless experience some problems. And beginning teachers typically experience more problems than experienced teachers. Why? For four reasons, says Valli (1992). First, beginning teachers have a strong tendency to imitate teachers they have had as students. The result is that they fail to develop effective personal approaches to teaching based on well-informed beliefs. Second, starting teachers tend to be isolated from other teachers; hence they have little emotional support during difficult times and little opportunity for tuition and guidance by more experienced and more expert teachers. Third, the novice teacher often finds it difficult to transfer what has been learned in teacher education programs to the solution of actual problems in the classroom. As a result, the teachers may put aside much of what they have learned, considering it irrelevant theory. Finally, many new teachers become overly concerned with discovering or applying the Correct Teaching Technique. Consequently, they fail to develop more spontaneous and creative—and often more effective—approaches.

SCHOOLING IN A WIDER CONTEXT

Those of us reared in areas in which school is universal and compulsory tend to become blasé about its role and its effects on society. We lose sight of the effect of schooling. Perhaps it would be a good thing to remind ourselves occasionally that ours is only one of the world's societies—and it is far from the most populous. Things are not everywhere as they are here; the contrast might highlight some of the differences that teaching and learning can make.

Consider, for example, that infant mortality in the United States is now less than 9 per 1,000 (U.S. Bureau of the Census, 1991). In parts of the nonindustrialized world, more than 100 infants per 1,000 die. In fact, more than 15 million of the world's infants die each year from preventable causes. Some 4 million die from diarrheal dehydration; almost as many die from vaccine-preventable diseases such as measles and tetanus (J. P. Grant, 1986). What does this have to do with education? A great deal. Research makes it clear that exposure to schooling in the Third World is related to a much higher probability of infant survival (Levine, 1987) and is significantly related to a reduction in birthrates as well. For example, mothers can be taught the simple hygiene that can prevent diarrhea, and they can be schooled in the inexpensive oral rehydration therapies that would save large numbers of lives.

It is clear that lack of schooling, illiteracy, poverty, and high mortality go hand in hand. Sadly, in most developing countries, especially in Africa, fewer than half of all children attend school (Tsang, 1988). For those who do attend school, the quality of education is extremely low, dropout rates are high, and the relative cost of education is very high. And although school enroll-

ments in Third World countries have increased approximately fivefold since 1950, lack of funds is seriously curtailing growth of schooling and is having a significant negative impact on the quality of education (Fuller & Heyneman, 1989).

It may be easy to imagine the effect of a high-quality, universal educational system in some remote Indian or African village; it is not so easy to see its effect closer to home. It might be a valuable exercise to imagine the eventual effect on our society were we to abandon universal schooling and instead turn our children into the streets.

MAIN POINTS

1.   Teaching skills are not hereditary; psychology can contribute significantly to their development. Specifically, psychology's knowledge about such topics as how students learn, what motivates them, and how they think and remember can help shape our beliefs. Beliefs (personal convictions based on knowledge and experience) underlie our teaching decisions.

2.   Psychology is the study of human behavior and experience. Various divisions of psychology are concerned with particular aspects of behavior (for example, developmental psychology, clinical psychology, and educational psychology).

3.   In psychology, as in most other disciplines, the principal means of discovering and of knowing is science. Science is as much an attitude as a collection of methods. It is an attitude that insists on precision, consistency, objectivity, and replicability. Its methods are designed to ensure these characteristics.

4.   Scientific facts are observations that are objective and replicable; theories are statements, the principal function of which is to summarize and explain related observations; laws are statements that are accurate beyond question; principles are statements that are probable rather than certain; and beliefs are private, personal convictions.

5.   Models are representations of the way things are (or should be) and are often *implied* in our theories and beliefs rather than explicitly stated. Important models in psychology are the organismic (we are like dynamic active organisms: responsive to internal forces) and the mechanistic (we are more like machines: highly predictable and responsive to external forces).

6.   Given the tremendous complexity and frequent unpredictability of human behavior, the theories and principles of psychology are not simple. In addition, they typically admit more exceptions than do the laws of the natural sciences.

7.   Teaching may be viewed as an ongoing sequence of problem solving and decision making. Part of the craft knowledge of expert teachers involves developing sequences of routines and strategies that allow them to solve or avert many classroom problems almost automatically. These techniques require a wealth of information about students, teaching, and learning, as well as some measure of art.

8.   Teaching empowers students (makes them capable) by giving them important information and skills, by fostering in them the feelings of personal power that come with social competence and self-esteem, and by developing in them the learning/thinking strategies that are essential for learning how to learn.

9. A simple but useful model describes the teaching process in terms of activities that occur before teaching (establishing goals, determining student readiness, selecting instructional strategies and collecting necessary materials, and planning for assessment and evaluation), activities that occur during teaching (implementation of teaching strategies), and activities that occur after teaching (assessing effectiveness of teaching strategies, determining the extent to which goals have been met, and reevaluating student readiness).

10. Educational psychology is the application of relevant psychological knowledge to educational theory and practice. Its principal usefulness is to answer such questions as how do people learn?

How can we increase motivation? How can we determine student readiness? What are the best teaching strategies for our objectives?

11. Teaching is not as lucrative as playing baseball or arranging to have wealthy parents. Teaching positions are sometimes scarce, and the demands and stresses of teaching sometimes drive young teachers out of the profession. But many stay and love it.

12. Given that most of us live where schooling is compulsory, it is easy to lose sight of the effect of education on our lives. Conditions in Third World countries underscore the relationship between lack of schooling and poverty, high infant mortality, and other forms of misery.

SUGGESTED READINGS

Educational psychology provides some of the answers, but not all. In his classic article, Coladarci argues that in addition to knowing and implementing the theories and suggestions of educational psychology, the teacher must innovate and experiment.

COLADARCI, A. P. (1956). The relevancy of educational psychology. *Educational Leadership, 13,* 489–492.

For a provocative and pertinent discussion of the role of scientific research in the behavioral sciences, see

McCAIN, G., & SEGAL, E. M. (1982). *The game of science* (4th ed.). Monterey, Calif.: Brooks/Cole.

Science is perhaps not the only way of knowing. In books that strive to crack our "cosmic eggs" (disrupt our world views) and that appeal to intuition as much as to reason, Pearce argues that science is not even the best way of knowing.

PEARCE, J. C. (1971). *The crack in the cosmic egg.* New York: Fawcett Books.

———. (1977). *Magical child.* New York: Bantam Books.

The following little booklet is an attempt to condense the results of educational research and squeeze from it a number of highly practical suggestions for teachers and parents:

U.S. DEPARTMENT OF EDUCATION. (1986). *What works: Research about teaching and learning.* Pueblo, Colo.: Consumer Information Center.

A detailed analysis of teaching as a contemporary career, with attention to the goals, functions, and philosophies of schools:

RYAN, K., & COOPER, J. M. (1988). *Those who can, teach* (5th ed.). Boston: Houghton Mifflin.

Bears are rather large, bobtailed mammals. They walk on the soles of their feet; eat flesh, roots, and other vegetable matter; and have five toes on each foot (Cameron, 1956).

part two | HUMAN DEVELOPMENT

It's all that the young can do for the old, to shock them and keep them up to date.

George Bernard Shaw, *Fanny's First Play*

But teachers cannot afford to be shocked too often by the behaviors of the young. If they are to teach them effectively, it's important that they know what to expect of them. Teachers should not be surprised at the six-year-old's occasional bewilderment in the face of the unfamiliar, nor should they be taken aback by the sometimes startling and often impractical logic of the adolescent. Much of growing up means becoming familiar with things; much of school learning involves learning how to use the mind well.

The two chapters in this second part trace the development of children through the school years. They look at the processes of human development and at the forces that shape us, and they examine the educational implications of our knowledge of how children develop.

The childhood shews the man,
As morning shews the day.
John Milton, *Paradise Lost*

As for being a General, well, at the age of four with
paper hats and wooden swords we're all Generals.
Only some of us never grow out of it.
Peter Ustinov, *Romanoff and Juliet*

chapter 2 | AN OVERVIEW OF HUMAN DEVELOPMENT

PREVIEW It seems clear that in order to teach children effectively it is useful to understand them. We don't expect our six-year-olds to understand Boolean logic, nor do we expect our teenagers to become excited at the prospect of being allowed to play on the swings if they color their drawing of mommy nicely, staying inside the lines. But what can six-year-olds understand? And what excites teenagers? This chapter presents the beginnings of answers for questions such as these in its summary of some of the important findings in the study of child development. It is important to keep in mind, however, that our discussion is necessarily limited to that mythical but convenient invention, the "average child." Your children are not likely to be "average"; they will need to be understood as individuals. Nevertheless, knowledge of the average may prove valuable in understanding the individual.

Excerpt from Raising the Kids, What?

When I was still very young, my father took me to my first fair. It completely overwhelmed me. I had never before heard or smelled so many things or seen so many colors or so much movement. Nor had I ever tasted cotton candy or candied apples, or touched an elephant. And I don't think I had ever actually seen a wild cow.

But what most impressed me about the fair was the "freak" show we attended at the end of the day. There I saw a man swallow an incredibly long and sharp sword without cutting himself and a woman who was sawed in half inside a box and then was magically put together again. Later, a midget stuffed flaming balls into his mouth and then spit them out, black and smoking, and a woman with tattoos over every inch of her body, or so she said, thrilled me with her display. For weeks after, I could

talk of little else. I now knew that there were things in this world that those less fortunate than I would not believe existed.

I am still fascinated by fairs, freaks, and fools.* When the fair came to our town one summer, I quickly offered to take my youngest, who was then seven. He was not overly enthusiastic, but I knew that this was partly because he likes to watch television on Saturdays and partly because he didn't yet know how wonderful fairs are.

So we went to the fair. And, to paraphrase an old song, all the wonderful things were there.

But my son didn't see them! He seemed unmoved by the sights, the sounds, the smells, and the tastes. And when we stood in front of the sideshow tent, listening to a man with a splendid voice urging

---

*PPC: I don't think you should make fun of those less fortunate. One of them might be offended.

Author: I mean fools in the sense of clowns. I used the term because of the alliteration. Besides, few of the other kinds of fools would actually read a book like this.

us to come in and see the two-headed calf, the woman with the skin of an elephant, the largest man in the whole world, and the one-handed midget concert pianist, my son didn't even look skeptical. He just looked bored.

"This is it," I said. "This is really what fairs are all about! Wait till you see this." And I dragged him into the tent in the wake of my enthusiasm.

Later that night, when we talked about the fair, I learned that my son had not seen a calf with the two heads or a strange woman with the soft gray folds of elephant skin. All he had seen was an unfortunate one-headed calf with a hint of a second head where its right ear should have been and a pathetic woman with a revolting skin disease. Nor had he seen a giant with a great rumbling voice. Instead, he had watched an unhappy, grotesquely obese man walk painfully across a barren stage, making plaintive breathing noises as he moved. And he had not heard heart-rending sonatas played by the one-handed midget; all he had heard was a handful of sad notes played on a tinny miniature piano.

And I had always thought there was magic in the fair. But he and I are from different worlds. His is far less naïve than mine. Television, among other things, has seen to that.

But where can he find magic these days?

CONCEPTS IN HUMAN DEVELOPMENT

Developmental psychology looks at changes that occur between conception and death. It describes human characteristics at different ages and tries to identify predictable differences among different ages and sexes and to explain the processes that account for developmental changes. To simplify, developmental psychology describes what it is like to be a seven-year-old, how seven-year-olds might be different from fourteen-year-olds, how seven-year-olds got to be the way they are, and how and why they will continue to change. This information is important to teachers, who must always be concerned with students' readiness, interests, and capabilities. Unfortunately, however, the information that developmental psychology provides us is not always simple and straightforward; it often must be qualified and is subject to many exceptions. Each of us is, after all, individual and unique.

Different Contexts

One factor particularly important to the developmental psychologist is the place and time in which individuals are born and raised. My son and I are clearly a case in point. We are of different worlds—of different contexts. As developmental psychologists would say, we are of different cohorts.

A **cohort** can be described as a group of individuals who were all born within the same period of time—say, the 1940s or the 1970s. Thus, a cohort is initially of a fixed size and composition, and it cannot grow in size after the time period that defines it has elapsed. Not only does it become smaller with the passage of time as members die but other predictable changes occur. For example, the proportion of males to females changes because males tend to die sooner than females throughout the world. Although there are 105 males born for every 100 females, the numbers of each still alive by early adulthood are approximately equal. But by age 65, only 69 males are still alive for every 100 females. These predictable changes have implications for understanding the lives of men and women.

From developmental psychology's point of view, the most important thing about a cohort is that its members have had a similar sequence of historical influences in their lives, particularly if their geographical, social, and other circumstances are also similar. In interpreting the conclusions of developmental psychology, we must keep in mind that many of these conclusions are based on research conducted with a small number of cohorts—often only one—and that they might not be valid for other cohorts. In our increasingly multicultural societies, differences among individuals are magnified, and the need for teachers to take these differences into account becomes increasingly important.

This chapter gives a brief overview of some important findings about human development. The next chapter deals more specifically with cognitive and social development.

Some Definitions

Development is the process whereby individuals adapt to their environments. It involves growth, maturation, and learning.

Growth refers to physical changes such as increases in height and weight. These changes are quantitative rather than qualitative; that is, they are changes in quantity or amount rather than transformations that result in different qualities.

Maturation, a somewhat less precise term than *growth*, describes changes that are relatively independent of the environment. Maturational changes are assumed to be closely related to the influences of heredity. In most areas of development, however, there is a very close interaction between heredity and environment. For example, learning to walk depends on the maturation of certain muscle groups and on increasing control over their movements (maturational developments), as well as on the opportunity to practice the various skills involved (environment, learning). Maturation is clearly illustrated by the changes in early adolescence that lead to sexual maturity (puberty)—changes collectively labeled "pubescence." Although their onset seems to be affected by environmental conditions (menarche—the onset of menstruation—occurred progressively earlier between 1850 and 1970, apparently because of nutritional factors; see Frisch & Revelle, 1970), the changes of pubescence are largely genetically programmed.

Learning is defined in terms of actual or potential changes in behavior as a result of experi-

ence. Thus, all relatively permanent changes in behavior that are not the result of maturation or of external factors, the effects of which are unrelated to environment (such as the temporary effects of drugs or fatigue), are examples of learning.

THE NATURE OF HUMAN DEVELOPMENT

This section briefly summarizes important knowledge in developmental psychology, in the form of nine principles of development. These principles are not an exhaustive summary of developmental psychology; rather, they have been selected mainly for their relevance to the teaching/learning process.

1. Influences on Development: Nature and Nurture

Development is influenced by both heredity (nature) and environment (nurture). We know, for example, that our genes are responsible for many of our physical characteristics, such as hair and eye color, facial features, and to some extent height and weight. But even here, the influences of heredity are not entirely simple and straightforward. Although some characteristics (for instance, hair and eye color) do appear to be entirely under the control of our genes, other characteristics (for instance, height and weight) clearly are also influenced by environmental factors.

The situation is far less clear for personality and intellectual characteristics than for physical characteristics. In fact, it has been extremely difficult to determine how important qualities such as intelligence and creativity are influenced by heredity and the extent to which they can be modified by the environment (see R. L. Linn, 1992). In attempting to clarify this question, many studies have focused on **identical twins** because, as Gould notes, they are "the only really adequate natural experiment for separating genetic from environmental effects in humans . . ."

(1981, p. 234). This is because identical (monozygotic) twins are genetically identical, a condition that is not true for any other pair of humans, including **fraternal** (dizygotic) **twins.** Therefore, if intelligence is genetically determined, identical twins should have almost identical intelligence test scores (almost but not exactly identical because we cannot measure intelligence completely accurately). But if intelligence is largely a function of the environment, ordinary siblings and fraternal twins should resemble each other about as closely as identical twins—and far more closely than identical twins who are brought up in separate homes.

Figure 2.1 presents a summary of studies of the relationship between intelligence and genetic relatedness. What does this figure reveal? First, note that the correlation coefficient (a measure of relationship that ranges from –1 to +1) for intelligence test scores is lowest for those who are least alike genetically (unrelated persons) and becomes progressively higher as the degree of genetic similarity increases. Intelligence is clearly influenced by heredity.

Note too, however, that the correlations also increase with degree of environmental similarity. Thus, identical twins reared together are more alike in measured intelligence than are those reared apart. Similarly, fraternal twins, who are no more alike genetically than are other siblings, nevertheless manifest higher correlations—presumably because their environments are more alike than are those of most siblings. After all, fraternal twins are of exactly the same age and are often exposed to the same experiences at about the same time.

The conclusion? As we stated at the beginning of this section, development is influenced by both heredity and environment. The two interact in complex and not clearly understood ways to determine what you and I become. What is most important about this principle, from an educational point of view, is that many of our characteristics can be influenced by the environment. And

although there is relatively little that we can do about heredity at this point, much of the environment still remains under our control. (See Chapter 7 for further discussion of the roles of heredity and environment relative to intelligence.)

2. Differential Growth Rates

Development occurs at different rates for different parts of the organism. This is not intended to mean that the left foot grows rapidly for a short while, then the right foot, and then one arm. It does mean, however, that various parts of the body, as well as some aspects of personality and cognitive and perceptual ability, grow at different rates and reach their maximum development at different times. For example, Bloom (1964) found that by the age of $2^{1}/_{2}$, humans have reached half their future height. He suggests that in the same way about half of a male's tendency to be aggressive toward others is established by age 3, and much of our intellectual potential has already been developed by age 6,[*] a fact that may be partly related to how and when the brain grows.

Investigations of brain development reveal several interesting and important facts. First, most of the **neurons** (nerve cells) that make up the human brain are formed during the prenatal period, although some additional neurons may form in the first few months after birth (Rosenzweig & Leiman, 1982). At birth, the infant's brain weighs approximately one-quarter of what it will weigh at its maximum, which is reached at about age twenty-five. Most of the increase in brain weight between birth and adulthood seems to be caused by the growth of axons and dendrites (the elongated portions of the nerve cell that permit neural transmission) and by myelination (the growth of a protective covering around the axon).

---

[*]Statements such as these are hypothetical approximations at best and refer to variation rather than to absolute amount. The important point is simply that major personality and intellectual characteristics appear to be strongly influenced (and perhaps partly determined) by early experiences.

Category		Correlation coefficient 0.0 0.1 0.2 0.3 0.4 0.5 0.6 0.7 0.8 0.9	No. of groups studied
Unrelated people	Reared apart	▮	4
	Reared together	▮▮▮▮▮	5
Foster parent-child		▮▮▮▮▮	3
Parent-child		▮▮▮▮▮▮▮	12
Siblings	Reared apart	▮▮▮▮▮▮	2
	Reared together	▮▮▮▮▮▮	35
Two-egg twins	Opposite sex	▮▮▮▮▮▮▮	9
	Like sex	▮▮▮▮▮▮▮	11
One-egg twins	Reared apart	▮▮▮▮▮▮▮▮	4
	Reared together	▮▮▮▮▮▮▮▮▮	14

FIGURE 2.1 Correlation coefficients for intelligence test scores from fifty-two studies. The high correlation for identical twins shows the strong genetic basis of measured intelligence. The greater correlation for siblings or twins reared together, compared with those reared apart, supports the view that environmental forces are also important in determining similarity of intelligence test scores. Adapted from L. Erlenmeyer-Kimling and L. F. Jarvik (1963), "Genetics and Intelligence: A Review," *Science, 142,* 1478. Copyright 1963 by the American Association for the Advancement of Science. Used by permission.

Second, brain growth also seems to be subject to varying rates. The brain does not grow at a uniform rate between conception and birth nor between birth and adulthood. Instead, it appears to grow in spurts. These growth spurts are reflected by increases in cranial (head) circumference. Examinations of head measurements have led Lewin (1975) to believe that a dramatic spurt in brain growth occurs during the later stages of fetal development. Evidence suggests that this period of rapid brain development is a critical period during which the effects of malnutrition can be especially severe—as can also be true during the first few months of infancy, during which the growth spurt continues (Parmelee & Sigman, 1983). It is not surprising that in the majority of the world's undeveloped nations, where malnutrition is most prevalent, scientists have noted smaller than average head circumference among children (Winick, 1976).

Epstein's (1978) examination of head circumference data leads him to the conclusion that significant and distinct spurts in brain growth take place during four periods between birth and adulthood: two to three months, two to three years, six to eight years, and fourteen to sixteen years for males and ten to twelve years for females. He notes as well that these spurts occur during periods that correspond closely with periods of major cognitive change, according to Piaget's theory (described in the next chapter), and suggests the possibility that physical changes in the brain

that accompany these growth spurts make cognitive development possible. Evidence to substantiate this supposition or to corroborate the consistency and significance of changes in cranial circumference is still scarce.

Another observation related to the principle of differential growth rates is **lateralization,** a term that refers to the fact that the two halves (hemispheres) of the brain do not exactly duplicate each other's functions. In newborns, the hemispheres do not seem to be highly specialized, but in early infancy, the **principle of opposite control** becomes evident. This principle is manifested in the fact that the right hemisphere is typically involved in sensations and movements of the left side of the body, and vice versa. Clear evidence of hemisphere asymmetry is also found in the fact that about 90 percent of all people are right-handed and only 10 percent left-handed (Halpern & Coren, 1990). This seems to have been true of our ancestral cave dwellers as well, as deduced from the fact that about 90 percent of all

primitive hand tracings are of the left hand (hence, presumably drawn by the right hand) (Springer & Deutsch, 1989).

Additional evidence of hemisphere specialization includes the observation that in the majority of individuals (95 percent of right-handed people and 70 percent of left-handed) the left hemisphere is somewhat more involved in language production functions (Bradshaw, 1989). However, this does not mean that the right hemisphere is *not* involved in language. In fact, when the left hemisphere suffers damage early in life, the right hemisphere frequently takes over language functions with little apparent subsequent difficulty. When damage is suffered later, however, recovery may not occur or may be more limited (Bradshaw, 1989).

Findings such as these have led some to speculate that in the majority of people the right hemisphere is more concerned with emotions and with the spatial and the temporal (for example, art and music) and that the left hemisphere is concerned more with logic, math, science, and language. Thus, individuals who are logical are sometimes described as "left-brain oriented," those who are more intuitive and artistic as "right brained." A number of researchers and theorists point out that our current educational practices emphasize left-brain functions, as is reflected in our preoccupation with verbal learning, mathematics, science, and logic (see, for example, Sonnier, 1985). Our schools neglect right-brain functions, they claim. Hence we should change our educational fare and philosophy to educate both halves of our students' brains. The phrase **holistic education** has been coined to represent this point of view. Unfortunately, investigating the dual function of the brain has proved difficult, and much of what passes for information is speculation rather than fact (Hellige, 1990).

To summarize the second principle: Development is not a uniform process for all features of an organism. The description of growth curves for development has led Bloom (1964) to postulate a principle that is of major importance for education. It is given here as principle 3.

3. Timing of Environmental Influences

Variations in environment have the greatest quantitative effect on a characteristic at its period of most rapid change and least effect on the characteristic at its period of least rapid change (Bloom, 1964, p. vii). This principle is most clearly illustrated with respect to physical growth. Twenty-four-year-old Rudolph, who was malnourished through much of his childhood and who is now five feet tall, is not likely to grow an additional foot as a result of a sudden change in his diet. In contrast, the eventual height of twenty-four-week-old Christianne is clearly more susceptible to the effects of dietary changes.

This principle also holds with respect to intellectual development. For example, brain growth seems highly vulnerable to malnutrition during growth spurts, especially during prenatal and early postnatal development. In addition, there is evidence that cognitive development may be most sensitive to environmental influences earlier rather than later in life. For example, Lee (1951) examined intelligence test scores of three groups of African-Americans living in Philadelphia, one of which included individuals who had been born in the south; the other two comprised individuals who had moved to Philadelphia either before first grade or at fourth grade. The greatest increases in intelligence test scores were for children who had moved from impoverished backgrounds to better school environments before first grade. In addition, the greatest changes occurred during the first few years. Not surprisingly, those born and raised in Philadelphia scored higher than the other two groups at all grades (see Figure 2.2).

Additional evidence suggesting that the timing of environmental influences can be very important is found in language acquisition: Infants and young preschoolers can easily learn two or more languages simultaneously and well, whereas adults experience more difficulty and less success.

To summarize: There are periods of rapid development of specific kinds; during these periods, environmental influences have the greatest effects. The implications of this principle for education are twofold: Educators need to identify periods of greatest and least rapid change, and they need to arrange for relevant experiences during periods of most rapid change. This line of thinking is illustrated in preschool programs such as Project Headstart, in which disadvantaged children are provided with experiences designed to allow them to catch up with more advantaged children. Although initial evaluations of these programs were not always positive (see, for instance, Bronfenbrenner, 1977), much of the pertinent research suffered from the extreme difficulty in measuring many of the important positive changes that can result from these programs. Typically, for example, research looks at obvious things, such as achievement on standardized tests, but fails to

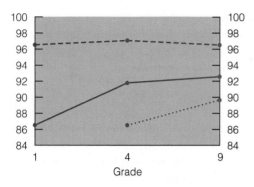

FIGURE 2.2 Changes in intelligence test scores on measures obtained in first, fourth, and ninth grades for African-American students born and raised in Philadelphia (dashed line), those born in the South who moved to Philadelphia in the first grade (solid line), and those who did not move to Philadelphia until the fourth grade (dotted line). Adapted from E. S. Lee, *American Sociological Review,* 1951, p. 231. Copyright 1951 by the American Sociological Association. Used by permission of the author.

take into account important social and emotional events, such as changes in self-concept, motivation, and so on.

Barnett and Escobar (1987) present a summary of some twenty studies that have investigated the effects of preschool intervention and the economic benefits of intervention in relation to its cost (in the jargon of the age, what economists call "cost effectiveness"). They conclude that many of these studies provide credible evidence that early intervention with disadvantaged children is not only educationally and socially beneficial but also economically sound.

4. Sequential Development

Development follows an orderly sequence. In fetal development, the heart appears and begins to function before the limbs reach their final form; the lips and gums form before the nasal passages do, the tail regresses before the permanent tooth buds form, and so on.

In motor development, children can lift their chins from a prone position before they can raise their chests, they can sit before they can stand, they can stand before they can crawl, and they can crawl before they can walk (Shirley, 1933).

In intellectual development, the same principle seems to apply, although the sequences are less obvious and the stages less distinct. Piaget's theory (see Chapter 3) is based on the assumption that human development is characterized by distinct sequential stages. For example, an analysis of changes in children's play behavior reveals two distinct developmental sequences—one dealing with the child's actual behavior in game situations and the other with the child's verbalized notions of rules. Specifically, until about age three, children do not understand the concept of rules, and they play as though there were none. Their play is "free play" in the sense that it is unencumbered by notions of what is permitted and what isn't.

During a second stage, lasting until age five or so, children have begun to imitate aspects of the rule-regulated play of adults, but the rules by which they play are idiosyncratic and constantly changing. They make rules up as they go along. But if asked about rules, they describe them as being external and unchangeable.

In the third stage (until age eleven or twelve), children realize that rules are inventions that can be changed. But their play behavior is again a contradiction of their beliefs in that they now follow rules rigidly, seldom (if ever) changing them. It is not until the fourth stage (beyond age eleven or twelve) that their play behavior finally reflects their understanding of the function of rules. Now, although they play according to rules, they occasionally change them by mutual consent. (See Table 2.1.)

The understanding of rules is only one small aspect of development that follows an orderly and predictable sequence. Piaget's investigations, described in Chapter 3, suggest that notions of reality, logical reasoning, understanding of time and space, and a wealth of important cogni-

TABLE 2.1 Piaget's Description of Children's Understanding and Use of Rules

APPROXIMATE AGE	DEGREE OF UNDERSTANDING	PLAY BEHAVIOR
Before 3	No understanding of rules	Do not play according to any rules
To 5 or so	Believe rules come from God (or some other high authority) and cannot be changed	Break and change rules constantly
To 11 or 12	Understand social nature of rules and that they can be changed	Do not change rules; adhere to them rigidly
After 11 or 12	Complete understanding of rules	Change rules by mutual consent

tive and perceptual events are sequential and predictable.

The observation that much of development follows an orderly and predictable sequence is especially valuable for teachers, who need to be concerned with the readiness of students. Teachers need to know when specific skills and abilities develop if they are to present children with tasks that are not impossible for them but are challenging enough to be interesting and to promote growth. As is made clear in the next chapter, it may also be extremely important to understand the factors that enhance—or that retard—development.

5. Developmental Stages

Development may be described in stages. Developmental theories are most often stage theories; that is, they describe important developmental events in terms of age-defined stages. Stage theories are based on the belief that although development is a relatively smooth, ongoing process, distinct and important changes nevertheless occur in a predictable sequence.

Stages are useful. They give us convenient places to "hang" our facts; they simplify our understanding, help our organization, and facilitate recall. They have been used extensively by theorists such as Freud, Erikson, and Piaget. Like theories, stages are invented by theorists to clarify and organize their observations. They are best evaluated in terms of their usefulness rather than their accuracy.

Given that stages are inventions, it is not surprising that the stages described by theorists such as Piaget, Freud, and Erikson are different; they are all expressions of different points of view, and they all describe different features of child development.

Stage theories are important for teachers because they provide information about the sequence of human development, about the most likely behaviors of children in different stages, and perhaps about the factors that facilitate transition from one stage to the next. We consider these matters again in the next chapter.

6. Correlation Versus Compensation

Correlation, not compensation, is the rule in development. A popular stereotype contradicts this principle. It assumes that those who are gifted in one area must not be nearly as well endowed in others. The egghead, the stereotype informs us, is a blundering social idiot, unattractive and frail, weak sighted, and completely useless at any kind of task requiring even the smallest degree of dexterity. The same stereotype insists that the athlete may be stunningly attractive but is remarkably stupid, spells with difficulty, cannot write a check without a lawyer to correct it, reads only simple comic books, and laughs uproariously at unfunny events.

Not so. In fact, the person who excels in one realm is more likely to excel in others. The corollary is that people who are below average in one area tend to be below average in other areas as well—and this too is true. Although there are obvious exceptions to this principle, it nevertheless serves as a useful guide in understanding the overall development of children.

7. Rate of Development

Development usually proceeds at the rate at which it started. A child who learns to walk and talk at an early age is more likely to be advanced later than is a child who begins developing more slowly. Bloom (1964) surveyed a large number of studies that, taken as a whole, suggest that human characteristics are remarkably stable. In other words, there is relatively little change in the rate of development after the initial period of rapid development that characterizes most physical and intellectual qualities.

8. Sex Differences

There are systematic, predictable differences in the development of boys and girls. From birth until early adolescence, boys are both taller and heavier than girls. But by about age 11, girls' average weight surpasses that of boys, and by age $11^1/_2$, the average girl is taller than the average boy. At about age 14, boys catch up and surpass girls—and remain taller and heavier for the rest of their lives (on average).

Girls have a temporary height and weight advantage over boys in early adolescence because girls mature sexually (reach **puberty**) earlier than boys. On average, they undergo the dramatic growth spurt of early adolescence, one of the first of the changes of **pubescence** (changes that lead to sexual maturity), about two years earlier than boys. These changes are accompanied by important hormonal changes that are evident not only in physical developments but also in changing interests and awakening sexuality.

The average adolescent girl has her first menstrual period—usually taken as a signal of puberty (sexual maturity)—at about age 12; the average boy reaches puberty at about age 14. But individuals are not averages; they are unique. For some girls, the changes of pubescence can begin at as young an age as 7—or quite a bit later.

Evidence suggests that early or late maturation can be a disadvantage when it puts the adolescent dramatically out of step with peers, especially if the changes (or lack of change) are seen as undesirable (Petersen, 1988) (see the case on page 35). Not surprisingly, early maturation is generally more positive for boys than girls, perhaps because the precocious boy's greater social maturity is seen as something to be admired and because male sexuality is still more acceptable than female sexuality. By the same token, boys who mature significantly later than average are sometimes more restless, more attention seeking, less confident, and less well adjusted than early maturers (Crockett & Petersen, 1987).

In addition to predictable sex differences in average age of maturation, there are other gender differences in interests and abilities. However, unlike maturational timetables, which are largely genetically controlled, differences in interests and abilities—where they exist—are largely a function of different experiences and different expectations. These gender differences are discussed in Chapter 3.

When she was in fourth grade, Sandra often spent hours in front of her mirror trying on different bulky sweaters and loose-fitting shirts, trying to make herself look *normal*. That's all she wanted. Just to look normal.

But no! Only nine, and she already had to let out her breath to fasten her bra—which was, in fact, her mother's bra. But she refused to get her own, a bigger one, because it seemed to her that maybe if she could hold them in tight in her mother's little bra, they wouldn't be so noticeable. She was, after all, only in fourth grade, and it didn't seem right that she should already have such big ones, almost like an infirmity, when all her friends were still nice and flat.

9. Individual Differences

Individuals vary greatly. This has to do with the fact that we are profoundly influenced by our different environments and that, excepting identical twins, each of us inherits different genetic characteristics. But no matter how different and unique each of us is, we can still make valid generalizations about human behavior and development. But—and this is extremely important—these generalizations apply to children as a group and not to any specific individual child. There is no normal, average child; the average child is a myth invented by grandmothers and investigated by psychologists.

The preceding developmental principles constitute an overview and summary of some educationally relevant statements that can be made about developmental processes. Even though they do not suggest highly specific instructional implications, they can nevertheless provide teachers with general concepts that might be useful for understanding students better.

There is, of course, far more to human development than can be summarized in nine principles. From the teacher's point of view, cognitive (intellectual) development is absolutely central to the teaching/learning process; it is dealt with in Chapter 3. Two other important topics for teachers are language development and moral development. We turn to these next.

LANGUAGE DEVELOPMENT

Our ability to communicate through **language** is one of the things that clearly separates us from other beasts—and not simply because language makes it possible for us to communicate with one another at levels of abstraction that we suspect are beyond the imaginations and the capacities of

BIZARRO　　　　　　　　By DAN PIRARO

these other beasts. Language separates us from wild and domestic beasts in at least two other, related ways: It provides us with a means for storing our knowledge and wisdom, and it allows us to transform that knowledge. More than this, language is what makes possible the universality of meanings and the sharing of human experience. And because it is the chief medium of instruction in schools, its importance can hardly be overestimated.

Language and Communication

Language is not synonymous with **communication**. Animals communicate, but they do not have language. A dog who gets its master's attention, walks to its dish and barks, looks its master in the eyes, and then begins to growl is communicating effectively. Animals that are not domesticated also communicate. Pronghorn antelope convey alarm by bristling their rump patches, white-tailed deer by flagging their long tails. Pheasants threaten rivals by crowing, elk by bugling, and moose by grunting. Hebb (1966) describes this type of behavior as communication through reflexive activity. The behavior of the dog, however, is an example of purposive communication, but it is still not language.

To communicate is to transmit or convey a message; it requires a sender and a receiver. To communicate through language is to make use of arbitrary sounds, gestures, or symbols in a purposeful manner to convey meaning. Further, the use of language involves sounds or other signs that can be combined or transformed to produce different meanings. A parrot, for example, can mimic a word or even a phrase and can be taught to speak a phrase so that its utterance will appear purposive. A parrot that says "You bore me" after a guest has been talking incessantly for two hours may appear to be using language in a purposive manner. But the parrot is not using the phrase with the intention of communicating meaning and cannot deliberately transform the phrase to

change its meaning. That would be the use of language as opposed to reflexive communication.

The Early Development of Language

In the course of babbling, infants may emit most of the sounds used in all the world's languages. How these sounds become organized into meaningful patterns of language is still a matter of some speculation.

One account of early language learning is based on what we know about the effects of reinforcement on behavior (described in Chapter 4). This explanation maintains that while babbling, the infant emits wordlike sounds, which tend to be reinforced by adults. As the frequency of these specific sounds increases, parents or siblings may repeat the infant's vocalizations, thus serving as models. Eventually, through reinforcement children learn to imitate the speech patterns of those around them. Were it not for this imitation and reinforcement, frequency and variety of speech sounds would probably decrease. This is borne out by the observation that deaf children make sounds much like those made by hearing children until about the age of six months; after that they utter few sounds, and not many of these are repetitive (Eilers & Oller, 1988).

Note that even though reinforcement may be a relatively good explanation for the early learning of speech sounds (**phonology**) and simple meanings (**semantics**), it is not an adequate explanation for either the rapidity with which children learn language or for the acquisition of complex **syntax** (sentence formation rules), **grammar** (rules of word classes and functions), and **pragmatics** (implicit rules governing conversation— for example, who should speak and when, and the meanings of pauses, intonations, gestures, and so on). These—phonology, semantics, syntax, grammar, and pragmatics—are the elements of language.

Researchers who have looked at the origins of language have been particularly interested in infants' first sounds and gestures and the interactions of infants and their caretakers. It seems clear that the ability to use and understand words develops through a complex series of such interactions, which Bruner (1983) labels the "language acquisition support system" (LASS). Among other things, this system involves learning how to make eye contact, how to direct attention through eye movements, and how to emphasize and communicate meaning through facial and other bodily gestures. (See the box entitled "More on Language Acquisition.")

For convenience and simplicity, the learning of language can be divided into a series of stages. Wood (1981) describes six stages, summarized in Table 2.2.

Six Stages. The prespeech stage spans most of the first year of life. Significant speech-related developments during this period include the development and refinement of gestures and noises such as cooing, babbling, and crying, largely through infant-caretaker interaction.

The second stage involves the appearance of the **holophrase**, or sentencelike word. This usually occurs by the age of twelve months. Although at this stage the child's utterances consist of a single word at a time, the meanings of the words plus nonverbal cues are sufficiently detailed that an adult would require an entire sentence to say the same thing. For example, the holophrase "cat," uttered in an unmistakably imperious tone by my nephew Eskabar, means very clearly, "Fetch me my ball and some ice cream and other good things, or I will screech very loudly and I will bite Boris's tail off again!"[*]

Two-word sentences (the third stage), made up primarily of modifiers joined to nouns or pronouns, appear by the age of eighteen months. At this stage, speech is still highly telegraphic; that is, complex meanings are squeezed into simple, and sometimes grammatically incorrect, two-word utterances. For example, the sentence "Mummy gone" may mean something as complex as "My dear mother is currently on a business trip in Chicago."

The fourth stage, multiple-word sentences, is reached between ages 2 and 2½. Sentences may now be five or more words long. Although they continue to be telegraphic, they make use of more grammatical variations to express different meanings, and they typically consist of appropriate subjects and predicates.

Between ages 2½ and 4, children learn to use progressively more complex grammatical structures (the fifth stage), culminating in adultlike structures in the late preschool years.

Note that although ages are assigned to each of these stages, these are simply approximations based on the average performance of large groups. Here, as in all areas of human development, it is normal for some to display a behavior earlier and others later. An average is not an expression of normality in the sense that those who deviate from it are abnormal; it is simply a mathematical indication of a point around which observations are distributed.

More on Language Acquisition

The learning theory and the reinforcement model advanced to explain children's language learning are partly correct but also inadequate. The incredible rapidity with which children acquire syntax and grammar during their third and fourth years, coupled with the fact that they make only a fraction of the mistakes they would be expected to make if they were learning through reinforcement alone, makes it unlikely that this is the complete explanation. Furthermore, their mistakes often result not from lack of proper models or lack of reinforcement but rather from the application of rules they have learned or

[*]PPC: Perhaps the author should choose an example that would be less likely to offend his relatives.

Author: Good idea. That's why I've changed my nephew's name to Eskabar. Boris, the cat, doesn't read.

TABLE 2.2 Stages of Grammatical Development in Children

STAGE OF DEVELOPMENT	NATURE OF DEVELOPMENT	SAMPLE UTTERANCES
1. Prespeech (before age 1)	Crying, cooing, babbling	Waaah, Dadadada
2. Sentencelike word or holophrase (by 12 months)	The word is combined with nonverbal cues (gestures and inflections).	Mommy (meaning: "Would you please come here, Mother.")
3. Two-word sentences (by 18 months)	Modifiers are joined to topic words to form declarative, interrogative, negative, and imperative structures.	Pretty baby (declarative) Where Daddy? (question) No play. (negative) More milk! (imperative)
4. Multiple-word sentences (by 2 to 2½ years)	Sentence includes a subject and a predicate.	She's a pretty baby. (declarative)
	Grammatical morphemes are used to change meanings (-ing or -ed, for example).	Where Daddy is? (question) I no can play. (negative) I want more milk! (imperative) I running. I runned.
5. More complex grammatical changes and word categories (between 2½ and 4 years)	Elements are added, embedded, and permuted within sentences. Word classes (nouns, verbs, and prepositions) are subdivided. Clauses are put together.	Read it, my book. (conjunction) Where is Daddy? (embedding) I can't play. (permutation) I would like some milk. (use of *some* with mass noun) Take me to the store. (use of preposition of place)
6. Adultlike structures (after 4 years)	Complex structural distinctions are made, as with *ask-tell* and *promise*.	Ask what time it is. He promised to help her.

Source: Based in part on B. S. Wood, *Children and Communication: Verbal and Nonverbal Language Development* (2nd ed.), 1981, p. 142. Reprinted by permission of Prentice-Hall, Inc., Englewood Cliffs, New Jersey.

invented. The irony is that their application of the rules is often logical and predictable, but our language presents so many exceptions that we cannot apply grammatical rules universally. Thus, children who say "I eated," "I was borned," "I dood it," and "I runned fast" are demonstrating that they are fine grammarians, even if they have not completely mastered the language.

These observations have led to biological theories of language learning—for example, Chomsky's theory of language acquisition device (LAD: 1957, 1965) and Nelson's rare event learning mechanism (RELM: 1989). What these biological theories have in common is that they try to account for the infant's apparent predisposition to learn language by assuming that we are born with a special language-learning capacity—a sort of prewired ability to recognize sounds, to produce them, and to invent grammars.

But LAD and RELM are really not explanations at all; they are just metaphors. They say, "We behave *as if* we had built-in language-learning wiring." They do not demonstrate the machinery or how it works. As Rice (1989) observes, no one has a completely satisfactory explanation of language learning.

Language and Intelligence

The **correlation** between verbal ability and measured intelligence is high. This means that if one ability is highly developed, the other is also likely to be highly developed—and vice versa (see Chapter 7 for a more complete explanation of correlation). This may be partly because most measures of intelligence are verbal. They usually require that children at least understand verbal directions, and they also often require oral or written responses. In addition, many tests measure the extent and sophistication of vocabulary. On the one hand, the very nature of intelligence tests probably accounts for at least some of the high correspondence between language and intelligence. On the other hand, the fact that verbal ability is given such an important role in these tests is an indication of its importance in our definitions of *intelligence* (see Chapter 7).

THE ROLE OF LANGUAGES IN EDUCATION

In 1982, almost 75 percent of the school-age population in the United States was white; Hispanic children accounted for only 10 percent of school-age children. However, projections are that by the year 2020 the percentage of white school-age Americans will have decreased to about 50 percent. Approximately half the remainder—that is, one out of every four children—will be Hispanics. The rest will be African-Americans (about 16.5 percent of school-age children) and other races

(Pallas, Natriello, & McDill, 1989). These changing demographics are due partly to lower birthrates among white families (14.8 per 1,000 population in 1989) than among blacks (22.1 per 1,000 in 1989) and other races (22.0 per 1,000 in 1989) (U.S. Bureau of the Census, 1991). In addition, immigration rates are much higher for nonwhites.

These projections are tremendously important for American education because if they are accurate, they will in all likelihood be reflected in dramatic changes in the school. Whereas in 1982 the majority of American schoolchildren spoke English—the dominant, standard, majority language—by 2020 English may not be nearly so dominant. By the same token, Spanish and so-called nonstandard forms of English, such as Black English, will have become far more common. What are the implications of these changes?

Nonstandard Languages

The languages that most majority-group people understand, speak, and read are referred to as **standard languages**; they are viewed as correct, acceptable language forms against which other forms of the same language can be compared. And the often explicit assumption that we make is that language forms that are nonstandard are inferior to the standard language. The varieties of English spoken by many African-Americans, by Hispanic Americans, by French Canadians, and by native Americans and Canadians are cases in point. We generally assume that these forms of language are inferior and that they are responsible for the frequent schooling problems experienced by those less proficient in standard English. However, the most plausible explanation for the poorer performance of those who speak a nonstandard English may not be that their language is less complex, less sophisticated, and less grammatical but simply that it is different. Because instruction in schools typically occurs in standard English and because evidence of achievement requires understanding of and expression in standard English, these children are clearly at a disadvantage (Baratz, 1969).

What, if anything, can—or should—be done to enhance the child's sophistication in the use of standard language? The first part of the question is simple; the second isn't. Several things can be done. One obvious solution is to emphasize standard English both in the home and in the school. Those who favor this approach argue that most commerce, both outside and inside school, is carried out in standard English and that those children who do not learn standard forms of the dominant language therefore will be at the same disadvantage outside school as they are in school. Another solution is to allow African-American children to use their nonstandard dialects, at least part of the time, in schools (Seymour, 1971). This would require that teachers also develop some proficiency in the nonstandard language.

What should be done is another matter. Such issues cannot always be resolved through either research or reason alone.

Second-Language Programs

As we have noted, because of differential birth and immigration rates, the demographic characteristics of contemporary societies are changing rapidly. As a result, increasing numbers of students come to school with limited English language proficiency. As Brisk (1991) notes, this was traditionally viewed as a problem with students—a problem for which schools need not accept any special responsibility. In some instances, the problem would rectify itself with exposure to traditional schooling, but in many cases students would simply fail. More recently, however, numerous bilingual or English as a Second Language (ESL) programs have been established. The main purpose of these programs, says Brisk, has been to prepare students to fit into the traditional, English-only school curriculum.

Brisk (1991) argues strongly that as students become increasingly multilingual and multicultural, schools need to become more responsive to their needs. This does not mean preparing students to fit into a traditional English-only curriculum so much as developing a curriculum that truly integrates the diversity of students whose language and cultural backgrounds are different. What schools should focus on, say Collett and Serrano (1992), is becoming truly inclusive—that is, schools that are truly multicultural rather than schools that simply admit students from diverse backgrounds and then try to make them all the same. Serafini (1991) argues that recognizing and encouraging diversity in schools, and valuing competence in more languages than simply English, may do much to reduce racism.

But there is another side to the argument. In the United States, powerful, well-funded, and highly vocal groups of English-only advocates argue that English should be designated the official language—as it has now been in at least eighteen states (Padilla, 1991). Many members of these groups—English Only, English First, and U.S. English, to name three—are firmly opposed to the use of public resources for bilingual education.

Other groups, notably English Plus, advocate expanding bilingual programs both for adults and for children. There is considerable tension surrounding the debate, notes McGroarty (1992). In fact, in the United States, bilingual education is mandated by law following court decisions that found that putting all children in English-speaking classes, regardless of their language and cultural background, does not amount to treating all children equally. In Canada, the right to instruction in both official languages is guaranteed in some provinces but not others. Most notable, Quebec's Bill 101 tends to entrench the use of only French in all public sectors in the province of Quebec (Padilla, 1991).

Immersion Programs. Research suggests that one of the best ways to learn a second language is not to take occasional lessons, private instruction, expensive audio- or videotape courses, or concentrated study but to become immersed in the language. In essence, **language immersion** involves entering an environment in which only the language that is to be learned is spoken. And there is ample evidence to suggest that if this occurs early enough (soon after the first language is firmly established), children can painlessly learn a second language and perhaps even a third and a fourth.

French and Spanish language-immersion programs are a mushrooming phenomenon in North America. Most immersion programs begin in preschool settings and continue through the elementary grades. In a typical program, teachers and teacher assistants speak only the immersion language in the first year; that is, the second language is not taught as a separate subject but is simply the language through which the regular curriculum is taught. In the second year, English is introduced for perhaps 10 percent of the school day. The percentage increases each year, until by sixth grade half the school day is conducted in English and half in the second language.

Research indicates that immersion programs can be extremely effective in teaching a second language (for example, Genesee, 1983, 1985). Participants quickly reach high levels of proficiency in understanding and speaking the second language, as well as in reading and writing, although the majority do not reach as high a level of proficiency as native speakers. In addition, perhaps only a small number will ever become what Diaz (1983) calls "balanced bilinguals" (individuals who are equally proficient in both languages). However, as Genesee (1985) points out, the language deficiencies of immersion students do not appear to interfere with their functional use of the second language. In addition, these students typically perform as well as students in conventional English programs in academic subjects such as mathematics, science, and social studies, as well as on measures of social and cognitive development. If the immersion program is entirely in the second language and students have not yet received instruction in English language arts, they do not, of course, do as well on measures of English literacy. But Genesee (1985) reports that within one year of receiving English instruction, they perform as well as children in monolingual English programs. In fact, research summarized by Lindholm and Aclan (1991) indicates that bilingual proficiency relates positively to high academic achievement.

Other Bilingual Programs. Language-immersion programs teach a second language by immersing students in the language. However, many bilingual programs use other approaches. For example, Lam (1992) describes six distinct types of bilingual programs used in schools. These include programs designed primarily to establish English-language competency, programs intended to develop a high level of competency in a second language as well as in English, and various other programs for students with special needs.

Effects of Learning a Second Language

There has been a staggering amount of research on the effects of bilingualism, says Cziko (1992). But the conclusions are neither clear nor simple. One of the problems, as Lam (1992) notes, is that some programs are exemplary and others not, some teachers are more effective than others, and some students learn more easily.

There are circumstances under which learning a second language may not be an entirely positive experience. Lambert (1975) coined the expression "subtractive bilingualism" to describe the situation in which learning a second language has a negative influence on the first. "Additive bilingualism" describes the opposite situation.

Research indicates that the circumstances under which learning a second language is most likely to be a negative experience involve minority-group children whose first language is a minority language. In such instances, the second language—the dominant, majority language—is extensively reinforced in the mass media and in society, whereas the minority language is not. This may be the case, for example, for French-speaking children in Canada or Hispanics in the United States who learn English as a second language in school. Because television and other media (and perhaps most community transactions) use English, the first language receives little support and reinforcement outside the home—and perhaps not even in the home. As a result, the first language tends to be seen as less valuable and is used at a less advanced level (Landry, 1987). Moreover, speakers of the minority language in the home are often poor models of that language. Thus, the Spanish or the French spoken at home might be more colloquial—less developed in terms of vocabulary, liberally sprinkled with English expressions, grammatically incorrect, and characterized by idiosyncratic pronunciation (Carey, 1987). And if the minority language is not part of children's schooling, they are unlikely to learn to read and write it. Ultimately, their first-language proficiency may be largely oral.

Learning a second language most often has a positive effect on children when the language learned is a minority language. This would be the case, for example, for English-speaking American or Canadian children enrolled in Spanish or French immersion programs. Growing evidence suggests that such programs are successful in developing a high level of proficiency in the second language and that they contribute to general academic achievement (Bialystok, 1988). In addition, they frequently strengthen the first language (Cummins & Swain, 1986).

There are, of course, numerous exceptions to these simple generalizations; real life is rarely as simple as our interpretations of research might suggest. But given the probability that our conclusions are more often correct than incorrect, there may be merit in Cummins's (1986) recommendation that the primary language of instruction for minority-group children be the minority language—and that the majority language be presented as a second language. And if our demographic projections are accurate, these issues may be far more pressing by the year 2020.

MORAL DEVELOPMENT

Many decades ago Piaget (1932) questioned children to find out what they knew about rules and laws, right and wrong, good and evil. He found that very young children do not behave according to abstract concepts of right and wrong but respond instead in terms of the immediate personal consequences of their behavior. In effect, the morality of young children is governed by the principles of pain and pleasure. Children consider good those behaviors that have pleasant consequences (or at least do not have unpleasant consequences); bad behaviors are those that have unpleasant consequences.

Piaget's label for this initial stage of moral development is "heteronomy." During this stage the child responds primarily to outside authority, which is the main source of rewards and punishments. This initial stage is followed by the appearance of more autonomous moral judgments. During the stage of "autonomy," behavior is guided more and more by internalized principles and ideals.

Kohlberg's Stages

Some three decades after Piaget's pioneering studies, Kohlberg (1964) undertook systematic investigations of moral beliefs and behaviors. His principal approach was to describe situations in which a person is faced with having to make a choice where the choice poses a moral dilemma. Subjects are asked how they would behave under similar circumstances and the reasons for their choice. Analysis of responses led Kohlberg to a description of three sequential levels of moral orientation, each of which is divided into two stages (see Table 2.3). In principle, these stages are similar to Piaget's description of a progression from heteronomy (control by others) to autonomy (self-control). Each of the levels and stages is described briefly here.

Level I: Preconventional. At the earliest level, children respond primarily in terms of the immediate hedonistic consequences of their behaviors and in terms of the powers of those who have authority over them. Preconventional reasoning may take two forms, described by Kohlberg as stages 1 and 2.

Stage 1: Punishment and Obedience Orientation. Behavior is designed to avoid punishment. The child believes that obedience is good in and of itself. Evaluation of the morality of an action is totally divorced from its more objective consequences but instead rests solely on its consequences to the actor. Behavior for which one is punished is bad; that for which one is rewarded must necessarily be good.

Stage 2: Instrumental and Hedonistic Orientation. This is the beginning of reciprocity ("Do for me and I will do for you"). The reciprocity characteristic of this stage is strikingly practical. Children will do something good for others only if they expect it to result in someone's doing something good for them in return. Their moral orientation remains largely hedonistic (pain and pleasure oriented).

Level II: Conventional. Conventional morality is a morality of conformity: Behaviors that are good are those that maintain established social order. This level reflects the increasing importance of peers and of social relations and is expressed in two stages.

Stage 3: "Good-Boy, Nice-Girl" Morality. Children judge their actions largely in terms of their role

in establishing and maintaining good relations with authority and with peers. Approval is all-important and is assumed to be the result of "being nice."

Stage 4: Law and Order. Morality is characterized by blind obedience. What is legal is, by definition, good. And the good person is the one who is aware of rules and obeys them unquestioningly.

Level III: Postconventional. At the highest level of moral reasoning, the individual makes a deliberate effort to clarify moral rules and principles and to arrive at self-defined notions of good and evil.

Stage 5: Morality of Social Contract. This stage retains an element of conformity to laws and legal systems but with the important difference that legal systems are interpreted as being good to the extent that they guarantee and protect individual rights. The individual can now evaluate laws in terms of social order and individual justice and is capable of reinterpreting and changing them.

Stage 6: Universal Ethical. The final stage of moral development is characterized by individually chosen ethical principles that serve as major unifying guides to behavior. Individual moral principles are highly abstract rather than concrete. They are not illustrated in rules like the Ten Commandments but are implicit in deep-seated convictions that guide behavior—for example, beliefs in justice or equality.

Kohlberg's Model Evaluated

Kohlberg's early research (1971) suggested that a child's progression through these stages is sequential and universal; that is, all children were assumed to progress through all stages in the same sequence. This did not mean, however, that all individuals eventually reached the sixth stage (self-determined principles) and that adults operated only on that level. In fact, a reanalysis of Kohlberg's original data using more careful

TABLE 2.3 Kohlberg's Levels of Morality

Kohlberg identified levels of moral judgment in children by describing to them situations involving a moral dilemma. One example is the story of Heinz, a man whose wife is dying but might be saved if given a drug discovered by a local pharmacist, who charges such an exorbitant price that Heinz can't pay. Should he steal the drug?

LEVEL 1: PRECONVENTIONAL	Stage 1: Punishment and obedience orientation	"If he steals the drug, he might go to jail." (Punishment.)
	Stage 2: Naïve instrumental hedonism	"He can steal the drug and save his wife, and he'll be with her when he gets out of jail." (Act motivated by its hedonistic consequences for the actor.)
LEVEL II: CONVENTIONAL	Stage 3: "Good-boy, nice-girl" morality	"People will understand if you steal the drug to save your wife, and they'll think you're cruel and a coward if you don't." (Reactions of others and the effects of the act on social relationships become important.)
	Stage 4: Law-and-order orientation	"It is the husband's duty to save his wife even if he feels guilty afterward for stealing the drug." (Institutions, law, duty, honor, and guilt motivate behavior.)
LEVEL III: POSTCONVENTIONAL	Stage 5: Morality of social contract	"The husband has a right to the drug even if he can't pay now. If the druggist won't charge it, the government should look after it." (Democratic laws guarantee individual rights; contracts are mutually beneficial.)
	Stage 6: Universal ethical*	"Although it is legally wrong to steal, the husband would be morally wrong not to steal to save his wife. A life is more precious than financial gain." (Conscience is individual. Laws are socially useful but not sacrosanct.)

Source: Based on L. Kohlberg (1971, 1980).

*Stage 6 is no longer included among Kohlberg's stages because none of his sample reached it. However, it is still described as a potential stage.

criteria found that only one-eighth of subjects (in their twenties) seemed capable of fifth-stage judgments. The same analysis found no evidence whatsoever of sixth-stage judgments (Colby & Kohlberg, 1984; Lapsley, 1990). Subsequently, Kohlberg has dropped the sixth stage from his description of moral development.

There have been criticisms of Kohlberg's stages. For example, Holstein (1976) found that many subjects skipped stages, reverted apparently randomly to earlier stages, or otherwise responded in ways that provided little evidence of stages. In addition, Holstein's female subjects often expressed moral judgments that appeared to be systematically different from those of male subjects. Furthermore, there is often such a lack of consistency among responses given by the same subject for different moral dilemmas that subjects cannot always be described as operating at one level rather than another (Fishkin, Keniston, & MacKinnon, 1973).

What this evidence suggests is that moral judgments depend not only on the ages of subjects but also on a host of other variables, including the intentions of the transgressor, previous experiences in similar situations, and the social, material, or personal consequences of the behavior (Eisenberg-Berg, 1979; Suls & Kalle, 1979).

Apart from the observation that progression through stages of moral development might not be as predictable and as systematic as Kohlberg suggested, Gilligan (1982) suggests that this research has at least two other important weaknesses. One is that Kohlberg's subjects were all males—and, as noted earlier, there is evidence of some sex differences in morality; the other is that the moral dilemmas that Kohlberg used may not always be immediately meaningful in the lives of children. It may be that our responses to hypothetical moral dilemmas ("What would you do if you were at war and you had the opportunity to shoot an enemy soldier who hasn't seen you and is unlikely to?") will be quite different from our actual behaviors, if we ever must in fact make a choice. It might also be that the dilemmas Kohlberg described are too complex for young children—and perhaps even for adolescents and adults. They require that a great deal of information be kept in mind, and they demand an analysis of complex situations involving a number of actors and circumstances. In fact, when moral dilemmas are made simpler, or when children and adolescents are observed in their normal, daily activities, investigators sometimes find evidence of

surprisingly sophisticated moral reasoning even at young ages (Darley & Shultz, 1990).

In an attempt to examine morality in women by means of meaningful moral dilemmas, Gilligan interviewed a sample of pregnant women struggling with a decision about abortion. All twenty-nine women in the sample had been referred by a counseling clinic for pregnant women. Twenty-one of these women subsequently had an abortion, four had their babies, one miscarried, and three remained undecided throughout the duration of the study. The study found that it is not so much the decision itself (to have or not to have the baby) that reflects the person's level of moral development as the person's reasons for the decision.

Gilligan identified three stages in the women's moral development. In the first stage, the woman is moved by selfish concerns ("This is what I need . . . what I want . . . what is important for my physical/psychological survival"). In the second stage, there is a transition from selfishness to greater responsibility toward others. This change is reflected in reasoning that is based not on simple, selfish survival but on a more objective morality (notions of what is right and wrong; specifically, a growing realization that caring for others rather than just for self is a form of "goodness"). The third stage reflects what Gilligan labels a "morality of nonviolence" toward self and others. This level of morality is reflected in the fact that the woman will now accept sole responsibility for her decision and that she bases this decision on the greatest good to self and others. The best moral decision at this level is the one that does the least harm to the greatest number of those for whom the woman is responsible.

In summary, Gilligan describes adult female moral development in terms of three stages, beginning with a selfish orientation, progressing through a period of increasing recognition of responsibility to others, and culminating at a level at which moral decisions reflect a desire to treat the self and others equally—that is, to do the greatest good (or the least harm) for the greatest number. At each of these three levels, what women respond to most when initially considering their moral dilemmas are the emotional and social implications of their decision for the self and subsequently the implications for others as well as for self. In contrast with Kohlberg's description of a male moral progression that moves from initial hedonistic selfishness toward a greater recognition of social and legal rights, Gilligan describes a female progression from selfishness toward greater recognition of responsibility to self and others.

Put another way, one of the important differences between male and female morality (as described by Kohlberg and Gilligan) is that moral progression in males tends toward the recognition and use of "universal ethical principles"; in contrast, women respond more to considerations of fairness and equality for self and others.

Additional corroboration of these sex differences is implicit in a number of studies that have found that girls frequently reach Kohlberg's third stage, morality of good relations, earlier than boys and remain at that level long after boys have gone on to the fourth stage, morality of law and order (see, for example, Turiel, 1974; Gilligan, Kohlberg, Lerner, & Belenky, 1971). One plausible explanation for this observation is that girls are more responsive to social relationships, more concerned with empathy and compassion, and more in touch with real life and less concerned with the hypothetical (Holstein, 1976). In contrast, boys are more concerned with law and order, social justice, and the abstract as opposed to the personally meaningful dimensions of morality.

Educational Implications of Moral Development

Knowledge of the progression of moral development can be of value to the teacher in several ways. First, knowing how and why children judge

things to be morally right or wrong relates directly to the types of rationalizations a teacher might offer children in exhorting them to "behave" and/or not to "misbehave." There is evidence, for example, that rationalizations that stress the object—"The toy might break"—are more effective for younger children than rationalizations that are more abstract—"You should not play with toys that belong to other children" (see Chapter 11). By extrapolation, the types of rationalizations that might be offered to adolescents would be quite different from those offered younger children. Also, the most meaningful rationalizations for girls might stress social relationships, empathy, and responsibility; the most meaningful rationalizations for boys might stress legal rights and social order.

A second application of knowledge of moral development is the actual teaching of morality. Unfortunately, little research has been devoted to the question of whether moral development can be promoted or accelerated in children. This is partly because early studies found little correspondence between actual behavior and moral and religious training (Hartshorne & May, 1928, for example). Specifically, these investigators found that immoral behaviors such as cheating were much less affected by religious training, apparent strength of conscience, and other abstract signs of "moral goodness" than by the probability of being caught. Given these widely accepted and highly pessimistic findings, it is not surprising that schools have traditionally paid little attention to the deliberate inculcation of virtues. However, Fodor (1972) has found that children identified as delinquents operate at a much lower level on the Kohlberg scales than nondelinquent children. And Kohlberg and Candee (1984) found that children at the higher stages of moral reasoning are more likely to be honest and to behave "morally." In other words, there does appear to be some correspondence between level of moral orientation and actual behavior. If this is the case, anything that the schools can do to promote progression through these stages might contribute directly to classroom control and indirectly to the development of better individuals.

What, precisely, can be done? Unfortunately, suggestions remain rather abstract (perhaps the next edition will be more concrete). Kohlberg (1964), for example, suggests that even though the content of moral rules can be taught, the attitudes necessary for behavior at each level result from a complete process of cognitive development and cannot themselves be taught. In addition, as Peters (1977) points out, Kohlberg's theory deals with the cognitive aspects of moral development, but it does not consider the affective components of morality. Hence, the theory itself does little to clarify the types of feelings that ought to be fostered if children are to develop morally.

Peters and other researchers have attempted to clarify this matter.

Peters (1977) argues that caring for others is perhaps the most important attitude involved in progressing from primitive levels of morality to self-determined principles. Similarly, McPhail, Ungoed-Thomas, and Chapman (1972) have developed a teaching program for adolescents designed to foster empathy and concern. Sullivan (1977) argues that the dimension of "care" often appears to be lost in contemporary society. He argues as well that the type of moral training most often characteristic of established, orthodox religions appears to serve as a motivator for attaining higher levels of moral reasoning (Sullivan & Quarter, 1972; Sullivan, 1977). Oser (1986) presents a strong argument for the use of a discursive approach whereby issues of morality and values are discussed, examined, and challenged and in which attempts are made to resolve moral conflicts.

In general, then, the implication of these findings and speculations is that teachers ought to attempt to develop in children care and concern for others and to encourage and reward behaviors that reflect virtues ordinarily associated with caring.

More concrete, Hoffman (1976) suggests four different kinds of experiences that can foster altruistic and caring behavior in children, some of which may suggest worthwhile classroom activities:

1. Situations in which children are allowed to experience unpleasantness rather than being overprotected

2. Role-playing experiences in which children are responsible for the care of others

3. Role-playing experiences in which children imagine themselves in the plight of others

4. Exposure to altruistic models

Teachers, says Giroux (1992), have played three different types of roles in the moral development of their students. The teacher as master is an advocate of good behavior and strong consciences. This role emphasizes teaching values and principles. The teacher as facilitator tries to help students develop and understand their own values, sometimes using discussion or other approaches such as value clarification programs. This role views the student rather than the teacher as the source of values. And the teacher as mentor is a guide and a friend, an enlightened leader, a source of vision and wisdom. The teacher as mentor is an example rather than a tutor.

Each role underlines the importance of the teacher's personal morality.

MAIN POINTS

1. Developmental psychology looks at characteristics at different ages, at predictable differences among age and sex groups, and at the processes that account for change between conception and death. Development can be viewed as comprising all changes attributable to maturation

(natural unfolding), growth (physical changes), and learning (the effects of experience).

2. A cohort is a group of individuals who were born during the same time period and who therefore are subject to the same historical influences.

3. Development results from the interaction of heredity and environment.

4. Development takes place at different rates for different features of the organism. For example, the brain seems to grow in spurts, with a major spurt occurring just before and just after birth (considered a critical period during which malnutrition can have serious consequences).

5. Environmental changes are most effective during the period of fastest growth and least effective during slowest growth. In practice, this principle favors early intervention, particularly with respect to such things as language development.

6. Development follows an orderly sequence, although the age at which various events occur can vary considerably from one child to another.

7. Development may be described in terms of arbitrary stages. Stages are useful inventions for organizing our observations about children.

8. Correlation, not compensation, is the rule in development.

9. Development usually proceeds at approximately the rate at which it started.

10. There are systematic, predictable differences in the development of boys and girls.

11. In spite of the generality of our developmental principles, individuals vary considerably.

12. The ability to use language for purposive communication is one of the things that most clearly separates us from other animals. The elements of language are phonology (speech sounds), semantics (meanings of sounds), syntax (sentence formation rules), grammar (word classes and functions), and pragmatics (implicit rules governing conversation).

13. The early development of language is facilitated by a complex network of caretaker-infant interaction, which includes learning how to make eye contact, how to direct attention through eye and body movements, the meanings of expressions and gestures, and so on.

14. Wood's six stages of language development are prespeech (before age 1, cooing and babbling), sentencelike word, or holophrase (by age 1), two-word sentence (by 18 months), multiple-word sentences containing subject and predicate (ages 2 to $2^1/_2$), more complex sentences and grammatical changes (by age 4), and adultlike structures (age 4 onward).

15. Nonstandard languages (different dialects of the dominant language, such as Black English) may place children at a disadvantage because school success typically requires a high level of proficiency in the dominant language.

16. Language-immersion programs appear to be among the most effective means of learning a second language. Evidence suggests that most immersion students develop a high degree of proficiency (although not perfection) in the second language and perform equally well in other subjects, including measures of literacy in the dominant language once it has been introduced and studied.

17. Bilingual school programs, mandated by law in many jurisdictions, are nevertheless a controversial and highly researched phenomenon. Some evidence suggests that learning a second language sometimes has a negative effect on knowledge of the first language (subtractive bilingualism), especially for minority-group children who learn the dominant, majority language as a second language. For native speakers of the dominant language, learning a second language is most often an additive experience that results in a relatively high level of proficiency in both languages.

18. Moral development in boys seems to proceed from a preconventional level (hedonistic and obe-

dience oriented) to a conventional level (conformity; desire to maintain good relationships). The postconventional level (individual principles of conduct) is seldom, if ever, reached by anyone. Moral development in girls may be tied more to social responsibility, empathy, and social relationships than to law and social order.

19. Knowledge of moral development might help teachers select the most effective rationalizations for different children. Also, it might be possible to foster moral growth through systematic educational programs.

SUGGESTED READINGS

For elaboration on and greater clarification of the developmental principles outlined in this chapter, you might consult the following textbooks:

LEFRANÇOIS, G. R. (1992). *Of children: An introduction to child development* (7th ed.). Belmont, Calif.: Wadsworth.

————. (1993). *The lifespan* (4th ed.). Belmont, Calif.: Wadsworth.

Language development is described in considerably more detail in

WOOD, B. S. (1981). *Children and communication: Verbal and nonverbal language development* (2nd ed.). Englewood Cliffs, N.J.: Prentice-Hall.

An excellent, current collection of chapters examining issues surrounding bilingual education is

PADILLA, A. M., FAIRCHILD, H. H., & VALADEZ, C. (Eds.). (1990). *Bilingual education: Issues and strategies.* Beverly Hills, Calif.: Sage.

The following is an excellent introduction to Kohlberg's theory:

KUHMERKER, L. (Ed.). (1991). *The Kohlberg legacy for the helping professions.* Birmingham, Ala.: Religious Education Press.

Folklore has it that many years ago in Switzerland, bears were worshipped because the faithful believed that they were descended—not from Adam and Eve—but from the bear (Engel, 1976).

*The parent who could see his boy as he really is would
shake his head and say: "Willie is no good: I'll sell
him."*
Stephen Leacock, *The Lot of the Schoolmaster*

*Youth will be served, every dog has his day, and mine
has been a fine one.*
George Borrow, *Lavengro*

Chapter 3 | EXPLANATIONS OF COGNITIVE DEVELOPMENT

Of the theories that have attempted to explain human development, those that look at the growth of mind are among the most important for teachers. This chapter describes these theories (specifically, those of Piaget and Vygotsky) and considers their educational implications. It looks as well at the development and significance of gender roles. And it gives us our first glimpse of **wild cows**.

Excerpt from Bear Tales (Book II): Valley of the Wild Cows

Imelda, the largest of the wild cows, had been the group's leader for almost as long as she could remember. It wasn't just that she was bigger, she reasoned; it was because she was a dang sight smarter, and besides, she was a born leader. No doubt.

Hadn't she been the first to use hair spray? She still fondly remembered the day. She had sprayed it on thick, and then she had shuffled her way out of the valley, and the force of the prairie wind just barely ruffled her coat. Hot damn! She had been proud.

And she'd been the only one of the bunch that had ever gotten hold of a truck, actually squished herself in behind the wheel, and tromped on the accelerator—double hot damn!!—spewing out a cloud of dust as she snaked across the prairie, until just by what seemed bad luck, the creek had come up smack in front of her, and she had drowned the truck forever, which Farmer Bob could no way ever figure out to this very day. But what did he know about wild cows anyway?

And wasn't that the very same muggy, take-your-clothes-off kind of day she'd figured out how it was a pretty hootin'-fine thing to do to go swimming? And everybody'd been swimming since then.

No doubt, Imelda was a leader. Absolutely no doubt. And there wasn't any way, you could bet all last summer's timothy grass on it, that she'd let the upstart Thomas show the bunch the way out of here, up toward the forest where she'd suggested they might want to spend the winter.

"What's his bloody qualifications?" she asked, getting right to the point in her characteristically blunt way. "Hey? What's his bedaggled qualifications?"

Some of the cows shuffled nervously in front of her, not wanting to look her in the eye, apparently

ashamed that they might have actually considered *following another leader. Others just chewed cud and looked bored, which Imelda knew didn't mean anything; that's just the way wild cows look a lot of the time, which is a very useful deception.*

But one, the admittedly sleazy Ramona, stared balefully at Imelda. "He's a guy wild cow," said she belligerently, looking at the others for signs of support. "They're supposed to be natural leaders."

"Bull!!" retorted Imelda. And she hauled off and kicked Ramona right in the gut.[*]

---

[*]PPC: Maybe this introduction goes too far. After all, educational psychology is a serious subject. Besides, I've never heard of wild cows.

Author: Dear reader: Your professor is not likely to ask you any questions about this chapter introduction. Those of you who are unrelentingly serious and determined should go immediately to the next section (Gender Roles).

Dear PPC: Wild cows are a real threat, so environmentally unfriendly are they. (If you don't believe this, see the introduction to chapters 4 and 5 . . . and others.)

GENDER ROLES

Gender roles are not all *bull*—although it may be that Imelda was right, that guy wild cows are not just *naturally* better leaders.

Gender roles are an important part of our lives. A **gender role** (also called a "sex role") is a learned pattern of behavior based on gender. Thus, there are masculine roles and feminine roles. These roles are defined in terms of the behaviors, personality characteristics, and attitudes that cultures find appropriate for each sex. The learning of behaviors according to one's gender is called **sex typing**.

That gender roles are largely learned becomes evident when we observe other cultures in which males and females sometimes behave (and think and feel) in ways quite different from males and females in our society. For example, in her investigations of three New Guinea tribes, Margaret Mead (1935) found a tribe, the Mundugumor, in which both men and women were ruthless, aggressive, and in other ways highly "masculine" (by our definition). In a second tribe, the Arapesh, both sexes were warm, emotional, noncompetitive, and unaggressive—in other words, both men and women were highly "feminine." And a third tribe, the Tchambuli, illustrated what Mead described as a "genuine reversal of the sex attitudes of our own culture" (p. 190).

The Nature of Male and Female Roles

When young children in our culture are asked which personality characteristics are masculine and which are feminine, they typically have no problem in creating similar lists of characteristics for each gender. Not only do they agree as to what boys and girls should be like, but they often agree that masculine traits are more desirable, as is shown dramatically in the "sex-change" study conducted by Tavris and Baumgartner (1983).

The study is simple and straightforward. Boys and girls were asked, "If you woke up tomorrow and discovered that you were a girl (boy), how would your life be different?" "Terrible," the boys answered. "That would be a catastrophe." "A disaster." "I would immediately commit suicide." "I would be very depressed." But the girls responded very differently. "Great," they said. "Now I can do what I want." "Now I can play sports." "Now I can be happy."

When, half a decade later, Intons-Peterson (1988) replicated this study using the same sex-change question, she reported no major changes and no surprises. Boys still responded negatively to the thought of becoming female. They saw girls as more passive, weaker, more restricted in their activities, more emotional, and burdened by menstruation. And although most females were content with their gender, the majority nevertheless responded to the sex-change question by describing what they saw as the highly positive aspects of being male. They viewed males as more active, less concerned with appearance, more aggressive, more athletic, and better able to travel and develop a career.

Parents, too, agree on proper behavior for boys and girls. In general, they feel that boys should be more aggressive, more boisterous, more adventurous, and less emotional and that girls should be more passive, more tender, more emotional, and less boisterous (Holland, Magoon, & Spokane, 1981).

In recent decades, there has been a strong reaction against the basic inequities of these roles and the stereotypes they foster, as well as against the injustices of traditionally male-dominated societies—societies that continue to favor males in spite of some notable progress toward sexual equality in recent years. For example, although the number of women working outside the home has increased dramatically—in the United States, 75 percent of all women aged 18 to 44 in 1989, compared with 13 percent in 1960 (U.S. Bureau of the Census, 1991)—jobs held by women are still not on a par with jobs held by men in terms of status, prestige, or income. In Canada, the average income for women is approximately 65 percent that of men (Statistics Canada, 1992); in the United States, it's about 63 percent (U.S. Bureau of the Census, 1991). And in 1990, women with four years of college could expect to earn only about $900 more per year than men who had not attended college—and less than two-thirds the wages of men who had attended college. (See Figure 3.1.)

Determinants of Gender Roles

Lynn (1974) suggests that three important factors are involved in determining sex roles: genetic (or biological), family-based, and cultural factors.

Genetic contributions to sex typing are evident in innate tendencies for the sexes to act, think, or feel differently. And although considerable evidence (including cross-cultural comparisons such as Mead's investigation of the three New Guinea tribes) suggests that many of the most obvious components of gender roles appear to be environmentally determined, there is

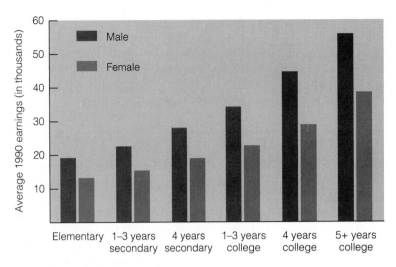

FIGURE 3.1 U.S. male and female earnings by educational attainment in 1988. Based on U.S. Bureau of the Census, 1992, p. 454.

nevertheless some compelling evidence that suggests that certain aspects of male-female differences have a biological basis. This is most notably true of **aggression**, for example, for which four separate lines of evidence support the notion of a genetic influence. First, greater aggressiveness is often found in males at a very young age, before environmental influences would be expected to have had a significant impact. Second, greater male aggressiveness is common among most cultures, Mead's testimony notwithstanding.[*] Third, most species of nonhuman primates (baboons, apes, chimpanzees) exhibit more aggressiveness among males than females. And fourth, injections of male hormones, particularly testosterone, can significantly increase manifestations of aggression; in fact, injections of testosterone in pregnant mothers have been shown to increase the subsequent aggressiveness of their female infants (Money & Erhardt, 1972).

However, in spite of the probable genetic contributions to greater aggressiveness in males, family and other cultural influences are also of significance. Considerable evidence suggests, for example, that parents treat manifestations of

aggression differently in their male and female children, encouraging it in the former and discouraging it in the latter (Russell & Ward, 1982). Similarly, teachers expect more aggressiveness in boys and are more likely to tolerate and even encourage it. In much the same way, we expect more emotionality from girls and consequently tolerate and encourage it in ways that we would find less appropriate for boys.

The Reality of Gender Differences

We have noted that parents, children, and society in general assume that there are differences in male and female roles. Most can describe the nature of these differences with little difficulty. But just because our naïve psychologies agree does not mean that they are always correct.

[*]In this connection, it is perhaps worth noting that following several years of interviewing many of the tribes that Mead studied, and following a painstaking analysis of her writings, Freeman (1983) suggests that much of her data is worthless—that she was so anxious to demonstrate the truth of her belief in the power of environments that she often overlooked evidence contrary to her beliefs and perhaps exaggerated evidence that she found more agreeable.

Following an early review of research on gender differences, Maccoby and Jacklin (1974) suggested four areas in which there are gender differences: (1) verbal ability, particularly in the early grades, favoring females; (2) mathematical ability, favoring males; (3) spatial-visual ability (evident in geographic orientation, for example), favoring males; and (4) aggression (lower among females).

But these differences no longer seem as clear in the 1990s as they did in 1974. In fact, sex differences among adolescents have declined dramatically in recent decades. There is mounting evidence that when early experiences are similar, many of these male-female differences are nonexistent (Tobias, 1982). Furthermore, even when differences are found, they tend to be modest and far from completely general (Deaux, 1985). Shepherd-Look (1982) reports that research now finds only trivial male-female differences in verbal performance, except among underprivileged populations. And Jacklin (1989) points out that differences in mathematics achievement are more closely related to students' anxiety about math, parents' stereotyped views of expected male-female performance, and the perceived value of the subject than to gender. In fact, a number of studies done in Hawaii report results that are directly opposed to those most often reported in North America. In those studies, girls typically perform better than boys on standardized mathematics tests (Brandon, Newton, & Hammond, 1987).

Still, contemporary research continues to find that on average males score higher than females on tests of general knowledge and mechanical reasoning; females score higher than males on tests of language usage (grammar and spelling). Significantly, there are no differences in measures of verbal ability, arithmetic, abstract reasoning, or memory span (Feingold, 1992). But, on the whole, males are more variable than females on most tests. That is, more are at the highest and at the lowest levels.

Implications of Gender Roles for Teachers

Teachers do, however, need to take some differences between the sexes into consideration. That some of these differences are not inevitable and that many are unjust might, in the final analysis, be quite irrelevant to the immediate business of being a teacher. Although teachers need to treat all children equally and fairly, this does not mean that all children need to be treated in exactly the same manner. If girls are less interested than boys in violent contact sports, it might be more than a little foolish to insist that they don shoulder pads and participate in the school's football games. And if their interest in the opposite sex manifests itself earlier, and if it sometimes expresses itself in different ways, that too needs to be taken into consideration. At the same time, however, there is a sometimes desperate need for teachers to be aware of and to eliminate the many flagrant and subtle instances of sex bias that still permeate our attitudes, our books, our schools, and our society.

See the case set in Ms. Fenna's fifth-grade class for snippets of gender inequities that persist in some of today's schools. These inequities are found in three areas, note Sadker, Sadker, and Klein (1991):

1. There is still sexism in school administration. At Wes Horman, the principal and vice principal are both male; the majority of teachers are female. In the United States in 1988, fewer than one-third of elementary school principals and 11 percent of high school principals were women (and about 4 percent of superintendents (Jones & Montenegro, 1988). Yet most teachers are female. And in recent years, female graduate students in education have outnumbered male graduate students (National Center for Education Statistics, 1989).

2. There is inequity in the treatment of students. Note that when Tom and Teddy called out, Ms. Fenna responded to them directly. But when Rosa echoed Tom, Ms. Fenna reprimanded her: "In this classroom we raise our hands," said she.

THE TIME: Early morning at Wes Horman School

THE PLACE: Ms. Fenna's fifth-grade class

Morning messages are just ending on the intercom. "And," says Mr. Sawchuk, school principal, "for noon detention in Mr. Busenius's office, the list is Ronald West, Frank Twolips, Eddie Mio, and Eddie Nyberg . . . and I hope there won't be any more by noon."

Ms. Fenna: "You heard that, Ronald?"

Ronald nods.

"Also," continues Mr. Sawchuk, "grade sixers who aren't going on the field trip: the boys will spend the day in Mr. Busenius's phys ed classes, and the girls will go to the art room . . . That's all."

Ms. Fenna: Now, class, I want you to open your math workbooks to page thirty-four, which we started yesterday, and finish the assignment on that page before we go on.

Tom Larsen: I finished mine. What can I do now?

Ms. Fenna: I'll come check it in a minute.

Rosa Donner: Me too.

Ms. Fenna: In this class, we raise our hand, Rosa.

Teddy Langevin: Can we read our *Tom Sawyers* if we're finished?

Ms. Fenna: How many are finished with page thirty-four?

Unusual? No. At virtually all educational levels, teachers interact more with male than with female students (Sadker & Sadker, 1986). On average, boys receive more instructional time and more attention from their teachers. They also receive more praise and more encouragement. And, like the detainees at Wes Horman School, they are also more often the subject of reprimands and punishment.

3. Sexual stereotypes are still found in books, in the curriculum, in classroom examples, and elsewhere. At Wes Horman school, boys who need looking after because they did not go on a field trip are sent to gym classes; girls are sent to the art room. And for those who have finished their arithmetic, the reading assignment is *Tom Sawyer*. Although "male hero" books are no longer as pervasive in schools as they once were, males are often portrayed as more dominant, girls as more helpless (Sadker, Sadker, & Klein, 1991).

It isn't sufficient simply to know that schools reflect much of the racism, the sexism, and other prejudices of society. Teachers (and principals)

need to be on guard constantly, lest they unconsciously propagate the same old stereotypes and the same inequities.

COGNITIVE DEVELOPMENT

Cognition, says my dictionary, is "the art or faculty of knowing." Hence, cognitive theorists are concerned with how we obtain, process, and use information. And *cognitive development* refers to the stages and processes involved in the child's intellectual development.

The remainder of this chapter looks at cognitive development. It pays particular attention to Jean Piaget's theory, which is the most influential child-development theory of this century. Piaget's approach looks at how the child's interaction with the environment leads to the development of cognitive abilities and cognitive structure. The chapter also looks at Vygotsky's theory, which is concerned more with how culture and language affect development.

BASIC PIAGETIAN IDEAS

Piaget's early training was in biology, not psychology. Accordingly, he approached the study of children as would a biologist, asking the two fundamental questions of the evolutionary biologist:

1. Which characteristics of the organisms under study enabled them to adapt to their environments?

2. What is the simplest, most accurate, and most useful way to classify living organisms?

Translated to a study of children, these questions become:

1. What are the characteristics of children that enable them to adapt to their environment?

2. What is the simplest, most accurate, and most useful way to classify or order child development?

Piaget's answers to these questions form the basis of his theory. They are now found in more than thirty books and several hundred articles.* Many of these answers result from the application of a special technique for studying children developed by Piaget: the **méthode clinique**. This is an interview approach in which the experimenter has a relatively clear idea of the questions to ask and of how to phrase them. However, using this approach, the investigator occasionally allows the child's answers to determine the next series of questions. Hence, the technique provides for the possibility that the child will give unexpected answers and that further questioning will lead to new discoveries about thinking.

Piaget's answers to the two questions of biology (briefly, what permits adaptation, and how can development be classified?) are complex and detailed but can be simplified—as they are here:

*Throughout a large part of his long career (he was active and prolific until his death in 1980, at the age of eighty-four), Piaget's closest associate and collaborator was Barbel Inhelder, who coauthored a large number of their publications and was sole author of many other books and articles.

Assimilation and Accommodation Permit Adaptation

The newborn child is a remarkable little sensing machine. Almost from birth, it can detect sounds, odors, sights, tastes, and touches; it can respond by squirming and wriggling, by crying, by flinging its limbs about and grasping things, and by sucking.

Characteristics of the Newborn. But can it think? Does it have a store of little ideas? of budding concepts? We can't answer these questions easily; the **neonate** (newborn) doesn't communicate well enough to tell us. But Piaget tells us that the child probably does not have ideas or concepts—does not think—in the sense that we ordinarily define these terms. The newborn does not have a store of memories or hopes or dreams—does not have a fund of information about which, and with which, to think.

But what this little sensing machine does have are the characteristics necessary for acquiring information. Flavell (1985) describes these characteristics somewhat like this: First, in order for the human system to acquire as much information as quickly as it does, it must be naturally predisposed to process an extraordinary amount of information, even when there is no tangible reinforcement (such as food) for doing so; that is, the system must be mainly intrinsically (internally) motivated—it must derive satisfaction from its own functioning and from its gradual acquisition of information.

Second, the human information-processing system must be preset to focus on the most informative—and therefore the most cognitively useful—aspects of the environment. Accordingly, the system must respond most strongly to novelty, surprise, and incongruity. It should search out the unexpected, for it is in the unexpected that the greatest amount of new information can be found. Similarly, it should be pretuned to attend to speech sounds and to make the hundreds of subtle distinctions that are so important in learning a language.

The human newborn that Jean Piaget describes is exactly such a system. It continually seeks out and responds to stimulation, and by so doing it gradually builds up a repertoire of behaviors and capabilities. The system is initially limited to a number of simple reflexive behaviors, such as sucking and grasping. Rapidly, however, these behaviors become more complex, more coordinated, and eventually purposeful. The process by which this occurs is **adaptation**. And, to answer the first question posed just before this section began, adaptation is made possible through the twin processes of **assimilation** and **accommodation**.

Assimilation and Accommodation. In Piaget's system, assimilation involves making a response that has already been acquired; accommodation is the modification of a response. Or, to put it another way, to assimilate is to respond in terms of preexisting information; it often involves ignoring some aspects of the situation in order to make it conform to aspects of the child's mental system. In contrast, to accommodate is to respond to external characteristics; as a result, it involves making changes in the child's mental system.

Imagine, if you will, an infant lying idly in her crib, not doing anything in particular. Now she waves her little hands seemingly haphazardly in the air, and one of them comes in contact with a pacifier that is fastened to her shirt by means of a safety pin and a length of purple ribbon. Her hand closes immediately around the familiar object, raises it into the air, and brings it unerringly to her mouth, which has already opened in anticipation and which closes greedily around the rubber end of the pacifier. Suck! Suck! Suck!

According to Piaget, there are **schemata** (singular: *schema*) involved here—mental representations of the infant's knowledge of pacifiers, including information concerning their suitability as objects to be grasped, to be transported toward the mouth, and to be sucked. The pacifier is being assimilated to these schemata; it is being understood and dealt with in terms of previous learning.

Imagine, now, that a generous grandmother replaces the infant's familiar old pacifier with a brand new one—one of those with the patented Easy Suck bulb on one end and the patented Easy Grab plastic knob on the other. The infant swings her tiny arms around again, until one pudgy little hand accidentally strikes the new object. Her hand closes on it at once; that's what hands are for. And again, her mouth begins to open; that's one of the important ways of exploring the world. Besides, in the very beginning, what can't be sucked isn't all that valuable.

But the Easy Grab knob is too large, the little girl's grip inadequate, and the new pacifier squirts away.

"Here, sweetie," grandmother purrs, shoving the object back into the child's hand. Now the infant's grip is rounder, more secure; subtle changes have occurred in the positioning of the fingers and in the pressure of the palm. In Piaget's terms, she has begun to accommodate the characteristics of this new object. She has adapted. As a result, the mental system—the arrangement of schemata—has changed in subtle ways.

Assimilation and accommodation are the processes that make adaptation possible throughout life. Note, however, that they are not separate and independent processes. All activity, Piaget maintains, involves both assimilation and accommodation. We cannot begin to make changes in schemata—to accommodate—without first having some basis for responding—that is, without having relevant previous learning to which we can assimilate new situations. Thus, all accommodation requires assimilation. At the same time, all instances of assimilation involve some degree of change to schemata, no matter how familiar the situation or how well learned the response—even if the change is no more significant than that the response will be a tiny fraction better learned and more readily accessible in the future.

In Piaget's system, it's important that there be a balance between assimilation and accommodation (he labels the process of maintaining this balance **equilibration**). If there is too much assimilation, there is no new learning; if there is too much accommodation (too much change), behavior becomes chaotic. In Flavell's (1985) terms, assimilation and accommodation are simply two sides of the same cognitive coin; both always occur together.

Human Development Consists of Stages

The answer to the second question on page 57 can only be outlined here; the details are given later in this chapter. Piaget conceives of human development as consisting of a series of stages, each characterized by certain kinds of behaviors and certain ways of thinking and solving problems. Piaget's descriptions of what he terms the "broad characteristics of intellectual functioning" constitute his answer to the second question. Put very simply, Piaget's theory classifies human development by describing the characteristics of the child's behavior at different ages. This description can be valuable in helping teachers understand their students; it is, in a sense, a description of how cognitive structure develops and changes.

PIAGETIAN COGNITIVE STRUCTURE

One of the principal tasks of theories of intellectual development (cognitive theories) is to describe both how we process perceptual (sensory) information to derive meaning from it and how we organize resulting meanings into long-term memory. In effect, the organization of our long-term memories defines what is meant by *cognitive structure*.

Piaget is a cognitive theorist. His principal interests relate to the origins of cognitive structure—specifically, to its development from birth to adulthood. For Piaget, as for other cognitive theorists, **cognitive structure** can be defined as

those properties of intellect that govern behavior. These properties are inferred rather than real—that is, a cognitive structure can neither be isolated and looked at nor described in concrete terms. It is, after all, only a metaphor.

In very young children, *structure* can be defined in terms of reflexes because these are the first "governors" of behavior. Piaget labels each reflex a "schema." Schemata become more firmly established as children assimilate objects to them, and schemata change as children accommodate to objects. A schema is usually named for the activity it represents. For example, there is a "sucking schema," a "looking schema," a "reaching schema," a "grasping schema," and, unfortunately, a "crying schema." Structure in later stages of development, usually after age seven or eight, is defined less in terms of overt acts than in terms of mental activity. By this age, children have internalized activities; that is, they can represent activities in thought. In addition, thought is subject to certain rules of logic. These rules, which are discussed in connection with the stage of concrete operations, define the term **operation.** In Piaget's system operations, or mental activities, are an outgrowth of real activities with concrete objects.

Cognitive structure governs behavior, and changes in behavior define stages of development; therefore, Piaget's description of development is really a description of cognitive structure at different ages. The details of these developmental changes are discussed next (see Table 3.1).

Sensorimotor Intelligence: Birth to Age Two

Piaget labeled the first two years of life the period of **sensorimotor intelligence.** It seemed to him that until the child develops some way of representing the world mentally, intelligent activity must be confined mainly to sensorimotor functions.

The child's world at birth is a world of the here and now, says Piaget. Objects exist when they

TABLE 3.1 Piaget's Stages of Cognitive Development

STAGE	APPROXIMATE AGE	SOME MAJOR CHARACTERISTICS
Sensorimotor	0–2 years	Motoric intelligence World of the here and now No language, no thought in early stages No notion of objective reality
Preoperational	2–7 years	Egocentric thought
Preconceptual	2–4 years	Reason dominated by perception
Intuitive	4–7 years	Intuitive rather than logical solutions Inability to conserve
Concrete operations	7–11 or 12 years	Ability to conserve Logic of classes and relations Understanding of numbers Thinking bound to concrete Development of reversibility in thought
Formal operations	11 or 12–14 or 15 years	Complete generality of thought Propositional thinking Ability to deal with the hypothetical Development of strong idealism

can be seen, heard, touched, tasted, or smelled; when they are removed from the infant's immediate sensory experience, they cease to be.

The Object Concept. One of the child's major achievements during the sensorimotor stage is the acquisition of what Piaget calls the **object concept**—the notion that objects have a permanence and identity of their own and that they continue to exist even when they are outside the child's immediate frame of reference.

Piaget (1954) devised an interesting and easily replicated experiment to trace the development of the object concept. It involves showing an attractive object to an infant and then hiding it. At the earliest level, children will not even look for the object; it does not exist when they can no longer see or touch it. Later, they will begin to search for the object if they saw it being hidden. It is usually not until around age one that children will search for an object they have not just seen.

Imitation. There is no language early in the sensorimotor period, but there is the beginning of symbolization. Piaget suggests that the internal representation of objects and events is brought about through **imitation**. *Thought* is defined as internalized activity; it begins when children can represent to themselves (in a sense, imitate) a real activity. The first step in this process of internalization involves activities relating to objects or events that are in the child's immediate presence. At a later stage, that of **deferred imitation**, the child can imitate in the absence of the object or event. This internal imitation is a symbolic representation of aspects of the environment. It is also the beginning of language because eventually words will come to replace more concrete actions or images as representatives. And, as J. M. Hunt notes (1961, p. 262), the more new things an infant has seen and the more new things he has heard, the more new things he is interested in seeing and hearing; the more variation in reality he has coped with, the greater is his capacity for coping.

In other words, the amount and variety of stimulation a child receives are instrumental in determining adaptation.

Accomplishments of the Sensorimotor Period. Among important accomplishments of the sensorimotor period is the acquisition of internally controlled schemes—the establishment of controlled internal representations of the world. In other words, by age two children have made the transition from a purely perceptual and motor representation of the world to a more symbolic representation. They have begun to distinguish between **perception** and conceptualization, but they will not perfect this distinction until much later.

A second accomplishment is the development of a concept of reality. Much of a child's development can be viewed in terms of how he or she organizes information about the world. It is evident that this information will be very much a function of what the child thinks the world is. As long as children don't know that the world continues to exist by itself, they are not likely to have a stable representation of it. Or perhaps it would be more accurate to say that as long as children don't have a stable representation system for the world, they cannot conceive of it when they are not actually experiencing it. In either case, the development of some notion of object constancy is absolutely essential for the child's further cognitive development.

A third accomplishment of this period is the development of some recognition of cause and effect. This is a logical prerequisite for the formation of intention because intention is seen in behavior that is engaged in deliberately because of its effect. Piaget sees intention as being inseparably linked with intelligence; for him, intelligent activity is activity that is, in fact, intentional.

Although these accomplishments describe the child at the end of the period of sensorimotor intelligence, they are not the general characteristics of that period. Those are implicit in the label given to the stage—"sensorimotor." In general, the first two years of a child's life are characterized by an **enactive** (Bruner, 1966), or motor, representation of the world. The next stage progresses from the perceptual/motor realm to the conceptual.

The Preoperational Period: Ages Two to Seven

The preoperational period is so called because children do not acquire operational (logical) thinking until around age seven. Before that age, their fumbling attempts at logic abound with contradictions and errors.

The period of **preoperational thinking** is often described in terms of two substages: the period of preconceptual thought and the period of intuitive thought.

Preconceptual Thought: Ages Two to Four

The period of **preconceptual thinking** is preconceptual not in the sense that children fail to use concepts but rather that the concepts they use are incomplete and sometimes illogical.

Preconcepts. Piaget illustrates this by describing his son's reaction to a snail. He had taken the boy for a walk one morning, and they had seen a snail going north. This humble creature had occasioned an expression from the child that can be imagined to have been phrased in the following manner:

"Papa! Cher Papa! Mon cher Papa!" (Swiss children like their fathers.) "Papa! Papa! Papa!" he repeated. "Voici un escargot."

To which Piaget probably replied, "Mon fils, mon fils, mon cher fils! Oui, mon fils, c'est un escargot!"

It was an interesting conversation, as father-and-son conversations go, but it was not remarkable. It happened, however, that a short while later they chanced upon another snail, whereupon the boy again turned to his father and said, "Papa! Cher Papa! Mon cher Papa! Mon Papa! Voici encore l'escargot! Regardez! Regardez!"[*]

This, Piaget says, is an example of preconceptual thinking. The child does not yet understand that similar objects define classes (all snails are snails) but are not identical (snail A is not snail B). In the same way, a child who is shown four different Santa Clauses in four different stores, all on the same day, and who still thinks there is one Santa Claus, is manifesting preconceptual thinking. She evidently knows something about the

concept "Santa Claus," because she can recognize one; but she does not know that objects with similar characteristics can all belong to the same class, yet each has an identity of its own. A young child who sees another child with a toy identical to one he has at home can hardly be blamed for insisting that he be given back *his* toy.

Transduction. Another feature of thinking in the preconceptual stage is labeled **transductive reasoning**. Whereas inductive reasoning proceeds from particular instances to a generalization, and deductive reasoning begins with the generalization and proceeds toward the particulars, transductive reasoning goes from particular instances to other particular instances. It is not a logical reasoning process, but it does occasionally lead to the correct answer. Consider, for example, the following transductive process:

A gives milk.

B gives milk.

Therefore, B is an A.

If A is a cow, and B is also a cow, then B is an A. If, however, A is a cow, but B is a goat, B is not

---

[*]PPC: Should this be translated?

Author: Dad! Dear Dad! My dear Dad! Dad! Dad! Dad! Here is a snail.

My son, my son, my dear son! Yes, my son, it is a snail!

Dad! Dear Dad! My dear Dad! My Dad! Here is the snail again! Look! Look!

an A. Surprising as it might sound, children do appear to reason in this way, as is evident when a child calls a dog "kitty" or a stranger "Daddy."

Intuitive Thought: Ages Four to Seven

After age four, the child's thinking becomes somewhat more logical, although it is still largely dominated by perception rather than by reason. Now it is governed by egocentricity, improper classification, and by intuition—-hence, it is **intuitive thinking**.

Egocentric. Piaget describes, for example, the answers given by children for this simple problem: Two dolls are placed side by side on a string. One is a girl doll, the other a boy. A screen is placed between the child and the experimenter, who are facing each other. The experimenter holds one end of the string in each hand so that the dolls are hidden behind the screen. The child is asked to predict which doll will come out first if the string is moved toward the right. Whether the child is correct or not, the boy doll is moved out and hidden again. The question is repeated; again the boy doll will come out on the same side. This time, or perhaps next time, but almost certainly before many more trials, the subject will predict that the other doll will come out. Why? "Because it's her turn. It isn't fair." This experiment clearly illustrates the role of **egocentrism** in the child's problem solving at the intuitive stage—the problem is interpreted only from the child's point of view.

Perception Dominated. A child is asked to take a bead and place it in one of two containers. As she does so, the experimenter places a bead in another container. They repeat this procedure until one of the containers is almost full. To confuse the child, the experimenter has used a low, flat dish, whereas the child's container is tall and narrow. The experimenter now asks, "Who has more beads, or do we both have the same number?" "I have more," the child says, "because they're higher." Or she might say, "You have more 'cause

they're bigger around." In either case, she will be answering in relation to the appearance of the containers. This reliance on perception, even when it conflicts with thought, is one of the major differences between children and adults.

Inability to Classify. Another striking characteristic of children's thinking during the intuitive period is their inability to classify. A five-year-old child is shown a collection of wooden beads, of which ten are brown and five are yellow. He acknowledges that all the beads are wooden but when asked whether there are as many, fewer, or the same number of brown beads as wooden beads, he says there are more. Piaget's explanation of this phenomenon is simply that asking children to consider the subclass destroys the larger class for them. In other words, children at this level understand that classes may contain many different but similar members (they would not make the preconceptual "escargot" error), but they do not yet understand that classes can be "nested," one inside the other, in hierarchies (as the class of brown beads is nested within that of wooden beads, each being separate but related).

Intuitive. The child's problem solving in this period is largely intuitive rather than logical. Whenever possible, mental images rather than rules or principles are used in arriving at answers, as is strikingly illustrated by Piaget's rotated-bead problem: Three different-colored beads are placed on a wire, and the wire is then inserted in a tube so that the child can no longer see the beads. She knows, however, that the red one is on the left, the yellow in the middle, and the blue on the right. She is then asked what the order of the beads will be if the tube is rotated through a half turn, a full turn, one-and-a-half turns, two turns, and so on. Young, preoperational children are likely to be thoroughly confused by the question; older children will solve it correctly so long as they can imagine the actual rotations—but they will not apply any rule to the solution of the problem (odd versus even number of turns, for example).

THE PLACE:
Marie King's second-grade classroom

THE SETTING:
A dinosaur expert from the Provincial Museum is visiting the class. He has brought a large, stuffed tyrannosaurus rex with him.

Expert: Dinosaurs are extinct. Does anyone know what that means?

Roseanne: Means there's no more.

Billy: Means they stink bad. (burst of laughter)

Ronald: Means they're all gone and all dead and there's no more, and . . . and I don't know.

Expert: That's right. It means there's no more. They're all gone. They're *extinct*.

Roseanne (very seriously, pointing to the stuffed tyrannosaurus rex): Is that a real dinosaur?

The thinking of the six- and seven-year-old, says Piaget, is more magical than ours. It does not draw as fine a line between reality and imagination; the logic that governs it is less compelling, more easily swayed.

The Marie King case above shows how it can be with magical thinking. Dinosaurs can be completely extinct, yet there remains the chilling possibility that there might still be a real one somewhere, maybe even in this classroom, today. When, later that day, the teacher asked this same class, apropos of something entirely different, "How many of you have ever seen a *real* dinosaur?" fully a third of those little grade 2 hands shot instantly in the air.

In summary, the thought processes of the intuitive period are not always entirely logical. Often, they are egocentric and dominated by perception. In addition, the child has not yet acquired the ability to classify or apply formal rules of logic for problem solving. And a final significant difference between thought at this period and thought during the subsequent period of concrete operations is that the preconceptual child has not yet acquired the ability to conserve. (See Figure 3.2 for a summary of preoperational thought.)

It would probably be wise for the reader who is not already familiar with Piaget to stop at this point. If you have available an electroencephalograph, a cardiograph, a thermometer, and a pupillometer (or any other graph or meter), these should be connected and read at once. Alpha waves, together with decelerated heart rate, abnormal temperature, and reduced pupil size, are symptoms of imminent **jargon shock**. This condition in advanced stages can be extremely detrimental to concentration and learning. Several hours of sleep or some other amusement may bring about a significant improvement.

If you don't have any of this sophisticated electronic gadgetry readily available, you can substitute a hand mirror. Hold the mirror up to your face, and look at your eyes. If they are closed, you are probably in the terminal stage of jargon shock.

Concrete Operations: Ages 7 to 11 or 12

An operation is a mental activity—a thought, in other words—that is subject to certain rules of logic. Before the stage of concrete operations, children are described as preoperational, not because they are incapable of thinking but because their thinking exhibits certain limitations. These limitations are related to children's reliance on perception, intuition, and egocentric tendencies rather than on reason.

But with the advent of **concrete operations,** children make a fundamentally important transition from a prelogical form of thought to thinking characterized by rules of logic. The operations that define thought at this stage apply to real, concrete objects and events—hence, the label. Concrete operations are distinguished most clearly from the preoperational period by the

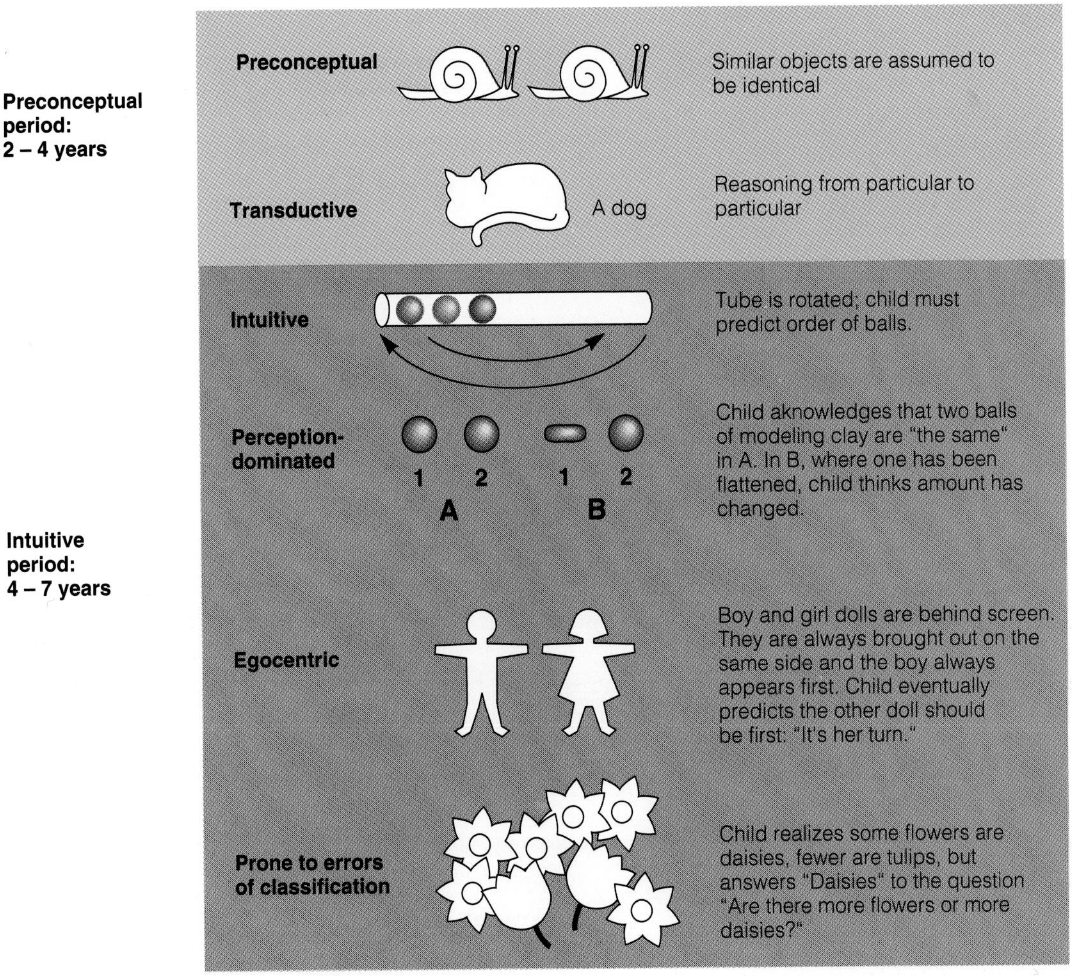

Preconceptual period: 2 – 4 years	**Preconceptual**	Similar objects are assumed to be identical
	Transductive	A dog — Reasoning from particular to particular
Intuitive period: 4 – 7 years	**Intuitive**	Tube is rotated; child must predict order of balls.
	Perception-dominated	Child aknowledges that two balls of modeling clay are "the same" in A. In B, where one has been flattened, child thinks amount has changed.
	Egocentric	Boy and girl dolls are behind screen. They are always brought out on the same side and the boy always appears first. Child eventually predicts the other doll should be first: "It's her turn."
	Prone to errors of classification	Child realizes some flowers are daisies, fewer are tulips, but answers "Daisies" to the question "Are there more flowers or more daisies?"

FIGURE 3.2 Some characteristics of preoperational thought.

appearance of one group of capabilities: the ability to conserve.

The Conservations. **Conservation** is "the realization that quantity or amount does not change when nothing has been added to or taken away from an object or a collection of objects, despite changes in form or spatial arrangement" (Lefrançois, 1966, p. 9). In the experiment cited earlier, in which children are asked whether the two containers have the same number of beads,

children do not demonstrate conservation until they realize that the numbers are equal.

A correct response to a conservation problem is evidence of one or more rules of logic that now govern and limit the child's thinking. Among these rules are **reversibility** and **identity**. The rule of reversibility specifies that for every operation (internalized action) there is an inverse operation that cancels it. Identity is the rule that states that for every operation there is another that leaves it unchanged. Both reversibility and identity can be

1. Conservation of number (age 6 or 7)

Two rows of counters are placed in one-to-one correspondence between the experimenter (E) and the subject (S):

O   O   O   O   O

O   O   O   O   O

One of the rows is then elongated or contracted:

S is asked which row has more counters or whether they still have the same number.

2. Conservation of length (age 6 or 7)

E places two sticks before the subject. The ends are aligned:

S is asked if they are the same length. One stick is then moved to the right:

The question is repeated.

3. Conservation of substance or mass (age 7 or 8)

Two modeling clay balls are presented to S. She is asked if they have the same amount of modeling clay in them. If S says no, she is asked to make them equal. (It is not at all uncommon for a young child simply to squeeze a ball in order to make it have less modeling clay.) One ball is then deformed.

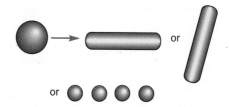

S is asked again whether they contain the same amount.

4. Conservation of area (age 9 or 10)

S is given a large piece of cardboard, identical to one that E has. Both represent playgrounds. Small wooden blocks represent buildings. S is asked to put a building on his playground every time E does so. After nine buildings have been scattered throughout both playgrounds, E moves his together in a corner.

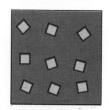

S is asked whether there is as much space (area) in his playground as in E's.

5. Conservation of liquid quantity (age 6 or 7)

S is presented with two identical containers filled to the same level with water.

FIGURE 3.3 Experimental procedures for conservation of six physical attributes.

illustrated by reference to the number system. The operation of addition can be reversed (and nullified) by subtraction (for example, 2 + 4 = 6; 6 − 4 = 2). The identity operator for addition is zero (that is, 2 + 0 + 0 + 0 = 2); for multiplication it is 1 (2 × 1 × 1 × 1 = 2).

The relevance of the operational rules to the thinking of a child at the concrete operations

One of the containers is then poured into a tall, thin tube, and the other is poured into a flat dish.

S is asked whether the amount of water in each remains equal.

6. Conservation of volume (age 11 or 12)
S is presented with a calibrated container filled with water

and two identical balls of modeling clay. One is squished and placed into the container; the other is lengthened.

S is asked to predict the level to which the water in the container will rise if the longer piece of clay replaces the squished piece.

stage can be illustrated by reference to any of the conservation problems. The child who has placed one bead in a tall container for every bead placed by the experimenter in a flat container—and who now maintains that there is the same number in each despite their appearances—may be reason-

ing as follows: (1) If the beads were taken out of the containers and placed again on the table, they would be as they were before (reversibility), or (2) nothing has been added to or taken away from either container, so there must still be the same number in each (identity).

There are as many conservations as there are perceptible quantitative attributes of objects. There is conservation of number, length, distance, area, volume, continuous substance, discontinuous substance, liquid substance, and so on. None of these conservations is achieved before the period of concrete operations; even then, some (volume, for example) will not be acquired until quite late in that period.

The experiments are interesting, and the results are often striking. Several experimental procedures for conservation are described in Figure 3.3, together with the approximate ages of attainment.

One of the intriguing things about conservation is that preoperational children can be made to contradict themselves many times without ever changing their minds. After the experiment on conservation of liquid quantity, for example, the experimenter can pour the water back into the original containers and repeat the question. The subject now acknowledges that they have the same amount—but the moment the water is again poured into the tall container and the flat one, the decision may be reversed.

In addition to conservation, children acquire three other abilities as they come into the stage of concrete operations: the abilities to classify, to seriate, and to deal with numbers.

Classification. To classify is to group objects according to their similarities and differences. The **classification** process involves incorporating subclasses into more general classes, while maintaining the identity of the subclasses. This process leads to the formation of what Piaget calls **hierarchies of classes** (Piaget, 1957). An example is given in Figure 3.4. The preoperational child's inability to deal with classes was illustrated in

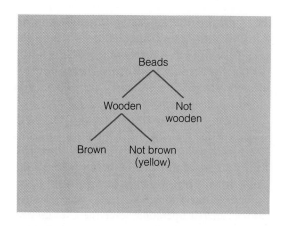

FIGURE 3.4 A hierarchy of classes.

that all the beads were wooden. The child no longer makes this error after reaching concrete operations.

Seriating. The ability to order objects in terms of some attribute is essential for an understanding of the properties of numbers. One experiment that Piaget conducted to investigate the understanding of **seriation** involves presenting children with two corresponding series, one containing dolls, the other canes. The problem is simply to arrange these as shown in Figure 3.5. When the objects are presented in random order, preoperational children cannot arrange the series in sequence. Typically, they compare only two objects at a time and fail to make an inference that is almost essential for the solution of the problem: If A is greater than B, and B is greater than C, A must be greater than C. Preoperational children do not hesitate to put C before A if they have just been comparing B and C.

the experiment involving the ten brown and five yellow wooden beads. Recall that at that stage the child thought there were more brown than wooden beads, even while acknowledging

FIGURE 3.5 Two ordered series.

Numbers. The ability to deal with numbers is simply a by-product of classification and seriation activities. A number involves classes in the sense that it represents a collection of objects (cardinal property of numbers); it involves seriation in the sense that it is ordered in relation to larger and smaller numbers (ordinal property of numbers).

To summarize, children at the stage of concrete operations can apply rules of logic to classes, to relations (series), and to numbers. In addition, their thinking has become relatively decentered; that is, it is no longer so egocentric or so perception bound. However, they are still incapable of applying rules of logic to objects or events that are not concrete. In other words, they deal only with the real or with that which they are capable of imagining. Their ready answer to the question "What if Johnny West had a short nose?" is "Johnny West does not have a short nose!"

Formal Operations: Ages 11 or 12 to 14 or 15

The final stage in the development of thought structures is labeled **formal operations**—*formal* because the subject matter with which children can now deal may be completely hypothetical, and their thinking may involve a formal set of rules of logic.

An example of the difference between the thinking of a child at the formal operations level and at the concrete level is provided by an item from Binet's reasoning test. The item deals with abstract relations. Edith is fairer than Susan; Edith is darker than Lilly; who is the darkest of the three? (If the reader has difficulty with this . . .) This problem is difficult not because it involves seriation (seriation has already been mastered in the stage of concrete operations) but because of the nature of the events that are to be ordered. If Edith, Susan, and Lilly were all standing in front of a ten-year-old subject, the subject could easily say, "Oh! Edith is fairer than Susan, and she is darker than Lilly—and Susan is the darkest." However, when the problem is not concrete but verbal, it cannot be solved until the child can handle propositions logically.

A second experiment that illustrates a distinction between formal and concrete thinking involves a number of colored disks. If subjects are asked to combine each color of disk with every other in all possible ways (that is, by twos, threes, and so on), a complete and systematic solution will not be achieved until the formal operations stage. Before this stage, the child will arrive at a large number of combinations but will not do so systematically and will therefore not exhaust all the possibilities. Piaget refers to the thought processes involved in the solution of this and of similar problems as "combinatorial thinking."

The development of formal operations in the school child is of particular significance because before this stage the child will understand many concepts incompletely or not at all. Such concepts as *proportion* and *heat* are ordinarily beyond the comprehension of a child at the level of concrete operations (see Lovell, 1968).

An important feature of formal operations is an increasing concern with the ideal. Once children are able to reason from the hypothetical to the real or from the actual to the hypothetical, they can conceive of worlds and societies that, hypothetically, have no ills. Having just discovered this boundless freedom of the mind to envisage the ideal, adolescents create their Utopias and rebel against the generation that has as yet been unable to make its Utopias realities.

Beyond Formal Operations

For a long time, developmental psychologists believed that the major intellectual changes of human development take place between birth and the end of adolescence. This model held that after adolescence there is a long period of relatively little change, a sort of plateau. This plateau is eventually followed by gradual decline in old age.

Piaget's description of intellectual development reflects this long-prevalent model. Thus, he describes intellectual growth in terms of changes reflected in identifiable stages. The last of these stages, formal operations, is a stage descriptive of adolescents; beyond that—nothing. . . .

But what of adults? Is adulthood merely a plateau followed by inevitable decline? Are no more positive changes possible?

The simple answer is no; we have invented a new model. Now we believe, with good evidence, that important positive changes come in adulthood—although these changes are not characteristic of everyone. Indeed, formal operations thinking is not characteristic of all adolescents or even of all adults. For some, thinking remains at the concrete stage all their lives; for others, thinking never even progresses beyond the intuitions of the preconceptual level.

But the truly adult thinker, Basseches (1984) informs us, does not think like the school child or the adolescent. Cognitive development, Basseches insists, continues after adolescence. But instead of becoming more logical—more unwaveringly rational—thinking becomes more relative, more attuned to conflict, and more sensitive to moral, ethical, social, and political realities. It is a form of thinking that Basseches terms *dialectical*. Dialectical thinking struggles to create meaning and order by resolving conflict. The dialectical thinker is always aware of other possibilities and recognizes that no solution is necessarily absolute and final.

Labouvie-Vief (1980) agrees. Formal logic, she informs us, might be entirely appropriate for some of the problems that children face, especially in schools. But it might be inadequate and perhaps even largely irrelevant for many of the problems that adults face. The most logical solution may well be entirely wrong, entirely inappropriate. Mature reasoning requires "concrete pragmatics"; that is, it must take into account what will work and what is acceptable—what is, in other words, pragmatic (Labouvie-Vief, 1986). The thinking of the truly wise person is not bound simply by logic—which is not to say that it is illogical. Instead, it is sensitive to a wide range of possibilities; it considers implications; it factors in social and moral realities.

In summary, Basseches, Labouvie-Vief, and others concerned with the intellectual growth of adults claim that Piaget's model is not adequate for describing adult thought processes. According to these theorists, adult cognitive growth may take the form of learning new ways to resolve a wide range of personal problems that could involve relationships, artistic activities, business transactions, religion—indeed, all of life. They argue that adult thinking is more sensitive to and tolerant of ambiguity and contradiction and that it is more likely to bring into play a variety of factors (for example, morality, social and political implications, economic considerations, and so on) in addition to simple logic.

PIAGET EVALUATED: THE CONTRIBUTIONS OF THE NEO-PIAGETIANS

Although Piaget's stature in developmental psychology is unequaled, he has a number of critics. Among the standard criticisms are that he has not used sufficiently large samples, sophisticated analyses, or adequate controls. The validity of these criticisms can be assessed by determining whether replications support his findings.

Replications. Of the many hundreds (or thousands) of studies that have attempted to replicate Piaget's findings, a majority provide at least some evidence that the sequence of intellectual stages is much as Piaget described, especially the sensorimotor period. However, many of these studies have found that North American and European children often reach Piaget's stages earlier than he had thought—although less privileged groups might reach them later (see, for example, Dasen, 1977).

There is somewhat less agreement with respect to sequencing and descriptions of major stages in later childhood and adolescence than there is for earlier stages. Here, there are two major criticisms: The first is that Piaget has drastically underestimated the cognitive achievements of the preschool child; the second is that he has overestimated the formal operations capabilities of adolescents (and even of adults).

Achievements of Preschoolers. With respect to the first criticism, the neo-Piagetians* are widely agreed that it is inappropriate and misleading to refer to the preschool child's mind as "preconceptual," "preoperational," or "prelogical" (see, for example, Case, 1985; Gelman, 1982; Flavell, 1985). Their research suggests that a number of significant cognitive achievements of this period were underemphasized or simply overlooked by Piaget. Among these are monumental advances in the child's ability to represent symbolically and to discover relationships among ideas. And perhaps the clearest illustration of children's impressive abilities with respect to discovering and working with relationships is their understanding of numbers.

Gelman (1982) and colleagues (Gelman, Meck, & Merkin, 1986) describe two kinds of knowledge about numbers that appear during the preschool period. The first kind is number abstraction skills. They give the child an understanding of number, or quantity—how many things there are in a collection of, for example, baby mice in one's pockets. A number of principles underlie number abstraction skills. These include the one-on-one principle (if you're going to count mice, you must assign one, and only one, number to every mouse that is to be counted), the stable order principle (the correct order for counting is one, two, three, four . . . and not one, three, four, two . . .), the cardinal order principle (the last number assigned is the one that indicates the quantity of the collection), the abstraction principle (absolutely anything and everything can be counted), and the order irrelevance principle (the order of counting is irrelevant to the final outcome of the counting operation).

These five number abstraction principles have to do with how to count, what to count, and what it means to count. Children as young as two or three often behave as though they understand these principles clearly, even though they might still make mistakes (often systematic errors) in their counting. The second kind of knowledge about numbers that appears during the preschool period relates to numerical reasoning principles. This is the knowledge that permits the child to reason about or predict the outcome of simple numerical operations such as adding to or taking from.

Number abstraction and numerical reasoning are important and complex cognitive activities. They serve as dramatic illustrations of the cognitive achievements of the preschool child, in sharp contrast to Piaget's description of the intuitive, egocentric, perception-dominated, prelogical, preoperational child.

Limits of Formal Operations. Some criticism of Piaget's stage of formal operations has been based on the observation that many people do not manifest such thinking during adolescence or even beyond (Papalia, 1972; Rubin, Attewell, Tierney, & Tumolo, 1973). Piaget (1972) has conceded that this stage may be less general than he originally had thought.

Another criticism of formal operations relates to errors that Piaget apparently made in his use of models of logic to describe adolescent thought. Ennis (1976, 1978), argues that Piaget's use of propositional logic involves redundant and unnecessary concepts, misuses the concept of propositions itself, and contains some errors of logic.

Summary. Fischer and Silvern (1985) argue that the evidence now available from neo-Piagetian research suggests a reformulation of developmental stages into eight levels (Fischer and Silvern consider *level* a more "modest" term than *stage*). The first four levels span infancy and are similar to Piaget's description of the stages of sensorimotor

---

*The neo-Piagetians are so called because their research stems largely from Piagetian ideas.

development; a single level (relations of a few representations) covers the entire preconceptual period; two levels cover concrete and formal operations, respectively; and a final level occurs in late adolescence. Some researchers also suggest that an additional level follows adolescence (for example, P. K. Arlin, 1975; Riegel, 1973).

In evaluating the importance and seriousness of these criticisms, it is important to keep in mind that Piaget's theory, like other theories, is simply a metaphor. Specifically, Piaget presents a philosophical/biological metaphor intended to explain intellectual adaptation through the growth of intellectual capabilities and functions. Many of the criticisms of his theory stem from a misunderstanding of the basic metaphors and intentions of the theory and from too narrow an application of its principles. In the final analysis, it may not be fundamentally important to the basic metaphor that some of the observations upon which it is based are inaccurate or that there are errors of logic, interpretation, or emphases in its description. Its explanatory strength and its practical utility may be far more important.

EDUCATIONAL IMPLICATIONS OF PIAGETIAN THEORY

Piaget's theory is a monument of cognitive-theory building in child development and has had (and continues to have) a profound impact on educational practices. Its most useful instructional applications relate to three topics: instructional theory, the acceleration of development, and the derivation of specific principles for teaching.

Instructional Theory

Robert Gagné (1985) describes an instructional model based on the notion that learning is hierarchical in the sense that higher-order skills and concepts depend on subordinate capabilities (described in Chapter 4). Hence, instruction based on this model always begins by analyzing what is

to be learned and arranging content into a hierarchy of tasks—a process called **task analysis**. Case (1975) suggests that Piaget's developmental theory can be combined with R. Gagné's instructional theory. Specifically, Piaget's theory can be used to assess the learner's developmental level and cognitive capabilities. Careful task analysis can reveal why certain tasks are too difficult—for example, for preoperational children—and might also suggest ways in which tasks can be structured to be more compatible with the student's developmental level.

Can Development Be Accelerated?

This question was of little direct concern to Piaget. He was concerned more with describing specific details of growth than with the factors that cause developmental changes. By implication, however, his theory supports the belief that a rich background of experiences should lead to the earlier appearance of more advanced ways of thinking.

Direct attempts to accelerate development have generally been aimed at the teaching of conservation behavior to young children. The results of the many studies on this subject are contradictory. Early attempts to teach conservation were not often successful (see, for example, Smedslund, 1961a–e). What appears to be one of the easiest teaching tasks possible—simply convincing a five-year-old child that an amount of modeling clay does not change unless something is added to or taken away from it—is next to impossible. And although several systematic training procedures have succeeded in accelerating the appearance of conservation behavior in young children, no evidence has yet been provided that this has a generally beneficial effect on other aspects of intellectual functioning (see, for example, Lefrançois, 1968; Côté, 1968). As Nagy and Griffiths (1982) conclude, "attempts to prescribe instructional strategies that accelerate intellectual development have borne little fruit" (p. 513). What is not clear is whether the general failure of these attempts is due to the fact that intellectual development cannot easily be accelerated or to the fact that we simply do not understand enough about the nature of intellectual development to devise more appropriate strategies.

Instructional Principles

The development of the child, insists Piaget (1961), does not occur independently of the child's surroundings and activities. To the contrary, it depends on four important factors.

First is equilibration, which, as we saw, is a natural tendency to maintain a balance between assimilation and accommodation. Put another way, equilibration involves an optimal balance between using old learning and behavior (assimilating) and making changes (accommodating). Equilibration accounts for adaptation and cognitive growth.

Second is maturation. *Maturation* refers to the gradual unfolding of genetically determined (or influenced) characteristics. For example, maturation is involved in the child's increasing control over speech-producing organs, even as it is involved in sexual development.

Third is active experience. In Piaget's view, development depends directly on the child's day-to-day activities and experiences with real objects and events.

Fourth is social interaction. Interaction with others is fundamental to the development of notions about others, about things, and about the self.

These four factors—equilibration, maturation, active experience, and social interaction—are the cornerstones of Piaget's system. Not surprisingly, they also suggest important instructional implications. Some of these implications are summarized here. They are not intended as recipes for classroom practice but rather as guiding principles for developing your own teaching style.

Providing Activity. To the extent that concepts arise from sensing and acting upon the environment (active experience), children should be in-volved in numerous real and relevant activities. For example, Piaget argues that the ability to deal with classes, relations, and numbers results from the activities of combining, separating, and setting up correspondences among real objects during the preoperational stage. Because children's natural methods of learning and of stabilizing what they know involve activity, much classroom learning should also involve activity. For Piaget, activity is not only physical activity but internalized mental activity. The point of this principle is twofold:

1. Provision should be made for a relatively large amount of physical activity in school, but obviously mental activity should be provided as well.

2. Provision should be made for relating learning to real objects and events, especially before the formal operations stage.

Providing Optimal Difficulty. To the extent that cognitive growth is facilitated by equilibration, schools should provide activities that encourage a balance between assimilation and accommodation. Recall that assimilation and accommodation are the child's two ways of interacting with the world; all activity involves both. Assimilation occurs when the child can react to new objects or events largely in terms of previous learning; accommodation involves modification or change. Assimilation requires that a situation be somewhat familiar; accommodation will take place only if the situation is, at the same time, somewhat strange. Therefore, what is required is an optimal discrepancy between new material and old learning. (This point is also made by other theorists—or example, Ausubel [1963] and Bruner [1966]; see Chapter 6.) By knowing a student's level of functioning, a teacher can more effectively and realistically determine which learning experiences are best for the individual.

Understanding How Children Think. Although it has always been recognized that there are some important differences between children and adults, Piaget, more than anyone, has demonstrated precisely what some of these differences are. When a child says that there is more water in a tall container than in a short, flat one, she truly believes what she is saying. When a row of disks is made shorter than a corresponding row, and the child changes his mind and says that now there are fewer disks in that row, he is not really contradicting himself because he sees no error and therefore no contradiction. When a second-grade student becomes completely confused by a verbal seriation problem—for example, "Frank Twolips has a shorter nose than Johnny West, and Johnny West has a longer nose than John George. Who has the longest nose?"—she is not being unintelligent.

These and other discoveries about the world of the young child should help teachers both to accept more easily the limitations of children's thought and to communicate more effectively with children.

Knowing Children's Limitations. A teacher needs to be aware of the limitations of children at different ages. Concepts of proportion cannot easily be taught to seven-year-olds—nor can conservation of volume be taught to five-year-olds. Even if this statement were proved false, it would probably still be true that the amount of time required to teach five-year-olds conservation of volume might be better spent teaching them to read. This is particularly true because they would probably acquire conservation of volume by themselves, but they would be less likely to learn to read without instruction.

Providing Social Interaction. One of the chief factors in making thought more objective is social interaction. The egocentric point of view of the young child is essentially one that does not recognize the views of others. Through social interaction, the child becomes aware of the ideas and opinions of peers and adults. Piaget contends that the socialization of thought, the development of moral rules as well as game rules, and even the development of logical thought processes are highly dependent on verbal interaction. The implication for teaching is that instructional methods should provide for learner-learner as well as teacher-learner interaction.

Assessing Students' Readiness. Detailed accounts of Piaget's experimental procedures and findings provide the classroom teacher with many informal and easily applied suggestions for assessing students' thought processes. It is not particularly difficult or time consuming, for example, to ascertain whether a child has acquired conservation of numbers or the ability to seriate. Both abilities are important for early instruction in mathematics.

Researchers have developed several scales to assess Piagetian concepts in children (for example, Pinard & Laurendeau, 1964; Goldschmid & Bentler, 1968; Uzgiris & Hunt, 1975). However, none of these scales has been widely used or standardized.

VYGOTSKY'S CULTURAL/ COGNITIVE THEORY

Theories such as Piaget's emphasize the role of interactions between the individual and others, as well as the role of innate tendencies and predispositions. In a sense, they attempt to account for both our biological and our social aspects. Another approach that places even more emphasis on social/cultural influences is that of Lev Vygotsky, the Russian psychologist.

The Man and His Ideas

A quick look at current writings in psychology might make one think that Vygotsky is a contemporary theorist. Almost all major textbooks have at least one or two references to him. And there are a significant number of new books dealing with his work, as well as new translations of his own books (for example, Wertsch, 1985; Vygotsky, 1986; Kozulin, 1990). But he is not contemporary in a literal sense; he has been dead for more than half a century (he died of tuberculosis in 1934 at the age of thirty-eight). And although he was already a major intellectual force in the Soviet Union by the time he was twenty-eight, his work was not well known outside that country until much later. It is interesting to contemplate what his contributions and his stature might have been had he lived as long as Piaget.

Three underlying themes unify Vygotsky's rather complex and far-reaching theory. The first theme is the importance of culture; the second is the central role of language; the third is what Vygotsky labels the "zone of proximal growth." We look at each of these briefly.

The Importance of Culture

Human development, says Vygotsky, is fundamentally different from that of animals. Why? Because humans use tools and symbols; as a result, we create **cultures**. And cultures are powerful things; they have a life of their own. They grow and change, and they exert tremendously powerful influences on each of us. Cultures specify what the end product of successful development is. They determine what we have to learn, the sorts of competencies we need to develop. We are not only culture producing, notes Bronfenbrenner (1989), but also culture produced.

Vygotsky makes an important distinction between what he calls "elementary mental functions" and "higher mental functions." Elementary functions are our natural, and therefore unlearned, capacities, such as attending and sensing. In the course of development, these elementary capacities are gradually transformed into higher mental functions such as problem solving and thinking, largely through the influence of culture. It is culture, after all, that makes language possible, and it is social processes that bring about the learning of language (referred to as *signs*). Language, or signs, ultimately make thought possible. Thus, during the preverbal stage of development, the infant's intelligence is a purely practical, purely natural capacity that is closely comparable to that of apes.*

The Role of Language

Language makes thought possible and regulates behavior. Vygotsky (1962) describes three stages in the development of the functions of speech: social, egocentric, and inner.

Social speech (or external speech) emerges first. Its function is largely to control the behavior of others (as in "I want juice!") or to express simple and sometimes poorly understood concepts.

Egocentric speech predominates from age three to age seven. It serves as a bridge between the primitive and highly public social speech of the first stage and the more sophisticated and highly private inner speech of the third stage. During this stage, children often talk to themselves in an apparent attempt to guide their own behavior. For example, they might speak about what they are doing as they do it. Unlike older children, however, they are likely to say things out loud (externalize) rather than silently, as though they believe that if language is to direct behavior, it must be spoken.

Inner speech is silent self-talk. It is characteristic of older children as well as adults. It is what William James (1890) called the "stream of consciousness." Our self-talk—our inner speech—is what tells us that we are alive and conscious. It permits us to direct our thinking and our behavior. More than this, it makes all higher mental functioning possible (see Table 3.2).

*PPC: How about bears? What is their intelligence like?

Author: They are possessed of a great wisdom, tempered by a savage cunning. They are accomplished dialectical thinkers, both pragmatic and poetic. They are pensive and somber, jovial and—in truth, Vygotsky does not say.

TABLE 3.2 Vygotsky's Theory of the Role of Language

STAGE	FUNCTION
Social (external) (to age 3)	Controls the behavior of others; expresses simple thoughts and emotions
Egocentric (3 to 7)	Bridge between external and inner speech; serves to control own behavior but spoken out loud
Inner (7 onward)	Self-talk; makes possible the direction of our thinking and our behavior; involved in all higher mental functioning

The Concept of a Zone of Proximal Growth

Higher mental functioning involves activities such as thinking, perceiving, organizing, and remembering. These functions originate in social activity and are inseparably linked with language, which is also a social phenomenon. In a very real sense, these higher mental functions define intelligence.

One of Vygotsky's strong interests was in maximizing intellectual development. He was far less interested in measuring past accomplishments or in assessing current levels of functioning than in arriving at some notion of potential for future development. Every child, he maintained, has a sphere or a zone of current capabilities—in Vygotsky's words, a **zone of proximal growth** (Belmont, 1989). Take, for example, two five-year-old children, who can both, under normal circumstances, answer questions that other average five-year-olds can also answer. Their mental ages might be said to correspond to their chronological ages, and their intelligence would be described as average. But if, when prompted, one of these children could successfully answer questions corresponding to a mental age of seven but the other could not, it would be accurate to say that the first child's zone of proximal growth is greater than the other's (that is, it spans a wider range of higher functions).

EDUCATIONAL IMPLICATIONS OF VYGOTSKY'S THEORY

Several educational implications can be derived from this brief overview of some of Vygotsky's principal theoretical beliefs. First, the theory highlights the importance of language in the development of higher mental functions. Vygotsky believed very strongly that language is a social and cultural phenomenon that is centrally involved in the development of thinking. Accordingly, schools can perhaps do a great deal to enhance the development of cognitive processes by paying special attention to the development of language.

Second, the theory stresses that cognitive development is profoundly influenced by cultural and social environments. Specifically, to the extent that the environment requires that the child perform at a level slightly in advance of current developmental level, progress will be enhanced. Vygotsky suggests that the level at which instructions and questions are phrased is extremely important. These, he argues, should be sufficiently ahead of the student's developmental level that they present a genuine intellectual challenge—but they must not be so far ahead of the child's current biological maturation and developmental level that they present too great a challenge (Valsiner, 1987).

In summary, Vygotsky's social/cognitive developmental theory underscores the role of culture and its most important invention, language, in the development of higher mental functions. Without culture, he argues, our intelligence would be comparable to that of apes[*]—hence, the fundamental role of education is cultural transmission.

We knew that. But we were perhaps not entirely aware of the theoretical underpinnings of this belief.

Do bears have a culture? Do wild cows?

MAIN POINTS

1. A theory is a systematic attempt to organize and interpret observations. It is best judged not in terms of accuracy and truthfulness but in terms of how well it reflects the facts, how consistent it is, and how useful it is for explaining and predicting.

2. Social learning refers to (a) learning that occurs in a social context—a process, and (b) the learning of social rules and conventions, of what is acceptable and what isn't—a product.

3. Gender roles are learned patterns of culturally approved masculine and feminine behaviors; they are a combined function of genetic, family-based, and cultural forces.

4. Traditional gender roles, which are changing slowly, reflect males as more aggressive, more boisterous, and more adventurous than girls. Both boys and girls tend to prefer male to female roles.

5. Sex differences, which typically have both genetic and environmental roots, are sometimes evident in the greater aggressiveness of males. In addition, there is a tendency for males to score slightly higher on tests of general knowledge and mechanical reasoning, and females, on tests of language usage. On a number of measures, male scores reflect more variability.

6. Sex differences in abilities are too trivial and too inconsistent to be important to teachers. What is important is that teachers be sensitive to both the interests of boys and girls and to the many instances of sexual bias that still permeate society.

7. Piaget's theory stems partly from his biological orientation and focuses on cognitive (intellectual) development. It describes the characteristics of human behavior that permit adaptation, and it classifies important intellectual events in terms of sequential developmental stages.

8. The newborn is an intrinsically motivated information-processing organism that acquires information and adapts through the joint processes of assimilation (making already acquired responses; making environmental stimulation conform to mental structure) and accommodation (modifying responses; making mental structure conform to environmental demands).

9. The sensorimotor period (birth to two years, the first of Piaget's four major developmental stages) is characterized by a sensory and motor representation of the world. Among the sensorimotor child's achievements are the learning of language, the acquisition of the object concept, the development of internally controlled representational schemes, and the recognition of cause-and-effect relationships.

10. The preoperational stage (ages 2 to 7) includes the preconceptual period (ages 2 to 4; reasoning is characteristically transductive—it proceeds from particular to particular)—and the intuitive period (ages 4 to 7; reasoning is egocentric, perception dominated, and intuitive).

11. The stage of concrete operations (ages 7 to 11 or 12) is marked by new skills relating to classifying, ordering, and dealing with numbers, as well as by the appearance of thought processes that are subject to some logical rules (identity and reversibility, for example) evident in the

[*]PPC: And bears?

Author: And perhaps to bears, too.

development of concepts of conservation (the realization that certain qualities of objects, such as weight or volume, do not change unless matter is added or subtracted).

12. During the formal operations stage (ages 11 or 12 to 14 or 15), the child becomes freed from concrete objects and events and can deal with the hypothetical.

13. Researchers such as Basseches (dialectical thinking) and Labouvie-Vief (pragmatic reasoning) argue that although formal operations may be appropriate for problems requiring nothing but logic, mature adult reasoning is more sensitive to and tolerant of ambiguity and contradiction and is more likely to consider the practical, social, ethical, and personal implications of decisions.

14. Replications of many of Piaget's experiments have tended to confirm the general sequence of stages up to formal operations, although Piaget may sometimes have underestimated children's capacities and the ages of some developmental accomplishments.

15. Piaget's description of the four factors involved in development (equilibration, maturation, social interaction, and active experience) suggest some important instructional principles, including the need to provide opportunities for student activity, to recognize that there is an optimal level of difficulty for new learning, and to be aware of the characteristics and limits of children's abilities.

16. Vygotsky's social/cognitive theory stresses the importance of culture and of its principal invention, language. Without culture, our intellectual functioning is limited to apelike, elementary mental functions; given culture and language, we become capable of higher mental functions involved in thinking, reasoning, remembering, and so on.

17. The child progresses through three stages in developing language functions: social (external) speech, predominant before age three or four, used largely to control others or to express simple concepts; egocentric speech (ages three to seven or so), which is self-talk that is spoken out loud and that has a role in controlling and directing the child's own behavior; and inner speech, marked by unspoken verbalizations that control thought and behavior.

18. Vygotsky's zone of proximal growth is the child's potential for development from the current level of mental functioning. Vygotsky emphasizes the importance of assessing potential rather than simply measuring past accomplishments. His theory presents a strong argument for language-related activities in schools and for instruction at the upper edge of the student's zone of proximal development—that is, for challenging instructional materials and methods.

SUGGESTED READINGS

The following is of particular value in understanding the logical thought processes of children in the concrete operations and formal operations stages:

INHELDER, B., & PIAGET, J. (1958). *The growth of logical thinking from childhood to adolescence.* New York: Basic Books.

Flavell's book is a highly readable and excellent analysis of cognitive development that deals in some detail with Piaget's theory, as well as with current developments in information processing and cognition. The book by Wadsworth is another clear account of Piaget.

FLAVELL, J. H. (1985). *Cognitive development* (2nd ed.). Englewood Cliffs, N.J.: Prentice-Hall.

WADSWORTH, B. J. (1989). *Piaget's theory of cognitive and affective development* (4th ed.). New York: Longman.

A comprehensive account of Vygotsky's theory is

WERTSCH, J. V. (1985). *Vygotsky and the social formation of mind.* Cambridge, Mass.: Harvard University Press.

Delayed implantation is one of the common features of brown and polar bears, badgers, mink, and a small number of other animals. The fertilized egg does not become implanted in the uterine wall shortly after conception, but may remain dormant for weeks and sometimes months. Although delayed implantation clearly has survival value, ensuring that the young will be born at the optimal time of the year, the mechanisms that delay embryonic development and later serve to trigger it are not understood (L. H. Matthews, 1969).

part three | LEARNING, THINKING, AND TEACHING

We know that you are mad with much learning.

Petronius, *Satyricon*

Learning is mostly what the educational process is all about. Fortunately, it does not ordinarily make us mad. The six chapters in the third part deal with learning and thinking, especially the instructional implications of what we know about these topics. Two of the chapters also look at intelligence, creativity, and other human characteristics that sometimes make us dramatically different from each other; this, too, has tremendous implications for teaching. And the last chapter in this part presents an antidote to the accusation that our sciences tend to mechanize and to dehumanize; it presents some humanistic approaches to teaching.

When I carefully consider the curious habits of dogs
I am compelled to conclude
That man is the superior animal.
When I consider the curious habits of man
I confess, my friend, I am puzzled.
Ezra Pound, *Meditatio*

Let such teach others who themselves excel.
Alexander Pope, *Essay on Criticism*

A little learning is a dangerous thing
Drink deep or taste not the Pierian spring
Alexander Pope, *Essay on Criticism*

Chapter 4 | BEHAVIORISTIC EXPLANATIONS OF LEARNING

For teachers, one of the most important questions about learning is which conditions lead most effectively to desirable changes in behavior. In other words, how can what we know about learning be applied to instruction? But before we can begin to answer this question, we must look at psychology's explanations of learning. This chapter presents the behaviorists' explanations—those that, among other things, have to do with how behavior is controlled by its consequences. Teachers control some of the consequences of students' behavior and in so doing they indirectly control students' behavior. But is it ethical to control a person's behavior by manipulation with rewards and punishments? This chapter addresses this question as well.

Excerpt from Bear Tales (Book II): Valley of the Wild Cows

So the wild cows headed up the Saskatchewan River, which Imelda thought was a blast 'cause she fancied herself a bit of an adventuress.

By Drowning Ford, they stopped for a drink, and some of the younger cows even went for a bit of a swim while the older ones rested or belched and chewed cud.

"Hot damn," said Imelda, loving how the herd tore the bank to rat dung and trampled it down, swirling black and mucky into the water, loving how the glacier blue current turned soupy thick and smelled of hot cow droppings. She'd never much cared for fish anyway.

Imelda belched loudly, and it wasn't cud this time, just hot whiskey because she had tossed back a couple of belts real quick when they first stopped, *but now she sipped more slowly, liking how her taste buds burned like they never did with grass, which she didn't really much like any more since she'd taken to drinking whiskey in the morning.*

"Ten more minutes," Imelda announced loudly, belching again. "Enough time for a cigar." One of the younger, horned cows passed the cigars around, which they all took and lit, spewing blue smoke rings in the air, laughing when the birds fell silent, gagging and staggering from their perches. Except Roseanne, who had been one beaut of a cow when she was younger, but now she was middle-aged and she had no wish to smoke at all. And she didn't drink either, which made the others more than a little suspicious.

Because she didn't even have an ulcer or cirrhosis or anything. "She's just dang contrary, is all, which ain't natural," Imelda muttered as she puffed on her cigar, resenting the look Roseanne gave her, which she thought might have been holier-than-thou.

But everybody knew Roseanne wasn't really holier at all because the wild cow philosophers, who were mostly grandmother wild cows, had a theory that normal cows like to drink whiskey and smoke cigars. And they like to stay close together, in bunches. Imelda knew the theory was right because, by dang, that's the way wild cows are.

"Let's move it," Imelda bellowed out of the corner of her mouth, lips clamped around her cigar. "To the forest!" Visions of wild strawberries and fiddlehead ferns danced in her head.

Roseanne trudged alone. Upwind. She didn't like the smell of whiskey or cigars. "Maybe," she thought sadly, "I don't much like the smell of wild cows either! I just don't fit any of the theories."

THE NATURE OF SCIENTIFIC THEORY

My aunt Lucy, who knew nothing about wild cow philosophers, had various theories about people. One of her theories was that kids grow up to become like whatever heroes they have when they're young. She used this theory to explain why Robert wound up in jail (his uncle Nesbitt, who was a hardened criminal, had been his boyhood hero). And she used the theory as an excuse for inviting every new teacher over for dinner as often as seemed proper and the local priest, too. She wanted to make sure Luke would have the right kind of heroes. And he turned out remarkably well, but Edward, his brother, who was always there when teachers and priests came for chicken and stuff, had to spend a few years being *corrected* as Aunt Lucy put it. "He doesn't fit my theory, that one," she explained.

In the same way, Roseanne doesn't fit wild cow theory very well. In fact, there are many of us who don't fit our naïve or implicit theories very well. However, some of us do, because our home-grown theories, like scientific theories, stem from observations—and some of our observations are accurate. But the big difference between the observations of the armchair theorist and those of scientists is that we can have more faith in scientific observations because science demands that observations be made with precision and objectivity that are beyond the patience of naïve theorists. In addition, the conclusions and generalizations of social scientists are likely to apply to a greater number of individuals. Whereas my aunt could, with profound conviction, base her conclusions about human nature on a single isolated instance, science insists on samples that are large enough and representative enough to justify making generalizations.

One final, important difference between naïve theories and those of science is that theorists like my aunt do not habitually take random or chance factors into account. Science, on the other hand, is guided by a mathematically precise model of probability. Accordingly, science is far more likely than my aunt to admit that certain outcomes and observations are due to chance (or at least to unknown factors), rather than to specific things like the manipulations of an experimenter or the presence of a priest or a teacher at Saturday night dinners.

As we saw in Chapter 1, a theory is a collection of related statements, the principal function of which is to summarize and explain observations. It is, in a sense, an invention designed to make sense of what we know or suspect. In addition, a good theory allows us to make predictions. Accordingly, we judge theories on the basis of how well they reflect the facts, how consistent and logical they are, how useful they are for explaining and for predicting, and how practical they are in suggesting how to solve problems or simply how to behave in certain situations.

In this chapter, we look at several theories that attempt to explain learning and that have important educational implications.

LEARNING

Learning is mostly what education is all about: Teachers teach and students learn. These are the two sides of the educational coin. (Actually,

Learning, psychology informs us, is the acquisition of information and knowledge, of skills and habits, and of attitudes and beliefs. It always involves a change in one of these areas—a change that is brought about by the learner's experiences. Take tying shoes, for example. This complex skill requires knowledge about how laces can be twisted and looped and pulled, hours of practice and experience, and maybe just a little luck as well.

education has more than two facets; teachers also learn, and students also sometimes teach.)

Defined

Learning is the acquisition of information and knowledge, of skills and habits, and of attitudes and beliefs. It always involves a change in one of these areas—a change that is brought about by the learner's experiences. Accordingly, psychologists define **learning** as all changes in behavior that result from experience, providing these changes are relatively permanent, do not result simply from growth or maturation, and are not the temporary effects of factors such as fatigue or drugs.

Disposition.   Not all changes involved in learning are obvious and observable. For example, learning often involves changes in the learner's **disposition**—that is, in the person's inclination to do or not to do something. Hence, changes in disposition have to do with motivation. Such changes cannot always be observed but are no less real or important.

Capability.   Learning involves not only changes in disposition but also changes in **capability**—that is, changes in the skills or knowledge required to do something (R. Gagné, 1985). Like changes in disposition, changes in capability cannot always be observed directly. To determine whether students' dispositions or capabilities have changed following instruction, teachers must give them an opportunity to engage in the relevant behavior. The inference that dispositions or capabilities have changed—in other words, that learning has occurred—will always be based on performance. If instruction affects learners in such a way that their behaviors after instruction are observably different from those before instruction, we can conclude that learning has occurred.

Performance. Although a teacher's estimates of student learning typically are based on students' **performance** (actual behavior), all sorts of learning may occur in school without necessarily being manifested in performance. For example, some students learn to like or dislike school, school subjects, teachers, or the sound of amateurish chalk-writing; however, they do not always manifest these dispositional changes in their actual behavior. Similarly, students are not always provided with opportunities to display changes in knowledge and skills leading to new capabilities—a subject about which we say more in Chapter 13 (on measurement and evaluation).

Because learning involves changes in both capabilities and dispositions—changes that will be manifested in performance, given the right situation—we can distinguish among various kinds of learning. For example, learning that involves muscular coordination and physical skills (**motor learning**) appears to be different from learning involving emotions (**affective learning**) or that involving information or ideas (**cognitive learning**). These three distinctions are based on fairly obvious differences among the responses involved. Learning may also be classified by reference to the conditions that lead to it—an approach adopted by R. Gagné (1977a) and described later in this chapter.

BEHAVIORISM AND COGNITIVISM

Two major groups of theories relate to learning: **behaviorism** and **cognitivism**. Differences between these two groups of **learning theories** relate mainly to the questions each tries to answer. Behaviorism tries to explain simple behaviors—observable and predictable responses. Accordingly, it is concerned mainly with conditions (called **stimuli**) that affect organisms and that may lead to behavior, as well as with simple behaviors themselves (**responses**). Behavior-oriented (or behavioristic) researchers attempt to discover the rules that govern the formation of relationships between stimuli and responses (the rules of **conditioning**). For this reason, **behavioristic theories** are often referred to as **stimulus-response (S-R) theories** or as **associationistic theories**.

In contrast to behaviorism, cognitive approaches deal mainly with questions relating to cognition, or knowing. Cognitive theorists are concerned with how we develop a fund of knowledge and how we eventually develop notions of ourselves as players of what Flavell (1985) calls the "game of cognition." Children's gradual development of an awareness of themselves as knowers, their growing awareness of the strategies they can use to acquire and process information, and their ability to direct their efforts and to evaluate their cognitive activities are aspects of **metacognition**. Put another way, *cognition* refers to knowing; *metacognition* refers to knowing about knowing. Cognition-oriented researchers attempt to understand the nature of information—how it is acquired and organized by learners; how it can be recalled, modified, applied, and analyzed; and how the learner understands, evaluates, and controls the activities involved in cognition. Piaget, whose theory is described in Chapter 3, is a good example of a cognitive theorist.

A third approach to understanding human behavior is **humanism**. Humanistic psychologists are concerned more with human individuality and uniqueness than with discovering general rules to explain human responses. They focus more on emotional development than on information processing or on stimuli and responses (see Table 4.1).

TABLE 4.1   Three Approaches to Learning

THEORY	MAJOR FOCUS	KEY VARIABLES/ CONCEPTS	REPRESENTATIVE THEORISTS	PRINCIPAL USEFULNESS FOR TEACHERS
BEHAVIORISM	Behavior	Stimuli Responses Reinforcement Punishment Behavior modification	Watson Guthrie Thorndike Skinner	Explains learning of skills and attitudes; emphasizes reinforcement
COGNITIVISM	Knowing	Decision making Understanding Cognitive structure Perception Information processes Memory	Ausubel Bruner Gagné, R. Piaget Sternberg	Explains development of understanding (meaning); emphasizes importance of meaningfulness and organization
HUMANISM	The person	Self-concept Self-actualization Self-worth	Maslow Rogers	Focuses on affective development; emphasizes adjustment and well-being

This chapter deals with some of the behaviorists' explanations of learning and their implications for teaching. Chapters 5 and 6 look at cognitive explanations. Chapter 9 discusses humanism.

CLASSICAL CONDITIONING

Some simple forms of learning require little information processing or understanding. They can occur unconsciously, and they apply to some kinds of animal learning as well as to human learning.

The case in Mrs. Grundy's classroom on page 88 illustrates one of the simplest forms of animal and human learning: **classical conditioning**. The qualifier *classical* is used simply to differentiate between this specific form of learning and other forms of learning loosely referred to as *conditioning* in ordinary speech.

Pavlov's Classical Conditioning

Ivan Pavlov, a Russian physiologist, was one of the first to draw attention to classical conditioning. He had noticed that the dogs in his laboratory began to salivate when they were about to be fed, even before they could see or smell the food. Strangely, they seemed to be salivating at the mere sight of their keeper or even when they simply heard his footsteps.

This simple observation led Pavlov to a series of well-known experiments. These experiments involved ringing a bell or sounding a buzzer—neither of which ordinarily leads to salivation—and then immediately presenting the dogs with food, a stimulus that does lead to salivation. Pavlov soon found that if the procedure was repeated often enough, the bell or buzzer alone began to elicit salivation.

In Pavlov's experiments, the bell is referred to as a **conditioned stimulus** (**CS**); the food is an

case **THE TIME:** 1848

THE PLACE:
Mrs. Evelyn Grundy's classroom in
Raleigh, North Carolina

THE SITUATION:
Six-year-old Robert has been
Misbehaving to Girls and Telling Lyes.

The prescribed total punishment for these offenses is eleven lashes.[*] But because there are two separate infractions involved, Mrs. Grundy doubles the punishment. She administers the lashes herself. And every time she raises the cane to strike Robert, she squeals hoarsely, a little like pig grunting. By the tenth lash, Robert has begun to flinch a little just before the cane hits. He cries out quite loudly when it lands.

Later that day, when Mrs. Grundy is passing out the spellers, her back turned to Edward, his ruler-propelled spitball catches her just behind the left ear. She grunts loudly. And Robert flinches.

*PPC: The punishment sounds a little extreme. Readers will think you're making this up. Are you?

Author: Nope. See Table 4.3 if you don't believe me.

---

unconditioned stimulus (**UCS**); and salivation in response to the food is an **unconditioned response** (**UCR**), whereas salivation in response to the bell or buzzer is a **conditioned response** (**CR**).

The Mrs. Grundy/Robert case is a simple illustration of classical conditioning, as is shown in Figure 4.1. In this example, the sound of the grunt serves as a conditioned stimulus. The fear reaction (flinch) is the initial unconditioned response; the pain of the cane serves as an unconditioned stimulus.

In general terms, a stimulus or situation that readily leads to a response can be paired with a **neutral stimulus** (one that does not lead to a response) to bring about classical conditioning. Note that this learning typically is unconscious; that is, learners do not respond to the conditioned stimulus because they become aware of the relationship between it and an unconditioned stimulus. In fact, classical conditioning can occur even for responses over which the subject ordinarily has no control. For example, the application of cold or hot packs directly to the skin can bring about constriction or dilation of blood vessels. If these stimuli are paired with a neutral stimulus such as a tone, the tone by itself will eventually lead to vascular constriction or dilation.

Watson's Behaviorism

According to Watson (1913, 1916), who was greatly influenced by the work of Pavlov, people are born with a limited number of reflexes. Learning, explained Watson, is just a matter of classical conditioning involving these reflexes. Hence, differences among people are entirely a function of their experiences. (This point of view, referred to as **environmentalism,** is discussed in more detail in Chapter 7.)

Watson's view was extremely influential in the early development of psychology in the United States. His insistence on precision, rigor, and objectivity—and his rejection of such previously popular but difficult-to-define (and -measure) terms as *mind, feeling,* and *sensation*—was very much in line with the scientific spirit of the times. In addition, the belief that what we become is a function of our experiences presents a just and egalitarian view of humans. If what we become is truly a function of the experiences to which we are subjected, we are in fact born equal. As Watson declared, any child can become a doctor or a judge. In fact, however, things are not quite that simple: Not everybody can become a doctor or a judge (see Chapter 7).

Before Conditioning

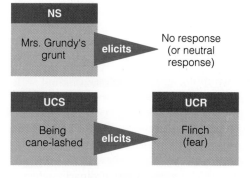

An unconditioned stimulus elicits an unconditioned fear response

Conditioning Process

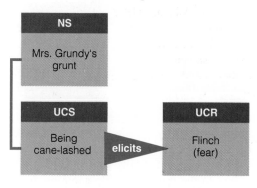

A neutral stimulus is repeatedly paired with the UCS

After Conditioning

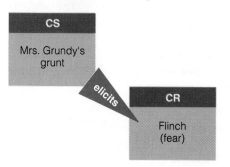

The previously neutral stimulus becomes a conditioned stimulus eliciting the conditioned response of fear

FIGURE 4.1 Classical conditioning. An initially neutral or pleasant stimulus (NS) is paired with an unconditioned, fear-producing stimulus (UCS) so that the subject is eventually *conditioned* to fear the previously neutral stimulus. Fear is now a conditioned response (CR) to a conditioned stimulus (CS).

Instructional Applications

Classical conditioning, especially of emotional reactions, occurs in all schools, virtually at all times, regardless of the other kinds of learning going on at the same time. And it is largely through these unconscious processes that students come to dislike schools, subjects, teachers, and related stimuli—or to like them. A school subject is a neutral stimulus that evokes little emotional response in the beginning, assuming that it is new to the student. The teacher, the classroom, or some other distinctive stimulus in the student's immediate environment may serve as a conditioning stimulus. This conditioning stimulus might be pleasant (a comfortable desk, a friendly teacher) or unpleasant (a cold, hard desk; a cold, hard teacher with a grating voice and squeaking chalk). Following successive pairings of the subject matter with this distinctive stimulus, the emotions (attitudes) associated with the stimulus become classically conditioned to some aspect of school. In short, students learn attitudes toward subjects, learning, school, and so on, largely as a function of classical conditioning. Thus, it is entirely possible to teach students mathematics while at the same time teaching them to dislike mathematics. Whereas learning mathematics is likely to involve cognitive processes (and perhaps some form of conditioning as well, particularly if repetitive skills are involved), learning to dislike mathematics may involve mainly classical conditioning (see Figure 4.2).

Thus, teachers need to know what is being paired with what in their classrooms, and they need to do whatever they can to maximize the number and potency of pleasant unconditioned stimuli and to minimize the unpleasant.

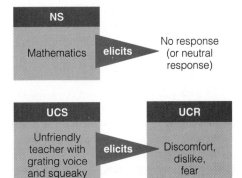

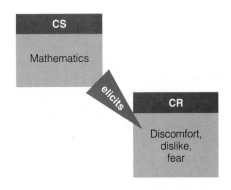

FIGURE 4.2 Classical conditioning of math phobia.

The old adage that learning should be fun is more than a schoolchild's frivolous plea; it follows directly from classical conditioning theory. A teacher who makes students smile and laugh while she has them repeat the 6-times table may, because of the variety of stimuli and responses being paired, succeed in teaching students (1) how to smile and laugh—a worthwhile undertaking in its own right, (2) to associate stimuli such as 6 × 7 with responses such as "forty-two"—a valuable piece of information, and (3) to like arithmetic—and the teacher, the school, the smell of chalk, the feel of a book's pages, and on and on.

What does a teacher who makes students suffer grimly through their multiplication tables teach?

Edward L. Thorndike's Connectionism

In attempting to explain the formation of relationships between stimuli, between responses, or between stimuli and responses, behaviorists can make one of two choices. They can maintain, as did Watson and Pavlov, that the simultaneous occurrence of events is sufficient to bring about learning. This reasoning is ordinarily referred to as a **contiguity** explanation. A second alternative, and one that was explicitly avoided by both Watson and Guthrie, is to explain the formation of S-R bonds by reference to the effects of the behavior. This explanation, introduced by Edward L. Thorndike and popularized by B. F. Skinner, is labeled a "reinforcement approach."

Thorndike defined *learning* as the formation of connections, or "bonds," between stimuli and responses. Accordingly, he labeled his learning theory **connectionism** (1949). In his words, learning involves "stamping in" S-R bonds; forgetting involves "stamping them out." Much of his theory deals specifically with the conditions that lead to the stamping in or stamping out of bonds. Put simply, Thorndike believed that it is the effect of a response that leads to learning or its absence (1911). One of his classic experiments used to illustrate this involved placing a hungry cat inside a cage and dangling a tasty bit of fish outside the cage. To escape from its cell and obtain the fish, the cat had to pull a looped string or perform some other mechanical feat.

The Laws of Learning. From these experiments, Thorndike (1913, 1932, 1933) derived two related conclusions about learning: the **law of effect** and the **law of multiple responses**. These are the basis of his theory.

The law of effect states that responses that occur just before a satisfying state of affairs tend to be stamped in (learned); those that occur before an annoying state of affairs tend to be stamped out. Thus, the law of effect means that learning is a function of the consequences of behavior rather than simply of contiguity. Thorndike later modified this law by asserting that pleasure is more potent for stamping in responses than pain is for stamping out responses. Whereas rewards strengthen behavior, punishment simply leads the learner to do something else.

The law of multiple responses is based on Thorndike's observation that when faced with a difficult problem for which they have no ready solution, individuals will engage in a variety of different responses until one response produces a satisfying effect. In other words, it is through trial and error that problems are solved. As a result of this law, Thorndike's theory came to be known as the theory of **trial-and-error learning**.

A third law, the **law of readiness**, recognizes that certain responses are more or less likely than others to be learned (stamped in), depending on the learner's readiness. Such factors as maturation and previous learning are clearly involved in determining whether learning is easy, difficult, or impossible. This important law provides the basis for Thorndike's definitions of **reward** and **punishment**. Specifically, it is the learner's readiness that determines whether a state of affairs is pleasant or not. Thorndike maintained that a pleasant state of affairs—a reward—results when a person is ready to do something and is allowed to do it. By the same token, not being allowed to do something when one is ready or being forced to do something when one is not ready results in an annoying state of affairs—punishment.

The importance of this law for teaching is readily apparent. It is clear that a child who is ready for a specific type of learning is far more likely to profit from such learning experiences than another who is not ready. What is not so obvious is precisely what is involved in being ready. Clearly, there are various types of readiness, some relating to physical maturation, some to the development of intellectual skills and the acquisition of important background information, and

some to motivation. Hence, to determine readiness, teachers must have some knowledge of children's emotional and intellectual development—topics covered in Chapters 2 and 3.

Instructional Applications

Much of Thorndike's research and writing was directed specifically toward applying his findings to education; not surprisingly, his theories are rich with instructional implications.

Rewarding Correct Trials. Perhaps most obvious are the implications of his belief that learning occurs through trial and error and results from the fact that the eventual correct response is rewarded—and therefore learned (stamped in). This belief leads directly to the principle that teachers and schools need to provide both ample opportunity for students to emit a variety of responses and that correct responses need to be rewarded. The theory also stresses that rewards and punishments need to be tailored to the situation and to the child and that, among other things, the child's readiness needs to be taken into consideration.

Establishing Attitudes. Other instructional implications of Thorndike's theory are to be found in a series of subsidiary laws that are part of the system. For example, the **law of set or attitude** states that people often respond to novel situations in terms of the **sets**, or attitudes, that they bring with them. This means that students can be taught that various aspects of a subject are related, and they will then react to new material as though it related to previously learned information. By the same token, students can be given a set to proceed as though the best way to learn is through rote memorization.

This law also implies that cultural background and immediate environment not only affect how a person responds but also determine what will be satisfying or annoying. For example, the student's environment may determine that

"That is the correct answer, Billy, but I'm afraid you don't win anything for it."

academic success will be satisfying—or that popularity will be more satisfying than academic success.

Attracting Attention. A second subsidiary law, the **law of prepotency of elements**, recognizes that people respond to the most significant or the most striking aspects of a stimulus situation and not necessarily to the entire situation. Obviously, students cannot and probably should not respond to all the sights and sounds that surround them at any given moment. Hence, teachers must be careful to stress (make prepotent) important aspects of the learning situation (for example, by underlining or **boldfacing**, through the use of color, through the use of voice and gestures, through repetition, and so on).

Generalizing. **Generalization** (sometimes referred to as **transfer**) is one of the important goals of education. Generalization occurs whenever a

previously learned response is used in a new situation—or when a new stimulus is reacted to as though it were familiar. When Tamy uses a multiplication rule she learned in school to determine how many packs of bubble gum two quarters will buy, she is generalizing. Thorndike believed that the transference of a response to a new stimulus is a function of the similarity between the two stimuli—hence, this subsidiary law is called the **law of response by analogy**.

Thorndike suggested that teachers can facilitate transfer by pointing out a variety of situations in which a single response (or rule) is applicable. He also emphasized the importance of pointing out connections among ideas. These connections, Thorndike insisted, are the basis of knowledge.

OPERANT CONDITIONING: B. F. SKINNER

By definition, behaviorists are concerned with behavior. They define learning in terms of changes in behavior and look to the environment for explanations of these changes. Their theories are **associationistic**; they deal with connections or associations that are formed among stimuli and responses. And, as we have seen, these theories make use of one or both of two principal classes of explanations for learning: those based on contiguity (simultaneity of stimulus and response events) and those based on the effects of behavior (reinforcement and punishment). Pavlov and Watson are contiguity theorists; Thorndike is a reinforcement theorist. So is Burrhus Frederic Skinner, one of the most influential psychologists of the twentieth century and the originator and chief spokesman for the theory of **operant conditioning**.

Respondent and Operant Behavior

Skinner accepted the existence and validity of classical conditioning. He claimed that many responses, called **elicited responses,** can be brought about by a stimulus and can become conditioned to other stimuli in the manner described by Pavlov and Watson. He labeled this behavior **respondent** because it occurs in response to a stimulus.

A second, much larger and more important class of behaviors, however, consists of behaviors that are not elicited by any known stimuli but are simply **emitted responses** of the organism. These are labeled **operants** because, in a sense, they are operations performed by the organism. Another way of making this distinction is to say that in the case of respondent behavior the organism is reacting to the environment, whereas in the case of operant behavior the organism acts upon the environment (see Table 4.2).

The distinction between respondent and operant behavior can be clarified further by examining some simple behaviors. Sneezing, blinking, being angry, afraid, or excited—these may all be respondents. What they have in common is that they are largely automatic and almost inevitable responses to specific situations. Put another way, they are responses that can reliably be elicited by specific stimuli. Such responses are learned through processes of classical conditioning.

In contrast, driving a car, writing a letter, singing, reading a book, and kissing a baby are generally operants (although these, too, may involve respondents, as when a red light leads me automatically to slam on the brakes). Their common characteristics are that they are deliberate and intentional. They occur not as inevitable responses to specific stimulation but as personally controlled actions (rather than reactions). And they are subject to the laws of operant conditioning.

Because it does not involve obvious stimuli operant conditioning is somewhat different from Thorndike's conception of learning and his law of effect. Whereas Thorndike believed that the effect of reinforcement is to strengthen the bond that exists between the stimulus and the response, Skinner declared that not only is the stimulus usually unknown but, in any case, it is irrelevant

TABLE 4.2 Classical and Operant Conditioning	
CLASSICAL (PAVLOVIAN)	OPERANT (SKINNERIAN)
Deals with respondents, which are *elicited* by stimuli (*reactions to* the environment)	Deals with operants, which are *emitted* as *instrumental* acts (*actions upon* the environment)

to the learning. The link is formed between response and reinforcement rather than between stimulus and response. Essentially, all that happens in operant learning is that when an emitted response is reinforced, the probability increases that it will be repeated.

Operant Conditioning Defined

Operant conditioning is most simply illustrated by reference to a typical Skinnerian experiment with a rat. In this experiment, a rat is placed in a **Skinner box,** a small, controlled environment (see Figure 4.3). The Skinner box is constructed to make certain responses highly probable and to make it possible for the experimenter to measure these responses and to punish or reward them. For our typical experiment, the box contains a lever, a light, an electric grid on the floor, and a food tray, all arranged in such a way that when the rat depresses the lever, the light goes on and a food pellet is released into the tray. Under these circumstances, most rats will quickly learn to depress the lever, and they will continue to do so for long periods of time, even if they do not receive a food pellet each time they work the lever. Similarly, rats can quickly be trained to avoid the lever if depressing it activates a mild electric current in the floor grid. However, if the electric current is constant and ceases only when the lever is depressed, rats will learn to depress it.

a	Light	c	Bar or lever	e	Rat
b	Food tray	d	Electric grid		

FIGURE 4.3 A Skinner box. From G. R. Lefrançois, *Psychological Theories and Human Learning* (2nd ed.). Copyright 1982 by Wadsworth, Inc. Reprinted by permission of Brooks/Cole Publishing Company, Monterey, California.

Most of the basic elements of Skinner's theory are evident in this situation. The rat's act of depressing the lever is an operant—an almost random behavior that is simply emitted rather than being elicited by a specific stimulus. The food pellets serve as reinforcement. Their availability increases the probability that whenever the rat finds itself in this situation, it will saunter over to the lever and depress it.

In general terms, operant conditioning is an increase in the probability that a response will occur again, this increase being a result of reinforcement (about which more is said shortly). Furthermore, Skinner's model of operant conditioning states that the reward, together with whatever **discriminated stimuli (SD*)** were present at

---

*Also referred to as *discriminative* stimuli; refers to those aspects of a situation (stimuli) that differentiate it from other situations.

the time of reinforcement, are stimuli that, after learning, may bring about the operant. For example, the rat's view (and smell) of the inside of the Skinner box may eventually serve as stimuli for lever-pressing behavior. (See Figure 4.4 for a model of operant learning and Figure 4.5 for some classroom examples.)

Principles of Operant Conditioning

One of Skinner's main concerns was to discover the relationship between reinforcement and behavior and to clarify how behavior is affected by its consequences.

Reinforcement. Skinner made an important distinction between two related terms: **reinforcer** and **reinforcement**. A reinforcer is a thing, or, in Skinnerian terms, a stimulus; reinforcement is the effect of this stimulus. For example, candy may be a reinforcer because it can be reinforcing and because it is a stimulus. A piece of candy, however, is not a reinforcement, although its effect on a person may be an example of reinforcement.

Although *reinforcement* may be defined in different ways (see, for example, Skinner, 1953), the most widely accepted definition is any stimulus that increases the probability that a response will occur. This definition makes it clear that it is the effect of a stimulus that determines whether it will be reinforcing. Thus, any given situation may be highly reinforcing for one person and highly unpleasant for another. First-grade students may react positively when they are presented with little gold stars in recognition of their work. College students whose professor offered them little stars might think, with some justification, that the professor was a little strange.

Reinforcers may be primary or generalized. A **primary reinforcer** is a stimulus that is reinforcing without the occurrence of learning and is ordinarily related to an unlearned need or drive: food, drink, sex. Presumably, people do not have to learn that these can feel good.

Before Conditioning

Stimulus Context: Classroom

Response	Response	Response
Read comic	Attend to teacher	Talk to neighbor

Various responses are emitted
in a certain stimulus context

Conditioning Process

Stimulus Context: Classroom

followed
by

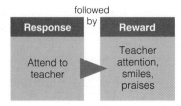

Response	Reward
Attend to teacher	Teacher attention, smiles, praises

One response is systematically reinforced

After Conditioning

Stimulus Context: Classroom

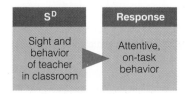

S^D	Response
Sight and behavior of teacher in classroom	Attentive, on-task behavior

The reinforced response becomes more frequent.
Stimuli accompanying the reward (discriminated
stimuli, or S^D) acquire control over the response

FIGURE 4.4 Operant conditioning in the classroom. Note that in operant conditioning, unlike classical conditioning, the original response is emitted rather than elicited by a stimulus. In this example, a variety of off-task and on-task behaviors are emitted. Reinforcement leads to the more frequent occurrence of on-task behaviors.

A **generalized reinforcer** is a previously neutral stimulus that, through repeated pairings with a number of other reinforcers in various situations, has become reinforcing for many behaviors. Prestige, money, and success are examples of extremely powerful generalized reinforcers.

Primary and generalized reinforcers can be positive or negative. A **positive reinforcer** is a stimulus that increases the probability of a response occurring when it is added to a situation. A **negative reinforcer** has the same effect as a result of being removed from the situation.

In the Skinner box example, food pellets are a positive reinforcer—as is the light. If, however, a mild current were turned on in the electric grid that runs through the floor of the box, and if this current were turned off only when the rat depressed the lever, turning off the current would be an example of a negative reinforcer.

Reinforcement and Punishment in the Classroom

In summary, there are two types of reinforcement. One involves presenting a pleasant stimulus (positive reinforcement; **reward**); the other involves removing an unpleasant stimulus (negative reinforcement; **relief**). In the same way, there are two types of punishment, each the converse of one type of reinforcement. On the one hand is the punishment that occurs when a pleasant stimulus is removed (**penalty**); on the other is the more familiar situation in which a noxious (unpleasant) stimulus is presented. Figure 4.6 summarizes these four possibilities; the sections that follow illustrate each in the classroom.

Positive Reinforcement (Reward). Examples of positive reinforcement in the classroom are so numerous and obvious as to make citing any one appear platitudinous. Whenever a teacher smiles at students, says something pleasant to them, commends them for their work, assigns high grades, selects someone for a special project, or tells a mother how clever her child is, the teacher is

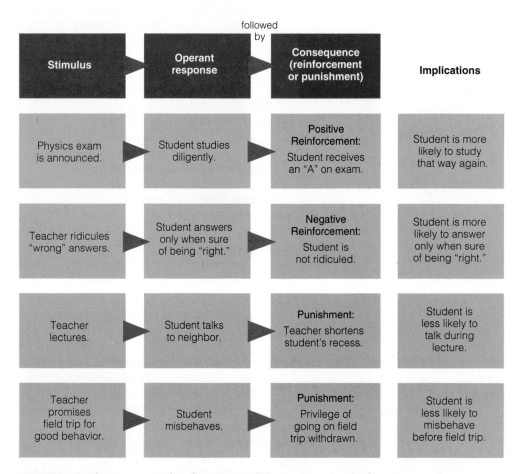

Stimulus Context: Classroom

Stimulus	Operant response	Consequence (reinforcement or punishment)	Implications
Physics exam is announced.	Student studies diligently.	**Positive Reinforcement:** Student receives an "A" on exam.	Student is more likely to study that way again.
Teacher ridicules "wrong" answers.	Student answers only when sure of being "right."	**Negative Reinforcement:** Student is not ridiculed.	Student is more likely to answer only when sure of being "right."
Teacher lectures.	Student talks to neighbor.	**Punishment:** Teacher shortens student's recess.	Student is less likely to talk during lecture.
Teacher promises field trip for good behavior.	Student misbehaves.	**Punishment:** Privilege of going on field trip withdrawn.	Student is less likely to misbehave before field trip.

(*followed by*)

FIGURE 4.5 Classroom examples of operant conditioning. Note that the first two examples (positive and negative reinforcement, respectively) lead to an *increase* in the likelihood of the response. The last two examples (both forms of punishment) lead to a *decrease* in the likelihood of the response. Note also that teachers may inadvertently reinforce maladaptive behaviors (second example).

using positive reinforcement. (See Chapter 11 for a more detailed discussion of various kinds of classroom reinforcement.)

Negative Reinforcement (Relief). Implicit or explicit threats of punishment, failure, detention, ridicule, parental anger, humiliation, and sundry other unpleasant eventualities make up the bulk of the modern, well-equipped teacher's arsenal of negative reinforcers. When these follow unruly, nonstudious, or otherwise unacceptable behaviors, they may be interpreted as punishment (the presentation of an unpleasant stimulus following undesirable behavior). When the threat of these possibilities is removed following acceptable behavior, they provide a clear example of negative

Nature of Stimulus Effect

	Pleasant	Unpleasant
Added to the situation	Positive reinforcement (reward) Louella is given a jelly bean for being "good."	Punishment I (punishment) Louella has her nose tweaked for being "bad."
Removed from the situation	Punishment II (penalty) Louella has her jelly bean taken away for being "bad."	Negative reinforcement (relief) Louella's nose is released because she says "I'm sorry."

(Application of Stimulus)

FIGURE 4.6 Reinforcement and punishment.

reinforcement (the removal of an unpleasant stimulus following desirable behavior). Negative and sometimes maladaptive behaviors, such as the tendency to escape or avoid situations, frequently result from the overzealous administration of negative reinforcement.

Punishment I. The first type of punishment involves presenting a noxious stimulus, usually in an attempt to eliminate some undesirable behavior. A classic example is the use of the lash in one North Carolina school in the year 1848 (see Table 4.3, and Mrs. Grundy's case, earlier in this chapter)—a practice that is no longer widely accepted.

Punishment II (Penalty). The second type of punishment involves the removal of a pleasant stimulus. The fairly common practice of detaining students after regular class hours, insofar as it removes the apparently pleasant privilege of going home, is an example of this type of punishment.

Effects of Reinforcement and Punishment. Reinforcement improves learning; it can easily be demonstrated that the behavior of animals and people can often be controlled through the careful use of reinforcement. That punishment has an equal, if opposite, effect is not nearly so obvious.

As Thorndike observed, pleasure is much more potent in stamping in responses than pain is in stamping them out.

In addition to objections based on ethical or humanitarian considerations are several other reasons why the use of punishment is an unsatisfactory means of behavior control. Among the most obvious is that punishment does not ordinarily illustrate or emphasize desirable behavior but simply draws attention to undesirable responses, so it is not very useful in a learning situation. A second objection is that punishment is often accompanied by highly undesirable emotional side effects that often are associated with the punisher rather than with the punished behavior. Third, punishment does not always lead to the elimination of a response but sometimes only to its suppression. In other words, a behavior is seldom forgotten as a result of punishment, although it may be avoided—sometimes only temporarily.

A last objection to punishment is a simple, practical one—it often does not work. Sears, Maccoby, and Lewin (1957) report that parents who punish their children severely for being aggressive are more likely than other parents to have aggressive children. And mothers who are unduly punitive when attempting to toilet train their

TABLE 4.3 Excerpt from a List of Punishments in a North Carolina School, 1848

NO.	RULES OF SCHOOL	LASHES
1	Boys and Girls Playing Together	4
3	Fighting	5
7	Playing at Cards at School	4
8	Climbing for Every Foot Over Three Feet Up a Tree	1
9	Telling Lyes	7
11	Nick Naming Each Other	4
16	For Misbehaving to Girls	10
19	For Drinking Spirituous Liquors at School	8
22	For Waring Long Finger Nails	2
27	Girls Going to Boy's Play Places	2
33	Wrestling at School	4
41	For Throwing Anything Harder than Your Trab Ball	4
42	For Every Word You Miss in Your Heart Lesson Without Good Excuse	1
47	For Going about the Barn or Doing Any Mischief about the Place	7

Source: From C. L. Coon. (1915). *North Carolina schools and academies.* Raleigh, N.C.: Edwards and Broughton.

children are more likely to have children who wet their beds. It appears, however, that overpermissive parents are as likely to have problems with their children as are those who make excessive use of physical punishment.

All of which is, indeed, valuable advice, whether it be interpreted by sages or by fools.[*]

Aversive Control

It should be stressed again that negative reinforcement and punishment describe two very different situations. The two are often confused because

[*]PPC: Perhaps Lefrançois should point out that the use of punishment is sometimes highly effective and highly appropriate. Or was it punishment that made a fool out of the bear who always used to face the front so sagely?

Author: I do in Chapter 11. And the bear is too smart to be a fool, although he is not yet a sage.

each usually involves unpleasant (noxious) stimuli. But whereas punishment results in a reduction in behavior, negative reinforcement, like positive reinforcement, *increases* the probability that a response will occur. Thus, a child can be encouraged to speak politely to teachers by being smiled at for saying "please" and "thank you" (positive reinforcement). Another child can be beaten with a cane (or threatened therewith) when pleases and thank yous are forgotten (punishment)—with the clear understanding that the cane will be put away only when behavior conforms to the teacher's standards of politeness (negative reinforcement). In the end, both children may be wonderfully polite. But which child, do you suppose, will like teachers and schools more?

Strange as it might seem, the use of negative reinforcement as a means of control is highly prevalent in today's schools, homes, and churches, as is the use of punishment. These methods of **aversive control** (in contrast to **positive control**) are evident in the use of low grades and verbal rebukes, in threats of punishment, in detention in schools, and in the unpleasant fates that await transgressors in most major religions. They are evident as well in our legal and judicial systems, which are extraordinarily punitive rather than rewarding. Material rewards for being good are seldom obvious, but criminality is clearly punished. In fact, the reward for being good frequently takes the form of not being punished. That, in a nutshell, is negative reinforcement.

It is difficult to determine which is more important in our daily lives—positive reinforcement or negative reinforcement. Nor is it always easy to separate the two in practice, daily life being considerably more tolerant of ambiguity than is psychological theory. Consider, for example, that I work to obtain the "good" things in life: food, prestige, power, and a soft, wet kiss. It seems obvious that I am controlled by positive reinforcement. Or is it true, as my grandmother suggested, that I am really working to prevent hunger, to escape from anonymity and helplessness, and to avoid loneliness?

The issue cannot easily be resolved, but it is worth noting that I am much more likely to be happy if positive rather than negative contingencies control my behavior. Indeed, **avoidance learning** and/or **escape learning** are among the most important consequences of aversive control. A child who performs well in school because of parental and teacher rewards probably likes school; another who performs well in order to escape parental wrath and school punishments will probably have quite different emotional reactions to school and may avoid further noncompulsory schooling or might even consider escaping from the situation.

Aversive control of behavior may have one additional, highly undesirable effect. When Ulrich and Azrin (1962) placed two rats in a situation in which they had to turn a wheel to avoid an electric shock, the rodents fell, tooth and nail, upon each other. Although each understood (in a primitive rat way, to be sure) that the source of their pain was the wheel and not the other rat, they insisted on behaving in a most unfriendly fashion.

It should be noted that the most dedicated proponents of applied behavioral techniques and principles strongly advocate the use of positive rather than aversive control methods. This was especially true of B. F. Skinner.

Schedules of Reinforcement

Through experiments with pigeons and rats, Skinner attempted to discover (1) the relationship between the type and amount of reinforcement used and the quality of learning achieved and (2) the relationship between the way reinforcement is administered and learning.

The first relationship cannot easily be determined because type and amount of reinforcement appear to affect individuals in unpredictable ways. It is clear from numerous experiments that even a very small reward will lead to effective learning and will maintain behavior over a long period. It is also clear that too much reward (satiation) may lead to a cessation of behavior. Several guidelines for the use of reinforcement are presented in Chapter 11. However, these should be interpreted cautiously.

The relationship between how reinforcement is administered (referred to as the **schedule of reinforcement**) and the resulting behavior can be investigated directly. Schedules invariably use either **continuous reinforcement** or **intermittent reinforcement** (also called "partial reinforcement"). In the first case, a reward is provided for every correct response (referred to as *every trial*). In the second case, only some of the trials are reinforced, in which case the experimenters have two options. They may choose to reinforce a certain proportion of trials (a **ratio schedule**), or they may base their schedule on the passage of time (an **interval schedule**). They might, for example, decide to reinforce one out of five correct responses, or they might reinforce one correct response for every fifteen-second lapse. In either case, they have two more options. They might choose to assign reinforcement in a predetermined fashion (**fixed schedule**) or in a more haphazard manner (**random** or **variable schedule**). Or, to really confuse things in proper psychological fashion, they might combine a number of these schedules and gleefully claim that they are using a mixed or **combined schedule**.

They have no more choices, fortunately . . . except maybe one. It is referred to as a **superstitious schedule**.

A superstitious schedule provides regular reinforcement no matter what the learner is doing. In fact, it's a fixed interval schedule without the provision that there has to be a correct response before reinforcement occurs. When Skinner (1948) left six pigeons on a superstitious schedule overnight (they received reinforcement at regular intervals no matter what they did), he found that by morning one bird had learned to turn clockwise just before each reinforcement, another pointed its head toward the corner, and several had learned to sway back and forth. Skinner suggests that we too learn "superstitious" behaviors as a result of reinforcement that occurs independently of what we do. For example, some of us frown when we're thinking or chew our hair or scratch our heads. Do we do these things because they actually help us think? Or do we do them because we happened to be doing them when we were reinforced (perhaps with a good idea) in the past?

The section on schedule of reinforcement may, at first glance, appear somewhat confusing. You are advised to read it again slowly and consult Figure 4.7. It is really quite simple. Experimenters have two choices: If they choose A, they have no more choices, but if they choose B, they have two new options. Each of these, in turn, offers two further options. And finally, the last four options may be combined, or the experimenter might throw in a superstitious schedule.

Schedules and Learning. Much of Skinner's work was directed toward discovering the relationship between various schedules of reinforcement and one of three measures of learning: **rate of learning**, **response rate**, and **extinction rate**. The most important results of these studies are reported here.

It appears that continuous reinforcement is most effective for increasing the initial rate of learning. When learning simple responses such as lever pressing, the rat might become confused and would almost certainly learn much more slowly if only some of its initial correct responses were reinforced. In terms of classroom practice, this means that initial learning, particularly for very young children, probably requires far more reinforcement than does later learning. Students often receive this reinforcement in the form of attention or knowledge that they are performing correctly.

Interestingly, although continuous reinforcement often leads to more rapid learning, it does not usually result in longer **retention** of what is learned. In fact, the rate of **extinction** for behavior that has been reinforced continuously is considerably faster than for behavior that has been reinforced intermittently. *Extinction* means the cessation of a response as a function of withholding reinforcement. The extinction rate is simply the time that elapses between the beginning of the nonreinforced period and the cessation of behavior.

The use of extinction in schools, often in the form of the withdrawal of attention in the case of unruly, attention-seeking behavior, is widespread and effective. Several illustrations are provided in Chapter 11.

In general, therefore, the best schedule would appear to consist initially of continuous reinforcement, followed later by intermittent reinforcement. Among the intermittent schedules, a random ratio arrangement ordinarily results in the slowest rate of extinction.

The rate of responding can also be brought under the control of the schedule used. Interest-

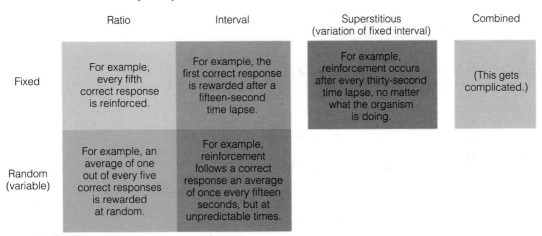

A. Continuous

| Every correct response is reinforced. |

B. Intermittent (Partial)

	Ratio	Interval	Superstitious (variation of fixed interval)	Combined
Fixed	For example, every fifth correct response is reinforced.	For example, the first correct response is rewarded after a fifteen-second time lapse.	For example, reinforcement occurs after every thirty-second time lapse, no matter what the organism is doing.	(This gets complicated.)
Random (variable)	For example, an average of one out of every five correct responses is rewarded at random.	For example, reinforcement follows a correct response an average of once every fifteen seconds, but at unpredictable times.		

FIGURE 4.7 Schedules of reinforcement. Each type of reinforcement tends to generate its own characteristic pattern of response.

ingly, the behavior of pigeons and rats often suggests that they have developed expectations about reward. A pigeon that has been taught to peck a disk and is reinforced for the first peck after a lapse of fifteen seconds (fixed interval) often completely ceases pecking immediately after being reinforced and resumes again just before the end of the fifteen-second interval. If, on the other hand, the pigeon is reinforced on a random ratio basis, its response rate will be uniformly high and constant, often as high as two thousand or more pecks an hour. (See Figure 4.8.)

Schedules and People. So! One can reinforce the behavior of rats and pigeons in a variety of clever ways and can note a number of consistent effects that this has on their ludicrously simple behaviors. From this, numerous graduate dissertations and great quantities of published research may be derived for the erudition of the scholars and the amazement of the people.

But what of human beings? How are they affected by schedules of reinforcement?

The answer seems to be: in much the same way as animals. Marquis (1941), for example, investigated the behavior of babies who were fed regularly (fixed interval schedule) and of others who were fed on demand. Not surprisingly, infants on fixed schedules showed a marked increase in activity just before feeding time. Bandura and Walters (1963) make the related observation that behaviors engaged in by young children who desire parental attention tend to be randomly reinforced—and tend, consequently, to be highly persistent. In the same way, the observation that extinction is more rapid in rats following

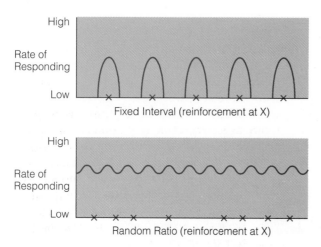

FIGURE 4.8 Pigeon pecking under two reinforcement schedules.

continuous reinforcement appears to be valid for human infants as well (Kass & Wilson, 1966).

There are many examples of the effects of schedules on people's behaviors. The fisherman who goes to the same stream time after time, although he rarely (but occasionally) catches fish, is demonstrating the persistence that results from an intermittent schedule of reinforcement. The small-town student who was at the top of her classes for eight years—but now finds herself being outdone in the fierce competition of a new school—ceases to study; she may be demonstrating the rapid extinction that follows continuous reinforcement. Knowing how schedules of reinforcement affect people's behaviors can be useful in a variety of practical situations—as the wife who occasionally but not too frequently praises her husband's appearance or his cooking will attest. He may continue to cook and to look good despite long sequences without reinforcement.

Shaping

A Skinnerian psychologist who wanted to train a rat to genuflect, turn three somersaults, and then stand briefly on its head with its tail pointing west might approach the rat's cage and watch carefully for the appearance of this complex sequence of operants. When the desired behaviors occurred, it would be a simple matter (theoretically, to be sure) to reinforce the behavior, thus increasing the probability that the sequence would be repeated. Unfortunately, both the psychologist and the rat likely would die of old age before the desired operants appeared.

Another, much better way of teaching rats using operant conditioning is called **shaping**. Shaping involves reinforcing the animal for every behavior that brings it slightly closer to the desired behavior. For example, if the objective is to teach the rat to genuflect, the experimenter might initially reinforce the rat every time its front quarters dipped slightly. Later, once the rat had learned to dip reliably and predictably, slight dips would no longer be reinforced but more pronounced dips would be. And if the reinforcements were accompanied by a distinctive stimulus such as a bell (a discriminated stimulus), eventually the rat might genuflect every time the psychologist rang the bell. Which would surely have amazed and confounded my grandmother!

For obvious reasons, shaping is also called the **differential reinforcement of successive approximations**. It is one of the most common techniques used in training performing animals. Does it have any relevance to the lives of humans?

Shaping and People. Yes. A great deal of human behavior is shaped through reinforcement. For example, as previously reinforcing activities become habitual and less rewarding, they tend to be modified. A motorcyclist may initially derive considerable reinforcement from the sensation of turning a sharp corner at high speed, but in time the sensation diminishes and the excitement decreases. And as the reinforcement begins to decrease, speed increases, imperceptibly but progressively. This is a clear illustration of shaping as a consequence of the outcome of behavior.

There are many examples of shaping in the classroom. Peer approval or disapproval, sometimes communicated in subtle, nonverbal ways, can drastically affect a student's behavior. The classroom clown would probably not continue to be a clown if no one paid any attention to her. Indeed, she might never have been shaped into a clown had her audience not reinforced her in the first place.

Generalization and Discrimination

Not all situations for which a specific operant is appropriate (or inappropriate) will be encountered by an individual while learning. Yet individuals do respond when faced with new situations. The behavioristic theorist explains this by reference to generalization or **discrimination**. Generalization, as we saw, involves making a response that would ordinarily be made under other, similar circumstances. Discrimination involves refraining from making the response in question because of some difference between this situation and other situations for which the response was clearly more appropriate. For example, children may learn very early in life that they will receive their mother's attention if they cry. This type of behavior is soon generalized from specific situations in which they have obtained their mother's attention to new situations in which they desire her attention. A wise mother can bring about discrimination learning simply by not paying attention to her child in those situations in which she does not want to be disturbed. While on the

phone, she might completely ignore her child's crying; soon the child will learn to discriminate between situations in which attention-getting behavior is not reinforced and other situations in which it is more likely to be reinforced.

Instructional Applications of Operant Principles

It is difficult to overestimate the relevance of the principles of operant learning to teaching. A classroom is in many ways like a gigantic Skinner box. It is so engineered that certain responses are more probable than others. For example, it is easier to sit at a desk than to lie on one—and it is easier to remain awake when sitting than when lying. And at the front of a million classrooms stand the powerful dispensers of reinforcement—the teachers. They smile or frown; they say "Good" or "Not good"; they give high grades or low grades; occasionally they grant special favors; at other times they withhold or cancel privileges. By means of this reinforcement and punishment, they shape the behavior of their students.

Drawing an analogy of a classroom, a teacher, and a student on the one hand and a Skinner box, a psychologist, and a rat on the other is somewhat unappealing and perhaps a little frightening (shades of Orwell's *1984*). Yet the analogy is relevant and potentially useful. Classroom teachers could often profit immensely from the discoveries of experimental psychologists.

One of the first direct results of the application of Skinner's theory to teaching was a renewed emphasis on **programmed instruction**—a topic discussed in some detail in Chapter 12.

Another application of the theory to **instruction** has taken the form of a serious criticism of education and of current teaching methods. In a 1965 article entitled "Why Teachers Fail," Skinner claimed that efforts to improve education seldom involve attempts to improve teaching as such and that teachers therefore continue to teach the way they themselves were taught. Chief among their methods are the techniques of aversive control—

the use of unpleasant stimuli, often for punishment but sometimes for negative reinforcement as well.

As alternatives to aversive control, Skinner suggests the obvious—positive reinforcement, together with "attractive and attention compelling" approaches to teaching. In addition, he presents numerous suggestions for the development of a **technology of teaching** in a book by that title (Skinner, 1968). Interestingly, some ten years later another behaviorist, Fred Keller (1978, p. 53) was to assert: "Never before in the history of mankind have we known so much about the learning process and the conditions under which an individual human being can be efficiently and happily trained." And others, such as Greer (1983), argue strongly that the effectiveness of behavioristic principles for teaching is not equaled by any other approach. The application of these principles requires that teachers become behavior analysts— that they dedicate themselves both to identifying and establishing environments that will lead to desirable behaviors and to providing reinforcement contingencies that will serve to maintain these behaviors. The success of such an approach has been demonstrated experimentally numerous times, perhaps most dramatically with mentally retarded, autistic, and other learning-disadvantaged children. A collective label for the application of these principles in education and in therapy is **behavior modification**. Specific behavior modification techniques are discussed in Chapter 11.

BEHAVIORISTIC CONTRIBUTIONS: A SUMMARY

"To satisfy the practical demands of education, theories of learning must be 'stood on their heads' so as to yield theories of teaching" (Gage, 1964, p. 269). Presumably, the same result would be obtained if students were asked to stand on their heads while the theories remained upright. Unfortunately, however, even as extreme a measure as standing these behavioristic theories on their heads would be unlikely to yield theories of teaching. On the other hand, they need be tilted only very slightly to produce a variety of principles of practical value—many of which have been mentioned and illustrated earlier in the chapter. For example, the notion that repetition is important for learning follows directly from Thorndike's laws as well as from what is known about classical conditioning. In Thorndike's system, the formation of bonds is a direct function of the number of times a stimulus and a response are paired and reinforced.

The importance of reinforcement is the second of the major instructional implications deriving from behavioristic theories. Skinner and Thorndike each made the principles of reinforcement cornerstones of their systems. And even in Watson's system, reinforcement may be important. Its effect may be to prevent the unlearning of a response by changing the stimulus situation so that the organism is prevented from making another response to the first stimulus. A number of specific conclusions by Thorndike have implications for educational practice:

1. Punishment is not very effective for eliminating undesirable behavior (Thorndike, 1932).

2. Interest in work and in improvement is conducive to learning (Thorndike, 1935).

3. Significance of subject matter and the attitude of the learner are important variables in school (Thorndike, 1935).

4. Repetition without reinforcement does not enhance learning (Thorndike, 1931).

Another Point of View

There are many others, however, who are quick to point out that behaviorism is not a universal cure for all our educational ills. Even if we were to agree that behavioristic principles should be applied whenever possible, we would soon discover that there are countless instances in which they cannot be applied very effectively at all. As H. Walker (1979) points out, teachers seldom control some

of the most powerful reinforcers that affect student behavior—for example, peer acceptance and praise, parental approval, and so on. What this means is that teachers are often relegated to using what are, at least for some students, the relatively weaker reinforcers—teacher approval and grades.

A second problem in the universal application of behavioristic principles in teaching is, as Brophy (1983) argues, that most of our instructional problems do not involve establishing a reinforcement schedule so as to maintain a desirable response but instead involve bringing about the response in the first place. This is quite unlike the Skinner box situation, in which the major problem has been to control and maintain a specific response through the manipulation of reinforcement and in which eliciting the response is often a minor problem.

A third problem is that although operant principles can be used to control maladaptive behavior, its application sometimes has serious limitations. Palardy (1991) points out that behavior modification techniques applied to behavior problems ignore the causes of misbehavior, place insufficient emphasis on prevention, and often do not have long-term benefits. However, he notes that these techniques *are* effective and that all teachers should be familiar with them; they simply are not sufficient *by themselves*. (More about specific behavior modification techniques in Chapter 11.)

That there are problems in applying behavioristic principles and that these principles are not easy solutions for all teaching problems should not blind us to their potential. Some of that potential is discussed in greater detail in Chapters 11 and 12.

BEYOND FREEDOM: A PHILOSOPHICAL ARGUMENT

If most significant human behaviors are controlled by reinforcement or the lack of it, it follows that we are controlled by our environments—that the freedom of which we are so proud is merely an illusion. If I awaken in the morning and decide to brush my teeth, am I really free to make the choice? Can I either brush or not brush according to the whim of the moment? Or am I bound by the dictates of past reinforcement (and/or punishment), real or imagined? In his book dealing with freedom and dignity, Skinner asserts that the autonomous person is a myth. "Autonomous man," he explains "is a device used to explain what we cannot explain in any other way. He has been constructed from our ignorance, and as our understanding increases, the very stuff of which he is composed vanishes" (Skinner, 1971, p. 200). We are controlled by our environment, says Skinner, but he reassures us that it is an environment of which we are almost totally in control—or at least an environment that is almost wholly of our own making. There is a fundamental difference between the two. An environment over which we have control implies an environment in which we are free, because we can change the reinforcement contingencies of that environment. An environment of our own making, but over which we have no immediate control, implies an environment in which we are not free. It may be that as a species, we have controlled our own destiny, but as individuals we do not control our own actions.

Skinner discusses at length the possibility of applying a science of human behavior for the benefit of humanity, an undertaking that would involve a degree of control over human behavior (Skinner, 1953, 1961). It is this aspect of his work that has met with the greatest resistance and has led some to speculate that Skinnerian behaviorism can as easily be made a weapon as a tool. The question is an ethical and moral one. The science exists, imperfect and incomplete as it is—and is sometimes used deliberately and systematically. Skinner (1961) describes, for example, how advertising uses emotional reinforcement by presenting alluring women in commercials and how motivational control is achieved by creating generalized reinforcers—as when a car becomes a powerful reinforcer by being equated with sex. He describes a society that controls through positive reinforcement in the form of wages, bribes, or tips—or that controls through drugs, such as "fear-reducers" for soldiers and steroids and cocaine for athletes.

But all of this began happening before Skinner, and, as he notes, "No theory changes what it is a theory about; man remains what he has always been" (1971, p. 215).

Nevertheless, this description of the human condition has come under severe attack from a wide variety of critics—as Skinner had predicted it would. In essence, he has questioned the control exercised by the "autonomous" person and has demonstrated the control exercised by the environment in an attempt to create a science of behavior. The approach itself brings into question the worth and dignity of people. "These are sweeping changes," Skinner said, "and those who are committed to traditional theories and practices naturally resist them" (1971, p. 21).

The dispute is essentially between humanistic psychologists (those concerned more with humanity, ideals, values, and emotions; see Chapter 9) and experiment-oriented psychologists (those more concerned with developing a relatively rigorous science of behavior). But the two positions are not really incompatible. "Man is much more than a dog," Skinner tells us, "but like a dog he is within range of scientific analysis" (1971, p. 21).

Is the fact that I can deliberately choose to lie to you proof that I am free?

SOCIAL LEARNING AND IMITATION

In psychology, the phrase **social learning** is often used without precise definition, as though everybody intuitively knows exactly what it means and all agree about that meaning.

Not so. In fact, the term is used in two ways. For some writers, it means all learning that occurs as a result of, or involves, social interaction. Others use the term to signify the type of learning that is involved in finding out what sorts of behaviors society accepts and expects, as well as those that are unacceptable. This difference in meanings is essentially a distinction between process and product. In other words, *social learning* might refer to the way in which learning occurs (that is, through social interaction) or to what is learned (the product: acceptable behaviors).

Socially Accepted Behaviors: The Product

Socially acceptable behavior varies both from culture to culture and from group to group within a single culture. For example, it is socially acceptable for students in some Asian countries to bow to their teachers and to offer them gifts. In most Western countries, a student who habitually bowed to teachers and offered gifts might embarrass both self and teacher.

Similarly, socially acceptable behavior is often a function of age and of sex. Young children are not expected to address teachers and other adults by their first names; they are expected to learn and obey an assortment of unwritten rules of respect and of social distance. In much the same way, some behaviors are socially expected—hence, culturally appropriate—for males but not for females and vice versa.

Probably one of the most important tasks of the home in the early years of a child's life, and later of the school, is to foster the development of appropriate behaviors—a process called **socialization**. This process involves transmitting the culture of a society to children and teaching them behaviors appropriate for their sex and social circumstance—or, in a more ideal world, teaching them that appropriateness of behaviors does not depend on sex.

Learning Social Behaviors: The Process

The central question from a developmental point of view is how the child learns socially acceptable behaviors. One answer is through imitation, the process of copying the behavior of others. Put simply, learning through imitation, sometimes referred to as **observational learning**, involves acquiring new responses or modifying old ones as a result of seeing a model do something. According to Bandura (1969), the processes involved in imitation are "one of the fundamental means by which new modes of behavior are acquired and existing patterns are modified . . ." (p. 118).

It is largely through the processes of social learning and imitation that fads and expressions sweep through countries: Overnight (almost), men begin to wear their hair long or short; short skirts are in, then out, then in . . . ; everyone is saying "yeah" or "outasight"; things are "cool" or "neat" and people are "beautiful."*

But these are trivial matters in the grand scheme of more cosmic events—although how to dress and what to say are by no means trivial in our more private, less cosmic, worlds. Social learning theory explains much more than our fads and expressions.

THE SOCIAL LEARNING THEORY OF BANDURA AND WALTERS

The social learning theory advanced by Bandura and Walters (1963) and by Bandura (1969, 1977) is based partly on a model of operant conditioning. But perhaps more important, it recognizes the fundamental importance of our ability to symbolize, to imagine, to ferret out cause-and-effect relationships, and to anticipate the outcomes of our behaviors. Accordingly, it is as much cognitive as behavioristic. The environment clearly affects our behavior, Bandura informs us; there is little doubt that we engage in many behaviors because of the reinforcing consequences

---

*PPC: Your faddish words are now a bit outdated. How about "totally" or one of the other valley girl expressions to add to the list?

Author: This is no longer a real young bear. He has almost stopped trying to keep up with fads. But he still thinks valley girl talk is like awesome, vertical, and totally tubular. Ya know? He has humongous appreciation for valleys, fer sure. But now he's told that valley girl talk is totally passé, which, since he had learned some of it, he finds just a little distressing.

of so doing. But reinforcement does not control us blindly; its effects depend largely on our awareness of the relationship between our behavior and its outcomes. As Bruner (1985) points out, it is not reinforcement that leads to or affects behavior directly, because reinforcement occurs after the behavior (sometimes considerably after). Rather, it is the individual's anticipation of consequences that immediately affects learning and behaving.

Our ability to symbolize and to anticipate is reflected not only in our ability to imagine the consequences of our behavior and therefore govern ourselves accordingly but also in our habit of deliberately arranging our environments so as to control some of the consequences of our actions. As Bandura (1977) puts it, "By arranging environmental inducements, generating cognitive supports, and producing consequences for their own actions, people are able to exercise some measure of control over their own behavior." Accordingly, one of Bandura's labels for his theory is **reciprocal determinism**.

The Theory Summarized

Bandura's position can be summarized in three statements:

1. Much human learning is a function of observing and imitating the behavior of others or of such symbolic models as fictional characters in books or television programs.

2. We learn to imitate by being reinforced for doing so; continued reinforcement maintains imitative behavior.

3. Some aspects of imitation (or observational learning) can therefore be explained in terms of operant conditioning principles.

The Prevalence of Imitation

Copying the behavior of others is a widespread phenomenon that is perhaps more obvious among nontechnological societies such as the Canadian Ojibwa. Until the turn of this century, the Ojibwa depended almost exclusively upon trapping, hunting, and fishing for their living. In Ojibwa tribes, young boys followed their fathers around trap lines as soon as they were physically able. For the first few years, they simply observed. Later, they would fashion their own weapons and traps and set their own snares as they had seen their fathers do. Whatever they bagged would be brought back to the father's lodge. If a boy had a sister, she would have learned how to prepare hides, meat, and fish, how to make clothing, how to erect shelters, and how to do the many other things she had seen her mother doing. When old enough, she would take care of her brother's catch, prepare his meals, and make his clothing.

In more technological societies such as ours, it is usually not possible to provide children with miniature working replicas of the tools used by their parents—nor is it possible for children to observe their parents at work. It would appear, then, that observational learning, although of some academic interest, could hardly be of much practical value for teachers.

Wrong. We may not learn to set traps or prepare furs from our parents, but we learn many other things from them—and from the wealth of other models that surround us.

Models. The term **model** may refer to an actual person whose behavior serves as a stimulus for an observer's response, or, as is more often the case in our society, it may refer to a **symbolic model**. Symbolic models include such things as oral or written instructions, pictures, mental images, cartoon or film characters, religious figures, and, not least important, the content and characters in books and television. For some children, symbolic models may be as important as real-life models. This is not to deny that peers, siblings, and parents serve as models or that teachers and other well-behaved people are held up as **exemplary models**. ("Why don't you behave like Dr. Lefrançois? See how nicely he sits in church with his eyes closed. He's praying for us, dear man."[*])

Sources of Reinforcement in Imitation

Imitation is reinforced in three ways. Direct reinforcement of the learner by the model is most evident in the early learning of children. It is not uncommon to hear parents exclaim over the behavior of their child simply because "he's doing it just like Daddy!"

A second source of reinforcement is the consequences of behavior, particularly if it is socially acceptable behavior that is effective in attaining a goal. Even though a child may learn to say "milk" partly as a function of imitation and partly as a function of her model's reinforcing her, she is not likely to go on saying "milk" unless someone gives her milk when she says it. It is in this sense that the consequences of behavior learned through observation can be reinforcing.

A third type of reinforcement is termed **vicarious reinforcement**. It involves deriving a kind of secondhand—hence, *vicarious*—reinforcement from observing someone else behave in a certain way. It is as though the observer assumes that the model does something because he or she derives reinforcement from that behavior. Therefore, in the observer's logic, anyone else engaged in the same behavior would receive the same reinforcement.

Interestingly, vicarious reinforcement can lead an observer to engage in ineffective behavior over a prolonged period of time. The fact that the behavior is maintained despite an apparent lack of direct reinforcement is evidence that some sort of vicarious reinforcement is involved. In fact, studies have shown that the administration of reward or punishment to a model has an effect on the behavior of observers similar to that which the direct administration of the reward or pun-

[*]PPC: I trust you are careful not to snore. . . .
Author: How cynical.

TABLE 4.4 Three Effects of Imitation

Modeling Effect	Acquiring *new* behavior as a result of observing a model
Inhibitory-Disinhibitory Effect	Ceasing or starting some *deviant* behavior as a result of seeing a model punished or rewarded for similar behavior
Eliciting Effect	Engaging in behavior *related* to that of a model

ishment would have. One such study (Bandura, 1962) involved exposing three groups of children to three different models. All models behaved aggressively toward an inflated plastic doll. The first model was rewarded for doing so, the second was punished, and the third received neither positive nor negative consequences. Subsequently, the model-rewarded group behaved significantly more aggressively than the model-punished group. The effect of reward and punishment on the models was transferred vicariously to the subjects.

The Effects of Imitation

Superficially, imitation seems to consist of little more than copying the behavior of a model. A closer examination of the responses involved, however, suggests that there are three categories of imitative behavior (Bandura & Walters, 1963; Bandura, 1977): the modeling effect, the inhibitory-disinhibitory effect, and the eliciting effect (see Table 4.4).

The **modeling effect** involves the acquisition of new responses. The **inhibitory-disinhibitory effect** involves the **inhibition** or the **disinhibition** of deviant responses, usually as a result of seeing a model punished or rewarded for the behavior. The **eliciting effect** involves behavior that is neither novel for the observer nor deviant; it is manifested when the observer engages in behavior related (but not identical) to that of the model.

The Modeling Effect. Whenever an observer acquires a new behavior as a result of seeing a model emit that behavior, the modeling effect is illustrated. The acquisition of novel aggressive responses has been extensively studied in laboratory situations, usually with nursery school children (Bandura, 1962; Bandura, Ross, & Ross, 1963). The typical experiment involves exposing the subjects to a real-life model or a cartoon or filmed model engaged in novel aggressive behavior directed toward a large inflated plastic doll. The model might punch the doll, strike it with a hammer, kick it, or sit on it. Control groups are exposed to the same model sitting quietly with the doll. The results of experiments such as this almost invariably illustrate the modeling effect. Children exposed to aggressive models are more aggressive than control groups when left with the dolls and also usually demonstrate imitative aggressive responses that are, in all likelihood, novel to them.

These experiments involve eliciting aggressive behavior in laboratory situations. The aggression is directed at an inanimate object. It might be argued that this is a far cry from aggression against real people in real life. Ethical considerations, however, prevent the use of babies instead of dolls in these experiments. It is therefore difficult to illustrate the acquisition of meaningful aggressive responses experimentally. However, studies of the effects of televised violence on children's behavior suggest that it may increase aggression in children, especially if the violence is realistic rather than slapstick (as in cartoons). But the extent and nature of the effects depend also on the child's personality and maturity (Collins, 1983). Similarly, prosocial television programs can sometimes have a positive effect on behavior (Cook et al., 1975).

Many other behaviors are also transmitted through imitation and are examples of modeling. The initial learning of socially appropriate behavior in primitive cultures such as that of the Ojibwa provides one illustration. Learning a language is also an example of modeling. This is especially obvious in the case of adults learning to speak a foreign language by imitating a teacher or an audiotape.

The Inhibitory-Disinhibitory Effect. This effect of imitation is particularly important for people who are concerned about deviant behavior. The inhibitory effect is the suppression of deviant behavior in an observer, usually as a result of seeing a model punished for engaging in the same behavior. The disinhibitory effect is the opposite; it occurs when an observer engages in previously learned deviant behavior, usually as a result of seeing a model rewarded (or at least not punished) for the same behavior.

As experimental evidence of disinhibition, Bandura and Walters (1963) cite studies in which viewing films led to aggression in children; the aggressive responses were not novel but were previously learned behaviors that the children had suppressed. Evidence from this research indicates that exposure to aggressive models may have a disinhibitory effect on young observers. Typically, the number of aggressive responses manifested by members of experimental groups is significantly higher than the number engaged in by the control groups. Also, the Bandura (1962) study that looked at the effects on observers of punishment or reward of the model showed that punishing a model inhibited similar behavior in observers and that rewards had an opposite, disinhibiting effect.

A related finding from the Bandura (1962) study is especially striking: When observers were offered rewards for behaving aggressively, all differences between the groups were wiped out! Now those who had been exposed to models who were punished for being aggressive nevertheless behaved as aggressively as those whose models had been rewarded for being aggressive. This observation is especially important in explaining why punishing those who misbehave often fails to discourage other transgressors. One of the reasons for punishing criminals is the hope that others will take heed and cease committing crimes. In other words, the intention is to *inhibit* criminal behavior by punishing a model. It follows from the Bandura experiment, however, that as long as subjects have their own incentives for criminal behavior, the model may just as well be rewarded as punished, as far as deterrence is concerned.

A series of sobering experiments illustrates that socially unacceptable behavior in adults can be disinhibited through the use of models (Walters, Llewellyn, & Acker, 1962; Walters & Llewellyn, 1963). These studies were modeled after the well-known Milgram (1963) obedience studies in which college students willingly administered what they thought were extremely dangerous, high-voltage electrical shocks to other students, simply because they had been told to do so by an experimenter. Results of the Milgram studies have often been used to explain various wartime atrocities perpetrated by apparently normal and gentle people who claimed they were simply obeying some powerful authority.

In the studies conducted by Walters and his associates, adult subjects were asked to participate in an experiment dealing with memory. Subjects were first shown one of two films: The first group saw a scene from the film *Rebel Without a Cause* in which two youths engage in a fight with knives; the second group saw adolescents engaged in artwork. All subjects were then asked to help with another experiment. This one involved administering a series of shocks to students in order to study the effects of punishment on learning. The student subjects involved in this learning experiment were actually confederates of the experimenters. The adults, who were the actual subjects, were made to sit in the confederate's chair and were administered one or two mild shocks so that they would know what the punishment was like. They were then seated at a control panel that consisted of two signal lights (one red and one green), a dial for selecting shock intensities, and a toggle switch for administering the shock. Instructions were simply to administer a shock whenever the red light went on, because it indicated that the subject had made an error.

These studies indicated that exposure to films with aggressive content significantly increases aggressive behavior, as revealed in the number and intensity of shocks the subjects were willing to give. (The students did not actually receive any shocks because one electrode was always disconnected before the experiment.)

The results of studies such as these, if they can be generalized, may be important for interpreting and predicting the probable effects of television violence—particularly in view of the fact that preschoolers spend more than one-third of their waking time watching television (Winn, 1985).

The Eliciting Effect. A third effect of imitation involves eliciting responses that do not necessarily precisely match those of the model (although they might) but that are related to the model's responses; that is, they belong to the same class of behavior. For example, a man might serve as a model of generosity if he works hard for civic organizations, at church activities, and at school functions. A number of his neighbors might be moved by his example to be generous in different ways. One might give money to local charities, a second might donate a prize for a church raffle, a third might give freely of advice. None of these observers imitates the model's behavior precisely, but each of them emits a response that is related to it in that it involves being generous.

Another illustration of the eliciting effect is the herd behaviors that are sometimes apparent in crowds at sporting events. One person's applause might elicit applause from the entire crowd, or one person's booing and hissing might elicit similar behavior from others. Similarly, when people begin to rise for the national anthem, the same behavior may be elicited in a great many who are not immediately aware of why they are standing. In each of these illustrations of the eliciting effect, no new behavior is involved (as is

Calvin and Hobbes

by Bill Watterson

the case in the modeling effect), and the behavior in question is not deviant (as it is in the inhibitory-disinhibitory effect).

The Processes of Observational Learning

Although reinforcement is implicated in learning through imitation, Bandura (1977) makes it clear that the effects of models are largely a result of what he refers to as their "informative function." In other words, from observing models we learn cognitively not only how to do certain things but also what the consequences of our actions are likely to be.

According to Bandura (1977), four distinct processes are involved in observational learning: attentional processes, retention processes, motor reproduction processes, and motivational processes (see Figure 4.9).

Attentional Processes. It is clear that we are not likely to learn much from models unless we pay attention to the significant features of the behaviors we want to learn. Clearly, many of the behaviors in which our models engage have no value for us; therefore, we pay little attention to them and do not learn them. For example, when I lived with my grandmother as a young adolescent, I was quite passionately interested in, among other things, trapping and snaring wild things for food and money. And when I had the opportunity

to go out into the woods with the renowned trapper George Ahenikue, I watched his every move like a hawk—how he walked, how he looked around, how and where he stopped, how he fashioned his sets and arranged his snares. These behaviors had high value for me.

But when I caught a rabbit who stupidly blundered into my snare, I paid little attention to the way my grandmother disjointed, sautéed, and stewed the beast; I just sat at the table and licked my chops in anticipation. The culinary preparation of the rabbit held no interest for me, although I relished the final result.

It wasn't until many years later, when I had a rabbit to prepare in my own kitchen, that I realized how little I had learned from my grandmother of the mysteries of the kitchen. Although I had watched her prepare dozens of rabbits, the behavior had not been sufficiently valuable for me to pay attention.

So I called my grandmother and I asked her about the stewing of snowshoe hares and jackrabbits, and she explained. Her explanation was every bit as much a model as her behavior might have been years earlier (had I been paying attention), but it was a symbolic model.

In addition to the affective and functional value of the behavior being modeled, a number of other factors affect attentional processes. These include the distinctiveness, the complexity, and the prevalence of the stimuli. Also, a number of

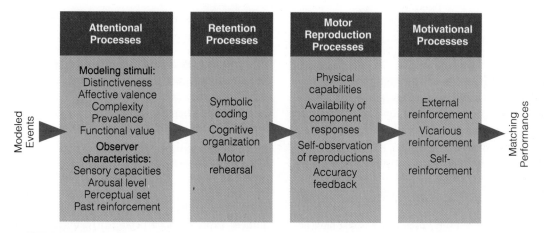

FIGURE 4.9 Component processes governing observational learning in social learning theory. From A. Bandura, *Social Learning Theory,* © 1977, p. 23. Reprinted by permission of Prentice-Hall, Inc., Englewood Cliffs, New Jersey.

characteristics of the learner are important, including arousal (motivation), perceptual set (readiness to observe), and history of previous reinforcement.

Retention Processes. Just as we must pay attention if we are to learn, so too must we remember what we have observed. Because the effects of imitation are usually delayed rather than immediate, we need some way of symbolizing, understanding, and organizing our observations.

According to Bandura (1977), observational learning involves two types of representation systems: visual (his term is *imaginal*) and verbal. For example, to learn a complex motor skill, it is sometimes useful to observe a model closely and store a visual sequence of the behavior. It is then possible to rehearse the desired behavior mentally. Bandura (1977) cites research indicating that mentally rehearsing a complex motor sequence (as in high jumping, diving, or gymnastics, for example) can significantly improve performance. He suggests that the best way to learn from a model is to organize and rehearse the observed behavior cognitively and then act it out.

Motor Reproduction Processes. Acting out a modeled behavior involves transforming symbolically represented (mentally visualized or imagined) actions into physical movements. Being able to do so successfully, of course, depends on essential physical capabilities; clearly, some of us will never be able to jump very high no matter how many models we observe. Accurate motor reproduction of an observed behavior depends also on the individual's ability both to monitor attempted reproductions and to use motor feedback to make corrections. Imitations of motor behavior are seldom perfect the first time—they must be refined. A coach might demonstrate repeatedly how a batter should stand, how she should hold the bat, how she should distribute and shift her weight, what her eyes and toes should do. But in the end, the truly good batter will have refined and perfected her batting through a long succession of trials (motor reproductions). These, however, are not blind trial-and-error reproductions repeated until the right one is accidentally found. Rather, they are carefully modeled trials that are evaluated and slowly modified as a function of feedback involving, among other things, how often contact is made with the ball, how far the ball goes when it is hit, and whether the coach smiles or frowns while watching the batter.

Motivational Processes. Much of what people observe and could learn is never manifested in their behavior. George Ahenikue, for example, was an important model for me with respect to setting snares for snowshoe hares; he knew a dozen clever little tricks for ensnaring them. I emulated as many of these tricks as I could. But he also knew a fantastic trick for blowing his nose. I have little doubt that I learned it; I remember it very clearly. But I don't do it. Ever. Put another way, I have acquired the behavior but do not perform it.

The distinction between acquisition and performance is important in social learning theory because, as we have noted, much of what is observed and presumably acquired is never performed. Whether the modeled behavior will ever be performed is a function of reinforcement or, perhaps more precisely, of anticipated reinforcement.

In summary, observational learning begins with a modeled event (perhaps a real-life model doing something, a verbal or symbolic model, or a combination of these) and culminates in some sort of matching performance on the part of the observer. Four processes intervene between the presentation of the model and the appearance of the modeled behavior. First, the observer must pay attention; second, the observer must represent the observed behavior cognitively, store it, and perhaps rehearse it; third, if the observer has the required capabilities, he or she reproduces and refines the observed behavior; and fourth, given appropriate motivational conditions (defined primarily in terms of anticipated reinforcement), the observer performs the learned behavior.

INSTRUCTIONAL IMPLICATIONS OF SOCIAL LEARNING

The greatest advantage that learning by imitation has over other forms of learning is that it provides a complete behavioral sequence for the learner. There is no need for successive approximations, for trial and error, or for association by contiguity. Nobody would put a person behind the wheel of a car and allow the person to learn to drive by trial and error alone. One might, on the other hand, teach driving to someone by presenting one or more models: exposure to a person driving, a driving manual, or a series of oral instructions. In this, as in many other types of learning, it would be foolhardy to permit people to learn only by doing.

A careful analysis of the processes involved in social learning suggests a number of considerations that might be important for teaching. For example, many of the factors associated with attentional processes (such as distinctiveness of stimuli, the learner's arousal level, history of past reinforcement, and so on) are at least partly under the teacher's control. Similarly, teachers can provide direction and opportunity for the activities involved in retention and in reproduction. And because the effects of reinforcement depend on our awareness of the connection between our behavior and its consequences, teachers can also exercise considerable influence on motivational processes. The deliberate use of social learning theory for changing and controlling behavior (sometimes included under the general term **behavior management**, or behavior modification) presents yet another important educational implication, considered in Chapter 11.

MAIN POINTS

1. Science demands that its theories be based on objective, replicable observations, that chance factors be taken into account, and that they be generalizable.

2. Learning involves all changes in behavior that result from experience, providing that these changes are relatively permanent, do not result simply from growth or maturation, and are not

the temporary effects of factors such as fatigue or drugs. Changes in disposition or capability are not always manifested in performance.

3. Behavioristic theories of learning are concerned with stimulus-response events and with the effects of repetition, contiguity, and reinforcement. Cognitive theories address problems relating to the organization of memory, information processing, problem solving, and metacognition (knowing about knowing).

4. Classical conditioning, described by Pavlov and Watson, involves the repeated pairing of a previously neutral stimulus (conditioned stimulus, or CS) with an effective stimulus (unconditioned stimulus, or UCS) so that the CS eventually brings about a response (conditioned response, or CR) similar to that for the unconditioned stimulus.

5. Classical conditioning is sometimes useful in explaining the learning of emotional responses. Hence, it is important for teachers to know what is being paired with what in schools and to maximize situations associated with positive emotions while minimizing those associated with negative feelings.

6. Watson's behaviorism is based on the notion that learning is a function of the classical conditioning of simple reflexes. Watson can be thought of as the champion of the conditioned reflex and of environmentalism—the belief that individual differences are attributable to experiences rather than to genetics.

7. Thorndike introduced the notion of reinforcement in learning theory through the law of effect, which asserts that responses followed by satisfaction tend to become linked to the stimuli that preceded them. According to Thorndike, learning involves stamping in S-R bonds, forgetting involves stamping out bonds. In the absence of previous learning, behavior will take the form of trial and error. Choice of responses attempted may be affected by set, by identical elements in stimulus situations, by classical conditioning, or by prepotent elements.

8. Among the educational implications of Thorndike's theory is his suggestion that one of the important goals of education is to teach for transfer (generalization) and to stress connections among ideas. He also emphasized the importance of students' readiness and of reinforcement, and he recognized the limited effectiveness of punishment.

9. Respondents result from a known stimulus; operants are simply emitted (respondents are reactions to; operants are actions upon). The Skinner box is a cagelike device used by Skinner to study the relationship between operants and reinforcement—ordinarily in rats or pigeons.

10. The model of operant conditioning maintains that when an operant is reinforced, the probability of its recurrence increases. A reinforcer is any stimulus that has the effect of increasing the probability that a response will occur. It may do so by being added to a situation (positive reinforcement; reward) or by being removed (negative reinforcement; relief).

11. Negative reinforcement is not punishment. The effect of punishment is to decrease, not increase, the probability that a response will occur. Punishment occurs when a pleasant stimulus is removed or an unpleasant one is introduced following behavior.

12. Aversive control involves the use of negative reinforcement (often in the form of removal of threats) and of punishment. The emotional consequences of positive control are usually more desirable.

13. Reinforcement may be administered continuously (for every correct response) or in a random or fixed manner relative to a ratio or interval basis (that is, it can be continuous, random ratio, random interval, fixed ratio, or fixed interval). In general, continuous schedules lead to faster learning, whereas intermittent schedules result in longer extinction periods.

14. Shaping may be used to teach animals novel behaviors or to alter human behavior in subtle

ways. It involves the differential reinforcement of successive approximations.

15. To generalize is to respond to similarities (make the same response in similar situations); to discriminate is to respond to differences (distinguish among situations in which identical responses are not appropriate).

16. Among the instructional implications that may be derived from these behavioristic theories are suggestions relating to the value of repetition, reinforcement, and punishment, as well as some practical suggestions for managing misbehavior.

17. There are those who believe that behavioristic principles can provide us with a technology of teaching that is more effective than any other approach and who lament the apparent reluctance of many educators to apply this technology. Others emphasize that the effectiveness of behavioristic approaches is limited, that teachers often control only the weaker reinforcers, and that many problems of instructing (organizing, sequencing, explaining, illustrating) cannot easily make use of behavioristic principles.

18. It is possible that we are not free, that we are controlled by our environment, and that we have only the illusion of freedom.

19. Most theories of social learning assume that imitation is a central process in determining behavior. Bandura's observational learning theory is based on the effects of reinforcement, on the observer's awareness of the connections between behavior and outcomes, and on the observer's ability to symbolize. It is a theory of reciprocal determinism (the environment determines behavior, but the individual chooses and alters the environment).

20. The term *model* refers to a person who serves as an example for another and to symbolic models (highly prevalent in technologically advanced societies), which include oral and written instructions, fictitious characters in books or films, television, and so on.

21. Sources of reinforcement in observational learning include direct reinforcement by the model, reinforcement as a consequence of behavior, and vicarious reinforcement (when the punishment or reward an observer thinks a model has received affects the observer's behavior).

22. Three effects of imitation include the modeling effect (the learning of novel responses), the inhibitory-disinhibitory effect (deviant behavior is disinhibited or suppressed, usually as a function of response consequences to the models), and the eliciting effect (the emission of responses that are related to those made by the model but that are neither novel nor deviant).

23. The effects of models are brought about largely through their informative function. They show us what to do, how to do it, and the most likely consequences of doing it.

24. Four processes are involved in observational learning: attentional processes (the observer pays attention to aspects of the model's behavior that are distinct and that have high value), retention processes (the observer symbolizes observations, stores them, and perhaps rehearses them mentally), motor-reproduction processes (the observer acts out the imitated behavior and refines it on the basis of feedback), and motivational processes (what has been learned may be manifested or not, depending on the learner's motivation).

SUGGESTED READINGS

Among the many attempts to apply learning theories to educational practice, the following three sources have been selected as the most representative and the most practical. Skinner's book is a collection of his papers on teaching, Lefrançois provides a simple explanation of early theories of learning, and Bell-Gredler

presents a useful look at the instructional implications of a variety of psychological theories.

SKINNER, B. F. (1968). *The technology of teaching*. New York: Appleton-Century-Crofts.

LEFRANÇOIS, G. R. (1982). *Psychological theories and human learning* (2nd ed.). Monterey, Calif.: Brooks/Cole.

BELL-GREDLER, M. E. (1986). *Learning and instruction: Theory into practice.* New York: Macmillan.

Skinner provides a highly readable and important behavioristic estimation of the human condition.

SKINNER, B. F. (1971). *Beyond freedom and dignity.* New York: Alfred A. Knopf.

The social development theory of Bandura and Walters is presented in the following:

BANDURA, A. (1977). *Social learning theory.* Morristown, N.J.: General Learning Press.

BANDURA, A., & WALTERS, R. (1963). *Social learning and personality development.* New York: Holt, Rinehart & Winston.

Hall and Kelson (1959) list exactly 130 subspecies and types of bears, ranging alphabetically from Ursus absarokus, *found in 1914 at the head of the Little Bighorn River in Montana, to* Ursus yesoensis.

I've a grand mind for forgetting, David.
Robert Louis Stevenson, *Kidnapped*

The Right Honorable gentleman is indebted to his memory for his jests and to his imagination for his facts.
Richard Brinsley Sheridan, speech in reply to Mr. Dundas

Chapter 5 | COGNITION AND MEMORY

Conditioning theories explain how stimuli, responses, and the consequences of behavior can become associated under certain circumstances. Accordingly, these theories are useful in explaining many relatively simple behaviors—and perhaps some complex behaviors as well. But how well do they explain the processes by which you and I can recognize, or at least contemplate, the role of, say, wild cows, in the grand scheme of things?

Excerpt from Bear Tales (Book III): Invasion of the Wild Cows

Wild cows have invaded the bear's forest. When he went to the stream at first light, he saw their droppings by the water, and he could not bring himself to drink. Now, with heavy heart, he follows their spoor across the forest floor. Wild cows are every bear's nightmare. While we imagine winning lotteries or being hugely loved heroes, bears fantasize about wild cow alarms that really work. Or, if they are mean hearted, they dream of wild cow plagues.

The bear sees where the bunch of wild cows has crossed the stream. In their spoor, in the trampled beds of wild strawberries and the uprooted clusters of daffodils, he finds confirmation of his greatest fears. He is tempted to stop and weep.

Early in the morning, the bear finds the herd. Some are playing cards, but most of them are lying in a small meadow. They have already filled the first of their stomachs. Now they belch and chew cud. The bear's stomach turns at the stench of the methane gases that fill the air.

It is a pretty, flowered meadow in which the wild cows lie. But the bear knows that the short-lived beauty of spring crocuses does not touch wild cows nor do the flame-orange wild tiger lilies. He knows they have no appreciation of sunrises or sunsets that they are neither awed when the storm clouds gather nor feel joy when the rains rejuvenate the land. They have no sense of mystery or of majesty, these wild cows; they recognize no sacred places. That is the source of the bear's sadness.

"There is no longer room for environmentally unfriendly creatures in our forest," mutters the bear. Can their behavior be changed through a conditioning process?, the bear muses as one of the wild cows throws her cards to the ground and stomps on them in a sudden display of childish rage. Can they be conditioned?, the bear wonders. Theoretically, yes, he answers. This would involve reinforcing them for

eating in a more restrained fashion, for refraining from lying on beds of clover and wild strawberries, and for changing their toilet habits. But he knows that none of this is likely to work in practice, simply because nobody has sufficient control over the things that reinforce wild cows. Or the things that punish them, either.

"Perhaps the best solution," concludes the bear, "is to reason with them, to get them to understand the impact of their behavior and to espouse values that emphasize the rights of others and the sanctity of the environment."

But he is overwhelmed by the problems of using a cognitive rather than a behavioristic approach with such creatures.

"I've been a cow all my life, honey. Don't ask me to change now."

COGNITIVISM

We saw in Chapter 4 that behaviorism, in its simplest sense, is the study of behavior and of the ways in which behavior is influenced by its consequences. In a behavioristic analysis of learning, the primary emphasis is on the external conditions that affect behavior. The typical unspoken assumption is that all learners are initially equal but the conditions to which they are exposed vary. This variance is what accounts for subsequent differences in behavior.

In contrast to behaviorism, cognitivism involves "the scientific study of mental events" (E. Gagné, 1985, p. 4). These mental events have to do with acquiring, processing, storing, and retrieving information. Accordingly, the primary emphasis in a cognitive analysis of learning is on the learner's **mental structure**, a **concept** that includes not only the learner's previous related knowledge but also the strategies that the learner might bring to bear on the current situation. In this view, the explicit assumption is that learners are far from equal. It is the individual's preexisting network of concepts, strategies, and understanding that makes experience meaningful.

Cognitivism, E. Hunt (1989) asserts, is a perspective rather than a discipline. It is a way of looking at things rather than a readily identifiable collection of findings. This way of looking at things is characterized by basic underlying beliefs that are apparent in the metaphors of cognitivism.

The Metaphors of Cognitivism

Historically, most scientists have been convinced that the successful completion of their searches would be a literal description of the way things actually are and a mathematically accurate system for relating causes and effects. Initially, there was little reason to suspect that science would one day discover phenomena that could only be described in such nebulous terms as *black hole*, *quark*, *node*, or *schema*. But science did uncover these phenomena and found itself at a loss to describe them literally and exactly; hence, these metaphors.

A metaphor is a comparison. It doesn't say, "This is that"; instead, it says, "It is interesting, or amusing, or useful, to look at this as though it were like that." Hence, a metaphor cannot be judged in terms of whether it is accurate but only in terms of whether it is useful—or interesting and amusing.

Perhaps more than any other approach in psychology, cognitivism uses metaphors. Its models are not meant to be exact descriptions of functions and processes; instead, they suggest, they compare, they draw analogies. And, as such, they cannot be judged in terms of their accuracy but, like other psychological theories, must instead be subjected to tests of usefulness and consistency.

A Definition. Cognitivism is defined in terms of cognition. *Cognition*, however, is not a simple concept. Literally, to cognize is to know; hence, cognition is knowing. As Neisser (1976, p. 1) puts it: "Cognition is the activity of knowing: the acquisition, organization, and use of knowledge." Or, in Glass, Holyoak, and Santa's words (1979, p. 2): "All our mental abilities—perceiving, remembering, reasoning—are organized into a complex system, the overall function of which is termed *cognition*." What is common to these and other definitions of *cognition* is that they emphasize the role of mental structure, or organization, in the processes of knowing. In other words, they deal with how mental representations are manipulated (E. Hunt, 1989). Not surprisingly, then, a major emphasis of cognitive approaches concerns the ways information is processed and stored. Note how dramatically this departs from the major emphasis of a behavioristic approach, which concentrates on behavior and its consequences.

A Computer Metaphor. Cognitivism's concern with information processing is closely related to the development of information-processing machines, more commonly called computers, and specifically to the branch of computer science concerned with artificial intelligence. This is the branch of computer science that attempts to make computers smarter. Raphael (1976) suggests several reasons why we might want to make computers smarter. Not the least of these is that a very smart computer can do some marvelous things for us and in the process free us to do other, equally marvelous things. But perhaps even more important, especially for those who study intelligence, a truly smart computer might clarify how our own information-processing systems—our minds—work. Scientists concerned with the second of these benefits typically use computers in one of two ways: to mimic the functioning of the

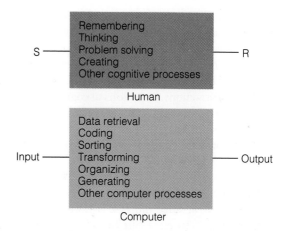

Human

Computer

FIGURE 5.1 A schematic parallel between human cognitive functioning and computer functioning. If S (stimulus) = input and R (response) = output, does it follow that the computer's memory and programs are accurate representations of human cognitive processes? From G. R. Lefrançois, *Psychological Theories and Human Learning* (2nd ed.). Copyright 1982 by Wadsworth, Inc. Reprinted by permission of Brooks/Cole Publishing Company, Monterey, California.

human mind or to generate models of human functioning. In these models, the brain, with its neurons and their networks of interconnections, might be compared to the chips and the storage and relay systems of computers. Or the processes involved in receiving, organizing, storing, and retrieving information might be compared to the programmed functions of the computer. In that case, it is the program rather than the computer itself that serves as a model for human functioning (Newell & Simon, 1972). See Figure 5.1.

Other Metaphors. The computer is clearly one of the metaphors of the cognitive sciences. This metaphor says, in effect, "It is useful to look at human cognitive functioning as though it functioned like a computer."

More common are approaches that invent their own metaphors—that look at cognitive functioning not in terms of something known, such as a computer, but in terms of something that is initially unknown and that requires that its characteristics be described. They use labels such as "knowledge base," "cognitive strategy," or "schema" for their metaphors. No one has seen a knowledge base, a cognitive strategy, or a schema; these are abstractions, inventions of cognitive theory. But each of these inventions can be described. And, once described, it is possible to say, "Learners behave as though they have a knowledge base and cognitive strategies."

Our current models of cognitive functioning—what are termed the *new cognitive sciences*—basically look at three things. First, they look at what Chi and Glaser (1980) call the **knowledge base**—the storehouse of information, concepts, and associations that we build up as we develop from children into adults. Second, they look at **cognitive strategies**—the processes by which information becomes part of the knowledge base, is retrieved from it, or is used. And third, they deal with the individual's awareness of self as a knower

and processor of information—with what is termed **metacognition**. We look at each of these aspects of the cognitive sciences in the sections of this chapter that follow. In Chapter 6 we look at the tremendous potential contribution of the cognitive sciences to education, especially in developing ways to teach and improve cognitive strategies.

A BASIC INFORMATION-PROCESSING MODEL

What Simon (1980) describes as an information-processing revolution in psychology, and specifically in learning theory, has led to a widely accepted basic model (Figure 5.2). This model, based largely on the work of Atkinson and Shiffrin (1968), portrays the human information processor in terms of three types of information storage: **short-term sensory storage** (sometimes called **sensory memory**), **short-term memory** (also called **working memory**), and **long-term**

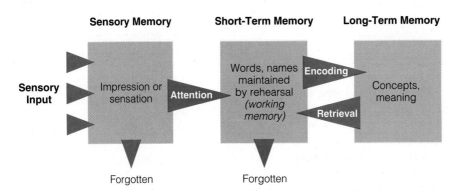

FIGURE 5.2 The three components of memory. Sensory information first enters sensory memory (*iconic* or *echoic* memory). From there it may go into short-term memory (also called *primary* or *working* memory), where it is available as a name or word (for example) as long as it is rehearsed. Some of the material in short-term memory may then be coded for long-term storage, where it might take the form of concepts. It is important to note that these three components of memory do not refer to three different locations in the brain or other parts of the nervous system but to how we remember—or, more precisely, to how we study memory. Adapted from G. R. Lefrançois, *Psychological Theories and Human Learning* (2nd ed.). Copyright 1982 by Wadsworth, Inc. Reprinted by permission of Brooks/Cole Publishing Company, Monterey, California.

memory. Each type of storage is distinct from the others primarily in terms of the nature and extent of the processing that information undergoes. In this context, **processing** refers to activities such as organizing, analyzing, synthesizing, rehearsing, and so on. In addition, the three types of storage differ in capacity and in the extent to which their contents are accessible.

The basic information-processing model of cognitive psychology does two related things: First, it provides us with an overall model of human **memory**. Second, it addresses a number of learning-related questions that are critically important for teachers—questions such as how information is organized and sorted, which teaching and learning methods can facilitate information processing, and how memory can be improved.

This basic information-processing model is examined in some detail in the pages that follow. Bear in mind, however, that what we are discussing is a model—a metaphor. It is not intended to be a literal description of the way things actually are stored in our brains.

Sensory Memory

The information-processing model attempts to represent how we acquire information, how we sort and organize it, and how we later retrieve it. The model is, in effect, a learning and memory model that begins with the raw material of all learning experiences: sensory sensation.

Our sensory systems (vision, hearing, taste, touch, smell) are sensitive to an overwhelmingly wide range of stimulation. Clearly, however, they respond to only a fraction of all available stimulation at any given time; the bulk of the information available in this stimulation is never actually processed—that is, it never actually becomes part of our **cognitive structure**. The label used for this is **sensory memory**, sometimes called "echoic" or "iconic" memory (Neisser, 1976). It refers to the fleeting (less than one second) and unconscious effect of stimulation to which we pay no attention.

Note that sensory memory is highly limited, both in terms of the length of time during which stimulus information is available for processing and in terms of the absolute amount of information available. Put another way, sensory memory is no more than the immediate sensory effect of a stimulus. If, without giving any prior instructions, I read you a list of numbers in a dry, professorial monotone and then ask you to repeat the numbers some ten seconds later, you are not likely to remember many of the numbers. But if I interrupt my reading and ask immediately, "What was the last number I read?" you will, in all likelihood, respond correctly. In fact, each of the numbers is stored in sensory memory for a very short period of time, but if it is not attended to or processed within a fraction of a second, it will no longer be available.

Short-Term Memory

The information-processing system of which cognitive psychology speaks makes use of a number of different activities with a common goal: making sense of significant sensation and, at the same time, ignoring or discarding more trivial matters. As we have seen, a great deal of sensory data that is not attended to does not go beyond immediate sensory memory. Paying attention is, in fact, one of the important activities of our information-processing system. It is the means by which information is transferred from sensory to short-term storage—hence, the importance of getting students' attention if teaching is to be effective.

In essence, short-term memory consists of what is in our immediate consciousness at any given time. As Calfee (1981) notes, it is a sort of scratch pad for thinking; it contains all that is in our immediate awareness. For this reason, short-term memory is often called **working memory**. The label draws attention to the function of this level of memory rather than simply to its duration.

One of the important characteristics of short-term memory is that it is highly limited in capacity. Following various memory experiments, Miller (1956) concluded that its average capacity

eidetic images

Sometimes when we remember something, we say, "I can picture it in my mind." But what, exactly, is it that we can "picture"? Most often, psychologists inform us, we see a sort of mental image—an imperfect representation from memory, subject to all the distortions and inaccuracies to which memory is prone. But there are those rare individuals whose mental images are more accurate—they possess eidetic imagery.

In effect, an eidetic image is a photographlike recollection of some stimulus—hence, the popular expression "photographic memory." People who have eidetic imagery are some-

Photo of *The Dream* by Henri Rousseau. 1910. Oil on canvas, 6′8¹/₂″ x 9′9¹/₂″. Collection, The Museum of Modern Art, New York. Gift of Nelson A. Rockefeller. Reprinted by permission.

is about seven discrete items (plus or minus two); that is, our immediate conscious awareness is limited to this capacity, and as additional items of information come in, they push out some that are already there.

Short-term memory lasts a matter of seconds (not minutes, hours, or days) and appears to be highly dependent on rehearsal. That is, for items to be maintained in short-term storage, they must be repeated (consciously thought about). In the absence of repetition, they quickly fade—usually before twenty seconds have elapsed.

The apparent limitations of short-term memory are not nearly as serious as they might at first seem. Although we cannot easily attend to more than seven discrete items, a process called **chunking** dramatically increases the capacity of short-term memory. In effect, a chunk is simply a group of related items of information. Thus, a single letter might be one of the seven items held times able to remember with amazing accuracy and detail. For example, in a typical investigation of eidetic imagery, subjects might be shown a picture, such as that reproduced here, for a brief period and then asked questions such as "How many oranges are there in the tree?" "How many stripes are there in the flute player's skirt?" "How many flowers can you see?" Investigations such as these reveal that some degree of eidetic imagery is not uncommon among young school-age children, but that it is far less common after adolescence (Ahsen, 1977a,b). These investigations also indicate that recall based on eidetic imagery is very much like looking at the actual picture. Those so gifted continue to "see" the picture after it is removed. When they are asked how many flowers they can see, their eye movements are similar to the eye movements of someone actually looking at the picture.

Contrary to popular opinion, eidetic imagery does not usually present any advantage in learning school-related tasks because it seldom involves any transference to long-term memory. In fact, the eidetic image is seldom available for recall even an hour later; typically, it fades within minutes. However, there are some recorded cases of remarkable, eideticlike memories that are not subject to the ravages of time. Among these, Luria's (1968) description of a young Russian known to us only as S is perhaps the best known. S went to Luria, a psychologist, because he was bewildered and confused. His mind was such a jumble of sights, sounds, and colors that he had difficulty following ordinary conversations. S's problem, quite simply, was an absolutely remarkable memory. On one occasion, Luria presented S with the array of numbers shown here. After spending three minutes examining the table, S was able to reproduce the numbers flawlessly in forty seconds. Within fifty seconds, he read off each of the four-digit numbers forming the first twelve horizontal rows, as well as the two-digit number in the last row. But what is even more remarkable is that even after several months had elapsed, during which time the table was never again presented, S could reproduce it flawlessly (although he took somewhat longer to "reimagine" the array).

But memories such as S's are exceptionally rare. Most of the memories with which teachers deal are more ordinary.

6	6	8	0
5	4	3	2
1	6	8	4
7	9	3	5
4	2	3	7
3	8	9	1
1	0	0	2
3	4	5	1
2	7	6	8
1	9	2	6
2	9	6	7
5	5	2	0
x	0	1	x

Table from *The Mind of a Mnemonist: A Little Book About a Vast Memory* by A. R. Luria, translated from the Russian by Lynn Solotaroff. Copyright 1968 by Basic Books, Inc., Publishers. Reprinted by permission of Michael Cole and Jonathan Cape Ltd.

in short-term memory, or it might be chunked with other letters to form a single word—which can, in turn, be one of seven items in short-term memory. To illustrate this phenomenon, Miller (1956) uses the analogy of a change purse that can hold only seven coins. If the purse holds seven pennies, its capacity is only seven cents. But if it holds seven quarters, seven fifty-cent pieces, or even seven gold coins, its capacity increases dramatically.

In summary, short-term memory is the ongoing availability of a small number of items, or chunks, of information in conscious awareness. Without continued rehearsal, these items are generally lost from memory within twenty seconds. The great usefulness of short-term memory is that it enables us to keep information in mind long enough to make sense of sequences of words and directions, to solve problems, and to make decisions.

Educational Applications of Short-Term Memory. The most common measure of short-term memory is to have subjects repeat a sequence of unrelated single-digit numbers they have just heard, a task that is common to a number of intelligence tests. Under these circumstances, adults and adolescents typically remember six or seven items (or sometimes nine or more). In contrast, six-year-olds are not likely to remember more than two or three.

These differences may be highly important for teachers. It may well be, as Siegler (1989) suggests, that certain problems are difficult or impossible for younger learners simply because they cannot keep in mind enough relevant information at one time—as might be the case, for example, if a young child were asked to add several numbers at once. Case, Haward, Lewis, and Hurst (1988) argue that one of the most serious limitations on the young child's ability to understand and solve problems is simply a limitation in the number of items that the child can retain in working memory for immediate availability.

Teachers have two courses of action in such cases. If many of the young child's cognitive limitations result from limited short-term memory capacity, teachers can either wait for appropriate changes in memory before progressing to more demanding tasks or take steps to improve the child's memory.

In practice, teachers most often resort to the first alternative; they simply wait for the child to mature. Recently, however, growing evidence suggests that it might be possible to teach certain aspects of cognitive strategies—such as rehearsal—that are important for short-term memory. (More about this later.)

Long-Term Memory

The type of memory that is clearly of greatest concern to educators is long-term memory. Long-term memory includes all our relatively stable information about the world—all that we know but that is not in our immediate consciousness. In fact, one important distinction between short-term and long-term memory is that short-term memory is an active, ongoing, conscious process, whereas long-term memory is a more passive, unconscious process. Accordingly, short-term memory is easily disrupted by external events—as we demonstrate every time we lose our "train of thought" because of some distraction. In contrast, long-term memory cannot easily be disrupted. If you know the capital of Finland today, you are likely to know it tomorrow, next month, and even next year.

As noted earlier, we transfer information from sensory storage to short-term storage through the process of attending, and we maintain it in short-term memory largely through rehearsal. But the transference of material from short-term to long-term memory involves more than simple rehearsal: It involves **encoding**, a process whereby meaning is derived from experience. To encode information is to transform or abstract it—to represent it in another form.

Encoding clearly involves information processing, an event that can occur at different levels. Craik and Lockhart (1972; Cermak & Craik, 1979), originators of the **levels of processing model**, suggest that memory results specifically from the level to which information is processed. Information that is not processed leaves only a momentary sensory impression (sensory memory), information that is merely rehearsed is available for seconds (short-term memory), and information that is processed to a greater degree finds its way into long-term memory. But not all material in long-term memory is processed to the same level. If, for example, subjects are asked to learn and remember a word, they can process it at a highly superficial level, paying attention only to its physical appearance. At a somewhat deeper level, they might pay attention to the word's pronunciation. And at the deepest level, they would take into account the word's meaning—a process called "semantic encoding" (Table 5.1 summarizes the characteristics of all three levels of memory.)

TABLE 5.1 Three Levels of Memory

	SENSORY	SHORT-TERM	LONG-TERM
ALTERNATE LABELS	Echoic or iconic	Primary or working	Secondary
DURATION	Less than 1 second	Less than 20 seconds	Indefinite
STABILITY	Fleeting	Easily disrupted	Not easily disrupted
CAPACITY	Limited	Limited (7 +/− 2 items)	Unlimited
GENERAL CHARACTERISTICS	Momentary, unconscious impression	Working memory; immediate consciousness; active, maintained by rehearsal	Knowledge base; associationistic; passive, the result of encoding

Cognitive Models of Long-Term Memory. One of the earliest models of long-term memory was described by Koffka (1935). It viewed the mind as something like a catalogue or a movie camera that records a sequential representation of all our experiences. From this representation, we later withdraw isolated memories as we need them, providing they have not been eradicated in the meantime. The fundamental characteristic of this model of memory is that it is nonassociationistic; that is, it views memory as consisting of isolated bits of information recorded sequentially.

Almost without exception, contemporary models of memory are associationistic. They are based on the fundamental notion that all items of information in our memories are associated in a variety of ways. And it is precisely because of these associations that we are able to recall things as impressively as we can. Unlike computer memories, which typically work on the basis of location (items are "addressed" in terms of location), our human memories seem to be addressed by content. Thus, a computer can retrieve and analyze information once it knows the particular place in storage that needs to be searched. In contrast, we need only know what to look for, rather than where, in order to find it.

Speculation about the nature of the associations that define human long-term memory have led to a number of abstract models and labels for describing memory. These models are essentially cognitive; that is, they relate to associations based on meaning or significance, rather than to behavioristic associations (for example, repetition and contiguity). This, of course, does not mean that repetition and contiguity are irrelevant. As Calfee (1981) points out, we know that the more often we encounter an idea or an experience, the more likely it is to be richly represented in memory and easily available. Similarly, experiences and ideas that often are encountered together are far more likely to be associated in memory. But what the cognitive, associationistic model stresses is that many ideas that are not presented frequently or in contiguity will be related in memory because of some association that has to do with their meaning.

Among the various metaphors for items in long-term memory are such terms as *nodes*,

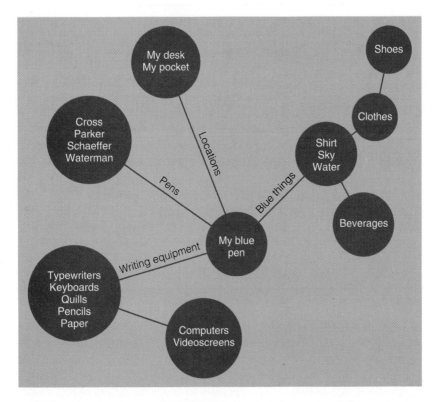

FIGURE 5.3 A model of a metaphor. Frame or node theory suggests that we remember abstractions—meanings and associations rather than specifics. Thus, my blue pen is depicted as a node embedded in a complex web of abstractions (for example, "blue things"), each of which relates to many other nodes that are not shown here. The complex of associated nodes is sometimes labeled a *frame*. From G. R. Lefrançois, *Psychological Theories and Human Learning* (2nd ed.). Copyright 1982 by Wadsworth, Inc. Reprinted by permission of Brooks/Cole Publishing Company, Monterey, California.

schemata, scripts, frames, networks, categories, coding systems, and *subsumers.* Some of these terms are defined and described in detail in the next chapter; several of them are described here to clarify the associationistic nature of long-term memory.

A node is literally a knot, a juncture, or a complication. As a metaphor for human memory, a node may be viewed as an intersection or juncture of concepts, ideas, or thoughts. It is simply a term for whatever it is that we can represent in our minds and that we are able to store and re-member. Its essential characteristic is that it represents ideas, thoughts, and the relationships among them. And terms such as *schema, frame,* and *network* are sometimes used to label the organization of memory. Thus, a frame or schema might be defined as a metaphor that represents how ideas or concepts (*nodes*) might be associated (see Figure 5.3). As Bransford (1979) argues, frame or schema models are actually models of the structure of knowledge. What cognitive psychology provides is a theory or model of what the educated mind is like.

Generative Versus Reproductive Memory. One important characteristic of long-term memory is that it appears to be partly constructive or generative, rather than reproductive; that is, what we remember is often a distortion of what we originally learned. In recalling a scene from a movie, for example, we tend to remember some of the major elements and to fill in whatever is missing. Thus, at least to some extent, we construct as well as reproduce; this is one reason why even eyewitnesses are not always accurate.

Loftus (1979) had subjects view a film in which a sports car was involved in an accident and subsequently asked them a series of questions about the accident. Some subjects were asked, "How fast was the sports car going when it passed the barn while traveling along the country road?" Other subjects were asked instead, "How fast was the sports car going while traveling along the country road?" When subjects were later asked whether they had seen the barn, 17 percent of those who had earlier been asked the first question claimed to remember seeing one; fewer than 3 percent of the others actually remembered a barn. In fact, there was no barn in the film.

As a result of this and a host of related studies, Loftus argues that much of what we remember has been modified by intervening events and dulled by the passage of time. In the end, perhaps fewer than half of us will be able to identify the thief; even fewer will remember the color of his hair or eyes. And some of us will remember things that we have never even experienced.

MEMORY PROCESSES

A number of important processes are involved in capturing a sensory impression and maintaining it in immediate awareness or transferring it to long-term storage from which it can later be retrieved. Because these processes have to do with knowing, they are cognitive processes. Three of the most important are rehearsal, elaboration, and organization. In addition, a number of specific strategies can be used with each process (Horton & Mills, 1984).

Rehearsal

Rehearsal, as we saw, is important in maintaining material in short-term memory (immediate consciousness), as well as in transferring it to long-term storage. To rehearse is to repeat. At a simple level, for example, rehearsal involves nothing more complex than naming something over and over again (repeating "seven, two, seven, five, five, five"). Most preschool children do not rehearse spontaneously and cannot easily be taught to do so (Flavell, 1985).

Elaboration

Elaboration is a cognitive process whereby material is extended or added to (elaborated) in order to make it more memorable. One way of elaborating material is to associate mental images with items to be remembered. Higbee (1977) suggests that because our memories are highly visual (photographs are more easily remembered than paragraphs), the use of mental images is an important aspect of most mnemonic systems (systems for remembering). Some of these systems are described later in this chapter.

Sometimes, elaboration involves forming associations between new material and material that is already well known. Research suggests that elaborations that relate to meaning are highly memorable. For example, when Bradshaw and Anderson (1982) asked subjects to recall sentences such as "The fat man read the sign," those who had elaborated the sentence to something like "The fat man read the sign warning of thin ice" performed significantly better than those who had not elaborated. Children younger than twelve do not deliberately elaborate to improve recall (Justice, 1985).

Organization

Organization as a memory process has to do with grouping, arranging, sorting, and relating material. Chunking—the placing of material into related classes—is one example of organization. Similarly, arranging material according to some logical system is an example of organization (for example, the characteristics of long-term memory on the one hand and those of short-term memory on the other).

The organizational strategies that are so important to long-term memory can be either extremely complex or quite simple. What most of them have in common, however, is that they are based on our recognition of similarities and differences. Humans (and perhaps other animals as well, although it is difficult to be certain) seem to have a tendency to see similarities and differences (as well as other relations) and to generalize from them. Put another way, we seem to be information-processing organisms whose function it is to make sense of all the data that surround us. One of the important methods we use for making sense of the world is to extract common elements from various experiences, thereby arriving at concepts or ideas that we can remember (Hintzman & Ludham, 1980).

In addition to this apparently natural tendency to look for relationships, there is evidence that many of our organizations of related concepts or ideas (many of our frames or schemata) result from the application of strategies we have learned. More than this, as we become aware of various strategies that we can use to make sense of the world (and to learn and remember), we also become aware of ourselves as organisms capable of learning and remembering. We learn things, and we learn about learning. Put another way, we develop metacognitive skills.

METACOGNITION

Young children are far less able to organize material than are older children and adults. More than

this, they are less aware of the importance of doing so. They are not yet reflective about themselves as knowers and have not yet recognized the special skills that allow them to extract information, to organize, to learn, and later to remember. Put another way, they know far less about knowing; they understand less about understanding (Flavell, 1985). In the current jargon, they have not yet developed the skills of **metacognition** or **metamemory**.

Metacognition is knowing about knowing. Similarly, metamemory involves knowing about remembering. Because knowing necessarily involves remembering, metacognition includes metamemory.

The skills of metacognition allow us to monitor our progress when we try to understand and learn something. They provide us with ways of estimating the effects of our efforts, and they allow us to predict the likelihood of being able to remember the material later. Metacognitive knowledge tells us that there are ways to organize material to make it easier to learn and remember, that some rehearsal and review strategies are more effective for one kind of material than another, and that some forms of learning require the deliberate application of certain strategies whereas others do not.

The Development of Metacognition

As we noted earlier, metacognitive skills seem to be largely absent in very young children. This does not mean that they make no use of cognitive strategies; it simply means that they are not aware of them and do not apply them consciously. By the same token, they are far less able to monitor, evaluate, and direct their own learning. In most instances, they do not realize that there are strategies that might make it easier to learn and remember. When Moynahan (1973) asked young children whether it would be easier to learn a categorized list of words or a randomly ordered list, children below third grade chose either list with approximately equal frequency. In contrast, older children almost invariably chose the categorized list; they knew more about knowing.

Among young children, there seems to be a greater spread between *memory behavior* and *memory knowledge*, note Borkowski, Milstead, and Hale (1988). For example, when questioned, children may reveal that they know specific learning (memory) strategies—for example, that grouping items makes it easier to remember them. However, when these same children are asked to learn lists of items, they make no use of the grouping strategy.

Specific strategies such as this can be taught to young children (Pressley, Forrest-Pressley, & Elliot-Faust, 1988). But children also need to be taught when they need to use the strategy. Unfortunately, as Borkowski and associates note, teachers are not often systematic about teaching the strategies of cognition. Instead, children are left to discover them on their own.

The Strategies of Cognition

We appear to have a natural tendency to extract generalities from experience, as well as to learn how to learn and remember. As we learn how to learn, we begin to see ourselves as players of Flavell's (1985) game of cognition, and we become aware of an increasing number and variety of strategies that can make us better players of this game. The object of the game of cognition is not to beat someone at something. Winners of this game are those who are successful in making sense of information and who can recall and use it effectively.

Some people play the game of cognition badly. They learn and remember with difficulty; much that they encounter is bewildering and frustrating. Others play the game well. They learn rapidly and with apparent ease; their understanding is often startling.

One difference between those who play the game of cognition well and those who play it less well may have to do with how clearly each understands the process of learning and remember-

ing—in other words, it has to do with the strategies of cognition. It may be that those who play the game best are those who have learned more about learning and who are better able to apply what they have learned.

A Definition. Simply defined, *cognitive strategies* are the tools of intellectual activity. With respect to school learning, E. Gagné (1985, p. 33) defines *cognitive strategies* as "goal-directed sequences of cognitive operations that lead from the student's comprehension of a question or instructions to the answer or other requested performance."

There are different kinds and levels of cognitive strategies, some of which appear to develop naturally. Many, however, are learned in schools, sometimes as a result of direct tuition but more often simply as a result of repeated exposure to certain types of problems that require specific types of strategies. In fact, one important function of schools is to provide learners not only with content but also with knowledge about ways to organize, analyze, synthesize, evaluate, create, and so on (Gagné & Dick, 1983). In other words, schools teach much more than content; they also teach students how to learn and remember—they teach cognitive strategies. Historically, most of this teaching (and learning) has occurred incidentally, in the course of teaching other things. Recently, however, a number of concerted attempts have been made to develop programs designed specifically to teach cognitive strategies. Several of these programs are reviewed in some detail later in this chapter.

Cognitive strategies allow us to learn, to solve problems, to study, and to understand. The strategy itself has little to do with the content of what we learn. It is a generalized approach, a "contentless" series of tactics or procedures (Gagné & Briggs, 1983). Accordingly, attempts to teach cognitive strategies are sometimes quite abstract and generalized, although they need not be. Indeed, Bransford Sherwood, Vye, and Rieser (1986) suggest that teachers relate cognitive strategies to specific subject areas and show students the importance of these techniques for solving problems in their own lives.

Learning/Thinking Strategies

The teaching/learning process has two broad classes of goals. Weinstein and Mayer (1986) describe these as goals relating to the products of learning and goals relating to the process of learning. Goals that relate to the products of learning are the *what* of the instructional process—the information being taught. Goals that have to do with the process of learning are the *how* of learning—the skills and strategies that can be used in acquiring and processing content; that is, they deal with learning to learn.

Cognitive psychology's most important current contribution to educational psychology is a renewed emphasis on the second of these major goals: learning to learn.

The phrase **learning/thinking strategy** is preferable to the expression "cognitive strategy" in this context. It is a broader term, including specific strategies such as rehearsing or elaborating as well as metacognition. In addition, it emphasizes that the strategies and processes involved in learning to learn are the very same processes that we ordinarily define as *thinking*. Put another way, learning/thinking strategies are the learner's information-processing/thinking tools.

A Description. And what, you may ask, are these learning/thinking strategies? Recall from earlier sections of this chapter that our basic information-processing model (the memory model) describes three main processes or activities involved in maintaining material in short-term memory and encoding and transferring it to long-term memory: rehearsal, elaboration, and organization. There are learning strategies, Weinstein and Mayer (1986) tell us, for each of these processes. Some are basic; others are more complex. Accordingly, there are basic rehearsal strategies, complex rehearsal strategies, basic elaboration strategies, complex elaboration strategies, basic organiza-

tional strategies, and complex organizational strategies.* And, in addition to these six classes of learning strategies, there are comprehension-monitoring strategies, which are essentially identical to what we have described as metacognitive skills, and affective and motivational strategies, which direct our attention, maintain our interest, and help us to relax and control impediments to learning and thinking (such as test anxiety).

Table 5.2 summarizes these eight classes of learning/thinking strategies and gives a simple example of each.

Educational Applications: Teaching Thinking

As we saw in Chapter 4, behavioristic approaches to learning lead to a number of instructional recommendations. Among other things, these approaches emphasize the importance of reinforcement and attempt to sort out the particular kinds and schedules of rewards and punishments that are most effective in the classroom. Later (in Chapter 11, for example), we will see that behaviorism has also led to specific techniques for behavior modification.

At first glance, the educational implications of the cognitive perspective seem quite different from those of behaviorism. After all, cognitivism is concerned much less with behavior, stimuli, rewards, and punishments than with thinking. It asks how children become thinkers and how we can make better, more critical, more creative thinkers of them.

The cognitive perspective suggests a two-pronged answer to these important questions. First, learners must develop an awareness of themselves as thinkers/learners/information processors;

---

*PPC: Terms such as *cognitive strategies, metacognition, learning/thinking strategies,* and *metacognitive strategies* are used in different ways in the literature. This can be very confusing. Maybe the bear could straighten things out, once and for all.

Author: Perhaps not once and for all, but for the time being, see the box entitled "Sorting It All Out Cognitively."

TABLE 5.2 Categories of Learning/Thinking Strategies

BASIC REHEARSAL STRATEGIES	Simple repetition: *hablo, hablas, habla, hablamos, hablais, hablan*
COMPLEX REHEARSAL STRATEGIES	Highlighting all the important points in a text
BASIC ELABORATION STRATEGIES	Forming mental images or other associations such as "*m*en *v*ery *e*asily *m*ake *j*ugs *s*erve *u*seful *n*octurnal *p*urposes" (the first letter of each word stands for a planet in the solar system)
COMPLEX ELABORATION STRATEGIES	Forming analogies, paraphrasing, summarizing, relating
BASIC ORGANIZATIONAL STRATEGIES	Grouping, classifying, ordering
COMPLEX ORGANIZATIONAL STRATEGIES	Identifying main ideas; developing concept-summarizing tables such as this one
COMPREHENSION-MONITORING STRATEGIES	Self-questioning; reciting main points; setting goals and checking progress toward those goals
AFFECTIVE AND MOTIVATIONAL STRATEGIES	Anticipating consequences of academic success (for example, a scholarship); deep breathing and other relaxation activities; positive thinking

Source: Based on C. E. Weinstein and R. E. Mayer, "The Teaching of Learning Strategies." In M. C. Wittrock (Ed.), *Handbook of Research on Teaching* (3rd ed.), New York: Macmillan, 1986, 315–327.

second, they must develop and practice the approaches and strategies involved in critical, creative, and effective thinking and problem solving. Put another way, the cognitive perspective argues that learners must develop metacognitive skills as well as appropriate cognitive strategies. These are the skills involved in learning to learn.

As we noted earlier, schools have traditionally devoted the bulk of their formal efforts to teaching specific curriculum content; the learning of cognitive strategies and the development of metacognitive awareness have been largely incidental—and sometimes accidental. Recently, however, an increasing number of researchers have developed programs designed specifically to develop cognitive skills in learners. Many of these programs are designed both to make students aware of the existence of cognitive strategies and to teach them to monitor and evaluate their use of these strategies. Such programs advocate a variety of approaches to teaching, including group learn-

ing (for example, cooperative learning), individual instruction (for example, teachers' questions designed to foster specific thinking skills), modeling procedures (in which, for example, a cognitive strategy is verbalized as it is being executed), and various programs in which learners are trained in the use of specific strategies (see, for example, Mulcahy, Peat, Andrews, Darko-Yeboah, & Marfo, 1990).

TEACHING THINKING

The best learners, argue Alexander and Judy (1988), are those who possess strategic as well as domain-specific (content) knowledge. Strategic knowledge deals with how to do things: how to solve problems, how to learn and memorize, how to understand, and perhaps most important, how to monitor, evaluate, and direct these activities as they occur.

sorting it all out cognitively

The following are some common, educationally relevant terms in the new cognitive sciences:

METACOGNITION
Knowing about knowing; our knowledge about our own cognitive processes and about cognitive processes in general. This knowledge permits us to select different approaches for learning and remembering; it allows us to monitor our cognitive activities and assess the likelihood of success; it suggests alternatives when necessary.

COGNITIVE STRATEGIES
The tools of cognitive behavior; goal-directed sequences of actions such as rehearsing, organizing, or elaborating; what we actually do to learn and remember.

LEARNING/THINKING STRATEGIES
A global term that includes both metacognitive and cognitive skills; the entire range of activities involved in learning and thinking.

SUMMARY
Learning/thinking strategies include metacognitive and cognitive strategies. Metacognitive skills are executive (control) skills; cognitive skills are nonexecutive (applied) skills.

ILLUSTRATION OF THE RELATIONSHIPS BETWEEN METACOGNITION AND COGNITION
I decide to learn the meanings of common, educationally relevant terms in the new cognitive sciences (setting a goal of which I suspect I am capable: a metacognitive experience). I begin to read this box (cognitive activity). I stop after two lines; I have a vague feeling that I have missed something (metacognitive experience). I read the lines again (cognitive activity). I sense that I am understanding (metacognition). I continue reading. I repeat each separate definition mentally once or twice (rehearsal, a cognitive strategy). Something tells me I am learning (metacognitive experience). I finish. I look at each term and silently repeat the definition (cognitive action). I am satisfied that I understand and will remember until tomorrow's quiz (metacognition).

Can students be taught these strategic or procedural skills? Can they be taught how to think and learn?

In a word, yes.

Learning How to Learn

Learning how to learn in schools is not entirely new. What is new is our attitude toward what it is that makes learning difficult or easy. Traditionally, we have simply assumed that the most important factor in learning is inherited or natural intelligence—recognizing, of course, that motivation, persistence, and other similar factors are important as well. Recently, however, our conceptions of intelligence have begun to change dramatically. We have begun to accept the view that among the important components of intelligent activity are cognitive functions that are largely acquired, not inherited.

Haywood and Switzky (1986) make a similar point. Intelligent behavior, they assert, requires two things: native ability (what we think of as innate intelligence) and cognitive functions. The important point is that whereas native ability is, by definition, genetic and therefore unmodifiable except by extreme measures, cognitive functions are acquired. Does it not follow that if they are learned, they can also be taught?

The simple answer is yes. And there is increasing evidence that this learning need not occur only incidentally—or even accidentally—as a by-product of school activities, the purposes of which are far removed from teaching students how to learn. A mushrooming new field of research involves looking for ways in which students can be taught not only the cognitive skills of rehearsing, elaborating, and organizing but also the metacognitive skills involved in monitoring their own levels of comprehension and in making other important decisions about their cognitive activities and their personal capabilities. Psychologists are being increasingly successful in discovering the rules, the strategies, and the objectives of this game of cognition that all of us are called upon to play. And, as a result, today's students may be far better players tomorrow than they would otherwise have been.

Researchers who have developed and investigated programs designed specifically to teach students how to learn and think have emphasized a variety of skills. Nickerson's (1988) review suggests that there have been at least seven identifiable emphases:

1. Basic operations such as classifying or generalizing

2. Domain-specific knowledge

3. Knowledge about reasoning principles such as logic

4. Knowledge about informal principles of thinking that might be used in problem solving

5. Metacognitive knowledge

6. Values such as fairness and objectivity

7. Personal beliefs (for example, about problems, about the world, about causes, and about the role of luck and effort)

These different emphases have led to the development of a variety of programs for teaching thinking. These programs typically take one of two different forms: stand-alone, in which cognitive skills are taught as a separate subject, and embedded, in which cognitive skills are taught within the context of subject matter. A third approach described by Prawat (1991), immersion, places more emphasis on ideas than on skills and processes but is really much like an embedded approach. Several programs are described briefly in the sections that follow.

Dansereau's Metastrategies

Dansereau and his associates have developed a stand-alone program designed to teach some general cognitive strategies to college students (Dansereau, 1985). These strategies apply mainly to verbal learning and are divided into two groups: primary and support strategies.

Primary strategies are information-processing skills for learning, storing and retrieving, and deriving meaning from textual material. They consist of such activities as using visual imagery, summarizing, paraphrasing, analyzing questions, and using context to facilitate recall. Support strategies are involved in maintaining an appropriate mind-set for learning and remembering. They include such metacognitive activities as setting goals, arranging schedules, monitoring comprehension, and self-evaluation.

A general program for studying devised by Dansereau and his associates is based directly on their analysis of metastrategies (strategies of metacognition). It is called MURDER, an acronym for the following sequential procedure: set your **mood**, read for **understanding, recall, digest information** (a procedure that involves recalling correctly, rehearsing, organizing, and storing), **expand knowledge** (involves elaboration through a process of self-inquiry), and **review mistakes**. MURDER is a somewhat more complex process than this brief description might imply. For example, a number of specific tactics are taught and practiced in connection with each of the major steps in the program (relaxation techniques associated with mood setting and imaging strategies associated with recall, for example). Studies of this program at the college level have generally shown increases in measures of cognitive functioning.

Feuerstein's Instrumental Enrichment

In practice, intelligence is most often assessed in terms of performance on tests that reveal how much a person has benefited from past experience. According to Reuven Feuerstein (1979), whose work is primarily on the topic of mental retardation, such tests represent a static rather than a dynamic view of intelligence: They reveal what the child has done rather than what the child can do in the future. They do not assess learning potential.

More useful measures of intelligence, Feuerstein argues, would do more than reflect what the child has done in the past; they would provide some estimate of capacity for benefiting from future experience. To this end, he has developed the Learning Potential Assessment Device (LPAD), which focuses on intellectual functioning—on cognitive processes—rather than simply on whether the child can answer correctly within a given time limit. The test allows the examiner to actually teach the child, to offer hints and clues, and to direct and help. Described as a dynamic rather than a static measure, it makes it possible both to identify strengths and detect absent or deficient cognitive functions. In Feuerstein's (1980) terms, it permits the construction of a "cognitive map" of the learner, which can serve as the basis for analyzing the cognitive functioning of what he calls "retarded performers" and as a blueprint for remediation.

Among Feuerstein's greatest contributions is the development of a complex and far-reaching series of activities and exercises designed to improve cognitive functioning. This program, Feuerstein's Instrumental Enrichment (FIE, sometimes abbreviated simply IE), is based squarely on the assumption that motivates all the learning-to-learn research: a strong belief in cognitive modifiability.

A logical outgrowth of the LPAD, the FIE program is largely content free; that is, it attempts to teach cognitive functioning rather than academic content. It is a clear example of a stand-alone program.

The FIE program uses a series of progressively more abstract paper-and-pencil exercises designed to help students identify strategies used in thinking and to encourage them to become aware of their use of those strategies. In all, there are more than five hundred pages of exercises—enough for a one-hour daily lesson over the course of several years.

Even though the FIE program was initially developed for use with "retarded performers" (Feuerstein deliberately avoids the term *mental retardation*), he argues that its principles are applicable to a wide range of ages and subjects. Use of the FIE program requires that teachers be specially trained.

Initial evaluation of the FIE materials involved a longitudinal experiment in which performance-retarded adolescents exposed to the FIE program were compared with similar adolescents in a more conventional, content-oriented enrichment program. Results were highly positive (Feuerstein, 1980).

Subsequent research in a number of countries, including Canada, the United States, Venezuela, and Israel, has been summarized by Savell, Twohig, and Rachford (1986). Although many of the studies they reviewed do not report clearly positive results—usually because of experiment-design inadequacies (such as lack of a control group) or shortcomings in applying the program—they nevertheless conclude that FIE has generally positive results. The most commonly reported cognitive gains are on nonverbal measures of intelligence and involve students between twelve and eighteen years old. Teachers in the most successful FIE programs had typically been given at least one week of training before the program, and students who were most likely to gain had been exposed to a minimum of eighty hours of FIE instruction. Gains were most likely to occur when FIE had been taught in conjunction with subjects of significant interest and importance to students.

SPELT

Another large-scale cognitive program is Mulcahy and associates' Strategies Program for Effective Learning/Thinking (SPELT) (Marfo, Mulcahy, Peat, Andrews, & Cho, 1991; Mulcahy, Kofi, Peat, Andrews, & Clifford, 1986). Described as a learning/thinking instructional program, SPELT is designed for use with all children—from learning disabled to gifted. Like FIE, it focuses on process rather than content. SPELT, unlike many other cognitive development programs such as Dansereau's metastrategies and FIE, is aimed at elementary and junior high school students rather than adolescents or college students.

One important difference between SPELT and FIE is that SPELT is an embedded rather than a stand-alone program. Embedded programs have the advantage of being more relevant to students and more easily applied because they are part of the regular curriculum. In addition, because they don't require a separate classroom period, they are less expensive and easier to schedule than stand-alone programs (Derry & Murphy, 1986).

SPELT has three major characteristics. First, its overriding goal is to involve the student actively in the learning process. It attempts to make students increasingly aware of their own cognitive processes and is geared toward discovery rather than reception learning.

Second, SPELT requires active teacher participation in identifying and discovering strategies as well as in devising methods for teaching them. Initially, teachers are presented with tested strategies and methods; after continuing in-service training, they are encouraged to develop their own.

Third, SPELT is designed to encourage students to recognize and generate their own cognitive strategies; that is, students are expected to become increasingly aware of their own intellectual processes and to become actively involved in developing and improving these processes. In short, they are encouraged to recognize and develop the tools they use in playing the game of cognition. The main objective of SPELT, says Mulcahy

(1991), is to develop autonomous learners—learners who have truly learned how to learn, who are in control of their own "cognitive as well as affective resources and activities" (p. 385).

The learning/thinking strategies developed and emphasized in SPELT cover a vast range—for example, general problem solving, math and reading strategies, memory strategies, study skills, test-taking strategies, mood-setting strategies, and general metacognitive strategies such as comprehension monitoring. In addition, special effort is made to develop social problem-solving strategies.

Implementation of SPELT occurs in three overlapping phases. In the first phase, students are taught a number of learning/thinking strategies by teachers trained in using and teaching these strategies. Instructional procedures in this phase are direct and teacher controlled. Their basic elements include motivating students, modeling the strategies, providing memorization and practice drills with feedback, and evaluating students' learning. The goal of this phase, as expressed by Peat, Mulcahy, and Darko-Yeboah (1989), is "metacognitive empowerment"—a condition that comes about as students become increasingly aware of the existence of cognitive strategies and of the contribution their systematic use can make to learning and problem solving.

The objectives of the second phase are to maintain the use of strategies learned in the first phase, to begin to evaluate the effectiveness of these strategies, and to modify and extend them to different content areas. The principal instructional method is no longer one of direct tuition but rather one of facilitating the application of previously learned strategies to new situations (teaching for transfer). The instructional method is now Socratic rather than direct; that is, students are encouraged to extend and apply strategies through an interactive question-and-answer process. Among the teacher's guidelines for questioning are the following: start with what is known, ask for more than one reason, ask students to describe steps in their reasoning

THE PLACE: Medicine Hat High School

THE TIME: 3:00 P.M. Friday

THE SETTING: The beginning of Orville Radcliffe's class, Life and Career Skills 10, taught to a tenth-grade class of low achievers—administratively labeled an "opportunity class"

THE LESSON: Personal banking

There is much noise and shuffling, much talking and restlessness. Little attentiveness. Mr. Radcliffe glances at his lesson notes. He reads the main heads:

The purposes of banks

Alternatives

Fluctuating interest rates

The cost of borrowing . . .

"Borrrrrrring!" Mr. Radcliffe acknowledges to himself. He clears his throat:

"Ahem," says he by way of getting their attention. It doesn't work.

"Today we're going to talk about personal banking," he mumbles uncertainly—soon, he knows, he will have lost them all until the bell rescues him.

But that's the lesson he prepared, and so he forges onward: "Take out your notebooks 'cause you should make notes, 'cause there'll be questions about this on the exam, especially about the effects of interest rates and all that . . ." He is wishing he had prepared a different lesson. . . .

---

processes, formulate general rules from specific cases, provide counterexamples or extreme cases, probe for differences among cases, and ask students to make predictions (Mulcahy, Peat, Andrews, Darko-Yeboah, & Marfo, 1990).

In the third phase of the SPELT program, the learner is encouraged to generate new cognitive strategies and to monitor and evaluate them. The principal instructional method continues to be that of Socratic dialogue. In contrast with the first phase, learning at this level is largely student rather than teacher controlled.

The SPELT program was evaluated during a three-year project involving some nine hundred gifted, average, and learning-disabled students in grades 4, 5, 7, and 8. Results were positive, especially for learning-disabled students and most notably at the fourth-grade level, at which reading comprehension and comprehension-monitoring skills improved most dramatically. Gifted students also benefited significantly. Use and awareness of cognitive strategies improved at all grade levels and for all groups. In addition, parents, teachers, and administrators responded favorably to the program. A year after termination of the experimental project, more than 85 percent of the teachers reported that they continued to use aspects of the program in their teaching.

A Conclusion

Dansereau's metastrategies, Feuerstein's Instrumental Enrichment, and Mulcahy and associates' SPELT are only three of a large number of learning/thinking programs being developed, modified, and evaluated (see, for example, Nickerson, 1988). Two things seem clear at this point: First, our attempts to teach students how to think and how to learn are not always as deliberate and as focused as they might be, and second, systematic programs can significantly improve learning and thinking for a variety of individuals and in many different contexts (French & French, 1991).

Although it would be premature to suggest that teachers should now begin using this or that program for this or that purpose, it is not at all premature to repeat many education critics' claim that the schools have not always done much to teach thinking and learning skills. The contemporary cognitive sciences are based on the assumption that much more can be done. They have also begun showing us how.

He struts to the front of the class, opens his briefcase flat on his desk so none of the students can see its contents—and then exclaims, "Now that's more like it!" while piling on his desk great stacks of money (well, maybe great stacks of newspaper cut just so, bound with elastics, with real bills on top).

"We don't get paid this much in a lifetime of teaching," says he. "But I've won the lottery!"

And together, Mr. Radcliffe and his class examine the various banking alternatives open to a lottery winner, the implications of each, and on and on. . . .

Among important cognitive strategies children learn are several having to do with remembering and, perhaps more important, retrieving from memory.

TEACHING FOR RETRIEVAL

Several characteristics of long-term memory are especially important for teachers: Material that is meaningful and well organized is learned more easily and remembered for longer periods of time than insignificant material. Events that are particularly striking tend to be recalled more easily and more clearly (Bower, 1981). Frequent rehearsal improves long-term recall. Visual material has a greater impact on memory than verbal material.

Each of the observations in the two cases at Medicine Hat High School on pages 138 and 139 suggests clear classroom implications.

The first lesson has little chance, especially with this class on a Friday afternoon. But the second might work wonderfully well—and might be remembered. It begins with material that is *striking*, it presents a situation that is *meaningful*, it provides opportunities for *relating* items of information, and for *emphasizing* concepts (perhaps with stacks of money), and it uses *visual* (and memorable) teaching aids. Nor will it be difficult to find opportunities for rehearsal and repetition. This is one lesson students might remember.

WHY WE CAN'T REMEMBER

One of the intriguing things about long-term memory is that, unlike short-term memory, it does not appear to have limits. Psychological research has not demonstrated that after a lifetime of learning our long-term memories become so crowded that we find ourselves incapable of learning new material until we have forgotten some of the old. Yet we do forget (or fail to remember) a great deal; knowing why we forget and what can be done to impede the process might be valuable for teachers.

Although no one knows precisely what the physiology of memory is or what happens when **forgetting** takes place, a number of theories have been advanced to explain these processes.

Fading

One theory holds that material that is not brought to mind frequently enough (that is not used) tends to fade from memory. I know at this moment that the oldest recorded age at which a woman has given birth to a live infant is fifty-seven. This fact was brought to my attention as I perused *The Guinness Book of World Records* in search of a record that I might break. Unless I review this information again, or have it brought to mind by someone or something, I probably won't remember it next year. It will have faded.

Distortion

Those memories that do not fade entirely are often distorted. It is now difficult for me to remember a specific sunset accurately; I have seen so many that even the most striking have become distorted until, in my memory of sunsets, there isn't a single one that looks very much different from any other. It's sad but true. My sunrises fare better (probably because I haven't seen as many). The notable unreliability of eyewitnesses (Loftus, 1979) is another illustration of memory distortion.

Suppression

It appears that people tend to forget events that are particularly unpleasant. One explanation for this phenomenon is Freud's belief that unpleasant memories filter into the subconscious mind, where the individual is not aware of them even though they may continue to have a profound effect on the person's emotional life.

Interference

The most popular theory of forgetting, and one that has direct relevance for teachers, says that interference from previous or subsequent learning is an important cause of forgetting. When previous learning interferes with current recall, **proactive inhibition** is said to occur; **retroactive inhibition** takes place when subsequent learning interferes with recall of previous learning. Teachers often have difficulty remembering the names of new students, especially if they have been teaching for a long time and have known many students with similar names. They confuse old names with new but similar faces. By the same token, once teachers have learned the names of all their current students, they sometimes find it difficult to remember the names of students from years past. The first case illustrates proactive inhibition; the second, retroactive inhibition.

Poor Retrieval

Some psychologists maintain that forgetting can often be accounted for by the inability to retrieve from memory rather than by simple memory loss, distortion, suppression, or interference. In other words, individuals appear not to remember simply because they are unable to find a way to recall an item of information from memory; presumably, they do not possess good **retrieval cues**.

Educational Implications

In summary, information may be forgotten because it has faded through disuse, because it has been distorted, suppressed, or interfered with, or because the individual does not have the proper retrieval cues. One important function of a teacher is to transmit information, attitudes, and skills that will not all be forgotten. Knowledge of why people forget can help in this task.

If students forget because of disuse (fading theory), teachers can provide repetition and review to remind them of important items. Similarly, the effects of distortion can be partially overcome by being careful to emphasize the most important and distinct (the most memorable) aspects of a situation.

Suppression theory does not suggest any simple educational applications. It is to be hoped that you will not provide your students with experiences that need to be suppressed. In any case, you would probably be ill advised to attempt to prevent suppression or to bring back to memory those experiences that have been suppressed.

Allowing time to elapse between lessons and organizing them to make use of similarities and differences may help overcome the effects of interference. And organizing material may partially overcome the retrieval problem, particularly if the organization facilitates the identification of relationships.

Using Similarities and Differences. Among the most important suggestions for increasing the ability to recall information are those relating to

"You simply associate each number with a word, such as 'Table' and 3,476,029."

the use of similarities and differences among items of information, a topic touched upon in the section on generalization and discrimination in Chapter 4. These topics are frequently treated under the heading of "transfer" (or "generalization"). The terms refer to the effects of old learning on new learning. Transfer can be either positive or negative. Positive transfer occurs when previous learning facilitates new learning and is sometimes evident in learning second languages. For example, it is easier to learn Latin if you know French than if you know only English; the similarities between French and Latin facilitate positive transfer. Negative transfer occurs when previous learning interferes with current learning; it is similar to proactive interference. Negative transfer occurs, for example, when you or I go to Bermuda, rent a motor scooter, and discover that all the traffic is on the wrong side of the street.

One obvious way to teach for positive transfer while at the same time eliminating negative transfer is, as suggested previously, to relate new material to old material, emphasizing similarities and differences. The similarities should facilitate positive transfer; knowledge of differences should minimize negative transfer.

Specific Memory Aids

In addition to these general approaches, there are a number of well-known techniques for improving memory. Many of these memory aids, or mnemonic devices, make use of specific retrieval cues.

Rhymes and Such. Rhymes, patterns, acronyms, and acrostics are common mnemonic devices. "Thirty days hath September . . ." is a simple rhyme without which many of us would not know how many days hath November. Similarly, the year in which Columbus sailed the ocean blue is nicely recalled by its little rhyme. The number "five million, five hundred fifty-one thousand, two hundred twelve" is considerably more difficult to remember than the number 555-1212; "triple five, double twelve" may be even easier. The mnemonic aid of chunking makes use of patterns.

Acronyms are letter cues that help to recall relatively complex material. *NATO, U.N.,* and *UNESCO* are popular acronyms. *Roy G. Biv* is another acronym, made up of the first letters of the words for the ordered colors of the visible light spectrum. Acrostics are similar to acronyms, except that they generally make use of sentences in which the first letter of each word represents an item of information to be remembered. Without the bizarre sentence "Men very easily make jugs serve useful nocturnal purposes," I would have considerable difficulty recalling the planets in order from the sun. "Every good boy does fine" is meaningful to beginning music students.

A number of more complex mnemonic techniques are described in detail by Higbee (1977) and are reviewed briefly here. All have one thing in common: They make extensive use of imagery. Recall that visual material appears to have a greater impact on memory and can be retrieved much more easily than most nonvisual material.

The Link System. The simplest of these techniques is the **link system**. It requires the subject to visualize the item to be remembered and to form a strong visual association (link) between it and other items to be remembered. It is easily illustrated with reference to a grocery list. (Once you have mastered this system, you need never write a grocery list again.) Suppose the list contains the following items: bread, salt, ketchup, dog food, and bananas. Visualize the first item. Concentrate on the picture that comes to mind first because it is likely to come to mind again when you think of bread. It might be bizarre, or it might be a simple image of a loaf or slice of bread. Now visualize the second item, salt, and form a visual link between the first image and the second. For example, you might see a slice of bread perched delicately on a large silver salt shaker. The salt shaker is dripping with ketchup being poured from a bottle held by a hungry dog with a banana in its ear. In most cases, you need not spend more than a few seconds with each image, nor should you rehearse them while you are learning the list.

The link system works amazingly well, although it has disadvantages. One is that it is sometimes difficult to remember the first item on the list. In that case, it might also be impossible to remember any of the other items because they are linked one to the other. This problem can be overcome by forming a visual association between the first item and a setting that is likely to remind you of the item. You might, for example, see the loaf of bread reclining in a grocery cart. A second disadvantage of the link system is that if you cannot recall one of the items, it is unlikely that you will recall any of the subsequent items.

The Loci System. A variation of the link system, the **loci system**, overcomes this second disadvantage. In effect, in the loci system you simply form associations between items you need to remember and places that are familiar to you and that you therefore can visualize clearly. Rooms in a familiar house make good loci (*locus* is Latin for *place*). You can quite easily "place" a grocery list in the rooms of a house simply by forming strong visual images of the objects, one in each of the rooms. The advantage of this system is that if you cannot remember what you placed in the hallway, you can always go to the bathroom.

The Phonetic System. A third mnemonic system, the **phonetic system**, is by far the most powerful, although it requires considerably more effort. Indeed, if you master this system, you could become a professional mnemonist. At the very least, you will impress your grandmother. The phonetic system allows you to recall items in order, backward, by twos, threes, fours, or—perhaps even more impressive—to recall any specific item (for example, the fourteenth item listed).

The first step in learning the system is to make an association between numbers and consonants. (Vowels do not count in the system.) Traditionally, the number 1 is represented by a letter such as *t* or *l*, because each has a single downstroke; the number 2 might be represented by an *n* because it has two downstrokes; 3 is *m* and 9 is *p* because each member of the pairs resembles the other. Once you have associated a letter with each digit, you can form words that represent numbers. Thus, the number 13 might be *tam*, *tome*, or *team* (remember, vowels don't count); the number 21 might be *nut* or *net*; and so on. The next step is simply to form a strong visual image of each of the words that correspond to numbers (1 through 25, for example). Having done so, you can stand on stage and have your audience describe or show you twenty-five items, which are recorded in order by your assistant, on a large chalkboard that remains out of your sight. By forming strong visual associations between each of these items and your number-linked words, you can recall all twenty-five items in any order or any specific item by its number of appearance. For example, if the twenty-first item the audience displays is a shoe, you visualize a shoe caught in a *net* (net representing 21).

This must have some classroom implication. Surely.

MAIN POINTS

1. Some of our learning involves apparently random behaviors (trial and error) and resulting reinforcement and punishment; behaviorism studies this type of learning. However, much of our learning seems to be guided by strategies, patterns, and hypotheses, as well as by a recognition of (or a search for) order and meaning in our experiences; these are the concerns of cognitive psychology, the primary emphasis of which is on the mental events involved in knowing, acquiring information, solving problems, and remembering.

2. Cognitive psychology looks at three things: knowledge base (the learner's storehouse of information), cognitive strategies (processes used in learning and thinking), and metacognition (awareness of the self as a knower and capacity to understand and monitor cognitive processes).

3. Computers, especially the branch dealing with artificial intelligence, present a useful model (metaphor) for human cognitive functioning. Another basic model of cognitive psychology describes the learner as a three-level information-processing-and-storage system in which the levels are labeled "sensory memory," "short-term memory," and "long-term memory."

4. Sensory storage is the immediate, unconscious, momentary availability of sensory data for processing, lasting only a fraction of a second.

5. Material to which we attend is processed into short-term (working) storage, where it is maintained for perhaps as long as twenty seconds. Without rehearsal, material fades quickly from short-term memory. Short-term memory capacity is seven (plus or minus two) items, some of which might include chunks of related material. Young children's sensory memories are limited to two or three items before age six.

6. Material is transferred from short-term to long-term memory through encoding (transforming or changing to abstract generalities and deriving meaning). Encoding involves three processes: rehearsal (repetition), elaboration (extending), and organization (relating, sorting).

7. Craik and Lockhart's levels-of-processing theory suggests that the extent and duration of memory result from the level to which information is processed. Thus, we are not conscious of material that is not processed, and it remains in sensory storage for only a fraction of a second; material that is attended to and rehearsed is held in short-term storage for a matter of seconds; material that is encoded finds its way into long-term memory.

8. A traditional model of long-term memory portrays the mind as a catalogue or movielike recording of a sequence of unrelated experiences. Contemporary models of long-term memory are associationistic; they hold that material in memory is organized according to relationships—that everything in memory is associated with something else.

9. Long-term memory does not simply reproduce events or images as a photograph does but instead generates or constructs as a painter does. It often forgets or distorts events that have happened, and it sometimes recalls events that have not.

10. As we learn about things (facts, problem-solving techniques, and so on), we also learn about learning. Knowledge about our own cognitive processes is metacognition. The skills of metacognition allow us to direct, monitor, evaluate, and modify our ongoing learning and thinking.

11. Cognitive (learning/thinking) strategies are the tools of cognitive behavior. Weinstein and Mayer describe eight classes of learning/thinking strategies: the first six are rehearsal, elaboration, and organizational strategies for either basic or complex problems; the last two are comprehension-monitoring strategies (strategies of metacognition) and affective (motivational) strategies.

12. Cognitivism asks how children become thinkers and how we can make better, more critical, more

creative thinkers of them. Part of its answer is by making them aware of themselves as knowers and information processors (metacognitive skills) and by teaching them specific cognitive strategies (for example, how to rehearse, organize, monitor, and so on).

13. Dansereau's metastrategies program for teaching thinking is a stand-alone approach (separate from ordinary curriculum content) that attempts to teach primary strategies (those used for learning, storing, and retrieving) and support strategies (those involved in maintaining mindset for learning) to college populations. MURDER (Mood, Understand, Recall, Digest, Expand, Review) is a Dansereau metastrategy.

14. Feuerstein's Instrumental Enrichment (FIE) program is based on the Learning Potential Assessment Device (LPAD), which attempts to assess the retarded performer's highest potential for achievement. It consists of paper-and-pencil exercises to develop cognitive strategies and was developed primarily for adolescents with performance deficits (below-average intelligence or normal intelligence with learning disabilities or cognitive deficiencies).

15. The Strategies Program for Effective Learning/Thinking (SPELT), developed by Mulcahy and associates, is an embedded program (designed for use within the context of ordinary curriculum) for elementary and junior high school students. It encourages teachers and students to identify and generate cognitive strategies in a variety of areas (general problem solving, social problem solving, math, reading, studying, test taking, mood setting, and general metacognitive strategies).

16. Useful strategies for teaching for retrieval emphasize meaningfulness, organization, visual imagery, rehearsal, and overlearning.

17. Theories of forgetting maintain that information is forgotten because it is unused, distorted, suppressed, or interfered with or because the individual has a poor retrieval system. These theories suggest that teachers should both emphasize distinct and important aspects of situations and stress similarities and differences in order to minimize interference and maximize transfer.

18. Mnemonic devices include rhymes, patterns, acrostics, and acronyms. More complex mnemonic techniques are the link system, the loci system, and the phonetic system. Each of these is based on the principle that visual imagery is an extremely powerful aid to memory.

SUGGESTED READINGS

Ellen Gagné's book is a clear and detailed description of contemporary cognitive psychology and its implications for education. The author looks at the application of cognitive science in specific subject areas.

GAGNÉ, E. D. (1985). *The cognitive psychology of school learning.* Boston: Little, Brown.

A very practical, classroom-oriented book that looks at how teachers can help students become more thoughtful is

BARELL, J. (1991). *Teaching for thoughtfulness: Classroom strategies to enhance intellectual development.* New York: Longman.

The following article presents a general overview of research in cognitive strategies training:

NICKERSON, R. S. (1988). On improving thinking through instruction. In E. Z. Rothkopf (Ed.), *Review of Research in Education* (Vol. 15). Washington, D.C.: American Educational Research Association.

Sternberg's book presents some of the flavor of current interest in cognitive strategies and includes various suggestions for improving intelligence.

STERNBERG, R. J. (1986). *Intelligence applied: Understanding and increasing your intellectual skills.* New York: Harcourt Brace Jovanovich.

A highly readable, informative, and practical discussion of memory and mnemonic aids is provided in

HIGBEE, K. L. (1977). *Your memory: How it works and how to improve it.* Englewood Cliffs, N.J.: Prentice-Hall.

The Eskimo believe that the soul of a wounded bear tarries near the spot where it leaves its body. Many taboos and propitiatory ceremonies are observed with regard to the slaughtering of the carcass and the consumption of the flesh (Engel, 1976, p. 69).

Some folks are wise, and some are otherwise.
Tobias Smollett, *Roderick Random*

*If a little knowledge is dangerous, where is the man
who has so much as to be out of danger?*
Thomas Henry Huxley, *Science and Culture*

Chapter 6 | COGNITIVE LEARNING IN SCHOOLS

PREVIEW Decision making, problem solving, analyzing, synthesizing, evaluating, and other manifestations of the cognitive functions that are involved in what we ordinarily think of as thinking—these all qualify as higher mental processes. This chapter discusses higher mental processes and presents two theoretical approaches to cognitive functions. Each leads to explicitly different instructional implications. Bruner's theory argues for discovery-oriented learning; Ausubel's makes a strong case for a more didactic approach. The merits of each are examined.

Excerpt from Raising the Kids, What?

Just when it looked like it would disappear at the end of the tunnel, the fat blue one turned, opened its great red mouth, and with an awesome crunch and a huge belch swallowed me whole.

My son, who was then seven, thought this was very funny. But when he started down the same tunnel, he quickly found himself wedged between another of the blue ones and three of the smaller, cowlike yellow ones. I saw him hesitate momentarily as the red mouth opened. "He's a goner too," I thought. But quick as an instant, he whirled behind the great blue monster and, before it could turn on him, pricked its scaly hide with his lance. It deflated at once with a loud "Chleb" (a sort of reverse belch), spraying the tunnel with a fine bluish mist that hid the cows and allowed him to escape into another room. There he soon encountered an army of three-legged things, each with a huge menacing eye and a single claw. Defying all odds, the boy leapt boldly over the first thing, scurried between the legs of the second, and ran smack into the third. Cackling insanely, it reached out with its single claw, grabbed him by the seat of the pants, and lifted him high in the air, holding him there, wriggling and screaming, until another of the fat, waddling, blue things appeared. Then it tossed him, almost carelessly it seemed, spinning through the air and into the huge red mouth.

"Belch!"

Another nightmare? No. Just a new computer game that we had purchased earlier that day and were now trying to learn—he because he enjoys playing these games, and I because surely an educational psychologist can squeeze out one or two lessons from learning a new computer game.

My first step in learning this game was to sit and read the directions—completely, carefully, and with the full benefit of years of experience in reading and following directions. My son's first step was to take the controls, start the game, and promptly get himself devoured by the blue thing with the red mouth—again and again and again, each time with a great crunch and a roaring belch. Distracted by this gruesome sound, I escaped to my study, where I could concentrate more easily. "Grip the control in either the right or left hand," I read, "and move the lever in any direction. Note how Varvok goes up, down, left, or right. Now spin the lever to make Varvok turn. See how his lance always points in front of him. To thrust with the lance, press the 'Fire' button on your control." And on and on, through more than a dozen pages describing how each of the creatures in the Caves of Zarool can move, in what way each is dangerous, and how each can be avoided, slain, or transformed into an ally. "Varvok's mission," the instructions informed me, "is to reach Zarool and slay him before he can finish his new formula, which will turn the moon into chocolate pudding and darken the Earth's nights."

"I will gladly make chocolate pudding of him," I chortled as I returned to the computer.

"What you have to do is get to the guy in the cave, Zarool," I explained as I took the controls. "You get past the blue ones by jumping behind them and spearing them, and you can jump over the yellow ones. The red ones throw big blobs of pudding, which you have to dodge unless you can get your spear into them. And the green ones . . . Here's a blue one. Watch as I spin. . . ."

"Chleb!"

OUTCOMES OF LEARNING: R. GAGNÉ

Sometimes there is clearly more involved in knowing than is made possible by reading, understanding, and remembering. The Caves of Zarool are a case in point. Although I knew with utmost clarity and precision the nature of each of Zarool's creatures—how each moves, attacks, destroys, and can itself be avoided, attacked, or destroyed,

although I knew the sequence of obstacles that Varvok must surmount in order to reach Zarool, and although I knew Zarool's only weak point (his right heel—like Achilles')—still, I apparently did not really know how to play the game. Yet my seven-year-old son, who had not read the directions and who therefore began to play the game from a totally different knowledge base, could nevertheless slay blue monsters, leap over the bristling, one-eyed, clawed ones, dodge through great clouds of flying puddings, and in the end threaten Zarool's very existence.

"Perhaps," I thought, ever the psychologist, "he has learned through trial, error, and reinforcement! And I have learned exactly the same thing but cognitively to begin with!" For example, his moves were clearly influenced by reinforcement (escaping from a creature or slaying it) and punishment (being captured, eaten, squished, chained to a cave wall, or otherwise disposed of). In addition, there appeared to be a great deal of trial and error involved in the learning, particularly in the early stages when he had little idea what the object of the game was or what obstacles there might be to attaining success. Surely this is an excellent example of learning through trial and error.

But as I watched him play and learn this game, it soon became apparent that real life is seldom as simple as our theories and that there might be more to my son's learning of the Caves of Zarool than can easily be explained by means of simple behavioristic theories. True, his behaviors continued to be responsive to the obvious rewards and punishments inflicted on poor chewed-up Varvok, but they also appeared to be guided by his increasing recognition of the strategies and patterns governing the behaviors of the various enemies. "Why did you move there?" I asked once, and he quickly answered, "Because I think they always come in threes, the orange ones, and right after is another of the big blues, and I can get behind it if I go that way. It's a lot like the Big Bang." Apparently his learning involved a

search for regularities (patterns and strategies), the generation of hypotheses ("If I move this way . . ."), and generalization from previous knowledge ("This is like the Big Bang"). In other words, his learning was at least partly cognitive.

There are at least five major domains of human capabilities related to learning, says Robert Gagné (1985): intellectual skills, verbal information, attitudes, motor skills, and cognitive strategies. These five domains represent, in effect, outcomes of the learning process. The practical usefulness of Gagné's instructional theory[*] derives largely from his analysis of the conditions most conducive to learning the capabilities represented by each of the five domains. Knowledge of these conditions, although still incomplete and speculative, can be valuable in suggesting appro-

priate instructional strategies. Accordingly, each of these categories is described in the sections that follow, together with the conditions believed to be conducive to their learning.

Intellectual Skills

Intellectual skills are the outcomes of learning. In one sense, these skills are the outcomes of the learning processes described earlier (classical and operant conditioning, for example); they also include more complex outcomes, such as the learning of discriminations, rules, and concepts.

Discrimination Learning. Learning discriminations involves acquiring the ability to differentiate among similar stimuli in order to respond correctly to them. As a simple example of discrimination learning in schools, consider the task of teaching students to discriminate between the letters *p* and *b*. One of the conditions necessary for discrimination learning is the presence of the

---

[*]Some writers, including Robert Gagné (Gagné & Dick, 1983), refer to this theory as the "Gagné-Briggs theory," since the publication of a major book by these two authors (Gagné & Briggs, 1983).

related individual sequences of responses, termed **chains**. In this case, these consist of the students' being able to say "bee" or "pee." Also, the individual chains must be repeated and reinforced, and distinctions among them must be highlighted. For example, the teacher might draw attention to the most obvious differences between the two letters and might also invent certain mnemonics that highlight these differences (for example, *b* looks like a boot and is also the first letter of that word).

Discrimination learning is prevalent in much school learning. Among other things, it is involved in learning to make different responses to printed letters, numbers, or words, in learning to differentiate among classes of things, and in learning to identify similar objects.

Concept Learning. Although discrimination learning and concept learning both involve responding to similarities and differences, it is generally true that discrimination is concerned more with differences, whereas concept learning is concerned more with detecting similarities. At a simple level, a concept is a notion or an idea that reflects the common characteristics of related events or objects. R. Gagné suggests that repeated experience with situations and events that present examples of the concept in question is one of the important external conditions that facilitate the learning of concepts. As an illustration, he describes a simple procedure whereby a child can be taught the meaning of the concept *odd*. The procedure involves presenting the child with a series of three objects; two are identical, the other is odd. The procedure continues with a variety of groups of objects and might involve placing a tangible reward (candy, for example) under the odd object or simply reinforcing the child verbally for selecting correctly. Subsequently, the teacher verifies the child's grasp of the concept by asking for additional examples.

The importance of concept learning can hardly be overemphasized. Concepts are essential elements of our thought processes; they are the substance of our views of the world; they enable us to make sense of both the world and our own behaviors. They reduce the complexity of the environment and make it possible to generalize, to make decisions, and to behave appropriately.

Rule Learning. Although concepts are fundamentally important, they are not sufficient. Clearly, students cannot be presented with all the different instances for which they will need a response. For example, if one of the instructional goals of a mathematics program is that students should be able to subtract 1,978 from 2,134, from 7,461, from 1,979, and so on, each of these instances need not (and probably cannot) be taught separately. Instead, a concept or a combination of concepts is used. This combination of concepts takes the form of a rule (which R. Gagné defines as a combination of two or more concepts). Rules reflect that which is systematic and predictable, thereby enabling us to respond to different situations in similar, rule-regulated ways. Spoken language offers numerous illustrations of rules. A child who says, "He jumps, cats jump, men jump, and rabbits jump" is obviously applying the rule that a verb preceded by a plural subject does not ordinarily end in *s*.

In discussing the external conditions that facilitate the learning of rules, R. Gagné suggests that instruction is typically verbal (Gagné & Briggs, 1983). In this case, the purpose of the instruction is usually to remind the learner of relevant concepts as well as to highlight important relationships among these concepts. As an illustration, Gagné and Briggs (1983) describe a situation in which a teacher presents students with a list of words, such as *made, fate, pale*, has them pronounce these words, and points out to them that the first vowel in each has a "long" sound. Following this, students are asked to pronounce *mad, fat*, and *pal*; then the instructor points out that the vowel has a "short" sound and also verbalizes the relevant rule. Alternatively, the teacher might simply present a variety of examples and encourage students, perhaps through appropriate questioning, to discover the rule for themselves.

Rules are what permit us to solve problems. In fact, R. Gagné refers to *problem solving* as a category of "higher-order rules." *Problem solving* refers to the thinking out of a solution to a problem by combining old rules to form new ones. It is the main reason for learning rules in the first place.

Numerous examples of problem solving can be drawn from people's daily activities. Whenever no previously learned rule is appropriate for the solution of a problem, problem solving may be said to take place (providing, of course, that the problem is in fact solved). A child who is learning to tie a shoe may combine several rules in order to succeed. The idea that laces go into holes and the notion that intertwined laces tend to cling together are rules that may be combined to form the higher-order rule: "Laced shoes with intertwined laces may be considered tied."

A condition clearly necessary for problem solving is the presence of the appropriate rules in the learner's repertoire. R. Gagné (1985) also describes some external conditions that appear to be useful for problem solving:

1. Verbal instructions or questions may be used to elicit the recall of relevant rules.

2. The direction of thought processes may also be guided by verbal instructions.

Many school subjects, says R. Gagné, consist of a hierarchy of information or skills. Understanding often requires mastery of essential subordinate capabilities and concepts. There is much that this lad must already know before he can understand the mysteries revealed by his magnifying glass.

Summary of Intellectual Skills

The preceding discussion of Robert Gagné's classification of intellectual skills shows how educational implications are derived from learning theory. For example, knowledge of the conditions that facilitate learning suggests specific instructional strategies.

R. Gagné (1977b) points out that many school subjects consist of a hierarchy of information or skills such that in order to understand higher levels, it is necessary to have mastered a number of subordinate capabilities. It follows that

instruction must proceed from the subordinate to the final task. The validity of this observation is perhaps clearest in subjects such as mathematics, in which solving higher-level problems requires mastery of a variety of subordinate skills.

Just as knowledge within a given content area may be described in terms of a hierarchical arrangement of subordinate capabilities, so may classes of learning skills. The learner must master lower levels before progressing to higher ones. In a nutshell, problem solving depends upon rules, which are derived from concepts, which require as prerequisites the learning of discriminations.

Discriminations depend upon either verbal associations or motor chains, both of which are derived from stimulus-response connections.

The instructional implications of this position can be summarized as follows:

- Content in a given area should be arranged in hierarchical fashion so that simpler abilities and concepts necessary for later learning are mastered first.

- Instructional goals should be analyzed in terms of the types of learning involved in their attainment. Instructional procedures should then be premised on knowledge of the conditions required for those types of learning.

Verbal Information

A great deal of the school learning that is of most direct concern to teachers takes the form of verbal information. In effect, verbal information is nothing more or less complicated than what is generally described as **knowledge**. An identifying characteristic of verbal information is that it can be expressed as a sentence or that it implies a sentence. Thus, the statement "Individuals of *Ursus arctos* are the true bears" and the single word *bear* are both expressions of verbal information; both presumably have meaning for whoever expresses them. This does not mean that verbal information is always learned and stored verbally. Much of our verbal information is derived from pictures and illustrations, perhaps from visions and dreams, but surely from our own behavior and that of others, as well as from the countless observations that we make in the course of our daily activities.

Quite apart from whatever practical value it might have, verbal information, says R. Gagné, is essential for acquiring further information. In addition, verbal information makes thinking possible. It's little wonder that schools devote so much time and energy to deciding which bodies of knowledge (verbal information) should be transmitted to students and how they can best be transmitted.

Many of the conditions that Robert Gagné describes as desirable external conditions for the acquisition of verbal information are similar to those described by Ausubel (discussed later in this chapter). Thus, R. Gagné mentions the importance of advance organizers and meaningful context. In addition, verbal information can often be made more meaningful by using photos, charts, illustrations, and other pictorial representations. Other useful instructional strategies are intended to ensure that learners pay attention and to facilitate recall and generalization. Thus, varying tone and emphasis in oral presentation and using attention-compelling instructional aids such as slides and films and a variety of other stimuli can be important attention-directing and -motivating features of teaching. (See Chapter 10 for a more complete discussion of motivation in the classroom.)

Attitudes

Educators throughout the world have a number of grand goals: We want to develop students who love life and learning, who respect the people, institutions, and ideas that we respect, and who want to be good citizens. In short, we want to develop students with positive attitudes. In fact, however, our educational systems teach attitudes only incidentally; they are aimed more toward teaching motor skills, verbal information, intellectual skills, and to some extent cognitive strategies. Why? Because an attitude is not an easy thing to teach, because it is a personal affective (emotional) reaction. In brief, an **attitude** is a positive or negative predisposition that has important motivational components. A positive attitude toward school, for example, implies not only liking school but trying to do well in school, to be liked by teachers, and to conform to the explicit and implicit goals of the school.

Attitudes are clearly affected by reinforcement. Students who have been most successful in school usually have more positive attitudes toward school than those who have not been successful (that is, have not been reinforced). And although this observation is obvious, teachers do not always behave as though they are fully aware of it. If you want your students to have positive attitudes toward whatever it is you are trying to teach them, it is imperative that they meet with success (reinforcement) rather than failure, particularly in their initial encounters with you and the subject you are teaching.

R. Gagné (1974) refers to Bandura's description of imitative learning as one of the principal indirect methods for teaching attitudes (see Chapter 4). Steps in the instructional sequence include selecting an appropriate model, preferably one with whom the student identifies (teachers are powerful models), arranging for the model to display personal choices reflecting the attitudes to be established, and drawing attention to the model's consequent reinforcement. If, for example, a teacher describes some small act of honesty that she engaged in and for which she was subsequently reinforced, either directly or simply through "feeling good" about her behavior, she has gone some distance toward developing positive attitudes toward honesty in her charges. Lest this sound too simplistic, let me hasten to point out that attitudes are subtle, pervasive, and powerful predispositions to think, act, and feel in certain ways; they are established in many ways and places (out of school as well as in it), and they are not nearly as easy to modify as the preceding discussion might imply.

Motor Skills

Motor skills are the many skills in our repertoires involving the execution of sequences of controlled muscular movements. Writing, typing, driving, walking, talking, dancing, and digging holes for outdoor toilets are motor skills. Some of these are important for school; others aren't. They can be taught through appropriate verbal instructions and demonstration (for example, "This is how you should sit in front of your computer . . . address the ball . . . grasp the shovel . . . hold the pencil . . . point your nose"), and they are perfected primarily through practice. Like other skills, motor skills are highly susceptible to reinforcement. Not only is reinforcement involved in determining whether a learner is likely to want to acquire a skill (in other words, whether the learner's attitude will be positive) but it is intimately involved in determining how well and how rapidly the skill will be learned and perfected. A word processor would learn very slowly if he could not see the results of his work. He would not correct his mistakes and would receive little reinforcement for a good performance.

Cognitive Strategies

Our intellectual functioning is guided by complex, highly personal strategies. These strategies govern how we pay attention, how we go about studying and organizing, and how we analyze, synthesize, and recall. In a sense, they result from the development of the elusive capabilities involved in learning how to think, to create, to discover, and to remember. In Chapter 5 we looked at a number of programs designed specifically to teach cognitive strategies such as those involved in rehearsing, organizing, and elaborating.

Summary of R. Gagné's Learning Outcomes

Table 6.1 summarizes Robert Gagné's classification of learning outcomes and of external conditions that appear to facilitate these outcomes. Knowledge of both conditions and outcomes can be of considerable value in helping teachers develop appropriate and effective instructional strategies. But the learning sequence is, in many respects, much more complex than our somewhat simplified discussions might imply. R. Gagné (1974) recognizes this greater complexity in a model of the act of learning, presented in Table 6.1. This model takes into consideration the

TABLE 6.1 Robert Gagné's Five Major Domains of Learning Outcomes, Some Illustrations, and Some Suggestions Pertinent to the Instructional Process

OUTCOMES OF LEARNING (MAJOR DOMAINS)	EXAMPLES	SUGGESTED CONDITIONS FOR FACILITATING OUTCOMES
1. INTELLECTUAL SKILLS		
Problem solving (Higher-order rules)	Learner determines optimal order of topics in an instructional sequence through experimentation.	Review of relevant rules; verbal instructions to aid in recall of rules; verbal instructions to direct thought processes
Rules	Learner demonstrates that metals expand when heated and contract when cooled.	Learner is made aware of desired learning outcome; review of relevant concepts; concrete examples
Concepts	Learner classifies objects in terms of size (shape, function, position, color).	Examples presented; learner actively involved in finding examples; reinforcement
Discriminations	Learner distinguishes among various printed letters of the alphabet.	Simultaneous presentation of stimuli to be discriminated; reinforcement (confirmation); repetition
2. VERBAL INFORMATION	Learner recalls information in writing or orally.	Advance organizers; meaningful context; instructional aids for motivation and retention
3. COGNITIVE STRATEGIES	Learner devises personal strategy for remembering complex verbal material.	Frequent presentation of novel and/or challenging problems
4. ATTITUDES	Learner selects among a choice of activities (subjects, teachers, schools).	Models; reinforcement; verbal guidance
5. MOTOR SKILLS	Learner writes (swims, walks, runs, flies).	Models; verbal directions; reinforcement (knowledge of results); practice

importance of motivational and attention-compelling factors, as well as retention and transfer.

COGNITIVE EXPLANATIONS

As we saw in Chapter 5, cognitive approaches to human behavior stress the importance of the learner's previous knowledge and skills. Unlike behaviorism, which tends to view all learners as initially equal—as equally susceptible to the effects of the consequences of behavior—cognitivism emphasizes that we often derive different meanings from experience, largely because we construct rather than discover meaning; consequently, we often learn different things.

Common to most cognitive theories is the basic assumption that the learner is a processor of information. Accordingly, these theories attempt to analyze learning in terms of what is often labeled **cognitive structure**. At a simple level, cognitive structure is the content of the mind. It includes concepts, relationships that the learner establishes among concepts, and strategies used in abstracting concepts and in organizing them in long-term memory. Terms such as *schema* or *script* are often used to describe cognitive structure.

Knowledge and Meaning

Cognitive theorists maintain that knowledge does not exist in a vacuum, but that it depends on relationships. As E. Gagné (1985) puts it: "All of a person's declarative knowledge can be conceptualized as a large network of interrelated propositions." In this context, **declarative knowledge** consists of all the facts we have learned and all the experiences we have had. In short, declarative knowledge involves knowing that something is the case. Declarative knowledge is contrasted with **procedural knowledge**, which involves knowing how to do something (that is, knowing a procedure for doing something). Procedural knowledge, too, derives its meaningfulness from interrelationships (Anderson, 1983).

Meaning Depends on Relationships. The idea that knowledge consists of networks of relationships is not new. Recall from Chapter 5 that our contemporary models of long-term memory are invariably associationistic; that is, they are models of relationships. What is new, however, is the recent upsurge of interest in exploring this idea in an effort to understand how we learn and know things and how we think. Thinking, according to this approach, involves the manipulation of what is represented mentally. In other words, it involves manipulating and forming relationships among items of information (E. Hunt, 1989). This chapter simplifies and illustrates this central idea and looks at some of its educational implications.

An Illustration. First, to simplify. Why do we say that knowledge and understanding depend on interrelationships among items of information? What does this concept mean?

Consider the following passage:

If the balloons popped, the sound wouldn't be able to carry since everything would be too far away from the correct floor. A closed window would also prevent the sound from carrying, since most buildings tend to be well insulated. Since the whole operation depends on a steady flow of electricity, a break in the middle of the wire would also cause problems. Of course, the fellow could shout, but the human voice is not loud enough to carry that far. An additional problem is that a string could break on the instrument. Then there would be no accompaniment to the message. It is clear that the best situation would involve less distance. Then there would be fewer potential problems. With face to face contact, the least number of things could go wrong. (Bransford & Johnson, 1973, pp. 392–393)

If you find this passage confusing and unclear, don't despair; so does almost everyone else. It's a frustrating experience because the language is clear and simple, the sentences are short and straightforward, none of the concepts is very difficult—yet the whole thing makes no sense.

Turn now to Figure 6.1 and glance at the illustration.

Schemata and Scripts. Now the passage makes sense. Why? Simply because the illustration provides a framework within which to understand; it activates what a number of cognitive psychologists refer to as a **schema**.

Schemata are metaphors for cognitive structure and functioning. They are like clusters of related items of knowledge that define concepts. They are what we know about things. For example, schemata relevant to understanding the balloon passage include, among other things, our knowledge that balloons filled with lighter-than-air substances will rise, our recognition of the musical equipment involved, and certain assumptions about the intentions and motives of the serenader and the serenadee. Note that each of these concepts is defined by one or more relationships (for example, the relationship between weight and falling or rising, the relationship between

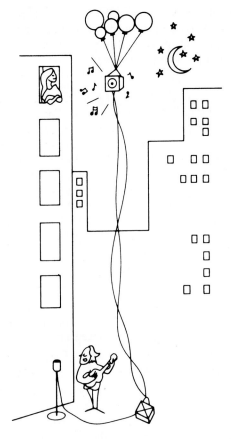

FIGURE 6.1 From J. D. Bransford and M. K. Johnson, "Consideration of Some Problems in Comprehension" (p. 394). In W. G. Chase (Ed.), *Visual Information Processing*. Copyright 1973 by Academic Press. Reprinted by permission of Academic Press, New York and J. D. Bransford.

musical sounds and a guitar, the presumed relationship between the individuals involved, and so on).

One aspect of schemata that is important for learning and remembering real-life things is called a **script**. Schank and Abelson (1977) describe script as that part of cognitive structure that deals with routines and sequences. We all know countless routines, countless scripts. We know, for example, that a sensible way to dress is to put on undergarments, socks, shirts, pants, and

shoes, more or less in that order. This is a verbal description of a common script. For dressing on a day like today in this somewhat harsh climate, I added putting on a heavy coat and gloves to my script—in that order. Had I wanted to be creative this morning and altered my script—say, by reversing it—I might have found dressing considerably more difficult and time consuming. And I would have had to wear my socks over my shoes and my shorts over my jeans, in which case I would probably not have been courageous or foolish enough to come in to the university.

Scripts, like schemata, deal with relationships. A script is, in a sense, an expression of sequential relationships. Scripts and schemata clearly have their uses. Nevertheless, they are still only metaphors that need to be made more concrete for our purposes.

Educational Applications of Cognitive Approaches

Cognitive approaches are concerned with how information is processed. Accordingly, these approaches look at how we derive information from the environment; how we organize and interpret this information, teasing out relationships in order to abstract meaning from our experiences; how we organize and store meaning; and how our thought processes make use of what we have stored.

From the educator's point of view, these concerns translate directly into a renewed emphasis on cognitive strategies and a recognition of the importance of relationships among items of information. Specifically, they suggest two things: First, the school's curriculum (and the teacher's presentation of that curriculum) needs to be organized to reveal and underline important relationships, and second, the school should pay systematic and deliberate attention to developing strategies that are involved in perceiving, interpreting, organizing, analyzing, evaluating, storing, and retrieving information.

A number of cognitively based theories reflect these two educational applications especially clearly. Among them are the theories of Jerome Bruner and David Ausubel. In many important ways these theories are similar, although they use different terms to describe the units and processes of cognitive organization.* There is, however, one important respect in which the theories are dramatically different from each other. Bruner advocates that learners be guided toward organizing material for themselves, once they have been provided with opportunities to discover relationships. In contrast, Ausubel argues that in most cases the teacher can organize the material and present it to the student in relatively final form. In other words, Bruner is a strong advocate of **discovery learning**; Ausubel argues for **reception learning.**

BRUNER'S THEORY: AN OVERVIEW

Cognitive psychology, as we already learned, assumes that the learner is an active information processor. It asks how the learner derives information from the environment, how information is organized and interpreted, and how it is used. Jerome Bruner's theory provides one set of answers for these questions—and for many other questions as well.

Bruner's cognitive theory describes learning and perception as information-processing activities that reflect our need to simplify and make sense of the environment (Bruner, 1973; Bruner, Goodnow, & Austin, 1956). These activities involve the formation of concepts (Bruner's term is **category**) that result from the abstraction of common elements among events and experiences. From these abstractions, we derive implicit rules that allow us to categorize (conceptualize) the world and discover a wealth of relationships among concepts. Bruner's metaphor for these relationships is called a **coding system**—a hierarchical arrangement of concepts of increasing (or decreasing) generality. Thus, our long-term memories—our relatively permanent store of knowledge, strategies, impressions, and so on—can be seen as a complex, highly associationistic arrangement of categories (concepts) and coding systems (see Figure 6.2).†

Discovery Learning: Bruner

As we saw in Chapter 3, one way to describe cognitive development is Piaget's notion that as a function of interacting with the environment (through assimilation and accommodation), the child gradually builds up a store of knowledge. In a very real sense, it is as though the learner *constructs* knowledge—in contrast with a situation in which the learner would be *given* that knowledge by someone else (parents or teachers, for example).

---

*PPC: Wouldn't the bear find life a lot easier if all cognitive theorists agreed to use the same clearly defined vocabulary, rather than so many insisting on inventing their own meanings or, perhaps worse, their own terms? Weren't *schema* and *schemata* and *script* and *cognitive structure* enough?

Author: Yes and no; no, those terms aren't enough, and yes, we need a variety of terms. Besides, the bear is an old bear; he's seen much jargon come and go. The meaning is in the meaning, not in the jargon. Do you get my meaning? (he adds slyly).

†PPC: There's no getting around the fact that this chapter is heavy going. (I just put the kettle on for more coffee.) How about some bears, cows, or cases?

Author: Okay. I have a cow warning I've been wanting to pass on in any case. So here's a clipping from the local newspaper. (This is true, I swear it.)

A 77-year-old farmer is in serious condition in a Graymont, Ill. hospital after being attacked by a gang of cows. Martin Duffy suffered a concussion and broken ribs after he was attacked, butted about and knocked unconscious by his own herd. Rescuers said Duffy had gone into his pasture to check on a cow due to deliver a calf when the attack occurred. "Apparently, Martin wanted the cow to move into the barn so she could have the calf in an enclosed area, but she did not want to move, and he approached her, she kicked him and he must have fallen down," said Mary Jo McSherry, one of the first on the scene. Other cows got excited too. "The cows were butting him with their heads. They had their heads down, pushing him, and when they would roll him, they would throw him up about three feet in the air." ("Cowed by Cows," 1992)

You've been warned.

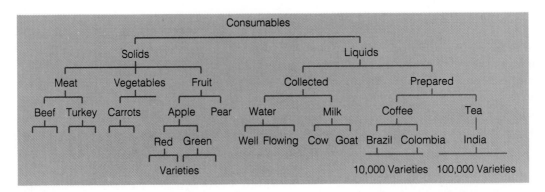

FIGURE 6.2 A coding system.

Bruner's theory is based on the same fundamental belief. We make up our own versions of reality, says Bruner (1986); we discover our own meanings (Bruner, 1990). And the functions of schools, he insists emphatically, should be to provide conditions that will foster the discovery of relationships; hence, his strong arguments for discovery learning in schools.

Discovery learning can be defined as the learning that takes place when students are not presented with subject matter in its final form but rather are required to organize it themselves. This requires learners to discover for themselves relationships that exist among items of information. In Bruner's theory, discovery is the formation of categories or, more often, the formation of coding systems, which are defined in terms of relationships (similarities and differences) that exist among objects and events.

The most important and most obvious characteristic of a discovery approach to teaching is that it requires far less teacher involvement and direction than most other methods. Note, however, that this does not imply that the teacher ceases to give any guidance once the initial problem has been presented. As Corno and Snow (1986) point out, teachers can offer a continuum of guidance (their phrase is "teacher mediation") by adapting their teaching to different students and different purposes. At one extreme, too little

or no mediation can leave students without the means for discovery; at the other extreme, constant direction and guidance from the teacher may remove all opportunity for self-direction and discovery by students.

The advantages of a discovery approach, claims Bruner, are that such learning facilitates transfer and retention, increases problem-solving ability, and increases motivation (Bruner, 1961a).

Conditions That Facilitate Discovery Learning. According to Bruner, four sets of conditions contribute to discovery learning: set, need state, mastery of specifics, and diversity of training. Awareness of each of these is important for teachers.

Set refers to a predisposition to react in certain ways. A discovery-oriented person is one whose customary approach to a problem is to look for relationships among items of information. One obvious way to affect set is through instructions. For example, a student can be encouraged to memorize subject matter as though it consisted of isolated bits of information simply by being told to do so. The same effect can also be produced by testing only for knowledge of isolated items of information. This is what Marton and Saljo (1984) call the "surface approach" to teaching and learning. It focuses on memorizing facts, completing tasks, and passing tests. On the other hand, students can be encouraged to look for relationships among items of information, either by being instructed to do so or by being told that they will be examined on their understanding of these relationships. This is Marton and Saljo's "deep approach." It focuses on relationships and on understanding.

Need state is the level of arousal, excitation, or alertness of the learner (see Chapter 10). Bruner suggests that a moderate level of arousal is more conducive to discovery learning than is either an excessively high or low level.

The degree of **mastery of specifics** refers to the extent of the learner's knowledge of specific, relevant information. Bruner argues that discovery (which is really the formation of generic codes) is not an accidental event. It is more likely to occur when the individual is well prepared. The wider the range of information learners possess, the more likely they are to find relationships within that information. Bruner's fourth variable, **diversity of training**, is related to this. Bruner argues that a learner who is exposed to information in a wide variety of circumstances is more likely to develop codes to organize that information.

Specific Educational Recommendations

Bruner's plea for the use of discovery-oriented techniques in schools is advanced in several articles and books (for example, *The Process of Education*, 1961b). In addition, renewed interest in discovery approaches to education can be seen in what is termed the **constructivist** approach to teaching (for example, Brown, Collins, & Duguid, 1989). This is a general term for approaches based on the assumption that students should build (construct) knowledge for themselves. Hence, constructivist approaches are basically discovery oriented. Similarly, the **conceptual change movement** is discovery oriented (see Farnham-Diggory, 1990; E. L. Smith, 1983). Conceptual change curricula present ideas that challenge the learner, that present problems and puzzles, and that ultimately result in a reorganization of knowledge (hence, *conceptual change*).

A number of specific recommendations and observations advanced by Bruner are especially important for discovery-oriented classrooms:

1. "... the curriculum of a subject should be determined by the most fundamental understanding that can be achieved of the underlying principles that give structure to that subject" (1961b, p. 31).

Bruner argues that knowledge of underlying principles and of the structure of a subject facilitates discovery because constructing knowledge requires knowledge of organizing principles. For example, it is much easier to arrive at a concept that relates *aspen, birch,* and *alder* once it has been discovered that they are all deciduous hardwoods. Indeed, it is the "peopleness" of individuals, the "treeness" of trees, and the "birdness" of birds that allows them to be reacted to in similar ways and that permits the learner to make inferences about specific people, trees, or birds—in Bruner's terms, that allows "going beyond the information given" (1957a). Bruner argues that unless the organization of the curriculum is such that it facilitates the formation of structure (coding systems), it will be learned with difficulty, it will not lend itself to transfer, and it will be remembered poorly.

2. "... any subject can be taught to any child in some honest form" (1961b, p. 52).

Bruner's critics have been quick to point out that not every concept can be taught to children of any age. For example, proportion probably cannot be understood by a four-year-old. Bruner's reply to this is that we should look at the possibility of teaching aspects of any subject at any age level. Perhaps some aspects of proportion can be taught to a four-year-old. The important question is how teaching can be made effective for very young children. Bruner's (1966) answer is that the form can be simplified and the mode of presentation geared to the simplest representational systems available. Because children progress from motor or sensory (**enactive**) representation to relatively concrete images (**iconic**), and finally to abstract (**symbolic**) representation, it follows that the sequence in teaching should be the same. In other words, if it is possible to present a subject so that a child can first experience it, then react to a concrete presentation of it, and finally symbolize it, that is the best instructional sequence.

3. A spiral curriculum that develops and redevelops topics at different grades is ideal for acquiring generic codes.

Bruner argues in several places (1961b, 1966) that spiral curricula are ideally suited to discovery. First, such a curriculum organizes subject matter according to principles, and it usually presents them systematically, from simplest to most complex. This progression parallels the development of coding systems. Second, a spiral curriculum involves the sort of repetition that is useful for constructing knowledge. To begin with, learners are exposed to the most general, most inclusive idea and then to a series of specific simple instances of concepts. As they discover relationships among these concepts, they build knowledge (coding systems) that is highly conducive to transfer, recall, and discovery.

4. ". . . a student should be given some training in recognizing the plausibility of guesses" (1961b, p. 64).

In this connection, Bruner speaks of the intuitive leap—the educated guess that is something more than a blind attempt but something less than simply making inferences or predictions on the basis of what is known about similar instances. An intuitive leap is less certain than that. Bruner argues persuasively that to discourage guessing is to stifle the process of discovery.

5. Aids to teaching (audiovisual, concrete, and so on) should be used.

One reason advanced to support this recommendation is that audiovisual aids provide students with direct or vicarious experiences and thus facilitate the formation of concepts. This relates directly to Bruner's suggestion that the best instructional sequence is often one that progresses in the same direction as the child's

representation of the world—that is, from enactive to iconic to symbolic (see the box, "Guided Discovery").

AUSUBEL'S THEORY: ANOTHER VIEW

Not all educators agree that discovery is the best approach. Perhaps most outspoken among those who advocate a different approach is David Ausubel (1963, 1977).

Overview

Ausubel has advanced a cognitive theory of learning that is specifically intended to deal almost exclusively with what he calls "meaningful verbal learning." More important from the point of view of educational psychology, Ausubel's work consists of a search for the "laws of meaningful classroom learning."

Meaning. According to Ausubel, an object has meaning when it elicits an image in the "content of consciousness" as a result of being related to something already known. Similarly, a concept acquires meaning when it is related to an idea that is already present in the mind. In other words, for a stimulus or concept to have meaning, there must be something in the learner's cognitive structure to which it can be related. For example, the word *car* has meaning for an individual only when it can be related to a mental representation of what cars are.

Learning. Meaningful learning, says Ausubel, requires that the learner have already learned associated concepts to which new material can be related—or, in Ausubel's terms, concepts that can "subsume" new learning. Learning therefore involves **subsumption**, of which there are two kinds. **Derivative subsumption** occurs when new material is so similar to what is already known that it could have been derived from it; **correlative subsumption** involves material that is sufficiently

guided discovery

Some school subjects lend themselves more readily to discovery-oriented techniques than do others. For example, some (though by no means all) scientific principles can be discovered by students in guided discovery situations that provide them with sufficient background information and the appropriate experimental equipment. Similarly, children on field trips can discover a variety of phenomena, although understanding and interpreting these phenomena (and even noticing them in the first place) often require considerable guidance.

The beginning teacher should not make the mistake of assuming that teaching through discovery implies letting students go out on their own with no more than the simple instruction to "discover." Not only must the processes of discovery be taught—through experience as well as through more didactic procedures—but the student must frequently be given guidance while in the process of discovering. The guidance need not ruin the discovery or destroy its magic.

As an example of discovery learning, Bruner (1961a) describes how a class of elementary school children is led to discover important relationships between human settlements and geographical features. Among other things, they are asked where they would es-

tablish a settlement if they were exploring an area for the first time. Their reasons for settling in certain areas rather than others gradually lead them to "discover" that major settlements should be at the confluence of rivers and near natural harbors. Thus, studying geography becomes an activity of discovering relationships between the environment and humans rather than simply of memorizing maps and related data.

Can the principle of the combustion engine be discovered by an eighth-grade class? Yes, it can. What might be the major features of a guided discovery lesson that you could design for this purpose?

---

novel that it requires some change in existing cognitive structure.

Cognitive Structure. Cognitive structure consists of more or less organized and stable concepts (or ideas) in a learner's "consciousness." Much like Bruner's, Ausubel's metaphor for cognitive structure assumes that this organization is hierarchical, with the most inclusive concept at the apex and increasingly specific concepts toward the base. Therefore, instruction should proceed from the most general and inclusive toward details of specific instances. This is somewhat like Bruner's notion that teaching should follow a sort of "spiral" curriculum in which the "big idea" (the most general concept) is presented first and then systematically revisited, perhaps over a period of years, at increasingly more complex levels of abstraction. The fundamental difference between Bruner and

Ausubel, with respect to their instructional theories, is that Ausubel argues that learners should be provided with organized information. Bruner, as we saw, maintains that students should be presented with specifics and allowed to discover their own organization (their own coding systems). For a summary of Ausubel's theory, see Table 6.2.

Expository Teaching: Ausubel

David Ausubel is an outspoken defender of expository teaching. He argues not only that expository teaching can lead to a high level of understanding and generality but also that discovery approaches are extremely time consuming without being demonstrably superior. In a review of the literature on discovery learning, Ausubel and Robinson (1969) conclude that research supporting such learning is virtually nonexistent. "Moreover,"

TABLE 6.2 Summary and Translation of Ausubel's Theory of Meaningful Verbal Learning

1. Subsumption may be *derivative* or *correlative*.	Learning (subsumption) involves either (a) relating new material to previously learned, highly similar material (derivative subsumption), or (b) extending previous knowledge to similar but new material (correlative subsumption).
2. Subsumption leads to a *hierarchical arrangement* of knowledge, from most general to most specific.	Learning leads to the meaningful elaboration of cognitive structure.
3. Remembering is *dissociative subsumption*.	Remembering requires being able to separate new learning from old.
4. Forgetting involves *zero dissociability*, or *obliterative subsumption*.	Forgetting occurs when material can no longer be differentiated from what is already in the mind.

they state, "it appears that enthusiasts of discovery methods have been supporting each other by citing one another's opinions and assertions as evidence and by generalizing extravagantly from questionable findings" (1969, p. 494).

Ausubel's emphasis on expository teaching and its outcome, reception learning, stems in part from the fact that most classroom learning seems to be of that type. In addition, meaningful verbal learning, with which his theory deals, occurs mainly in the course of expository teaching. He argues that this type of learning is not passive and does not stifle creativity or encourage rote learning. Indeed, meaningful verbal learning is anything but rote. It involves relating new material to existing structure, whereas rote learning involves ingesting isolated bits of information.

Ausubel advances some general recommendations for the planning and presentation of subject matter. These take the form of a discussion of the variables involved in subsumption: advance organizers, discriminability, and meaningfulness.

Advance Organizers. **Advance organizers** are complex sets of ideas or concepts given to the learner before the material to be learned is presented. It is meant to provide cognitive structure to which the new learning can be anchored (sub-

sumed). Another function of an organizer is to increase recall (prevent loss of what Ausubel calls **dissociability**—the ability to separate concepts). (Ausubel's phrase for forgetting is **obliterative subsumption**.) The use of advance organizers is called for, then, under two circumstances: when students have no relevant information to which they can relate the new learning and when relevant subsuming information is already present but is not likely to be recognized as relevant by the learner (Ausubel & Robinson, 1969).

Grippin and Peters (1984) describe four characteristics of advance organizers. First, advance organizers are presented before the lesson. Second, they are designed to bring to mind prior knowledge that is relevant to the lesson (to activate related **subsumers**). Third, advance organizers are presented at a higher level of abstraction than the material presented later. Put another way, advance organizers ordinarily consist of subsuming concepts, which are, by definition, more generic than subsumed concepts. Finally, advance organizers make explicit the connection between prior knowledge and the lesson to be presented.

Ausubel describes two different types of organizers—one to be used when the material is completely new and the other when it is somewhat familiar. The first is termed an **expository**

As part of a science lesson, a teacher wishes to familiarize her students with the many breeds of cows. Her students already know what cows are; they also know colors. But they do not know that an Aberdeen Angus is a sleek-looking black cow. She tells them so. Is this likely to be meaningful learning? What type of subsumption is involved?

This same teacher now wishes to teach her class what a zebra is. She tells them what it is; she compares it with horses, donkeys, mules, and—being resourceful—asses; she then shows them a picture of a zebra. What type of subsumption is involved here?

Why would the simple statement that a zebra is an herbivorous, black-and-white African animal be almost meaningless for urban, North American children who have never seen a zebra in books or on television?

---

organizer because it presents a description or exposition of relevant concepts. The second is called a **comparative organizer** because it is likely to make use of similarities and differences in new material and existing cognitive structure.

An expository organizer in a lesson on gold, for example, might describe the general, defining characteristics of metals before the lesson on the specific qualities of gold. The organizer is intended to provide concepts (subsumers) to which the new material can be related.

There are a number of examples of comparative organizers in this text. Many take the form of brief introductory sections that compare material about to be presented with material previously discussed. Some of the chapter previews are organizers of this kind. Recall that at the beginning of this chapter we associated Bruner with discovery learning and Ausubel with reception learning before actually discussing their theories—another advance organizer. Of necessity, a textbook is primarily expository (although parts of it may lead to a type of guided discovery)—hence, the frequent use of organizers in most textbooks.

In the classroom, teachers sometimes unconsciously make use of something very much like advance organizers when they summarize earlier lessons before beginning a new presentation. However, these summaries often fail to make the connection between new and old learning sufficiently explicit, nor are they abstract enough to qualify as advance organizers in the sense in which Ausubel uses the expression. A summary is often simply a summary—an accounting of the things that have been taught before. An advance organizer is more abstract; it draws from previous learning an idea—a concept—that is general enough to subsume the new material to be taught. (See, for example, Mr. Eddie Lemming's unit on gold and other precious metals.)

Notice how Eddie Lemming's lesson is preceded by a single, very abstract concept: the principle of supply and demand. Notice, too, that there is a promise to relate this concept to the question that constitutes the substance of today's lesson: Why is gold so expensive? The students have been reminded of a single, abstract, highly generic, stable concept upon which to anchor their new learning.

Research that has examined the effectiveness of advance organizers has often used organizers much like this one, sometimes presented in the form of a written paragraph, sometimes described by the teacher, sometimes elicited from students. Typically, the subsequent performance of a group of students that was given advance organizers is compared with that of a control group given the lesson without the advance organizer.

The results of much of this research are not entirely clear. Some researchers have found that advance organizers provide no measurable advantage (for example, Clawson & Barnes, 1973); others report significant positive effects (for example, Gabel, Kogan, & Sherwood, 1980). White and Tisher (1986) note evidence suggesting that students who lack relevant prior knowledge are most likely to benefit from the use of advance organizers and that this may well explain the contradictions among studies. In addition, the fact that teaching strategies such as these do not always lead to immediately measurable effects should not be taken as clear evidence that they are a waste of time. Many good things that teachers do are never measured—and perhaps they should not be.

Perhaps, just perhaps, the long-term effects of a single propitiously presented advance organizer might become apparent years later when the student, now an adult, correctly answers the $20-million question on a television game show. Or maybe the long-term effects will become evident in the bankrupt investor's recollection that gold is not really a useful metal, that the demand for it is rather artificial, and that the supply is quite abundant after all.

Discriminability. In Ausubel's theory, a major variable in determining the stability of what is learned is the ease with which new material can be discriminated from previous learning. He observes that information closely resembling previous knowledge (derivative subsumption) is quickly forgotten, whereas dissimilar material (correlative subsumption) tends to be retained longer. It follows from this that teaching techniques that highlight the differences between new material and old learning will lead to longer retention. At the same time, it is still necessary to relate the new to the old in order to facilitate subsumption (learning). Hence, comparing information in terms of similarities and differences should help both learning and retention. Also, the stability and clarity of the subsuming idea directly relate to the ease with which new material can be both incorporated with it and dissociated from it.

Making Learning Meaningful. Ausubel's emphasis on reception learning as opposed to discovery learning is partly based on his belief that the most desirable kind of learning is meaningful, as opposed to rote. This does not mean that discovery techniques do not lead to meaningful learning. However, Ausubel believes that expository approaches have some advantages, especially in terms of the efficient use of the learner's time.

THE PLACE:
Carmel Mid Valley School

THE SETTING:
Introduction to Mr. Eddie Lemming's
seventh-grade unit on gold and other
precious metals.

Lemming: So can anyone tell me why turbo-charged WZ 222As are so expensive?

Bruce: Is it 'cause they cost more to make?

Lemming: Well, no, Bruce, not really. That'd be a good reason, though, if they did cost more.

Jack: 'Cause everybody wants one?

Sally: 'Cause there's not enough for everyone who wants one?

Lemming: Right. Right. You're both right.

Jack: It's like you said before, about workers and their pay. Too much demand.

Sally: And too little supply.

Lemming: Supply and demand. Keep that in mind. If nobody wants a thing, or if there's a lot of it, it won't cost very much. Like your textbook. Everybody wants it, so it costs an arm and a leg! Heh, heh. Supply and demand. Now, today we're going to talk about gold! Pretty exciting stuff, gold! And pretty expensive. Is that because of supply? demand? something else? Let's see what we can find out. . . .

Meaningfulness is defined in terms of the relationship between new learning and existing cognitive structure (knowledge). This definition has a number of implications for teachers' behavior, some of which are suggested by the preceding discussion on advance organizers.

To begin with, meaning may derive directly from associations that exist among ideas, events, or objects. However, there will be no meaning unless the learner is aware of the association. For example, students can quite easily learn to pronounce and spell words that do not relate to any of their existing ideas and thus are meaningless to them. It seems clear that a new concept will have meaning if it relates to both the learner's past experiences and other ideas being learned.

The important point is that meaning is not an intangible property of objects or concepts themselves. Ausubel contends that no idea, concept, or object is meaningful in and of itself; it is meaningful only in relation to a learner. The implication for teaching, therefore, is that the teacher should present no new material until the learner is ready to understand it. And understanding requires appropriate cognitive structure. Consequently, much of the teacher's effort should be directed at providing the student with background information, frequently through the use of advance organizers (see the box, "Meaningless Learning").

RECONCILING DISCOVERY AND RECEPTION APPROACHES

It is not difficult to reconcile the two apparently divergent views presented in this chapter; they are not nearly so different as their juxtaposition here might make them seem. In fact, in many ways they are simply different emphases. Neither is necessarily superior to the other, and neither needs to be used to the exclusion of the other. Clearly, both have their uses. Even Ausubel suggests that discovery learning can be useful (Ausubel & Robinson, 1969). For example, it can be used with younger learners who do not yet have a large store of information to which new learning can be related. When this is the case, expository approaches are not always highly meaningful.

Discovery can also be used to test the meaningfulness of new learning. For example, learners

meaningless learning

"Learning involves the subsumption of meaningful material to existing cognitive structure through derivative or correlative means."

This particular pearl of psychological wisdom is undoubtedly meaningful to you but only because you know through previous learning what derivative and correlative subsumption are, what meaningful material is, and what type of beast cognitive structure is. For anyone who did not already know these terms, the sentence would be meaningless.

It is remarkably easy for teachers to fall into the trap of asking students to learn material that is meaningless for them because they do not have the required background information. One widely cited example of this is the use of white, middle-class-oriented readers for children from non-white, poor neighborhoods, or, as was the case in the Arctic until recently, for Eskimo children. The Eskimo children, who had never seen a city, an automobile, a telephone, or an indoor toilet, were asked to learn to read sentences similar to "John goes for a drive," "Fire fighters, police officers, and college professors are our friends." (Now, of course, many Eskimos have satellite dishes and access to hundreds of television channels, so their cultural isolation has been much reduced.)

Do you remember learning that a demagogue is "an unprincipled politician who panders to the emotions and prejudices of the populace"? That the center of the Earth is "in a stage of igneous fusion"? That the closest star is "several billion light-years away"? How meaningful was this information?

might be asked to generate (that is, discover) instances in which some new learning might be applicable—for example, a new principle in arithmetic. In fact, Ausubel argues that discovery learning is essential in problem solving if students are to demonstrate that they understand what they have learned. Furthermore, says Ausubel, there are indications that students more readily apply to new situations information that they discover, as opposed to material that is presented to them in final form. In addition, discovery approaches might be more motivating than expository approaches, and self-learning might be more intrinsically satisfying.

Although Ausubel accepts the usefulness of a discovery approach in some instances, he remains a strong advocate of expository teaching. He argues that most learning is of the reception variety and that any alternative would be highly inefficient in terms of the time involved, the cost incurred, and the benefits that accrue to the learner. Relatively little school learning can be discovered by a student, says Ausubel, not only because it would take too long but also because students are not always capable of discovering much that is significant. Even subjects that apparently lend themselves to discovery approaches can often be mastered as well and faster if the information is given to the learner in relatively final form. Ausubel believes that after the age of eleven or twelve, the learner possesses enough background information to understand many new concepts clearly if they are explained simply. After this age, Ausubel contends, asking a student to "discover" is largely a waste of time.

Scientific Comparisons

Because a number of studies have attempted to compare discovery-oriented and reception-oriented approaches to teaching and learning, it should be possible to evaluate the two without relying solely on opinion, conjecture, or theoretical speculation. However, that is not really the case because the research does not consistently support one approach over the other and is often confusing and contradictory. Why? Partly because different studies often use different criteria for assessing the effectiveness of different approaches. For example, some studies look at speed of learning, others are concerned with retention; some attempt to assess transfer, and others look at affective or motivational changes in learners.

Another reason that the conclusions of teaching-outcome studies are sometimes contradictory is that it is often impossible to control (and therefore to equate or compare) the approaches used in different studies—or sometimes even within a single study. Not only are students and classes dramatically different from one another but so are teachers. A well-prepared expository lesson might be extremely effective when presented by Mr. Joneskowski, but Ms. Rudifesk might present the same lesson poorly. By the same token, one fifth-grade class might respond exceptionally well to a discovery lesson, whereas another might be totally confused by the same lesson presented by the same teacher.

Some Studies. Studies that have attempted to evaluate the effectiveness of a single approach (rather than comparing two different approaches) have not led to clear conclusions, either. Among these are a large number of studies that have looked at the contribution of advance organizers to learning, retention, and transfer. Grippin and Peters (1984) point out that about half these studies indicate that the use of organizers makes a significant difference; the other half find that learning is just as effective without the use of organizers. However, good organizers are effective more often than not.

Mayer (1979) suggests that the most effective organizers are those that (1) allow the student to generate all or most of the logical relationships in the material to be learned, (2) point out clear relationships between familiar and less familiar material, (3) are relatively simple to learn and use, and (4) are used in situations in which the learner would not spontaneously use an organizer, perhaps because of inexperience or inability to recall relevant information.

The effectiveness of discovery approaches has also been researched. Here, too, there is often confusion and contradiction, resulting in part from inconsistent definition, inappropriate measurement, and uncontrolled (and often uncontrollable) differences among teachers and students. However, even strong advocates of other approaches generally concede that discovery approaches can be highly effective in a variety of circumstances (see, for example, Corno & Snow, 1986).

Some Conclusions. What, then, should the teacher conclude? Should teachers use mostly discovery or mostly expository approaches? The simple answer is that the question is not as simple as it sounds, nor are the choices as clear. A good teacher will, of course, use both.

Disturbing as it might be for those who prefer the uncomplicated comfort of a black or white position, in a great many instances it is impossible to use only one instructional approach to the complete exclusion of others. Johnny, intensely motivated to discover the mating habits of that noble barnyard fowl, the turkey, runs to the local library and finds a learned exposition on the turkey. From this exposition he learns a bewildering amount. Discovery learning? In contrast, Frank's teacher, a recent reception-learning convert, presents a brilliant exposition of the mating habits of turkeys to his bench-bound students. During the course of this exposition, it occurs to Frank that turkeys have been unnecessarily and unjustly demeaned in recent times, as is evident in the popular expression, "You turkey!" In the course of his inspired musings, he discovers that there is little reason not to rank turkeys with eagles as birds worthy of our respect and admiration. Reception learning?

The confusion arising from these illustrations may be lessened by the realization that learning is what students do and teaching is what teachers do. A teacher who emphasizes discovery will try to arrange the teaching/learning situation so that students are encouraged to experiment, to think, to gather information, and, most important, to arrive at their own organization of that information. Teachers who emphasize expository teaching will be more concerned with organizing information so that it is immediately meaningful for students and therefore becomes a stable part of their existing cognitive structure. In the end, however, it is the student who learns. And, in spite of a teacher's emphases to the contrary, students may discover new information and new relationships for themselves, or they may discover no more than a structured exposition ready to be learned and assimilated as is.

CURRENT DEVELOPMENTS AND EMPHASES

The juxtaposition of apparently opposing points of view is sometimes a useful teaching device. It highlights differences and, if Ausubel is correct, makes the points of view more memorable—more easily dissociated from each other.

But there is also a disadvantage to this approach: It exaggerates differences and masks similarities. It leaves the impression that the points of view are more different and the theorists more adamant in their beliefs than is actually the case.

This chapter is a case in point. Juxtaposing the theories of Bruner and Ausubel has underlined the differences between them—especially the discovery-versus-expository debate. At the same time, this approach has perhaps glossed over important points of agreement between them—especially the conviction of each that the key to successful cognitive processing is to be found in the learner's organization of knowledge. Both positions are, after all, unwaveringly cognitive. Both present a view of the learner as an active, information-processing organism for whom the environment is meaningful to the extent that new material can be related to existing cognitive structure. Furthermore, the descriptions that each theory provides of the formation of cognitive structure are similar, even though their language is different (*categories* and *coding systems* on the one hand; *subsumers* and *subsumption* on the other). And, as we have seen, in the final analysis discovery and reception learning are not totally incompatible approaches to teaching and learning. As described by Bruner and Ausubel, each is intended to lead to the acquisition of meaningful concepts, to maximize transfer, retention, and motivation, and to reduce the extent to which school learning is a passive exercise in rote learning.

Cognitive Apprenticeship

An educational model that attempts to pull together these different emphases is termed **cognitive apprenticeship** (Collins, Brown, & Newman, 1989). This model views the learner as an apprentice in much the same sense as novices who are apprenticed to experts to learn new trades and skills. In the cognitive sphere, the experts are parents, siblings, other peers, or adults and, most important, teachers. Within this model, the role of the teacher is less to fill the learner's mind with information, facts, figures, procedures, and so on than to present examples, to invite the student to explore, to provide guidance and encouragement. The model suggests that teachers need to be concerned with developing a variety of cognitive strategies so that students are equipped to explore, organize, discover, and learn on their own. It advocates the use of techniques such as modeling (showing students how to do things), coaching (guiding specific aspects of the student's performance), scaffolding (providing support so that students can accomplish tasks that would otherwise be too difficult), **fading** (removing support so that students can assume responsibility for solving problems and learning as soon as possible), and articulation and reflection (asking students to verbalize their behaviors and especially their thought processes). This last technique is similar to Mulcahy's (1991) use of Socratic dialogue, a series of questions and answers designed to lead learners to become aware of their own thought processes and cognitive strategies.

Three principles guide the sequencing of material in Collins, Brown, and Newman's (1989) model of cognitive apprenticeship. The first, *global before local*, refers to the belief that learners should be provided with an overall view of what is to be learned or performed *before* they begin to work on specifics. In practice, the *global* aspect of the instruction might take the form of a summary, an overview, a completed activity, a final rendition. In this sense, the global-before-local principle is similar to Ausubel's use of advance organizers.

Second, the model suggests that material should be presented in order of simplest to most complex—very much in line with Bruner's notion that learners should begin with the simplest examples of concepts and proceed to more general, more inclusive concepts.

Third, to increase transfer and meaningfulness of learning, the model suggests that once acquired, knowledge and skills should be applied in an ever increasing diversity of situations. Collins, Brown, and Newman (1989) note that much that we learn from textbooks, lectures, and labs is never applied outside these situations, often because we don't know when or how to make applications. In this sense our knowledge is "inert" rather than active.

Empowerment

It is worth repeating again the one-sentence summary of one of the most important of educational objectives, first presented in Chapter 1: The goal of education is to empower students. As we saw, to empower is to enable, to give power. At a simple level, education empowers students by providing them with skills and knowledge that enable them to do important things they could not otherwise do (for example, read newspapers, write love poems, add up the money in one's pocket or purse, and so on). At a deeper level, education empowers by contributing to the development of cognitive content and intellectual processes; that is, it empowers by teaching people actual things (content) as well as by teaching them how to think (process). And finally, education empowers by developing in students the sort of power that comes with feelings of social, intellectual, and personal competence.

Misconceptions and Their Effects on Learning

Cognitive psychology's attention to how the student learns and understands has led to some important discoveries about the ways students think. For example, it seems that many students (and many teachers as well) sometimes find it difficult to understand what might otherwise be relatively simple concepts and principles, simply because they have learned, and incorporated into their cognitive structures, certain stubborn misconceptions that interfere with learning (sometimes referred to as *alternative conceptions*, a less negative term). Evidence suggests that more than three-quarters of fifth-grade students believe that eyes actually see objects—rather than responding to reflected light that travels in straight lines and bounces off various objects (Anderson & Smith, 1984). Similarly, elementary school children who readily state that the Earth is round often have a conception different from what you or I might have of what a round Earth means (Nussbaum, 1979). Some see it as a flat round thing, something like a cookie, perhaps surrounded by water; others conceive of the Earth as a huge globular object with the ground near the bottom of the globe, the sky at the top, and air in between. In much the same way, some teacher trainees report that the insulating coating on electrical wires is designed to keep electrons from escaping from their pathway (West, 1988). And Lockhead (1985) found that more than three-quarters of college students don't really understand ninth-grade algebra, even if they can correctly manipulate algebraic symbols and equations.

These and a large number of related studies have been concerned primarily with what students don't know—or, more precisely, with what they think they know that is not only fundamentally incorrect but is also such a basic part of cognitive structure in specific subjects like physics or mathematics that it interferes with learning. Ramsden (1988a) reports numerous studies that indicate how persistent these misconceptions are.

Among the implications of these studies is the need for teachers to be aware of their students' naïve and misleading beliefs and to take pains to correct them (Calfee & Drum, 1986). Advance organizers, questioning, verbalizing solutions to problems, and related activities might be used for this purpose. Ramsden (1988b) suggests that today's teacher needs to adopt a relational view of teaching. This view emphasizes that learning is about changing conceptions rather than simply about the addition of more facts. Accordingly, teachers need to be concerned as much with the processes of learning—with learning how to learn—as with its content. They also need to focus on the relationship between the subject matter and the learner rather than simply on the relationship between teaching methods and test performance. In Nickerson's words, "it should be the goal of education to help people become competent knowers, thinkers, and learners" (1988, p. 34). Or in Bruner's words: "The salvation is in learning how to go about learning . . ." (1985, p. 8).

Effective Teaching

Benjamin Bloom (1984) believes that one important current challenge for educational research is to devise instructional procedures that are as effective with entire classes as one-to-one tutorials are with single students. His review of the literature finds that a one-to-one tutorial is by far the most effective method of instruction available. In fact, if given good tutoring, the average student can be expected to achieve at somewhere around the ninety-eighth percentile in a group of comparable students taught in a conventional classroom setting. In other words, in a tutorial situation, an average student will outperform 98 percent of students in ordinary classrooms! The potential for higher achievement is apparently there; only the method is lacking. Finding that method (or methods) is the challenge.

Some Implications of Instructional Research

Robert Gagné's ideas, summarized earlier in this chapter, are an excellent example of how learning theory can be related directly to educational practice. For every type of learning, R. Gagné describes instructional procedures that might be most effective.

Educational literature abounds with other examples of how findings and theories about learning can be translated into instructional practice. In fact, Glaser and Bassok (1989) note that research on instruction can no longer be easily separated from research on cognitive processes.

What kind of research is this?

There is a great deal of it, spanning a wide variety of age and grade levels and involving many subjects and instructional procedures. As a result, it is not easily described or summarized. For our purposes, however, the most important research is that which has looked at the effects of specific, theory-derived instructional procedures on the performance of learners. Often, the research has involved elaborate, relatively long-term experimental, school-based programs (see Rosenshine & Stevens, 1986, or Glaser & Bassok, 1989, for summaries and reviews).

More important, what does the research tell us?

Two Undisputed Facts. Alexander and Judy (1988) claim the research tells us many things, among which are two findings they describe as "undisputed facts." First, the more the learner knows about a specific subject (that is, the more domain-specific knowledge there is in the individual's cognitive structure), the better the learner will understand and remember. Second, learners who are most adept at monitoring and controlling their cognitive activities typically do better than other learners who are less skilled players of Flavell's (1985) game of cognition.

These two undisputed findings have profound implications for teachers' behavior. The finding about those with the greatest amount of domain-specific prior learning (as opposed to more general information) highlights the importance of advance preparation for learning. It also emphasizes the cumulative and hierarchical nature of much of our learning, and it lends support to the contention that both lessons and curricula need to present material so that new understanding builds on a firm base of knowledge and skills. It makes no difference whether we use the language of a Bruner (numerous, varied instances of concepts need to be presented so that the learner can discover coding systems that will permit going beyond the information given); of an Ausubel (learners need to be given—and reminded of—stable, relevant subsuming concepts so that there will be something in cognitive structure to give meaning to new learning and to which new learning can be firmly anchored); or of a Robert Gagné (the content in any given subject area needs to be presented hierarchically so that essential subordinate skills and understanding are available). In the final analysis, the instructional implications of each of these differently worded and somewhat jargon-laden statements are much the same: Understanding depends very much on what we already know. It isn't a particularly startling revelation, but it is a fundamentally important one.

The second of Alexander and Judy's (1988) undisputed facts—that learners who are best at monitoring and controlling their cognitive strategies perform better—also has clear instructional implications: Specifically, teachers must devote more time and energy to teaching the skills and strategies of thinking and learning.

Other Findings. In addition to these two findings (which relate to the role of previous learning in achieving understanding and to the role of self-monitored cognitive strategies), cognitive research on learning presents several other findings that are relevant to instruction. Among these, Shuell (1986) includes cognitive psychology's emphasis on the active nature of learning (in contrast to a more passive view that stresses the importance of response consequences) and its concern with comprehension (rather than simply with performance). Another important line of cognitive research, mentioned earlier, deals with the role of the learner's preconceived and often incorrect notions. As Nickerson notes, "an approach to instruction that ignores [learner misconceptions] is likely to fail" (1988, p. 35).

Conclusions of Research into Effective Teaching

Rosenshine and Stevens (1986) summarize a number of experimental studies that have looked at the effectiveness of theory-generated instructional programs in schools. In general, these studies show that it is possible to train teachers to follow specific instructional procedures and that students exposed to experimental programs often outperform comparable control groups on a variety of measures.

The studies reviewed by Rosenshine and Stevens (1986, p. 377) suggest that effective teaching is characterized by a number of behaviors that can be taught and encouraged in teachers. Specifically, the most effective teachers, with respect to teaching well-structured subjects, are those who

1. start their lessons with a brief review of prerequisite learning,

2. begin by stating the lesson's goals,

3. present material in small steps, allowing students to practice between steps,

4. give explicit and detailed instructions and explanations,

5. allow all students to practice lessons actively,

6. ask many questions to check students' understanding and obtain responses from all students,

7. provide students with immediate guidance for initial practice,

8. provide systematic feedback and correct students' errors as they occur, and

9. provide clear and explicit instructions for seat work and monitor students' performance as necessary.

Rosenshine and Stevens caution that these teaching procedures do not apply to all students at all times. As noted, they are most applicable to well-structured content that can be presented in small steps, for which the teacher can provide detailed and explicit instructions, allow for students to practice with immediate corrective feedback, and so on. But when the lesson deals with more abstract, less structured content (such as morality and ethics, creative writing, politics, and so on), different teaching approaches are necessary.

MAIN POINTS

1. R. Gagné classifies learning outcomes in five major domains: intellectual skills, verbal information, cognitive strategies, attitudes, and motor skills.

2. Intellectual skills (learning discriminations, rules, and concepts) are hierarchical in that higher-level skills depend upon lower-level skills. Discriminations result from the ability to respond differentially to similar stimuli. Concepts involve responding to similarities and are best explained by reference to cognitive theories. Rules, which are statements of relationships among concepts, enable us to predict and organize and may be combined to solve complex problems.

3. Verbal information (knowledge) can be expressed in sentence form and is indispensable to conversation and other ordinary daily activities, as well as to acquiring information and to thinking.

4. Attitudes are affective predispositions to make certain choices or to behave in certain ways, given a choice of behaviors. They therefore have important motivational properties.

5. Motor skills, such as typing and writing, involve the execution of controlled sequences of muscular movements.

6. R. Gagné defines *cognitive strategies* as including both metacognitive and cognitive skills. Metacognitive skills such as comprehension monitoring relate to knowing about knowing; cognitive skills are what we actually do when we learn, think, and remember—rehearsing or elaborating, for example.

7. Cognitive theories stress the importance of the individual learner's cognitive structure and look at how information is processed, organized, and recalled. Cognitive theories think of knowledge as consisting of vast networks of relationships. Declarative knowledge consists of all the facts we have learned (things that are or have been); procedural knowledge involves knowing how to do something. Schemata are metaphors for cognitive structure and functioning. They may be thought of as clusters of knowledge that define concepts. Scripts are the aspects of schemata that deal with routines and sequences.

8. Cognitive psychology's principal tenets suggest that (a) the curriculum needs to be organized to reveal and emphasize relationships, and (b) schools should pay deliberate attention to developing strategies for organizing and using knowledge.

9. Bruner's cognitive theory describes learning and perception as information-processing activities that involve the formation of concepts (categories) that result from abstracting commonalities among events and experiences. Hierarchical arrangements of related categories are referred to as *coding systems*. Coding systems are important for retention, discovery, and transfer.

10. Bruner is a strong proponent of discovery approaches to instruction, which require the learner to structure information by discovering the relationships that exist among concepts or principles. He argues that discovery leads to higher degrees of transfer and longer retention. It also increases motivation and leads to the development of problem-solving skills.

11. Discovery learning is affected by four general conditions: set (predisposition to learn in a given way), need state (degree of arousal), mastery of specifics (amount and detail of learning), and diversity of training (variety of conditions under which learning takes place).

12. Bruner presents arguments in favor of a spiral curriculum, the teaching of difficult subjects in simplified but honest form to younger students, the organization of a curriculum around themes or underlying principles, the encouragement of plausible guesses, and the use of aids in teaching.

13. Renewed interest in discovery approaches are found in constructivist approaches (based on the assumption that students construct knowledge) and in the conceptual change movement (based on the recognition that teachers should be more concerned with the learners' concepts and cognitive strategies that lead to conceptual change than simply with factual information).

14. Ausubel's theory is a cognitive attempt to explain meaningful verbal learning. It is concerned largely with arriving at laws of classroom learning. He defines *meaning* as involving a relationship between new material and old material (cognitive structure). Cognitive structure consists of hierarchically organized concepts (subsumers) arranged much as categories are arranged in Bruner's coding systems.

15. To learn is to subsume material to existing cognitive structure. This may take the form of deriving material from preexisting structure (derivative subsumption), or it may involve material that is an extension of what is already known (correlative subsumption). Loss of ability to recall (to dissociate new material from old) is obliterative subsumption.

16. Ausubel argues that discovery learning is highly time consuming and often impossible. His most important instructional technique involves the use of advance organizers—highly generic concepts presented before the lesson, designed to bring to mind relevant prior knowledge, and intended to clarify the relationships between new and old learning.

17. Discovery methods and expository teaching are not mutually exclusive. Both are useful. Ausubel suggests that discovery may have advantages for teaching in the early grades, for testing meaningfulness and problem solving, for ensuring transferability, and for establishing intrinsic motivation. In the end, teaching is what teachers do, and learning is what students do. Discovery teaching does not always lead to discovery learning—and vice versa.

18. Although Bruner and Ausubel present points of view that are opposite in many respects, both present a fundamentally cognitive view of the learner as an active, information-processing organism whose efforts to derive meaning from the environment are closely related to the development of associated networks of concepts. Their recommendations for instruction are intended to lead to the acquisition of meaningful concepts, to maximize transfer, retention, and motivation, and to reduce passive rote learning.

19. The cognitive apprenticeship model suggests a relatively complex role for today's teacher—one that recognizes a wide diversity of desired learning outcomes (procedural as well as declarative knowledge, for example), a range of different instructional approaches (including modeling, coaching, scaffolding, fading, articulation, and re-flection), and some important sequencing principles (global before local, from simplest to most complex, and toward increasing diversity).

20. An important objective of education is to empower students by providing them with knowledge, skills, and confidence.

21. Occasionally, what students don't know, or the inaccurate and misleading things they are convinced they do know, interfere with learning and understanding, hence the importance of advance organizers, questioning, and other approaches in ensuring that all learners have appropriate prerequisite knowledge and skills for new learning.

22. Two findings from cognitive research have important implications for effective teaching: (a) The more background knowledge a learner has about a subject, the more effective the learning (domain-specific knowledge), and (b) learners who are most skilled at monitoring and controlling their use of cognitive strategies learn and solve problems (use strategic knowledge) most effectively.

23. The most effective teachers for well-structured material are those who (a) begin by reviewing (often using advance organizers), (b) state goals clearly at the beginning, and (c) present material in small, detailed, and explicit steps with both ample opportunity for practice and systematic feedback during the lesson and during seat work.

24. Bloom's challenge is to find an instructional method(s) as effective for an entire class as a one-on-one tutorial is for a single student. "The salvation is in learning how to go about learning" (Bruner, 1985, p. 8).

SUGGESTED READINGS

Original sources are among the best references for approaches to learning theory such as Bruner's and Ausubel's. The following references are clear presentations of Bruner's theories and educational recommendations:

BRUNER, J. S. (1957). On going beyond the information given. In *Contemporary Approaches to Cognition*. Cambridge, Mass.: Harvard University Press.

———. (1961). *The process of education*. Cambridge, Mass.: Harvard University Press.

———. (1990). *Acts of meaning.* Cambridge, Mass.: Harvard University Press.

BRUNER, J. S., GOODNOW, J. J., & AUSTIN, G. A. (1956). *A study of thinking.* New York: Wiley.

The psychological theories of Ausubel are best explained in

AUSUBEL, D. P. (1968). *Educational psychology: A cognitive view.* New York: Holt, Rinehart & Winston.

An excellent collection of articles dealing with the application of cognitive research in teaching, especially with respect to science, is

RAMSDEN, P. (1988). Studying learning: Improving teaching. In P. Ramsden (Ed.), *Improving Learning: New Perspectives.* London: Kogan Page.

Farnham-Diggory's book is highly recommended for the contemporary teacher concerned about the intellectual development of learners; Biggs's book is a shorter collection of articles that attempt to relate current cognitive science to teaching and learning.

FARNHAM-DIGGORY, S. (1992). *Cognitive processes in education* (2nd ed.). New York: HarperCollins.

BIGGS, J. B. (1991). *Teaching for learning: The view from cognitive psychology.* Hawthorn, Australia: The Australian Council for Educational Research.

The much feared grizzly bear (Ursus horribilis) *weighs about nine hundred pounds at maturity. Many "experts" consider the grizzly to be a species of the brown bear* (Ursus arctos). *The grizzly's prodigal strength is attested to by one bear that moved an 850-pound trap one quarter of a mile and then escaped (Soper, 1964).*

I will not Reason and Compare: my business is to Create.
William Blake, *Jerusalem*

Since when was genius found respectable?
Elizabeth Barrett Browning, *Aurora Leigh*

Chapter 7 | INTELLIGENCE AND CREATIVITY

PREVIEW Intelligence and creativity, those nebulous and ill-defined characteristics, are among the most prized of our "possessions"—and perhaps among the most useful as well. This chapter examines the meanings of these terms, the forces that shape the qualities they represent, and some of the methods that have been devised to assess them. In addition, the chapter looks at the relationship between creativity and intelligence. Is it possible to be creative but stupid? to be intelligent but totally devoid of creative talent?

Excerpt from Bear Tales (Book III): Invasion of the Wild Cows

The bear lies next to a chokecherry bush on a small rise above the meadow. The wild cows are in plain view, but they're downwind, and the smell of their gases is faint. The cows pay no attention to the bear. Some of them play cards while they chew cud; others sip whiskey or do their hair. One of them has gotten hold of a truck and is spinning endless donuts through the meadow, ripping through the spring clover and the wild strawberries. The big one slouches against a tree blowing smoke rings and belching like everything is perfect. No wonder; she's just beaten the crap out of a young bull.

But the bear knows nothing's perfect anymore. He's been watching the cows, studying them, trying to understand more clearly what dangers they represent. He sees them building their overblown fires on chilly evenings, savaging the forest. It ticks him off because he knows they don't really need the fires, that they're just a wild cow indulgence.

That isn't all. These wild cows think it's clever to use hair sprays from cans that have chlorofluorocarbon propellants. They think this makes them look sweet. "It's a bloody affectation," mutters the bear. "Ugly, stupid wild cows."

He doesn't yet understand fully the power of trends. He knows, because he's seen it, that today's trendy wild cow is no longer satisfied simply to eat and chew cud and make calves. Now she likes to sip whiskey from styrofoam cups while she sits around the blazing fires! And she likes to smoke and belch great clouds of methane gas and generally run amok. And dance.

To quote the bear again, "Bloody wild cows!"

It really upsets the bear that wild cows don't care. Sometimes, when he remembers the songs of birds he can't hear anymore, he weeps. "It's those damn wild cow philosophers," he moans. Wild cow philosophers reassure the populace with meaningless axioms, like "Every problem contains its own solution!" So wild cows think the technology they worship will solve the world's problems when those problems are serious enough to need solving.

Wild cow philosophers are wrong, insists the bear. This problem does not contain its own solution. Technology's values, he says, are driven too much by economics. And even if this weren't true, he argues, the wild cows have gotten us into a mess that technology can't solve.

"Our creativity and our intelligence are our only hope for salvation," the bear says. "But first, we have to get rid of wild cows."[*]

VIEWS OF INTELLIGENCE

The second most frequently used and least understood term in education is **intelligence**; first place goes to the term **creativity**.

Wagner and Sternberg (1984) suggest that there are basically three different views of intelligence. They label the first the "psychometric view." Historically, it has been the most common approach to understanding intelligence. *Psychometrics* refers to the measurement of psychological functions; hence, the psychometric view of intelligence is that which is based on a measurement approach.

The second view is Piaget's. This perspective sees intelligence as an active process involving progressive adaptation through the interplay of assimilation and accommodation. The results of intelligent activity are manifested in cognitive structure. The principal characteristics of cognitive structure change with age; the changes are the essential features of Piaget's developmental theory.

The third view of intelligence is the informa-

---

[*]PPC: What is all this about wild cows? What does it mean? Why is the author doing this?

Editor: It's clearly a metaphor. Fortunately, your author has responded to this inquiry—in the glossary, under **wild cow**. Check it out. You might also want to check out **bear**.

tion-processing view. Like Piaget's approach, it is more qualitative than quantitative. That is, it seeks to describe the important characteristics of intelligence in terms of processes rather than to measure its products.

We looked at Piaget's theory in Chapter 3; here we discuss the psychometric approach, and we look at two approaches related to the information-processing view: Gardner's "multiple intelligences" and Sternberg's "componential theory."

Psychometric Definitions of Intelligence

There are a tremendous variety of measurement-based (psychometric) definitions of *intelligence*; here are four of them:

1. "Intelligence is what the tests test" (Boring, 1923, p. 35).

2. "The global and aggregate capacity of an individual to think rationally, to act purposefully, and to deal effectively with his environment" (Wechsler, 1958, p. 7).

3. "Intelligence A: The innate potential for cognitive development." . . . "Intelligence B: A general or average level of development of ability to perceive, to learn, to solve problems, to think, to adapt" (Hebb, 1966, p. 332).

4. To Hebb's definition, West and MacArthur added another dimension, labeled Intelligence A[1]: "The present potential of an individual for future development of intelligent behavior, assuming optimum future treatment adapted to bring out that potential" (1964, p. 18).

The first definition ("intelligence is what the tests test") is not meant to be facetious. It is at once an admission that intelligence is a difficult concept to define and an assertion that intelligence tests are useful if the scores they provide are related to success on tasks we think require intelligence. Whatever they measure can then be called "intelligence," even if its exact nature is unknown.

The second definition ("global and aggregate capacity") defines intelligence in terms of clear thinking, purposeful activity, and effective interaction with the environment. Wechsler sees intelligence as a "global" capacity. This view is advanced in distinction to the view held by Spearman (1927) and Thurstone (1938), among others, that intelligence is not a single characteristic but instead consists of a number of separate abilities or factors. Guilford (1959), whose work is reviewed later in this chapter in the section on creativity, advances a similar view.

The third and fourth definitions make some useful distinctions among different types of intelligence. As Vygotsky (1986) points out, people are born with different potentials for development—what Hebb calls "intelligence A." However, conventional measures of intelligence assess "intelligence B"—current level of development—rather than intelligence A. Inferences about potential are then based on measures of current performance. In contrast, Vygotsky's approach to measuring intelligence, as well as Feuerstein's (1980), gives test subjects hints and suggestions in an effort to arrive at a better estimate of *potential* performance.

In another psychometric approach, Cattell (1971) makes an important distinction between two kinds of intelligence. On the one hand, certain capabilities seem to underlie much of our intelligent behavior. These capabilities are essentially nonverbal and are unaffected by culture or experience; Cattell labels them **fluid abilities**. Measures such as general reasoning, memory, attention span, and analysis of figures reflect fluid abilities.

In contrast with fluid abilities is a grouping of intellectual abilities that are primarily verbal and that are highly influenced by culture, experience, and education. These **crystallized abilities** are reflected in vocabulary tests, tests of general information, and arithmetic skills. Not surprisingly, performance on crystallized measures tends to increase with age, sometimes into very old age (Horn & Donaldson, 1980). In contrast, fluid abilities seem to be more dependent on physio-

logical structures and more susceptible to the ravages of age; they typically show declines in old age (Horn, 1976).

A Synthesis. How, then, should we define intelligence? Is it what the tests test? a global and aggregate sort of thing? a two-sided thing involving what is potential as well as what is actual? a different two-sided thing involving relatively "pure" capabilities on the one hand and capabilities that are highly affected by experience on the other? Or should we use a combination of all these definitions? As Vernon (1969) observes, when we speak of intelligence, we often mean any one of three things or a combination thereof: a genetic capacity (presumably reflected in fluid intelligence or in Hebb's intelligence A), a test score (derived from any of a large number of different intelligence tests), or observed behavior (reflected in Hebb's intelligence B).

Or should we, as Das (1992) argues, abandon the search for this elusive but measurable thing called "general intelligence" (commonly abbreviated **g**)? "If I were a young psychologist," says Das, "I wouldn't waste my life looking for g . . ." (p. 137). Not only does trying to rank people on a single scale of merit like general intelligence fail to take into consideration the tremendous variation of interests, skills, and capabilities of different individuals but it is politically dangerous. It leads too easily to the conclusion that such and such a race is intellectually inferior, especially if we assume that intelligence is largely genetically determined—as do Jensen (1980) and Rushton (1988).

Instead, says Das, we have to look at three aspects of intelligence: the processes and components of intelligent behavior, the individual's competence in relation to the person's culture and age, and the possibility of improving competence through training and experience.

Gardner's Multiple Intelligences

From the teacher's point of view, the recognition that high competence and talent may be

TABLE 7.1 The Seven Intelligences

INTELLIGENCE	POSSIBLE OCCUPATION	CORE COMPONENTS
Logical-mathematical	Scientist Mathematician	Sensitivity to and capacity to discern logical or numerical patterns; ability to handle long chains of reasoning
Linguistic	Poet Journalist	Sensitivity to the sounds, rhythms, and meanings of words; sensitivity to the different functions of language
Musical	Composer Violinist	Abilities to produce and appreciate rhythm, pitch, and timbre; appreciation of the forms of musical expressiveness
Spatial	Navigator Sculptor	Capacities to perceive the visual-spatial world accurately and to manipulate the mental representations that result
Bodily kinesthetic	Dancer Athlete	Abilities to control one's body movements and to handle objects skillfully
Interpersonal	Therapist Salesperson	Capacities to discern and respond appropriately to the moods, temperaments, motivations, and desires of other people
Intrapersonal	Person with detailed accurate self-knowledge	Access to one's own feelings and the ability to discriminate among them and draw upon them to guide behavior; knowledge of one's own strengths, weaknesses, desires, and intelligences

Source: From H. Gardner and T. Hatch (1989). Multiple intelligences go to school: Educational implications of the theory of multiple intelligences. *Educational Researcher,* Vol. 18, No. 8, pp. 4–10.

manifested in some but not necessarily all areas of human functioning is important. It underlines the need to encourage the development of competencies in those areas where the individual might be especially gifted and to provide support and assistance in other areas.

Gardner (1983) suggests that we have not one but seven largely unrelated kinds of intelligences. These multiple intelligences are manifested in competence in seven distinct areas: logical-mathematical, linguistic, musical, spatial, bodily kinesthetic, interpersonal, and intrapersonal (see Table 7.1).

Attempts to assess each of these seven capabilities are difficult for two reasons, claim Gardner and Hatch (1989). First, most of our experience in measuring intelligence involves mathematical, linguistic, and logical tasks. Their view of multiple intelligence requires the development of a range of new tasks to tap competencies such as bodily kinesthetic, the intrapersonal, and the interpersonal.

Second, it now seems clear that intelligence cannot easily be separated from culture and background. As a result, assessing these multiple intelligences requires taking into consideration the

intelligence in other species

We generally assume that of all animals on Earth, we are by far the most intelligent and the most inventive. As evidence, we point proudly to our increasing mastery of nature, and we contrast with this the perennial struggle for survival of those less gifted than we.* So viewed, we appear to be the creature that has adapted best to the environment—and this, the ability to adapt, is a useful definition of intelligence.

Ironically, we—the self-designated wise ones—do not have the largest brain of the earthly species. Indeed, the adult male brain weighs a mere 3¼ pounds. The female brain weighs approximately 10 percent less—not even 3 pounds. This, compared with the 13-pound elephant brain or the brain of a whale, which in some cases weighs 19 pounds,

is relatively unimpressive. However, given the strong likelihood that the absolute weight of the brain is less related to intelligent behavior than is the ratio of brain to body weight, we still retain the advantage. Our brain-to-body-weight ratio is approximately 1 to 50; that of the whale and elephant approaches 1 to 1,000. However, some small monkeys have even better brain-to-body-weight ratios—as high as 1 to 18. But in these cases, the absolute size of the brain is so small that it probably cannot do much more than handle simple physiological functioning. The dolphin, on the other hand, is not inordinately large—in fact, it often weighs no more than an adult man. Yet its average brain weight is a full 3³⁄₄ pounds. This fact has led to a great deal of specula-

tion and research on the dolphin's intelligence—research that has not yet succeeded in determining how intelligent the dolphin really is.

Although a fairly accurate ranking of species in terms of intelligence may be based on their brain-to-body-weight ratios, such a crude indicator of intelligence does not appear to be of any real value in gauging the subtle but significant differences that exist between geniuses and less gifted individuals within the human species. For this, instruments labeled "intelligence tests" are commonly used. Not only are these tests generally unsuitable for nonhumans but also they are often suitable only for very specific groups within the human species.

*And we point, less proudly, to our dwindling supply of irreplaceable resources, to our idiotic penchant for polluting the environment, to our unreasoning failure to control our numbers, and to the increasing risk of nuclear self-annihilation.

---

extent to which social background influences the child's competence, interest, and even willingness in the testing situation.

"Even so," conclude Gardner and Hatch, "the goal of detecting distinctive human strengths, and using them as a basis for engagement and learning, may prove to be worthwhile. . ." (1989, p. 9).

Sternberg's View

The information-processing view of intelligence stresses the importance of the strategies and

processes involved in knowing. Accordingly, it is a cognitive perspective. In its simplest form, this perspective maintains that one of the important components of intelligent activity is cognitive functions. And most important from the teacher's point of view is the widely held belief that these functions are largely acquired. As was discussed in Chapter 5, functions that are acquired (that is, functions that are learned) can be taught. That, in a nutshell, is the rationale underlying the cognitive strategies programs currently being developed and tested.

Contextual Intelligence. A good representative of the information-processing approach to intelligence is Sternberg's (1984a, 1984b, 1986) contextual and componential theory. The theory is contextual in that it defines intelligence in terms of adaptation to a particular environment. In Sternberg's words, intelligence is the "purposive selection and shaping of and adaptation to real-world environments relevant to one's life" (1984a, p. 312). One important feature of this definition is that it emphasizes the individual's control over the environment. It says, in effect, that intelligent individuals exercise control over their environments not only by changing and molding significant aspects of them but also by selecting them in the first place. Thus, it would be quite stupid (or at least moderately unintelligent) of someone who is tone deaf to select a career in music or for someone who suffers from severe vertigo to buy a home high on a cliff.

How can we measure contextual intelligence? Sternberg says that one way is simply to ask people what is considered intelligent and stupid in their culture. After all, contextual intelligence is simply an indication of how well a person adapts in a specific environment—and people who live in that environment may be expected to be the best sources of information about what is required for effective adaptation. Not surprisingly, an analysis of the responses of people in North American cultures to the question of what makes up intelligent behavior reveals three broad groupings of abilities that best describe intelligent people: practical problem-solving ability, verbal ability, and social competence. In other cultures, responses might be different.

One advantage of a contextual view of intelligence is that it highlights the importance of the individual's success in coping with the ordinary demands of life in the social and physical context; that is, it removes intelligence from the realm of the abstract and theoretical and brings it to a more concrete, more easily understood level. But this view also has a number of disadvantages. First, it is too inclusive. Because all adaptive behaviors are intelligent, almost all behaviors are potentially intelligent (even if they are perhaps somewhat stupid in one context, they may be adaptive in some other context). Second, the contextualist view does not adequately describe the processes and structures that underlie intelligence; instead, it describes intelligence in terms of the characteristics and effects of behavior.

A Componential View. As a response to these weaknesses, Sternberg (1986) has proposed a componential theory of human intelligence. This theory identifies three separate components of intelligence (see Figure 7.1). First are the components involved in metacognition—that is, in planning, monitoring, and evaluating cognitive performance. These are labeled **metacomponents**. They include what Sternberg also calls "executive skills"—those used in making decisions about which cognitive activities to use and in monitoring and evaluating the results of these ongoing activities. Conventional measures of intelligence typically do not measure metacomponents.

Second, there are **performance components**. These are processes that are actually used in carrying out tasks. They include inductive reasoning, encoding, analyzing, remembering, paying attention, and so on. Note that these processes are what Cattell defines as *fluid abilities*. They appear to be relatively independent of experience and more dependent on innate factors. Sternberg suggests that a number of conventional intelligence tests that measure fluid intelligence can also serve as good measures of performance components.

The third of Sternberg's three components of intelligence are the **knowledge-acquisition components**. Sternberg (1984c) identifies three processes that are important for acquiring new information: selective encoding (separating relevant from irrelevant information), selective combination (combining selected information with other information so as to make it meaningful), and selective comparison (deriving meaning from new information by relating it to previous learning).

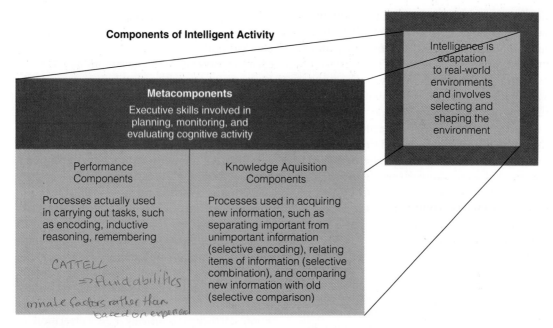

Components of Intelligent Activity

Metacomponents
Executive skills involved in planning, monitoring, and evaluating cognitive activity

Intelligence is adaptation to real-world environments and involves selecting and shaping the environment

Performance Components

Processes actually used in carrying out tasks, such as encoding, inductive reasoning, remembering

CATTELL
=> fluid abilities
innate factors rather than based on experience

Knowledge Aquisition Components

Processes used in acquiring new information, such as separating important from unimportant information (selective encoding), relating items of information (selective combination), and comparing new information with old (selective comparison)

FIGURE 7.1 Sternberg's information-processing view of intelligence defines *intelligence* as adaptation to the real world (a contextual view). Adaptation is made possible through cognitive processes such as planning and monitoring intellectual activity (metacomponents), actually carrying out cognitive activity (performance components), and learning (knowledge-acquisition components).

Summary

In summary, there are three separate views of intelligence. The psychometric view looks at intelligence as a phenomenon that is evident in the individual's performance on tasks assumed to require intelligent behavior and that can therefore be measured by a carefully selected assortment of these tasks. Piaget's view describes what he terms "intelligence in action." He sees intelligence as an ongoing adaptive process involving the interplay of assimilation and accommodation and resulting in the gradual development of cognitive structure. And the information-processing view is concerned with the cognitive processes that underlie intelligent behavior.

Current approaches to intelligence have two things in common: They stress processes more than products, and they recognize the diversity of skills and capabilities that compose intelligence. Thus, Gardner and Hatch describe seven separate and presumably relatively independent intelligences—although they do admit that research might discover these to be more closely related than the theory suggests (Gardner & Hatch, 1989). And Sternberg presents a contextualist definition of *intelligence* (intelligent behavior is behavior that is adaptive in a particular context) and argues that intelligence consists of three components: Metacomponents have to do with metacognition (planning, organizing, monitoring, and selecting processing strategies), performance components are processes that are actually used in carrying out a task (encoding, inductive reasoning, and so on), and knowledge-acquisition components have to do with acquiring new information (separating the important from the unimportant, relating items of new information, and comparing new information with old knowledge).

From the teacher's point of view, intelligence is an important concept, both to the extent that it relates to school achievement and to the extent that it may sometimes require teachers to modify their instructional strategies. And from a practical point of view, teachers will most often obtain evidence of intelligence from the actual performance of their students and somewhat less often from more formal measures of intelligence.

The Concept of Correlation

In fact, good teachers are sometimes remarkably good at estimating the IQs of their students without measuring them. The correlation between teachers' estimates and actual measures is on the order of 0.55, reports Follman (1991). What does that mean?

Correlation is a frequently used term that is not always clearly understood. Two or more **variables** (properties that can vary) correlate if there is some correspondence between them. Size of shoe correlates with size of sock, income correlates with standard of living, size of house correlates with number of windows, and drunkenness correlates with alcohol consumption. These are all examples of **positive correlation**: As one variable increases, so does its correlate. The inverse relationship, labeled **negative correlation**, can also hold: Number of wild animals correlates with number of people, amount of pollutants in water correlates with number of fish, and sobriety correlates with alcohol consumption. In each of these cases, as one variable increases, the other decreases; therefore, each is an example of negative correlation.

The index (or coefficient) of correlation most often used ranges in value from −1.00 to +1.00. Each extreme indicates perfect correlation, whereas zero indicates complete lack of relatedness (see Figure 7.2). The symbol used for a correlation coefficient is usually r. A correlation of 0.55, as Follman (1991) found, between IQ scores and teachers' estimates of intelligence means that there is a relatively high probability that if a teacher estimates a student's IQ as being high (or low), testing will reveal that it is high (or low).

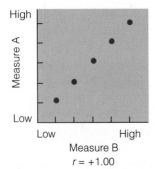
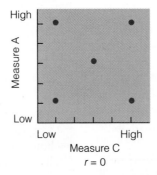
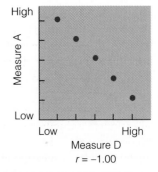

FIGURE 7.2 Representations of correlation (r), which indicate the extent to which two measures tend to vary together. The *direction* of the relationship (positive or negative) is shown by the *sign* of the correlation coefficient (plus or minus). The *strength* of the relationship is indicated by the *magnitude* of the correlation coefficient: The closer r is to ± 1, the stronger the observed relationship; the closer it is to 0, the weaker the relationship. In this example, scores on Measure A correlate perfectly with scores on Measures B and D and not at all with scores on Measure C.

It is important not to make an inference of causality solely on the basis of correlation. Even though any two variables that vary together correlate, variation in one does not necessarily *cause* the other to vary. It is true, for example, that there is a high positive correlation between the number of liquor outlets in urban areas and the number of churches in those same areas. However, some people would prefer to think that one does not cause the other.

Intelligence and Achievement

One assumption underlying the construction of most intelligence tests is that intelligence is related to successful performance of school tasks. It is not surprising, therefore, that these tests correlate relatively highly with measures of school achievement. In fact, intelligence tests and achievement tests both measure much the same sorts of things—that is, both measure the effects of previous learning (achievement), and both typically are highly verbal. The principal differences between the two are that intelligence tests sample from a wider range of behaviors and (to some degree) emphasize the ability to apply knowledge and skills to new problems; in contrast, achievement tests tend to be limited to specific content areas or subjects.

Conventional intelligence tests, particularly the kinds of paper-and-pencil group tests that are most commonly used in classrooms, do not measure innate capacity except by remote inference; that is, psychologists sometimes make the inference that those who do well on these tests have higher innate capacity for learning than those who do less well. In fact, however, what the tests actually provide is a measure of the learning experiences that subjects have had, as well as a crude measure of how much they have profited from these experiences. Vygotsky (1986) and Feuerstein (1979) both argue that in order to measure learning potential, subjects must be placed in sit-

"If his I.Q. is based on guessing the right answers, perhaps we could assume he'll go through life being a remarkably successful guesser."

uations in which they must learn rather than in situations in which their past learning is tapped—hence, the use of hints and clues in Feuerstein's measurement of aptitude (the LPAD, described in Chapter 5).

In view of the close relationship between what achievement tests and intelligence tests measure, it is not surprising that the correlation between the two ranges from 0.30 to 0.80 over a large number of studies (see Barrett & Depinet, 1991). It would appear, then, that knowledge of a student's score on an intelligence test may be of considerable value to a teacher. Unfortunately, as is pointed out later in this chapter, intelligence test scores are not usually very valuable in predicting how a specific individual will perform. Their results are notably unreliable: Scores fluctuate widely for the same individual from one test to another, and for any individual they may not accurately reflect future or past performance. However, they can be of considerable value in predicting how well *groups* of students are likely to do.

Accordingly, they are often used for grouping students for instruction and counseling purposes. Keep in mind, however, that intelligence is only one factor that correlates with school success. Previous success is an even better predictor of future success.

Myths Concerning IQ

Teachers who make use of intelligence tests should be aware of their limitations and of the myths that frequently surround the concept of **intelligence quotient** (**IQ**).

Misconception 1. IQ is a fixed, magical, mysterious, and constant something possessed in greater or lesser amounts by everyone. This myth is evident in the question "What's your IQ?" or the expression "My IQ is . . ." In fact, the numerical index of intelligence known as the IQ is simply a score obtained by an individual in a specific testing situation and on a specific "intelligence" test. Intelligence tests have (a sometimes disputable) **validity**. A test is valid to the extent that it measures what it claims to measure; hence, an intelligence test is valid if it measures intelligence and nothing else. In addition, none has perfect **reliability**. (See Chapter 13 for a discussion of reliability and validity.) The accuracy (reliability) with which intelligence tests measure whatever it is that they do in fact measure varies considerably. This variation, technically known as the "error of measurement," is such that any teacher looking at a specific intelligence quotient should reason: "This score of 130 means that this student probably has a measured IQ that ranges somewhere between 120 and 140."

Also, research increasingly points to the fact that measured IQ is *not* fixed. True, there is a substantial correlation between measures of intelligence taken after early childhood and those obtained later. Bloom (1964) reports correlations as high as about 0.80 between measures at age 5 and measures at age 17—and even higher correlations for measures obtained after age 8 and those in early adulthood. And Gustafsson and Undheim

(1992) found high stability of factors that underly measured intelligence. But there is mounting evidence that interaction with new technologies (such as computers or even calculators) is *increasing* measured intelligence (Salomon, Perkins, & Globerson, 1991). And there is also striking evidence that schooling increases intelligence. In Husén and Tuijnman's words, "Child IQ has an effect on schooling outcomes [and] also schooling per se has a substantial effect on IQ test scores" (1991, p. 22). The effect may be even more evident with the implementation of new cognitive strategies curricula that aim to develop cognitive competence (see Chapter 5).

Misconception 2. Intelligence tests measure all the important things. In fact, most intelligence tests measure relatively limited kinds of abilities—typically, the ability to work with abstract ideas and symbols. They seldom tap interpersonal skills, athletic ability, creativity, and a variety of other desirable human attributes. As Weinberg (1989) notes, they do not reveal many important things about human cognition. For example, most measures of intelligence do not tell us anything about social intelligence, motivation, adaptive skills, or emotion.

Misconception 3. Intelligence tests are impersonal, impartial, and fair. Not so. Many intelligence tests are culturally biased; that is, they tend to favor children whose backgrounds are similar to that of the sample that was used as the norm for the test. In North America that sample has usually consisted of white, middle-class children, which explains why many intelligence tests are unfair for a variety of minority groups. However, the most recent revisions of such tests as the Stanford-Binet and the Wechsler have expanded their standardization samples to include minority groups in a representative way. Accordingly, they are now fairer to minorities.

A number of other tests—none of them widely used in practice, though some are used more extensively in research—attempt to minimize cultural bias. Such tests, sometimes labeled

That intelligence tests measure all the important things is one of our common myths. In fact, most intelligence tests measure relatively limited kinds of abilities—typically the ability to work with abstract ideas and symbols. An intelligence test would tell us very little about this girl's ability to create something with such an uncanny resemblance to Mr. Su Yee, her neighbor. Nor would they tell us much about her interpersonal skills, her athletic ability, or a wide variety of her other important characteristics.

"culture-fair," or, more accurately, "culture-reduced," are typically nonverbal. They attempt to tap intellectual functions through problems involving pictures or abstract designs (for example, the Ravens Progressive Matrices Test). One important approach to overcoming some of the cultural biases in testing is Mercer's **System of Multicultural Pluralistic Assessment** (**SOMPA**, 1979; Mercer & Lewis, 1978), which is described later in this chapter.

True. IQ is related to success, both in school and in life—although a number of psychologists have argued to the contrary. For example, Thorndike and Hagen (1977) and Cohen (1972) point out that although the correlation between intelligence test scores and school achievement is substantial,

previous achievement correlates even more highly with future achievement than does IQ. And McClelland (1973) argues strongly that intelligence test scores bear little relationship to success in life or in careers. But, following a detailed review of the research, Barrett and Depinet conclude, "The evidence from these varied scientific studies leads again and again to the same conclusion: Intelligence and aptitude tests are positively related to job performance" (1991, p. 1016).

INTELLIGENCE TESTS

A wide variety of intelligence tests are available, most of which yield a score referred to as the *IQ*. The average IQ of a randomly selected group of people on most tests is about 100. Approximately

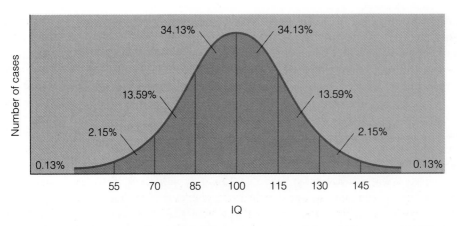

FIGURE 7.3 A normal curve depicting the theoretical distribution of IQ scores among humans. (Average score is 100; 68.26 percent of the population score between 85 and 115; only 2.28 percent score either above 130 or below 70.) Actual scores for a population may vary somewhat from this theoretical distribution.

two-thirds of the population score between 85 and 115. About 11 percent score above 120, and 1.6 percent score above 140. Figure 7.3 depicts the distribution of measured intelligence in a normal population.

There are two general types of intelligence tests: group and individual. The former are administered simultaneously to a group of test subjects; the latter require individual administration. Typically, **group tests** are paper-and-pencil tests. There are many more of them than there are individual tests, probably because group tests are inexpensive and widely used. Unfortunately, their validity and reliability are often poor. **Individual tests,** in contrast, are much more expensive in terms of equipment and administrative time. The scores they yield are sometimes more reliable, however, and they often provide greater insight into intellectual processes. They are particularly valuable in diagnosing specific learning problems in children. It is relatively rare, for example, to find school systems that base decisions to put students in "special" classrooms or programs simply on a group assessment. Typically, an individual assessment is required after initial screening with

a group measure, partly to determine whether the test has been fair to the student.

Group tests can usually be administered and scored by any reasonably competent classroom teacher. However, the administration of individual tests with few exceptions requires a great deal of training and skill. Brief descriptions of some of the most commonly used individual and group tests are given here. For more information, consult *Tests in Print* (Mitchell, 1983).

Individual Intelligence Tests

Individual intelligence tests, as we saw, are administered to a single student at one time, usually by a trained examiner.

Peabody Picture Vocabulary Test–Revised (PPVT–R). This is among the most easily administered and scored individual intelligence tests. It is an untimed test, usually requiring fifteen minutes or less per subject. It consists simply of having the subject point to the one picture out of four that represents a word that has been read by the examiner. There are two forms of the test (L and M), each consisting of 175 words (plates) arranged from easiest to most difficult. After six consecutive incorrect answers, the test is discontinued. An intelligence score can then be computed on the basis of the subject's age and the level of the last correct response.

Revised Stanford-Binet. The Stanford-Binet is among the best-known and most widely used individual measures of intelligence. A relatively high degree of training and competence is required to administer it. It consists of a wide variety of different tests graded in difficulty so as to correspond to various age levels. It yields a score that can be converted to an IQ. A recent revision of the Stanford-Binet (4th ed., Thorndike, Hagen, & Sattler, 1985) yields scores in four separate areas: verbal reasoning, quantitative reasoning, abstract/visual reasoning, and short-term memory. It also provides a composite score that is described as a measure of "adaptive ability" and is interpreted in much the same way as an IQ.

Wechsler Intelligence Scale for Children (3rd. Ed.) (WISC-III). This individual test is similar to the Stanford-Binet, but it is somewhat easier to administer. It also yields scores on a number of specific tests (for example, vocabulary, block design, digit span, comprehension) and two major "intelligence" scores—one verbal and one performance. These can be combined to yield what is referred to as a "full-scale IQ score." There is an adult version of this test as well as a preschool version. Various subtests of the WISC-III are described in Table 7.2.

System of Multicultural Pluralistic Assessment (SOMPA). In several instances in this chapter, the point is made that many intelligence tests are unfair to those from ethnic and social groups outside the white middle-class majority. Indeed, several court decisions in the United States have recognized this fact. For example, in *Diana v. California State Board of Education*, twelve Mexican-American children claimed that they had been improperly placed in classes for the mentally re-

tarded on the basis of testing that was conducted in a language other than their native one. Specifically, these children had been administered standard English versions of the Wechsler scales and of the Stanford-Binet. The judgment—in favor of the plaintiffs—ordered that the children be retested by someone fluent in Spanish, that greater emphasis be placed on nonverbal parts of the tests, and that new tests be developed for Spanish-speaking children.

This and a number of related court cases have had several effects on testing in schools. One not entirely beneficial effect has been to discourage the use of tests. It is probably a lot better to rely on tests, however biased they might be, than to rely on the judgments of teachers and other professionals who are not allowed the assistance of test results. Biases in tests are fixed and therefore perhaps detectable and measurable; human biases are no less real, but they are more subtle—and therefore harder to detect and control.

Another effect of these court cases has been to stimulate the development of new tests and new approaches to testing. Among these is Mercer's SOMPA (System of Multicultural Pluralistic Assessment: Mercer, 1979; Mercer & Lewis, 1978, 1979). The SOMPA consists of a battery of ten separate individual measures. These measures reflect assessments in three areas, which Mercer refers to as "models": the medical model, the social system model, and the pluralistic model. Measures relating to the medical model attempt to determine whether the child is biologically normal. These measures include tests of visual and auditory acuity, measures of physical dexterity and motor coordination, and indexes of health and physical development. Measures relating to the social system model are intended to determine whether the child is socially "normal"—that is, whether the child behaves in expected ways in social situations. The WISC-III and a test labeled the Adaptive Behavior Inventory for Children (ABIC) are used to measure functioning in the social system. Mercer's assumption is that children who fall in the bottom 3 percent of the

TABLE 7.2 The Wechsler Intelligence Scale for Children (WISC-III)

VERBAL SCALE

1. *General information.* Questions relating to information most children have the opportunity to acquire (M*)

2. *General comprehension.* Questions designed to assess child's understanding of why certain things are done as they are (M)

3. *Arithmetic.* Oral arithmetic problems (M)

4. *Similarities.* Child indicates how certain things are alike. (M)

5. *Vocabulary.* Child gives meaning of words of increasing difficulty. (M)

6. *Digit span.* Child repeats orally presented sequence of numbers, in order and reversed. (S*)

PERFORMANCE SCALE

1. *Picture completion.* Child indicates what is missing from pictures. (M)

2. *Picture arrangement.* Child must arrange series of pictures to tell a story. (M)

3. *Block design.* Child is required to copy a design with colored blocks exactly. (M)

4. *Object assembly.* Subjects must assemble puzzles. (M)

5. *Coding.* Child follows a key to pair symbols with digits. (M)

6. *Mazes.* Child traces way out of mazes with a pencil. (S)

7. *Symbol Search.* Child performs symbol location task that measures mental processing speed and visual search skills. (S)

*(M) Mandatory
 (S) Supplementary

WISC-III will not behave as expected in school. In her terms, their school functioning levels will be abnormally low.

The pluralistic model is of particular interest because it considers the child's cultural and social background in attempting to determine the probability of his or her success in school. The principal measure used here is the WISC-III, administered in the usual fashion but with different standards. Specifically, Mercer administered the WISC-III to a California standardization sample consisting of 456 African-Americans, 520 Hispanic-Americans, and 604 whites. As expected, Hispanics and African-Americans scored significantly lower than the white groups—91.9 and 88.4 were the average full-scale IQs for Hispanics and blacks, respectively, compared with 103.1 for the whites. Combining these norms with information relating to the child's family (family size, family income, family structure, and socioeconomic status), Mercer developed a formula for predicting the likelihood of the child's success in school. This prediction, labeled an "estimated learning potential (ELP) score," is pluralistic in that it attempts to take into account social and ethnic background as well as measured potential.

Sattler (1982) has criticized the SOMPA on the grounds that the California sample is not nationally representative, there is insufficient evidence that predictions based on the SOMPA are more valid than those based solely on the WISC-III, and there is some question about the wisdom of using a medical model in making educational decisions.

There is recent evidence, however, that the SOMPA may be effective for some important purposes. For example, Matthew, Golin, Moore, and Baker (1992) used the SOMPA to identify a group of African-American children as gifted; none of these children had been so identified using the usual unadjusted measures. Yet on various measures of cognitive processes, they performed as well as groups of gifted children identified in the usual manner. And after they had been in a gifted program for seven months, there were no significant differences between the group identified using the SOMPA approach and other students.

Group Intelligence Tests

Group tests of intelligence are usually paper-and-pencil tests that can be administered to a large group at one time. Only a few examples of the hundreds of tests available are described briefly here.

Draw a Person Test. This interesting measure of intelligence, developed by Goodenough (1926) and later revised by Harris (1963) and Naglieri (1988), is based on the assumption that children's drawings reflect their conceptual sophistication. The child is simply asked to draw the best person possible; no time limit is imposed (see Figure 7.4). Drawings are scored primarily on the basis of detail and accuracy, according to a well-defined set of criteria. Tables for converting raw scores to IQ scores are provided.

Cognitive Abilities Test (CogAT). This is a widely used, multilevel, paper-and-pencil test suitable for grades 3 through 13. It yields three scores—verbal, quantitative, and nonverbal—as well as a composite IQ score. The test includes tables for converting individual scores to percentile scores based on the performance of other children at the same grade level. (A percentile indicates the percentage of cases that fall at or below a given point. For example, a student who scores at the seventy-fifth percentile has performed as well or better than 75 percent of students in the same grade.)

Otis-Lennon School Ability Test. A test designed to assess school-related ability, the Otis-Lennon consists of five levels of items suitable for grades 1 through 12. Items are intermingled (for example, vocabulary, reasoning, numerical, and other items are in mixed order) and are presented in order of increasing difficulty. The test yields a sin-

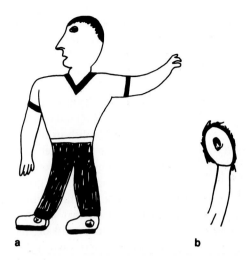

a   **b**

FIGURE 7.4 Two examples of the Goodenough-Harris Drawing Test. Both subjects were boys aged $10^{3}/_{4}$ years. The raw scores and IQ equivalents, respectively, for the drawings are (a) 41 and 110; (b) 4 and 54. The child who drew b also had a low Stanford-Binet IQ score. From the Goodenough-Harris Drawing Test. Copyright © 1963 by Harcourt Brace & Company. Reproduced by permission. All rights reserved.

gle standardized score labeled a "school ability index" (SAI).

Uses of Intelligence Tests

Although still used in many school systems, intelligence tests are no longer routinely administered to all students everywhere. This is partly because of a strong antitest movement among parents and others and partly because of a growing recognition of the potential weaknesses and abuses of testing.

Chief among the purposes for which intelligence tests are used are counseling, career guidance, class placement, and diagnosis for remedial or enrichment purposes. There is little doubt that when skillfully administered and intelligently interpreted, they can be of considerable value for any and all of these purposes. Unfortunately, they are not always skillfully administered and intelligently interpreted.

A number of important cautions should be kept in mind when interpreting the results of intelligence tests, most of them related to the misconceptions described earlier. For example, teachers need to remember that the validity and reliability of all measures of intelligence are less than perfect. If Johnny's measured IQ today is 120 and Frank's is 115, it would be foolish in the extreme to conclude that Johnny is more intelligent than Frank and that he should therefore be granted the privilege of studying with the group called the "Orioles" rather than with the "White-Breasted Kites." It might well be that Johnny's measured IQ next month would be 110 or that Frank's measured IQ on another test today would be 130. It is, in fact, precisely the relative imprecision of measured IQ that has served to justify the secrecy that sometimes surrounds the IQ. Unfortunately, the concept of IQ is not at all well understood by parents; perhaps even more unfortunate, it is often not well understood by educators.

Teachers need to keep in mind, too, that intelligence is not a fixed and unchanging characteristic. As we saw, formal schooling and continued interaction with things like television sets and computers *increase* intelligence.

What these cautions mean is that a teacher's decisions based on test results should be tentative and subject to continual review, that students should not be labeled on the basis of limited and changing samplings of their behavior, and that, in short, good sense should prevail here as it should elsewhere.

DETERMINANTS OF INTELLIGENCE

Intelligence doesn't just happen; it has a cause. And the causes of intelligence are also the causes of stupidity because one is the absence of the other. The assumption that human characteristics result from the interplay of heredity and environment is discussed in Chapter 2 (also see the box, "Experience and Intelligence: A Debate," on pages 196–197). As we see there, the debate has by no

"We realize you do better on your I.Q. tests than you do in anything else, but you just cannot major in I.Q."

means ended, although a great deal of evidence has been gathered on both sides. Heredity versus environment is clearly no longer an important question. More important questions have to do with *how* individuals and environments interact during development, with the processes that account for intellectual change, and with how deficits can be remedied and gifts fostered.

The Rubber-Band Hypothesis

One of the better analogies advanced to describe the interaction of heredity and environment is Stern's rubber-band hypothesis. It compares innate potential for intellectual development to a rubber band. Intelligence at any time is reflected by the length of the band. Obviously, a short piece (poorer genetic background) can be stretched; with a great deal of effort it can be stretched a long way. The forces that exert the pull on the band, or that fail to, are environmental. Hence, genetic and environmental forces interact in such a way that less environmental stimulation may be required for average development if genetic

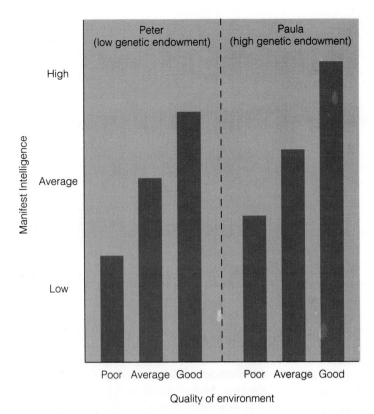

FIGURE 7.5 The Stern hypothesis: Individuals with different inherited potentials for intellectual development (genetic endowment) can manifest below-average, average, or above-average intelligence as a function of environmental forces.

endowment is high. The reverse is also true. One of the functions of schools is to stretch rubber bands (see Figure 7.5).

The Effect of Families

Some evidence suggests that family size and birth order may influence manifested intelligence of children. More than a century ago, for example, Galton (1869) observed a preponderance of first-born children among the great scientists that Britain had produced. Since then, many studies have revealed that firstborn and only children (who are necessarily also firstborn) speak more articulately and at a younger age than later-born

children (Koch, 1955), score higher on measures of intellectual performance, have a higher need for achievement (Altus, 1967), perform better academically (Zajonc, 1976), and are more likely to attend college and to achieve eminence (Velandia, Grandon, & Page, 1978).

A closer examination of birth-order data suggests, however, that the contribution of birth order to such things as academic achievement or intelligence is negligible at best; at worst, birth order may make no contribution whatsoever. Following a massive investigation of nine thousand high school graduates and their brothers and sisters (more than thirty-thousand subjects), Hauser

experience and intelligence: a debate

The most important question from an educator's point of view is whether the child's experiences can increase intelligence. A sample of the research relevant to this question, and relevant to the general nature-nurture question, is summarized here in the form of an imaginary debate between John Watson (a champion of environmentalism) and Francis Galton (who believed that intelligence is entirely inherited). The debate is replete with glaring anachronisms. In order to know all that they claim to know, Galton and Watson would both have to be older than 100.

Galton: My dear Watson, if you will simply open your mind to the problem, I can demonstrate for you beyond any doubt that heredity is the most powerful factor in development. As I said in Eighteen Sixty-Nine, "I have no patience with the hypothesis occasionally expressed, and often implied, especially in tales written to teach children to be good, that babies are born pretty much alike. . . ."

Watson: Give me a dozen . . .

Galton: You have said that before. Consider, if you will, the numerous twins studies that have been performed. As you know, identical twins are genetically exactly alike, whereas fraternal twins are as dissimilar as any two siblings. Burt's famous Nineteen Fifty-Eight study shows that the intelligence test scores of identical twins, whether reared together or apart, display considerably higher correlation than the scores of fraternal twins. I have no doubt that if we had more reliable measures of intelligence, the correlations would be higher still. Bloom summarized this study — on page sixty-nine in his Nineteen Fifty-Four book—along with four others. They all show the same thing.

Watson: Whoa now! That is a highly prejudiced interpretation. If you look at the Nineteen Thirty-Seven Newman, Freeman, and Holzinger study—and that one too is in Bloom's summary—if you look at that study, you'll see just where environment comes in. Why do you suppose it is that the correlation for twins reared together is always considerably higher than for twins reared apart? Ha! What do you say to that?

Galton: I say that studies involving the measurement of intelligence in people are highly suspect. Now, take rats, for example.

Watson: That's irrelevant!

Galton: It is not! Now you just hold on and listen here for a minute. In Nineteen Forty, R. C. Tryon did a fascinating study, and it proves you wrong. Do you know it?

Watson: You mean Tryon's study?

Galton: Yes.

Watson: No.

Galton: I thought not. You don't read much, do you? You're just a popularizer. What Tryon did was take one hundred forty-two rats and run them through a seventeen-unit maze nineteen times. The brightest rat made, I forget . . . about twenty errors [actually, he made fourteen] and the dullest made two hundred errors. [Again Galton is wrong. The dullest rat made 174 errors.] The brightest rats were then bred with each other, and the dull males were given dull females. That usually happens to people, too. Heh! Heh! Well, after repeating the same procedure for only eight

and Sewell (1985) found that birth order made absolutely no difference. They did find, however, that size of "sibship" (number of brothers and sisters) has a negative effect on schooling. In other words, the larger the family, the more likely that academic achievement will be lower.

The relationship between family size and academic achievement, as well as that between family size and performance on intelligence tests, has been corroborated in a number of studies. In an generations, a remarkable thing began to happen. The dullest rats in the bright group consistently made fewer errors than the brightest rats in the dull group. In other words, the brightest rats in the dull group were duller than the dullest rats in the bright group—or the dullest rats in the bright group were . . . you know. Imagine what we could do with people. John Humphrey Noyes would have done it if the American government hadn't outlawed polygamy. [Noyes set up a religious, communal, free-love group in Oneida, New York, in the late nineteenth century. He practiced selective breeding with the aim of producing a super race but had to disband the group when polygamy was outlawed in the 1880s.]

Watson: So that's the kind of ridiculous evidence you base your eugenic movement on. [*Eugenics* is the term for the practice of selective breeding.] Let me tell you about a rat study, seeing as you're the one who brought it up. Hebb in Nineteen Forty-Seven and Krech, Rosenzweig, and Bennett—in Nineteen Sixty, 'Sixty-Two, and 'Sixty-Six—

provide evidence that randomly selected rats can be significantly affected by environment. In the first case, Hebb showed in Nineteen Forty-Seven that rats raised as pets did better than laboratory rats on maze tests. Krech, Rosenzweig, and Bennett, in Nineteen Sixty-Two, even changed the brain chemistry of rats by enriching their environments. And if you don't think that's enough evidence, consider Heyns's Nineteen Sixty-Seven work in South Africa. He's been affecting the intelligence of babies by using vacuum cleaners.

Galton: Whoa, there, whoa! Vacuum cleaners! You're going a little far.

Watson: That's what you think. It was reported in *Woman's Own* on February Fourth, Nineteen Sixty-Seven.

Galton: You read *Woman's Own?*

Watson: My wife does. Anyway, what Heyns did was set up a decompression unit using a vacuum cleaner motor. He put this plastic bubblelike thing over the woman's abdomen and sucked the air out. It relieves all kinds of aches

and pains and makes babies brighter, too.

Galton: It sounds like a gimmick to me. Jensen reviewed the research in Nineteen Sixty-Eight, and he concluded genes determine intelligence.

Watson: Well, the optimistic point of view for a teacher to have is certainly mine. You can't do anything about genetics, but you can change the environment . . . and that's what schools should be doing. That's what acceleration is and television for kids and books and programs for gifted kids . . .

Galton: Don't get carried away, Watson. Your point of view might be more optimistic, but it's less accurate. I'm a scientist, not a philosopher.

The argument ends with Watson's wife calling him in to wash dishes.

But the debate continues, although most scientists now believe that both heredity and environment are important, that their relative influences cannot easily be separated, and that the important question in any case is not what the effects of these factors might be but how they affect intelligence (Anastasi, 1958).

attempt to explain these relationships, Zajonc (1975, 1976, 1986) and Zajonc and Markus (1975) suggest that one important influence on intellectual development is the intellectual climate of the home. Furthermore, they provide a

simple formula, based on the **confluence model**, for determining the approximate intellectual climate of a home.

According to this model, each family member is assigned a value related to age: Parents are worth

30 points each; newborn infants, zero; and all other children, values that range from zero to 30. The index of intellectual climate is then calculated by averaging values assigned to each individual in the family. For example, a firstborn child is born into an intellectual climate valued at 30 plus 30 (when there are 2 parents) plus zero (for the infant), divided by 3 (this equals 20, for those whose calculators are not functioning). A child born later or born into a large family in which there are many young children would be born into a family with a lower index of intellectual climate. The Zajonc-Markus model predicts, simply, that measured intelligence for large groups will be related to the intellectual climate index. And there is, in fact, some evidence that this is the case (see, for example, Grotevant, Scarr, & Weinberg, 1977).

Do these observations support the notion that family size and birth order are among the important influences on intelligence? Zajonc and Markus argue yes (1975); however, more recent analyses suggest that they are only partly correct.

Most evidence does not question the conclusion that family size correlates inversely with measured intelligence (larger families equal lower intelligence), although this correlation is not always very high or very general. What is often questioned, however, is whether the most important variable is family size. In one of several large-scale and systematic investigations of this type, Page and Grandon (1979) found pretty much the same correlations that Zajonc and Markus and others had previously reported. But they also found that when the variables of social class and race were included, correlations of these factors with manifested intelligence were even more significant than that of family size. Put more simply, in most studies that found a high correlation of family size, birth order, and intelligence, researchers did not consider the fact that large families tend to be more common in lower social classes, in certain ethnic minorities, and among those who are less well educated. And perhaps the "intellectual climate" in large families is more a function of ethnic, social, and educational variables than of family size per se.

The most reasonable conclusion at this point is probably that many variables are influential in determining intellectual development. Among the important variables are genetic forces (over which we have relatively little control) and such environmental variables as formal schooling and interactions among children and their parents and siblings, as well as between children and technological aspects of society.

All of which is far from simple.

Finally, it should always be kept in mind that the grand conclusions of social science are most often based on the average performance of large groups of individuals. Invariably, within these groups are many individuals whose behavior contradicts the conclusion at every turn. In other words, there are geniuses among large families and among all social and ethnic groups, even as there are fools, morons, and idiots everywhere.[*]

CREATIVITY

A great deal of attention has been devoted to the subject of creativity in the past several decades, particularly following the work of J. P. Guilford (1950, 1959, 1962). However, the central question in creativity research and speculation—what is creativity?—remains largely unsolved. Few people agree on an answer.

While conversing with George Bernard Shaw, his biographer, Stephen Winsten, alluded to the proverbial hairsbreadth that separates genius from madness: "The matter-of-fact man prefers to think of the creative man as defective, or at least akin to madness." To which Shaw replied, "Most of them are, most of them are. I am probably the only sane exception" (1949, p. 103).

Although we no longer fear the creative person as openly as we might once have, uneasiness and uncertainty remain. As Cross, Coleman, and Terhaar-Yonkers (1991) put it, creativity is still

[*]PPC: Is the bear a cynic? Does he mean this?
Author: Older bears are often cynical.

stigmatized in our society, and those who are exceptional are often subjected to tremendous pressure to conform—to behave like those who are more ordinary.

Are creative people nonconformists, eccentrics, radicals, and fools—or are they ordinary people? The answer is probably that there are some of both, but that there really is no mystical or magical quality about creativity. Like intelligence, it is a quality of humans and of human behavior—a quality possessed by everyone. Just as low intelligence is stupidity, so low creativity is ordinariness. There are few geniuses as identified by tests of intelligence; there are also few very highly creative people.

Problems in Defining Creativity

Creativity is not easily defined. The following are three of many definitions:

1. Creativity involves fluency, flexibility, and originality (Guilford, 1959).

2. Creativity is "the forming of associative elements into new combinations which either meet specified requirements or are in some ways useful. The more mutually remote the elements of the new combination, the more creative the process of solution" (Mednick, 1962, p. 221).

3. Creativity results in "a novel work that is accepted as tenable or useful or satisfying by a significant group of others at some point in time" (Stein, in Parnes and Harding [eds.], 1962, p. 86).

Consider the three examples presented in the cases of Réné Choumard, Joseph Lalonde, and Rollie Wozny on page 198. Each of these people is creative by one definition but not the others. Réné is creative according to Guilford. His behavior is original, and he shows remarkable verbal fluency and flexibility. However, he is not creative according to Mednick and Stein. Joseph, in contrast, meets Mednick's criteria for creativity—highly remote associations satisfying his own

specifications. We might even assume that he is original, fluent, and flexible. But he does not produce anything "tenable or useful or satisfying." But Rollie Wozny, the scientist, does. Yet his behavior is not original; rather, it is clumsy—and he makes no remote associations whatsoever.

This discussion highlights the confusion that makes defining and assessing creativity so difficult. The problem is partly resolved by accepting that *creativity* is a global term and that it does not necessarily represent only one event or quality. If we distinguish among the creative *process*, the creative *product*, and the creative *person*, many of the contradictions implicit in earlier formulations disappear. Réné is a creative person who doesn't produce anything; Joseph uses a creative process but also produces nothing creative; the scientist neither is creative nor uses a creative process, but he produces something valuable.

These distinctions, although useful, solve only part of the problem because they are not reflected in current attempts to measure creativity. The inference continues to be made, at least implicitly, that creative personalities and processes can be identified and assessed on the basis of products that are judged to be creative.

How to Identify the Gifted

From an educational point of view, it's important to be able to define *creativity* and *giftedness* so that we can identify and select students for special programs. Accordingly, many school systems lump together various categories such as "creative," "talented," and "gifted" under a single label (such as "talented and gifted" or simply "gifted") and provide specific criteria for identifying students who belong to this group. The most often used criterion is, not surprisingly, measured intelligence expressed in the form of an IQ—and the most common cutoff is 130; that is, all students whose measured IQ is 130 or more would qualify as gifted (Humphreys, 1985). (Programs for the gifted are reviewed in the next chapter.)

A number of problems are associated with defining creativity or giftedness solely (or even primarily) in terms of intelligence (Hoge, 1988). In the first place, as is shown in a later section, independent measures of creativity do not correlate at all well with measured intelligence. In the second place, given the rather unimpressive validity and reliability of our intelligence tests, their use for selecting students for special programs is often unfair. On the other side of the coin, these tests may be considerably fairer than teachers who are forced to rely only on their intuitive judgments.

One interesting approach to defining creativity and giftedness is taken by Gardner (1983), who, as we saw earlier in this chapter, speaks of seven largely unrelated kinds of intelligence. He believes that creativity (or giftedness) can occur in any one of these domains and that it represents the highest level of functioning in each. Thus, it is possible to be highly gifted in one aspect but not in any other—as may be evident among the musi-cally or the scientifically gifted. Wallach (1985) has a similar point of view, arguing that creativity can be manifested in excellence in any specific domain.

The argument that creativity is largely domain specific is not shared by all researchers. Many believe that although giftedness is often manifested in one domain rather than another, certain general underlying qualities make it possible for the creative person to be described as generally creative. And perhaps it is possible to measure these qualities.

Measuring Creativity

One of the simplest (and most unreliable) ways of identifying creative talent is to have teachers rate students. Gallagher (1960) cites research indicating that teachers miss approximately 20 percent of the most highly creative students. As Shaklee (1992) points out, teachers often don't recognize giftedness in students who are not the higher-achieving school or class leaders. Furthermore, says Shaklee, most schools confine children to a lock-step curriculum that is not likely to foster the development of giftedness or to permit its recognition.

Another method for identifying creativity is to use one of several tests available for that purpose. Among the most common of these are tests first proposed by Guilford (1950) and developed by Torrance (1966, 1974: Torrance Tests of Creative Thinking). These tests are based on the assumption that creative ability comprises several separate factors, among which are fluency, flexibility, and originality. Tasks have been designed that encourage the production of a variety of responses, which can then be scored in terms of these and other factors. One such test is the Unusual Uses Test, in which subjects are asked to think of as many uses as they can for an ordinary object, such as a brick or a nylon stocking. Responses are counted to arrive at an index of fluency. Flexibility is measured by counting the number of shifts among classes of response. For example, a brick might be used for building a house, a planter, a road, and so on. Each response scores for fluency but not for flexibility. A shift from this category of uses to one involving throwing the brick would illustrate flexibility. Originality is scored on the basis of the number of responses that are either statistically rare or are judged unusual by the experimenter. A statistically rare response might be one that occurs less than 5 percent of the time. (See Table 7.3.)

Some more recent tests of creativity try to assess cognitive processes thought to be involved in creative behavior (for example, Urban & Jellen, 1986). However, these are used mainly in research and in the development of theory rather than in school settings where teachers and administrators need to identify the gifted and the talented. As is pointed out in the next chapter, gifted children are most often identified solely on the basis of academic achievement and measured intelligence—in spite of the fact that official criteria for giftedness typically include high aptitude in other areas such as creativity, leadership, psychomotor ability, and visual or performing arts.

THE CONNECTIONS BETWEEN CREATIVITY AND INTELLIGENCE

Because measured intelligence is often used to select gifted children for special programs, it's important to determine the relationship between high intelligence and high creativity.

One of the classic studies in this area is that reported by Getzels and Jackson (1962), who found that creative students were not necessarily the most intelligent—although they often achieved as well in school as those who were more intelligent. Interestingly, however, the highly creative students were not as well liked by the teachers.

Unfortunately, findings from the Getzels and Jackson study cannot easily be generalized. The mean IQ in the school from which the subjects were chosen was an astounding 132. The mean IQ for the groups described as "high creative, low IQ" was a more-than-respectable 127. With such a limited range in intelligence test scores, it is doubtful that any relationship between creativity and intelligence would be found, even if it existed. Besides, any findings from a study such as this might well apply only to especially intelligent children.

A related study (Wallach & Kogan, 1965) also identified four groups of students classified as high or low on intelligence and creativity, respectively. The purpose of this study was to identify characteristics that might be different among the four groups. Results of the study are summarized in Figure 7.6. They indicate that highly creative but less intelligent students are most frustrated with school and that highly intelligent but less creative students are addicted to school and well liked by their teachers. Keep in mind, however, that these four groups represent extremes of measured intelligence and creativity. The vast majority of students are not extreme. In addition, these general descriptions of school adjustment and

TABLE 7.3 Sample Answers and Scoring Procedure for One Item from a Test of Creativity

Item	How many uses can you think of for a nylon stocking?
Answers	♦ wear on feet
	♥ ♠ wear over face
	♦ wear on hands when it's cold
	♦ ♥ to make rugs
	♦ ♥ make clothes
	♦ ♥ ♠ make upholstery
	♦ ♥ to hang flower pots
	♦ ♥ hang mobiles
	♦ ♥ ♠ make Christmas decorations
	♦ ♥ use as a sling
	♦ ♥ to tie up robbers
	♦ ♥ ♠ cover broken windowpanes
	♦ ♥ ♠ use as ballast in a dirigible
	♦ ♥ make a fishing net
Scoring	♦ Fluency: 14 (total number of different responses)
	♥ Flexibility: 10 (number of shifts from one class to another)
	♠ Originality: 5 (number of responses that were unusual or occurred less than 5 percent of the time in the entire sample)

personality characteristics are just that—general descriptions. Even with groups as highly select as these, there are numerous individual exceptions.

No conclusive statements can yet be made concerning the correlation between creativity and intelligence—although there is a relatively high correlation between *measured* creativity and IQ scores (McCleod & Cropley, 1989). Torrance states, for example, that "if we were to identify children as gifted simply on the basis of intelligence tests, we would eliminate from consideration approximately 70 percent of the most creative" (1962, p. 5).

Another View: Guilford's Model

It seems clear that talents and gifts can manifest themselves in a variety of different areas. So, too, can deficits. Yet many of our theories of intelligence, and our models of mental functioning, fail to take this into account.

One exception is J. P. Guilford's (1959, 1967) model of the intellect. This unusual representation is relevant both to intelligence and creativity. The model is organized around three main aspects of intellectual functioning: operations, products, and content. All abilities, says Guilford, involve a combination of these three aspects of functioning. Because there are 4 different kinds of content, 5 different operations, and 6 different types of products, there are at least 120 distinct human abilities (see Figure 7.7).

The Three Faces of Intellect. Guilford's multifactor theory of intelligence is most easily understood by looking at the three aspects of intellectual functioning:

1. **Operations**. An operation is a major intellectual process. The term includes such activities as knowing, discovering, or being aware (cognition), retrieving from storage (memory), generating multiple responses (divergent thinking),

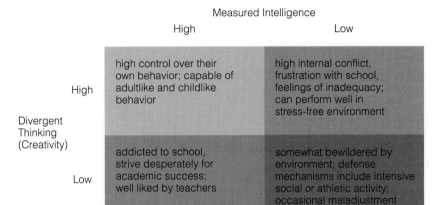

Measured Intelligence

		High	Low
Divergent Thinking (Creativity)	High	high control over their own behavior; capable of adultlike and childlike behavior	high internal conflict, frustration with school, feelings of inadequacy; can perform well in stress-free environment
	Low	addicted to school, strive desperately for academic success; well liked by teachers	somewhat bewildered by environment; defense mechanisms include intensive social or athletic activity; occasional maladjustment

FIGURE 7.6 Characteristics of children identified as high and low on measures of intelligence and of divergent thinking (creativity). Based on studies reported by Wallach and Kogan, 1965.

arriving at a single, accepted solution (convergent thinking), and judging the appropriateness of information or decisions (evaluation).

2. **Content**. An operation is performed upon certain kinds of information. This information, or content, may be figural, symbolic, semantic, or behavioral. Figural content is concrete information, such as images. Symbolic content is information in the form of arbitrary signs, such as numbers or codes. Semantic content is information in the form of word meanings. And behavioral content is nonverbal information involved in human interaction—for example, emotion.

3. **Products**. Applying an operation to content yields a product—the form that information takes once it is processed. Products include single, segregated items of information (units), sets of items grouped by virtue of their common properties (classes), connections between items of information (relations), organizations of information (systems), changes of information (transformations), and extrapolations or predictions from information (implications).

The two operations that have stimulated the most research and interest are convergent and divergent thinking. These are also the two operations most closely related to creativity and intelligence. **Convergent thinking** involves producing one correct solution to a problem; it is a crucial factor in intelligence testing. **Divergent thinking** involves producing multiple solutions or hypotheses; it is central in the creative process. In fact, the phrase "divergent thinking" is often used as a synonym for creative thinking.

Guilford's model, like Gardner's theory of multiple intelligences, is based on the assumption that intelligence is not a single trait but a collection of separate abilities. This viewpoint resolves the apparent contradiction among some of the studies that have examined the relationship between creativity and intelligence. If intelligence is defined in terms of the entire structure, and if creativity involves only some of the 120 abilities described in the model, it is likely that there will be some correlation between the two. At the same time, it is also likely that this correlation will vary from very low to very high, according to the individual's pattern of abilities.

Implications for the Teacher. Guilford's model of the intellect has a number of important implica-

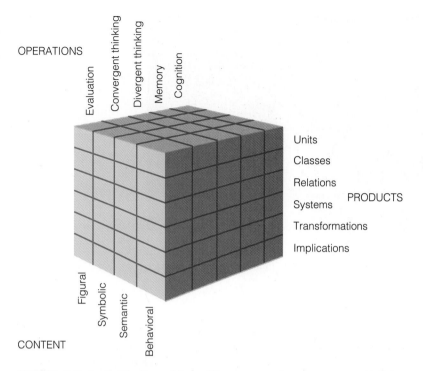

OPERATIONS

Evaluation
Convergent thinking
Divergent thinking
Memory
Cognition

Units
Classes
Relations
Systems   PRODUCTS
Transformations
Implications

Figural
Symbolic
Semantic
Behavioral

CONTENT

FIGURE 7.7 In Guilford's model, intelligence comprises 120 separate abilities, each of which represents a combination of a specific operation, content, and product. From J. P. Guilford, "Three Faces of Intellect," *American Psychologist*, Vol. 14, 1959, pp. 469–479. Copyright 1959 by the American Psychological Association and reproduced by permission.

tions for the teaching/learning process. To begin with, the model draws attention to both the complexity of intellectual processes and the variety of forms in which these processes can be expressed. By so doing, it highlights the crucial role that the instructional process can play in intellectual development. If, for example, teachers always require that students remember content as presented, only memory operations are being emphasized. And if, as is often the case, only semantic content is involved, figural, symbolic, and behavioral content are being overlooked.

In short, consideration of this model makes it apparent that the classroom teacher and the educational process bear considerable responsibility for the intellectual development of students and that this development may well be shortchanged if only the traditional, highly limited operations, products, and content are attended to. Although schools have traditionally fostered the development of a variety of abilities in children—providing repeated practice in psychomotor skills, mathematics, verbal skills, social skills, and so on—teachers have not always systematically attended to the development of some of the more complex abilities, such as those involved in creative thinking (divergent thinking), evaluating, arriving at implications, and so on. Programs designed to foster learning/thinking strategies are an attempt to correct this failure.

It is alarming to note that the school dropout rate for gifted adolescents is often higher than that of the general population (McMann & Oliver, 1988). There are a number of possible rea-

In schools there may be many Beethovens and Mozarts, Picassos and Dalis, Shakespeares and Hemingways whose special talents remain unrecognized and undeveloped. Is another Bobby Fischer here, among these boys?

sons for this, including the frustration that may result when school programs do not permit adequate expression and development of special abilities. In addition, Kanchier (1988) suggests that the expectations that gifted adolescents have of themselves—and that others have for them—may affect some of them negatively.

Current educational practice and beliefs typically insist that identifying and teaching those who have disabilities requires special training. But, it is sad to note, we are strangely ambivalent about what should be done to identify and teach those who are highly gifted.

There is an important distinction to be made between inherent and functional abilities. In our schools, there may be many Raphaels, Da Vincis, Mozarts, and Einsteins unrecognized and undeveloped, disguised as ordinary people, totally unaware of their inherent abilities. Only in the right circumstances and with the right environmental demands will these talents become functional. Perhaps it would help if schools demanded more evaluation, implication, divergent thinking, and so on.

MAIN POINTS

1. There are three basic views of intelligence: the psychometric (based on measurement concepts), the Piagetian (based on child-environment interaction), and the information-processing (based on cognitive processes).

2. Psychometrically, intelligence is seen as an adaptive quality sometimes defined in terms of what intelligence tests measure, or in terms of an underlying general ability (g) that is merely potential or that might be manifested in behavior.

3. Cattell describes fluid abilities (basic, non-verbal, and unaffected by experience) and crystallized abilities (primarily verbal, highly influenced by culture and education). Gardner describes seven unrelated, multiple intelligences.

4. Sternberg's information-processing view of intelligence includes a contextual subtheory (in-telligence is defined in terms of adaptation to a specific environmental context) and a three-component subtheory that looks at meta-components (executive processes involved in selecting cognitive activities, monitoring them, and evaluating their results); performance components (activities actually used in carrying out cognitive tasks); and knowledge-acquisition components (activities involved in acquiring new information).

5. A correlation coefficient is an index of relationship between variables. It is a function of covariation—not of causal relatedness. The most common correlation index (r) varies from -1.00 to $+1.00$.

6. Intelligence tests typically correlate quite well with school achievement. Conventional measures of intelligence do not measure innate capacity so much as the extent to which the individual has profited from past learning experiences. In addition, they are less than perfectly valid (do not always measure only what they purport to measure) or reliable (do not always measure consistently); they typically do not tap a number of important qualities, such as interpersonal skills, creativity, and athletic ability; and many are biased against social and ethnic minorities.

7. Intelligence tests usually yield an IQ score ranging from perhaps 50 to 160 and averaging about 100 in an unselected population. They are ordinarily group (Draw a Person Test, the Cognitive Abilities Test [CogAT], and the Otis-Lennon School Abilities Test) or individual (Peabody Picture Vocabulary Test–R, the revised Stanford-Binet, and the Wechsler scales). Individual tests require trained testers, consume a great deal of time, and are consequently far more expensive, but they are more valid and reliable for important educational decisions.

8. The SOMPA (System of Multicultural Pluralistic Assessment) uses a collection of measures to assess biological and social normality and to derive an estimated learning potential (ELP) score on the basis of WISC-III scores standardized on ethnic minority samples, taking into account important family variables.

9. Both creativity and intelligence appear to be a function of an interaction between heredity and environment. Family size and configuration also play a role, as do ethnic background and social class. None of these factors necessarily causes high or low intelligence; they are merely related to manifested intelligence.

10. The rubber-band hypothesis is an analogy that compares innate potential for learning to a rubber band: It can be stretched by a good environment, but it will shrivel in a poorer environment. In this analogy, the final length of the band (after it has been stretched by experience) reflects measured intelligence.

11. Although birth order and family size have sometimes been associated with intelligence and academic achievement (firstborns and only children are favored), associated social and ethnic factors are most important. The intellectual climate of the home, says Zajonc, is a function of family size and position in the family.

12. Creativity is defined in various, apparently contradictory ways. Much of the contradiction disappears when the creative product, process, and person are considered separately.

13. Creative, talented, and gifted individuals are often identified in terms of performance on measures of intelligence (for example, an IQ of 130 or more). Gardner suggests that creativity is simply the highest level of functioning in any one (or more) of the domains of our multiple intelligences.

14. Creativity can be measured by using teacher or pupil ratings or by using some of the tests de-

veloped for this purpose (for example, the Torrance Tests of Creative Ability).

15. Creativity and intelligence may or may not be highly related. It is likely that relatively high intelligence is required for superior creative effort. Above a certain point, however, personality and social factors are probably more important than purely intellectual ones.

16. Guilford's model describes human intellectual functioning in terms of operations (major intellectual processes such as knowing and remembering) that are applied to content (cognitive information in the form of numbers, symbols, or words, for example) to yield a product (the result of processing information, describable in terms of forms such as units, classes, relations, or implications). The model yields 120 separate abilities.

17. Divergent and convergent thinking are two important operations in Guilford's model. Divergent thinking relates to creativity; convergent thinking is more closely related to the types of processes required for successful performance on intelligence tests.

SUGGESTED READINGS

The following two books present an important information-processing view of intelligence:

STERNBERG, R. J. (1985). *Beyond IQ: A triarchic theory of human intelligence.* New York: Cambridge University Press.

———. (1986). *Intelligence applied: Understanding and increasing your intellectual skills.* New York: Harcourt Brace Jovanovich.

For a sensitive look at giftedness and numerous practical suggestions for fostering excellence in the home and the school, see

CLARK, B. (1983). *Growing up gifted: Developing the potential of children at home and at school* (2nd ed.). Columbus, Ohio: Merrill.

Current thinking and research in creativity are summarized in

CROPLEY, A. J. (1992). *More ways than one: Fostering creativity.* Norwood, N.J.: Ablex.

STERNBERG, R. J. (Ed.). (1988). *The nature of creativity: Contemporary psychological perspectives.* Cambridge, Mass.: Cambridge University Press.

Guilford's structure of intellect is described in a 1959 article, which has been reprinted in countless books of readings and in his 1967 book.

GUILFORD, J. P. (1959). Three faces of intellect. *American Psychologist, 14,* 469–479.

———. (1967). *The nature of human intelligence.* New York: McGraw-Hill.

A useful overview of intelligence measures, with detailed comparisons and evaluations of the Stanford-Binet and WISC-III, is

KAMPHAUS, R. W. (1993). *Clinical assessment of children's intelligence.* Boston: Allyn & Bacon.

During hibernation, all the metabolic processes are slowed to an absolute minimum. The animal is exceedingly torpid and approaches death as closely as possible without actually dying. Bears do not truly hibernate, although they do "den-up" during severe weather (L. H. Matthews, 1969).

How dull it is to pause, to make an end,
To rust unburnished, not to shine in use!
As tho' to breathe were life.
Alfred, Lord Tennyson, *Ulysses*

Ah, yes! I wrote the "Purple Cow"—
I'm sorry, now, I wrote it!
But I can tell you anyhow,
I'll kill you if you quote it!
Gelett Burgess, *Burgess Nonsense Book, The Purple Cow*

chapter 8 | TEACHING GIFTED AND EXCEPTIONAL CHILDREN

PREVIEW Today's school is vastly different from my father's school—or my childhood school. And not just because of the appearance of new-fangled technologies like computers but maybe more because today's average, ordinary classroom typically contains a sometimes bewildering diversity of students. For one thing, North American societies are becoming increasingly multicultural; for another, legislation now mandates that wherever possible, exceptional children be educated in ordinary classrooms with more average students. As a result, the teacher's roles and responsibilities have become increasingly complex, as we see in this chapter.

Excerpt from Learn 'Em Well

"Suppose," my father said, "suppose you have a wild cow . . . no, make that a demented goose. . . ." Some of us chuckled a bit, squirming forward in our seats to get closer and not miss anything. My father often began his lessons that way, especially when we were hot and sweaty and unsettled from recess. All he had to say was something like "suppose"—a rich word, pregnant with implications—and we would collectively draw a quick breath and listen for what was to come next. And when, in the same short sentence, he would wave in front of us an image like that of a wild cow or a demented goose, he had us—attention riveted, unwavering.

"A demented, cross-eyed goose," he continued. "A goose with a completely unnatural passion for Ford cars." Robert tittered suddenly, loudly, perhaps knowing or suspecting something about demented geese or unnatural passions of which the rest of us were not yet aware.

"Now suppose this crazy goose is flying along at thirty miles an hour and he looks down and sees that he just happens to be over a nice Ford that's going in the same direction, only it's just going twenty miles an hour. Well, the goose is tempted to go right down and get closer to this Ford." Robert tittered once more.

"But," my father continued, "when the goose looks out in the distance with his crossed eyes, he sees another Ford. This other Ford is exactly one hundred twenty miles away and it's coming directly toward the first Ford at a steady speed of forty miles an hour.

"Well, our mad goose immediately leaves the first Ford and flies straight toward the second one at thirty miles an hour. But when he gets to the second Ford, he remembers the first, changes his mind, and turns right around. Without slowing down a bit, he flies right back to the first Ford. Well, as I told you, this goose is a little strange, so when he gets back to

the first Ford, he turns around again and flies right back to the second, always at thirty miles an hour and always without slowing down—back and forth and back and forth, honking madly and looking in both directions at once with his crossed eyes, until finally the two Fords run smack into each other!

"The question is," my dad announced into the expectant silence—and we knew that we had again been seduced into a math problem—"the question is, how far will that goose have flown before the two cars run into each other?"

Stan raised his hand at once. "I know the answer! Can I tell it?"

"Just write it down and hand it to me." We knew that Stan's answer would be correct, although I couldn't for the life of me see how he could have figured it out so fast. Most of the rest of us wrestled with the problem, writing numbers, dividing, multiplying, drawing lines, trying to figure out how many turns the goose would make, how much shorter each one would be. For his part, Robert drew exquisite replicas of two Ford cars, one in each of the bottom corners of a sheet of paper. Then he sketched a clearly delirious cross-eyed goose in one upper corner, drew a line from that corner to the other, curved the line down and back part of the way, curved it back again (but a shorter distance this time), and continued doing this, back and forth, until he had drawn what looked like a continuous series of diminishing esses down to the bottom center of the page. He then measured this line with a ruler and a string and announced, "Three hundred and seventy-four miles—give or take a few." There was something about demented geese that Robert apparently did not know.

THE TALENTED AND THE GIFTED

"That is an excellent goose!" my dad announced. He seemed truly proud, as if he were somehow responsible for the fact that Robert could draw and paint so well. "May I show it to the others, even if the goose didn't fly quite three hundred seventy-four miles?"* And even Robert was proud. One of my father's greatest gifts as a teacher was that he

recognized gifts and talents in others and that he encouraged these attributes and made their owners feel proud.

Education does not always recognize giftedness and talent. One problem is that historically, with some notable exceptions, most school jurisdictions have not offered special programs for gifted children. And those that have were never quite certain about which children to include in these programs. As Adamson (1983) notes, our "fuzzy" concept of giftedness might include superior academic achievement, high measured intelligence, exceptionally rapid learning, evidence of a single extraordinary ability or talent, or combinations of these.

Giftedness Defined

Like creativity, *giftedness* is not easy to define. Unfortunately, however, a fuzzy concept of giftedness is of little value to teachers and school administrators who need to identify students for gifted programs.

Public Law 91-230. The concept of giftedness was clarified somewhat in 1969, following the passage of U.S. Public Law 91-230. A section of this law (806) relates directly to the gifted and talented and includes the following definition:

> Gifted and talented children are those . . . who by virtue of outstanding abilities are capable of high performance. These are children who require differentiated educational programs and/or services beyond those normally provided by the regular school programs in order to realize their contribution to society.

The law goes on to state that capacity for high performance may be defined in terms of demonstrated achievement and/or potential for achievement in one or more of the following aptitudes and abilities:

*PPC: How far did the goose fly?

Author: I don't remember. But I could figure it out. Now, to reach the second Ford the first time . . .

1. General intellectual ability
2. Specific academic aptitude
3. Creative or productive thinking
4. Leadership ability
5. Visual and performing arts
6. Psychomotor ability

Interestingly, a modification of this legislation in 1978 deletes the category "psychomotor ability" as a means of identifying gifted children. This was done not because children who are exceptional in this area are not considered gifted but simply because psychomotor giftedness is generally evident in superior athletics, an area that is well funded under other programs (Harrington, Harrington, & Karns, 1991).

Defining giftedness and establishing criteria for admission to this group is particularly important where special programs are available for gifted and talented children. The definition and criteria we use determine which children will be eligible for special programs. By the same token, they determine which children are not eligible— that is, they implicitly label a large group of children "not gifted." There are, as Hoge (1988) notes, important ethical and equity issues here, particularly in light of the serious problems with the procedures used to identify gifted children.

Identifying Gifted Children. In practice, those who are gifted are typically identified through their performance on group intelligence tests, through teachers' nominations—usually as a function of superior achievement in schools— and perhaps through an individual intelligence test. But a great deal of ambiguity and confusion surrounds the use of intelligence tests. As we saw in Chapter 7, what these tests measure isn't entirely clear; what we do know is that they tell us very little about some important things, such as motivation, persistence, and other personality variables. And they don't measure very accurately.

In effect, then, what happens in practice with respect to identifying gifted children often does not reflect official definitions of giftedness. In the majority of cases, general intellectual ability and academic achievement are taken into consideration, but these are only two of the six criteria identified by U.S. Public Law 91-230 (today only five criteria remain, psychomotor ability having been deleted). Although special talents and abilities in the other criteria (creative ability, leadership qualities, and talents in visual and performing arts) may affect teachers' nominations, they are seldom part of formal identification procedures.

Many researchers have attempted to develop assessment procedures and definitions of giftedness that reflect these concerns. Renzulli, Reis, and Smith (1981), for example, define giftedness in terms of a variety of characteristics. They suggest, however, that from the teacher's point of view, giftedness can be recognized in terms of a combination of three things—either demonstrated or potential:

1. High ability (might be evident in high achievement and/or high measured intelligence)
2. High creativity (sometimes evident in production of novel ideas or in problem-solving ability)
3. High commitment (manifested in a high level of persistence and task completion)

Renzulli's Scale for Rating Behavioral Characteristics of Superior Students gives teachers a preliminary instrument for identifying gifted and talented students (Renzulli, 1986). Such instruments are essential if teachers and administrators are to identify candidates for special programs fairly.

Prevalence of Giftedness. Estimates are that somewhere between 3 and 5 percent of the school population might be considered gifted on the basis of these criteria (S. P. Marland, 1972). However, special programs are provided for nowhere near this proportion of students (Harrington,

Harrington, & Karns, 1991). And a number of researchers (Renzulli, 1982, for example) argue that this estimate is far too conservative, that as many as 20 percent or more of all children have the *potential* to be gifted.

Overlooking Culturally Different Gifted Learners. Among the gifted who are systematically overlooked are a number of identifiable groups. Perhaps most obvious are the culturally different, for whom the usual measures of achievement and potential are sometimes highly inappropriate. For example, Kitano (1991) notes that minority groups are underrepresented in gifted programs in spite of education's growing concern about meeting the needs of these children. And Matthew, Golin, Moore, and Baker (1992) report that the use of the SOMPA, a testing procedure deliberately designed to be fairer to ethnic minorities, results in the identification of gifted children who would otherwise be missed by more conventional testing practices (see Chapter 7 for more information on the SOMPA).

Gifted children who are culturally different also are often overlooked because many of them are underachievers (Wilgosh, 1991). Because they don't do as well as majority-group children in ordinary classroom programs, they are hardly likely to be viewed as potentially gifted. Similarly, Urban (1991) reports that gifted youngsters who have behavior disorders are seldom found in programs for the gifted.

There are four principal reasons why many gifted youngsters are overlooked, reports Shaklee (1992): (1) our definitions are too limiting, (2) there is confusion about identifying gifted learners as well as about the options available for them, (3) we place too much emphasis on biased measures of ability and achievement, and (4) there are insufficient programs for gifted learners.

Programs for the Gifted

Following the passage of PL 91-230, a massive survey of programs for the gifted and talented was undertaken in the United States. The survey, which involved thousands of parents and educators, revealed several things. One was that the education of the gifted and talented was typically perceived as a very low-priority issue: Only twenty-one states had any legislation to provide facilities for the gifted, and in most cases this legislation represented intent rather than concrete action. Another revelation was that those programs that did exist typically did not reach the gifted and talented from ethnic and social minorities and that there were some serious problems in identifying the gifted and talented (S. P. Marland, 1972).

A similar survey, conducted some six years after the passage of PL 91-230, found that all but eight states had some type of legislation concerning programs for the gifted and talented. And the National Research Center on the Gifted and Talented has been receiving nearly $10 million per year since 1990 to direct and coordinate research on the gifted and to establish gifted programs (Harrington, Harrington, & Karns, 1991). However, the majority of states (and provinces) still provide services to relatively small numbers of children in this category—a situation that may be attributed to lack of funding, lack of trained personnel, and lack of widely accepted procedures and criteria for identifying the gifted and talented. Sadly, an observation made by Terman (1925) more than six decades ago might still be true today: When comparing potential and achievement, we find that the most "retarded" group in our schools is the highly gifted.

Acceleration Versus Enrichment. There are two approaches to educating the gifted: **acceleration** and **enrichment.** The terms are essentially self-explanatory. Programs that accelerate simply move students more rapidly through the conventional curriculum, exposing them to the same material as other students. Programs that enrich provide gifted students with additional and different school experiences in an attempt to deepen and broaden their knowledge and capabilities.

The enrichment approach is well illustrated by Renzulli's (1977) enrichment model, also called the "revolving door" model (Renzulli, Reis, & Smith, 1981). This model advocates selecting gifted individuals on the basis of three characteristics: high academic ability, high creative potential, and high motivation. No rigorous cutoff scores are used; instead, all students whose achievement or apparent potential places them in the upper 25 percent of students in the school are designated as talented. Any of these students may then enter enrichment programs and drop out of them as they wish (hence, the revolving door). The programs vary according to the expressed interests of the students. When they identify a project and commit themselves to it, they are allowed to enter a resource room and work on the project.

The acceleration approach is perhaps best illustrated by Stanley's (1976) radical acceleration model, developed primarily for students gifted in mathematics. It attempts to compress the ordinary curriculum so as to enable gifted individuals to master a course of studies in a fraction of the time ordinarily required. Subsequently, many of these accelerated youngsters are enrolled in university-sponsored courses for additional acceleration.

The relative merits of acceleration and enrichment have long been debated among educators. One of the most common arguments against acceleration is that it might be harmful to move students much beyond their social and psychological levels of development. Educators have been concerned that one effect of accelerating gifted students might be that they would eventually no longer "fit in" socially with their peers—a possibility that might have harmful consequences. Interestingly, the most common argument for enrichment is precisely the argument used against acceleration; that is, educators simply assume that enrichment will not have the same social and psychological implications as acceleration. After all, enrichment does not remove gifted children from their age and grade levels as does acceleration; it simply provides them with an opportunity to deepen and broaden their knowledge at each level.

Horowitz and O'Brien (1986) point out that research has not yet established that one of these methods is superior to the other. It does seem clear, however, that most acceleration programs do not lead to negative social or emotional consequences (Janos & Robinson, 1985). And it may well be that the best programs are sufficiently flexible that they can include both acceleration and enrichment according to the needs of the learners.

Mentoring and Tutoring. An increasing number of programs for the gifted use **mentors** or **tutors**. A mentor is an individual who serves as a sort of intellectual and psychological guide. Mentoring implies a close relationship within which the mentor may be a role model, consultant, adviser, source of wisdom—even a sort of protector. Hence, the term *protégé* to signify the one who is mentored (Jacobi, 1991). A tutor, on the other hand, is a teacher rather than a mentor; but unlike the regular classroom teacher, the tutor teaches *only one* student at a time.

Tutoring, says Bloom (1984), is clearly the most effective way to teach. His review of the research suggests that one-on-one tutoring will move the average learner from the middle of the pack (where, by definition, average learners are found) to about the ninety-eighth percentile. In addition, tutoring has beneficial effects on the tutors themselves—they develop more positive attitudes and gain in understanding. And it has beneficial effects on children identified as being at risk of failure (Snow & Swanson, 1992).

Mentoring, which requires a more encompassing relationship between two individuals, seems to have become more common in education in recent years. For example, a large number of school jurisdictions have instituted mentor programs wherein expert teachers are designated as mentors to assist the early development of novice teachers. Little (1990) notes there is little research to support the assumption that mentoring is highly effective in this situation. Similarly, mentoring programs are used at some universities, especially at the graduate, but also at the undergraduate, level. Again, there is little systematic research to indicate that mentoring relationships have a beneficial effect at universities (see Jacobi, 1991). However, in a study of creativity, Torrance (1984) found that students who had mentors benefited significantly in terms of creative achievement.

Individual Education Plans (IEPs). Another approach to the education of the gifted involves self-directed and independent study, often using learning/thinking strategies of the kind mentioned in Chapter 3. Some self-directed study programs also use **individual education plans (IEPs),** individually designed for students according to their special needs and talents. IEPs are widely used for special-needs children, their use having been mandated in the United States by a 1975 law (PL 94-142). (IEPs are described and illustrated later in this chapter.) Torrance (1986) notes that IEPs are becoming more popular for use with gifted children, for whom the plans usually involve a combination of approaches and materials such as self-directed study, mentoring, enrichment, perhaps acceleration, and programs for development of learning/thinking strategies and motivation.

Special Schools. In addition to these approaches to the education of the gifted, a number of schools cater solely to these children, as do Saturday and summer programs and a variety of community or university enrichment programs. Some of their offerings can sometimes be included in IEPs designed for gifted children.

In spite of these special programs, many gifted and talented children—like many whose gifts and talents are less than average—are in regular classrooms and lack access to any formal "special" education. This does not mean, however, that there is nothing that teachers of regular classes can (or should) do for them. In fact, as we discuss later in this chapter, mainstreaming legislation now makes it mandatory for many children who would otherwise receive special instruction to spend most of their time in regular classrooms. It has therefore become necessary for teachers in regular classrooms to learn about exceptionality and about what they can do for these children. Many suggestions included in this chapter are appropriate for both ordinary students and for those who are more extraordinary.

PROMOTING CREATIVITY AND GIFTEDNESS

"In the final analysis," write Harrington, Harrington, and Karns, "[we] must provide educational challenge for [our] bright people or else tomorrow we will be led by the mediocre, and on the day after, by the incompetent" (1991, p. 41).

Do schools do what they can (or should) for the gifted and creative? Perhaps not, if Ms. Bourgeois' class is any indication (see the case on page 213). Cropley (1992) suggests it might be. The behaviors and personalities most characteristic of the highly creative, he notes, are not the qualities most preferred by teachers. Schools are geared toward developing students who are obedient, accepting of other people's ideas, popular, punctual, courteous, and respectful. And academic success is fostered by memorization and the ability to recognize and replicate accepted answers and procedures. Note that flexibility, risk taking, originality, inventiveness, and nonconformity are absent in these lists. Claire, like all other students in her class, was expected to learn a simple odd-even rule and to repeat it when asked.

A *good* teacher would not have responded as Ms. Bourgeois did. Not only was she unwilling to consider the possibility that Claire's response might have merit—or at the very least, to have her explain her response—but she resorted to name calling.

THE SETTING: Ms. Adèle Bourgeois' Grade 3 arithmetic class. The class has been learning odd and even numbers.

Ms. Bourgeois: So who can tell me, you should all know this by now, which numbers between one and ten can be divided by two?

Thomas: All the even ones. Two, four, six, eight, and ten!

Ms. Bourgeois: Very good, Thomas. That's exactly right.

Claire: That's not right.

Ms. Bourgeois (slightly angry): What's that, Claire?

Claire: That's not right. I mean, not just the even numbers.

Ms. Bourgeois (quite angry): You always think you know better than the book, don't you?

Claire (more timidly, but sticking to her guns): But the odd ones too. My dad said . . .

Ms. Bourgeois: Your dad isn't the teacher, smarty pants. How d'you suppose you'd divide five by two, huh? Weren't you paying any attention at all when we talked about how all even numbers can be divided by two?

Claire, red-faced, shrugs and whispers "two-and-a-half" too softly for Ms. Bourgeois to hear.

As the world's problems multiply, the need for creativity becomes ever more pressing and more apparent—as does the need for teachers to learn how they can contribute to the development of the gifted and creative.

What Teachers Can Do: Some Techniques

After you have been teaching for a while, it might be a good idea to pause and ask yourself what it is that you have been teaching. If you are honest (as most teachers are), you will probably find that you have been teaching information relating to one or more conveniently labeled and categorized bodies of knowledge that we call "subjects" and perhaps a number of practical skills related to reading, writing, and manipulating numbers. You might also note that some of your students, some of the time, have also begun to learn how to understand and appreciate, how to analyze and synthesize. Some will show signs of being able to compare and summarize, will perhaps even know how to interpret and criticize, find and test assumptions, and observe and classify.

Sadly, however, unless you are one of those rare teachers who have taken pains to work toward these ends, or unless you are part of an experimental project designed to develop learning/thinking strategies (see Chapter 5), most of this learning will have occurred incidentally—almost accidentally.

Although we have long paid lip service to the desirability of developing creative and thinking skills in students, schools have paid little attention to programs deliberately designed to foster these skills. In fact, we have naïvely assumed that the abilities involved in creating and thinking are largely innate. Worse yet, we have assumed that systematic exposure to increasingly large bodies of information and increasingly difficult problems and concepts would automatically develop the ability to think. With respect to creativity, we have been less certain; we have preferred, instead, to assume that some have it and others don't. At the same time, we have assumed that the worst thing a teacher might do with respect to creativity is to stifle it and that the best thing a teacher might do is not stifle it.

But there are specific things teachers can do to teach students different ways of thinking and perhaps to foster creative thinking. Among them are a number of different problem-solving techniques.

Brainstorming. Brainstorming, for example, is among the most common group approaches for solving problems creatively. Developed by Alex Osborn (1957), **brainstorming** is a technique for

producing a wide variety of solutions while deliberately suspending judgment about the appropriateness of any of them. This, the principle of deferred evaluation, is the most important characteristic of brainstorming—and, in fact, of most approaches to creative thinking. Putting off evaluation is an extremely difficult thing for inexperienced problem solvers to do, but it leads to the production of 23 to 177 percent more good-quality solutions than when simply following instructions to "produce good ideas" (Parnes, 1962). Delaying evaluation allows much greater scope in the responses emitted. Evaluation during production has a dampening effect on both groups and individuals.

In a brainstorming session, several rules are followed closely:

1. Criticism of a contributed idea is absolutely barred (deferred evaluation).

2. Modification or combination with other ideas is encouraged.

3. A large quantity of ideas is sought.

4. Unusual, remote, or wild ideas are sought.

In industry, a brainstorming session may last for two or more hours and involve five to twelve people from a wide variety of backgrounds. The leader explains the rules, describes the problem to be solved, and the session begins. Ideally, it is a free-wheeling, wide-ranging affair, with ideas coming rapidly from all sources. All forms of evaluation are forbidden. Evaluative comments such as "that sounds good" or "no, that won't work," ridicule, laughter, or nonverbal expressions of either admiration or disgust are stopped immediately. Habitual offenders may even be removed from the group.

During a brainstorming session, a number of specific aids to creativity are used. Most common are checklists used to stimulate ideas. For example, Parnes (1967) provides a checklist of nine actions that could be applied to a variety of problems. Each of these nine possibilities is illustrated here with reference to the question, "How many suggestions can you make for different ways to manage a classroom?"

1. *Other uses.* The class might be used as something other than a learning situation. For

example, students might be given the responsibility for entertaining the school at a social evening.

2. *Adapt.* Adaptation involves using ideas from other sources; perhaps the class could be run like a factory, like a prison, or like a playground.

3. *Modify.* Modification suggests changing the composition of the class, changing teaching methods, or changing the approach to discipline problems.

4. *Magnify.* Class size could be increased, as could the number of teachers, number of assignments, or magnitude of punishment or reinforcement.

5. *"Minify."* Class size could be decreased, as could the number of assignments, number of reprimands, or number of school days.

6. *Substitute.* A new teacher might be substituted, the entire class might be exchanged, or a few members of the class might be replaced by students from other classes.

7. *Rearrange.* The physical setup of the room could be changed, or the seating plan could be rearranged to separate troublemakers.

8. *Reverse.* Perhaps the desks should all face the rear. Or the teacher might face the front as a sort of reversal. Another reversal would be to have the students take turns teaching.

9. *Combine.* A combination of the previous suggestions might provide a solution. Or the teaching/learning function could be combined with other functions, such as entertainment, problem solving, or discussion of noncurricular topics of interest.

The Gordon Technique. A slight modification of brainstorming, the **Gordon technique,** differs from brainstorming in that it presents participants with an abstraction of a problem rather than with a complete, detailed problem (W. J. J. Gordon, 1961). For example, if the problem is one of parking cars in New York, the leader of a Gordon group might begin by saying, "The problem today is one of storing things. How many ways can you think of for storing things?" Such an approach sometimes leads to ideas that would not otherwise occur (for example, "put them in bags," "pile them up," "hang them," "can them," "put them on conveyer belts," "fold them," "put them in boxes," "cut them up," and so on).

Later in the session, the leader of the group begins to narrow the problem down. The next step might be to say, "The things to be stored are quite large." Later, more restrictions will be specified: "The objects cannot be folded or cut up," and so on.

Morphological Analysis. This procedure, described by Osborn (1957) and Arnold (1962), was originated by Fritz Zwicky of Aero-Jet Corporation. It involves dividing a problem into a number of independent variables, thinking of as many potential solutions as possible for each one, and then combining the results in all possible ways. Arnold illustrates **morphological analysis** using the problem of developing a new type of vehicle. Three different aspects of this problem are (1) the type of vehicle, (2) the type of power, and (3) the medium in which the vehicle will be used. Each of these aspects lends itself to various solutions. For example, the type of vehicle might be a cart, a sling, a rocket, a box, and so on. Figure 8.1 presents 180 potential solutions for the problem; there are thousands more. Some of these have already been invented; some are completely impractical; others might be worth pursuing. Imagine, for example, a sling-type vehicle, drawn by horses, going through oil; or imagine an atomic rocket going through a tube.

Lateral Thinking. According to de Bono (1970), if you want to dig a hole deeper, it is necessary to dig vertically. But if the object is to have a hole that, so to speak, covers different ground, you have to dig laterally. In the same way, if the object

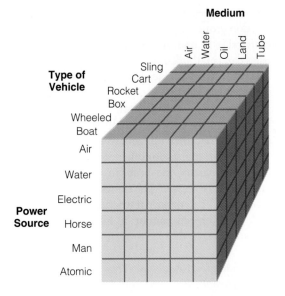

FIGURE 8.1 A model of morphological analysis for the "problem" of developing a new vehicle. One hundred and eighty possible "solutions" are shown.

is to discover more about something or to arrive at a conventional, accepted, "convergent" solution to a problem, **vertical thinking** is entirely appropriate; but if the object is to find unusual, divergent, creative solutions for problems, **lateral thinking** would be better. De Bono argues that lateral thinking is a way of using the mind that leads to creative thinking and to creative solutions but that it is not the same thing as creative thinking. He maintains that although lateral thinking is closely related to insight, creativity, and humor, these last three can only be prayed for, whereas lateral thinking can be developed deliberately. Accordingly, he has devised a program for teaching lateral thinking, as well as one designed just to teach thinking (de Bono, 1976).

Unlike brainstorming and other techniques designed to foster creative behavior, de Bono's program for teaching lateral thinking does not require students to solve specific problems; instead, it encourages them to develop new ways to approach all problems. In de Bono's words, it

attempts to teach "lateral" rather than "vertical" approaches.

Many exercises in de Bono's program are similar to items used on various tests of creativity. Students might be presented with various geometric designs, for example, and asked to describe them in as many ways as possible. Other activities are designed to encourage students to ask why, to suspend judgment, to identify and challenge assumptions, to brainstorm, to produce analogies, and so on. Throughout, emphasis is on creating new ideas and challenging old ones, but care is taken to assure that the learner does not overemphasize the negation of the old. Negation, de Bono says, is one of the principal techniques in vertical thinking because "logical" thinking is based on negation and selection, with the major role being played by rejection. Hence, the centrality of a word such as *no* in logical (vertical) thinking.

Lateral thinking does not have a central word—that is, it didn't. In addition to offering a large number of exercises, de Bono also presents his students with a new word, *po,* intended to be to lateral thinking what *no* is to vertical thinking. The word *yes* is clearly unsuitable, for it implies uncritical acceptance. But the word *po* is entirely suitable; it means nothing and everything. It is a word that permits us to do or say anything, a word that requires no justification, a word that de Bono terms the "laxative" of language and thinking. *Po* is neither affirmation nor negation; it is simply an invitation to think laterally. As such, it is an invitation to examine, challenge, modify, combine, brainstorm, or analogize. Po might have some place in your teaching.

Conceptual Models. Education, we argued in Chapter 1, must do far more than simply teach facts and procedures. Students should not only learn; they should also learn how to learn. Although they need to accumulate facts and formulas, they should also grow in their ability and in their willingness to think. One of the grand goals of all education, we insisted, is to empower students; that is, students should be given the skills, the attitudes, and the

If the object is to find unusual, divergent, creative solutions for problems, says de Bono, students need to be encouraged to engage in *lateral thinking*. This involves questioning and challenging old ideas. It also involves being open to surprises and to new answers.

information that will enable them to deal most effectively with life—that will empower them to solve their problems (as well as yours and mine).

To be truly empowered, students must also be creative. Mayer asks the question, "What can be done to empower students to be creative when they are faced with problems?" (1989, p. 43). One important answer, he claims, can be found in the use of conceptual models as an instructional technique.

A conceptual model is a verbal or graphic presentation designed to assist the learner in developing a clear and useful mental representation of whatever is being studied. It is, as Mayer (1989) puts it, a special form of advance organizer of the kind we discussed in connection with Ausubel's theory (see Chapter 6).

Figure 8.2 is an example of a conceptual model that includes the most important elements required to understand how radar functions. Students who were allowed to examine this model for one minute before a short lecture on radar later recalled 57 percent more of the important concepts than did students who had been given the lecture without the model. Perhaps more important, students who had examined the conceptual model were able to produce solutions that were 83 percent more accurate than the other group's for problems that required transferring what they had learned to new situations. Put another way, these students were able to use what they had learned creatively in the sense that they could then apply it to new situations.

1. TRANSMISSION: A pulse travels from an antenna.

2. REFLECTION: The pulse bounces off a remote object.

3. RECEPTION: The pulse returns to the receiver.

4. MEASUREMENT: The difference between the time out and the time back tells the total time traveled.

5. CONVERSION: The time can be converted to a measure of distance because the pulse travels at a constant speed.

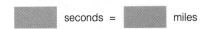

⬛ seconds = ⬛ miles

FIGURE 8.2 A conceptual model of how radar functions. Adapted from R. E. Mayer (1989), "Models for Understanding." *Review of Educational Research, 59,* 1, 43–64. Copyright 1989 by the American Educational Research Association. Reprinted by permission of the publisher.

Mayer (1989) cites a number of other studies that support the argument that conceptual models significantly increase students' creative solutions to problems not presented in the initial lesson. In addition, models of this kind increase recall of important concepts, although they tend to decrease rote, or verbatim, recall. Like Ausubel's advance organizers, conceptual models provide the learner with important concepts that organize previous learning and that provide essential elements of cognitive structure to which new material can be related.

From the teacher's point of view, it is important to know both how to devise models and which models are most likely to be effective. Mayer (1989) describes a number of characteristics of good conceptual models.

First, such a model is complete in the sense that it contains all essential aspects of a system, so that the learner sees and understands how the system works. At the same time, the model needs to be both concise (so that it doesn't overwhelm with detail) and coherent (so that it makes sense). The model must be concrete in that it deals with events and functions that are familiar to the learner, but it also needs to be conceptual in that it deals with meaningful ideas. It goes almost without saying that it must also be correct. And finally, a good conceptual model must be considerate in that it takes into consideration the learner's sophistication and level of understanding.

Clearly, there might have been better terms with which to describe the characteristics of conceptual models most likely to lead to understanding and creativity, but note that in the alliteration is a useful mnemonic.*

Research with conceptual models suggests that they can be particularly effective in science, especially when there is a need to explain how a system (such as radar) works. Mayer (1989) suggests that visual models are also highly effective for organizing and recalling lists.

"Better learning," argues Papert, "will not come from finding better ways for the teacher to *instruct,* but from giving the learner better opportunities to *construct*" (1990, p. 3). Computer programming (with *Logo,* for example) is one way to

*PPC: I'm not sure all students will understand this. Even those who know what alliteration is may not c the relevance of this sentence. Do you get it?

Author: [Groan]

construct—to make models; making graphic representations with paper and pencil is another; inventing mental models is yet another. This new constructionist emphasis in teaching and learning encourages learners to discover and build their own representations, their own models.

Classroom Climate and the Creative and Gifted

Encouraging exceptionality in students needs to go far beyond occasionally making use of specific techniques developed to encourage creative problem solving or lateral thinking. Lowe (1983) suggests that creative teaching and learning stem from a belief in the importance of self-initiated learning, from flexible and nonauthoritarian instructional methods, and from approaches that value reasoning, questioning, and the manipulation of ideas and materials. Creativity and high achievement are fostered by teachers (and parents) who have an attitude that recognizes and encourages individuality and creativity in students (Fahrmeler, 1991) and by a culture that rewards rather than punishes those who are gifted (Scott, 1991). Schools that reflect these values might also do much to foster the development of gifted—talented—creative youngsters.

Haddon and Lytton (1968) contrasted two types of schools, which they labeled "formal" and "informal." The formal schools were characterized by an authoritarian approach to learning and teaching, whereas the informal schools tended to emphasize self-initiated learning and greater student participation. Not surprisingly, students in informal schools consistently did better on measures of creative thinking than did students of comparable intelligence and socioeconomic status who attended the formal schools. Similar results were found in relatively unstructured classrooms (informal classes) where students spent time programming computers using *Logo* (see Chapter 12). These students typically did better on subsequent measures of creativity (Clements, 1991).

One important aspect of classroom climate is the extent to which students perceive school activities as cooperative or competitive. Adams (1968) reports that students tested under noncompetitive conditions score higher on tests of spontaneous flexibility than do those tested under competitive conditions. Further, if the examiner is warm and receptive, students do even better. These findings have been corroborated in a large number of studies, twenty-eight of which are reviewed and summarized by Slavin (1980). Among other things, the studies indicate that cooperative teaching methods (in which students work in small groups and receive rewards based on group rather than individual performance) lead to "increased student achievement, positive race relations in desegregated schools, mutual concern among students, student self-esteem, and other positive outcomes" (p. 315). (See Chapter 9 for a detailed discussion of cooperative learning.)

Teachers' Attitudes and Creativity

Some evidence suggests that humanistic approaches to teaching are more likely to lead to creativity among students. Research reviewed in Chapter 9, for example, indicates that open education often leads to higher creativity scores, but it also often leads to lower scores on standardized achievement tests. Similarly, Turner and Denny (1969) found that warm, spontaneous, and caring teachers are more likely to encourage creative behavior in their students than are teachers characterized as highly organized and businesslike.

It should be kept in mind, however, that humanistic concerns and attitudes are not clearly and irrevocably incompatible with businesslike approaches to learning. The important variables are probably not specific teaching methods so much as teachers' attitudes and other personality characteristics.

Torrance (1962) gives a list of suggestions for teacher attitudes and behaviors designed to promote creativity in students. Consider how each might be implemented in the classroom:

1. Value creative thinking.
2. Make children more sensitive to environmental stimuli.
3. Encourage manipulation of objects and ideas.
4. Teach how to test each idea systematically.
5. Develop tolerance of new ideas.
6. Beware of forcing a set pattern.
7. Develop a creative classroom atmosphere.
8. Teach children to value their creative thinking.
9. Teach skills for avoiding peer sanctions.
10. Give information about the creative process.
11. Dispel the sense of awe of masterpieces.
12. Encourage self-initiated learning.
13. Create "thorns in the flesh" (that is, awareness of problems).
14. Create necessities for creative thinking.
15. Provide for active and quiet periods.
16. Make available resources for working out ideas.
17. Encourage the habit of working out the full implications of ideas.
18. Develop constructive criticism—not just criticism.
19. Encourage the acquisition of knowledge in a variety of fields.
20. Develop adventurous teachers.

In contrast with these behaviors and attitudes that might foster creativity, Hallman (1967) lists some common inhibitors of creativity:

- Pressure to conform
- Authoritarian attitudes and environments
- A teacher with a rigid personality
- Ridicule and sarcasm
- Overemphasis on evaluation
- Excessive quests for certainty
- Hostility toward divergent personalities
- Overemphasis on success
- Intolerance of playful attitudes

It follows that if these behaviors discourage creativity, their opposites might promote it. This list suggests what not to do—as opposed to Torrance's list, which suggests what a teacher should do. Both, taken in combination, can serve as useful guides for teacher behavior.

Teaching Styles and Creativity

In a global sense, a teaching style is an identifiable and related group of teaching activities. Thus, researchers speak of styles that reflect specific methods of instructing (for example, the lecturing style, the questioning style, the role-playing style). Or they speak of styles that reflect the teacher's predominant relationship with students or the major roles that each assumes (for example, authoritarian versus democratic, teacher centered versus pupil centered, traditional versus progressive). Research has also examined several broad classifications, such as formal-informal styles or direct-indirect styles.

Although teaching style often reflects a teacher's personality, it also reflects many other factors, including personal philosophy, educational goals, the influences of teacher-training programs, maturity, wisdom, and the use of inspiring or less inspiring textbooks. Nor do most teachers invariably display only a single style. For example, most use a variety of instructional procedures and choose different ones depending on the lesson being taught, who the learners are, the amount of preparation time and resources available, and other factors. However, many teachers have a definite tendency to be more formal than informal (or vice versa) or to use more direct rather than less direct approaches to instruction.

From the teacher's point of view, it may be important to know the likely effects of these different styles on students' achievement, on students' motivation, and on the development of the skills and attitudes related to being thoughtful and creative.

Formal-Informal Styles. One of the broadest classifications of teaching styles describes formal and informal styles (Bennett, 1976). Teachers whose styles are most formal teach each subject separately, emphasize individual rather than group work, assign class seating, restrict students' movement, emphasize assessment and achievement, and make extensive use of external motivators such as grades. Those whose styles are more informal tend to integrate subjects, provide students with considerable freedom in determining their activities, typically allow students to select their seating, do not emphasize tests and academic achievement, and tend to rely on internal sources of motivation like self-satisfaction.

Do these styles significantly affect students' achievement? Research suggests that they do. As we see in Chapter 12, formal styles are associated with higher academic achievement than are informal styles. However, informal styles may be associated with higher levels of creativity.

Direct-Indirect Styles. Flanders (1970) describes two types of teacher-learner verbal interaction that define direct and indirect teaching styles. The direct style is in some ways much like the formal style just described. Teachers whose behavior reflects this style direct classroom activity: They lecture, elaborate their opinions, give directions, and criticize or justify on the basis of their authority and that of others. In contrast, the indirect teaching style involves asking questions rather than providing information and is characterized by an acceptance of the student's feelings and attitudes, by the encouragement of student-initiated behaviors and opinions, and by the solicitation of ideas from students. Flanders's analysis of teacher-student classroom interaction led him to conclude that the direct style predominates in approximately two-thirds of all classrooms.

Research that has evaluated both direct and indirect teaching styles reports mixed results—perhaps, as Silvernail (1979) notes, because using verbal interaction alone to evaluate teaching style oversimplifies a complex situation. In some situations and for some students, a direct style may be best; in different situations or for different students, indirect styles may be superior.

In spite of these ambiguous conclusions, a number of specific characteristics of teaching styles are clearly related to the outcomes of the educational process. As we have seen elsewhere in this text, such things as praise, feedback, criticism, advance organizers or conceptual models, classroom climate, and cooperative reward structures all relate importantly to student achievement and perhaps to creativity and thoughtfulness as well.

Teachers' Expectations and Students' Performance

There are numerous examples of self-fulfilling prophecies—of situations in which what we expect will happen does. Sometimes we assume that our expectations somehow affect outcomes. But surely, there are just as many examples of situations in which what we expect does *not* happen. Do the expectations of teachers have any effect on the behaviors of their students?

The Research. The classic study of teacher expectations is Rosenthal and Jacobson's (1968a, 1968b) "Oak School" experiment. Teachers in this school were told that they were participating in the validation of a new test designed to predict academic "blooming." They were told that children, especially slow achievers, often show sudden intellectual spurts and that the new test could identify "spurters." But the tests that the Oak School children were given were actually only intelligence tests (the Flanagan Tests of General Ability). These were administered in the spring; the following September, the teachers were given false information about the test results. Specifically, they were casually given the names of students designated as "spurters" but actually chosen randomly from the student body. This group comprised about 20 percent of the school's population. The only difference, then, between the "spurters" and other students (control groups) was that the teachers had reason to expect increased performance on the part of the "spurters."

Amazingly, report Rosenthal and Jacobson, their expectations were fulfilled. What is more surprising is that not only did academic achievement—which is to some degree under a teacher's control—increase but so did intellectual ability as measured by the Flanagan tests. The most dramatic "spurts" were for first-grade students, probably those who had the greatest room for improvement. In addition, indications are that intelligence is more malleable at an earlier age (see Chapter 2).

The results of the Rosenthal and Jacobson study were later questioned by many reviewers (see Wineburg, 1987; Rosenthal, 1987). In particular, critics question the analyses used, alleging frequent misjudging, misrecording, and misrepresentation of data. Furthermore, numerous attempted replications have failed. But others have not.

Brophy and Good (1974) reviewed sixty attempted replications and concluded that many were confusing and inconclusive and that none provided strong evidence of results as dramatic as those first reported by Rosenthal and Jacobson. But, they hasten to point out, many of these studies reveal quite consistent patterns of expectations among teachers and these expectations are probably linked in important ways to such crucial things as the student's self-concept and self-esteem, as well as to achievement.

Similarly, Braun (1976) reviewed a wealth of teacher-expectation literature and also found remarkably consistent patterns for teachers' expectations. It seems that teachers often develop more positive expectations (with respect to academic achievement) for children who come from higher socioeconomic backgrounds, who are obedient and compliant, who are attractive, and who sit close to the teacher and speak clearly. And there is

evidence, as well, that expectations might be communicated in subtle but measurable ways. For example, Brophy and Good (1974) report that some teachers pay less attention to lower achievers, give them less time to answer questions, and are more likely to criticize their answers than identical answers given by higher achievers.

Other investigations continue to clarify the conditions under which teachers' expectations develop and the effects they might have on the teaching/learning process. For example, Rolison and Medway (1985) found that both the type of label applied to the student and the information the teacher has about the student's recent performance are important in determining the teacher's expectations. Teachers had higher expectations for students labeled "learning disabled" than for those labeled "mentally retarded"; they also had higher expectations for students whose recent performance showed an ascending rather than a descending pattern. Babad (1985) reports a significant bias in the grading of worksheets by teachers relative to whether or not teachers believe the work to have been done by excellent or weak students.

Implications of Research on Expectations. Obviously, the conclusion that teachers' expectations undeniably and consistently affect pupils' behavior is not fully warranted by the evidence. It appears, nevertheless, that teachers do develop expectations and that these may be important (see, for example, Means, Moore, Gagné, and Hauck, 1979). In some instances, negative expectations may adversely affect students' behavior or teachers' assessments—just as positive expectations might have more positive effects. As Bardwell (1984) notes, positive expectations might do much to increase students' motivation and, indirectly, students' performance.

Another Possibility. Clearly, positive expectations don't always have beneficial effects, nor are the effects of negative expectations always negative. Is the opposite possible?

Goldenberg (1992) describes an investigation in which nine students were studied during their first year of school. Two of these students, both Hispanic-American girls who shared the same first-grade teacher, had scored poorly on a scale of reading readiness—which would predict that each would do poorly in first-grade reading achievement. Unaware of their nearly identical reading readiness scores, the teacher had high expectations for one girl but low expectations for the other.

But the teacher was wrong. In fact, the girl for whom the teacher had high expectations did poorly; the other did remarkably well. Amazing? No, claims Goldenberg. These apparently contradictory results are easily explained by the fact that the teacher provided more assistance, more personal attention, more support for the girl for whom she had the lowest expectations—having determined that this girl needed the additional help. The most reasonable conclusion, argues Goldenberg, is that what matters most is not what the teacher *expects* but rather what the teacher *does*. Negative expectations might lead one teacher to give up on a student, to pay little attention, to provide no help, perhaps even to stop interacting with that student—and the self-fulfilling effects of the expectation may seem clear. But another teacher might react as did the Hispanic girl's teacher, with additional assistance and attention; the final results might be in direct opposition to expectations.

OTHER FACES OF EXCEPTIONALITY

Most of the human population is what we consider normal or average—in spite of the fact that each of us is different from every other. But there are some who, in one or more ways, are different from the average.

Among them are those about whom we have been talking: those who are far more intelligent, far more creative. There are others who are endowed with superior motor skills or outstanding physical appearance; others are socially gifted.

These are individuals for whom the label "exceptional" is appropriate.

Unfortunately, there is another dimension of exceptionality—one that includes those less intelligent, less creative; those with physical and motor disabilities; those with emotional and adjustment problems. In short, the term *exceptional* applies equally to those to whom nature and nurture have been noticeably generous and to those to whom they have been much less kind.

Public Law 94-142

Knowing how to identify exceptional children—and knowing, as well, how to administer the programs and resources available for them—has always been an essential part of the training of special education teachers. These are teachers whose express function is to provide educational services for children with disabilities.

In recent years, however, the special needs of exceptional children have also become important to the regular classroom teacher—particularly since the passage of Public Law 94-142 in 1975. This law was in part an attempt to correct some of the injustices that have sometimes existed in the treatment of exceptional children. Among other things, the law requires that school jurisdictions provide special services for qualified children in the "least restrictive environment" possible (Macmillan, Keogh, & Jones, 1986). In most instances, this environment has been judged to be the regular classroom, this being why an increasing number of teachers must now deal with exceptional children. Placing special-needs children in regular classrooms is termed **mainstreaming.** (Mainstreaming is discussed in the next section.)

Major Provisions of PL 94-142. In addition to the provision for education in the "least restrictive environment," Public Law 94-142 brought about a number of other significant changes in the schools' treatment of exceptionality by stipulating that

1. Extensive effort be made to identify disabled children using procedures that are not racially or culturally biased.

2. Parents have a right to be informed *and* to grant or withhold consent regarding assessment and educational plans for special-needs children.

3. School jurisdictions are compelled to provide special services for children who need them *at no cost* to parents or guardians.

4. A written individual education program (IEP) must be provided for *every* disabled child. (IEPs are described in a later section.)

For obvious reasons, PL 94-142 is often described as the "Bill of Rights for the disabled." But even though it has done a tremendous amount to reduce bias and unfair practices in the treatment of exceptional children, it has also presented some real difficulties of interpretation and implementation for educators. IEPs, for example, are difficult and time consuming to prepare and are therefore extremely costly, and they have not proved popular. Nor is it always easy or even possible to find tests for specific forms of exceptionality or to find tests in the child's native language. In addition, the law's most obvious practical manifestation—mainstreaming—has not been entirely without controversy.

Mainstreaming. Mainstreaming, the placement of exceptional children in ordinary rather than in "special" segregated classrooms, is a direct result of the passage of PL 94-142. In addition, it resulted from at least two other related events in the field of special education. The first involves the recognition—sometimes by courts of law—that many who had been labeled "emotionally disturbed" or "mentally retarded" and who had therefore not been admitted into regular classrooms were indeed capable of learning and functioning effectively when given access to these classrooms. At the same time, a relatively new classification of student was introduced: the "learning disabled." This category, often loosely defined, generally includes individuals who do not have obvious disabilities (blindness, deafness, or profound mental retardation, for example) and have therefore not been eligible for special classes but have not functioned well in regular classrooms.

Thus, there is, on the one hand, a recognition that some "special" children have been mislabeled and that, even if they have not been mislabeled, they can benefit from regular classroom experiences. On the other hand, educators now recognize that there are a number of children in regular classrooms for whom special attention would be highly desirable.

But subsequent research did not always confirm these earlier findings. Although some children did not fare as well in special classrooms, others seemed to do much better (see, for example, Budoff & Gottlieb, 1976; Semmel, Gottlieb, & Robinson, 1979).

Most recent research on mainstreaming—often labeled "inclusion" or "inclusive education"—indicates that the needs of special students can be met in regular classrooms (McDonald, 1993). And evidence is mounting that the self-concepts and social adjustment of children who are mainstreamed are more positive than those of segregated children (Macmillan, Keogh, & Jones, 1986). Mainstreaming nevertheless remains highly controversial (Chester, 1992). This is at least partly because inclusion of special-needs children in regular classrooms is expensive and difficult for school administrators, given legal requirements concerning unbiased and extensive testing and the need to consult parents and obtain their consent. In addition, integration complicates the lives of teachers. And not all teachers are well prepared, both in terms of personality characteristics and in terms of training, to deal intelligently and effectively with inclusive classrooms. The inclusive classroom requires changes in teacher education programs, with considerably more emphasis on identifying and providing programs for disabled and gifted children (see the case about Robert Goldberg on page 225).

It is perhaps not surprising that Chester found that teachers in inclusive classrooms are relatively likely to rate their learning disabled students as "underachieving, uninterested, non-studious, not striving for success, ashamed, and lacking in self confidence" (1992, p. 93). Strikingly, non-learning-disabled students in these same classrooms rated the learning-disabled students significantly more positively than did the teachers, giving them negative ratings only with respect to popularity and self-confidence. And, in fact, research indicates that learning-disabled students do have lower self-concepts than average children, whether they are mainstreamed or not (Chapman, 1988).

Individualized Education Programs (IEPs). Individualized education programs (sometimes called Individualized Program Plans or IPPs) are written programs, mandated by law and required for every disabled child. In inclusive (mainstreamed) classes, IEPs are often prepared by the classroom teacher, sometimes in consultation with a number of others. And they are almost invariably implemented by the teacher, although sometimes with the assistance of one or more specialists. Hence, it is essential that all teachers know what is required in these plans, how to interpret them, and how to prepare them.

A number of steps typically occur before an IEP is prepared. First, someone—often a teacher, sometimes a parent—becomes aware that a student might require special services. Following this, *if parents consent,* the student may be referred for assessment, perhaps by school personnel, sometimes by outside agencies. PL 94-142 mandates that an interdisciplinary assessment team be employed to determine whether comprehensive assessment is required. Assessment may involve various diagnostic and achievement tests. If the final decision is that the student requires special services, an IEP is prepared—often by the assessment team in consultation with the teacher *and* the parents.

Public Law 94-142 stipulates that IEPs must contain (1) a statement of annual goals, as well as of shorter-range objectives, (2) the expected duration of the program, including specific dates, and (3) evaluation procedures that will be used to determine whether the program's goals are being met. An example of an IEP is provided in Figure 8.3.

Not all exceptional children have their needs met only by their teachers and entirely in regular classrooms. Some may stay in a regular classroom, but the regular teacher may be assisted by an aide, an assistant teacher, or an itinerant specialist; others may be sent to a special resource room for part of each day or week; some may be in special classrooms part of the time and in a regular classroom for the remainder of the time; some may be in a special class full time. Still others may be in residential schools (some of the deaf or blind, for example) or in hospitals or other institutions.

STRATHCONA COUNTY BOARD OF EDUCATION
INDIVIDUALIZED EDUCATIONAL PLAN

NAME OF STUDENT Thea Murray

GRADE ECS **SCHOOL** Wye

DATE October 1, 1989

TEACHER C. Munoz

POSITION Special Needs Aide

IEP TEAM MEMBERS

POSITION	SIGNATURE
Teacher	
Assistant Principal	
Counsellor	
Speech Clinician	

PROGRAM GOAL(S)	INSTRUCTIONAL OBJECTIVES	STRATEGY/MATERIALS/ RESOURCES	DATE START	DATE END	EVALUATION CRITERIA	PLACEMENT/PERSON RESPONSIBLE
1. develop intelligibility	– to improve intelligibility *(handwritten:* NB "r" "b" following l as in library)	– through one-to-one assistance, provide Thea with the correct speech model – have Thea repeat the model speech – provide Thea with the opportunity to interact with her peers with appropriate levels of intelligibility	Oct. 3 *(handwritten:* check "got" – use of "timed" at intended word "forgot" – is syntax also)	June 28	– ongoing assessment notes will be kept on on-going basis – periodic reassessment by L. Brent	– C. Munoz – E. Takata – H. Murphy – L. Brent * * L. Brent is responsible to train the assigned teacher aide to carry out the appropriate assistance program for goals 1–4.
2. develop correct production of /L/	– to improve production of /L/ *(handwritten:* much improved)	– through one-to-one assistance, provide Thea with the correct speech model – have Thea repeat the model speech – encourage Thea to find words with 'L' in her environment – provide Thea with the opportunity to interact with her peers with appropriate /L/ usage	Oct. 3	June 28		

FIGURE 8.3 Sample Individual Educational Plan (IEP). Reprinted by permission of Strathcona County School.

STRATHCONA COUNTY BOARD OF EDUCATION

INDIVIDUALIZED EDUCATIONAL PLAN

NAME OF STUDENT ___Thea Murray___   GRADE ___ECS___   SCHOOL ___Wye___   TEACHER ___C. Munoz___

PROGRAM GOALS (S)	INSTRUCTIONAL OBJECTIVES	STRATEGY/MATERIALS/ RESOURCES	DATE START	DATE END	EVALUATION CRITERIA	PLACEMENT/PERSON RESPONSIBLE
3. develop receptive and expressive syntax	– to improve receptive and expressive syntax	– through one-to-one assistance, provide Thea with the correct speech model – have Thea repeat the model speech – provide Thea with the opportunity to interact with her peers with appropriate receptive and expressive syntax	Oct. 3	June 28		
4. develop fine motor skills	– to improve fine motor skills	– through one-to-one assistance, Thea will participate in a variety of fine motor skills including pasting, painting, drawing, manipulating, etc.	Oct. 3	June 28	– ongoing assessment – progress relative to expected performance	

i.e., "I don't got a turn".

Second objective improved – vert using more not where not intended.

FIGURE 8.3 (continued)

Dimensions of Exceptionality

Given the classroom teacher's role in identifying and providing services for children with special needs, it has become increasingly important for teachers to be familiar with the various manifestations of exceptionality they are most likely to encounter.

Exceptionality, as we saw, has two dimensions: the exceptionally gifted and those who are disabled.* Exceptionalities are identified in each of the three main areas of human functioning—the cognitive, the physical, and the social-emotional. In each area, abilities range continuously from some point just noticeably beyond the average to the furthest extreme in either direction. People at the extreme of the negative end include, for example, the severely mentally disabled, those with severe multiple physical disabilities (such as being blind, deaf, and quadriplegic), and those with serious emotional disorders (such as schizophrenia).

PL 94-142 provides an important official definition for the term *handicapped*: "Handicapped children means those evaluated as being mentally retarded, hard-of-hearing, deaf, speech impaired, visually handicapped, seriously emotionally disturbed, orthopedically impaired, other health impaired, deaf-blind, multihandicapped, or as having specific learning disabilities, who because of these impairments need special education and related services" (U.S. Office of Education, 1977, p. 42478).

*PPC: I noted the Bear is now using *disabled* where he used *handicapped* in the previous edition. I know that *disabled* is more acceptable, but it too strikes me as more negative than necessary. Many of my special education colleagues now use the word *challenged*. Might that be better?

Author: In even earlier editions, other terms such as *deficient* were often used. And before the Bear, words like *idiot, imbecile,* and *moron* were widely accepted psychological terms. Now these terms are carefully avoided (except when speaking of stupid cretins like wild cows). Terms such as these often have highly negative connotations and are quite uninformative. Maybe, as you suggest, *challenged* would be better. It's certainly more emotionally neutral. But it's also stunningly vague.

The sections that follow examine exceptionality of three major kinds—physical, cognitive (intellectual), and social (emotional)—with special emphasis on cognitive disabilities, which often are more relevant for the regular classroom teacher (see Figure 8.4). Teachers who major in special education would be expected to know much more than can be included in these few pages.

Physical Exceptionality. At one extreme among the physically exceptional are those who are endowed with superior capabilities that might be manifested in athletic skills and in other activities requiring motor coordination, strength, rhythm, and so on. At the other extreme are those with physical disabilities, sensory deficits, cerebral palsy, or a number of diseases that might or might not lead to problems in school. Among these, blindness and deafness may require special assistance beyond the capabilities and resources of the regular classroom teacher. On occasion, however, corrective devices (glasses and hearing aids) and special learning aids (large-print books, for example) can be used within the regular classroom in compliance with mainstreaming regulations.

Social-Emotional Exceptionality. At the positive end of this dimension of exceptionality are those more socially adept, better adjusted, more immune to the stresses and tensions of life than are ordinary individuals. These exceptional individuals often go unrecognized and unheralded, although they might on occasion be envied.

At the other extreme are those variously described as "behavior-disordered," "emotionally disturbed," or "socially maladjusted." What these labels have in common is that each describes individuals who are troubled and often unhappy and who are also usually a source of difficulty for teachers, peers, parents, and others (Whelan, 1978). Estimates of the prevalence of emotional disorders vary from 2 to 20 percent of the total school population, depending on the criteria used and on whether both mild and more severe cases are included (Kelly, Bullock, & Dykes, 1977).

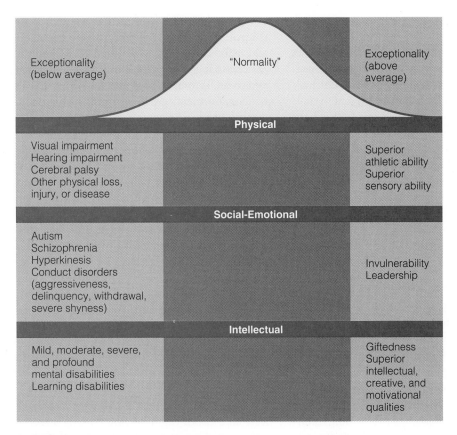

FIGURE 8.4 Dimensions of exceptionality.

For the most severe manifestations of emotional disturbance (for schizophrenia, for example), institutional care is generally required. In many cases, however, children who might be described as suffering from emotional disorders continue to function in regular classrooms.

For instance, attention deficit hyperactivity disorder (ADHD) (commonly called "hyperactivity") does not generally require special services outside the school. ADHD children are characterized by a variety of persistent symptoms, the most common of which are extreme difficulty in sustaining attention, a very high level of physical activity, and high levels of vocalization (Platzman et al., 1992). In school, such children, the majority of whom are boys, are easily distracted, inatten-

tive, fidgety, loud, and restless. Not surprisingly, they are often a problem for teachers.

Attempts to change the behavior of ADHD children through counseling or reinforcement programs have had only limited success (Gordon, Thomason, Cooper, & Ivers, 1991). As a result, ADHD is most often treated medically with Ritalin, a psychostimulant, amphetaminelike drug that has the paradoxical (contrary to expectations) effect of sedating rather than stimulating these children. Because of the behavior problems associated with high activity in schools, some children who do *not* have ADHD are nevertheless diagnosed as such and prescribed Ritalin. Unfortunately, Ritalin can have some negative effects (emotional and physical), although these are rare when the child has been properly diagnosed (Guffey, 1991).

A variety of other personality and conduct disorders (sometimes manifested in lying, cheating, extreme insolence, and other socially maladaptive behaviors) occasionally present serious management and teaching problems for teachers. In most cases, however, such students remain in regular classrooms, barring some major transgression of school regulations or some criminal activity that might lead to expulsion from school and/or to detention in an institution for juvenile offenders.

Intellectual Exceptionality. On the one hand are the gifted and creative, about whom we spoke earlier in this chapter; on the other are children who have significant difficulty in learning some, if not all, things learned relatively easily by others. This dimension of exceptionality includes two important categories: the mentally disabled (or retarded) and the learning disabled.

Mental retardation is defined by the American Association on Mental Deficiency (AAMD) as follows: "Mental retardation refers to significantly subaverage general intellectual functioning resulting in or associated with concurrent impairments in adaptive behavior and manifested during the developmental period" (Grossman, 1983). Figure 8.5 presents some commonly used classification schemes for mental retardation. Note that the labels are based primarily on performance on standard measures of intelligence, most commonly the Stanford-Binet. In practice, approximately 1 percent of the general population appears to be mentally disabled—when level of adaptive behavior is taken into account (Mercer, 1979). This is why it is so important to take adaptation into consideration (Edgerton, 1979).

The causes of mental retardation are so varied that classification is almost always done in terms of degree rather than cause. Nevertheless, researchers often identify two groups of causes: those that are *organic*, whether they be pre- or postnatal, and the *familial* (Zigler & Hodapp,

1991). Organic causes of mental retardation include cerebral injury, chromosomal aberrations and defects such as Down's syndrome, maternal infections at critical periods of fetal development, and so on. Familial causes include inadequate genetic endowment, growing up in unstimulating environments, or a combination of environmental and genetic factors.

The largest group of retarded children is only mildly or moderately disabled. Only some of these children are identified as intellectually impaired before they have been in school for a period of time. Many are eventually capable of acceptable academic achievement in elementary school. The majority are usually mainstreamed.

Severe and profound mental impairment are generally associated with highly limited motor learning—virtually no communication skills in the case of profound impairment and only rudimentary skills for the severely impaired—and institutionalization throughout life. In the case of profound retardation, institutional care is usually of a custodial nature, involving feeding and clothing.

Whereas intellectual impairment usually affects all areas of cognitive functioning, a second class of intellectual exceptionality manifests itself in only a few areas of functioning—and frequently, only in one. This class includes children who, in the absence of any perceptible physical or emotional disturbance, nevertheless experience significant difficulty in learning specific skills. These children have sometimes been described as suffering from a learning dysfunction, hyperactivity, cerebral dysfunction, minimal brain damage, perceptual disabilities, dyslexia, perceptual disability, or simply as being slow learners.

A. O. Ross (1976) notes that most of these terms are nonspecific, often confusing, and sometimes meaningless. Largely for this reason, Samuel Kirk proposed the term **learning disability** in 1963. It soon became widely popular and is now used to describe a variety of conditions, including academic retardation; specific learning problems associated with single subject areas,

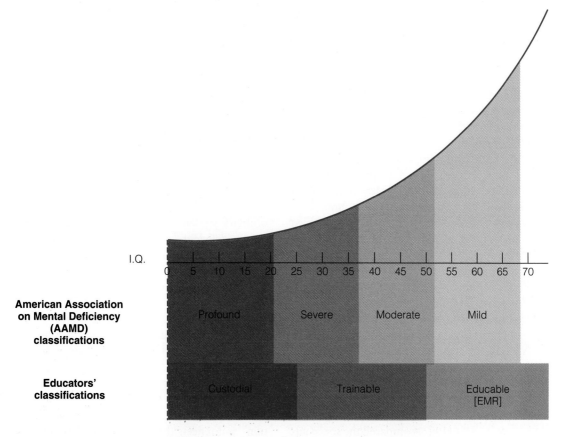

I.Q.

| 0 | 5 | 10 | 15 | 20 | 25 | 30 | 35 | 40 | 45 | 50 | 55 | 60 | 65 | 70 |

**American Association
on Mental Deficiency
(AAMD)
classifications**

| Profound | Severe | Moderate | Mild |

**Educators'
classifications**

| Custodial | Trainable | Educable
[EMR] |

FIGURE 8.5 Two common classification schemes for mental disabilities. (Note that these classifications are based entirely on measured IQ. In practice, adaptive skills would also be taken into account.) The AAMD classifications shown here are based on the Stanford-Binet or Cattell tests. The Wechsler scales have a different distribution and therefore different cutoff points: 55–69, mild; 40–54, moderate; 25–39, severe; below 25, profound.

such as reading or arithmetic, and manifested in uneven patterns of development; some central nervous system dysfunctions; and all other learning problems not due to mental retardation, environmental disadvantage, or emotional disturbance (Morsink, 1985).

The identifying characteristic of learning disabilities, according to government regulations, is a significant discrepancy between IQ and achievement, caused by problems in such basic psychological processes as remembering and perceiving.

Children whose ability to learn is generally depressed or who suffer from environmental deprivation, emotional problems, or sensory defects are specifically excluded from the category of the learning disabled. But, as Shepard, Smith, and Vojir (1983) found following a survey of eight hundred children classified as learning disabled, many supposedly learning-disabled children have characteristics that do not conform to the definitions found in government regulations. In fact, more than half this sample had emotional disorders, mild retardation, or specific language problems; they should not have been classified as learning disabled. Unfortunately, this misclassification may lead to the use of inappropriate treatment strategies with some of these children. It will almost certainly confound the results of research designed to investigate the incidence of learning disabilities and the effectiveness of various treatments.

Given this evidence of widespread faulty classification, it is perhaps not surprising that the number of children identified as learning disabled more than doubled between 1978 and 1983 (Kavale & Forness, 1985). The learning disabled now make up roughly two-thirds of all students requiring special education in the United States—almost 4 percent of the total school population (Myers & Hammill, 1990).

In most instances, learning disabilities are treated in the context of the regular classroom, often with the help and advice of learning-disability specialists. These children are not typically different from other children in regular classrooms, other than for the specific learning difficulty they experience. Most of the learning disabled are well adjusted, and well liked. When Juvonen and Bear (1992) compared the social adjustment of learning-disabled children with that of non-learning-disabled children, they found no differences between the two in the proportion of each ranked as well liked or as rejected on sociometric scales.

Here, as in other areas of exceptionality, the onus of initial identification rests with the classroom teacher. In fact, the teacher's opinion is sometimes relied on in place of more formal—and more expensive—testing. Unfortunately, as Clarizio (1992) reports, the regular classroom teacher's opinion is often the *most* influential data with respect to determining whether a child is learning disabled. Yet the results of Clarizio's research indicate that relying solely on teachers' judgments would nearly *double* the number of students identified as learning disabled, resulting in a huge number of false identifications. Hence, the need for clear definition and strict adherence to accepted criteria when identifying *all* special-needs children.

Identifying Exceptional Children

Macmillan and Meyers (1979) note that mild mental retardation, learning disabilities, and emotional disturbances are seldom identified before the child goes to school. A number of stages appear to be common in the identification of each of these manifestations of exceptionality.

Initially, these children begin school as ordinary students. Some will achieve at a sufficiently deficient level that they may be kept in first grade an extra year, a practice that seems to be more common for the mildly retarded from lower socioeconomic backgrounds (Mercer, 1973).

The next stage described by Mercer begins when the teacher realizes that the child has not progressed sufficiently to be promoted to the next grade. At this point, the decision is made to refer the child for further diagnosis. In some cases, the child may simply be promoted to the next grade—an action that is called a "social promotion" and reflects the school's reluctance to separate children from age peers.

Lynch, Simms, von Hippel, and Shuchat (1978) provide a number of suggestions to help teachers in the early stages of tentative diagnosis—when the important decision is whether professional assessment is warranted. First, teachers are urged to learn to observe carefully in order to identify children who seem "difficult," hard to get along with, or slow. Having identified these children, teachers can attempt to determine what might work with them and can try several different approaches. Frequently, it turns out that there is no problem.

Second, Lynch, Simms, von Hippel, and Shuchat suggest that teachers ask themselves key questions such as does the child learn so slowly, or is the child's adaptive behavior (ability to use language, to play with other children, and to be

identifying exceptionality

Some extremes of exceptionality are obvious and can easily be detected by parents and others not specifically trained in such things. However, most instances of exceptionality are not extreme, and their diagnosis and assessment are often difficult.

Although the final diagnosis and assessment of an exceptionality that requires special intervention are usually made by a professional team following extensive testing, initial identification of those in need of further evaluation is often made by parents or teachers; hence, it is useful to know what to look for. However, parents and others need to be extremely cautious in their tentative judgments of exceptionality, especially in cases in which children (and sometimes adults) experience mild problems with subjects such as reading or arithmetic. It is extremely easy to misinterpret a common learning problem as evidence of a learning disability or mental retardation.

Some symptoms parents and teachers might notice are listed here. Further assessment and evaluation, or referral, can usually be provided by school psychologists.

Cerebral Palsy—Diagnosis is made by a physician. Symptoms can include any, none, or most of the following and can range from very mild to very severe:

uneven gait

jerky movements

speech problems

rigidity

drooling

balance problems

uncontrolled fluttering movements

involuntary facial gestures

shaking movements

possible convulsions

Epilepsy—Diagnosis requires medical assessment. Observable symptoms are seizures. In petit mal, seizures are momentary lapses of attention lasting only seconds and may be accompanied by fluttering of the eyelids and suspension of activity. Grand mal seizures (also called "fits," "attacks," or "convulsions") may involve sudden stiffening, falling, thrashing around, and moaning. Seizures may last only a few seconds and seldom last more than five minutes. Seizures that last longer require urgent medical attention.

hearing problems

frequent earaches

inattentiveness

speech problems

high volume on TV or radio

failure to respond

discharge from one or both ears

child turns head to listen

speaks in abnormally loud voice

Vision Problems

rubbing of eyes

redness of eyes

headaches

difficulty seeing chalkboard

squinting

high sensitivity to light

holds material close to see

Schizophrenia—Requires psychiatric diagnosis. May be characterized by one or more of the following:

aloofness

refusal to cuddle

self-injurious behavior (head banging, for example)

no verbal communication

repetitive behaviors (twirling, rocking, for example)

abnormal object attachments

insensitivity to pain

poor balance

withdrawal

extreme distress when faced with change

high sensitivity to pain

poor coordination

Attention Deficit Hyperactivity Disorder—Primarily a male disorder.

continued

Characterized by at least eight of the following characteristics, present for at least six months and before the age of seven, and more frequent and severe than in most other children of the same mental age:

often fidgets

difficulty remaining seated

easily distracted

difficulty awaiting turn

often blurts out answers

difficulty following instructions

difficulty sustaining attention

shifts often from one activity to another

difficulty playing quietly

talks excessively

often interrupts

often does not seem to listen

often loses things

often takes physical risks

Conduct and Personality Disorders—These disorders require psychological or psychiatric assessment. They span a wide range of behaviors and symptoms, some of which might include the following (note that only extreme and persistent manifestations of these behaviors would be considered disorders):

high aggressiveness and hostility

extreme withdrawal and social isolation

extreme shyness

lying

stealing

temper tantrums

highly negative self-concept

Mental Disabilities—Diagnosis and assessment require administration of individual intelligence tests by a trained psychologist. The most obvious feature is deficient ability to learn, ranging from mild to severe; defined in terms of significantly sub-average performance on intelligence tests (IQ below 70) and deficits in adaptive behavior. Early symptoms of moderate to severe disabilities include:

significant developmental lag in learning to crawl, walk, and talk

failure to learn developmental tasks such as eating, dressing, tying shoes

poor motor coordination

markedly inferior verbal skills

Mild Retardation—Ordinarily, this is not detected before school age; once in school, the child may show the following symptoms:

significant difficulty in learning

problems with short-term memory

language deficits

motor problems

short attention span

Learning Disabilities—Identification and assessment are difficult even for trained professionals. Learning disabilities may be manifested in:

uneven pattern of academic achievement

academic retardation

learning problems not related to intelligence or environmental disadvantage

specific learning problems in language-related subjects or arithmetic

erratic spelling

frequent failure to recognize simple words

confusion of letters or numbers

persistent difficulty with simple arithmetic computations

inattentiveness, impulsivity, mood shifts

poor visual memory

reasonably independent) so poor that the child cannot participate fully with the other children?

Third, and very important, teachers must be careful to distinguish between exceptionality and simple cultural differences. Very intelligent children whose dominant language and values are significantly different from those of the mainstream can sometimes appear less than normally bright.

Fourth, just as it is important to distinguish between the culturally different and those in need of special education, it is also important to recognize normal individual differences in temperament, motivation, interests, and so on. And teachers must always be aware of the possibility that difficulties between themselves and certain children might have to do with differences in personal style rather than with specific failings in the children.

Once teachers have determined that there is a real possibility of a problem requiring special attention, the next stage is to obtain professional help. Subsequent diagnosis—typically undertaken by professionals—usually involves assessments using prescribed instruments and consultation among members of an interdisciplinary team. Following diagnosis, remedial action will depend on the specific diagnosis, especially for learning disabilities, for which remedial prescriptions are based on as detailed a diagnosis as possible. As we saw, most children diagnosed as having mild mental retardation, an emotional disturbance, or a learning disability will continue to attend regular classes, although they may also be segregated for group or individual special services. For each of these children, an IEP will need to be prepared and implemented. (See box entitled "Identifying Exceptionality.")

Labels in Special Education

"Learning disabled," "educable mentally retarded," "attention deficit hyperactivity disorder"—these and their highly common letter substitutes, LD, EMR, and ADHD, respectively, are widely used labels in special education. But they are just that: labels. Labels do nothing more than name; they don't explain anything. To say that Eric has difficulty recognizing numbers *because* he is LD might mislead us into thinking we understand *why* Eric hesitates and struggles when he picks up the six of spades. But all the label "LD" tells us is that Eric's behavior manifests a combination of symptoms that we have agreed to label "LD." The label can be useful because it permits us to communicate with one another, and it gives us some basis for developing educational programs for children like Eric.

Still, labels do have disadvantages, and many argue against their use. Common arguments insist that labels are often unfair (given the social and cultural biases of intelligence tests), that they lead to lower expectations and thus present an additional disadvantage to those who are labeled, and that there is a remarkable lack of homogeneity among those who are given identical labels (Macmillan & Meyers, 1979). In addition, there is a growing tendency to treat disabled children as *quantitatively* rather than *qualitatively* different from normal children. The use of generally pejorative labels is clearly incompatible with this trend.

We have come some distance from labels that were once as widely accepted as those we use today: "idiot," "moron," "imbecile," "cretin" . . .

MAIN POINTS

1. U.S. federal regulations define the talented and gifted as children who are identified by professionals as being capable of high performance by virtue of outstanding capabilities that might be reflected in general intellectual ability, specific academic aptitude, creative or productive thinking, leadership or artistic talent. In practice, these children are often nominated by teachers and

identified on the basis of ability and achievement measures. The culturally different are often overlooked and are underrepresented among programs for the gifted.

2. The two main approaches to educating the talented and gifted are acceleration, in which students progress through the conventional curriculum at an accelerated pace (for example, Stanley's radical acceleration), and enrichment, in which students explore the conventional curriculum in greater depth and breadth (for example, Renzulli's revolving door model). Other approaches include mentoring, self-directed and independent study, the use of individual education plans (IEPs), the establishment of special schools, and the provision of special out-of-school programs and courses.

3. Brainstorming is a group approach for producing ideas and solving problems, using the principle of deferred evaluation. The Gordon technique is a slight modification of brainstorming that begins with an abstraction of the problem. Morphological analysis involves dividing a problem into its attributes and brainstorming each of these. De Bono presents a number of practical suggestions for developing skills involved in lateral (creative) and vertical (logical) thinking. The use of conceptual models can also increase creative thinking and problem solving.

4. Classroom climate is related to creative behavior. Students in formal schools have lower scores on creativity measures than do their counterparts in informal schools; warm, receptive teachers are more likely to encourage creativity, and severe competition is detrimental to creative performance.

5. Teaching styles are related groups of teaching activities. Formal styles (structured, teacher controlled, achievement oriented, emphasizing individual work) often lead to higher academic achievement. Informal styles (student centered, integrative, intrinsically motivated—characteristics of open classrooms) are frequently associated with lower academic achievement and are some-

times associated with higher creativity and motivation. Results of research comparing direct styles (teacher controlled, lecture dominated, authority driven) with indirect styles (student centered, question oriented) are somewhat ambiguous.

6. Disputed evidence shows that teachers' expectations can serve as self-fulfilling prophecies and affect students' performance positively or negatively in accordance with expectations. Expectations are often higher for students from higher socioeconomic levels, for obedient children, for students with the most positive labels (for example, "learning disabled" rather than "mentally retarded"), and for those who sit front and center and speak clearly. There is also the opposite possibility—that low expectations might lead teachers to provide additional help for a student, thus leading to higher achievement.

7. *Exceptionality* describes significant deviation from the norm in cognitive, social-emotional, or physical functioning. It can be either positive (associated with superior functioning) or negative (related to deficits in functioning).

8. In addition to mandating education in the "least restrictive environment" (mainstreaming, in other words), Public Law 94-142 attempted to establish the child's right to due process (classification and assessment procedures and all school records open to parents and subject to appeal and independent evaluation), to protect children from biased and discriminatory testing (more than one assessment procedure must be used, and tests must be presented in the child's native language), and to assure that all children in need of special programs are given systematic programs with clear goals and built-in evaluation procedures (individual education plans, or IEPs).

9. Mainstreaming (also called "integration" or "inclusion") attempts to meet the needs of exceptional children in the regular classroom. IEPs must be prepared for all special-needs children, following assessment and parental involvement and consent. These include statements of goals, duration of the program, and evaluation procedures.

10. Physical exceptionality may be manifested in exceptional athletic ability, for example; at the other extreme, it may be manifested in a variety of sensory or motor impairments, physical disabilities, diseases, and so on.

11. Social-emotional exceptionality in its negative sense includes manifestations of emotional disturbance, behavioral disorders, and attention deficit hyperactivity disorder (ADHD), among others. All but the most severe forms of social-emotional exceptionality are ordinarily dealt with in the regular classroom.

12. Mental retardation is characterized by a marked depression in general ability to learn and may vary from mild to profound. Learning disabilities generally refer to more specific learning impairments, often manifested in difficulties with reading or arithmetic.

13. Initial identification of exceptionality is often made by classroom teachers after the child has begun school. Mild retardation and learning disabilities are seldom diagnosed before this time.

14. Labels are useful in categorizing children and in providing for their special needs. But they simply name rather than explain. It is best if the names are not pejorative.

SUGGESTED READINGS

The following two references should be of particular value for teachers concerned with the creative behavior of their students. The first has been translated into many different languages and continues to be popular. The second is a collection of papers dealing with novel, technologically oriented, constructionist approaches to teaching thinking. Many of these approaches reflect the use of what this chapter terms conceptual models:

OSBORN, A. (1957). *Applied imagination.* New York: Charles Scribner's.

HAREL, I. (Ed.). (1990). *Constructionist learning.* Cambridge, Mass.: MIT Media Laboratory.

Cropley's short book is a useful analysis of current thinking and research in creativity. The last three chapters deal specifically with approaches that foster creativity in the classroom.

CROPLEY, A. J. (1992). *More ways than one: Fostering creativity.* Norwood, N.J.: Ablex.

A practical classroom guide for the teacher in an inclusive (main-streamed) classroom is

HANKO, G. (1990). *Special needs in ordinary classrooms: Supporting teachers* (2nd ed.). Oxford, England: Blackwell.

A detailed look at learning disabilities, with emphasis on practical strategies for teachers, is included in

MYERS, P. I., & HAMMILL, D. D. (1990). *Learning disabilities: Basic concepts, assessment practices, and instructional strategies* (4th ed.). Austin, Texas: pro-ed.

Far more comprehensive introductions to special education than can be provided here are found in general textbooks such as

HARING, N. G., & MCCORMICK (Eds.). (1990). *Exceptional children and youth* (5th ed.). Columbus, Ohio: Merrill.

HALLAHAN, D. P., & KAUFFMAN, J. M. (1991). *Exceptional children: Introduction to special education* (5th ed.). Boston: Allyn & Bacon.

In the summer, a bear's heart normally beats approximately forty times per minute. In winter, when the bear is denned up, heart rate may drop as low as ten beats per minute. Amazingly, extreme cold rouses the bear as readily as does warmth. If this were not the case, many bears would freeze to death because it is necessary for the bear to awaken and warm up when the temperature drops too low (L. H. Matthews, 1969).

I am going to where life is more like life than it is here.
Sean O'Casey, *Cock-a-Doodle Donkey*

There is surely a piece of divinity in us, something that was before the elements, and owes no homage unto the sun.
Sir Thomas Browne, *Religio Medici*

Chapter 9 | HUMANISTIC APPROACHES TO TEACHING

PREVIEW Humanism objects to what is sometimes interpreted as the mechanistic, dehumanizing, and inhumane emphases of "traditional" approaches to psychology and education. It urges adoption of new attitudes, concepts, and approaches in these fields. This chapter describes the fundamental characteristics of humanistic approaches to understanding people and to teaching. The most important point it makes is that humanism, behaviorism, and cognitivism are not incompatible. You can be all the good things that humanism implies and still make use of the knowledge offered by other approaches.

Excerpt from Don't Lie to Grammaw

When I was a young student, I believed that psychologists had devious ways of peering into our minds and that they could, if they wanted to, easily uncover all sorts of dark or juicy secrets hidden there. So I studied psychology, absolutely convinced there was little about human and animal behavior that a clever psychologist could not explain to everyone's satisfaction. And, as a budding psychologist, I brought explanations home to my grandmother. I told her why pigs lie in their muddy wallows on hot summer days; why chickens crow in the morning and roost at night. I explained to her why cows always go into the same stall and why horses stand with their backs to a storm.

But she saw no magic in my explanations, my grandmother. "If I were a pig," she said, "I'd lie in the mud. And if I were a chicken I'd crow in the morning and roost at night."

"But . . ."

"And if I were a cow," she continued, keeping me from telling her how my explanations were still bang-on . . . "if I were a cow, I'd be a wild cow. I'd never go into stalls!"

"But the point," I said (brilliantly, I thought), "is that you're not a pig, a chicken, or a cow. You're a people, and we have explanations for that too!" Quickly, I launched into a wonderful behavioristic explanation of Frank's fear of cats and Louise's embarrassing attachment to the tattered remains of a dirty green baby blanket.

"But," countered my grandmother, "what about why Frank isn't scared of dogs, and he was bitten about eight times? And cats hardly ever bit him. And what about how Louise doesn't even like any other blankets or pillows? And why doesn't Lucy like her baby blanket?"

A practiced skeptic, my grandmother could always ask questions more rapidly than I could answer them. And although I had enough of the beginnings of some answers to eventually convince her that Skinner, Freud, Piaget, and others each had important and useful things to say about Frank's fear of cats and Louise's love of a dirty rag, there was no way I could ever convince her that they, or I, knew more about Frank or Louise than she did.

As my grandmother so pointedly put it, "I personally know pigs that don't care to wallow in mud, chickens that never roost or crow, cows that park their arses wherever, and horses so contrary they'll face whichever way they bloody please."

My grandmother was a humanist. *

HUMANISTIC PSYCHOLOGY

Humanistic psychology is concerned with the uniqueness, the individuality, the humanity of each individual. It is an orientation that readily admits that some people smile when they wallow in mud, some turn up their noses but endure the embarrassment, and others find such behavior quite unacceptable. In more human terms, it is an orientation based on the fundamental observation that although we might resemble each other in many important ways, each of us is quite different from every other. Our uniqueness is our "self." And self is the most central concept in humanistic psychology. Three passages in this text (in Chapter 1, here, and the Epilogue) make the point that a science of humans tends to dehumanize people. This point is especially appropriate here because the approach discussed in this chapter attempts to humanize people.

Humanism Versus Other Views

The conflict between humanism and behavioristic or cognitive approaches owes to orientations

that are fundamentally different in terms of their most basic beliefs and attitudes toward human beings. In a nutshell, what humanists object to is what they see as the technological orientation of approaches such as behaviorism. In its most extreme form, this technological orientation asserts that certain identifiable teaching processes, when used with such and such a type of student for such and such a kind of content, will predictably result in the attainment of specific, previously identified, and clearly intended objectives.

Humanists object strongly to this process-product orientation. As Shulman (1986) observes, they see it as focusing too strongly on techniques that "should" be practiced by teachers and as placing far too much emphasis on the measurable outcomes of the teaching/learning process, especially in terms of gains on standardized tests. They are alarmed that the conclusions and recommendations of process-product research have often been used by school authorities as a basis for evaluating school systems, teachers, and teaching.

The humanistic view emphasizes two things: the uniqueness of the pupil and the autonomy of the teacher. If teaching is both an art and a science—as we claimed in Chapter 1—humanists are on the side of art and behaviorists on the side of science.

But before we rush forward to describe what it is the humanists have to say, it is important to note that our use of terms in this section, and in much of this chapter, is almost shamefully loose and general. Real life is not so simple. Behaviorists are not often as technology oriented as an exaggerated humanistic description of their views might suggest; nor are all process-product researchers behaviorists, or cognitivists. In fact, later in this chapter we look at two important and quite specific instructional methods (one based on learning styles and the other on cooperative learning), each of which reflects much of the humanist's concern with the individual and with emotional growth but each of which is fundamentally concerned with both the processes and

*PPC: Don't you think the language is a little strong, especially for a grandmother? After all, some students reading this have had pretty sheltered lives.

Author: That's the way she talked. If she felt like it. Sheltered students, please don't take offense.

On second thought, if you want to take offense . . .

the products of instruction. The results of process-product research do not really suggest that teachers should ideally be quasirobotic classroom mechanics who repair cognitive and behavioral deficits and impairments and produce wonderful little academic achievers.

Keep in mind that most educators do not fall neatly into the humanist, the behaviorist, and the cognitive camps. Most are quite eclectic; they borrow from here and there.

So what we do in this chapter is stretch the truth on two counts: We exaggerate the differences between humanism and, especially, behaviorism; and we pretend that all that is not clearly humanistic is, by default, behavioristic. Exaggeration can be a useful pedagogical device—so long as you are not deceived.*

ROGERIAN PHENOMENOLOGICAL THEORY

As an introduction to humanism, we look first at a summary of those aspects of the writing of Carl Rogers that deal with personality and behavior; then we look at several approaches to education that reflect humanistic orientations. (Rogers is among the most influential theorists in this area; Abraham Maslow, another important humanist, is discussed in Chapter 10.)

Rogers's writings are based not so much on objective data as on his answers for questions

---

*PPC: This is an important point. Perhaps you should repeat it.

Author: Okay: Exaggeration can be a useful pedagogical device—so long as you are not deceived.

PPC: That's not what I meant. Can you make the point in a different way, to make it more memorable?

Author: Okay. Real life is seldom like the simple black-and-white pictures that we draw to depict our little theories and our precious ideological stances. We are still like children using crude wooden pencils. In our drawings we miss all the color, most of the nuances, and thousands of other poses that we could have drawn. We draw only frozen stick-men and stick-women, but we think we have drawn something with a soul.

---

such as what individuals think about the world. How do they feel? How do they perceive their relationships to others? Thus, Rogers's theory contrasts sharply with the more rigorous approaches of other theorists. And it provides the teacher with a different way of looking at and communicating with students.

Important Terms

Different terms are used to describe the various emphases of Rogerian theory. The first, **client-centered therapy** (also called **person-centered therapy**), describes several aspects of the system. It indicates, first, that the theory is a therapeutic one; that is, it is designed to be useful to a counselor who deals with behavioral and emotional problems. Second, the label highlights the major difference between this and other approaches to **counseling**—namely, that the counseling procedures revolve around the person. It proposes client-centered as opposed to **directive therapy.** The counselor's role in client-centered therapy is accordingly deemphasized; instead of giving advice or solving problems for clients, the therapist sets the stage so that clients themselves define their problems, react to them, and take steps toward their solution. (The process is actually much more complex than it may seem from the preceding statements; see Rogers, 1951.)

The second term is **phenomenology**, a term that denotes concern with the world as it is perceived by an individual, rather than as it may actually be. Rogerian theory is phenomenological in that it is concerned primarily with the individual's own view of the world—that is, with the world as a person sees it rather than as it appears to others.

The third term is **humanism**. Humanism in literature, philosophy, and psychology has historically been concerned with human worth, with individuality, with humanity, and with the individual's right to determine personal actions. Accordingly, the development of human potential tends to be highly valued while the attainment of material goals is deemphasized. Rogers's description of **self-actualization** as the end toward which all humans strive is a clear expression of humanistic concerns. In addition, his encouragement of client-centered therapy is compatible with the humanist's emphasis on self-determination. Indeed, the question of self-determination versus external control, together with a consideration of the ethical and practical problems of applying a science of behavior, was the subject of a debate by Rogers and Skinner (1956).

The Behavior-Control Debate: Rogers Versus Skinner

The central issue in this debate concerns the application of behavior control techniques for personal control in social groups, for educational procedures, and for control by governments. Skinner argues strongly for abandoning techniques of aversive control (see Chapter 4) and for consciously and openly applying techniques of positive control toward the betterment of society. (This topic was the subject of his novel, *Walden II* [1948], an account of a fictitious society developed through the application of a behavioral technology.)

But, claims Rogers, Skinner underestimates the problem of power by making the false assumption that techniques of social control will be used in the better interests of society. Furthermore, he fails to specify goals for this behavioral technology. Rogers dismisses Skinner's claim that if behavioral scientists experiment with society, "eventually the practices which make for the greatest biological and psychological strength of the group will presumably survive" (Skinner, 1955, p. 549). Rogers argues instead that a society's goals should be concerned primarily with the process of "becoming," with achieving worth and dignity, with being creative—in short, with the process of self-actualization.

The debate resolves no issues; it simply exposes the fundamental conflict between those who favor human control (for our benefit)

through the thoughtful application of a science of behavior and those who believe that science should be used not to change or control us but simply to enhance our capacity for self-control and self-determination.

Principles of Rogers's Theory

In the eleventh chapter of *Client-Centered Therapy* (1951), Rogers presents an integrated account of his position in the form of nineteen propositions. The most important of these are summarized here. (Also, see Table 9.1.) An understanding of these principles is important for understanding the rationale underlying the various approaches to humanistic education described later in this chapter.

Principle 1. Every individual is the center of a continually changing world of experience. This, one of the most fundamental assertions of the phenomenologist, recognizes two features of human functioning that are particularly important for the teacher. First, it implies that for any individual, the significant aspects of the environment consist of the world of *private* experience. Second, it suggests not only that the individual's phenomenological world is private but also that it can never be completely known by anyone else. Consider, for example, the simple complaint of a child to his mother after waking up from a nightmare: "Mama, I'm scared." The fear that the child expresses is a real and significant aspect of his world, and his mother may draw on her own stored-up memories of past fears to imagine how her son feels. But she cannot really know his fear. The phenomenological world is private.

Principle 2. The organism reacts to a field as it is experienced and perceived. This perceptual field is, for the individual, reality. This proposition makes the point that reality is the **phenomenal field** (the individual's immediate consciousness), and because this field is defined in terms of the individual's private experience, reality is also

TABLE 9.1 Major Characteristics of Human Personality According to Rogers (1951)

1. *Reality is phenomenological.*	The significant aspects of reality consist of the world of private experience. Our realities are therefore completely individualistic. They can be *intuited* but not *known* by others.
2. *Behavior is motivated by a need to self-actualize.*	Each of us has a basic tendency to strive toward becoming a complete, healthy, competent individual through a process characterized by self-government, self-regulation, and autonomy.
3. *Behavior occurs within the context of personal realities.*	The best way to understand a person's behavior is by attempting to adopt his or her point of view; hence, humanism emphasizes the importance of open communication.
4. *The self is constructed by the individual.*	We discover who we are on the basis of direct experiences and on the basis of beliefs and values that we incorporate in our self-concepts from information provided by people who communicate to us what we are.
5. *Our behaviors conform with our notions of self.*	In general, we select behaviors that do not contradict who and what we think we are.

private. Therefore, what is real for one individual is not necessarily real for another. A student who likes her teacher, no matter how unbearable that teacher appears to other students, has a likable teacher in her phenomenal field—and her behavior toward that teacher will reflect this reality. This is why it is important for a teacher to understand that students perceive their worlds in different ways. It is no accident that the teacher who seems to understand students best is often described as empathetic (able to intuit how others feel).

Principle 3. The organism has one basic tendency and goal—to actualize, maintain, and enhance the experiencing organism. It is neither necessary nor useful to list a variety of needs, drives, or goals to account for human behavior; we strive for only one goal—self-actualization. Rogers admits that "it is difficult to find words for this proposition" (1951, p. 488). Indeed, having found the central word, *self-actualization,* he is now left with the problem of defining it.

One way of defining self-actualization is to say that it involves becoming whatever one can become through activities determined by oneself (Maslow, 1970). In other words, to actualize oneself is to develop one's potentialities. Rogers attempts to clarify this definition by describing some characteristics of the process of self-actualization.

Self-actualization is, first, a directional process in the sense that it tends toward maturation, increasing competence, survival, reproduction, and so on. Interestingly, all are goals; each has, at some time, been described as a more or less important motivation-related objective of human functioning. For Rogers, however, these goals are merely tendencies that characterize an overriding process.

Self-actualization is also directional in that it is assumed to move toward increasing "self-government, self-regulation, and autonomy." At the same time it moves away from "heteronymous control, or control by external forces" (Rogers, 1951, p. 488). This is one reason for the basic

incompatibility between behavior control in a Skinnerian sense and the process of growth in a Rogerian sense.

In summary, Rogers believes that humans have an inner, directing need to develop themselves in the direction of healthy, competent, and creative functioning. This notion is absolutely basic to an understanding of the humanist's view of people as essentially good and forever striving toward a better state. It leads logically to the Rogerian belief that occasional less-than-healthy functioning is a result of experiences.

Principle 4. The best vantage point for understanding behavior is from the internal frame of reference of an individual.

The individual's reality is private and personal, says Rogers. No one can really know it. But if we are to come close to understanding someone else, we have to try to adopt their point of view— as Arnold Jackson was forced to when confronted with the question "Are you sure it's *his* problem?" (see the case about Arnold Jackson on page 245). Rogers claims that much of our inability to un-

derstand behavior results from our failure to recognize that responses are meaningful only from the individual's own point of view.

Principle 5. As a result of interacting with the environment, and especially with other people, we develop notions of who and what we are. In other words, we begin to construct notions of "self." The self is a consistent pattern of beliefs we have about our "I" or "me." As we receive feedback about ourselves from others, we incorporate this information into our concept of self. Most children receive signs at a very early age from parents and others indicating that they are lovable and good. Consequently, notions of themselves as being good become part of their perceived selves. In the same manner, a child may learn that he is "cute" from the comments of others; he may also learn that he is anything but cute ("My, my, look at that kid's nose, will you!"). As a result of receiving high grades, a student may develop a concept of self that includes the belief that she is intelligent. Conversely, she may come to think of herself as being stupid if the information she receives is negative.

Arnold Jackson, who has now been teaching for thirteen years, about his first year teaching:

I was only twenty-two and I had this grade ten class, and, I'll admit, I was scared. What scared me most was I might have bad discipline, they wouldn't listen to me. So I watched real hard for misbehavior and rebellion because I was determined I'd wipe it out quick.

Well, there was this student, big guy named Randy, a bit older than all the others, and he wasn't doing very well. He'd already failed at least once but I think twice, and he could never answer any questions in class, and I just knew he was going to be trouble.

Which he was. Only maybe the second or third day of English class, and already he was slouched down in his seat, his legs sprawled way out into the aisle. So I straightened him out, just a quick, firm, verbal reprimand—which worked, but I had to do it twice more that class, and again the next day, until, finally, totally exasperated, I just walked down the aisle, put my foot under his outstretched leg, and flung it back under his desk.

At that moment, he looked at me like raw hate, and I knew I'd got me a bad enemy. And from there, it just seemed to get worse, day by day. Every time I looked at him in class, it's like he was doing something else, mostly not paying attention, deliberately not handing in his assignments on time, slouching his feet out in the aisle, and then drawing them back quickly as if he'd just thought of it.

Finally, I talked to Franklin Lohde, the vice principal who was pretty well in charge of discipline in the school. I explained to him how Randy'd been behaving. "He's got a real problem," I concluded. And I'll never forget what Franklin Lohde said:

"You sure it's his problem?" he said.

"What?"

"You sure it's his problem—that he's deliberately inattentive and defiant? Or is it maybe your problem?"

That one simple question turned me right around, turned my whole career around for sure. It made me think maybe I should ask, is this really Randy's problem? Is it possible there's a problem only because in *my* mind I think there is? Is it possible maybe this big kid slouches not because he doesn't have respect but just because he's so big in that desk? The more I thought about it, the more it made sense that maybe Randy didn't deliberately decide not to finish his work, but maybe he just couldn't.

I started to see him, and a lot of my other students, in a completely different way, almost like asking well, what would that feel like or be like if I was them?

Two important sources of information are related to the development of the self. The first is the child's direct experiences—experiences of being loved and wanted and of feeling good as a result, experiences of being hurt and the consequent realization that the self does not like to be hurt, experiences of gratification (for example, eating) together with the realization that gratification is pleasant. These direct experiences lead to the development of an awareness of self. The child also experiences self-related events indirectly, often by being told things ("You're real smart, Guy. Good boy"). These experiences too contribute to the development of self-notions.

Sometimes an individual's direct and indirect experiences are contradictory and lead to conflicting notions of the self. Consider, for example, the student whose indirect experiences have led him to believe that he is academically gifted (that is, his mother has often said to him, "You're academically gifted, son") but whose direct experience is that he constantly fails in school. The resolution of this conflict may take several forms. One, of course, involves accepting the direct evidence and concluding that he is not especially brilliant. An alternative would be for him to accept the indirect value and distort his perception of direct experience. He might, for example, conclude that he is, indeed, quite brilliant but that his teachers don't like him. Or he might look for additional information to resolve the dilemma. Rogers suggests that the seeds for later maladaptive behavior are often found in the early failure to resolve the conflicting pictures of self that emerge from direct experience and what he terms *introjected values*.

Principle 6. Most of the ways of behaving that are adopted by the organism are those that are consistent with the concept of self. Consider, for example, the man who thinks of himself as a gifted orator and who has been invited to address the local chapter of the Ear Realignment and Onion Society (EROS). This proposition predicts clearly that in line with his image of self, this individual will accept the invitation. By the same token, a man who thinks of himself as inhibited and verbally inept would be likely to turn down such an invitation. In both these cases, and indeed in most instances of human behavior, the activity selected is compatible with the self-image.

Consider what happens, however, when the image of self is somewhat distorted—when, for example, the person who believes himself to be a gifted speaker has derived this notion not from direct experience (that is, applause following past orations) but from the words of his wise and ancient grandmother: "You shpeak zo vell, Ludvig, you mus be a gud spichmakerrr." In line with his self-image, he accepts the invitation; but as the day approaches, he becomes afraid—not consciously but organically. This individual may suddenly find himself physically ill in a literal sense. How can a sick man be expected to address a large audience of ear realigners and onion lovers? Indeed, to refuse to do so, when ill, is quite congruent with this man's image of self-as-great-orator. In Rogers's words, "The behavior which is adopted is such that it satisfies the organic need, but it takes channels which are consistent with the concept of self" (1951, p. 588). This—the organism's attempt to satisfy a "real" need that is not consistent with the image of self—is assumed to be one of the primary sources of neurotic behavior in humans.

Evaluation of Rogerian Phenomenology

Many aspects of Rogers's views of behavior are intuitively correct. It seems obvious that each individual perceives the world in a manner not experienced by anyone else. It also seems obvious that to understand others completely, it may be useful to adopt their points of view. Admittedly, however, some aspects of the propositions are not so obvious, and the meanings of terms such as *self-actualization* are not always clear. Nor are Rogers's conclusions about human behavior necessarily as general as he implies.

Rogers's approach is clearly "soft-nosed"; it is not based on rigorous, replicable research. Nevertheless, its merits in the progress of science may be considerable; even very speculative theorizing can sometimes generate fruitful ideas. Also, the theory has had considerable impact on counseling and teaching.

The important question now should not be whether this is a correct view of humanity but rather whether this is a useful way to look at humanity. It is.

INSTRUCTIONAL IMPLICATIONS OF HUMANISTIC THEORY

In line with their basic beliefs, humanists such as Rogers, Maslow (1970), and Combs (1982) present a strong plea for **student-centered teaching.** They advocate a philosophy of teaching in which students are given a far more important role in curriculum decisions than has traditionally been the case. They argue, as well, that teachers should be learning facilitators rather than didactic instructors and that to be successful as learning facilitators, they must be trained to be sensitive and caring, genuine and empathetic.

Not surprisingly, humanistic approaches to education emphasize healthy social and personal

As an alternative to Skinner's behavioral technology, Rogers proposes the following five-point model for the control of human behavior (Rogers & Skinner, 1956, pp. 1063–1064):

1. It is possible for us to choose to value humanity as a self-actualizing process of becoming—and also to value creativity and the processes by which we acquire knowledge.

2. Science can help us discover the conditions that lead to the development of these processes and may provide better ways of achieving these purposes.

3. It is possible for individuals or groups to set the conditions for growth without resorting to a great deal of external control or power. Current knowledge suggests that the only authority necessary is the authority to establish certain qualities of interpersonal relationship.

4. Exposed to these conditions, individuals become more self-responsible, make progress in self-actualization, become more flexible, and become more creatively adaptive.

5. Choosing these humanistic values would lead to the beginnings of a social system in which values, knowledge, adaptive skills, and even the concept of science would be continually changing and growing. The emphasis would be upon the human being as a process of becoming.

development and, at the same time, deemphasize rigorous, performance-oriented, test-dominated approaches to subject matter. They strongly advocate providing students with experiences of success rather than failure; their orientation is toward discovery rather than reception learning. The humanistic view of human functioning accepts individuals for what they are, respects their feelings and aspirations, and holds that every person has the right to self-determination. Such a view of the student leads naturally to child-centered schools.

But the child-centered school is not concerned solely with the emotional and personal development of the child—although it sometimes seems that way, partly because its emphasis is on affective growth and partly because this aspect of the humanistic movement has been exaggerated as a reaction against more rigorous approaches. Most humanistic programs, several of which are described next, are responsive to the important requirements of curricula. After all, even the most self-actualized of individuals may

still need to know how to read, write, and name the major capitals of Europe. Indeed, becoming self-actualized—that is, becoming all that one can and should be—may well depend on both knowledge of the 3Rs and the wealth of cognitive and metacognitive strategies that our new cognitive instructional sciences use to build their programs. Clearly, cognitive concerns can also be part of a thoughtful, humanistic approach to teaching.

Humanistic Movements in Education

The thinking exemplified in humanistic theory has become part of the so-called third-force psychology—the other two forces being behavioristic S-R theory and Freudian theory. In education, third-force psychology represents a movement pervaded by (1) a belief in the uniqueness and importance of the human individual and (2) a strong reaction against overly mechanistic and dehumanizing approaches to understanding humans.

The humanistic movement in education is represented by such writers as Purkey (1984), Combs (1982), Kohl (1969), T. Gordon (1974), Postman and Weingartner (1971), and many others, and by a variety of unconventional alternative approaches to education that go by labels such as "free schools," "open classrooms," "process education," and "community-centered education." The rationale for these methods is based on a genuine concern for the welfare of children—and a firm belief that this approach is better for that welfare—and the conviction that current methods of schooling leave much to be desired. Thus, in his description of an alternative to traditional schooling, Dennison speaks of the profound beneficial effects of that alternative on the lives of students. He also criticizes (very politely) the "military discipline, the schedules, the punishments and rewards, the standardization" of more conventional approaches (1969, p. 9). His book, however, like many similar books, is not in itself a criticism of existing educational methods but rather an attempt to describe an approach that might be better. "There is no need to add to the criticism of our public schools," Dennison informs us. "The critique is extensive and can hardly be improved upon" (p. 3).

Principles of Humanistic Education

The concerns of humanistic education and those of the more traditional schools are basically compatible. All schools are concerned with the current and future welfare of students; all recognize the worth and the rights of the individual; all pay lip service to such human and humane values as openness, honesty, selflessness, and altruism. The conflict between humanistic and traditional approaches exists whenever the pressure of large numbers, regimentation, anonymity, and competition for academic success leave little time and energy for unpressured communication, for the exploration of values, or for the development of affect and self. As was noted earlier, however, nothing prevents you

from being a humanistic teacher in a traditional classroom situation.

Humanistic approaches to education are highly varied, although the current literature suggests that they have a number of things in common. Knowledge of these commonalities might be of value for teachers. More detailed information than can be included here might be of even greater value (see the list of suggested readings at the end of this chapter).

Common Emphases.   Most humanistic approaches share a number of common emphases (see Table 9.2). Chief among them is a greater attention to thinking and feeling than to the acquisition of knowledge (see, for example, Simpson & Gray, 1976). In this respect they are sometimes quite different from more traditional approaches. Postman and Weingartner (1971), advocates of a "soft revolution," present a number of provocative suggestions for effecting change in the direction of greater freedom and creativity. Many of their suggestions are intended for students rather than for teachers, however, and many are more radical than is typical of the humanistic literature in general.

A second common emphasis of humanistic approaches is on development of notions of self and individual identity. Representative of this emphasis are books by Borton (1970), Satir (1972), and Purkey (1984). Borton presents a highly humanistic, three-phase teaching model designed to identify students' concerns, so that students might be reached as individuals and still taught in a systematic fashion compatible with traditional schools. Labels for these three phases form the title of Borton's book: *Reach, Touch, and Teach.* Purkey, also concerned with the developing self-concepts of students, draws an interesting and useful distinction between teachers (and teachers' behaviors) that are "inviting" and those that are "disinviting." One of his major premises is that there are more students who are disinvited than disadvantaged; disinvitation is often communicated to the child through a teacher's apparent

TABLE 9.2 Common Emphases of Humanistic Approaches to Education

1. *Affect*	Much greater emphasis on feeling and thinking and less on the acquisition of information
2. *Self-Concept*	Explicit concern with the development of positive self-concepts in children
3. *Communication*	Attention to the development of positive human relationships and honest interpersonal communication
4. *Personal Values*	Recognition of the importance of personal values, and an attempt to facilitate the development of positive values

indifference and through failure to respond to students as people. A teacher invites students by communicating to them (in any of numerous different ways) that they are valuable, able, and self-directed and by expecting behaviors and achievements that are compatible with their worth and their self-directedness—in short, by having and communicating highly positive feelings about students. Examples of disinvitations are listed in the box entitled "Disinvited Students."

A third major emphasis is on communication. T. Gordon's (1974) Teacher Effectiveness Training (TET) program illustrates this emphasis. It presents teachers with specific advice on methods of bringing about good teacher-learner relationships, and it is based on the notion that teachers should be taught the principles and skills of "effective human relations, honest interpersonal communication, [and] constructive conflict resolution" (1974, p. ix).

A final emphasis shared by most humanistic approaches is the recognition and development of personal values. Students are encouraged to know themselves and express themselves, to strive toward feelings of self-identity, to actualize themselves. Simon, Howe, and Kirschenbaum (1972), for example, present teachers with seventy-nine specific strategies aimed at the elaboration and clarification of values in students.

Common Instructional Methods. These four common emphases—affect, self-development,

communication, and values—lend themselves to a number of instructional methods more readily than do the more traditional emphases on mastery of academic content, good citizenship, and sportsmanship. Thus, group process approaches, rooted in the sensitivity group and encounter group movements (sometimes referred to collectively as "growth groups"), are common instructional approaches in humanistic education. In groups, students can be encouraged to express their feelings more openly, to discover and clarify these feelings, to explore interpersonal relationships, and to articulate their personal value systems. Various communication games can enhance the genuineness and openness of interpersonal relationships. Role-playing games also offer a way to explore emotions and human relationships.

General descriptions of humanistic classrooms are often of limited value to the prospective teacher, particularly in relation to the nitty-gritty of classroom activity. Such descriptions pay less attention to the details of the instructional process than to the personal qualities of teachers and to teachers' attitudes toward children. In short, although advocates of humanistic approaches to teaching present appealing and sometimes highly convincing arguments for humanizing the teaching/learning process, they too often leave the novice teacher short of methods and strategies. Unfortunately, they also often leave the novice with the impression that the traditional classroom and the more humanistic classroom

disinvited students

Purkey (1984) presents a strong argument for the encouragement of teacher behaviors that *invite* students to see themselves as valuable, responsible, worthwhile, and important people. It would be naïve to assume that all teachers have attitudes toward students that lend themselves to inviting behaviors. Listed here is a sample of experiences that are clearly *disinviting* in that they label students as irresponsible, incapable, or worthless—and sometimes all three (from Purkey, 1984).

The teacher said I didn't want to learn, that I just wanted to cause trouble.

She told the class we were discipline problems and were not to be trusted.

The teacher put me out in the hall for everyone to laugh at.

They put me in the dummy class, and it had SPECIAL EDUCATION painted right on the door.

The teacher said to me in front of the whole class: "I really don't think you're that stupid!"

When the principal hit me he said it was the only language I understood.

She said I was worse than my brother, and I don't even have a brother.

My name is Bill Dill, but the teacher always called me "Dill Pickle" and laughed.

I transferred to a new school after it had started. When I appeared at the teacher's doorway, she said, "Oh, no, not another one!"

---

are quite incompatible and that the latter should replace the former.

Perhaps the most important contribution humanistic concerns can make to teachers' preparation is in the realm of attitudes rather than methods. The humanistic educator strives toward a real caring for people, toward open and effective communication, and toward genuineness, empathy, and warmth. But these are vague terms, and vagueness is not what we need; we need examples and methods.

In the final sections of this chapter, we look at three alternatives to traditional education. The first—open education—is most concerned with the affective (emotional) development of students and, by that token, is most clearly humanistic. The other two alternatives—learning styles approaches and cooperative learning—although also driven by some of the humanist's concerns for the individual, retain more emphasis on academic and cognitive growth.

THREE HUMANISTIC CLASSROOM APPROACHES

Although learning is a natural process schools are not naturally conducive to learning. Children are compelled to attend; they have little choice in the content of a curriculum whose value may not be apparent; they must share the teacher's time and other resources with peers; classmates differ from one another in ability and experience, requiring many of them to deal with an instructional tempo not suited to their interest or preparation; and they are governed by a set of rules about personal acts such as talking, moving around, and attending to physical needs. In short, schools are not user-friendly (Hess & Azuma, 1991, p. 2).

Different cultures do react differently to the sometimes poor fit between students and schools. The Japanese culture, claim Hess and Azuma (1991), is most likely to require that students change to conform to the demands of the system.

In contrast, North American cultures are more likely to try to make changes in the system to conform to the needs and wishes of students.

In spite of this, most classrooms in North America are what we might term *traditional*—that is, they are very much like the not very "user-friendly" school described by Hess and Azuma. We know what these classrooms are like; most of us have been through them. And most of us, given that we are here in this rarefied academic atmosphere—you there and me here—have not been treated too badly by this thing called "traditional education."

But that alternatives exist is what this chapter is all about. In the sections that follow we look at three of them.

The Open Classroom

Several decades ago, a phenomenon called "open education," or the "open classroom," became something of a North American fad. The open classroom differs from the traditional classroom in a number of important ways. First, the principal goals of open education are not the kinds of goals—specifically, individual growth, critical thinking, self-reliance, cooperation, and a commitment to lifelong learning—that are ordinarily sought in traditional classrooms (Walberg, 1986). Second, in open education, the most important person is the student, not the teacher. And third, the open classroom typically does not adhere to the same curriculum-bound, age-/grade-locked system that typifies the traditional school but is instead far more informal.

The flavor of open education is perhaps best conveyed by Dennison's (1969) description of an open classroom. He describes an approach that emphasizes student-centered and intensive but relaxed teacher-pupil contact (made possible in his example by the extremely low teacher-pupil ratio). It is an approach that deemphasizes schedules—following Rousseau's notion that time is not meant to be saved but to be lost (Dennison, 1969, p. 13). The philosophy of open education, as expressed by Dennison, is that a school should be concerned with the lives of its children rather than with education in a narrow sense, that abolishing conventional classroom routines can lead to important insights about the roles of emotions and other features of the human condition, and that running an elementary school can be a very simple thing once it is removed from "the unworkable centralization and the lust for control that permeates every bureaucratic institution" (p. 9).

It is impossible, in this short section, to fully convey the atmosphere that permeates the type of school of which Dennison speaks. Indeed, it seems futile and perhaps misleading to describe such a school as one that has no administrators, no report cards, no competitive examinations, and extremely modest facilities; where every child is treated with "consideration and justice"; where the unfolding lives of the children are the primary concern. Whereas this is an accurate description of the school, it is only a partial description. As Kohl (1969, p. 15) points out, it is difficult to say exactly what an open classroom is. Similarly, it is difficult to say what freedom is or to draw the line between chaos and student-determined order, between rebelliousness and the legitimate expression of individual rights, between nonproductive time wasting and the productive waste (or use) of time for activities outside the curriculum.

Open education is now rare in North America. Interestingly, however, most of the many studies that evaluated this approach and compared it with more traditional approaches found that open education was usually effective in reaching its most important goals; that is, students exposed to open classrooms typically had better self-concepts and were more creative and cooperative (see, for example, Horwitz, 1979). However, these gains were usually at the expense of academic achievement as defined by more traditional measures.

The Learning Styles Approach

In discussing traditional education, Dunn and Griggs claim: "The system works well for some, but not for others" (1988, p. 1). Why?

Different Styles. Because, Dunn and Griggs explain, some students do not learn at all well in the morning but perform very well in the afternoon. Some work well in bright, noisy environments; others do their best work in quiet places with subdued lighting. Some excel with highly structured, teacher-directed instructional methods; others do far better in informal, unstructured environments. Some students need and want to be told what to do and when and how to do it; others perform best when working on their own initiative. In short, each student has a personal and unique **learning style.**

Unfortunately, traditional schools do not often take individual learning styles into account. As a result, they reward students whose personal styles happen to match that for which the traditional school was designed—and, by the same token, they unwittingly punish those whose rhythms are sounded on a different drum. Students whose biological rhythms make it difficult to concentrate in the morning must nevertheless come to school and sit through the same offerings as everyone else. Those who respond best to visual stimuli—or to tactile stimulation—are forced to listen as much as those who are more responsive to auditory stimuli. Children with shorter attention spans are compelled to sit as long as those who are not so easily distracted.

This situation is not fair, argue Dunn and Griggs; it is not an optimal learning situation. Schools, they insist, must take into account these fundamentally important differences in learning styles. But how?

Adapting Schools to Styles. First, schools need to develop a profile of each student's learning styles. A number of instruments are available for this purpose, including Gregorc's (1982) Style Delin-eator and Renzulli and Smith's (1978) Learning Styles Inventory. The Gregorc instrument provides a measure of perceptual strengths (how people obtain information, including a concrete/abstract dimension) and differentiates among learners on the basis of their predispositions toward reason, emotion, and intuition. It also looks at the individual's preferred ways of dealing with and ordering information.

The Renzulli and Smith inventory is designed to help teachers customize their instructional procedures to match individual learners' attitudes toward such common instructional procedures as lectures, simulations, discussions, projects, games, drills, recitations, peer teaching, independent study, and programmed instruction.

Identifying individual learning styles is only the beginning; dramatic changes are required in schools and in teachers' behavior if schools are to be truly responsive to students' individual differences. Dunn and Griggs (1988) visited ten schools at which attention to learning styles had become the determining factor in educational offerings. Although there were many differences among these schools, they had a number of things in common. A description of these is, in a sense, an idealized description of a humanistic school.

The Learning Styles-Driven School. This idealized school gives learners an almost staggering assortment of options. It allows children to work alone on soft carpets or to work in groups at conference tables. It provides highly structured teacher-presented lessons, peer teaching, programmed instruction, computer-assisted instruction, and self-learning. It rotates presentation of core subjects so that they are offered at all times of the day, including early in the morning and later in the afternoon. It allows students to take examinations and do projects at times that are compatible with their biological rhythms.

The idealized humanistic, learning style-driven school is identifiable not only by its attention to differences among individual learners but also by its values and objectives. Far more than the traditional school, it stresses students' involvement at all stages of learning, and it emphasizes problem solving and creativity.

Finally, this idealized school's most common instructional technique, especially for presenting new material, is a highly participatory, cooperative, small-group approach that is sometimes called **circles of knowledge.** This approach is described in the next section, which discusses cooperative learning.

This brief description of the translation of learning styles information into classroom practice cannot do justice to the complexity of the topic. There is no single, best program that we can describe simply and accurately; programs continue to change and develop. As we noted, most require profound changes in schools and in teachers, and the changes required must be continual. They involve experimentation in and modification and clarification of programs, as well as refocusing of objectives and of efforts, and on and on.

Evaluation. We cannot begin to evaluate the effectiveness of this approach, other than very tentatively. Dunn and Griggs (1988) report that in the ten learning styles-driven schools they visited, learners performed exceptionally well on a variety of measures of academic performance. Some had won national awards, and many had succeeded in passing subjects they had previously failed. And most said they liked—no, loved—school.

Snow and Swanson (1992) note that current lists of learning styles, and the instruments used to measure them, are unorganized, lengthy, and include a large range of habits, personality characteristics, and abilities. And research has not yet established whether any of them are useful.

Perhaps when the bear is a very, very old bear, history will look back and say, "Hey, that learning styles stuff just before the turn of the millennium was another one of those educational fads, like open schools and teaching machines." Or maybe, just maybe, history's judgment will be "Hey, just before the millennium—that's when it all started."

Cooperative Learning

According to Johnson, Johnson, Holubec, and Roy, teachers have three basic choices: "In every classroom teachers may structure lessons so that students are in a win-lose struggle to see who is best. They can also allow students to learn on their own, individually, or they can arrange students in pairs or small groups to help each other master the assigned material" (1984, p. 1).

Unfortunately, these authors claim, most students see schools as competitive because that is how grades are typically assigned. Not everyone can do well; in order to achieve at the highest level, students must compete with, and outachieve, the others. And when schools are not competitive, they are most often individualistic; that is, students are urged to work toward the attainment of their own individual goals—without help, proudly and independently!

A simple way of distinguishing among these three alternatives is in terms of rewards (Bossert, 1988). In a cooperative situation, the individual is rewarded in proportion to others in the group; in a competitive situation, individual rewards are inversely related to those others receive; and in an individualistic situation, there is no relationship among individual rewards.

Occasionally, some schools present a few activities that are cooperative. Only rarely do schools and teachers make cooperative learning a fundamental part of their instruction. Schools that do, claim Schniedewind and Davidson (1988), are humanistic schools because cooperative learning is essentially a humanistic approach to education. It combines the cognitive and affective aspects of learning, and it emphasizes participation and active engagement, both of which are humanistic concerns. But perhaps more than other explicitly humanistic approaches, cooperative learning also stresses academic achievement and clearly defined curricular goals. In most schools that use cooperative learning methods, students do not have the unstructured freedom that they might be given in an open classroom, nor does the system cater to their personal strengths and preferences as it might in a school organized to respond to individual learning styles.

The Rationale for Cooperative Learning. Why is it important to learn to cooperate? Advocates of this approach present a variety of reasons. Among the most compelling is the nagging suspicion that it is our only hope for salvation—that if we do not learn to cooperate, we and our planet are doomed.

There are other reasons why we must learn to cooperate—if survival does not seem sufficiently important, or if our doom seems too distant, or if we simply prefer not to think about it. Cooperation, Bossert (1988) tells us, is the cornerstone of modern democracy. Nations cannot be governed without cooperation among leaders; cooperation is essential for political and economic survival.

At a more immediate level, teaching cooperation in the schools might do much to reduce students' dependence on teachers and to decrease divisiveness and prejudice among students. Cooperative learning, Johnson and associates (1984) claim, may resolve two important crises: declining academic performance and pervasive feelings of alienation, isolation, purposelessness, and social unease among students.

Another reason for using cooperative learning is that *it works*. In Snow and Swanson's words, "The evidence clearly shows its effectiveness in achieving cognitive goals, but the methods also promote more positive attitudes toward school, improved student self-esteem, and improved relations among different types of students" (1992, p. 612).

Finally, students *prefer* cooperative approaches. When researchers asked students from three different cultures (Germany, Canada, and Iran) which approach to learning they most preferred, they chose cooperative learning (Huber, Sorrentino, Davidson, Epplier, & Roth, 1992).

Cooperative Learning Defined. Cooperative learning occurs when students work together to achieve a common goal. Unlike competitive learning, rewards depend not on doing better than someone else but on doing well with someone else.

Although there are a variety of approaches to cooperative learning in the classroom, most have a number of features in common (Johnson, Johnson, Holubec, & Roy, 1984). To begin with, cooperative learning requires face-to-face interaction among group members—usually four to six students. Second, the relationship among group members can be described as one of positive interdependence; that is, members must cooperate in allocating resources, assigning roles, and dividing labor if they are to achieve their goals. Third, cooperative learning usually assigns some degree of individual responsibility for sharing, cooperating, and learning. Accordingly, various techniques are used to ensure that goals and rewards are contingent on the performance and contribution of all group members. Finally, cooperative learning involves the use of interpersonal and small group skills, such as those involved in taking turns, facilitating, collaborating, and so on.

Bossert (1988) describes a large number of cooperative group activities that have been developed and used in schools. They have a variety of names but are sometimes included under the generic labels "circles of knowledge," or "circles of learning." Although each activity is distinct from the others, all share the common features described earlier, the most important of which is the interdependence of group members.

Learning Together. In learning together, groups of four to six students are given a lesson or worksheet that they must learn or complete together. Members must help each other to ensure that everyone learns the lesson or completes the assignment. Members of each group are also encouraged to help other groups once they have completed the assignment. Praise is given for cooperating and finishing the assignment. In this approach, there is no competition among groups.

Student Teams–Achievement Divisions (STAD). STAD is one of several forms of student "team learning," in which individual groups are teams that compete against one another. In STAD, students are divided into heterogeneous teams of four to six students. Ideally, each team includes high- and low-ability children, children of different ethnic backgrounds, and children of both sexes. New material is typically presented to the class using conventional approaches like lectures, discussions, and videos. Following this, groups are given material to study and worksheets to complete. They can work on these individually, in pairs, or in larger groups. They are encouraged to help each other and to make sure that everybody understands and knows the material. At the end of the study period, which typically lasts a week, students write quizzes based on that week's material—individually, and without helping each other. Team scores are then calculated. And although recognition is given to teams that obtain the highest total scores, winning teams are those whose individuals *improved* the most. In that way, lower-achieving students can contribute as much as more able students (sometimes even more) to the team's total score.

STAD produces dramatic changes in the classroom, claims Slavin. "[Students] begin to see learning activities as social instead of isolated, fun instead of boring, under their own control instead of the teacher's" (1983, p. 7). Also, he claims, they now help each other learn instead of resenting those who learn more easily or making fun of those who learn with more difficulty.

Teams–Games–Tournaments (TGT). TGT begins in exactly the same way as STAD, with the same teams, instructional sessions, and cooperative learning sequence. The difference is that at the end, students engage in tournaments rather than in quizzes. In these tournaments, team members are assigned not as a group, but as individuals, to a table. Each table consists of three competitors of approximately equal ability (as selected by instructors). Games occur at all tables simultaneously and involve drawing numbered cards, trying to answer questions corresponding to the numbers on the cards, and challenging incorrect answers. Players retain cards when they answer (or challenge) correctly and lose them for incorrect challenges. At the end of the game (or period), points are assigned according to the number of cards in each player's possession, and total tournament points are computed for each *team.*

More complete rules for TGT can be found in Slavin (1983). Materials for STAD and TGT are available for a wide range of subjects in elementary and secondary schools from The Johns Hopkins Team Learning Project, Center for Social Organization School, Johns Hopkins University, 3505 North Charles St., Baltimore, Md. 21218 (410-338-8249).

Jigsaw. In "jigsaw," the material to be learned is divided into separate units. Individual members of the group are then given separate parts of the whole to learn, and they must teach what they have learned to other members of the group. No one member is given sufficient information to solve the problem at hand or complete the assignment in question, but when all the information is put together—Voilà!* The jigsaw is complete.

Group Investigation. Group investigation, described by Sharan and Sharan (1992), is a cooperative technique that combines academic scholarship and inquiry with the principles of cooperation. Using this approach, students in a class select an area for study, typically some problem that lends itself to investigation. The area is then divided into subtopics, and the class divides itself into small groups of investigators on the basis of shared interest in a topic. Each group then formulates a plan by which to investigate and assigns responsibilities. Members can now work individually, in pairs, or as larger groups. Having completed their inquiry—perhaps over a period

*PPC: Ha! Ha! A bilingual bear!
The Bear: But of course!

of some weeks—group members meet and share the fruits of their investigations. They decide, as well, how to present their integrated information to other members of the class. Finally, all groups meet for the final sharing of information. Throughout the process, teachers are involved in guiding students, helping them with both the academic skills required for successful inquiry and the social skills involved in group processes.

Reciprocal Teaching. Palincsar and Brown (1984) describe a cooperative learning technique based on the principle that a good way of learning is to teach. In reciprocal teaching, students and teachers take turns being teacher. Material taught is typically from written text, but students-as-teachers are taught specific procedures designed to develop strategies involved in questioning, clarifying, summarizing, and predicting. Mosston and Ashworth (1990) describe a similar approach (they call it the "reciprocal style") in which pairs of students guide each other's learning and performance in structured situations.

Implementation of Cooperative Learning Techniques. The techniques just described are only a few of the many that have been developed and evaluated. For those interested in still more approaches, the Suggested Readings section at the end of this chapter lists important sources of information.

Unlike the learning styles approach, cooperative learning does not require a major restructuring of the school day or a reordering of curriculum offerings. Whereas the learning styles approach attempts to cater to individual differences in learning styles and learning preferences, cooperative group methods typically include all students simultaneously. In fact, one advantage of cooperative approaches is that they foster cooperation among students with different strengths and weaknesses and perhaps those of different ethnic backgrounds, ages, and sexes.

Cooperative learning techniques are most often introduced as an adjunct to regular classroom offerings. In a typical situation, they might be used for sixty or ninety minutes a day. However, the most vocal advocates of this approach recommend that as much as 70 percent of class time involve cooperative activities, with 20 percent devoted to individualistic approaches and only 10 percent to competitive activities (Johnson & Johnson, 1975).

Although cooperative approaches normally make up only a small part of the total curriculum, their implementation usually requires careful preparation of material. Depending on the specific approach used, the teacher will need to prepare worksheets, questions, resource materials, and so on, all carefully structured to foster cooperation while promoting learning.

Evaluation of Cooperative Learning. How well do these cooperative techniques work? Johnson, Maruyama, Johnson, Nelson, and Skon (1981) analyzed 122 studies that had examined cooperative learning. Most of these studies contain direct comparisons between specific cooperative approaches and traditional classroom instruction. Johnson and associates conclude that cooperative learning leads to better achievement at virtually all grade and age levels studied and for all subjects. They suggest that increases in achievement occur because group discussion and cooperation promote discovery, lead to the development of higher-quality cognitive strategies, increase motivation to learn, increase comprehension by requiring students to teach each other, enrich the learning experience by blending students of a variety of ability levels and experiences, and promote highly positive relationships among group members. This last statement is also supported by results of a study involving a school with a mixture of Israeli and Arab students in which students exposed to a cooperative approach not only performed better academically than those exposed only to a traditional approach but also displayed far fewer signs of ethnic tension in their language (Sharan & Shachar, 1988).

In general, the research reviewed by Bossert (1988) supports this positive evaluation. Cooperative learning approaches most often result in measurably superior academic performance, higher motivation, greater interest in school, and better relations among students. He suggests, however, that the positive academic effects of cooperative learning may owe more to the fact that lessons typically are more highly structured and more systematic than simply to peer interaction.

Why Cooperation Works. Dividing classes into groups may not always be the most effective way to teach. In fact, on occasion, and for some students, it does not work. It is possible for students to work *in* groups but not *as* groups. Students working *in* but not *as* groups can easily waste time talking about irrelevant matters or develop procedures wherein some group members dominate and others are ignored.

Slavin (1990b) suggests two things are necessary for cooperative learning to work: incentive to cooperate and individual accountability. In most applications of cooperative learning, group recognition and/or interteam competition provide the incentive. And there is individual accountability to the extent that group or team performance depends on the performance of each individual in the group.

Vygotsky's (1978) theory suggests yet another reason why cooperative learning might work. Learning, he claimed, is highly dependent on social interaction. To a large extent, it depends on interactions with others who are better informed, and the results of learning are manifested in social interaction as well. Furthermore, learning—and all higher mental processes—depend on language. One of the great contributions of cooperative group learning is that it fosters the development and exercise of language skills.

To Cooperate? Or Not? Cooperative learning, it seems, can be highly effective in imparting academic content and strategies and also seems to have beneficial effects on the social development and interpersonal relationships of students.

Mueller (1992) reports that it also enhances self-esteem and the learner's sense of purpose and autonomy. Does this mean that all teachers and schools should now become cooperative—that is, *entirely* cooperative?

Bossert (1988) advises caution. Even though it seems clear that cooperative approaches have substantial academic and social benefits, they also have some disadvantages. For example, low-achieving students are sometimes embarrassed by their performances and ashamed of the fact that they lower the group's score. As a result, they may become progressively more reluctant to participate in cooperative activities as their motivation and self-concepts deteriorate. The long-term effects of this situation might be lower achievement for these students—and perhaps lower achievement for their groups as well. However, the use of performance improvement as the basis for scores, as is done in STAD and TGT, may do much to invalidate this caution.

Bossert also cautions that those who advocate that cooperative techniques should be the dominant feature of classroom activity may be overlooking the possibility that one reason cooperative learning is effective is precisely because it presents a clear contrast to conventional classroom procedures. The shifts in attention and in procedures required of students serve to increase concentration, to motivate, and ultimately to enhance performance. But if all or most classroom activity were cooperative, these shifts might not occur, and performance might not improve so dramatically—if at all.

Finally, Bossert argues that even though it is important for children to learn to cooperate with one another, it is also important to learn competitive and individualistic skills.

SOME REACTIONS TO HUMANISTIC EDUCATION

To the extent that humanistic education represents concern for the individual lives and self-concepts of students and concern for the healthiest

and happiest development of human potential, it is beyond reproach. All teachers *must* be humanistic.

However, humanistic education too often appears to deal with vague qualities and speculative conclusions. Terms such as *authentic, open, real, genuine, fully functioning,* and *meaningful* are often meaningless. How do you distinguish between an authentic experience and one that is not authentic? between a genuine teacher and an impostor? between a fully functioning student and one who is only three-quarters functioning? Unfortunately, although these terms are vague, they seem to represent good things and are therefore highly appealing. Equally unfortunate, the things they represent cannot be easily defined or measured, and as a consequence the evidence upon which advocates of humanistic reforms base their arguments is not always convincing.

Perhaps the most telling criticism of general humanistic approaches to teaching is that most are highly dependent upon the personal qualities and skills of individual teachers. More conventional approaches to classroom practice are, in this respect, much more "teacher proof."

These criticisms are not entirely fair, however. They apply primarily to global approaches to humanistic education, such as those represented by "open" (or what have sometimes been called "free") schools. As we saw earlier, evidence from research suggests that although students who emerge from these schools appear to be more creative and more cooperative and have better self-concepts, these gains typically come at the expense of academic achievement. A large-scale evaluation in the United States found that these students performed more poorly than comparison groups on almost all achievement measures (Kennedy, 1978) (although few of these measures tap creative thinking skills, the ability to reason logically, or other important personality characteristics). Perhaps it is not surprising that most of these schools have now closed. We should note, however, that various forms of nongraded schools (no age/grade placement and no graded report cards) can have positive effects on student achievement (Gutiérrez & Slavin, 1992). But these schools are somewhat different from open schools in that they typically present a structured curriculum but in an ungraded, no-fail environment.

These criticisms of humanistic education—of vagueness, overattention to affective growth, and disregard of both standard curricula and cognitive development—are not relevant with respect to two expressions of humanistic concerns detailed in this chapter: learning styles-oriented schools and cooperative learning. As we saw, both approaches can lead to superior academic achievement. Interestingly, among the important techniques of learning styles schools are the group methods that define cooperative learning.

It is extremely important to bear in mind that humanism is not a specific educational technique, although it manifests itself most clearly in specific techniques. In effect, humanism is an educational philosophy characterized by the sorts of admirable attitudes toward students and toward educational goals that should be characteristic of all teachers. These attitudes, as mentioned earlier, are not subject to the same criticisms that have been applied so generously to specific humanistic approaches to education. In the end, it may not be important to copy the models or take the advice presented by the more visible of humanistic educators. What is important is that you genuinely care about students as people.

THE LAST WORD—FROM WATSON!

It may seem strange to conclude a discussion of humanism by referring to the recognized initiator and principal spokesman of the position usually considered most directly opposed to humanism. Interestingly, however, some of the writings of John B. Watson describe a highly humanistic society. More than six decades ago, Watson concluded a book with a section entitled "Behaviorism as a Guide for All Future Experimental Ethics" (1930, pp. 303–304):

> Behaviorism ought to be a science that prepares men and women for understanding the principles of their own behavior. It ought to make men and women eager to rearrange their own lives, and especially eager to prepare themselves to bring up their own children in a healthy way. I wish I could picture for you what a rich and wonderful individual we could make of every healthy child if only we could let it shape itself properly and then provide for it a universe in which it could exercise that organization—a universe unshackled by legendary folklore of happenings thousands of years ago; unhampered by disgraceful political history; free of foolish customs and conventions which have no significance in themselves, yet which hem the individual in like taut steel bands. I am not asking here for revolution; I am not asking people to go out to some God-forsaken place, form a colony, go naked and live a communal life, nor am I asking for a change to a diet of roots and herbs. I am not asking for "free love." I am trying to dangle a stimulus in front of you, a verbal stimulus which, if acted upon, will gradually change this universe. For the universe will change if you bring up your children, not in the freedom of the libertine, but in behavioristic freedom—a freedom which we cannot even picture in words, so little do we know

of it. Will not these children in turn, with their better ways of living and thinking, replace us as society and in turn bring up their children in a still more scientific way, until the world finally becomes a place fit for human habitation?

MAIN POINTS

1. Humanistic psychology is concerned with the uniqueness, the worth, and the dignity of the self. It presents an ideological conflict with the more mechanistic orientation of other approaches. It also objects to the school's emphasis on academic achievement and its neglect of affective growth.

2. Carl Rogers's theory is phenomenological (the phenomenal world is the environment as it is perceived by one individual), humanistic (concerned with the individual, with self-actualization), and student centered. His position is opposed to Skinner's expressed concern with control through the application of the principles of operant learning.

3. Rogers believes that an individual's real world is private (phenomenological), the purpose of behavior is to achieve self-actualization (development of maximum potential), self-actualization is related to healthy and creative functioning, and the development of the "self" results from interactions with the world (direct experience) and from values about the "me" that are borrowed from the actions of other people (indirect experience).

4. Rogerian theory suggests that in order to promote full, healthy functioning, schools should be student centered. The instructional procedures that Rogers sees as best for these schools are discovery oriented.

5. The major emphases of humanistic approaches are the development of self, the clarification of values, openness, honesty, and self-determination.

6. Open education is most concerned with the affective growth of students—with critical thinking, self-reliance, and commitment to learning. It is student rather than teacher centered. Research suggests that graduates of open schools may be more creative, more cooperative, and have better self-concepts—but they usually fare less well on traditional academic measures.

7. Learning styles are individual preferences and strengths as they relate to the best conditions for learning (for example, morning versus evening; visual, auditory, or kinesthetic; individual versus group; structured versus unstructured; and so on).

8. Learning styles-driven schools develop profiles for individual students and attempt to match instructional methods, curriculum offerings, scheduling, and other aspects of instruction to each learner's personal style. Students in learning styles schools appear to do very well on standard academic measures.

9. Cooperative learning involves small-group techniques structured so that learners are rewarded for the group's results but are nevertheless individually responsible for learning and for helping other members of the group to learn. It is characterized by face-to-face interaction, positive interdependence, individual responsibility, and the use of interpersonal and small-group skills.

10. Some techniques for cooperative learning include learning together (pure cooperation, common goal, no intergroup competition), Student Teams–Achievement Divisions (STAD) (groups are teams that compete against each other on the basis of performance improvement), Teams–Games–Tournaments (TGT) (STAD-like procedure but with three-member head-to-head competitions following learning), jigsaw (each group member given only part of the information; interaction with whole required to solve a problem or learn a lesson), group investigation (whole class investigates single inquiry-type problem by dividing in groups for investigation and coming

together to integrate and share), and reciprocal teaching (students take turns teaching and learning or performing or doing).

11. Evidence suggests that cooperative learning techniques lead to superior academic achievement, high motivation, and the enhancement of social skills. These positive effects may be due partly to the greater curriculum structure required for cooperative learning and to the contrast these approaches present to the traditional classroom. They may also be due to the language and social skills they foster.

12. General humanistic approaches to education are often highly dependent upon individual teachers' qualities and sometimes use vague and speculative terms. Humanism in education is less vulnerable to criticism as an attitude or philosophy than as a technique—and as an attitude it is perhaps more valuable to teachers. In this sense, all teachers should be humanistic.

SUGGESTED READINGS

Rogers's attempt to apply his theories and beliefs to education is expressed in

ROGERS, C. R. (1969). *Freedom to learn*. Columbus, Ohio: Merrill.

Among numerous humanistic books for teachers and students are the following:

BORTON, T. (1970). *Reach, touch, and teach: Student concerns and process education*. New York: McGraw-Hill.

PURKEY, W. W. (1984). *Inviting school success: A self-concept approach to teaching and learning* (2nd ed.). Belmont, Calif.: Wadsworth.

SIMPSON, E. L., & GRAY, M. A. (1976). *Humanistic education: An interpretation*. Cambridge, Mass.: Ballinger.

The learning styles approach to education is well described in

DUNN, R., & GRIGGS, S. A. (1988). *Learning styles: Quiet revolution in American secondary schools*. Reston, Va.: National Association of Secondary School Principals.

The book by D. W. Johnson and associates is an excellent description of cooperative learning and of a number of different schools that use this approach. Rhoades and McCabe present a brief and useful guidebook for the teacher wishing to initiate cooperative activities in the classroom. Sharan and Sharan describe cooperative group investigation in the classroom. The Slavin book is a brief but practical overview of team-learning approaches such as STAD and TGT.

JOHNSON, D. W., JOHNSON, R. T., HOLUBEC, E. J., ROY, P. (1984). *Circles of learning: Cooperation in the classroom*. Alexandria, Va.: Association for Supervision and Curriculum Development.

RHOADES, J., & MCCABE, M. E. (1985). *Simple cooperation in the classroom*. Willits, Calif.: ITA Publications.

SLAVIN, R. E. (1983). *Student team learning: An overview and practical guide*. Washington, D.C.: National Education Association.

SHARAN, Y., & SHARAN, S. (1992). *Expanding cooperative learning through group investigation*. New York: Columbia University, Teachers College Press.

The Laplanders venerated the bear and called it the Dog of God. The Norwegians called it "the old man with the fur cloak" (Engel, 1976).

part four | MORE EFFECTIVE INSTRUCTION

I have measured out my life with coffee spoons.
T. S. Eliot, *Love Song of J. Alfred Prufrock*

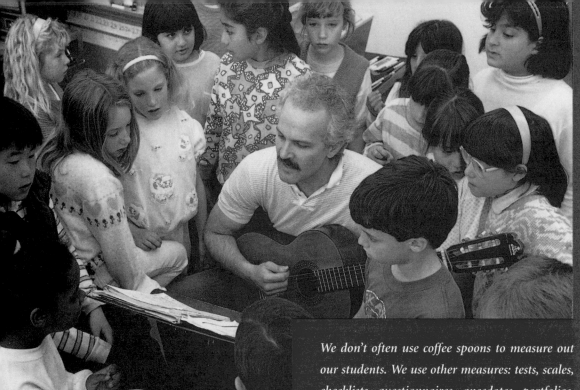

We don't often use coffee spoons to measure out our students. We use other measures: tests, scales, checklists, questionnaires, anecdotes, portfolios, observations . . . and on and on. Teaching is not a simple business. There are hundreds of choices to be made. And the nitty-gritty of classroom practice requires much more than what we have gleaned from educational psychology and reported in the preceding chapters. Among other things, it demands of the teacher interpersonal and management skills of the highest order; it requires patience and imagination, a measure of genius and a touch of humility, enthusiasm and warmth, and other good things often more characteristic of angels than of teachers. The four chapters in the last part discuss these and related topics.

Boredom is a sign of satisfied ignorance, blunted apprehension, crass sympathies, dull understanding, feeble powers of attention and irreclaimable weakness of character.
James Bridie, *Mr. Bolfry*

Persons attempting to find a motive in this narrative will be prosecuted; persons attempting to find a moral in it will be banished; persons attempting to find a plot in it will be shot.
Mark Twain, *Huckleberry Finn*, Introduction

chapter 10 | MOTIVATION AND TEACHING

PREVIEW My grandmother, an astute observer of human affairs, spent much of her knitting and quilting time in quiet contemplation of human motives. "Why do geese go south and ravens stay?" she would mutter as her needles clicked. "Why did Réné go out in the storm?" "Why does Frank study so hard and Lucille won't do zip?" "Why doesn't Robert want to go to school anymore?" This chapter might have been of some value to her, although the questions it examines are surely no more important than the questions she asked. But it does provide some answers for why we do or don't do things and some suggestions for teachers whose role in motivating students can hardly be overstated.

Excerpt from Bear Tales (Book IV): Wild Cow Parties

Imelda didn't trust the bear. She never had, right from the very beginning. It wasn't that she was afraid for the calves or anybody. He was so old, she knew she could whack the feathers out of him any time she cared to. Besides, she had rightly guessed, he was a vegetarian.

A bloody vegetarian bear—imagine!!

But he spent too dang much time watching them, and she couldn't for the life of her figure why. And the way he looked at them, the way he held himself, is what bothered her most. At first, she thought there was something wrong with his neck, the way his head always pointed toward the front, like maybe he couldn't turn it around. But later she saw him turn in all kinds of directions, always with that sad-eyed look like he carried the weight of the world on his stooped shoulders. Some kind of pervert bear, she thought.

"Join us for a drink?" she invited him anyway, thinking, what the hell, let's all party. But he turned his grizzled snoot skyward as though offended and lurched up the hillside to the little ledge where he spent most of his days.

"Some day, I'm gonna bloody go up there," Imelda promised herself, pouring a long draft from the big jug.

God, good whiskey, sweet cigars, scads of trees yet to burn, and every night, party like there's no tomorrow . . . Imelda belched contentedly. . . .

And then Thomas, the boy wild cow, roared down the meadow in Farmer Joe's pickup, which Farmer Joe kept finding in fields he couldn't for the life of him remember parking in, and Thomas pulled three awful impressive do-nuts right on the edge where some of the cows were dancing, spraying them with mud and torn sedges and sweet grasses so that they all laughed, being in such a party mood, all of them. . . .

And Ramona, who they sometimes called "you sleaze, you," but mostly in fun, sashayed over to the truck when it stopped and sort of leaned on it, not really looking at Thomas but letting him know she was watching him anyway, so when he opened the door, she just slipped right in, sort-of nonchalant. . . .

"Hold it right there," Imelda roared, grinding her cigar into the mud. "Where d'you think you're going, you slut?" And it wasn't Ramona she was talking to; everybody knew it was Thomas.

"Just for a little ride," he half whined, his gut still sore from where Imelda'd kicked him last time. "Just for a little ride. That's all."

"I don't bloody believe you," said Imelda, yanking Thomas's door open. "I think you got ulterior motives."

MOTIVES: EXPLANATIONS FOR BEHAVIOR

Ulterior motives—a strange and wicked disorder from which even I have sometimes suffered. You see, ulterior motives are, by definition, hidden and unknown; they do not show themselves. More than once I have wished that my true motives had been more obvious—had been more apparent to others.

In this chapter we look not at motives that are ulterior but at those that are more obvious. Motives are what move us; they are our reasons for doing the things we do. As Dweck (1986) notes, motives are the causes of all our goal-directed activity. They explain the *why* of our behavior, whereas learning theories are more concerned with the *how* and the *what*.

From the teacher's point of view, the most important motives are those relevant to learning and achievement. The teacher needs to be especially concerned with why some students expend a great deal of effort in achievement situations and others do not.

Keith and Cool (1992) tried to determine some of the factors that most contributed to the achievement scores of more than 25,000 students.

Teachers need to understand why some students expend a great deal of effort in achievement situations and why others don't—and why some activities are more likely than others to capture and maintain student interest.

Not surprisingly, the strongest direct effect they found was for ability. Two factors had strong indirect effects: **motivation** and quality of instruction. "It appears," conclude Keith and Cool, "that students enrolled in a high-quality school and curriculum are more highly motivated by that curriculum. . . . Students with high academic motivation take more academic course work . . . and do more homework . . . and as a result, achieve at a higher level" (1992, p. 215).

The importance to the teacher of understanding motivation and the factors that affect it can hardly be overemphasized. Uguroglu and Walberg (1979) estimate that motivation accounts for a proportion of student achievement sufficient to be the difference between success and failure. And recent research makes it clear that a wide variety of classroom variables have a direct effect on students' motivation—variables such as "classroom organizational, instructional and climatic variables, including task structure, task complexity, grouping practices, evaluation techniques, locus of responsibility for learning, and quality of teacher-student and student-student relationships" (D. B. Matthews, 1991).

This chapter explores various explanations for human behavior, with special emphasis on how each factor listed by Matthews can affect students' motivation. Initially, it touches briefly on some historical approaches to motivation, then it outlines a psychological theory that has physiological underpinnings (arousal theory). Finally, it moves to a series of more detailed discussions of contemporary views of motivation, organized according to the three major models discussed in earlier chapters: behaviorism, humanism, and cognitivism. Keep in mind that these divisions continue to be artificial and therefore somewhat misleading. As we study them, we sometimes feel compelled to judge them and choose only one among them. But different theories are simply reflections of different world views and different underlying emphases and metaphors. One is not correct and the others incorrect; rather, something of each may be useful for our different purposes.

HISTORICAL VIEWS OF HUMAN MOTIVATION

History, as is often its custom, can teach us about an assortment of past beliefs, not all of which are relevant to our current views. Nevertheless, something in these historical views often may be useful to our understanding of human behavior in general and of children in particular. In the case of one of the first views of human motivation—that concerning instincts—what history can tell us may be more relevant to our understanding of animals than of people.

Instincts

When Zoe, our dog, gave birth to her first litter, four-year-old Laurier watched bug eyed as the bitch eased each little pup in turn from its sac, nipped its umbilical cord close to its belly, ate the afterbirth, and nudged it toward her nipples. "Where'd she learn to do that?" he asked. But she hadn't learned; somehow, she already knew. How to birth pups was one of the **instincts** with which she was born.

A Definition. Instincts are innate, complex, species-specific, relatively unmodifiable behavior patterns. What do these terms mean?

> *Innate:* Instinctual behaviors are not learned but are genetically determined.

> *Complex:* Behaviors such as blinking in response to air blown in the eye, sucking behavior, and other simple behaviors of which we are capable at birth are not instincts; they are *reflexes.* Instincts are more complex groupings of behaviors such as those involved in courting or nesting among some birds.

> *Species specific:* Instincts are general within species. Thus *all* wild ducks are characterized by a migratory instinct, and *all* bears (except for polar bears) by the urge to den up in winter.

> *Relatively unmodifiable:* Because instincts are largely innate, they are not much affected by the environment—although, in the absence of some environmental experiences, instinctual behaviors can be changed somewhat. For example, female rats reared in deprived environments do not exhibit the maternal and nesting instincts characteristic of female rats reared normally.

"Mother" Lorenz.

Human Instincts. There are many examples of instinctual behavior patterns among animals, most having to do with nesting, migration, and mating—all behaviors related to survival. The question is whether people engage in behavior that can be similarly explained in terms of instincts.

Some early theorists thought so. For example, L. L. Bernard (1924) listed some six thousand human instincts, ranging from the common ones (sexual, maternal) to remote inclinations, such as the tendency "to avoid eating apples that grow in one's own garden" (p. 212).

The obvious disadvantage of this approach is that naming an instinct neither explains a behavior nor predicts it. At best, the whole process is entirely circular. If humans make love, it is obvious that we have an instinct for doing so. Why, then, does one make love? Well, because one has this instinct, you see. How do we know that this instinct exists? Well, because people make love. And so on, ad infinitum.

Currently, the notion of instinct is applied more to animal than to human behavior, although a related phenomenon, **imprinting,** is sometimes linked to some features of infant development. Imprinting is the appearance of complex behaviors, apparently as a result of exposure to an appropriate object or event (releaser) at a **critical period** in the animal's life. For example, newly hatched ducklings will follow the first moving object they encounter and become attached to it. Fortunately, this object is usually the mother duck. Lorenz (1952) reports, however, the case of a greylag goose that imprinted on him and followed him around like a dog. Much to his embarrassment, when it matured it insisted on foisting its affections on him during mating season.[*]

Although there do not appear to be critical

*PPC: Among other demonstrations of undying love, Lorenz's birds persisted in depositing beakfuls of minced worms in his ears. Lorenz did not reciprocate.

Author: Yecch!

periods in the infant's life during which it must be exposed to appropriate experiences in order to have some behavior imprinted, researchers such as Bowlby (1982) suggest that the first six months might be a *sensitive* period during which a parent or other caregiver must be present for the infant to develop strong attachment bonds.

Psychological Hedonism

A second historical explanation of human motivation is psychological hedonism, the belief that we act so as to avoid pain and obtain pleasure. Unfortunately, psychological hedonism does little to explain behavior because it does not specify those conditions that are pleasurable or painful. Even if it is true that the pain/pleasure principle governs our activities, we can predict and control these activities only if we know what gives pleasure and what gives pain.

Need-Drive Theories

Need-drive theories offer one way to define pain and pleasure. **Needs** are states of deficiency or lack within an organism. **Drives** are the energies or the tendencies to react that are aroused by needs. For example, we have a need for food; this need gives rise to a hunger drive.

If we assume that satisfying needs is pleasant and that a state of need is unpleasant, the relationship between need theory and psychological hedonism is obvious: The identification and description of needs make clear the nature of pain and pleasure. A list of needs is a list of conditions that when satisfied are pleasant and when unsatisfied are unpleasant.

Needs can be divided into two broad categories: psychological and physiological. **Physiological needs** are manifested in actual tissue changes; **psychological needs** are more closely related to mental functioning. Other differences between the two categories are that psychological needs are never completely satisfied, whereas physiological needs can be. In addition, psychological needs are probably more often *learned* than are physiological needs. Physiological needs include the need for food, water, sleep and rest, activity, and sex. Psychological needs include the need for affection, belonging, achievement, independence, social recognition, and self-esteem.

Summary and Implications of Historical Approaches to Motivation

From the teacher's point of view, the most useful explanations of motivation are those that provide us with the greatest insight about the circumstances under which students will be most interested in doing certain things—and least interested as well.

Explanations such as those based on instincts may be valuable explanations for a bear's habit of denning up in the winter, but they tell us little about why Robert will study all night before his science exam or why Sam will watch television instead and will then have to explain how he forgot all about the exam.

Nor does psychological hedonism tell us much about Sam or Robert. True, the belief that we do things that we expect will lead to pleasant outcomes—and that we avoid behaviors that lead elsewhere—does little violence to our naïve convictions about human behavior. But, as we saw, the belief by itself explains little; we need to know what is pleasant and unpleasant.

Theories about needs and drives begin to spell out some of the conditions and outcomes we find pleasant or unpleasant. We know that people who are hungry and thirsty will go to extraordinary lengths to obtain food and drink. People who are lonely may also go to staggering lengths to ease their solitude.

Teachers need to be aware of needs in their students. It is clear, for example, that certain basic biological needs must be satisfied if the teaching/learning process is to be effective. A hungry or thirsty student is almost certain to find concentration difficult. By the same token, a hungry teacher is probably seldom as effective as a well-fed one. Other basic needs, such as the need for sex, are not likely to present a serious problem for younger students; the same cannot be said about adolescents or about teachers— young or old.

Because most children's basic needs are adequately taken care of in our society, teachers are not often called upon to walk around with a bag of cookies and a jug of milk. Psychological needs are quite another matter. Recall that these include the need for affection, for belonging, for achievement, for social recognition, and for self-esteem. A useful exercise for a prospective teacher might be to consider what a "bag" filled with the wherewithal to satisfy these needs would look like. Teachers who through their actions can give each student a sense of accomplishment and belonging are probably carrying such a bag.

AROUSAL: A PHYSIOLOGICAL/ PSYCHOLOGICAL THEORY

Arousal is both a psychological and a physiological concept. Psychologically, it refers to alertness or attentiveness. It is, in a sense, the individual's degree of wakefulness. At the lowest levels of arousal, the individual is asleep (or in a coma) and is totally inattentive; at higher levels of arousal, the individual is intensely aware and alert; at still higher levels of arousal, the individual might be in a state of panic or shock.

Accompanying these psychological states— ranging from sleep to panic—are underlying physiological changes evident in the functioning of the sympathetic nervous system. At the lowest levels of arousal, respiration and heart rate, brain wave activity, conductivity of the skin to electricity, and so on, are all at low levels. But with increasing arousal, respiration and heart rate may increase, the skin's electrical conductivity increases as a function of perspiration, and brain wave activity changes in predictable ways.

Sources of Arousal

The main sources of arousal are the **distance receptors**—hearing and vision—but arousal may be affected by all other sources of stimulation, including activity of the brain. Some properties of stimuli—meaningfulness, intensity, surprisingness, novelty, and complexity (Berlyne, 1960)— make them more arousal inducing than others. Therefore, amount of stimulation is probably less critical in determining level of activation than the nature of stimulation.

Arousal and Motivation

The relationship between arousal and motivation is expressed in two assumptions:

Assumption 1. For any given activity, for an individual there is a level of arousal at which performance will be optimal. Certain activities can best be performed under conditions of relatively high arousal, whereas others are best performed under conditions of lower arousal. Activities such as sleeping or resting, or activities involving routine, habitual responses such as counting one's fingers or driving a car, do not ordinarily require a high level of arousal. On the other hand, intense, concentrated activities such as taking examinations require higher levels of arousal.

The relationship between arousal level and performance is illustrated in Figure 10.1 (Hebb, 1955). At the lowest level of arousal—sleep— there is little or no response to external stimulation. Try asking a sleeping person where Moose Jaw is. *Nada*. Ask her again just as she is waking up. "What the #$@#%##?" As she becomes more fully awake, she may respond correctly (if she knows the answer). But if in your zeal for observing the relationship between arousal and behavior you go ahead and set your subject's house on fire, awaken her with a bucket of cold water, inform her that her house is on fire, and then ask her what the capital of Iran is, you will probably observe the ineffectiveness of behavior that accompanies excessive arousal.

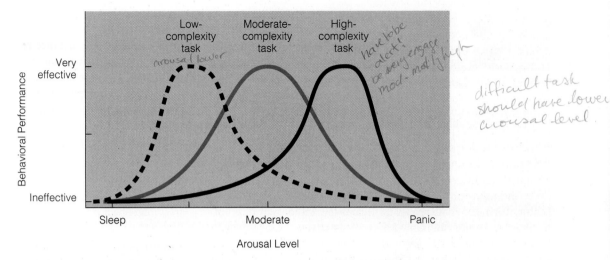

FIGURE 10.1 The relationship between behavioral performance and arousal level. The level of arousal that is optimal for effective behavior varies with the complexity of the task.

People under great stress often engage in inappropriate behavior. There are the tragic examples of panic-stricken people in crowds trampling one another to death in their haste to escape danger (Schultz, 1964). There are the studies of Marshall (cited by Bruner, 1957b), who found that fewer than one-quarter of the infantrymen in combat during World War II actually fired their rifles when under heavy fire. Fortunately, the enemy probably did no better.

Assumption 2. An individual behaves in such a way as to maintain the level of arousal that is most nearly optimal for ongoing behavior. In other words, if arousal level is too low, the individual will seek to increase it; if it is too high he or she will attempt to lower it. For example, when people experience great fear, their first reaction may be to flee the object of their fear. The effect is to reduce arousal level. When people are bored, their level of arousal is probably too low. They may then engage in more stimulating activity: reading, sports (participating or observing), or, if they are students, daydreaming. The effect should be an increase in arousal level.

Arousal and Learning

Like effective behavior, maximally effective learning takes place under conditions of optimal arousal. Low levels of arousal are characterized by low attentiveness—and less effective learning. As a teacher, you can illustrate this point. Prepare a good lesson full of content, write it out, and read it to your class very slowly in a soothing monotone. Then deliver the same lesson to another, comparable class in your usual, "today" kind of style. Test the relative retention of your two classes. It is little wonder that common synonyms for the term *motivating* are expressions such as "interesting," "captivating," "arousing," "moving," "useful," "involving," "stimulating," "compelling," "attention getting," "challenging," and "curiosity whetting."

When Arousal Is Too High: Anxiety and Learning

One manifestation of increasing arousal is anxiety—a feeling characterized by varying degrees of fear and worry. Research on anxiety and its relationship to learning (and more specifically to

biofeedback

If we care to, we can determine the texture of objects by touching them, their colors by looking, their sounds by listening, their smells, their tastes. . . . Our senses permit us to detect external feedback—information that comes back to us from "out there." But under normal circumstances, we know little of the internal functioning of our nervous systems; we have little biological feedback. However, psychology has invented ways of giving us **biofeedback** and has conducted experiments to determine whether subjects can learn to control their own arousal.

In one kind of experiment, subjects are connected to an electroencephalogram recorder, also called a "polygraph" or "alpha recorder" (or sometimes a "lie detector").

Simple alpha recorders differentiate between alpha (normal, resting arousal level) and beta (more vigilant, excited) brain waves. The object of the experiment is to have the subject control brain functioning and increase the proportion of alpha waves.

It has repeatedly been demonstrated that this is quite possible without any direct instructions, using the principles of operant conditioning. Whenever subjects emit a sufficient proportion of alpha waves, a tone sounds. Because they have been told that the object is to keep the tone going as long as they can, the sound serves as reinforcement. Eventually, most subjects find that they can reach the "alpha state" much more easily than they could originally. Interestingly, practitioners of Zen,

yoga, and transcendental meditation can, through the practice of their respective meditative techniques, arrive at similar states of low arousal—a condition that is believed to be highly conducive to physical and mental health.

Biofeedback instruments and techniques are being used to bring about relaxation, to treat migraine headaches, to deal with mental and emotional problems involving tension and anxiety, and in the treatment and prevention of cardiovascular problems such as hypertension (Parloff, London, & Wolfe, 1986). They are also being used in attempts to train children with attention deficit hyperactivity disorder (ADHD) to develop control over aspects of their brain functioning (Lubar, 1991).

---

performance on tests) dates back more than four decades but has been quite sporadic and unsystematic. However, recent years have seen a marked upsurge in research on the nature of anxiety, its relationship to performance, and techniques that can be used to reduce it. Much of this research is of a psychiatric nature, because anxiety is implicated in many mental disorders (American Psychiatric Association, 1987). Research that deals more specifically with anxiety and education is reviewed briefly here.

Text Anxiety. Sarason (1959, 1961, 1972, 1980) was among the first to show that anxiety related to test taking decreases test performance. This important finding has been well documented by

subsequent research. Hembree (1988) summarized 562 separate studies that have investigated **test anxiety.** The conclusion is clear, claims Hembree: Test anxiety causes poor test performance. In addition, it is related to lower self-esteem. Females tend to be somewhat more test anxious than males, although their greater anxiety does not manifest itself in lower performance. Research also indicates that in addition to performing less well on tests, highly anxious students do not profit as much from instruction. In other words, anxiety appears to have a detrimental effect not only on test taking but on learning as well (McKeachie, 1984). This observation is apparently true for a wide variety of instructional methods. However, highly anxious students tend to learn better with the more highly structured instructional approaches, such as programmed learning, computer-assisted instruction, and teacher-directed lessons in which student interaction is not expected or required (see Resnick, 1981). Thus, high anxiety does not always mean poorer test performance—although it often does (see J. H. Mueller, 1992a, 1992b).

Reducing Anxiety. Following an extensive review, G. S. Tryon (1980) concludes that many different anxiety-reducing techniques can work. Most of these techniques are aimed at changing students' attitudes about their personal competence and at focusing attention on the tasks at hand rather than on feelings of worry. Accordingly, they often take the form of attempting to develop learning/thinking strategies (McKeachie, Pintrich, & Lin, 1985).

Other possibilities for reducing anxiety, suggested by Hill and Wigfield (1984), include a variety of changes in instructional and evaluation procedures. For example, teachers can reduce time pressure on students by providing more time for assignments and tests and by teaching students simple time management strategies. They can also try to prevent failure by changing the difficulty level of assignments and tests, thereby matching them more carefully to students' skill levels.

Hembree's review of 562 studies indicates that many of these approaches are effective in reducing test anxiety and that improved performance typically follows anxiety reduction. In light of these findings, he argues that tests such as intelligence or standardized achievement measures—and even teacher-made examinations—consistently underestimate the abilities of test-anxious students—at least after fifth grade. Before this time, test anxiety is not ordinarily a significant factor in test performance.

The implications of these findings are twofold: First, steps should be taken to reduce test anxiety for highly anxious students, both through treatment programs and through changes in test-taking directions. And second, education needs to conduct research to discover ways to prevent test anxiety from developing in the first place.

Controlling Arousal in the Classroom

The relevance of arousal theory for education depends on the teacher's control over variables that affect arousal. Ideally, all students in a given class would be working at a moderate level of arousal. Students who are asleep, nearing sleep, or just waking up are at too low a level of arousal for most classroom activities; those who show signs of panic and impending flight are at too high a level.

The really central question for teachers is how arousal level can be controlled.

We saw that the primary sources of arousal are the distance receptors, but all other sources of stimulation also have some effect. Furthermore, it is less the amount than the intensity, meaningfulness, novelty, and complexity of stimulation that affect arousal. There are other factors as well. Degree of risk or personal involvement is probably directly related to arousal level, as is illustrated by the arousing effects of risk-taking behavior.

Teachers control a significant part of the stimulation to which students are exposed. The intensity, meaningfulness, and complexity of what teachers say, of what they do, of how they look, and of what they write all directly affect the attention (arousal) of their students. They can keep students at an uncomfortably high level of arousal by overemphasizing testing, making tasks unrealistically difficult, using threats, or presenting material that is too complex—and students may reduce that arousal by withdrawing attention and effort. Teachers can also keep students at too low a level of arousal by failing to present meaningful material in a stimulating manner—and again students may cease to pay attention.

The important thing for a teacher to remember is that arousal increases in proportion to the intensity, meaningfulness, novelty, and complexity of stimulation. Presenting Napoleon Bonaparte in the

Boris Randolph, a good teacher, as recollected by Elizabeth, teacher in training:

He had a wealth of knowledge of history, and he would allow ten minutes at the beginning of each class for questions on any topic relating to history, not just the specific time frame we were dealing with in class. After an extensive unit on Napoleon, he presented to us a man who was dressed as the Emperor Napoleon. We were given the entire class period to question "Napoleon" about his life, his career, and the state of France and Europe during his reign. The gentleman who disguised himself as Napoleon was a history professor at the local university so he was able to correctly answer our questions. This man also came to us as Adolph Hitler, Joseph Stalin, and Otto Von Bismarck.

classroom is clearly novel, meaningful, and highly motivating (see the case set in Boris Randolph's class above). Similarly, all changes in teachers' behavior that intensify the meaningfulness and novelty of stimuli may also increase attention. One key feature of highly arousing (motivating) approaches to classroom teaching is clearly *variety*.

THE BEHAVIORISTIC APPROACH

Motivational theories can be categorized in much the same way as approaches to learning: behavioristic, humanistic, and cognitive. Recall that behaviorism is concerned with how the consequences of behavior regulate and control actions; that humanism is concerned with the autonomy, the dignity, and the worth of the self; and that cognitivism deals with how we know, think, and remember. Accordingly, behavioristic approaches emphasize extrinsic or external motives such as those having to do with praise and reward; humanistic approaches emphasize the importance of intrinsic or internal motives such as those related to the need to be autonomous, to develop competence, to actualize potential; cognitive approaches emphasize the individual's need to know and understand.

Reinforcement in the Classroom

Psychological hedonism—the pain/pleasure principle—is a simple summary of the most basic behavioristic motivational principle: We behave to obtain pleasure and avoid pain. However, as we saw earlier, pain and pleasure are subjective emotional evaluations that are not easily admitted into a rigidly behavioristic position. Instead, the behaviorist attempts to identify situations (stimuli) that have the effect of increasing the probability of a behavior. These positive reinforcers can then be used in various ways to bring about desirable behaviors and sometimes to eliminate those that are less desirable.

Positive and negative reinforcement (and sometimes punishment as well) is used in virtually all classrooms, even by the most humanistic or cognitively oriented of teachers. Teachers praise and admonish students, they give high and low grades, they smile and frown. These and a thousand other indicators of approval or disapproval are examples of reinforcement techniques. As is made clear in Chapter 4 and again in Chapters 11 and 12, there is much in behavioristic theory that can be usefully applied to instruction.

But we are not simply hungry rats in some experiment, Weiner (1984) informs us. If we look into the classroom, we will see that behavior is informed—that it is driven by cognitions and by emotions and that it is both logical and illogical.

It should come as no surprise that current applications of reinforcement theory in the classroom take the student's thinking into account. As Stipek (1988) notes, the most powerful reinforcers for students are stimuli such as praise, the effectiveness of which clearly depend on the student's interpretations of the teacher's behavior.

Praise. Praise is not like food in an empty belly, warm and pleasurable even in the absence of learning. Rather, it is a complex event that says not only "you have done well" but also "you have behaved in a socially approved manner." Praise—and its absence, too—give us fundamentally important information with which to build notions of self. It says things about how worthwhile and competent we are. And, as is made clear shortly, these are fundamentally important concepts in human motivation.

But teachers do not always use praise well. Brophy (1981) notes that much teacher praise is determined not so much by the student's actual behavior as by the teacher's perception of what the student needs. As a result, praise is often used too infrequently to be effective, or it is used so often as to be almost meaningless. Praise used in these ways is not clearly contingent (dependent) upon a specific desired behavior, as a good reinforcer is, nor is it sufficiently credible to be very rewarding.

Brophy suggests that if it is to be effective, teacher praise should not be too frequent, and there are a number of ways in which it can be made far more effective. Most of these suggestions reflect principles discussed in Chapter 4. For example, praise should be contingent upon some specific behavior, it should be credible, and it should be informative. In addition, it should focus on the student's efforts. It should not be random and unsystematic, nor should it reward mere participation rather than quality of performance. (See Table 10.1 for a summary of Brophy's suggestions.)

Although reinforcement (in the form of praise and otherwise) is used extensively by virtually all teachers, some object to its systematic and deliberate use because they sense that there might be something mechanistic and dehumanizing about the systematic application of rewards and punishments (termed **extrinsic reinforcement**) to shape behavior. Others object because they fear that if students are trained to respond too readily to extrinsic reinforcers, they might become too dependent on them. And some humanists fear that such students will never learn to listen to their own motives—to their intrinsic and fundamentally human urge to excel, to become something worthwhile and actualized.

HUMANISTIC MOTIVES

But there is an important difference between extrinsic rewards, like tiny gold stars and high grades, and praise. Praise is simply a verbal affirmation that the student has done well. Many contemporary researchers argue that external rewards serve to decrease **intrinsic** (or internal) **motivation;** in contrast, praise may have the opposite effect (Fair & Silvestri, 1992). In this sense, praise is more humanistic than gold stars.

Humanistic psychology's concern with intrinsic motives is evident in Maslow's (1970) theory of human needs and especially in his conception of self-actualization.

Basic Needs and Metaneeds

Maslow proposes two general need systems: the basic needs and the **metaneeds.**

Basic Needs. The basic needs consist of

physiological needs, the basic biological needs—for example, the need for food, water, and temperature regulation;

safety needs, needs that are manifested in people's efforts to maintain sociable, predictable, orderly, and therefore nonthreatening environments;

love and belongingness needs, the need to develop relationships involving reciprocal affection; the need to be a member of a group; and

self-esteem needs, the need for cultivating and maintaining a high opinion of oneself; the need to have others hold one in high esteem.

TABLE 10.1 Guidelines for Effective Praise

EFFECTIVE PRAISE	INEFFECTIVE PRAISE
1. Is delivered contingently	1. Is delivered randomly or unsystematically
2. Specifies the particulars of the accomplishment	2. Is restricted to global positive reactions
3. Shows spontaneity, variety, and other signs of credibility; suggests clear attention to the student's accomplishment	3. Shows a bland uniformity that suggests a conditioned response made with minimal attention
4. Rewards attainment of specified performance criteria (which can include effort criteria, however)	4. Rewards mere participation without consideration of performance processes or outcomes
5. Provides information to students about their competence or the value of their accomplishments	5. Provides no information at all or gives students information about their status
6. Orients students toward better appreciation of their own task-related behavior and thinking about problem solving	6. Orients students toward comparing themselves with others and thinking about competing
7. Uses students' own prior accomplishments as the context for describing current accomplishments	7. Uses the accomplishments of peers as the context for describing student's current accomplishments
8. Is given in recognition of noteworthy effort or success at difficult (for *this* student) tasks	8. Is given without regard to the effort expended or the meaning of the accomplishment (for *this* student)
9. Attributes success to effort and ability, implying that similar successes can be expected in the future	9. Attributes success to ability alone or to external factors such as luck or ease of task
10. Fosters endogenous attributions (students believe that they expend effort on the task because they enjoy the task and/or want to develop task-relevant skills)	10. Fosters exogenous attributions (students believe that they expend effort on the task for external reasons—to please the teacher, win a competition or reward, and so on)
11. Focuses students' attention on their own task-relevant behavior	11. Focuses students' attention on the teacher as an external authority figure who is manipulating them
12. Fosters appreciation of and desirable attributions about task-relevant behavior after the process is completed	12. Intrudes into the ongoing process, distracting attention from task-relevant behavior

Source: From J. Brophy, "Teacher Praise: A Functional Analysis," *Review of Educational Research, 51,* No. 1, 5–32 (p. 26). Copyright 1981 by the American Educational Research Association. Reprinted by permission of the publisher.

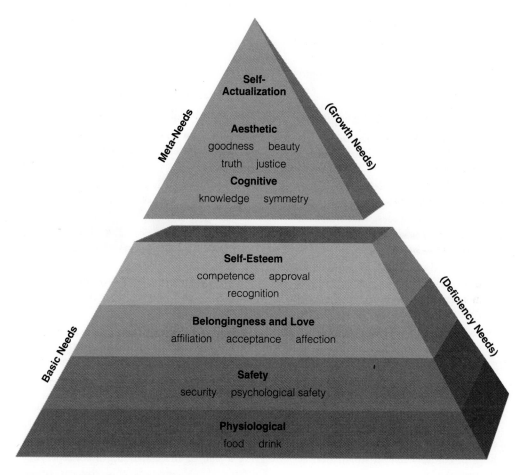

FIGURE 10.2 Maslow's hierarchy of needs.

These needs are hierarchical in the sense that higher-level needs will be attended to only after lower-level needs are satisfied (see Figure 10.2). When people need food, they are not likely to be concerned with love or with self-esteem. History provides striking examples of the potency of lower-level needs. In the 1933 famine in Eastern (Soviet) Ukraine, for example, in which at least 4.5 million people died, more than half the victims were infants. In the words of one of the survivors ("Ukrainian Famine Survivors," 1983):

All you think about is food. It's your one, your only, your all-consuming thought. You have no sympathy for anyone else. A sister feels nothing for her brother; a brother feels nothing for his sister; parents don't feel anything for their children. You become like a hungry animal. You will throw yourself on food like a hungry animal. That's what you're like when you're hungry. All human behavior, all moral behavior collapses.

Metaneeds. Maslow's basic needs are also termed *deficiency needs* because they motivate (lead to behavior) when the organism has a deficiency with respect to a need (for example, lacks food or water). The metaneeds are termed *growth needs* because they motivate behaviors that result not from deficiencies but from our tendencies toward growth. The growth will be attended to only after the basic needs are reasonably satisfied.

The metaneeds include aesthetic and cognitive urges associated with such virtues as truth and goodness, the acquisition of knowledge, and the appreciation of beauty, order, and symmetry. The highest need in Maslow's system is our tendency toward self-actualization—the unfolding and fulfillment of self.

Recall from Chapter 9 that self-actualization is a process rather than a state. It is a process of growth—of becoming—a process that most humanistic psychologists consider absolutely central to the healthy experience of being human. And although such abstractions as beauty, goodness, truth, and self-actualization are difficult to describe and even more difficult to examine in a scientific way, they do represent motivating concerns and processes for a great many individuals.

Competence Motivation

R. W. White (1959) argues that one of our most important intrinsic needs is the need to feel competent. **Competence motivation** is manifested in the child's struggle to perform competently and in the feelings of confidence and worth that accompany successful performance.

R. W. White believes that competence motivation is especially important in species such as ours in which individuals are born with so few innate competencies. Unlike the young of many nonhuman species, our infants cannot run or hide, they cannot feed themselves; they have little recognition of enemies or of danger. Perhaps even more important, they know few of the signals, gestures, and sounds they need to master to communicate competently. To be human is to learn a thousand competencies.

Competence motivation, suggests White, explains a tremendous range of behaviors engaged in by children. It is the drive for competence—for mastery—that explains curiosity and information-seeking behavior. Competence motivation is

"How about that? I recently became my own person, too."

evident in the repetitive, circular reactions of Piaget's infant (see Chapter 3); it also explains why schoolchildren practice skills over and over again until they achieve competence.

R. W. White explains the child's struggles for competence in terms of the feelings of pride and efficacy (personal effectiveness) that result from mastering a skill or understanding a concept. Albert Bandura (1986) expands this concept of **self-efficacy** in a theory that is as much cognitive as humanistic (it's often labeled a "social/cognitive theory"). We look at self-efficacy later in this chapter.

Implications of Humanistic Orientations

Humanistic approaches to motivation emphasize internal or intrinsic factors that affect behavior. As we saw in Chapter 9, humanistic schools are child rather than teacher or subject centered. Their emphasis is on affective growth and on the development of self-concept. At the same time, however, humanistic concerns need not be incompatible with more traditional values that emphasize curriculum content and the development of basic skills.

Three educational alternatives that illustrate humanistic concerns are open education, learning styles schools, and cooperative learning. These alternatives translate into practice some of the educational implications of humanistic approaches to motivation (see Chapter 9 for a discussion of their strengths and weaknesses).

The greatest contribution of humanistic approaches to instructional practice is embodied perhaps less in specific recommendations for the nitty-gritty of classroom practice than in teachers' attitudes toward students. The humanistic educator is a concerned individual who places great value on the personal development of students. Accordingly, self-actualization is one of the important goals of humanistic instruction—as is the concomitant development of positive feelings about the self and about personal effectiveness and competence (self-efficacy). As a case in point, consider the case set in Miss Cook's class on page 281.

COGNITIVE VIEWS OF MOTIVATION

Once again, it's important to realize that our categories in psychology are seldom as neat as we would like; the real world is not as simple as the models we invent to represent it. For example, aspects of R. W. White's competence motivation theory are every bit as cognitive as they are humanistic, and in some ways they are behavioristic as well. And some of the theories we consider in this section have behavioristic and humanistic overtones as well.

The earliest accounts of motivation viewed the human organism as a passive being, unmoved and unmoving in the absence of external or internal conditions that define needs, drives, and arousal levels, that trigger instinctual or primitive learned behavior, or that are clearly associated with pain or pleasure. In other words, early psychology has, inadvertently or otherwise, described an organism that is highly reactive but considerably less active. Hence, the contention that older theories have painted an overly passive and mechanical picture of human beings.

Newer approaches are clearly more cognitive and social. We are seen not as victims of internal or external prods moving us willy-nilly through our daily activities but as organisms whose ongoing activity is mediated largely by conscious evaluation, anticipation, and emotion. Bolles (1974), agreeing with one of Freud's basic beliefs, makes the point that there are no unmotivated behaviors; thus, motivation is not some special force that should be isolated and classified as needs are isolated and listed. It is simply a characteristic of ongoing behavior. And perhaps the single most important feature of human motivation is our ability to delay gratification (Mischel & Baker, 1975). So much of our behavior is motivated by our anticipations of distant outcomes that the analysis of human behavior in terms of those conditions that seem relevant to the behavior of very young children is often fruitless for schoolchildren and adults. We can delay gratification by virtue of some uniquely human abilities involved in thinking, imagining, and verbalizing. It is through a study of these ongoing cognitive processes that social/cognitive theorists such as Bandura search for understanding and explanations.

Self-Efficacy

One of the most important aspects of the information we have about ourselves, Bandura (1986, 1991) informs us, concerns our estimates of our personal effectiveness—our self-efficacy. The most efficacious people are those who can most effectively deal with situations—in other words, those who are most competent. Accordingly, self-efficacy has two related components: The first has to do with the skills—the actual competencies—that are required for successful performance; the second has to do with the individual's personal estimates of competence.

Personal estimates of competence are extremely important in education. As Zimmerman, Bandura, and Martinez-Pons put it, "Numerous studies have shown that students with a high sense of academic efficacy display greater persistence, effort, and intrinsic interest in their academic learning and performance" (1992, p. 664). Accordingly, it is important for teachers to understand the origins of judgments of self-efficacy. Much of what teachers do—and can do—has an effect on self-efficacy.

Influences on Self-Efficacy Judgments. Bandura (1986) identifies four important influences on a person's judgments of self-efficacy (or personal competence). He labels these "enactive," "vicarious," "persuasory," and "emotive" influences.

Enactive influences are evident in the results of the individual's own actions. Whether a person is habitually successful in a given task clearly influences personal judgments of competence. Those who are never successful are less likely to have highly positive evaluations of self-efficacy than are those who most often succeed. It does not follow, however, that success is invariably attributed to personal competence and inevitably results in high self-efficacy judgments. As we see later, some individuals habitually attribute their successes to good fortune or to other factors over which they have no control, rather than to their own competence and effort. By the same token, these individuals take little personal blame for their failures, attributing them instead to bad luck (see the later section on attribution theories for more information).

A second influence on self-efficacy judgments is vicarious (secondhand); it has to do with observing the performance of others. Clearly, if we see that others around us always produce nicer paintings than we do, we are not likely to develop high evaluations of our artistic competence. Similarly, children who always receive the poorest grades—or the highest—are being provided with comparative information that might be highly instrumental in determining their judgments of personal worth.

Bandura (1981) suggests that the most important comparisons for making judgments of personal competence are those the child makes with peers. It is not particularly helpful for my self-concept to beat the trousers off a twelve-year-old at racquet ball. It would be considerably more informative (and unlikely) to decimate the local champion.

Vicarious sources of influence on self-judgments are most important in competitive school situations—which means, of course, that they are important in most school situations because, as we saw earlier, most are competitive. In more cooperative settings, however, comparisons with peers are not nearly so important.

Persuasion can also sometimes be an important source of information about competence. Those who lack confidence—and whose self-efficacy judgments are therefore presumably low—can sometimes be persuaded to do things they would otherwise be reluctant to do. Implicit in the persuasion ("Come on, Emily, play your bandura* for us") is a positive judgment ("You play your bandura so well, Emily").

The fourth source of influence on judgments of self-efficacy is labeled "emotive" and has to do with *arousal*. As we saw in an earlier section of this chapter, arousal refers to alertness or vigilance and ranges from sleep or comatose states to states of high, intense alertness or even panic.

High arousal, Bandura (1986) suggests, can affect self-judgments in different ways. For example, great fear might lead to judgments of low personal competence. A mountain climber overcome by fear might decide he is incapable of continuing—as might a person about to speak in public. In contrast, great fear might lead a hiker to judge that she is capable of outrunning a bear.

In summary, our feelings of competence are a combined function of the results of our behavior (enactive influence: our successes and failures tell us much about how competent we are), our comparisons with others (vicarious influence: our

---

*PPC: I don't get this. Are you trying to make fun of Albert Bandura?

Author: Not really. A bandura is an ancient, many-stringed Ukrainian musical instrument. It looks a little like what we might imagine an angel's harp looks like.

performance is as good as, better than, or poorer
than that of others), the persuasions of others
(persuasory influence: when others persuade us,
their behavior tells us positive things about our
competence), and the intensity of arousal (emotive influence: judgments of competence can be
raised or lowered by the intensity of an immediate
emotional reaction).

Importance of Self-Efficacy Judgments. Notions
of self-efficacy or competence are especially important in motivating behavior. Schunk (1984)
points out that under most circumstances, children (and adults as well) do not spontaneously
undertake activities in which they expect to perform badly. Thus, judgments of self-efficacy affect
our choices of activities and settings. In addition,
they also influence the amount of effort we are
likely to expend. Normally, if our expectations
of success are high (that is, if our judgments of
self-efficacy—of competence—are high), we will
willingly expend considerably more effort on a
given task. If, on the other hand, our expectations
of success are low, we may not devote nearly as
much time and effort to the task.

Self-efficacy judgments have also been shown
to be related to goals. Zimmerman, Bandura, and
Martinez-Pons (1992) showed that students set
their academic goals in relation to notions of their
self-efficacy for academic achievement. Children
who do not see themselves as being effective
learners set lower goals for themselves than do
those who have higher estimates of self-efficacy.

Goals are especially important, says Bandura
(1986), because they set the criteria for personal
failure or success. Reaching them, or failing to, is
therefore accompanied by strong emotional reaction. Hence, the goals learners set for themselves
are powerful sources of motivation.

Judgments of efficacy also motivate our behavior by influencing our thoughts and our emotions. Those whose judgments of personal competence are low are far more likely to evaluate
themselves negatively and to suffer from poorer
self-esteem. Significantly, Coopersmith's (1967)
research with adolescent boys indicates that positive self-concepts are closely related to success
both in school and in interpersonal affairs.

It follows that highly favorable judgments of
competence (high self-efficacy), together with accompanying positive evaluations of the self (positive self-esteem), can be extremely important positive influences on a child's behavior in school. By
the same token, low self-efficacy judgments may
have highly negative effects.

Attribution Theories

Success and failure clearly affect our judgments of
personal competence—of self-efficacy. But we are
not simple, highly predictable creatures, you and
I; we don't necessarily react to our failures or successes in exactly the same way. It very much depends, says Weiner (1986), on our personalities—
specifically, on one aspect of our personalities:
our locus of control. *Locus* (meaning place) *of*

control refers to the causes to which we attribute our behaviors. Some of us are internally oriented; others are externally oriented.

Locus of Control: Internal Versus External Orientations. If I am internally oriented, I might attribute my successes and failures to my ability, to my effort, or to some combination of the two. The important point is that I am attributing my performance to causes for which I assume a high degree of personal responsibility.

But if I am externally oriented, I am more likely to attribute my performance to factors over which I have no control and for which I therefore have no responsibility—namely, luck or task difficulty. Thus, if I fail, I might assume that the task was too difficult or that I was unlucky (or both); conversely, if I succeed, I might attribute my success to the easiness of the task or to luck (see Figure 10.3).

Clearly, there are other causes to which performance can be attributed (mood, illness, or fatigue, for example), but these are more personal, more variable, and not easily amenable to scientific investigation.

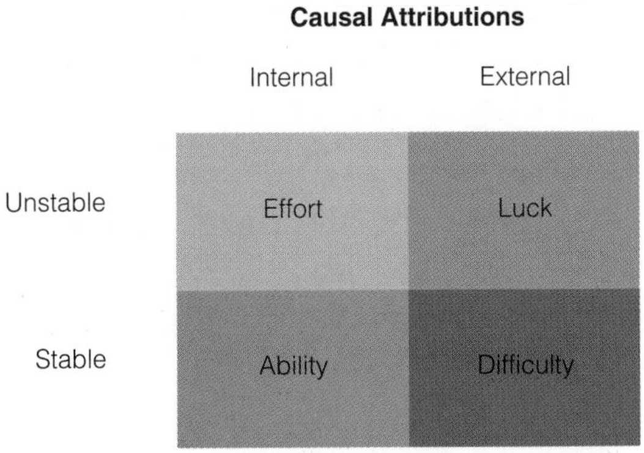

Development of Attribution Tendencies. The tendency to attribute success and failure to either internal or external causes seems to be a relatively predictable and stable personality characteristic. However, it is less apparent in children younger than nine, who have not yet differentiated between such factors as ability and effort. Nicholls (1978) reports that these children equate effort with intelligence; they believe that smart people are those who work hard (and consequently succeed). At the age of nine or ten, the child begins to consider ability as a separate factor that contributes to success. But even at this age, smartness is still equated with hard work. By age eleven, however, the child typically shares our intuitive notions about the distinctions among ability, luck, effort, and task difficulty.

Performance Versus Learning (Mastery) Goals. Children, Dweck (1986) informs us, seem to be-

Causal Attributions

FIGURE 10.3 Attributions for success and failure. Our explanations of why we succeed or fail may be internal or external; in addition, they may involve causes that are either stable or unstable.

have as though they subscribed intuitively to one of two views of intelligence: the entity theory or the incremental theory. If they subscribe to the entity theory, they behave as though they believe that intelligence is fixed and unchanging. Accordingly, their achievement goals are performance oriented; that is, they will be moved to obtain favorable judgments about their competence (about their ability) and to avoid unfavorable judgments. On the other hand, if they subscribe to the incremental theory, they behave as though they believe that intelligence is malleable. Accordingly, the goals of their achievement-oriented behavior will be mastery or learning goals rather than performance goals; that is, they will focus on effort and will attempt to increase their competence.

Dweck's analysis of attribution research strongly suggests that students whose basic orientation is toward performance goals (have a view of intelligence as being fixed) need to have extremely high confidence in their ability to be willing to accept challenges—that is, to be oriented toward mastery. Students whose confidence is lower are more likely to be characterized by what Dweck describes as "helplessness," primarily because they see failure as a direct reflection of their ability. In contrast, students who are oriented

TABLE 10.2 Achievement Goals and Achievement Behavior

THEORY OF INTELLIGENCE	GOAL ORIENTATION	CONFIDENCE IN PRESENT ABILITY	BEHAVIOR PATTERN
Entity theory (Intelligence is fixed.)	*Performance goal* (Goal is to gain positive judgments/avoid negative judgments of competence.)	*If high*	*Mastery oriented* (Seeks challenge; high persistence)
		If low	*Helpless* (Avoids challenge; low persistence)
Incremental theory (Intelligence is malleable.)	*Learning goal* (Goal is to increase competence.)	*If high or low*	*Mastery oriented* (Seeks challenge that fosters learning; high persistence)

Source: Adapted from C. S. Dweck (1986), "Motivational Processes Affecting Learning." *American Psychologist, 41,* 1040–1048.

toward mastery (those who view intelligence as malleable) are far more likely to seek challenges and to be persistent; that is, when students view ability as being a function of effort, they are more likely to strive toward high achievement because for them the cost of failure is not as high as it is for those who see ability as fixed and unchangeable. (See Table 10.2.)

Attribution and Achievement Motivation. The implications of attribution theory for understanding students' behavior become clearer when considered in relation to what is termed *achievement motivation.* Some individuals behave as though they have a high need to achieve, to be successful, to reach some standard of excellence; others behave as though they are more afraid of failing than desirous of success (McClelland, Atkinson, Clark, & Lowell, 1953). Research indicates that individuals who score high on measures of achievement motivation also tend to be the high achievers in school (Atkinson & Raynor, 1978).

Other relevant findings are that high-need

achievers are typically moderate risk takers. They attempt tasks that are moderately difficult, thus providing themselves with a challenge while keeping their probability of success fairly high (McClelland, 1958; J. W. Thomas, 1980). In contrast, low-need achievers typically attempt tasks that are quite difficult or quite easy. Why?

The answer may lie in attribution theory. If I attempt a very difficult task and fail, I will probably attribute my failure to task difficulty, a factor over which I have no control; hence, I will assume no personal responsibility and therefore experience no negative affect (emotion). If I am successful, there is again little positive affect because my success is not due to factors over which I have any control but to external factors. Moderate risk takers, on the other hand, can attribute success to skill or effort; similarly, they can attribute failure to personal factors. In either case, there is considerably more emotional involvement in the outcomes of their performances (see Figures 10.4 and 10.5).

It appears reasonable to suppose, then, that high-need achievers will tend to be internally oriented, whereas low-need achievers will more

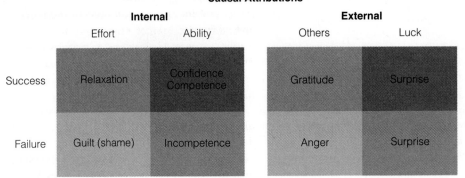

Causal Attributions

	Internal		External	
	Effort	Ability	Others	Luck
Success	Relaxation	Confidence Competence	Gratitude	Surprise
Failure	Guilt (shame)	Incompetence	Anger	Surprise

FIGURE 10.4 Relations between causal attributions and feelings associated with success and failure.

likely attribute their performance to external factors. This supposition is, in fact, borne out by research (Greene, 1985; Wittrock, 1986).

CLASSROOM APPLICATIONS OF COGNITIVE VIEWS

Cognitive approaches to understanding motivation have a wealth of educational implications. This is not surprising because many of these approaches have been developed specifically in order to understand achievement in the classroom.

Increasing Achievement Needs

Assuming that high-achievement needs are desirable, can they be increased in students? Yes, say Alschuler (1972) and others (for example, McClelland & Winter, 1969; Andrews & Debus, 1978) who have devised achievement programs for use in schools and with adults in economically deprived circumstances. These programs typically provide learners with a series of situations in which they are invited to take risks, make predictions about their performance, modify their predictions on the basis of ongoing feedback, and earn or lose points or token money on the basis of their performance. Among the objectives of these programs are to encourage learners to make use of information concerning their previous perfor-

mance, to arrive at realistic goals, and to assume personal responsibility for their performance. Indications are that these programs can be quite successful, both in increasing measured need for achievement and in improving actual performance (Alschuler, 1972).

Changing Attributions

We know that attributions are related to motivation and performance and that internally oriented individuals typically manifest higher achievement orientation and set more realistic goals. Can externally oriented individuals be made more internal?

A number of attribution-changing programs have been developed and investigated. As Wittrock (1986) notes, the major objective of most of these programs is to move students in the direction of effort attributions; that is, the programs attempt to lead students to the understanding that their successes and failures ought to be attributed to their personal efforts. For example, de Charms's (1972) program attempts to teach students to shift their locus of control from an external orientation—in which they see themselves as helpless "pawns" who have no responsibility for their own learning and achievement—to an internal orientation, in which they perceive themselves as "origins" and assume greater responsibility for the outcomes of their behavior. Similarly, a program

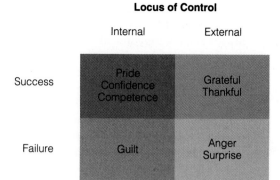

Locus of Control

	Internal	External
Success	Pride Confidence Competence	Grateful Thankful
Failure	Guilt	Anger Surprise

FIGURE 10.5 Relations between locus of control and feelings associated with success and failure.

developed by McCombs (1982) attempts to develop motivation not only by changing the student's attributions to internal causes but also by teaching cognitive strategies and metacognitive skills. It follows that as students become more adept at the management of these skills and strategies (as they learn more about learning), they will also begin to realize that they can exercise a great deal of control over learning and achievement—that it isn't all just a matter of luck and faith.

In most school-related tasks, luck should have little bearing on performance, although there are those students who will invoke that lady repeatedly in any case. They blame her when they have studied the wrong sections, inadvertently misaligned their answer sheets, or had the misfortune of being presented with inferior teachers. Teachers can exercise some control over the other three major categories to which performance outcomes can be attributed (effort, ability, and task difficulty), but luck can only be left to chance.

It should come as no great surprise that repeated failures are likely to have a negative effect on self-concept and on feelings of competence and that individuals who have failed more than they have succeeded will be reluctant to attribute their failures to lack of ability. Indeed, it appears reasonable to predict that repeated failures will contribute to external attribution and corre-

sponding feelings of powerlessness. By the same token, repeated successes in tasks of moderate or high difficulty (rather than tasks too absurdly simple) are most likely to lead to positive self-concepts, feelings of competence, acceptance of personal responsibility for performance, and high achievement drives.

The key phrase undoubtedly is "personal responsibility." To the extent that students accept personal responsibility for their performance they will be emotionally involved, success will enhance their self-concepts, motivational forces will be largely intrinsic rather than extrinsic, and the problems of classroom management (discussed in the next chapter) will become interesting pedagogical problems rather than discipline problems.

Changing Achievement Goals

Goal theory, a new emphasis in cognitive explanations of motivation, looks at how the individual's goals affect behavior. An achievement goal, says Ames (1992), is a pattern of beliefs and attributions that produces an intention to do or accomplish something. Goal theory is based on two important observations, which have been mentioned earlier in this chapter:

1. Students who believe that the outcomes of their behaviors result from personal effort tend to develop mastery goals—goals that focus on the intrinsic value of the learning. (Recall that Dweck also labeled these "learning goals.") Such students focus on developing skills, understanding their work, becoming more competent, in short, mastering what they study. Mastery goals are associated with high need for achievement, with risk taking, and with positive attitudes toward learning (see Ames, 1992).

2. Students who believe that behavioral outcomes are a function of ability rather than effort develop performance goals. Their focus is on doing better than others, on achieving public recognition, on succeeding according to external norms. Learning and understanding are

secondary for these students; doing well (performing) is all-important. Performance goals are associated with the avoidance of challenging tasks, use of short-term learning strategies, and negative affect following failure.

These two goal orientations are strongly influenced by whether students perceive classrooms as being oriented toward mastery. And that perception, says Ames (1992), is affected by at least three aspects of the classroom experience: tasks, evaluation, and authority. In an analysis of these three factors are numerous suggestions for teacher behaviors that might enhance student motivation (see Blumenfeld, 1992):

- Tasks. "Embedded in tasks," says Ames, "is information that students use to make judgments about their ability, their willingness to apply effortful strategies, and their feelings of satisfaction" (1992, p. 263). There are at least three important motivational dimensions of tasks: variety, challenge, and meaningfulness.

    Variety, notes Blumenfeld (1992), is associated with sustained motivation. And when tasks are defined in terms of specific, short-term goals, students are more likely to decide they can accomplish them with reasonable effort (to see themselves as efficacious). Similarly, tasks that are personally involving are less likely to lead students to compare their performance with that of others—and less likely to lead to performance goals.

- Evaluation. One of the surest ways to develop a performance orientation is to use evaluation procedures that emphasize ability and that underline comparisons among students. When the focus in classrooms is on students' products and on correctness and memorization, rather than on the processes of learning and on comprehension, students soon become performance oriented.

    Social comparisons are among the most obvious of performance-oriented evaluation procedures. They are evident, says Ames (1992), in the practice of making public the highest and lowest scores, of singling out students' papers and performances, of displaying students' achievements. The effect on those who do not compare favorably can be devastating.

    There are evaluation practices such as criterion-referenced assessment or portfolios, described in Chapter 13, that avoid the most direct forms of social comparison, and that might contribute significantly to the development of more intrinsically motivated, mastery goals.

- Authority. The extent to which teachers give students meaningful choices is directly related to students' mastery orientation. Research reviewed by Ames (1992) suggests that teachers who provide students with meaningful opportunities for autonomy are more likely to foster mastery orientations. Teachers who are highly controlling and who make all important decisions encourage performance goals. Ames notes that in most contemporary classrooms, students have little opportunity to make meaningful decisions regarding curriculum, methods and pace of studying, or assessment.

A Review of the Cognitive View

Why do some learners set challenging but attainable goals and others not? Why do some persist in the face of difficulty, but others don't? How can teachers keep students interested?

Big questions, these, with no short or simple answers. But we have too little space here to be long winded and no wish to be complex. So what follows is only a little bit of an answer squeezed from the contemporary cognitive view we have just reviewed.

The learner, this view insists, is first of all a reflective, thinking being (that is, a cognitive being). In this view, motivation boils down to the individual learner's decisions about goals, how these decisions result from and interact with some of the learner's beliefs, and how the learner's behavior is guided by both beliefs and goals. In a sense, it is as though the learner evaluates self in terms of wishes, inclinations, and abilities and evaluates goals in terms of likely rewards. And, as we have seen, for some learners, intrinsic rewards (often associated with mastery or learning) are more important than external rewards (often associated with performance or product).

We asked what is important. The cognitive view suggests that the student's self-evaluation is one thing that is important. Believing that we are bright and capable—and loved because we are lovable—is fundamentally important to each of us. Most of our lives, Kegan (1982) says, we struggle to be meaningful—to mean something to others. If we mean nothing, that is the measure of our personal worth.

Do teachers affect students' self-evaluations? Clearly, yes. Much of what teachers do—and can do—directly and indirectly influences students' perceptions of their competence and their meaningfulness. But the classroom factors that contribute to these evaluations do not mold them in simple ways. As Marshall and Weinstein (1984) put it, influences are complex and interactive. Often students' self-evaluations are based at least in part on comparisons with other students. But many factors (in complex interaction) are involved in the final evaluation. For example, in most competitive situations, success increases self-evaluations of ability; failure has the opposite effect. But if children are each given different tasks, the opportunity for comparison is much less than if all work on identical tasks. In much the same way, whole-class instructional procedures often provide more opportunity for direct comparisons than do small-group approaches such as those often used in cooperative learning.

In addition, students' self-evaluations clearly depend on the outcomes of their behaviors and

Drawing by Schoenbaum; © 1989 The New Yorker Magazine, Inc.

on the responses of teachers and others. Other things being equal, success leads to positive self-evaluations more often than does failure. And teachers' responses to students are typically loaded with information. Gestures, attention, facial expressions, grades, and verbal comments are just a few sources of information that tell the student, "Gee, you're pretty dumb, kid" (or worse), or that say, "Hey, way to go!"

Unfortunately, not everyone can do very well. In fact, not everyone is equally competent. But, as Marshall and Weinstein (1984) put it, the outcome of social comparisons need not always be negative for low achievers. If teachers and students alike see competence and intelligence as a matter of accumulating skills and knowledge through effort (Dweck's incremental theory), rather than as a fixed, unchangeable quality (entity theory), those who achieve less well need not suffer from unfavorable comparisons. Teachers who hold these views, claim Marshall and Weinstein, will favor noncompetitive learning, flexible grouping, mastery-oriented learning, and comparisons of a student's current performance with previous performance instead of with the current performance of others.

MAIN POINTS

1. Theories of motivation attempt to answer questions about the initiation, the direction, and the reinforcement of behavior. These answers are tremendously significant for education.

2. Instinct theory as applied to human behavior is largely of historical rather than current interest. Instincts are complex, unlearned patterns of behavior common to an entire species.

3. Psychological hedonism recognizes that people usually behave so as to achieve pleasure and avoid pain. Need theories offer one definition of pain and pleasure: The satisfaction of a need (physical or psychological) is assumed to be pleasant; not to satisfy a need is unpleasant.

4. Increasing arousal is defined by physiological changes (for example, in respiration and heart rate) accompanied by increasing alertness or wakefulness. Amount, intensity, meaningfulness, surprisingness, and complexity of stimulation are directly related to the level of arousal. There is an optimal level of arousal for maximally effective behavior, and the individual will behave in such a way as to maintain arousal level at or near the optimal.

5. One responsibility of teachers is to maintain moderate levels of arousal in students. Overly high arousal, sometimes manifested in anxiety, often has a detrimental effect on students' learning and performance. In particular, test anxiety has repeatedly been shown to decrease grades. Highly anxious students do better when exposed to instructional methods that are more structured, less demanding of public interaction, and consequently less anxiety arousing.

6. Humanistic approaches emphasize intrinsic (internal) motives such as those relating to autonomy, competence, and self-actualization; behavioristic approaches emphasize extrinsic (external) motives such as those relating to rewards and punishments. The humanistic educator is especially concerned with both the personal development of students and the enhancement of positive self-concepts.

7. Praise is an important classroom reinforcer. Teachers often use praise infrequently, unsystematically, and more in response to their perceptions of a student's needs than in response to the student's actual behavior.

8. Maslow's humanistic theory presents a hierarchical arrangement of need systems, with physiological needs at the lowest level and the need for self-actualization at the highest. R. W. White believes that an intrinsic need to develop competence motivation is an important human motive.

9. Traditional theories of motivation present a passive view of humans. More cognitive theories describe humans as active, exploring, evaluating organisms capable of delaying gratification and of explaining the outcomes of their own behaviors.

10. Bandura suggests that ideas of self-efficacy (of personal effectiveness) are important in determining which behaviors will be undertaken (children are least likely to attempt activities in which they expect failure) and the amount of effort that will be expended (greater if success is anticipated). Judgments of self-efficacy are affected by enactive influences (successful outcomes increase positive judgments), vicarious influences (comparisons with others), persuasory influences (persuasion by others), and emotive influences (high arousal can increase or decrease judgments of self-efficacy).

11. Weiner's attribution theory of motivation is based on the assumption that individuals attribute their successes or failures to internal (ability and effort) or external (difficulty or luck) factors. Individuals with a high need for achievement tend to attribute their performances to internal factors, thus accepting personal responsibility for their successes and failures. Those with a lower need for achievement are more likely to attribute their performances to external factors over which they have no control.

12. Dweck suggests that children who subscribe to the entity theory (intelligence is fixed) tend to be oriented toward performance goals (product

oriented; outcome reflects ability). They will be mastery oriented only if their confidence in their ability is very high; otherwise, they are likely to avoid challenges and be characterized by helplessness rather than a mastery orientation. Children who subscribe to the incremental theory (intelligence increases with effort) are more likely to be oriented toward mastery (learning) goals, focus on effort, seek challenges, and be mastery oriented.

13. Students whose need for achievement is high are typically more internally oriented (have an internal locus of control) and consequently are more likely to accept personal responsibility for the outcomes of their efforts. Achievement orientation can be modified by specific training programs. These programs typically invite children to take risks, make predictions, modify predictions, establish realistic goals, and assume personal responsibility for the results of their behaviors.

14. Attribution-changing programs attempt to move students in the direction of making more effort attributions—that is, attributing successes and failures to the results of effort rather than to causes over which the individual has no personal control.

15. Most cognitively oriented, motivation-driven classroom interventions attempt to foster the development of mastery rather than performance goals by manipulating factors such as tasks (variety, personal meaningfulness, surmountable challenges foster commitment and persistence), evaluation (social comparisons encourage performance orientations), and authority (opportunities for meaningful autonomy enhance commitment and mastery goals).

SUGGESTED READINGS

A practical guide to motivating students in school, with particular attention to the development of achievement motivation, is the following:

STIPEK, D. J. (1988). *Motivation to learn: From theory to practice.* Englewood Cliffs, N.J.: Prentice-Hall.

For a fascinating account of the effect of high arousal on human behavior, see

SCHULTZ, D. P. (1964). *Panic behavior.* New York: Random House.

Cognitive theories of motivation are presented clearly at a sophisticated level in the following book:

WEINER, B. (1986). *An attributional theory of motivation and emotion.* New York: Springer-Verlag.

McClelland's theories of motivation are described in considerable detail in the following two books. The first, a collection of writings by some of McClelland's most outstanding former students, is both a tribute to McClelland and an elaboration of many of his ideas. The second is a detailed analysis of the relationship between achievement and attribution theory.

STEWARD, A. J. (Ed). (1982). *Motivation and society.* San Francisco: Jossey-Bass.

HECKHAUSEN, H., SCHMALT, H., & SCHNEIDER, K. (1985). *Achievement motivation in perspective* (M. Woodruff & R. Wicklund, Trans.). New York: Academic Press.

Bandura's book is an excellent overview of current cognitive approaches to motivation; the Ames and Ames collection of articles, and especially the more recent Ames article, look specifically at the application of cognitive motivational concepts to the classroom.

BANDURA, A. (1991). Social cognitive theory of self-regulation. *Organizational Behavior and Human Performance, 50,* 248–287.

AMES, R., & AMES, C. (Eds.). (1984). *Research on motivation in education (Vol. I): Student motivation.* New York: Academic Press.

AMES, C. (1992). Classrooms: Goals, structures, and student motivation. *Journal of Educational Psychology, 84,* 261–271.

The brown bear (Ursus arctos) *is still found in small numbers in very limited mountainous areas of western Europe, in Russia, Asia, India, and northern China, as well as in North America. It is extinct in the British Isles (Southern, 1964).*

Most people sell their souls and live with a good conscience on the proceeds.
Logan Pearsall Smith, *Afterthoughts*

Few men have virtues to withstand the highest bidder.
George Washington, *Moral Maxims*

Oh wad some power the giftie gie us
To see oursels as other see us!
It wad frae monie a blunder free us
An' foolish notion.
Robert Burns, *To a Louse*

Chapter 11 | CLASSROOM MANAGEMENT

PREVIEW It may not come as a surprise to you that one of the principal reasons for teachers' unhappiness and premature retirement is discipline problems. This chapter, one of the more practical chapters in this text, outlines a number of strategies and principles that might be effective in preventing and/or correcting disruptive behavior in the classroom. It looks too at the application of behavior modification in the classroom. The single most important point it makes is that here, as in medicine, prevention is far more valuable than correction.

Excerpt from Learn 'Em Well

In the second grade, I tried to make a hole in my rubber eraser by holding a freshly sharpened pencil against it and hitting the pencil with my ruler. It didn't work, but it made interesting noises that I had been warned I shouldn't keep on making. So the teacher, my father, called me to the front of the class and administered the strap once on each of my small hands.

In the fourth grade, I was kept after school and asked to scrub the inside walls of the outhouse, where someone had discovered an offensive bit of graffiti penciled above the small hole (there was a larger one). I might have remained convinced to this day that God does watch all transgressors and reports directly to their teachers had I not remembered later that the spelling test we had been given that afternoon had contained most of the words found in the graffiti. In those days, I spelled turkey "t-e-r-k-e-e."

In the eighth grade, I had to write "I will not squirt ink on Louise" 150 times. I don't remember why I had to write "I will not squirt ink on Louise," though it now strikes me that these words might be a nice title for a song.

In the ninth grade, I had to write "I will not write about wild cows or draw their pictures" 250 times. I remember why.

I escaped unscathed from the tenth grade, having fallen in love with a sweet young thing who seemed to prize academic excellence, cooperation, and love of teachers. I cooperated, tried to excel, and almost succeeded in loving my teacher.

In the eleventh grade, I fell out of love and into a small gang of village terrorists. We placed thumbtacks on our teacher's chair, glued her books to her desk, painted her class register, and aimed missiles at her back in between barely suppressed fits of hysterical giggles. Elsewhere, we broke light bulbs, "borrowed" horses for insane bareback romps along the lake shore, and distributed dead chickens on doorsteps in the middle of dark winter nights. Various unimaginative disciplinary measures did little to dampen our enthusiasm, though most of us eventually tired of regular noon-hour and after-school detention.

In the twelfth grade, they sent me to a private boarding school—a place for bright kids, I was told, although I did hear one of my cousins remark unkindly, "He's always been a discipline problem."

DISCIPLINE AND CLASSROOM MANAGEMENT

Some of the various meanings of the term *discipline* are evident in these common statements:

> One of the reasons she's a good teacher is that she maintains such good discipline.

> They had to be disciplined again after they released the pigeons in the classroom.

> Now, Jack, for example, is a well-disciplined young man.

> What sort of discipline do you use in your classroom?

Although the term **discipline** is used frequently by teachers, administrators, and students, it is not always the correct word. Often, **classroom management** would be better.

In Kounin's words, discipline is simply "how a teacher handles misbehavior" (1970, p. v). As such, discipline includes a wide range of options such as punishments of various kinds, behavior modification programs, and various kinds of classroom management practices. *Classroom management* is a more inclusive term than *discipline*. It refers to the arrangement of classroom activities to facilitate teaching and learning. Hence, classroom management may include procedures designed to prevent misbehavior or to deal with it—in other words, classroom management includes discipline. In addition, it includes a wealth of procedures, routines, and practices that have much less to do with discipline than with teaching and learning.

Clearly, management and disciplinary acts may occur simultaneously or in close sequence, depending on the requirements of the immediate situation. Accordingly, this chapter discusses classroom management and discipline together. The emphasis throughout is on the practical and ethical aspects of disciplinary and management processes, rather than on the distinctions between the two. As Doyle notes, some educators view management as a prerequisite to instruction—something to "get out of the way so that teaching can occur" (1986, p. 394). Exactly the same thing may be said about discipline—that is, some educators view discipline as something that must be taken care of so that teaching can occur.

Not so. Neither classroom management nor classroom discipline can be "taken care of" and then put aside so that instruction and learning can take place. Rather, both are centrally involved in the ongoing process of teaching.

Discipline problems are one of the principal reasons for teachers' failure and stress (Blase & Pajak, 1985). Not surprisingly, then, the topic of classroom management is one of the primary preoccupations of many teachers. Unfortunately, however, the emphasis in teacher-training programs has traditionally been on authority and control—that is, on the disciplinary aspects of classroom management. Teachers are given lists of classroom management techniques designed to develop obedience and compliance in their students—rather than techniques designed to develop creative problem solvers, self-regulated risk takers, and independent thinkers who respond to their own intrinsic rewards rather than to pressure to achieve high grades.

This chapter deals with both aspects of classroom management: first, the facilitation of learning and second, the prevention and correction of misbehaviors.

CHARACTERISTICS OF THE CLASSROOM

To put the subjects of this chapter into perspective, it is important to consider the environment (the context) in which teaching and learning occur—and the teacher manages.

In the same way that the "average student" is an abstraction that does not exist in the real world, there is no "average class." Every class is unique. Each has its special blend of personalities that interact with one another, and with the personality and style of the teacher, to create its own dynamic ecology—that is, its own ever-changing environment. Some classrooms are filled with obedient and compliant children; others are riddled with violence. Each day, note McCaslin and Good (1992), some 135,000 children in the United States bring guns to school! Thousands of others have been suspended or are on detention; thousands more are in institutions for juvenile offenders.

Some classes are a complex mix of different ethnic groups, different abilities, different language skills, different interests; others are a homogeneous collection of majority-group children. Some include only children of highly similar abilities and interests; others are inclusive classes, characterized by an unpredictable mix of special needs.

Yet, says Doyle (1979), certain characteristics are descriptive of most classes and need to be taken into account in the business of teaching students and managing classes. These include the fact that classes are multidimensional. As we have just noted, they can include a variety of individuals participating in many different activities and working toward a number of goals. In addition, many of the different events in the classroom are simultaneous. Seldom is only one thing happening at a time. Even when they are engaged in direct, whole-class instruction, teachers may recognize different degrees of attentiveness among individual students and different behaviors (or misbehaviors) that may require them to interrupt the instructional process. As they phrase questions, they must also make decisions about who will answer, assess the pace of the lesson relative to time constraints, and constantly monitor individual students for signs of inattention or for potentially disruptive behaviors.

Classroom events are not only multidimensional and simultaneous but also immediate; that is, many of the events that occur simultaneously in the classroom require a teacher's immediate response. Decisions must be made and implemented rapidly if the flow of classroom activity is to remain smooth and purposeful.

Finally, and perhaps most important, given the immediacy, the multidimensionality, and the simultaneity of classroom events, their course at any given moment is highly unpredictable.

To manage such an environment—one that demands a continuous, rapid sequence of immediate decisions and is as complex and unpredictable as a classroom—requires a special set of managerial skills. These skills are tempered, of course, by the teacher's personal philosophy and teaching style and should be consistent with sound pedagogical principles gleaned from writings in educational psychology—or from the mutterings of old bears. It is not a simple task.

But it is not a completely overwhelming task either—although it might seem that way to the beginning teacher. Expert teachers do not need to consciously analyze all the elements simultaneously present in the classroom; they don't need to deliberately and sequentially monitor and appraise the immediate activities of each student, responding when necessary and all the while maintaining a wonderful pedagogical flow, never failing to recognize and capitalize on those brief, unpredictable opportunities that recent jargon labels "teachable moments." The expert teacher, Kagan (1988) tells us, does all these things, many of them unconsciously. Such teachers develop sequences of routines and strategies that become almost automatic.

Can the skills and the strategies used by expert teachers be learned?

In a word, yes. Some skills and strategies have been identified, and simply being aware of them might prove helpful to beginning teachers. For example, certain important pedagogical (instructional or teaching) skills concern sequencing, structuring, and managing the content of instruction. Many of these skills can be gleaned from what psychology knows about learning and development, and many are described in the chapters of this text.

But teaching is more than organizing content. Teaching also requires important classroom management skills having to do with paying attention to students and being aware of ongoing classroom events. Copeland (1987), who labels these "multiple-attention and vigilance skills," has devised a computer-simulated class in which it is possible to detect and evaluate these skills in teachers and to relate them to what goes on in real classrooms. As we see later in this chapter, some teachers are more "with it" than others; they are more aware of what is going on in their classrooms and are better able to direct the flow of activities to keep students on-task (involved) and interested. And as Eisner (1982) puts it, some teachers are more gifted in the art, although not necessarily the science, of teaching. Such teachers can more skillfully build the classroom environments—the contexts—that are most conducive to learning and to happiness—and least conducive to management and discipline problems.

In addition to the artistic, pedagogical, and "with-it-ness" skills that teachers require are a wealth of specific strategies and potential responses to classroom events that can be learned and applied in the discipline and management of classes. These strategies and responses are the subject of this chapter.

THE ETHICS OF CONTROL

The term *control* is highly—and unjustifiably—unpopular. Some of its unpopularity can be traced to educational and philosophical writings that have addressed issues of freedom, self-determination, self-worth, individuality, and other humanistic concerns—those often equated with liberal and permissive child rearing and educational methods. These concerns define much of the spirit of our times; no teacher wants to be conservative and restrictive. And there is little doubt that the deliberate exercise of control is restrictive. Is control therefore unethical?

There is, of course, no simple answer. If there were, there would be little controversy, and behaviorists and humanists would have much less about which to disagree.

Consider, first, that control is not only inevitable but necessary. Teachers, by virtue of their position and by virtue of their duties, have control. Indeed, it is not at all unreasonable to insist, as M. Marland (1975) does, that the exercise of control is one of the teacher's most important duties. We are not speaking here of a fear-enforced control that might have been characteristic of some of yesterday's schools. Control can be achieved, or at least facilitated, in a variety of gentle ways, some of which can be learned.

Parents too control their children (or at least try), often by setting limits for their behavior. Part of the successful socialization process requires that children be prevented from engaging in behaviors that might be injurious to themselves or to others. Thus, parents do not permit their children to play with dinner as it is cooking on the stove, to insert knives in electrical outlets, to jump off ladders, or to discharge firearms in the garage. Less extreme instances of control involve the teaching of socially appropriate behavior, of values and morals—of "shoulds" and "should nots." It is less by accident than by virtue of parental control that children learn not to deface walls, steal other people's property, or kill the neighbor's dog. In short, certain standards of behavior are learned at least partly as a function of parental control. Whether such control involves reinforcement, punishment, models, reasoning, or a combination of these and other strategies cannot hide the fact that control is being exercised.

The classroom situation is not really very different. Teachers have often been described as acting *in loco parentis*—in the place of parents. They are urged to act in all ways as might a wise, judicious, and loving parent. And there is, in fact, no great incompatibility between values held in highest esteem by those who describe themselves as humanists and the techniques of behavior control that have been described by science. Love, empathy, warmth, genuineness, and honesty can go a long way toward ensuring a classroom climate conducive to learning and development. In spite of these highly desirable qualities, however, discipline problems are not uncommon in classrooms. That teachers should judiciously administer rewards and punishment in an effort to maintain an effective educational environment does not mean that they care less for their students; indeed, it might well indicate that they care more.

CLASSROOM MANAGEMENT STRATEGIES

In the classroom, as in medicine, prevention should be valued more highly than correction. And it is reassuring that research is paying increasing attention to the methods by which teachers might prevent the occurrence of discipline problems (see, for example, Doyle, 1986). Perhaps the most important (though not entirely surprising) finding of this research is that the degree of order in a classroom depends far less on the frequency and insistence with which the teacher acts to maintain or restore order than on the nature of ongoing classroom activity. In the current jargon of classroom management, the strength of the primary vector—the principal ongoing stream of activity—is most influential in establishing and maintaining order (Kounin, 1970).

The second most important finding of this research concerns the timing of a teacher's interventions. The most successful classroom managers are those teachers who seem to anticipate most accurately when misbehaviors are likely to occur and intervene early to prevent them. In addition, the most effective interventions are subtle, brief, and often almost private, and as a result they do not interfere with ongoing classroom activities (Erickson & Mohatt, 1982).

Preventive strategies greatly depend on classroom management—that is, on the arrangement of classroom activities to facilitate teaching and learning. It is not difficult to find advice intended to help teachers manage the classroom in order to avoid discipline problems. Much of this advice is based on the collective experience of successful teachers and on the systematic observation of teachers in their classrooms. For what it might be worth to you, this chapter presents a distillation of such advice. Bear in mind, however, that the teacher's personality is probably the single most important factor in the classroom situation. Students find reasons to like or to dislike teachers in the combination of elusive and abstract qualities that define personality. Some traits can be learned, but desirable personality characteristics cannot, and thus they are not discussed further in this chapter. Not everybody should be a teacher. If you do not genuinely love children, and if they don't like you very much either, . . . please.

Kounin's Management Model

What successful teachers do to prevent misbehavior, says Kounin (1970), is probably more important than whatever they might do to handle misbehavior once it has occurred. Following detailed analysis of teachers' behavior in actual classrooms, he describes a handful of specific behaviors that appear to be closely related to successful classroom management, and he identifies a number of teacher behaviors more likely to lead to student misbehaviors.

With-It-Ness. The most successful teachers, says Kounin, seem to be more aware than less successful teachers of what is going on in their classrooms, of who is responsible for infractions of rules, and of when intervention is necessary. These teachers are more with it. **With-it-ness** is important for maintaining order in the classroom. A teacher who is "with it" knows what is going on and is more likely to be respected by students.

Precisely what with-it-ness is and how it can be developed are important matters for the teacher. Unfortunately, we know little about its development, although we may know more about its nature. Kounin (1970) arrived at teacher with-it-ness scores by looking at how often a teacher successfully directed a student to **desist**—that is, to stop engaging in some "off-task" behavior. Teachers with the highest scores were those whose "desists" were on target and on time (neither too early nor too late). Teachers who were less with it tended to instruct the wrong students to desist, or they tended to deliver their desist requests either after an off-task behavior had been going on for some time or too far ahead of its occurrence.

In an attempt to define *with-it-ness* in concrete terms, Borg (1973) identifies several components of with-it "teacher desist behaviors." According to Borg, the most with-it teachers suggest some alternative, on-task behavior rather than simply requesting cessation of the off-task behavior, praise on-task behavior while ignoring concurrent off-task activities, and provide descriptions of desirable behaviors or of relevant classroom rules. In addition, the most effective desists are timely (they occur before the misbehavior spreads and/or intensifies) and on target (they are directed toward the principal wrongdoer). Also, highly effective teachers seemed more aware of what Kounin calls the "ripple effect." The ripple effect is simply the tendency of the effects of a teacher's behavior to spread to an entire class. For example, a teacher's desists directed toward me ("Stop eating your pencil, Guy, or I'll just have to strap you. Again") always seemed to ripple over and work for Luc Doré, who would immediately stop doing whatever he had been doing. He feared the strap even more than I did.

Kounin's (1970) research on teacher with-it-ness led to the conclusion that timely and on-target desists are associated with less deviant behavior in the classroom and more involvement in classroom activities. This conclusion was later corroborated in a study by Brophy and Evertson (1976) and again in research conducted by Copeland (1987). In Copeland's study, teachers interacted with a computer simulation of a classroom situation. The simulation allowed the investigator to assess teachers' multiple-attention and vigilance skills—described in much the same terms as Kounin's with-it-ness. Teachers were then observed in their classrooms, and measures were obtained of the extent to which their students remained on-task or were disruptive. Copeland reports that the highest on-task scores were associated with high teacher vigilance and attentiveness.

Overlapping. Classrooms, as we noted earlier, are characterized by multiple sequences of events occurring simultaneously.

Successful teachers, says Kounin, are able to deal with several matters occurring at one time— a situation termed **overlapping.** Overlapping occurs in two different kinds of situations: when a desist is required in the course of a lesson or when something intrudes on the flow of the lesson. Both situations are illustrated in the case set in Dennis Kightly's class on page 297. The bathroom request is a mild intrusion but one that would have been disruptive had Kightly interrupted himself to say, "Yes, okay, you can go to the bathroom, Sam." And the interception of the Evelyn West note is a nondisruptive desist—again, a situation that would have been clearly disruptive had Kightly interrupted himself (as Ms. Regina Donnelly typically does in her class) and said, "Evelyn West! Would you like to read that note out loud to the class?"

The guiding principle in dealing with overlapping, notes Kounin, is that the ongoing flow of classroom activities be interrupted as little as possible.

Smoothness and Momentum. Successful teachers keep the pace of classroom activity flowing smoothly. This means not only that the teacher

THE PLACE: Walnut Creek Elementary

THE SETTING: Dennis Kightly's sixth-grade class

THE SITUATION: Mr. Kightly is reading a passage from Charles Dickens's *A Christmas Carol*:

". . . At length the hour of shutting up the counting-house arrived. With an ill-will Scrooge dismounted from his stool, and tacitly admitted the fact to the expectant clerk in the Tank, who instantly snuffed his candle out, and put on his hat.

" 'You'll want all day to-morrow, I suppose?' said Scrooge. . . ."

While reading, the very with-it Mr. Kightly notices that Sam Taylor, who today has a touch of the galloping something, has raised his hand tentatively in the beginning of the signal that means, "Sorry but I gotta go quick." At the same time, he sees that Evelyn West has just completed a note and is reaching to pass it to her cousin, Mary West.

" 'If quite convenient, sir . . .' "

Mr. Kightly continues, at the same time nodding almost imperceptibly to Sam, who immediately lurches, bent over, from his desk.

" 'It's not convenient,' said Scrooge, 'and it's not fair. If I was to stop half-a-crown . . .' "

By now Mr. Kightly has reached Evelyn's desk. He intercepts the message in midair, returns to his desk, and drops it in the wastebasket without missing a beat.

" 'for it, you'd think yourself ill-used . . .' " (Dickens, 1843/1986, p. 23)

must be able to deal with overlapping but also that transitions between classroom activities occur smoothly. Kounin reports that a normal school day contains an average of more than thirty-three major changes in learning activities (not including nonacademic transitions such as going to recess or lunch). These include transitions from one subject to another, as well as transitions from one major activity to another within lessons (say, from listening to reading, from reading to writing, from individual work to group activity).

Good teachers, says Kounin, have smooth transitions that maintain the momentum of classroom activities. In fact, reports Kounin, jerky transitions and lesson interruptions are among the principal causes of students' inattentiveness, restlessness, and misbehavior. He describes several major causes of lesson slowdown or interruption, or of what he terms "jerky transitions." His observations yielded a number of typical classroom behaviors, for which Kounin proposes specific labels:

- "Stimulus-boundedness"—the teacher's attention is interrupted by some extraneous stimulus; for example, if Mr. Kightly had interrupted his reading when he saw Evelyn West writing her note, and said, "That reminds me. I want each of you to write a note to your parents about getting permission to get back late from the field trip on Friday. So remind me after I finish this story."

- "Thrusts"—the teacher interrupts students' activities without prior signal and without consideration for their readiness.

- "Dangles"—the teacher interrupts an ongoing activity and then returns to it again.

- "Truncations"—the teacher does not return to the original activity after being interrupted.

- "Flip-flops"—the teacher makes a transition from one activity to a second and then flip-flops back to the first activity, as though he has changed his mind.

- "Overdwelling"—the teacher spends far more time than necessary on some aspect of a lesson or perhaps with some aspect of a student's behavior (or, more often, misbehavior); this is a type of lesson slowdown.

- "Fragmentation"—the teacher breaks down an activity (or a group of students) in such a way that individuals are required to wait unnecessarily, resulting in a lesson slowdown; for example, a teacher has students come to the chalkboard, one at a time, to complete a simple arithmetic problem—"Now it's your turn, Bobby"—while the others wait their turns. But if there is nothing to be learned from watching Bobby, all students might come up at once, greatly reducing waiting time and improving the momentum of the lesson.

Maintaining Focus. The most important factor in determining classroom order is not the frequency or strength of teachers' interventions so much as the nature of ongoing classroom activity.

Researchers inform us that there are perhaps eleven (Berliner, 1983), perhaps seventeen (Stodolsky, 1984), or perhaps a less definite number of different classroom activities. These include seat work, student presentations, small-group activities, discussions, recitations, demonstrations, lectures, giving instructions, tutoring, and so on. In the elementary school, an activity typically lasts somewhere between ten and twenty minutes; in the higher grades, an activity often lasts somewhat longer. Between activities are transitions, also sometimes considered a type of activity.

In an extensive study of student involvement and classroom activity, Gump (1969) found that small-group activities led by the teacher brought about the greatest involvement. In contrast, student presentations elicited the least student involvement—at least on the part of nonpresenters. Subsequently, a number of researchers have reported that involvement is lowest when students are doing seat work and highest when teachers are actively leading the class (see, for example, R. P. Ross, 1984; Burns, 1984). Accordingly, disruptions and misbehaviors are most likely to occur during seat work, during student presentations, and during transitions.

Kounin (1970) describes three different ways by which successful teachers attempt to maintain students' focus on ongoing activities. First, they develop ways of making each student accountable—usually by having each individual in the class demonstrate some product or some competence or understanding. Second, they use "group-alerting" cues, which are signals designed to maintain attention or alertness. Asking questions at random and keeping children in suspense about who will be called upon next are common group-alerting cues. Third, students' focus can be maintained through the format of classroom activities. Lesson formats that require only one student to perform at a time (as in reading, for example) often lead to inattentiveness on the part of other students. One lesson format to counteract this requires other students to do something else *while* one student is reading (for example, answer a question, think of a question, listen for an answer).

The Result? "A management system based on Kounin's principles," write McCaslin and Good, "provides expectations and understandings around which there is generally shared meaning between teachers and students, although teacher behaviors will be interpreted variously by individual students. The system allows the class to function in a relatively smooth and predictable way" (1992, p. 13).

But classes—and teachers—are quite different one from another. And students change with age, so that management principles that work well with very young children don't work at all well with older children. As McCaslin and Good (1992) point out, teachers' rules, behaviors, and expectations need to be flexible and sometimes need to change dramatically. Certainly, if one of the important objectives of education is to develop independent thinkers, the continued application of teacher-determined rules and procedures may be quite inappropriate.

The literature suggests a number of other teacher behaviors that might be important for successful classroom management *and* that might contribute to effective learning.

Marland's Suggestions

For example, M. Marland (1975) lists several teacher characteristics and behaviors that present a somewhat humanistic approach to the classroom.

Caring for Children. It's important, says Marland, not only to care for children but to let them know they are cared for. In this connection, one obvious but highly useful classroom strategy is to memorize pupils' names as soon as possible. More important, perhaps, is to learn as much as you can about each student. Relevant information can be obtained from conversations with other teachers (but beware of their prejudices and the consequent expectations that you might develop), from records, from involvement in extracurricular activities, and from parents and others. The children you teach should be more than just names and faces. The extent to which you care about them is reflected in the knowledge and understanding that you have of each. And the evidence suggests that the depth of your caring also affects how much they care about you and about each other.

Setting Rules. Classroom management and discipline would be much simpler if we could just give teachers a clear and simple list of rules and regulations that should govern all students in classrooms—complete with prescribed punishments for violation of these rules.

It's not quite so simple. Rules for student conduct are not and should not be fixed and absolute. Instead, they must be relative to teachers, to situations, and to students. Because of their different temperaments and styles, not all teachers expect or approve of similar student behaviors. Nor should teachers expect conformity to the same rules among students of widely differing ages and experience. And the rules of conduct imposed in a physical education class are quite different from those imposed during a recitation or a final examination.

Despite the relativity of rules, research suggests a number of generally valid observations. Probably the most important is that effective classroom management depends to a large extent on the successful establishment of rules and procedures early in the school year (Doyle, 1986). However, because rules are highly relative to situations, they are not usually established formally; that is, teachers seldom tell students that this is a rule and that is a rule and that is another rule and so on. Instead, as Hargreaves, Hester, and Mellor (1975) note, students tend to learn most rules indirectly, often when infractions of those rules occur. Many rules are never made explicit but are simply implied by the teacher's interventions.

In contrast, many routines are taught explicitly and directly. Particularly in the elementary grades, such routines are indispensable to the smooth operation of the class and govern the activities of teachers and students. They specify where books and supplies are to be kept, how questions are to be asked and answered, how games are to be played, where reading circles are to be placed, and dozens of other details of classroom activity. The establishment of such routines is an important aspect of classroom management that provides a context within which learning can be greatly facilitated.

Routines need to be established early in the school year. As Doyle (1986) observes, the most successful classroom managers are those who, in a sense, hover over activities at the beginning of the year, guiding and directing students until procedures have become routine and the routines have been learned and accepted by all students. Although rules and routines need to be predictable and consistent, this does not mean that they must always be enforced inflexibly. Even in the highly controlled, one-room bush school that I attended, the "no talking" and "no leaving your desk without permission" rules occasionally could be bent and sometimes broken.

I remember this happening one day when a bear ambled across the schoolyard and the teacher (my father) allowed the entire class to crowd up against the windows and watch. Later that day, he delivered a marvelous lesson on how bears socialize in the woods beyond the river, how they den up in the winter to dream of wild cows, and what their cubs look like when they are first born.

For days after that, I kept looking out the window, hoping to see a bear. Even now, years later, when I'm bored and tired I sometimes catch myself looking for a bear through my window. . . .

But there are no places for bears here. There is only concrete.

Giving Legitimate Praise. M. Marland (1975) advises that teachers arrange situations so that they can make frequent but legitimate use of praise and that they observe some simple guidelines concerning the use of praise and criticism. Praise, given its effect on self-esteem and self-concept, should be public. On occasion, it should be communicated to parents and other interested adults as well. Criticism, in contrast, also because of its effects on self-esteem and self-concept, should be given privately.

In addition, both praise and criticism should be specific rather than general. As we saw in Chapter 10, research clearly demonstrates that praise and punishment that are not contingent on behavior or that are not clearly related to a specific behavior are much less likely to be effective. Thus, Marland suggests that a student should not be admonished in general terms such as "Behave yourself" or "Be good." Instead, students should be directed to engage in a specific behavior and given a reason for that behavior. For example, the teacher might say, "Please put down your water pistol and your hunting knife because you are disturbing the class." Presumably, the rule relating to the inadvisability of disturbing the class will already have been explained and justified and the penalties for repeated infraction of that rule will have been made explicit.

Using Humor. The effectiveness of humor is often overlooked by teachers who do not consider themselves spontaneously humorous. And teacher-training facilities have not gone out of their way to encourage prospective teachers to learn either how to make others laugh or, perhaps most important, how to laugh at themselves. Potentially explosive confrontations can often be avoided by turning aside an implied student challenge with a skillful and humorous parry.

Consider, for example, Ms. Howard, who, because of her reputation for maintaining order in the classroom, has been assigned a ninth-grade class that might generously be described as predelinquent. (Less generous descriptions are entirely inappropriate in a polite textbook.) On the first day of class, she is challenged. One Rodney Phillips, closely modeled after a popular television personality who is himself modeled after a stereotype of the 1950s, finds an excusable error in Ms. Howard's arithmetic computations on the chalkboard. "She can't even add proper and they call her a teacher," he says for the benefit of his classmates. Whereupon Ms. Howard immediately falls to her knees and, in an amateurish imitation of the television hero, prays loudly to some undisclosed source to "Make me perfect again like I used to be!" Laughter that might otherwise have been directed at her is now with her. Ms. Howard simply has the knack of not taking herself too seriously.

Shaping the Learning Environment. Everything involved in teacher-learner interactions and in the teaching/learning environment can facilitate or impede classroom discipline. M. Marland (1975) suggests various ways to personalize the learning environment. For instance, there is something impersonal and cold about the traditional, dominating position of the teacher's desk at the front-center of the class. Similarly, students' desks traditionally are aligned in straight, even-length rows with uniform spaces front, back, and sides. Eyes front! Of course, certain definite advantages are inherent in this traditional placement, not the least of which are that there must be some focal point for students'

Mrs. Fitzsimmons, a good teacher, as recollected by George, teacher in training:

In grade three, Mrs. Fitzsimmons designed a "city" in which my fellow students and I could actively take part. Every two weeks we elected a mayor who was given privileges such as opening the "city gate" so the students could come into the classroom. Along the outside edges of the classroom we set up stores, restaurants, offices, and a zoo with large cardboard boxes, assigning students to each vocation. The currency in "our city" was silver-painted bottle caps with numbers; merchandise in the store was brought from home. If we behaved well all day and lessons were completed, we were given time to transact in "our city," which was a learning experience in itself. By rewarding good behavior there was peer pressure to pay attention. As we got older, extra credit assignments were given to those who had completed their work and could be a distraction in the classroom.

---

attention and that it is considerably easier for students to look to the front to see their teacher than it is to look to the rear. My eleventh-grade teacher moved her desk to the back of the room—not because she was experimenting with ways to personalize the classroom environment but because she could more easily watch those among us who had already dedicated their lives to mischief. We suspected as well that she had tired of being bombarded with our crude, elastic-propelled spitballs.

M. Marland's advice that the learning environment be personalized goes beyond a search for a more "personal" arrangement of desks. It includes those small decorative touches that are often more visible in the early rather than the later grades. Posters, charts, wall hangings, and other instructional and/or decorative objects need not be provided solely by the school and by teachers but might also be provided by students.

Classroom climate is more than the physical environment. As was shown in Chapter 8, for example, creativity appears to be fostered in certain climates (warm, friendly, and so on) and to be impeded in others (cold, authoritarian). So, too, certain classroom climates are more conducive to preventive discipline than others. Glasser (1969), for example, says that discipline problems will be minimized in warm, personal environments in which all students are accepted as capable.

The case set in Mrs. Fitzsimmons's classroom (see above) is one example of a personally meaningful classroom environment, which also involves the use of some reinforcement principles for classroom management and learning.

Webster's Democratic Procedures

Webster (1968) offers a number of principles to guide teachers in their efforts to maintain a nonautocratic form of classroom order. One primary goal of these principles is to promote the development of self-discipline in students. The principles are based on what Webster describes as the 3Rs of good discipline: reason, respect, and relevance. Thus, discipline should be reasonable and interpreted as such by students; it should reflect one of the most important of society's values, respect for individuals; and it should be relevant to the behaviors giving rise to disciplinary action. Several of the principles listed by Webster are shown in Table 11.1.

Even though there is little that is surprising, obscure, or difficult about Webster's advice, it is nevertheless valuable. It is all too easy to act "instinctively" when faced with a discipline problem. And although the teacher's instincts might often be entirely appropriate, there might be occasions when other behaviors would have been considerably more appropriate. Perhaps knowledge of these principles can increase instances of appropriate action.

TABLE 11.1 Webster's Principles of Nonautocratic Order

1. Teachers must make sure that all students understand rules and standards and the reasons for their existence.

2. The first violation of a rule should lead to a warning, a discussion of alternative ways of behaving, and clarification of the consequences of repeated infractions.

3. Teachers should endeavor to discover the causes underlying misbehavior.

4. Whenever possible, teachers should address students in private regarding their misbehavior.

5. Sarcasm, ridicule, and other forms of discipline that lead to public humiliation should be avoided.

6. When teachers make mistakes (if they ever do), they should apologize.

7. The punishment should fit the crime. Minor infractions should not bring about harsh punishment.

8. Extra class work and assignments, academic tests, and other school-related activities should never be used as a form of punishment.

From S. W. Webster. (1968). *Discipline in the classroom: Basic principles and problems.* New York: Chandler, p. 50.

A Foundation for Preventive Discipline

Like Webster, Grossnickle and Sesko (1990) provide a list of ten procedures they consider an important basis for classroom management. Many of these have been mentioned earlier in this chapter but are worth repeating in this simple, organized form:

1. *Establish clear behavior guidelines.* Expectations, standards, and rules should be clear to teachers, students, *and* parents. Preferably, they should be written and distributed to all concerned.

2. *Adopt a teamwork approach.* Teachers, administrators, and parents are a team and should all work together to support, follow, and enforce agreed-upon management procedures.

3. *Design a complete discipline ladder.* This is a clear description of available *corrective* disciplinary measures and the order in which they are to be invoked (for example, first an in-class warning, followed, in order and if necessary, by an after-class conference, a phone

call to parents, referral to the principal, help from counselors . . .).

4. *Teach self-management and self-discipline.* This is a gradual process but an essential function of schools.

5. *Invite good discipline.*

6. *Focus on students' success and self-esteem.*

7. *Implement firm, fair, and calm enforcement.*

8. *Plan lessons thoroughly.*

9. *Continually monitor the classroom environment.*

10. *Minimize problems early.*

Creating a Context for Preventive Classroom Management

The preceding sections might seem a little like a catalog from which a clever teacher might select an assortment of tricks and tactics for managing classrooms, all the while keeping students happily on-task. But good teaching is not so simple; in teaching, there are no recipes that, when followed one-two-three, always lead where they are intended.

Good teaching—which implies effective classroom management—requires far more than the deliberate and judicious application of principles and tactics in specific classroom situations. As we saw at the beginning of this chapter, classes are characterized by a multiplicity of often unpredictable events occurring simultaneously; they demand of the teacher an exceptional level of attention and vigilance (with-it-ness). And they require as well an ongoing series of instantaneous decisions and their immediate implementation.

In addition to the ongoing decision making and problem solving that good teaching requires, it involves a large number of decisions that are made in advance. These might be in response to specific, immediate questions, such as "What do I teach next?" "What assignments are appropriate for this unit?" "How should I arrange the seats in my classroom?" Or they might be in response to more global questions, such as "Should I incorporate cooperative learning activities in my classroom?" "Should I involve students in decisions about rules?" "Should I include programs designed to increase prosocial behavior?" "Should I emphasize a whole-class, teacher-directed teaching style?" "Should I implement more small-group learning activities?" And so on.

The important point is that learning and classroom management occur in a classroom context that is determined by at least four influences: the blend of students that compose the class, the teacher's beliefs and personality, the teacher's application of the science that texts such as this provide, and a measure of art.

You may have some control over the third and fourth of these influences but not over the first two. You cannot easily change your beliefs and personality, and you are not likely to be allowed to select students for your classes. Still, enough is under your control to make worthwhile the struggle to become the best teacher you can. All that relates to good and effective teaching also relates to maintaining classroom order.

CORRECTIVE STRATEGIES FOR THE CLASSROOM

Even enormously effective teachers are sometimes called upon to deal with disturbances and disruptions in the classroom. That this should be the case does not necessarily mean that the teacher is a failure, that the system is at fault, or that teacher-training institutions have been remiss. Although each of these might be wholly or partly responsible, the point is not to lay the blame but to deal with the situation.

In dealing with any disciplinary problem, two concerns are of paramount importance. The first is that the individual not be harmed—that whatever the teacher does is done in the best interests of the student, with full consideration of that person's self-esteem and humanity. The second is that the disciplinary measures invoked should be applied in the interests of the entire group. In short, the teacher as a humanitarian practitioner of skills (with a little art, to be sure) must strike a delicate balance between the well being of the group and that of the individual. The resolution is not always simple.

A variety of corrective strategies are available to the teacher. **Behavior modification** refers specifically to strategies predicated on behaviorist learning theory. These include the use of reinforcement, models, extinction, and punishment. In addition, some applications of behavior modification use principles of cognitive theory; these are labeled "cognitive behavior modification." Examples of each of these strategies is discussed here with specific reference to discipline problems.

Behavior Modification

The immediate objective of corrective discipline is to change or eliminate a particular behavior. Reinforcement and punishment are among the most common elements of corrective discipline. Not surprisingly, then, the strategies of corrective discipline often use principles of conditioning theory (described in Chapter 4). Collectively, these strategies are labeled "behavior modification"—or sometimes "behavior management" or "behavioral intervention."

Presland (1989) describes the most common sequence for a behavioral intervention program for an individual student:

1. Defining the problem: Often a written list is developed of behaviors that are too frequent (speaking out in class) or too infrequent (volunteering answers for questions). The student might be involved in this step.

2. Measuring the problem: The teacher attempts to determine how serious (frequent or infrequent) the behavior actually is, perhaps by counting occurrences.

3. Determining antecedents and consequences: What conditions precede the behavior? What are its apparent consequences? In other words, how is it triggered and what reinforces it?

4. Deciding whether and how to change antecedents and consequences: Are there existing consequences that serve to reinforce a too-frequent behavior? Are there new consequences that might reinforce an infrequent behavior? For example, one of the consequences of undesirable behavior might be increased teacher attention. This might serve to maintain the behavior. If so, teacher inattention might have the opposite effect. Similarly, increased teacher attention for less frequent but more desirable behaviors might increase their frequency.

5. Planning and implementing the intervention: Having determined behaviors in need of change and having identified certain antecedents (stimuli) and consequences (potential reinforcers) associated with them, it's now possible to devise a program designed to modify the behavior in question. The program should specify, often in contract with the student, how antecedents and consequences will be used and how the student will be involved.

6. Following up: Following the program's implementation, the teacher (and student) evaluate its effectiveness and determine whether additional or different intervention is desirable.

Systematic Reinforcement Programs

Applying positive reinforcement as a corrective strategy often involves rewarding behaviors that run counter to those that are a problem. Instead of focusing on eliminating undesired responses, the teacher focuses on reinforcing the opposite behavior. For example, if a teacher's attention reinforces Sally's disruptive behavior (for example, speaking out during other students' recitations), one reinforcement strategy that is often effective is to pay attention when the student is not being disruptive and to ignore her when she calls out inappropriately.

Teachers have at their disposal a wide variety of potent reinforcers, not the least important of which are praise, smiles, grades, and attention. When these social reinforcers prove ineffective, more elaborate reinforcement systems can be established. The best known are token systems whereby students earn points or tokens for good behavior and sometimes lose them for less desirable behavior. The tokens can later be exchanged for tangible rewards.

An Example of a Token System. Psychology journals offer numerous examples of the use of positive reinforcement in the classroom. For example, O'Leary and Becker (1967) describe a study in which a token system of reinforcement was used in conjunction with social approval in order to eliminate deviant responses and encourage acceptable classroom behavior. The subjects were 17 nine-year-olds. (Although these students were of average intelligence, they had been classified as emotionally disturbed and placed in a special classroom.) The experimental procedure, which lasted for a year, involved writing a number of instructions on the chalkboard (for example, "Desk clear," "Face the front," "Do not talk") and then assigning each student a daily score based on observance of the rules. The scores were entered in a record book on each student's desk and could be totaled and exchanged for small toys and trinkets at any time. Additional reinforcement was provided for each child by the teacher's comments (for example, "I like the way you held your hand up before talking today"). The success of the project was evaluated by comparing incidents of deviant behavior before the program and at its completion. The evidence suggests that it was highly effective.*

Although the effectiveness of reinforcement in establishing and maintaining acceptable behaviors can hardly be disputed, there are a number of problems involved in the systematic use of token systems. The establishment of such a system requires a great deal of time and care and presents some real problems in selecting reinforcers for which tokens can be exchanged. In addition, several studies have found tokens ineffective for some students and distracting for others (Kazdin & Bootzin, 1972). Some students spend so much time counting and sorting their tokens that they experience considerable difficulty attending to the tasks desired of them.

Other Examples. One frequently used alternative to token systems, called the "Premack principle," simply allows students who have behaved appropriately (or who have not behaved inappropriately) to engage in some reinforcing activity—one that the child enjoys. Thus, one child might be permitted free time for reading, another for painting, another for running around the gym. (A later section describes the Premack principle in more detail.)

Another interesting alternative is presented by Nay, Schulman, Bailey, and Huntsinger (1976), who used tape to demarcate an area of approximately one square yard around each student's desk. These areas were described as the students' personal spaces, to be named and decorated by

them and to be occupied by them alone. The experiment addressed two types of deviant behaviors: leaving one's desk at inappropriate times and speaking out. Unambiguous signals were placed at the front of the class to indicate when leaving one's territory and speaking were not allowed. A red light was the signal prohibiting leaving; a figure with the lips closed signaled "no talking." When walking quietly around the room, obtaining supplies, or leaving personal territory for some other reason was permitted, a green light replaced the red light; similarly, when children were permitted to talk quietly, a figure with the lips open was placed at the front. The assumption of the experiment was that being allowed to remain in one's territory is reinforcing, particularly if infractions of rules result in one's removal from that territory. Accordingly, desks were set aside in an area labeled "no-man's land," and children guilty of leaving their seats or of talking when these activities were prohibited were sent to one of these desks for a twenty-minute period. Further infractions in "no-man's land" resulted in a longer exile from home territory. Strikingly, after several weeks, disruptive behavior had virtually been eliminated in a class that had previously threatened to pose some severe discipline problems.

Some Limitations. In spite of the apparent effectiveness of some systematic behavior modification programs as corrective disciplinary strategies, it should be noted that many are difficult or impractical in ordinary classrooms (Hughes, 1988). In addition, as Lepper (1981) has demonstrated, the excessive use of reinforcement can have harmful effects on subsequent motivation. In one representative experiment, Lepper and Greene (1975) asked two groups of children to solve a number of geometric puzzles. One group was told that they would be allowed to play with some attractive toys as a reward; the other was also allowed to play with the puzzles but was not led beforehand to expect a reward. Later, children were observed unobtrusively to see whether any of them spontaneously played with the puzzles,

*The procedure described here involved both positive reinforcement and extinction. In fact, most programs based on behavior modification make use of a combination of techniques.

which were freely available in the classroom. As is shown in Figure 11.1, significantly more of those who had not expected a reward continued to be motivated to play with the puzzles.

Why? Lepper and Greene suggest that the most reasonable explanation is a cognitive one. It is important for us to try to make sense of our behaviors—to understand why we do things. Typically, we resort to two classes of explanations for our behaviors: extrinsic or intrinsic causes; that is, we generally recognize that we do things for certain external rewards (money, prestige, being allowed to play with toys), for internal rewards (satisfaction, sense of accomplishment, personal interest), or sometimes for both internal and external rewards. When external rewards are large and obvious, our motivation becomes largely extrinsic, but when we expect no great extrinsic rewards, we must look to intrinsic causes. Thus, children who expect reinforcement can understand and justify their behavior in terms of extrinsic factors; those who do not expect external rewards must justify their behavior in terms of such things as the pleasure and enjoyment associated with it. Children who do not expect rewards are subsequently more highly motivated (intrinsically motivated) to continue the activity. To the extent that this observation is true, there may clearly be some danger associated with the indiscriminate and excessive use of external rewards. And, as we saw in Chapter 10, children who are intrinsically motivated tend to be mastery oriented. Not only do these children achieve at a higher level but their emphasis is on learning and understanding, rather than simply on performing and competing. Hence, the advisability of encouraging intrinsic motivation.

Intrinsic Reinforcement. Although **intrinsic reinforcement** is not under a teacher's direct control, the teacher can nevertheless structure learning situations in ways that are more likely to lead to intrinsic satisfaction. Presenting students with tasks that are too difficult is not likely to lead to satisfaction with learning. Likewise, excessively

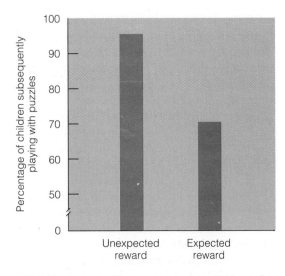

FIGURE 11.1 Significantly more of the children who had not expected a reward showed intrinsic interest by subsequently playing with the geometric puzzles. Based on data from M. R. Lepper and D. Greene (1975), "Turning Play into Work: Effects of Adult Surveillance and Extrinsic Rewards on Children's Intrinsic Motivation," *Journal of Personality and Social Psychology, 31,* 479–486.

simple tasks are not self-reinforcing. As we saw in Chapter 10, teachers can foster an intrinsic (mastery) orientation by manipulating tasks (personal involvement in challenging but achievable tasks), type of evaluation (social comparisons foster a performance orientation and a reliance on extrinsic sources of reinforcement like grades), and use of authority (providing students with opportunities for meaningful autonomy—say in determining questions worth investigating—fosters an intrinsic orientation).

The teacher's use of external rewards, especially in the early grades, is another potential source of influence on intrinsic reinforcement. If rewards are initially administered for behaviors related to learning, it follows that the process of learning may acquire the characteristics of a generalized reinforcer. In fact, it is customary in structured teaching programs based on reinforcement principles to use external rewards only in the initial stages of the program (see, for example, Meacham & Wiesen, 1969; Hewett, 1968). It is assumed that intrinsic reinforcement will eventually suffice to maintain the behavior.

Extrinsic Reinforcement. Among the extrinsic reinforcers most commonly used in the classroom are attention, praise, tokens, stars, grades, and promotion. Another important and apparently quite effective source of reinforcement is defined by the **Premack principle** (Premack, 1965), which states that behavior that ordinarily occurs frequently can be used to reinforce less frequent behavior. Parents and teachers use this principle constantly: A child is allowed to play outside *after* eating supper; a student is permitted to read a library book *after* completing an assignment.

Bijou and Sturges (1959) classify extrinsic reinforcers according to five categories: "consumables," "manipulatables," "visual and auditory stimuli," "social stimuli," and "tokens." It is interesting, and potentially valuable, to consider the use of each of these in the classroom. Consumables are relatively inconvenient. A teacher walking around a classroom with a bag of cookies, dispensing them as she observes desirable student behavior, might occasion some concern among parents. Manipulatables, objects such as toys or trinkets, can be used successfully, particularly with young children. Reinforcing auditory and visual stimuli are less likely to be readily available to a teacher. Such reinforcers are signals that have been given reinforcing properties. For example, if a teacher told students that he would ring a bell every time he was happy with them, the bell would be an auditory reinforcer. This is not to be confused with social reinforcers, which take the form of praise, approval, or simply attention, and which are by far the most prevalent and powerful reinforcers available to a teacher. In this connection, it should also be kept in mind that peer approval is often as powerful or more powerful a reinforcer than teacher approval. Tokens, check marks, or stars are sometimes used as direct ex-trinsic reinforcement for desirable behavior. In a token system, it is not uncommon to arrange for tokens to be exchanged for other reinforcers: consumables, manipulatables, or perhaps time for some pleasant activity.

Parents as Reinforcers. Teachers are not the only ones who have control over reinforcers that are important to the lives and learning of their students. Indeed, parents also are administrators of what can be particularly powerful rewards—and punishments, too.

Barth (1979) reviews several dozen studies in which investigators deliberately and systematically enlisted the help of parents in providing reinforcement for school-related activities. These studies involved students in group homes, in special classes, and in ordinary classes. Reinforcers varied from tokens and social praise to consumables and special privileges and were administered for an extremely wide range of behaviors. In many cases, money was also used as a reinforcer. For example, students would earn varying amounts of money for different school grades—and sometimes would lose money for failing to complete assignments or for getting low grades.

Taken as a whole, the studies reviewed by Barth indicate that home-based reinforcement can be extremely influential in bringing about measurable and significant positive changes, both in behavior and in academic achievement, for many students in a wide range of subjects and situations.

Seven Principles for Using Reinforcement. Michael (1967) describes seven principles that should be kept in mind when attempting to control behavior through its consequences. Some of these have been discussed earlier, but all are important enough to bear repeating.

First, the consequences of behavior, whether rewarding or punishing, are defined only in terms of their effect on the learner. Teachers should not always assume that a stimulus they consider pleasant for a student will strengthen behavior. Peer attention, for example, is generally strongly reinforcing; for a very inhibited student, however, peer attention may be quite punishing. Nor can a teacher simply ask students what is reinforcing for them, because this might well render some reinforcers almost meaningless. If, for example, students were to indicate that praise was reinforcing, subsequent praise might be interpreted as less genuine and hence would be less reinforcing.

A useful concept in relation to this first principle (that reinforcement is highly individualistic) is that of the **reinforcement menu,** introduced by Addison and Homme (1966). Based largely on the Premack principle, a reinforcement menu is a list of potentially reinforcing activities from which the student is allowed to select following some behavior that merits reinforcement. Table 11.2 presents one example of a reinforcement menu. Interestingly, however, research with very young children (between two and six years) indicates that rewards selected by experimenters are sometimes *more* effective than rewards children are allowed to select for themselves (Baer, Tishelman, Degler, Osnes, & Stokes, 1992).

The second principle states that the effects of reinforcement are automatic; that is, the teacher need not explain to students that if they learn well, they will receive some specific reinforcement that will then lead them to study even harder. The point is that if students do learn and consequently are reinforced, they will probably study even harder without ever having discussed this marvelous phenomenon with their teacher. However, as Kalish (1981) points out, praise (or punishment) by itself, especially for young children, is not as effective as praise accompanied by a description of what was done to deserve praise or by an explanation of why it is deserved.

The third principle stresses that reinforcement or punishment should be closely related to the desirable (or undesirable) behavior. In other words, teachers must have some short-range goals clearly in mind so that they can reinforce behavior that matches those goals.

TABLE 11.2 A Reinforcement Menu*

REWARD	COST
1. One free period in the library	10
2. One free period in class	10
3. One day off from clean-up duty	5
4. Lunch with Ms. Clements (the teacher)	15
5. Lunch prepared by Ms. Clements	25
6. Extra help with one subject	2
7. Get to choose the game for gym	10
8. Get to sit anywhere in class for one day	3

*Members of a fifth-grade class could purchase activities from this menu, using points earned in school-related activities.

Fourth, reinforcement should be consistent. This does not mean that reinforcement must occur for every correct response. It does mean, however, that a specific behavior should not be reinforced one time and punished the next.

Fifth, consequences should follow behavior closely. Delayed reward or punishment is much less effective than immediate consequences. Adherence to this principle is clearly one of the major strengths of programmed instruction in which learners receive knowledge of results immediately (discussed in Chapter 12). Another implication of this principle is that the period of time between giving a quiz and returning the results should be kept as short as possible.

The sixth of Michael's principles is that the amount and potency of reinforcement necessary for behavioral change is usually underestimated. This is particularly true for the early stages of learning.

The seventh principle relates to the structuring of a learning situation. It maintains that the student's work should be set up as a series of clear steps, each of which can be reinforced. Programmed instruction (see Chapter 12) can meet this requirement much more easily than can a classroom teacher who is responsible for a relatively large number of students.

Modeling

Teachers make unconscious use of the various effects of models throughout their teaching careers. It is inevitable that they should be models for students and that students should also be models for each other. The deliberate and systematic use of models is perhaps rarer, but it can be highly effective.

Recall from Chapter 4 that one effect of models is the suppression or reappearance of previously suppressed deviant behavior. This effect, labeled the **inhibitory-disinhibitory effect,** apparently occurs as a result of seeing a model being punished or rewarded for deviant behavior.

The inhibitory effect is common in schools. It is, in fact, what Kounin calls the ripple effect. When a teacher selects for punishment one offender from among a group of offenders, the hope is that the effects of the punishment will spread to the remainder of the group. This is why leaders are often punished for the transgressions of their followers.

Extinction

Animal studies indicate that responses maintained by reinforcement can usually be eliminated through the complete withdrawal of reinforcement—usually but not always. For example, a pigeon that has been taught to peck at a disk for its food will usually cease to peck when food is no longer provided as a consequence of disk pecking. But some pigeons will continue to peck at the disk indefinitely, even when the pecking no longer leads to reinforcement. A humanist might simply insist that to be a pigeon is to peck and that a fully actualized pigeon gets high by pecking disks and remains unmoved by the crass material rewards that might move other pigeons. Others might argue that pigeons have a biological predisposi-

Punishments used by teachers include facial gestures of disapproval, reprimands, detention, unpleasant activities, time-outs, and, occasionally, physical punishment. Verbal reprimands, such as this teacher is using, are not subject to the same criticisms as physical punishment.

tion for pecking. Whatever the reason might be, it remains true that not all behaviors can be extinguished through the removal of reinforcement. Furthermore, many disruptive behaviors in the classroom are reinforced by peers rather than by teachers. To the extent that teachers are not in control of relevant reinforcers, there is little that they can do to remove them.

More optimistically, some disruptive behaviors appear to be maintained by teacher attention, in which case it might be a relatively simple matter to cease paying attention. However, the matter might not be quite so simple if the behavior in question is highly disruptive of class activities. But

there are other alternatives, the most common of
which is punishment.

Punishment

Punishment can take a variety of forms. Recall
from Chapter 4 that there are, in principle, two
distinct types of punishment: The first involves the
presentation of a noxious (unpleasant) stimulus;
the second involves the removal of a pleasant stimulus and was illustrated in the Nay and associates
study (1976) in which students were removed
from their territories for infraction of rules.

Specific punishments used by teachers include facial gestures of disapproval, reprimands,
detention, unpleasant activities, time-outs, and,
occasionally, physical punishment (see the case set
in Mrs. Neigel's classroom above). There are many
passionate objectors to the use of punishment and
a number of practical objections as well. At the
same time, there is a need to reexamine the effectiveness of various forms of punishment.

Physical Punishment. Physical punishment is the
use of physical force to bring about pain. Often, it
is also associated with fear and humiliation.

Although physical punishment is no longer
nearly so common as it was some decades ago,
McFadden, Marsh, Price, and Hwang (1992) report that it is still used in a large number of
schools. Interestingly, courts as high as the U.S.
Supreme Court have affirmed the rights of schools
to use corporal punishment, providing it is not
grossly excessive. In contrast, some apparently
milder forms of punishment such as suspension
and expulsion present schools with much clearer
legal liabilities because a number of courts have
ruled that to suspend students is to deprive them
of their rights to an education.

McFadden and associates (1992) looked at
4,391 discipline files from 9 Florida schools.
These schools had clear written rules concerning
violations and disciplinary options. For example,
they identified 25 different classes of infractions
ranging from serious (assault, possession of
weapons), which were quite rare, to mild (bother-
ing others). They found that 7 categories of violations accounted for more than 80 percent of all
misbehaviors. And the most common punishment for misbehaviors requiring counselor or
principal intervention was in-school suspension;
second most common, strikingly, was corporal
punishment; third, suspension from school.

McFadden and associates (1992) also report
marked race and gender bias in the application of
corporal punishment. Not only did males account
for more offenses than females but physical punishment was administered for a higher proportion of these offenses. Similarly, some 45 percent
of all African-American students referred were
punished physically but only 22 percent of the
white students and 23 percent of the Hispanics.

Interestingly, punishment seemed to have little effect on recidivism (repetition of offenses) in
these schools. The large majority of the students
referred for punishment in these schools were repeat offenders. As McFadden and associates put
it, "punishments may actually serve to increase

the frequencies of the very behaviors they are intended to eliminate" (1992, p. 145).

The Case Against Punishment. That it does not often work is one of the important objections to the use of punishment. In addition, there are some obvious ethical and humanitarian objections and a number of more practical ones. Among these is the observation that punishment by itself draws attention to socially undesirable behavior but fails to illustrate suitable alternatives. (Note that punishment used in conjunction with reasoning and other corrective measures need not be subject to the same objection.)

Additional evidence suggests that punishment sometimes has effects opposite of those intended. This is particularly obvious when parents or teachers attempt to eliminate aggressive or violent behavior through physical punishment, as we saw in the McFadden and associates study (1992). In effect, those who punish violence with violence provide a model of **aggression** for the child—a model that might be interpreted to mean that aggressiveness is permissible under certain circumstances.

Other objections to the use of punishment are described by Clarizio and Yelon (1974, p. 50) as follows: First, punishment does not eliminate an undesirable response, although it might result in its suppression or in a reduction in its frequency. Second, punishment may have unpleasant emotional side effects that are themselves maladaptive (for example, fear, anxiety, and tension). Finally, punishment is a source of frustration and may therefore lead to other undesirable or maladaptive behaviors.

The Case for Punishment. Most of the objections just cited apply only to one type of punishment: the presentation of unpleasant stimuli. Furthermore, these objections are most applicable to physical punishment and much less applicable to verbal punishment. The forms of punishment that involve the removal of pleasant stimuli (for example, loss of privileges) are not subject to the same practical and philosophical objections and should be considered legitimate methods by which teachers can maintain the degree of control essential for humane and personal teaching.

The case to be made for punishment can be based on a number of studies demonstrating that punitive methods can be effective in suppressing disruptive and sometimes dangerous behaviors (Parke, 1974). Some situations demand immediate and decisive intervention and do not lend themselves to the more gentle strategies of reinforcement, modeling, and reasoning. A child caught lighting matches and touching them to the draperies may be reasoned with and physically removed, but if he persists in burning the curtains at every opportunity, punishment may well be in order.

Although reinforcement, modeling, and reasoning have proved highly effective for promoting desirable behaviors, it is extremely difficult for a child to learn to recognize unacceptable behaviors simply by generalizing in reverse from situations that have been reinforced (Ausubel, 1958). In many cases, then, punishment of specific behaviors can be highly informative. And even though considerable evidence shows that punishment administered by an otherwise warm and loving parent is more effective than punishment administered by a habitually cold and distant parent (Aronfreed, 1968), no evidence shows that punishment administered by a loving parent disrupts emotional bonds between parent and child (Walters & Grusec, 1977).

One theoretical objection to the use of punishment is that it does not work—that although it might serve to suppress behavior or reduce its frequency, it does not lead to the elimination (extinction) of a response. Consider, however, that a punisher's intent clearly is to suppress a behavior; complete elimination is, in fact, absolutely irrelevant. If Johnny has been punished for burning curtains, we should not dare hope that he will, as a result, have forgotten how to burn curtains. But we are justified in hoping that he will refrain from doing so in the future.

Interestingly, most of the data that we have regarding punishment is derived from animal studies. For obvious reasons, it is easier to do research with animals than with children (although even the lowly rat is now treated with considerably more respect than was once the case). It is possible to administer electric shocks to animals; there are no directly comparable stimuli that can be used with children. Hence, controlled research of the effects of punishment on children typically use "annoyers" such as loud buzzers. Evidence from a number of studies suggests that these annoyers can be effective in suppressing unwanted behavior. (In many of these experiments, children are asked not to play with a toy; the buzzer sounds if they do.)

This section is not meant to minimize the dangers of punishment. Several important points need to be made. The most important is that most researchers and theorists remain virtually unanimous in their rejection of physical punishment. Not only is physical punishment a humiliating violation of the person but it presents a highly undesirable model. If your task were to teach children that the best way to obtain what they want is by force, excessive use of physical punishment might well be your best teaching method.

If we do reject physical punishment (in practice, the rejection is far from complete), a number of alternatives remain. The least objectionable are those involving the withdrawal of reinforcement.

If you are like most teachers, you are likely to make use of both major types of punishment in your classroom: withdrawal of pleasant consequences and the administration of unpleasant consequences. A careful review of the punishment literature and of humanistic counterarguments reveals that three effective forms of punishment that do not have the disadvantages usually associated with punishment are reprimands, time-outs, and response cost.

Reprimands

Reprimands can be mild or harsh, they can be verbal or nonverbal, and they can be administered by teachers, parents, or peers. A simple no is a verbal reprimand; a negative head shake is a nonverbal reprimand.

Frequency of Use. Reprimands are the most common form of punishment, both in the home and in school. This is not particularly surprising given that reprimands are simply expressions of disapproval. As such, they are available to anyone in power, and they are extremely easy to administer. Furthermore, given our social natures, reprimands can influence us in a way that they cannot influence most animals.

Researchers have compared the frequency of praise and of reprimands by teachers. In a large-scale survey, M. A. White (1975) found that the proportion of praise and reprimands changes markedly through school. Praise is more frequent than reprimands during first and second grade; in subsequent grades, reprimands are more common. The actual rate of reprimands through the remaining elementary and junior high school grades was approximately one every two minutes but dropped to about half that rate in high school. In college, it drops even more drastically. M. A. White also found that reprimands are somewhat more common with respect to students of lower ability.

Effectiveness. Van Houten and Doleys (1983) reviewed a number of studies that have examined the effectiveness of reprimands and the particular qualities that increase their effectiveness. The majority of these studies found reprimands to be highly effective. Among other things, verbal reprimands that identify the undesirable behavior and provide specific rationales for doing (or not doing) something are more effective than reprimands that simply express disapproval (a point that we stressed earlier). For example, it is more effective to say, "Robert, please do not stick out your tongue because you distract the other children and you confuse me when I'm trying to explain something" than to say, "Don't do that, Robert!"

Investigations of reprimands also reveal that those given at a closer distance are more effective than those given from far away. In a study conducted by Van Houten, Nau, MacKenzie-Keating, Sameoto, and Colavecchia (1982), students were reprimanded from a distance of 1 meter or 7 meters (approximately $3\frac{1}{4}$ feet or 23 feet). Tone and intensity of reprimand were kept constant. Reprimands from a distance of 1 meter were more effective.

Loud and Soft Reprimands.

Research examining the effects of reprimand intensity has produced contradictory results. In one series of studies (O'Leary & Becker, 1968; O'Leary, Kaufman, Kass, & Drabman, 1974), soft reprimands, audible only to the student being reprimanded, were found to be more effective than loud reprimands audible to the entire class. However, Van Houten and Doleys (1983) report that higher-intensity (loud) reprimands often are more effective than soft reprimands and that the O'Leary results might be due not to the intensity of the reprimands but to the fact that soft reprimands were always delivered in closer proximity to the student. In addition, being in close proximity to the student increases the possibility that the teacher will reinforce the reprimand by means of eye contact and other nonverbal gestures that have been found to increase the effectiveness of reprimands.

Whether soft reprimands are as effective or more effective as loud reprimands may be less important than some other considerations. Recall the advice given earlier about praise and punishment: Because of the effect on the child's self-concept, praise should be public (loud) and criticism should be private. Also, because reprimands are typically used either to prevent or to stop behaviors that threaten classroom activity, the most successful reprimands consist of simple, unobtrusive squelches such as "shh," "wait," "no," or simply a look or gesture. Reprimands such as these have the advantage of minimizing disruption of the class.

Limitations.

Reprimands of the type discussed in this section are clearly not always appropriate or effective for the most severe instances of disruptive behavior. Those who engage in crimes such as physical violence, robbery, drug use and sale, rape, and vandalism in schools are likely to sneer at gentle reprimands. For these behaviors, more drastic measures are clearly warranted. In most cases, these misbehaviors occur in corridors, lunchrooms, washrooms, and playgrounds rather than in the classroom, and they are sufficiently rare in most schools that when they occur, they are usually dealt with by school administrators. The most common misbehaviors the classroom teacher must deal with on a daily basis are truancy, tardiness, inattentiveness, talking, and forgetting books and assignments (Doyle, 1986). For these misbehaviors, a simple reprimand might suffice—or perhaps a time-out or response-cost procedure might work.

Time-Outs

In a **time-out** students are removed from a situation in which they would ordinarily expect reinforcement and are placed in a situation in which they cannot be reinforced. For example, if classroom activities are such that the students like to be in class, being removed from the classroom for a time-out may be interpreted as a form of punishment.

Brantner and Doherty (1983) distinguish among three different time-out procedures that the classroom teacher might use. The first involves **isolation.** This is clearly illustrated when a child is physically removed from the area of reinforcement (typically, the classroom; perhaps also the playground, the lunchroom, or the library) and isolated in a different place. Although isolation is not entirely uncommon in schools, it is somewhat controversial because it violates our more humanistic values. It reminds us of the types of seclusion that have sometimes been used with criminals.

A second time-out procedure does not isolate misbehaving children but simply excludes them from ongoing activities. A common **exclusion** time-out procedure in a school might require a child to sit at the back of the room, facing in the opposite direction or perhaps sitting behind a screen.

The third time-out procedure is labeled **nonexclusion.** In this, the mildest of the three, the child is removed from the ongoing activity (removed from the immediate source of reinforcement) and is required to observe others engaging in the activity. The child might, for example, be asked to stand apart from a game (or at the side of the class) and simply watch.

Following a thorough review of the time-out literature, Brantner and Doherty (1983) conclude that this is an extremely common classroom management practice but that research results are too few and too inconsistent to identify the characteristics of effective time-out procedures. In addition, although time-out procedures are generally effective, they do not always work.

Response Cost

When students have been given tangible reinforcers for good behavior but stand to lose some of these reinforcers for disruptive behaviors, the loss is referred to as **response cost.** It too constitutes a mild form of punishment—similar to preventing a child who has misbehaved from watching television. Response-cost systems are frequently used in token-reinforcement programs. An experiment reported by Kaufman and O'Leary (1972) clearly illustrates the difference between a response-cost method and a reinforcement system. The experiment was conducted in two classes in a children's unit of a psychiatric hospital. In one class, students earned points for good behavior (token reinforcement); in a second class, children were awarded all their points at the beginning of a class period and had points sub-

tracted from their total for specific misbehaviors. Although both methods were highly effective in reducing disruptive behavior, neither was more effective than the other.

Pazulinec, Meyerrose, and Sajwaj (1983) report that the majority of studies of the effectiveness of response-cost procedures have found positive results. Such procedures successfully reduce disruptive classroom behavior and bring about significant increases in class achievement and in performance on standardized tests. Among the relative advantages of response-cost procedures for classroom management is that they do not remove the child from the learning situation (as time-out procedures typically do). In addition, they are usually combined with a reinforcement procedure (use of tokens, for example) and can therefore derive benefit from the many advantages of reinforcement.

COGNITIVE BEHAVIOR MODIFICATION

Behavior modification (also termed *behavioral intervention* or *behavior management*) focuses not on what the student *has* or *is* but on what the student *does*. This is true of management techniques based on the principles of behavioristic conditioning theories—such as those we have been considering in this chapter—and of an approach that merges cognitive with behavioristic principles.

Changing Cognitions

Cognitive behavior modification is based on the recognition that what we *think* is fundamentally important to what we do. As Meichenbaum (1977) notes, the effects of the consequences of our behavior may have more to do with our ability to imagine and to anticipate these consequences than with the consequences themselves. I know clearly that I am hurrying as I write these words this evening because I have not yet eaten, and I can predict and anticipate that when I am done, I will be able to go to where I can eat. I don't hurry like some mindless rat simply because I have been conditioned to expect food at the end of my labors; I hurry because I *see* lasagna on the table of my reason.

Accordingly, the cognitive behavior therapist looks not just at external behaviors but at cognitions (thoughts). The causes of behavior, says Hughes (1988), are "cognitive mediating processes." And our cognitions, our thoughts, are subject to change in the same way as are our behaviors.

In essence, cognitive behavior modification uses the principles of behavior modification *and* incorporates cognitive activities (thinking processes) in an effort to bring about change (Hughes, 1988).

An Illustration

Cognitive behavior modification is well illustrated in Meichenbaum and Goodman's (1971) attempt to reduce the impulsivity of overly active children. They devised a five-step cognitive behavior modification training procedure using a simple line-drawing task:

1. The experimenter performed the task, serving as a model, and speaking out loud throughout the performance. The verbalization focused on the problem, responses to the problem, and monitoring of ongoing activity (the "cognitive modeling" phase):

   Okay, what is it I have to do? You want me to copy the picture with the different lines. I have to go slow and be careful. Okay, draw the line down, down, good; then to the right, that's it; now down some more and to the left. Good, I'm doing fine so far. Remember go slow. Now back up again. No, I was supposed to go down. That's okay. Just erase the line carefully . . . Good. Even if I make an error I can go on slowly and carefully. Okay, I have to go down now. Finished. I did it. (p. 117)

2. The child is asked to perform the same task but is guided by the experimenter while doing so.

3. The child performs the task while speaking "self-instructions" out loud.

4. The child performs the task but only whispers the directions.

5. The child performs the task, guided only by silent "inner speech."

These five steps were used with progressively more difficult tasks during four different sessions. Subsequently, impulsive children appeared to have become more reflective. They took more time to complete tasks and committed significantly fewer errors while doing so.

One important characteristic of cognitive behavior modification is an emphasis on our ability to think—to reason. In fact, reasoning, although often used less systematically than might be appropriate for a cognitive behavior modification program, is one of the most effective—and most common—classroom management strategies.

Reasoning

Reasoning is one of the most important alternatives to the more direct forms of corrective intervention. Essentially, to reason is to provide rational explanations; hence, reasoning as a corrective strategy involves presenting children with reasons for not engaging in deviant behavior and/or reasons for engaging in some alternative behavior. There is a fundamental difference between saying to a student, "Don't snap your fingers because you are distracting the others and making it difficult for them to study," and saying, "Don't snap your fingers or you will have to stay after school." The first uses reasoning; the second involves a threat of punishment. Note, however, that the first statement, while appealing to reason, might also be interpreted as implying a threat, depending on the child's prior experience with the person attempting the correction. If children have learned through experience that the likely consequences of not acceding to authority's wishes, no matter how reasonably those wishes might be phrased, is some form of punishment, the effectiveness of reason might well be due to the implied threat.

Reasoning is considerably more appealing to parents and teachers than are most other disciplinary alternatives. It seems somehow more humane to deal with children on an intellectual level than to deal with them from our positions of power as dispensers of rewards and punishments. And, happily, research and good sense both confirm our suspicions that reasoning can be an effective means of controlling or correcting student behavior.

Effectiveness of Different Reasons. A number of researchers have investigated the comparative effectiveness of various kinds of reasons that might be given children to prevent them from engaging in some behavior. In a typical experimental situation, children are asked not to play with a toy and are then left alone with that toy; they have no reason to believe that they will be admonished if they do play with the toy. Investigators give the children specific reasons for not playing with the toy.

Parke (1974) reports that rationales that stress the object ("The toy might break") are more effective for younger children than are more abstract rationales relating to rights of possession ("You should not play with toys that belong to others"). However, Hoffman (1970) found that for older children rationales that emphasize the consequences of their behavior for other people ("other-oriented induction") are more persuasive than rationales that emphasize the consequences to the child. In other words, if the experimenter says, "Do not play with that toy because you will make the child it belongs to unhappy," subjects are more likely not to play with the toy than if the experimenter says, "Do not play with that toy because it might break and that would make you unhappy."

Walters and Grusec (1977) also argue that reasoning that arouses empathy for others is usually more effective than reasoning that focuses on personal consequences, particularly after the age of six. Thus, with advancing intellectual and moral development, children are more likely to respond to rationales relating to abstractions and ideals and to become less concerned with immediate objective consequences. This observation is further corroborated by what is known about the sequence of moral development in children (see Chapter 2). The implications of the foregoing observations are obvious: It is wise to provide younger children with specific, concrete reasons for requests that are made of them. After children have reached school age, however, more abstract rationales are preferable. Perhaps most important, rationales that are other directed and that consequently arouse empathy for others appear to be most effective.

Why Reason? In addition to humanitarian and ethical considerations that clearly favor reasoning over punishing, reasoning is preferable to punishment for several practical reasons. First, a punishing agent provides a model of aggressiveness for the learner. In effect, the punisher's activities signify that one acceptable method of dealing with difficult situations is through the assertion of power in punitive form. Reasoning provides a rather different model. To reason with a child—to provide a rationale for required behavior—is to say, in effect, that one way to cope with difficulty is the deliberate application of thought.

A second advantage of a reasoning strategy is that such an approach lends itself naturally to the description of alternative acceptable behaviors. In other words, reasoning need not be restricted to providing rationales for why a behavior should not be engaged in but can also be directed toward explaining why certain behaviors should be undertaken. Various forms of altruistic and prosocial behavior (cooperation, sharing, helping) cannot easily be taught by punitive means but instead lend themselves more easily to the use of models, reasoning, reinforcement, or a combination of these.

FROM DISCIPLINE TO MORALITY

The first part of this chapter has intentionally emphasized preventive and management strategies, rather than corrective strategies, in the hope that with proper attention to the aspects of teacher-learner interaction that are conducive to enthusiasm, warmth, and caring, seriously disruptive behavior will be infrequent and the need for corrective action rare. As a result, the teacher may have more time and energy to address the larger but sometimes less visible problems of social adjustment, self-discipline, and moral development.

Rules and regulations in a classroom exist primarily to ensure the order necessary for teaching and learning, but they have other effects as well. School is more than preparation for later life; it is a fundamental part of the child's immediate life. And it is perhaps fortunate that, in many respects, schools mirror the larger society. The penalties for infraction of school rules might not be as harsh as those that apply to the infraction of society's laws, but the rewards for compliance are no less. And although we might strenuously object that schools should not teach compliance, we must nevertheless admit that society would be incredibly more chaotic than it sometimes appears to be were it not that most of us have learned to live within social, legal, and moral prescriptions, that we have learned how to resolve a majority of our conflicts without resorting to knives, guns, and fists, and that we behave in morally acceptable ways most of the time.

It is probably somewhat presumptuous of schools to assume that the development of high moral standards, the internalization of values, and the development of principles and ideals will result incidentally from the experiences that life provides for children—that nothing can, or should, be done deliberately to foster their development.

In fact, it is likely that much is accomplished incidentally by wise and sensitive teachers who might accomplish much more were they to address themselves deliberately to the development of character. A grab-bag expression for values, moral strength, principles, and virtues, *character* is an ill-defined and rare term in today's social sciences. Otherwise, these sciences might have more advice to offer the teacher who is concerned with more than classroom management and the curriculum-bound teaching/learning process.

Prosocial Programs

Humanistic approaches to education represent several attempts to cater directly to children's social and emotional needs and to help them develop the social skills that are useful and necessary for effective interaction with others. The humanistic emphasis on affective education points clearly in this direction, as do the various group-process approaches that have become popular in humanistic schools, as well as a handful of values-clarification and conflict management programs developed for use in schools.

Conflict Management. Palmares and Logan (1975) have developed an extensive curriculum, both audiovisual and textual, intended to teach children a variety of methods they can use to resolve conflicts. Many of these methods are used spontaneously by children and are learned incidentally as a function of the give-and-take of social interaction. However, some children experience more difficulty than others in acquiring these social skills. For these children, the program should prove particularly effective.

Among the conflict resolution skills taught by the program are negotiating, compromising, taking turns, explaining, listening, apologizing, soliciting intervention, using humor, and invoking chance (for example, flipping a coin). Seventeen specific strategies are developed, fourteen of which are primarily positive and clearly useful in adult interaction as well. Three are more negative (violence, flight, and tattling), although they too might occasionally be resorted to.

An Experimental Prosocial Program. A more general approach to developing prosocial behavior is illustrated by an experimental program implemented and evaluated during a five-year period in three elementary schools (Solomon, Watson, Delucchi, Schaps, & Battistich, 1988). The program emphasizes commitment to accepted and shared values, a sense of community, and the development of concern and care. It includes five separate kinds of activities for students. Among the most important of these are small-group cooperative activities of the kind described by Johnson, Johnson, Holubec, and Roy (1984) and intended primarily to develop values associated with fairness, respect, responsibility, and helping one another.

The second aspect of the program, developmental discipline, is a student-centered approach to classroom management and discipline wherein students are given an opportunity to participate in formulating and enforcing rules. The emphasis is on understanding the principles that underlie rules, and the goal is to foster student development toward autonomy.

A third component of the Solomon and associates (1988) program involves activities promoting social understanding and is exemplified in instances in which the teacher uses classroom situations to discuss and reinforce prosocial values. In addition, role-playing games, formal discussions, books, films, and other activities are used to increase children's sensitivity to one another and to promote tolerance of differences.

Fourth, the program encourages activities that involve highlighting prosocial values. For example, teachers are instructed to draw attention to instances of prosocial behavior in the class-room, such as sharing and comforting. Films, books, and other models of prosocial behavior are also used.

The fifth component of this program stresses helping activities. It consists of encouraging children to engage directly in prosocial behaviors by helping one another and their community. To this end, "buddy" systems and tutoring programs are set up, and various school and community-improvement activities are organized.

This program was evaluated by comparing students in three experimental schools with comparable students in three other schools. The results? In the authors' words, "[The program] had substantial positive effects on children's interpersonal behavior in the classroom (without impeding their achievement)" (Solomon, Watson, Delucchi, Schaps, & Battistich, 1988, p. 545). Children in these programs were found to be more supportive, more cooperative, friendlier, and more helpful toward one another than comparable children not in the program.

Although implementing this program required that teachers undertake week-long training sessions, attend weekly and monthly meetings, and be provided with considerable supportive material, elements of the program can profitably be incorporated in any classroom. As Solomon and associates (1988) note, two general aspects of life in the classroom seem clearly related to the development of prosocial values and behaviors: One is the establishment of a warm teacher-student relationship; the other is the provision of opportunities for cooperation and collaboration among students.

Intentionally or otherwise, schools do much to teach children how to get along with one another. Unfortunately, students sometimes learn *not* to get along instead. Perhaps if teachers attend to these two things—the teacher-student relationship and interstudent cooperation—schools will intentionally do much more that is positive.

MAIN POINTS

1. The expression "classroom management" refers to the arrangement of classroom activities to facilitate teaching and learning; *discipline* relates to the interventions made necessary by student behaviors that disrupt (or threaten to disrupt) classroom activities.

2. Events in the classroom context are multidimensional (many individuals, many activities, many goals), simultaneous (many events occurring at any one time), immediate (many events require instant teacher decision and action), and unpredictable (the course of classroom events cannot easily be predicted). Hence, managing classes requires special pedagogical and information-processing (vigilance and with-it-ness) skills, many of which eventually become unconscious and automatic.

3. Despite some valid ethical and humanitarian objections to control, to the extent that teachers act in loco parentis and care for their students, discipline is necessary.

4. Kounin describes these important characteristics of successful classroom management: with-it-ness (timely, noninterruptive, on-target desists); overlapping (responding effectively to potential classroom disruptions *without* interrupting ongoing activity); smoothness and momentum (as opposed to jerky transitions and interruptions caused by stimulus-boundedness, thrusts, dangles, truncations, flip-flops, or slowdowns); maintaining focus (by making students accountable, using group-alerting cues, and using lesson formats that involve all students).

5. Other important classroom management strategies include establishing routines, learning students' names, setting rules, applying rules consistently, arranging frequent occasions for the legitimate use of praise, using humor, and paying attention to classroom environment and climate. Webster's democratic discipline is based on reason, relevance, and respect, guided by a number of obvious but often overlooked principles.

6. Behavioral intervention applies behavioristic principles in order to change behavior and typically involves specific steps: define the problem, measure it, determine response antecedents and consequences, decide how these can be changed, plan and implement intervention, and follow up (evaluate and terminate or perhaps modify the program).

7. Systematic reinforcement programs in schools typically use positive reinforcement, sometimes in the form of tokens or a combination of teacher praise and other tangible rewards (such as the Premack principle that calls for a desirable activity to be used as a reinforcer). Some evidence suggests that excessive reliance on external rewards may have a dampening effect on intrinsic motivation as reflected in the student's subsequent interest and motivation.

8. Extrinsic reinforcers include consumables, manipulatables, visual and auditory stimuli, social stimuli, tokens, and items on reinforcement menus (lists of rewards from which students select). The teacher's attention is extremely important. Important principles governing the use of reinforcement in the classroom include these: Reinforcement is individualistic (defined only in terms of its effects on the individual); its effects are automatic; reinforcement and punishment should be consistent, should be related closely to the relevant behavior, and should occur as soon as possible; the amount of reinforcement required should not be underestimated; and students' work should be organized in such a way that it is possible to reinforce small steps frequently.

9. Models provide children with standards of appropriate behavior. On occasion, punished models may serve to inhibit deviant behaviors as well. Perhaps the most important classroom model is the teacher.

10. Extinction involves an attempt to eliminate undesirable behavior through the withdrawal of reinforcement.

11. Punishment involves the presentation of an unpleasant stimulus or the removal of a pleasant stimulus as a consequence of behavior. Among objections to the use of punishment are claims that it does not always work, that it presents an undesirable model of violence, that it might have undesirable emotional side effects, and that it might lead to maladaptive behaviors through the introduction of frustration. Research indicates that punishment may suppress undesirable behaviors and that it may be particularly appropriate in cases in which it is necessary for a child to learn about behaviors that are not permitted.

12. Reprimands (expressions of disapproval, generally verbal but sometimes nonverbal) are among the most common of classroom punishments. Those that provide reasonable rationales for doing or not doing something and that are delivered in close proximity are most effective.

13. Time-out punishment is the removal of a student from a reinforcing situation to another situation in which the same reinforcement is not possible. It might involve isolation (physical removal), exclusion (removal of the child from ongoing activities but not from the classroom), or nonexclusion (removal of the child from the ongoing activity to a place where the child is required to continue observing the activity). Response cost is punishment in which previously earned reinforcers are lost as a consequence of undesirable behavior.

14. Cognitive behavior modification uses the principles of behavioral intervention *and* the person's thoughts (cognitions) to change behavior. Often, it attempts to make people aware of their thought processes and of the reasons for their behaviors.

15. Reasoning, often in combination with other disciplinary measures, appears to be a highly effective and humane way of handling classroom problems. Concrete reasons appear to be more effective with younger children; abstract reasons work better with older children. In addition, reasons that appeal to the effect of behavior on others are particularly successful and may be important in developing higher levels of moral orientation.

16. In addition to maintaining classroom order, teachers should also attend to the development of social and affective skills in children. Humanistic educators suggest that teachers should also pay attention to students' emotional and moral development, perhaps by using specific prosocial programs and techniques.

SUGGESTED READINGS

The following is a little booklet that lists ten specific methods or "building blocks" for establishing preventive discipline in a classroom. It also includes practical checklists of 38 do's and 7 don'ts.

GROSSNICKLE, D. R., & SESKO, F. P. (1990). *Preventive discipline for effective teaching and learning.* Reston, Va.: National Association of Secondary School Principals.

An excellent guide to the application of behavior management principles in the school is Ward's short book. The O'Banion and Whaley book is a useful introduction to the systematic use of reward and punishment in attempts to change behavior using behavioral "contracting."

WARD, W. D. (1991). *Applied behavior analysis in the classroom: The development of student competence.* Springfield, Ill: Charles C Thomas.

O'BANION, D. R., & WHALEY, D. L. (1981). *Behavior contracting: Arranging contingencies of reinforcement.* New York: Springer.

A comprehensive analysis of research on punishment, its effectiveness, and its uses is detailed in

AXELROD, S., APSCHE, J. (Eds.). (1983). *The effects of punishment on human behavior.* New York: Academic Press.

The book by Fenstermacher and Soltis is a thought-provoking analysis of three different approaches to teaching and classroom management.

FENSTERMACHER, G. D., & SOLTIS, J. F. (1992). *Approaches to teaching.* New York: Teachers College Press.

Bears are extremely confident and capable climbers, particularly when young. With increasing weight, however, they trust only the stoutest of branches, although a fall is not likely to prove disastrous. Polar bears, for example, can climb an almost sheer ice wall and will then routinely jump down from heights of fifteen to twenty feet. And this in spite of their ponderous weights. One bear reportedly dived more than fifty feet into the water to escape hunting dogs and then set off in the direction of the closest land mass—an impressive twenty-two miles away (Perry, 1966; L. H. Matthews, 1969).

I am a Bear of Very Little Brain, and long words Bother me.

a. a. milne, *Winnie-the-Pooh*

Madam, I have been looking for a person who disliked gravy all my life; let us swear eternal friendship.

Sydney Smith, *Memoirs*

Chapter 12 | INDIVIDUALIZING INSTRUCTION

PREVIEW My Funk and Wagnall's tells me that technology is the application of science and of technical advances in industry, the arts, and other fields. Education is presumably among these other fields, and this, the twelfth chapter, is this textbook's technology chapter. It details the application of science (to the extent that psychology is a science) and of technical advances in the business of educating. Accordingly, this chapter describes programmed instruction, the use of computers in education, and specific teaching techniques founded on distinct theoretical principles.

Excerpt from Bear Tales (Book V): Wild Cow Instruction

The bear lies curled on his ledge just below the crest of the ridge overlooking the valley, his black snoot nuzzled between his paws, his eyes half closed. It's one of the sacred places the wild cows have not yet spoiled. They probably think no green plants could grow on a slope so steep, although one day the big one dragged her whiskied carcass half-way up the hill before giving up and going back for a fresh whiskey. She had no idea about the spring at the back of the ledge or about the fiddlehead ferns along the edge.

The bear doesn't eat these ferns. He sniffs them, and sometimes he licks the dew from their curled heads, but something in his pagan soul prevents him from curling his tongue around their stalks and wrenching them into his mouth. He sees magic in their unfurling and hears poetry in their gracefulness. On his ledge, the bear is a poet; sometimes he can hear the music of the fiddlehead ferns.

But today wild cows are dancing on the valley floor below. They dance in groups of four, tails intertwined, shuffling back and forth in time to the heavy rhythms of the cousset drums. Those who don't care to dance lounge with their whiskeys around the perimeter of the dance area, making lewd remarks about the dancers. Or they dive and swim and muck about in the stream. The stench of cigars and of methane gases rises from the valley, and the bear is no longer able to smell the ferns or the freshness of his spring. He is no longer a poet.

Unexpectedly, the bear wonders about the taste of wild cow meat. But because he's a vegetarian by choice, the thought revolts him; it makes him sick right there on the ledge.

The bear is not ordinarily a complainer. True, wild cows make him angry—in his words, "They tick me off, disgusting cows!"—but he's not a complainer; he's a doer!

Suddenly, the bear stands on his ledge. "Listen up, cows!" he yells. But the insistent drumming of the coussets and the low mooing of the wild cows, who don't know the lyrics but are simply mooing in accompaniment, drown out the bear's cry.

"Listen up!" the bear roars. Some of the wild cows turn toward the ledge. They see the bear standing above them, waiting for silence.

The bear is a terrific teacher; he has wonderful presence, and he knows how to handle a class of wild cows. "I have some important things to teach you," he says. The wild cows grow silent. The bear smiles. He'll teach them about the world. He'll instill in them respect for their environment. Eventually, they'll be environmentally friendly, these wild cows!!

The bear looks his class over. Where to start? What to do? Clearly, there are some intelligent wild cows here. They have that keen look in their bovine eyes and an especially attentive posture. There is an alertness and a readiness about them.

Sadly, there are others who are neither so intelligent nor so interested. Many have not yet understood the seriousness of the bear's call; they don't sense the strength of his presence. They keep on smoking and drinking whiskey.

The bear, remarkable teacher that he is, knows at once that not all wild cows can be taught in exactly the same way.

MAKING THE LESSON FIT THE STUDENT

Some very ordinary classes are a lot like a bunch of wild cows. Some students are bright, alert, inquisitive, and interested; others are less capable or less interested—or both. There are times when, if the lesson does not fit *all* the students, many may learn but some will undoubtedly continue to dance and drink whiskey—metaphorically, of course. What can an ordinary classroom teacher do to individualize instruction?

One solution is for the teacher to spend time with each student individually, responding to the student's immediate needs and interests, explaining, probing, imparting strategies, and doing other things good teachers do. Unfortunately, teacher-pupil ratios, the time available, and the demands of the curriculum make this a difficult and often impractical solution.

Ability Grouping

A second solution is to "track" the class. **Tracking** involves separating the class into ability or interest groups and then providing different instructional experiences for each group. Tracking students into high- and low-ability classes was once a relatively common way of attempting to match school offerings more closely to students' differences. However, the bulk of the research indicates that being assigned to a low track often has negative effects on the achievement, self-esteem, and motivation of students (see Snow & Swanson, 1992). And, although being placed in a high track may have a positive effect on some students, Slavin (1990a) reviewed twenty-nine studies of tracking effects and concludes that tracking has essentially *no* effect, either positive or negative.

Given the doubtful, or negative, effects of ability grouping, and given also that inclusion (mainstreaming) is mandated by law, tracking is now rarely seen in North American schools.

Other solutions, discussed in some detail later in this chapter, include the use of computers that can interact with students and can sometimes modify instructional programs according to students' responses; specially designed teaching programs (programmed instruction), which can be presented in text form or by means of computers; and any of a number of relatively elaborate, theory-based instructional systems, such as PSI (personalized system of instruction) or IGE (individually guided education).

The Learning Styles Approach

Another solution, perhaps the one that goes furthest toward making the lesson fit the student, is the learning styles approach discussed in Chapter

9 (see Dunn & Griggs, 1988). The learning styles philosophy recognizes that students learn in different ways—that each has a unique learning style. Some students learn well in the morning; others awaken reluctantly and don't function well until later in the day.* Some excel with highly structured, teacher-directed, whole-class approaches; others perform much better with less-structured, self-initiated, individual approaches; still others achieve better in small-group, cooperative settings. Some students prefer to work in bright, well-lit surroundings with loud music; others require quiet, more subdued environments. Some learners have a marked preference for the visual or the auditory mode, some respond better than others to praise or criticism, some have longer attention spans than others . . . and on and on.

To truly individualize instruction, advocates of learning styles approaches argue, it is necessary to develop a profile of each learner. This profile provides a detailed description of strengths and weaknesses, as well as of preferences and dislikes. Schools and classes can then be tailored to cater to each individual's style. As we saw in Chapter 9, in practice this approach requires a tremendous assortment of alternatives. Core school subjects must be presented at different times of the day; classes must be organized so that individuals can select among small-group, individual, or whole-class approaches; rewards must be restructured so that classes include individual, cooperative, and competitive situations; and instructional materials must be developed to appeal to visual, auditory, and kinesthetic sensory modes.

Individualizing Instruction in the Regular Classroom

Truly individualizing instruction as completely as is suggested by a learning styles approach is diffi-

*PPC: We'd have a lazy bunch of students if we let them sleep all morning just because that's their learning style.

Author: The bear is not lazy, but he sleeps all winter. That's his *life*style.

Although there often isn't enough time, money, or energy to implement completely individualized programs for all students, individualization on a more limited scale is possible in every classroom. Individualization of instruction does not mean that all students work individually at all times throughout the school day. But it does mean that whenever possible the teacher takes into consideration the needs, strengths, weaknesses, and wishes of individual students.

cult or impossible for many practical reasons. Even if everyone concerned were convinced that this is the best of all possible instructional alternatives, in most instances there simply isn't enough time, money, or energy to implement all aspects of the program. But individualization on a more limited scale is possible in virtually every classroom. In fact, not only is it possible but it is essential, especially in the now common inclusive classroom that may include any number of children with unique special needs.

Mr. Stewin, my grade 3 and 4 teacher, always made sure he knew what each student was most interested in and he found ways of letting us work on these interesting subjects, sometimes alone and sometimes in groups. For example, some of us were quite interested in native people, so he had us research a particular tribe and then build articles that they would have used. We then buried them in the school yard, and another team of students had to dig them up and assess their lifestyle. Then we got together and more or less taught the rest of the class about this tribe.

Keep in mind that individualization of instruction does not mean that all students work individually at all times throughout the school day. What individualization means is that instructional methods, class organization, evaluation procedures, and other components of the teaching/learning process are selected and modified in response to learners' characteristics, course and lesson goals, and practical constraints. In practice, this usually means that some students are exposed to different experiences at least some of the time; some of these experiences might well be individual, but many will occur in small groups. And even in classes in which the teacher individualizes instruction, much can take place in whole-class situations (see the case set in Edward Stewin's classroom above).

Among the instructional methods available to teachers are lecturing, discussing, reciting, questioning, facilitating guided discovery, using small- or large-group strategies, tutoring, peer teaching, and so on. Each has advantages for different purposes, but even the methods that research has identified as potentially "best" (for example, one-to-one tutoring; Bloom, 1984) cannot, for practical reasons, be used exclusively. Even the methods represented by such global terms as *lecturing, discussing,* and so on are virtually never used to the exclusion of all other methods by any teacher worth even slightly more than his or her salt. Thus, teachers do not typically lecture or discuss; they present lessons, an activity that involves talking, listening, questioning, demonstrating, using instructional materials, and sometimes standing on one's ear or nose. These activities might be directed toward an entire class of students (large or small), a single student, or a handful of students, or they might alternate among the various possibilities. And they might occur in connection with any of a number of specific techniques that have been developed to individualize, to systematize, to computerize, and/or to personalize instruction.

Several of these techniques, some derived directly from specific psychological theory and experimentation, are described in the remainder of this chapter: programmed instruction, computer-assisted instruction (CAI), mastery learning, Keller's personalized system of instruction (PSI), individually guided education (IGE), and individually prescribed instruction (IPI). Aspects of the methods and principles of each of these approaches might be profitably incorporated in the increasingly sophisticated arsenal of every contemporary teacher.

PROGRAMMED INSTRUCTION

The term **programmed instruction** can be used in a general sense to describe any organized **autoinstructional device**—that is, any device that presents information in such a way that the learner can acquire it without the help of a teacher. In this sense, textbooks are a kind of programmed material, as are computers. A more specific definition of programmed instruction, however, limits it to material that is specifically designed to be autoinstructional and is arranged according to one of two patterns, linear or branching, or a combination of the two. Skinner

(1954) is usually associated with the **linear program,** whereas Crowder (1961, 1963) introduced the **branching program.**

Linear Programs

The Skinnerian or linear program is one in which all learners move through the same material in exactly the same sequence. But they progress at their own rate; thus does it individualize.

Linear programs are based directly on an operant conditioning model. They present material that leads the student to emit a correct response and that provides reinforcement for that response. In effect, the students' responses are operants, and the knowledge that they have responded correctly is a reinforcer. Accordingly, linear programs have the following characteristics that ensure that a student will almost always answer correctly:

1. The material is broken down into small steps, referred to as **frames,** which are presented in logical sequence. Each frame consists of a minimal amount of information so that a student can remember this information from frame to frame.

2. Students are required to make frequent responses—usually one in every frame and often as many as four or five in one frame. They are given **prompts** to ensure that they answer correctly.

3. Linear programs provide immediate **knowledge of results.** Students know at once whether they have answered correctly. This knowledge is assumed to act as reinforcement. Kaess and Zeaman (1960) have demonstrated that positive feedback (that is, knowledge that one is correct) is more effective than negative feedback (knowledge that one is wrong). Because linear programs attempt, through the use of prompts and small frames, to ensure that few errors are made, most of the feedback is positive.

To try your hand at a linear program, see the box entitled, "Piagetian Jargon: A Linear Program," and follow the directions.

Branching Programs

Crowder or branching programs present learners with much longer frames than linear programs (sometimes an entire page at a time), and unlike linear programs, they require learners to select from among several alternative answers rather than making up their own. But the most striking difference between the two is that in branching programs, not all students go through the program in exactly the same way. Students who give all responses correctly go through in the shortest way possible. Students who make errors receive remedial instruction and further clarification. Typically, learners who answer incorrectly are sent to a **remedial frame** or sequence of frames and eventually return to the main branch. They then proceed from there (see Figure 12.1). An example of a branching program is presented in the box entitled "Bear Tracking: A Branching Program" on pages 330–331.

Usefulness of Programmed Instruction

Instructional programs, as originally conceived and developed, are largely of historical interest only, although some of their principles may be useful in ordinary classrooms. Markle and Tiemann (1974; Markle, 1978) point out that these principles constitute the rudiments of an instructional theory that can be applied to simple tasks of motor learning or to highly complex cognitive learning tasks. The three fundamental concepts of

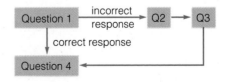

FIGURE 12.1 A branching program.

piagetian Jargon: a linear program

Directions: Fold a sheet of paper or use a strip of cardboard to cover the answers, which are given in the right-hand margin. With the answers covered, read frame 1 and write your answer in the blank provided. Move the paper or cardboard down to check your answer before proceeding to frame 2.

1. Jean Piaget has developed a theory that deals with human adaptation. It is a developmental theory of human _____ .

   adaptation

2. As children learn to cope with their environment and to deal effectively with it, they can be said to be _____ to it.

   adapting

3. Adaptation therefore involves interacting with the environment. The process of adaptation is one of organism-environment _____ .

   interaction

4. One of the central features of Piaget's developmental theory is that it attempts to explain _____ through interaction.

   adaptation

5. Interaction takes place through the interplay of two complementary processes: One involves reacting to the environment in terms of a previously learned response. This process is called assimilation. Assimilation involves a _____ learned response.

   previously

6. Whenever children use an object for some activity they have already learned, they are said to be *assimilating* that object to their previous learning. For example, when Jennifer sucks a pacifier, she is _____ the pacifier to the activity of sucking.

   assimilating

7. Sam is given a paper doll. He looks at it curiously and then puts it in his mouth and eats it. He has _____ the doll to the activity of eating.

   assimilated

8. Assimilation is one of the two processes involved in interacting with the environment. It is part of the process of _____ .

   adapting or adaptation

9. Adaptation involves two processes. The first is assimilation. The second is called *accommodation.* It occurs whenever a change in behavior results from interacting with the environment. Accommodation involves a _____ in behavior.

   change or modification

10. When children cannot assimilate a new object to activities that are already part of their repertoire, they must _____ to them.

    accommodate

11. Johnny West was presented with a very long pacifier on the occasion of his first birthday. Before that time he had been sucking a short "bulb" pacifier. The long pacifier matched his nose. He had to elongate his mouth considerably more than usual in order to suck this new pacifier. Johnny West had to _____ to the new pacifier.

    accommodate

12. If Johnny West had been given his old, short pacifier, he could more easily have _____ it to the activity of sucking.

    assimilated

13. . . . .

this programmed instruction theory are active responding, errorless learning, and immediate feedback. Applying these principles to classroom practice involves presenting small units of information so as to maximize immediate comprehension and minimize the number of errors students make while learning, providing for continual student involvement through active responding, and providing students with immediate confirmation of correct responses. And although it is very time consuming to structure lessons in as logical a sequence as programs require, such a sequence can be conducive to learning.

THE COMPUTER AND INSTRUCTION

Some principles of programmed instruction are also evident in another development that can contribute dramatically to individualizing instruction—the use of computers in schools.

The Computer Revolution

"The computer revolution is upon us!" we are told almost daily—and have been told for some time now. A big word, *revolution*. Small wonder that so many of us should wonder what this computer revolution is, whether it actually is upon us, and whether it is good or bad.

The Third Wave. Yes, the computer revolution is upon us, according to Alvin Toffler (1980), who earlier (1970) warned us that the coming of this revolution might send many of us into a state of shock. Toffler sees the computer revolution as the "third wave" in a series of monumental changes that have swept over humanity. The first wave, which occurred more than ten thousand years ago, was the agricultural revolution—a revolution that transformed our hunting and foraging ancestors into domesticators of animals and growers of food, changing the very meaning of what it was to be human in those times. The second wave, far

more recent in our history, was the industrial revolution, the ultimate effects of which were to transform our workplaces, our homes, and the very fabric of our lives. Only history can ultimately tell us how profound will be the effect of the third wave—the computer revolution that is sweeping over us now.

Resistance to the Revolution. "Tomorrow," writes Wilson (1988), "we're going to need to do something entirely different. And that's frightening because people have to let go of who they think they are. A good caterpillar only wants to know how to be a better caterpillar. 'A butterfly?' she says. 'No way you're going to get me up in one of those things' " (p. 14).

Some teachers, and some students, simply want to be good caterpillars. They are uneasy about the computer, afraid of the changes the revolution might require. But there are signs of change. Kristiansen (1992) studied teachers' attitudes toward computers in education over a twenty-year period (1970 to 1990) and found marked increases in acceptance of, even enthusiasm for, computers in school—and a dramatic decline in fear. Yet even today, many college students suffer from varying degrees of "technophobia"—they are apprehensive of the new computer technologies—and more of these are females than males (Bernhard, 1992).

All this may well change, however, as today's generation of children grows. When Todman and Lawrenson (1992) compared nine-year-olds with first-year psychology students, they not only found that the children were less anxious about computers than the college students but also that they had significantly more experience with them. For them, the new technologies will not seem anything like a revolution.

Evidence of the Revolution. Evidence of the computer revolution is all around us. Some two decades ago, I wrote the first edition of this book using a 25-cent ballpoint pen and two dozen pads of yellow paper. Now I write to you on a computer

bear tracking: a branching program

Objectives: After you have read this program, you should be able to:

1. recognize a forest

2. recognize a bear's tracks

3. recognize a bear

4. recognize a bunch of wild cows

5. run very rapidly in all directions

Note: Because only part of the program is presented here, only the first two objectives can be attained.

Directions: Read each frame very carefully; reread it if it appears confusing. Then select what you think best completes the statement presented, and follow the directions that correspond to that answer.

1. A forest is a collection of trees. It is a large collection of trees, just as a city is a large collection of people. A wood is a small collection of trees, just as a town is a small collection of people. A bush is a collection of small trees. What is a collection of small people? Never mind. Bears are often found in large collections of trees.

   If you were looking for a bear, you would go to:
   (a) a large collection of people.
   (b) a forest.
   (c) an ocean.
   If you answered (a), go to frame 10.
   If you answered (b), go to frame 3.
   If you answered (c), go to frame 7.

2. Correct. Good. Now that you have found a forest, you must find some tracks. Remember, a bear's tracks look like this:

After you have found the tracks, follow them. Somewhere, a bear is standing in them. If you find these tracks:

you should go
(a) N.
(b) S.
(c) E or W.
If you said (a), go to frame 8.
If you said (b), go to frame 12.
If you said (c), go to frame 4.

3. You are correct. Bears are often found in forests. Occasionally, however, bears are also found elsewhere. You should keep this in mind. The best way to find a bear is to do two things: First, look for a forest: second, look for a bear's tracks. They look something like this:

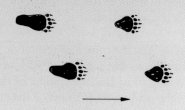

The best way of finding a bear is to:
(a) look for an ocean.
(b) look for its tracks.
(c) look for a forest.
If you answered (a), go to frame 7.
If you answered (b), go to frame 9.
If you answered (c), go to frame 2.

4. Your answer is incorrect, but it may not be unwise. If you are afraid of bears, you might even consider going south. Go to frame 12 to see what would happen if you went south.

5. It is obvious that you are afraid of bears. Your instructions are to go directly to your local university library (do not pass Go, do not collect $200, heh, heh). You are asked to read about counterconditioning, paying special attention to systematic desensitization. If you can afford to, you might consider hiring this textbook's author as a therapist. If you can't afford me, hire someone else.

6. Good! Good! You should do something else. But first you must return to the large collection of people. Having done that. . . .

   (Now go to frame 13.)

7. You are not paying attention. Go back to frame 1 and start again.

8. Good. You noticed the arrow. You may eventually see a bear. It is interesting, don't you think, that a bear always stands facing toward the front of its tracks, *sniffing around?* This makes it a lot easier to locate. After you have found the bear, you will have to make a decision:

   Will you:
   (a) stop and pray?
   (b) run home?
   (c) do something else?

If you said (a), go to frame 11.
If you said (b), go to frame 5.
If you said (c), go to frame 6.

9. That is not correct. If you begin to look for a bear's tracks before finding a forest, you may never find either track or bear. Go back to frame 3.

10. That is not correct. A large collection of people is a city. Bears are not usually found in cities, but they are often found in large collections of trees (forests). You might waste a lot of time looking for bears in cities. Now go back and read frame 1 again.

11. Piety is an admirable quality in a student, but it is not the desired response here. You might seriously consider, at this point, whether you really want to track bears. If you are sure that you do, you are instructed to begin with frame 1.

12. Stop! You are going in the wrong direction. A bear faces toward the front of its tracks. This is an important point. Now you may go back to frame 2, or you might want to rest for a minute before continuing. You may do so, but you should probably begin at frame 1 when you are well again.

13. The beginning of this program is included here simply as an illustration of a branching program. Frustrated would-be bear trackers are invited to consult their local library—or you can hire me as a guide (high-quality service at reasonable rates).

linked to a laser printer—and linked as well to a university computer, a library system, and an assortment of databases. Not that there were no computers then—quite the contrary, there were quite a number, and surprising as it might seem, in many important ways they were not very different from today's computers in terms of their capabilities. But some important differences between first-generation computers and today's computers account for the revolution. Chief among those differences are the reduced size and price of today's desktop, or personal, computers, made possible by the microchip, a fingernail-size wafer that contains all of the computer's processing units. Now people (and schools) can own personal computers as easily as they can own television sets. In addition, today's personal computer is far easier to operate than its grandparents. It is, in the jargon of the trade, far more "user friendly." Small wonder that personal computers proliferate on the market. But what will their effect be on education?

The Potential Effects of Computers in Education

Computer enthusiasts and other optimists predict sweeping, somewhat radical, and highly beneficial effects of the widespread introduction of computers into schools.

Positive Effects. Among other things, they see schools becoming a part of large information exchange-and-retrieval systems in which individual students will have virtually instant access to an almost unlimited quantity of high-quality information. Some also predict that smaller, friendlier, more personal schools will again proliferate once the resource disadvantages that sometimes characterize smaller schools disappear with the coming of the computer (Coburn et al., 1982). Some of these enthusiasts insist that problems with reading, writing, and arithmetic will end as people master the new computer skills. Indeed, some go so far as to suggest that many of the ill effects

of television will be replaced by the creative activities encouraged by computers and that family ties will be strengthened as more and more of the third-wave generation are able to work from their homes, linked to their offices (if there still are such things) and to the world via spun-glass fibers, gold filaments, infrared rays, or more mundane telephone lines.

Less Positive Possibilities. There is, of course, a less optimistic view of the likely impact of computers. This view suggests that our basic computational skills may decline dramatically as computers take care of our computational needs, that reading skills are likely to suffer as children spend more time being amused by computers and their fantasy games and less time reading, and that violence may increase as a function of computer-based video games, the predominant themes of which are violent. Others believe that computers are not likely to make knowledge and power more accessible to the masses but rather to have the opposite effect.

Parsons (1983), for example, argues that according to our best historical evidence, computers are more likely to increase than to decrease the gap between the haves and the have-nots. And, in fact, it seems clear that at least in the first decades of the computer in the school, poor and ethnic-minority students (and females) have had less access to computers than wealthier, ethnic-majority students (and males) (Sutton, 1991).

Also, says Parsons, computer enthusiasts are sometimes guilty of exaggerating and misrepresenting the benefits of computers in education. For example, he points out that these enthusiasts use the term *interaction* widely and inaccurately. Parsons sees interaction as a "meeting of minds," a sort of sharing of meaning (exemplified in conversation or in reading a book). Typically, however, interaction with a computer is quite different: It primarily involves the giving of information. Furthermore, in spite of the fact that computers often are described as "expert" systems of one kind or another, they do not resemble the human experts in most fields (doctors, lawyers, professors, psychiatrists); computers are generally ill-equipped to provide us with advice—information, yes, but advice only occasionally.

In the final analysis, these opposing optimistic and pessimistic views of how computers are likely to affect our lives are no more than speculation—based perhaps on reason and probability but certainly based also on hope and fear. What will come to pass in the end may not be affected a great deal by our often premature speculations. From the teacher's point of view, given the invasion of the computer in our lives and our schools, what is most important is to understand the uses of the computer that will provide the greatest benefits to students.

Uses of Computers in Education

With their peculiar tendency toward jargon and acronyms, educators have given us a whole series of computer-related expressions: CAI (computer-assisted instruction), CML (computer-managed learning), CBE (computer-based education), CAT (computer-assisted training), CBT (computer-based testing), CBT again (computer-based training), CMI (computer-managed instruction), CMT (computer-managed training), and CAL (computer-assisted learning). Of these, *CAI* is perhaps the most general term, although there are indications that it is being replaced by ICAI (intelligent computer-assisted instruction) or ITS (intelligent tutoring system).

Basically, there are three related things students can do with computers; they can learn *about* them, they can learn *with* them, and they can use them simply as tools.

Computer Literacy. Learning about computers is what computer literacy is all about. In the same way as learning something about cars is essential for most of us whose daily activities require that we drive, learning something about computers may well be essential for today's children who will in all likelihood be required to do far more with computers than we are.

Or will tomorrow's computers, like today's computerized banking machines, be so simplistic that even the nearly illiterate will be able to operate them? Will they be "dumbed down" like fast-food cash registers with pictures of tiny hamburgers on their keys?

Computers as Tools. Computers can be useful tools in the management of schools. Not only can they simplify routine clerical tasks such as registering students, storing data, solving scheduling problems, issuing report cards, and so on but they can also be used as computing and writing instruments.

Computers can also be useful word-processing and computing tools for students. And they can be extremely important sources of information, given their enormous information storage-and-retrieval capacities. When connected to the appropriate databanks, a computer terminal can give us almost instant access to the most encyclopedic and current information available. For example, the computer can be used as a source of advice on career decisions. Their great advantage in career guidance is that they can store a tremendous wealth of information concerning career opportunities and requirements that relate to a rapidly changing job market. They handle routine career-related questions quickly and efficiently, and they can be programmed to find relationships in a student's achievement, aptitude, and interests and the likelihood of success in various careers. Many career advice computer programs are now available and widely used in schools. Many of these provide information on thousands of careers, and most are designed to be used with the personal computers found most commonly in homes and schools.

Although these are extremely valuable functions, they are associated with the actual business of instruction more remotely than some of the computer's other uses.

Computers for Drill and Practice. Computers can be used as a sort of teaching machine—as an ultrasophisticated piece of audiovisual equipment designed to present programs or lessons, with or without the assistance of teachers. For example, the first uses of the computer in education were often to present Skinnerian or branching programs. The computer is particularly suitable for presenting programs individually, as well as for repetitive, drill-type exercises (in mathematics or language learning, for example). Used for these purposes, computers can do a great deal to free the classroom teacher for other activities that computers do not do as well.

Research indicates that these relatively unimaginative uses of computers are expensive and work better for lower- than higher-ability students but that they are effective for many students, that they can result in time savings, and that students' attitudes toward computers are generally positive (Scott, Cole, & Engel, 1992).

Simulations. Happily, the computer's uses are not limited to drill and practice exercises but include simulations as well. For example, programs are available that mimic the circulatory system, a chemical laboratory, or the in-flight responses of a Boeing 737. Simulations allow the learner to discover the results of specific responses without the risk and expense of actually performing them. Thus in using a computer-controlled simulator, a pilot can learn that a particularly unlucky combination of aileron and rudder movements can cause a crash—without actually destroying either a multimillion-dollar aircraft or several lives.

At a less dramatic level, a clever simulation of a chemical laboratory might allow students to discover the potentially disastrous effects of combining, chilling, heating, pressurizing, or eating different chemicals, without losing a school building or a human body in the process.

One benefit of computer simulation is that it can be used for teaching problem-solving skills. For example, Woodward, Carnine, and Gersten (1988) presented students with a commercial program called Health Ways. This program presents information about factors that contribute to health and survival and simulates the probable outcomes of different combinations of these factors. The program presents learners with different profiles (basic information about an individual, including age, occupation, heredity, and so on) and asks them to manipulate important variables to increase life expectancy. In the Woodward, Carnine, and Gersten study, students who had used the Health Ways computer program were compared with students in a control group given the same information in a structured teaching format that included enrichment instruction and exercises instead of the computer simulation program. After a twelve-day instructional sequence, members of the experimental group outperformed those in the control group, not only with respect to factual knowledge but also in solving health-related problems.

Virtual Reality Simulations. Imagine you are a student studying ancient Mayan civilizations. Today, you have chosen to explore a Mayan ruin. You climb the precipitous slope of the main pyramid's north face, skipping along the lower steps, then clawing your way up to where the ancient stones have crumbled. Finally, you stand on top. Deliberately, you look in each of the four directions. Now you take out your compass, turn it so that it points to 280 degrees, and search the jungle for signs of the opening into the sacrificial cenote. Finding it, you switch to "museum mode" and explore a database, complete with photographs, filled with information on Mayan sacrifices and related topics.

Possible? Almost, with interactive videodisk environments used to produce what is termed virtual reality (VR). VR describes a particular kind of computer-learner relationship ("interface," in computer jargon) wherein the learner experiences aspects of an environment and makes choices or moves within that environment in such a way that the experience seems almost real (hence the label "virtual reality"). In the VR system described by Ferrington and Loge (1992), individuals wear the computer's display systems on their heads in the form of a system that looks something like a helmet and goggles. This system presents the individual with three-dimensional visual and corresponding auditory displays and includes sensors that respond to the user's movements. If users look up, they might see the sky; to the left, another landscape; to the right, yet another. Furthermore, users make choices suggested by the visual display by manipulating an icon (termed a *puppet*) that appears on the visual display. The puppet is controlled by a "dataglove" that is so engineered that finger and hand movements are translated directly into corresponding movements of the puppet. Thus, the user can open doors, grasp and move objects, and point in any direction to "move" in that direction.

Although virtual reality systems are still largely experimental, various interactive instructional/entertainment programs are available—including the Mayan program, called *Palenque,* just described (Wilson & Talley, 1990). Although it doesn't use headset receivers or datagloves, it presents learners with individual point-of-view camera angles and permits a variety of choices of places to explore physically, or of other modes such as "museum," which then permits still further choices such as different "rooms" within the museum (Kozma, 1991).

The simulations that VR systems might make possible are staggering to contemplate.

Integrated Learning Systems. Computer-based courses are widely available for a tremendous variety of topics and ages. Delivery systems might include a computing center and a number of student terminals or might consist of one or more stand-alone units, each with its own computer and terminal. Typically, the learner interacts with the computer program by means of a monitor and a typewriter keyboard or some other control device such as a mouse or a joystick. This physical paraphernalia is collectively labeled **hardware;** the programs, which are really the brains of the computer—its information, instructions, and capabilities—are termed **software,** or sometimes *courseware.*

The phrase "integrated learning system" (ILS) is used to refer to any of a variety of computer-based learning systems typically developed for mass marketing. The systems typically include hardware and software and may also involve links with external databases (Scott, Cole, & Engel, 1992). For example, McCullough (1992) describes an integrated learning system at Graham Elementary School in Shelby, N.C., that was created by Computer Systems Research, Inc. (a division of CTB-Macmillan-McGraw Hill). This courseware provides various programs and activities in the three basic areas: reading, writing, and arithmetic. This ILS allows for different levels of objectives and activities and permits ongoing evaluation of students' performance. As a result, it also provides for diagnosis and automatically prescribes a series of courses for each student. Most ILS programs such as this one emphasize course content rather than the student's cognitive processes. Few approach the current ideal in the field of computer applications to education: intelligent systems.

Intelligent Tutor Systems (ITS). An intelligent tutor system is a program that takes into account the learner's strengths and weakness and modifies its offerings accordingly—very much as a good teacher does. Intelligent tutor systems try to determine what a student knows (or needs to know) on the basis of the student's interactions with the system—that is, typically on the basis of the student's answers. The system then draws from its databases experiences and instructions that will be most effective given this student and the goals programmed into the system.

Intelligent tutor systems are best described in terms of five separate aspects or "modules" (Farnham-Diggory, 1992; Scott, Cole, & Engel, 1992). The "expert module" is the source of knowledge—in computer jargon, a database. Like a good teacher, the ITS's database allows it to select from its expert knowledge information and activities that are appropriate for specific learners. Hence, it is a far more complex database than would be found in most integrated learning systems.

The "student module" is the computer's representation of what the student is like. This representation is built from the student's responses but must necessarily be based on certain preconceptions about learners that are built into the system. The system also has to be designed so that it can obtain information it needs about the learner. That is, just as a good human tutor asks the learner to explain an answer, so too might an ITS—and it would then use this information to make qualitative judgments about the learner.

The "instructional module" consists of pedagogical, or teaching, rules built into the system. The rules might take forms such as, "If a student qualified as X gives response (explanation) A, then . . ."

The communication component consists of the interface, or link, between student and machine. It includes the ways in which the learner can interact with the system (a keyboard, a mouse, a joystick, a finger) and the ways in which the system can interact with the learner (visual display, auditory signals).

ITS systems are still largely experimental. One of the major problems, notes Farnham-Diggory (1992), is that computers do not process human language as we do; they cannot easily, in their own words so to speak, explain the meaning of a prose passage—or comment sincerely on the learner's new shoes.

Logo. Another fundamentally important use of the computer is evident in the learning of programming skills. As Papert (1980, 1987) has shown, these skills can be learned by very young children—children who program computers rather than being programmed by them.

"If you've ever watched youngsters use Nintendo and other computer games," Soloman tells us, "you know there are powerful forces at work—concentration, commitment, and control. Schools need to harness that power. . ."(1992, p. 10). Teaching children to program computers seems to be one way to harness that power.

In order to teach young children how to program computers, Papert and his associates have developed a simple computer language, **Logo,** which is powerful enough to let children explore the world of differential equations or move to an understanding of *Hypercard,* a Macintosh courseware package (Yoder, 1992), but simple enough to enable children with no mathematical sophistication whatsoever to explore the world of plane geometry. For this purpose, *Logo* (which runs on most personal computers) introduces the turtle—a triangular little creature on the computer monitor that can be moved by means of ordinary words rather than the more abstract and complex terminology of most computer languages. For example, the child simply types FORWARD 50 to make the turtle move straight ahead fifty little turtle-steps, dragging a "pen" behind it so that you can see its path; FORWARD 50 RIGHT 90 FORWARD 50 makes it go ahead fifty steps, turn to the right, and go forward another fifty steps at right angles to the first path. It is only a short child-step from here to the design of a complete square and but one small additional step to learn that all the instructions required for making this square can be shortened because they involve repetition (REPEAT 4 FORWARD 50 RIGHT 90) and can be given a name—such as SQUARE. Subsequently, when the child types SQUARE, the turtle draws a square. The child has easily and painlessly created a simple program.

As the child learns new instructions and continues to "play turtle," the programs can become more complex and the designs of plane geometry more intricate. Playing turtle simply involves imagining how the turtle will respond to all the combinations of instructions possible. Thus can a child learn to program the computer to draw a cartoon figure, a house, a tree, an anything. Thus, too, can the child learn geometry, mathematics, the systematic and clear thinking required to write programs, and other aspects of what has come to be called **computer literacy.** If the effects of the computer revolution are anywhere near the magnitude of the agricultural and industrial revolutions, those who remain computer illiterates may be swept under and drowned by the third wave.

Computer Applications Evaluated

Among the advantages of computers are their impressive memory capacities, the rapidity and accuracy with which they can deliver information, their problem-solving and computation capabilities, and the versatility of their presentation modes. Computers also present a number of advantages not directly related to their role in assisting instruction—advantages that have relatively little to do with how they are used to help in the ordinary business of teaching (and learning) the conventional curriculum. These advantages have to do with the computer's unique qualities and with the cognitive processes it can foster. As Olson (1985) notes, computers are "tools of the intellect" that require a degree of explicitness and precision in the use of language—and, therefore, in thinking—that is not found in ordinary conversation. Computers do not understand ambiguous statements; they are not programmed to guess or to "read between the lines." Instead, they respond logically and rationally. As a result, to be intelligent in the computer society—to be truly computer literate—requires learning how to be completely explicit, context free, repeatable, logical, and rational (Calfee, 1985). This type of communication is quite different from our natural, spoken language, which tends to be highly implicit, specific to context, idiosyncratic, and intuitive.

Better or Not? Because of the important differences between computers and other instructional media such as teachers, texts, and television, Salomon and Gardner (1986) caution against attempting to evaluate computer-related instruction by asking such naïve and largely uninformative questions as "Does it teach better than . . . ?" The important point in evaluations is the recognition that computers both do things that are different from other instructional methods and do them differently as well. For example, computers allow us to teach programming and perhaps to foster the types of cognitive processes involved in programming. As M. C. Linn (1985) puts it, the function of programming courses is to teach problem solving as well as programming. In much the same way, Papert's *Logo* is designed to teach students how to learn (as well as to teach them *Logo*). And subsequent assessments reveal that children who became skilled in Logo not only increased their mastery of metacognitive skills but improved in measured creativity as well (Salomon & Gardner, 1986).

A comprehensive review of evaluations of **computer-assisted instruction (CAI)** at the college level looked at fifty-nine separate studies (Kulik, Kulik, & Cohen, 1980). Although this global review does not offer direct comparisons of different CAI programs, it does provide additional evidence that CAI in general produces significant positive changes in both achievement and attitude among college students. It should be noted, however, that these changes are very small. More encouraging is the finding of Kulik and associates that CAI substantially reduces instruction time.

Revolution or Not? But are we in the midst of a computer revolution in education and in society at large? *Revolution* implies sudden, dynamic, sweeping changes that ultimately transform significant aspects of our lives. Looking back through the ages, social historians have no difficulty identifying and naming revolutions: the agricultural, the industrial, the French. We recognize these revolutions clearly; sometimes we even think we understand them.

But recognizing current social change—or predicting future change—is more difficult. We are too much a part of our cultures to easily sense change in them. Perhaps we are too much a part of the change itself.

Computers, Papert (1987) tells us, are a fundamental part of our culture. They are more than simply tools that we can use for various purposes; they change our very way of thinking and acting. We are part of the computer revolution, and as a result, perhaps we do not see it very clearly.

But if a computer revolution is actually happening in education, it certainly doesn't seem sudden. Laurillard (1988) notes that computers should provide an excellent learning environment for our students, given their amazing powers for storing, retrieving, and processing information and in light of their interactive capabilities. However, in her words, "computer assisted learning has never become a principal teaching method at any level of education" (p. 215).

We have now had a full two decades to examine the use of computers in schools and to incorporate them in our programs, says Laurillard. Yet those who advocate their use must continue to rely on their promise rather than on evidence of what they have done.

In fact, however, students have *not* had wide access to computers until recently, so we have not really had two decades to develop their educational uses or to assess their impact. It is only during the last few years that computers have become sufficiently compact and affordable to be widely available—in some schools and homes, although by no means all.

Change in education is seldom rapid—especially from the perspective of those who are part of it. In the end, history might look back and judge that, yes, this was a sudden and most dramatic revolution that produced a truly marvelous outcome. The ultimate contributions of computer-based instructional systems may be even greater than we can yet imagine. All the caterpillars might yet decide they really do want to go up in that thing called a butterfly.

It is also possible that historians will look back and say, "There was no revolution of any kind back there near the end of the twentieth century. There was only the rather slow proliferation of that primitive tool they called the computer. Of course, now it's obsolete."

INDIVIDUALIZED INSTRUCTIONAL PROGRAMS

Programmed instruction—in all its variations, with or without computers—is but one of the instructional modes that clearly reflect the influence of psychological theory on education. There are more. Among them, perhaps no others have received greater attention than Bloom's suggestions for **mastery learning** and Keller's outline for a **personalized system of instruction** (**PSI**), sometimes called "the Keller plan." Also well known are **individually prescribed instruction** (**IPI**) and **individually guided instruction** (**IGE**).

Basic Assumptions

These approaches have much in common. Most important, each is based on a fundamental assumption: There are faster learners and slower learners (Bloom, 1976). Accordingly, aptitude is primarily a function of the speed with which a student acquires information, concepts, or skills. So long as all students receive identical instruction, the correlation between aptitude and achievement will be high. In other words, with identical instruction, faster students will achieve better, and slower students will achieve at a lower level. However, if each student is presented with optimal learning conditions, the relationship between aptitude and achievement will be very slight, and most learners will reach the same level. In Bloom's terminology, all learners, provided they are given optimal instruction, will achieve mastery of important objectives. If all learners master the same material, differences among them will be minimal, and the relationship of achievement to aptitude will be negligible.

A second important assumption of most individualized instructional systems is that learning requires constant evaluation, not so that the learner can be graded but to guide the learning/instruction process. This type of evaluation, termed *formative,* is not to be confused with more formal evaluation provided at the end of a unit or course, termed *summative.* Whereas **summative evaluation** is intended primarily to provide a grade, **formative evaluation** is an essential diagnostic tool in the teaching process. In both Bloom's and Keller's systems, for example, the attainment of a specific grade is not the most important criterion; mastery of course objectives is.

Bloom's Mastery Learning

Bloom's **mastery learning model** is based largely on John B. Carroll's (1963) model of school learning. Simply stated, this model specifies that degree of learning is primarily a function of the time spent learning relative to the amount of time required to learn. Amount of time required is, in turn, a function of both aptitude and quality of instruction received.

Carroll's emphasis is on providing all learners with both high-quality instruction and the time required to learn. His objective is "equality of opportunity," which contrasts with Bloom's objective of "equality of attainment" (Carroll, 1989, p. 30).

Bloom's basic notion is that it is possible to analyze any learning sequence in order to specify a number of specific objectives and to teach in such a way that most, if not all, students attain these objectives. Although the teaching methods suggested by Bloom are not fundamentally different from those ordinarily used by teachers, they differ in two important respects: First, they are directed specifically toward the mastery of previously identified objectives, and second, they make extensive use of formative evaluation to diagnose learners' difficulties, to suggest modifications in instructional strategies, and to identify subject areas in which more time needs to be spent. A third important characteristic of Bloom's mastery learning is that it requires the use of a great variety of systematic and deliberate corrective procedures in conjunction with formative evaluation (Bloom, 1987). Among these corrective procedures are study sessions, individualized tutoring, reteaching, students helping each other in small, cooperative groups, and a selection of alternative instructional materials in a variety of forms, such as programs, films, audiotapes, and so on. (See Table 12.1.)

One final characteristic of Bloom's mastery learning is the provision that classes typically progress from one unit to another as a group. This is accomplished by providing enrichment for students who master course objectives first. Thus, the pace of progress through the curriculum is determined largely by those who require the longest time to reach mastery. Ultimately, all students who have mastered course objectives are given "A's"; those who have not succeeded are given "I's" (for incomplete, but meaning "mastery in the making"). No students fail in this system.

Keller's Personalized System of Instruction (PSI)

The Keller PSI plan is an elaboration of Bloom's mastery learning (Keller, 1968). Originally developed for teaching introductory psychology at the college level, the **personalized system of instruction** has since been used in a variety of college courses. And although its applicability at the elementary or secondary school level has not been extensively demonstrated, the principles upon which it is based and the methods it suggests might prove useful there as well.

Essentially, a PSI approach requires that the course be broken down into small units, that appropriate instructional materials be developed for each of these units, and that students be allowed to take as much time as necessary to learn each unit. Whenever students feel they are ready, they are given a short unit quiz, the quiz is marked immediately, and they are told whether they need to

TABLE 12.1 Basic Elements of Bloom's Mastery Learning

UNDERLYING ASSUMPTIONS	1. There are *faster* learners and *slower* learners (not *better* learners and *poorer* learners).
	2. Learning requires constant *formative* evaluation, designed specifically to guide the teaching/learning process.
BROAD CHARACTERISTICS OF TEACHING METHODS	1. Instruction is directed toward the attainment of specific, explicit, and previously identified objectives.
	2. Instruction is guided by the results of formative evaluation.
	3. Numerous *corrective* instructional procedures in the form of study sessions, cooperative student groups, individualized tutoring, reteaching, and alternative instructional materials are provided.

spend more time studying the same unit or whether they can proceed to the next unit. At the end of the course, an examination covering all material is given.

Unlike mastery learning, the Keller plan does not advocate the use of traditional instructional methods, nor does it rely as heavily on corrective procedures, although alternative learning materials are available. Instead, the onus for mastering a unit rests largely on the student. In many cases, the unit in question corresponds to a chapter in a textbook and/or to a programmed version of the same material. Tutoring often occurs after a student proctor marks the unit quiz, but it is not an essential part of the course. Nor, indeed, is the traditional lecture. In fact, students attend lectures only after they have successfully completed specified units. Lectures are intended to serve as reinforcement for success rather than as a basis for it.

Keller's PSI, like Bloom's mastery learning, is designed to provide experiences of success for all learners. And although both approaches recognize important individual differences among learners, they contradict the ancient belief that there are good and bad learners—faster or slower, perhaps, but not better or poorer. Accordingly, each approach attempts to provide learning experiences that will optimize the attainment of specific objectives for each learner. Those objectives might be behavioral or performance objectives or a specified score on a quiz.

The advantages claimed for approaches such as these center on the attention that each pays to individual differences in learning rate. Whereas traditional approaches to instruction and evaluation almost necessitate that those who learn more slowly than their age/grade peers will often fail, these highly individualized approaches ensure that almost all students will eventually succeed.

Another advantage of mastery approaches may be increased student motivation. As Stallings and Stipek (1986) note, repeated exposure to a mastery approach should lead students to the expectation that they will succeed if they work hard enough. It follows that students who are externally oriented may, as a result, eventually become more internally oriented and consequently more willing to accept challenges (see Chapter 10).

Individually Prescribed Instruction (IPI)

To individualize teaching is to make it more responsive to the needs and the characteristics of the individual learner. This does not mean that instruction must occur only in a private, individual setting and in a self-paced situation (Anderson & Block, 1977). The essential requirement is simply that some of the characteristics of instruction (such as level of material presented, mode of presentation, and instructional goals) take into account at least some of the student's characteristics (such as aptitude, interest, and previous achievement). **Individually prescribed instruction,** for example, is a complex system based on the reorganization of the entire curriculum for each subject into a large number of sequential units, each with its own objectives and tests. Students work individually on a unit, making extensive use of written materials. Once they have completed a unit, they take the accompanying test; if their performance is satisfactory, they proceed to the next unit. Units are essentially ungraded so that a learner can progress as rapidly or as slowly as ability and inclination allow. Thus at any one time, students in what would otherwise be a single grade might be working at levels that elsewhere would fall within a wide spread of grades (Scanlon, Weinberger, & Weiler, 1970). In fact, IPI's advocates claim that this is one of the chief advantages of the system.

Individually Guided Education (IGE)

IGE originated at the University of Wisconsin in the early 1970s. Like IPI, it requires a reorganization of school systems, for it too is based on the principle of ungraded schools. In addition, **individually guided education** makes use of teams of teachers, extensive workshops to coordinate the objectives and activities of teachers, a systematic program of home and school cooperation, individual programming for students, and ongoing research to develop and improve IGE materials (Klausmeier, Rossmiller, & Saily, 1977; Haney & Sorenson, 1977). Both IGE and IPI use their own curriculum materials or extensively modify existing materials. Partly for this reason, both can involve considerable expense, particularly in their early stages.

Individualized Instruction Evaluated

Do individualized approaches to instruction work? In a word, yes. But to say that they work better than more conventional approaches all (or even most) of the time would require more convincing evidence than we now have. Approaches such as IGE and IPI, which require extensive reorganization of schools and school systems, cannot easily be compared to more traditional instructional methods. As Walker and Schaffarzick (1974) point out, the "new" approaches are usually slightly superior in some respects, perhaps somewhat inferior in others, and not very different in most.

Investigations of Keller's PSI at the college level and of Bloom's mastery learning primarily in elementary schools have found these approaches to be quite effective, both in terms of reaching course goals and in terms of general attitude toward course work. In a review of studies that have investigated the effectiveness of mastery approaches, Slavin (1987) found a number of studies with positive results—and several showed no advantage for mastery learning. Bloom (1987) suggests that results are usually positive when students make full use of the "corrective feedback" process that is part of formative evaluation.

Kulik, Kulik, and Bangert-Drowns (1990) subsequently analyzed 108 investigations of mastery learning. Their conclusion: In general, mastery learning increases achievement, most notably for weaker students. In fact, average increases for all groups were from approximately the fiftieth to the seventieth percentile. In addition, mastery learning has positive effects on students' attitudes toward school. On the other hand, self-paced mastery programs are associated with lower completion rates in college courses.

Kulik, Kulik, and Cohen also analyzed seventy-five studies that compared Keller's PSI with conventional approaches (see Figure 12.2 for one comparison). Their conclusion: "The analysis establishes that PSI generally produces superior student achievement, less variation in achievement,

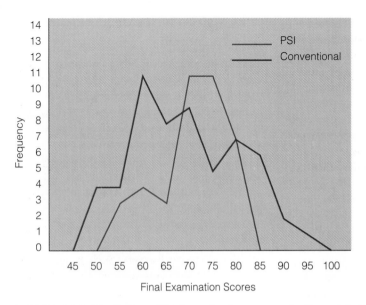

FIGURE 12.2 Distribution of final examination averages for forty-eight PSI and forty-eight conventional classes (PSI = personalized system of instruction). From J. A. Kulik, C. C. Kulik, and P. A. Cohen, "A Meta-analysis of Outcome Studies of Keller's Personalized System of Instruction," *American Psychologist, 34,* 307–318. Copyright 1979 by the American Psychological Association. Reprinted with permission of the authors.

and higher student ratings in college courses, but does not affect course withdrawal or student study time in these courses" (1979, p. 307).

Lest we madly run off selling another educational panacea, it should be noted that PSI and mastery learning have their faults and weaknesses as well and that not all evaluations are as positive and as optimistic as that of Kulik and associates. For example, a number of researchers have noted that student attrition is often higher with these methods than with more conventional approaches (Robin, 1976). And other critics have observed that an emphasis on the mastery of objectives that all (or most) learners can achieve might, in fact, penalize the fast learner (M. Arlin, 1984). At best, such a system does not maximize the faster learner's achievement; at worst, it leads to boredom, destroys motivation, and renders meaningless the assignment of grades because all

who work long enough obtain "A's." Furthermore, we cannot completely discount the possibility that undue emphasis on specifiable objectives might restrict the teaching/learning process and prevent the occurrence of important incidental learning—and that it might, in fact, lead to an extrinsically motivated, performance-based orientation rather than a mastery orientation.

In one of the most comprehensive investigations of individualized instruction in secondary schools, Bangert, Kulik, and Kulik (1983) analyzed and summarized the findings of fifty-one separate studies. Each study had measured the effectiveness of instructional methods involving the division of the curriculum into units, the use of "learning activity packages," students working at their own rate, and formative testing before moving to the next level of work. Thus, the summary included studies of IPI, IGE, and PSI, among other approaches. The summary indicates that individualized instruction has a modest but positive effect on school achievement in secondary grades but that it does not affect attitude toward subject matter, self-esteem, or measures of abstract thinking ability.

As Bangert and associates note, the results of this study are quite different from those reported by Bloom (1987) or those summarized by Kulik and associates (1979). Note, however, that the earlier analysis dealt with research at the college level; this one deals with the secondary school level. It appears that individualized instruction has far more positive results at the college level than it does in secondary schools—a fact that might be explained partly in terms of the characteristics of college students compared with those of secondary school students. These characteristics might include greater maturity, greater motivation, better study skills, and more appropriate cognitive strategies.

In summary, individualized instruction is at least as effective as more conventional approaches in secondary schools and often is significantly more effective at the college level. In general, the approaches require considerable effort on the part of schools and teachers with respect to systematizing and simplifying instruction. And they demand that schools and teachers make a conscious effort to specify their immediate goals and sometimes also their long-range goals. Among their virtues, these approaches provide important experiences of success for learners who might otherwise lack them by making it possible for learners of all aptitudes to master units and courses. In addition to these and other positive features of systematic individualized instruction, the greatest contribution of this approach may turn out to lie in the impetus it provides for research on attribute-treatment interaction (ATI). Such research is designed to uncover the relationships among specific instructional modes, identifiable learner characteristics, and the attainment of instructional goals.

ATTRIBUTE-TREATMENT INTERACTION

Approaches such as Keller's PSI and Bloom's mastery learning are based on the assumption that all learners can achieve the same instructional goals—that each is capable of mastery. However, they also recognize that some people learn faster than others and that some need more assistance. Even approaches that try to minimize the importance of differences in learners' characteristics must, in the end, recognize that these differences are sometimes quite important.

Other programs, such as learning styles approaches, are based directly on a recognition of differences among learners. Such programs require information about the relationship between learners' characteristics and specific instructional methods—or what is termed **attribute-treatment interaction** (Cronbach & Snow, 1977).

The basic premise of attribute-treatment research is simple: Specific instructional methods are better for students with a particular characteristic, whereas different instructional methods might be better for students with other characteristics. Put another way, an attribute-treatment interaction exists whenever the effectiveness of instruction (the treatment) is shown to depend, at least in part, on the learner's characteristics. The ultimate goal of attribute-treatment research is to identify the best combinations of attributes and treatments.

Findings and Conclusions

Researchers have looked at numerous student characteristics (including anxiety, dependence, conformity, various dimensions of intellectual abilities, and many others) and have attempted to relate these to various instructional methods (such as lecturing, small-group interaction, programs, computers, demonstrations) and to various characteristics of each of these—including, for example, whether the approach is structured or unstructured (Ross, Rakow, & Bush, 1980; Whitener, 1989).

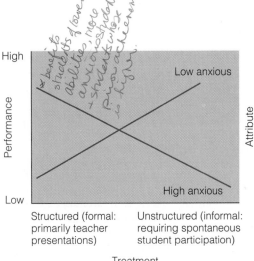

Handwritten annotations on figure:
benefits of lower ability + more anxious students + students whose prior achievement is higher

(left margin, vertical handwritten text:) high anxious

Performance (vertical axis, High to Low)

High
Low anxious
High anxious
Low

Attribute (right vertical axis)

Structured (formal: primarily teacher presentations)   Unstructured (informal: requiring spontaneous student participation)

Treatment

FIGURE 12.3 A schematic representation of an attribute-treatment interaction—specifically, an interaction between anxiety and degree of structure in teaching method. Note that highly anxious students tend to perform better with more structured approaches, but that the opposite is true of students who are less anxious.

Although findings from ATI studies are by no means clear and simple, researchers advance several tentative conclusions. One of the most replicated findings is the interaction between anxiety and the degree to which an instructional method is structured or requires active learner participation. Specifically, highly anxious students do better with instructional approaches that do not require a high degree of student interaction but instead are more "teacher centered" (see, for example, Snow & Swanson, 1992; see Figure 12.3). Similarly, there appears to be an interaction between general ability and structure, such that students of lower ability do relatively better with highly structured approaches (such as programmed instruction) that use small steps together with frequent responding and reinforcement (Swing & Peterson, 1982). This interaction may result in part from the fact that highly structured approaches reduce information-processing requirements—that is, they demand fewer cognitive strategies of the learner (Resnick, 1981).

Recall that Kulik, Kulik, and Bangert-Drowns (1990) also found that mastery learning tended to be more effective with lower-ability students.

Whitener (1989) also reports an interaction between prior achievement (as opposed to aptitude) and lesson structure. Highly structured lessons increase the difference between high and low achievers; in contrast, self-paced, relatively unstructured lessons tend to decrease that difference. In effect, what this means is that higher achievers benefit more than lower achievers from an increase in instructional structure.

In conclusion, then, at least three separate interactions between lesson structure and student attributes have been uncovered by research. Specifically, highly structured approaches benefit students of lower ability, more anxious students, and students whose prior achievement is higher.

Some Cautions. Several important cautions are in order. First, these conclusions are extremely tentative at best. Furthermore, simple summaries of complex studies tend to make the results seem far clearer and more definite than they actually are. In fact, the results of research on attribute-treatment interaction are highly inconsistent and often contradictory. As a case in point, consider that two of our three conclusions are almost contradictory: Students of lower ability do better with highly structured approaches, but higher-achieving students also improve more with increasing structure than do students who have previously achieved at a lower level.

Interestingly, when students' preferences are taken into account in an attempt to discover the best combinations of attributes and teaching approaches, the picture becomes more confused rather than clearer. For example, research tells us (tentatively to be sure) that students of lower ability tend to perform better in more highly structured classroom environments, but that the opposite is true of higher-ability students (Snow & Lohman, 1984). However, R. E. Clark (1982) found that lower-ability students prefer unstructured and highly permissive classrooms—perhaps because their lack of achievement is more likely to go unnoticed in this environment. In contrast, better students express a strong preference for highly structured approaches—approaches that make it unnecessary for them to plan and think and that they suspect will make it easier for them to direct their efforts and achieve well. Thus, students' preferences directly contradict what research suggests is best for them.

Ability and Achievement. If this sounds impossibly complex to you, do not despair. Its complexity and lack of clarity mean that no very valuable suggestions can yet be derived and applied directly to classroom practice (Pintrich, Cross, Kozma, & McKeachie, 1986). Besides, as Gagné and Dick (1983) observe, measures of relationships uncovered thus far have been extremely modest. In the end, the most powerful variables related to school achievement continue to be intellectual ability and previous school achievement. Consequently, the most fruitful approach to matching instruction to students' characteristics is probably one that takes these two variables into account. And that is what happens, at least to a small degree, when students are sorted into groups on the basis of achievement and sometimes of ability. We should not be misled into thinking, however, that these two variables—achievement and ability—account for most of the variation in observed student achievement. In fact, they account for only about 25 percent of the variation; some of the remaining 75 percent is linked to other factors such as home background, type and quality of instruction, and personality characteristics, particularly as they are reflected in motivation and attitudes (Bloom, 1976).

MAIN POINTS

1. Tracking (ability grouping) is uncommon and may have negative effects on members of lower groups and sometimes zero effects on other groups. Learning styles approaches attempt to tailor a variety of instructional features—instructional method, teaching mode, curriculum, evaluation, and rewards—to individual students' strengths and weaknesses.

2. A program is a sequential arrangement of information in small steps (frames), each of which requires the learner to make a response that is then reinforced through immediate feedback (knowledge of results). A linear program (Skinner) requires all learners to progress through the same material in exactly the same sequence and to construct their own responses; a branching program (Crowder) requires learners to select an answer and then directs them to the next frame on the basis of that answer. Those who make errors are provided with further help.

3. The optimistic view of the computer revolution suggests that computers will provide students with immediate access to high-quality information; may lead to smaller, friendlier, and more personal schools; can reduce problems with basic reading, writing, and mathematical skills; and might do a great deal to counter the negative effects of television. A more pessimistic view suggests that computers may lead to a decline in computational and reading skills; might encourage violence; might help widen the gap between the haves and the have-nots; might lead us to rely on "expert" computer systems, the expertise of which rests on information rather than on wisdom; and might depersonalize schools. Some resist the apparent revolution.

4. Computers are used in schools to teach computer literacy; as tools to manage instructional programs (data storage and analysis, for example), obtain information (databases), provide career information, and for word processing and computation; for drill and practice instructional exercises; for simulations, including possibilities opened up by virtual reality; for computational purposes; as

sophisticated "teaching machines" or audiovisual aids to present programs, sometimes in integrated learning systems; and as intelligent tutoring systems (ITS) in which the computer modifies its interactions on the basis of its analysis of the student. Students can also be taught to program computers, with resulting cognitive benefits.

5. Bloom's mastery learning is based on the assumption that most learners are capable of mastering important school objectives, but that some people require more time and more nearly optimal instruction than others. This "no-fail" program breaks the curriculum into small units that must be mastered before the student proceeds.

6. Keller's personalized system of instruction (PSI), closely related to Bloom's mastery learning, is designed for teaching at the college level. It places the onus for attainment of unit and course objectives primarily on the student. Students are allowed to repeat unit quizzes until they reach a specified performance criterion and then progress to the next unit.

7. Individually guided education (IGE) and individually prescribed instruction (IPI) require the reorganization of entire school systems because both are nongraded approaches. In IPI, the entire school curriculum is divided into small units, each with related tests. Students work individually on each unit and progress to the next whenever they are successful on the accompanying test. In IGE, students also work individually on specially prepared and sequenced material. IGE uses teams of teachers and home and school programs, as well as workshops and research programs designed to improve instructional materials and approaches.

8. Evaluations of these approaches to individualizing instruction indicate that they typically have positive effects on achievement and attitudes. They are sometimes associated with higher student attrition, however.

9. Attempts to individualize instruction have also taken the form of studies of attribute-treatment interactions. Such interactions exist when there is a consistent relationship between the effectiveness of an instructional approach and some identifiable characteristic (or grouping of characteristics) of the learners.

10. The clearest example of an attribute-treatment interaction involves anxiety and instructional structure. Specifically, highly anxious students often do better with structured approaches (programmed instruction or highly didactic teacher presentations in which students are not required to participate extensively). Also, lower-ability students perform better under highly structured conditions. But conclusions about attribute-treatment interactions are tentative at best. These interactions are typically modest. In the final analysis, the two variables that appear to be most highly related to school success are ability and previous achievement.

11. A bear always faces the front of its tracks.

SUGGESTED READINGS

The following book should be of practical assistance to students who wish to explore programmed instruction more carefully:

MARKLE, S. M. (1964). *Good frames and bad: A grammar of frame writing.* New York: Wiley.

Papert's book presents an important vision of the potential of computers in the cognitive development of children. The book by Merrill and associates is a clear and comprehensive survey of the various uses to which computers can be put in education.

PAPERT, S. (1980). *Mindstorms: Children, computers, and powerful ideas.* New York: Basic Books.

MERRILL, P. F., HAMMONS, K., TOLMAN, M. N., CHRISTENSEN, L., VINCENT, B. R., & REYNOLDS, P. L. (1992). *Computers in education* (2nd ed.). Boston: Allyn & Bacon.

Classic references for PSI and Bloom's mastery learning include

BLOOM, B. S. (1976). *Human characteristics and school learning.* New York: McGraw-Hill.

KELLER, F. S. (1968). Good-bye, teacher. . . . *Journal of Applied Behavior Analysis, 1,* 79–89.

An excellent collection of many of the best of Benjamin Bloom's articles and presentations appears in

BLOOM, B. S. (1981). *All our children learning: A primer for parents, teachers, and other educators.* New York: McGraw-Hill.

The following article gives both a historical and a current view of computers in education:

SCOTT, T., COLE, M., & ENGEL, M. (1992). Computers and education: A cultural constructivist perspective. In G. Grant (Ed.), *Review of research in education* (Vol. 18). Washington, D.C.: American Educational Research Association.

The following booklet is an interesting and potentially useful attempt to translate research about teaching into practical applied principles. It presents forty-one findings, with explanatory comments and practical suggestions relating to each.

U.S. DEPARTMENT OF EDUCATION. (1986). *What works: Research about teaching and learning.* Pueblo, Colo.: Consumer Information Center.

Seals are the staple food of the polar bear. Infant seals are particularly easy to capture when they are still in the aglos (calving dens). The aglo is a small ice cave hollowed out by a mother seal and accessible only from the water. It is covered with a three- to five-foot layer of snow and a thick cover of ice. The polar bear can scent aglos from a remarkable distance. Having found one, the bear rapidly excavates the overburden of snow with quick blows of paws and then attempts to break through the ice by rearing up and smashing downward with both front paws. If the ice is too thick, the bear may move back a short distance, run toward the aglo, leap high in the air, and come thundering down with all four paws, crashing noisily through the ice. It is then a simple matter to reach inside and pull out the squirming infant (Perry, 1966).

All animals are equal, but some animals are more equal than others.

George Orwell, *Animal Farm*

The low man goes on adding one to one
  His hundred's soon hit:
This high man, aiming at a million
  Misses a unit.

Robert Browning, *A Grammarian's Funeral*

Chapter 13 | MEASUREMENT AND EVALUATION

PREVIEW In spite of the intuitive appeal of "schools without failures," "schools without tests," and other hypothetical situations in which everyone is highly motivated, absolutely dedicated, and deliriously happy, the nitty-gritty of classroom practice sometimes (perhaps frequently) requires assessment. This chapter describes the various methods by which students' and teachers' performance can be measured and evaluated, why assessment is important, some of the abuses and misuses of assessment procedures, and some trends toward new assessment procedures.

Excerpt from Bear Tales (Book V) Wild Cow Instruction

"Listen up, cows," the bear says. He feels like a missionary; he's an environmental crusader. "Listen up," he repeats. The cousset drums fall silent, the dancing stops. The last of the wild cows drags herself from the water. The cows stand on the floor of the valley below the bear's ledge.

"Listen up. Pay attention. You there," he says to the brindle-faced wild cow. "Yes, you," he says as the cow pulls the cigar from her lips and raises her eyebrows as though to ask, "You mean me?"

"Pay attention," the bear repeats. He's terrific. What a teacher! Some of the cows shuffle their feet as though anxious for the bear to continue. When the cow with the crooked horn slurps her whiskey too noisily, the others glare at her. She looks embarrassed and puts her cup down. She looks toward the bear, but he can tell that her mind isn't on the lesson, that she's still thinking about her whiskey; she has that glazed look.

"We're going to play a game," the bear says, suddenly inspired. He has always known much about the science of teaching, but at this very moment he learns something new about the art. A tremor of excitement rumbles through the group. The cow with the crooked horn stubs her cigar on the ground. Her eyes are no longer glazed; for the moment, she has forgotten about the whiskey. Several of the cows whose tails are still intertwined from the dance now pull apart. They shuffle their feet, but it isn't the rhythms of the dance that move them; it's the voice of the teacher, the promise of his lesson.

"A wonderful game," the bear says. He has to think fast, but that's what makes teaching so exciting. "Line up," he says, "starting over there by the spruce." He points to his left, toward the tree against which the cows have constructed a temporary bar. On the bar are brown whiskey jugs and a

Calvin and Hobbes

by Bill Watterson

Panel 1: IT SAYS HERE THAT BY THE AGE OF SIX ...

Panel 2: .. MOST CHILDREN HAVE SEEN A MILLION MURDERS ON TELEVISION.

Panel 3: I FIND THAT VERY DISTURBING!

Panel 4: IT MEANS I'VE BEEN WATCHING ALL THE WRONG CHANNELS.

crock of water for those who like to cut their whiskey. On the tree next to the mirror behind the bar, someone has nailed a styrofoam-cup dispenser. There are aerosol cans of hair spray on a shelf below the mirror.

"Start with the shortest. I want the shortest cow closest to the spruce tree. Yes, right up next to the bar," the bear says. "Put the second shortest cow . . . yes, stand next in line. And so on. . . . That's it."

There is much shuffling and jostling, much standing next to each other to gauge the top of the other's head, much arguing. The bear intervenes as necessary. "If you two are exactly the same height," he asks once, "what would be a fair way to decide who should stand next in line?" He balances a coin on his nose as he asks the question. He's such a marvelous teacher.

"Before we begin the game, I need to know a lot more about each of you," the bear says, the structure of the lesson unfolding in his mind. He recognizes this as a special pedagogical moment; he is filled with a wonderful feeling. He already has in mind the rudiments of a game that will lead the wild cows to a new environmental consciousness. It is a cooperative team game, with just enough interteam competition to pique the wild cows' interest.

Before the game begins, the bear must help the cows divide themselves into groups. For this task, he needs to know something of their individual abilities. He needs to measure their intelligence and their prior learning. He needs to evaluate their commit-

ment, assess their interests and motivation, and judge their personalities. Quickly, the bear decides which tests he will use to assess the wild cows. He's very excited; measurement and evaluation do that to him. He feels like such a pedagogue!!

The cow with the crooked horn stands in line. She's a short cow; as a result, she's very close to the bar. She's bored. "Enough of this crap," she finally mutters. She goes to the bar, pours herself a cup of whiskey, and lights up a fresh cigar. One of the cousset drums draws her attention, and her rump begins to twitch rhythmically, and the air fills with the odor of methane gas.

The bear notices. "This is not yet an environmentally friendly cow," he thinks sardonically. "But by God I'll measure and evaluate her too!"

MEASUREMENT AND EVALUATION IN SCHOOLS

A statement such as, "The cow with the crooked horn is environmentally unfriendly" illustrates **evaluation**. The statement, "The brindle-face is fifty-two inches high" is an example of **measurement**. Measurement involves the use of an instrument (for example, a ruler or tape measure) to assess a specific quantity; to evaluate is to judge certain qualities—to place a *value* on them. In general, measuring is a more precise and more objective procedure; evaluating is less precise and

The Instructional Process

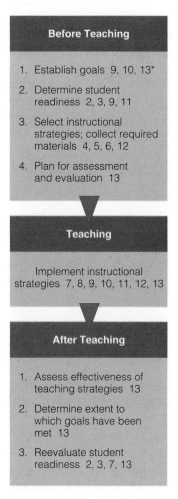

Before Teaching

1. Establish goals 9, 10, 13*

2. Determine student readiness 2, 3, 9, 11

3. Select instructional strategies; collect required materials 4, 5, 6, 12

4. Plan for assessment and evaluation 13

Teaching

Implement instructional strategies 7, 8, 9, 10, 11, 12, 13

After Teaching

1. Assess effectiveness of teaching strategies 13

2. Determine extent to which goals have been met 13

3. Reevaluate student readiness 2, 3, 7, 13

*Chapters containing relevant information

FIGURE 13.1 A three-stage model of the teaching process.

more subjective. The term **assessment** is often used as a synonym for *evaluation.*

Both measurement and evaluation are important parts of the instructional process. As we saw in Chapter 1, instruction can be described as a sequence of procedures conducted before teaching, during teaching, and after teaching (see Fig-

ure 13.1). In the before-teaching phase, measurement and evaluation may be involved in placing students, in selecting instructional procedures, and in determining students' readiness. Plans for final assessment and evaluation should also be made at this stage. During the teaching phase, assessment might be used to determine whether goals are being met, as a basis for modifying instructional procedures, or as a learning event. And in the after-teaching phase, measurement and evaluation are used not only to determine the extent to which instructional goals have been met but also to assess the effectiveness of instructional strategies and to reevaluate students' placement and readiness. Measurement is being used when actual tests are used; it is essentially a quantitative process. Evaluation is being used when teachers make decisions concerning the adequacy of instructional procedures, the readiness of students, and the extent to which curriculum goals are being met; it is a more qualitative process.

Evaluation need not be based on measurement. Indeed, much teacher assessment of students' behavior is not based on measurement. The countless value judgments made by teachers about the abilities of students, their motivation, their persistence, their pleasantness, and so on are often examples of evaluation without measurement. In addition, a number of important assessment procedures such as exhibitions and **portfolios** frequently do not involve tests.

In this chapter, as in most other educational writing, the terms *assessment* and *evaluation* are used interchangeably to include any or a combination of subjective valuations, measurement with tests, or appraisal by some other means.

The Importance of Educational Assessment

Because evaluation is a central component of each stage of the teaching model presented in Figure 13.1, it might be expected that assessment procedures would occupy a significant portion of classroom time.

Prevalence. This is in fact the case. Gullickson (1985) reports that an average of 5 to 15 percent of class time is actually spent on tests. (In lower elementary grades, the percentage is closer to 5; in high school, it is closer to 15.)

In addition to time spent actually writing, correcting, and going over tests, a tremendous range of other evaluative activities fills school days: asking students questions, commenting on students' responses and presentations, evaluating nontest performances in such subject areas as art, drama, music, and writing, informal observations of ongoing student work, correcting and grading homework assignments, evaluating written work, informal assessments of attitudes and efforts, and many more. In fact, the bulk of the teacher's evaluations, especially in lower elementary grades, is based on informal observation and on grading of assignments and performance rather than on test results.

Effect on Students. How do these evaluative procedures affect students? Profoundly. In fact, it is difficult to overestimate the influence of evaluation on students' behavior. Ramsden (1988a) argues that students' beliefs about assessment are among the most important influences on learning. He explains that the types of assessments used determine what students study and how they learn. Sadly, our most common approaches to evaluation encourage a passive form of learning in which rote memorization of facts and formulas is heavily rewarded. Put another way, there are two broad approaches to learning: a surface approach that emphasizes memorization of unrelated facts and a deep approach that involves a deliberate and active search for underlying principles and concepts and that attempts to discover relationships (Crooks, 1988). Because our tests emphasize the simple, surface components of curriculum content and largely ignore the more complex, deeper aspects of knowledge, the surface components are what students learn.

How do we change surface approaches to deep ones? How do we get learners to pay attention to relationships and principles, and how do we get them to achieve understanding instead of memorization?

This text provides several possible answers. For example, there are programs with the express goals of teaching thinking, developing cognitive strategies, imparting learning/thinking skills, or developing metacognitive awareness. And there are cognitive learning theories, such as those described by Bruner and by Ausubel, that emphasize meaningfulness and comprehension while de-emphasizing "meaningless rote learning." These theories provide a number of recommendations for helping students attend to the underlying structures of knowledge, to relationships, and to meaningfulness.

But perhaps, in Elton and Laurillard's words, "the quickest way to change student learning is to change the assessment system" (1979, p. 100) because in the final analysis students try to learn what teachers test, not what teachers suggest is important. It is not sufficient to pay lip service to the importance of complex cognitive processes such as synthesizing or evaluating, or what Bruner calls "going beyond the information given." If teacher-made tests and final examinations ask students only to repeat what they have read in textbooks or heard in class, that is what students will learn to learn.

The point is clear: Teachers must evaluate students on the right things; that is, they must evaluate students on those things they consider most important—the things they want students to learn.

A second point should also be clear: Evaluation needs to be fair, consistent, and reliable. Whenever possible it should be based on the best measurements available, although often it will also result from informal observation.

There is much that an expert teacher should know about measurement. Read on. . . .

SCALES OF MEASUREMENT

A number of different ways of measuring—or scales of measurement—are appropriate for measuring different things (see Table 13.1). The

TABLE 13.1 Four Scales of Measurement

SCALE	CHARACTERISTICS AND FUNCTIONS	EXAMPLE
Nominal	Names: places things in categories	Labeling reading groups "Giraffes," "Zebras," and "Goats"
Ordinal	Ranks: tells us about relative amount (more than/less than)	Being in first grade, second grade, third grade, and so on
Interval	Measures in equal intervals: has an arbitrary zero; permits precise measurement of change, but not comparison of absolute amounts	Most psychological and educational measurement; we *assume* that score intervals are equal
Ratio	Provides true zero and equal intervals: permits comparison of absolute amounts	Weight, height

crudest and least informative scale of measurement is a **nominal scale**. As its label implies, this level of measurement simply names. The numbers on the backs of football players or descriptive categories such as "blue" and "red" or "house" and "barn" are examples of nominal measurement. They tell us nothing about amount but only indicate the categories to which things belong.

At a more advanced level, **ordinal scales** permit us to rank, or order, individuals on the basis of the characteristics we measure. For example, tasting different beverages might allow us to rank them in terms of sweetness. The ranking (or ordinal scale) tells us nothing about absolute amount of sweetness but does give us some information about relative amounts.

The third measurement scale, the **interval scale,** allows us to measure quantity in intervals that vary in fixed, predictable ways. We measure temperature using interval scales. We can therefore say that a change from 0 to 10 degrees is equivalent to a change from 10 to 20 degrees or to a change from 20 to 30 degrees. But what the interval scale does not permit us to do is to say that 20 degrees is twice as hot (or half as cold) as 10 degrees or that 30 degrees is three times as hot as 10 degrees. To be able to compare amounts in this way, we need to measure characteristics that conform to a **ratio scale**. A ratio scale has a true (rather than an arbitrary) zero. In a temperature scale, for example, the zero is completely arbitrary. It could have been set at any temperature—and is, in fact, set at different points on the Fahrenheit and the Celsius scales. Weight, age, and height, on the other hand, have exact, nonarbitrary zeros. And six feet *is* twice the length of three feet.

Most of our measurement in psychology and education makes use of interval scales, although most of what we measure doesn't really fit this scale; that is, we assume that the difference between 60 and 70 percent on our tests is roughly equivalent to the difference between 40 and 50 percent. The emphasis should be on the word *roughly*. In most instances, we have little evidence to support this assumption of equivalency.

Although most measurement in education uses an interval scale, virtually none of it is direct; that is, no instruments have yet been devised that measure knowledge (or intelligence) directly, as a ruler measures length or a scale measures weight. Measurement in education is like estimating temperature: The measure is inferred from the observation that a column of mercury or alcohol rises or descends in a hollow glass tube; achievement is inferred from changes in behavior. Knowledge is not directly measurable, but we assume that some of its effects on behavior are.

MEASUREMENT AND EDUCATIONAL GOALS

The relationship between measurement in schools and educational goals is simple: Goals are what tell the teacher not only what to teach but also which behaviors need to be evaluated. We cannot assess the effectiveness of our instructional procedures unless we know what they are intended to accomplish, and we cannot determine what they have accomplished without assessment.

A comprehensive theory of instruction, argue Glaser and Bassok (1989), must pay attention to at least three important aspects of the teaching/learning process: (1) describing the desired outcomes of the learning process—the knowledge and skills that learners are to acquire, (2) analyzing the pre-instruction state of the learner's knowledge and skills, and (3) suggesting the means by which the learner can be guided to make the transition from the pre-instruction state to the desired outcomes of instruction.

As we saw in Chapter 1, the desired outcomes or objectives of education can be expressed in broad terms such as "The goal of education is to develop decent, worthwhile citizens" or "The goal of education is to empower students." Among broad educational goals recently advanced by a president of the United States is the following statement:

> By the year 2000, American students will leave grades four, eight, and twelve having demonstrated competency in challenging subject matter including English, mathematics, science, history, and geography; and every school in America will ensure that all students learn to use their minds well, so that they may be prepared for responsible citizenship, further learning, and productive employment in our modern economy. (George Bush, cited in R. Walker, 1990, p. 16)

Although general statements of objectives such as these are useful in guiding the development of curriculum and in influencing the behavior of administrators and students, they are not nearly so useful in the day-to-day business of teaching as are more specific instructional objectives.

INSTRUCTIONAL OBJECTIVES

Instructional objectives are statements about the type of performance that can be expected of students once they have completed a lesson, a unit, or a course. Note that objectives do not describe the course itself but instead describe the intended performance of students. Because performance implies behavior, the phrase "behavioral objectives" is sometimes used interchangeably with "instructional objectives."

Instructional Objectives and Teachers' Accountability

In recent years a renewed emphasis on the use of instructional objectives in schools has become apparent. This emphasis stems not only from the recognition of their importance in teaching but also from a growing concern with what is called "teacher accountability." The phrase implies that teachers should in some way be held accountable for their performance in the classroom—accountable perhaps to students, perhaps to parents, but most certainly to the administrative authorities who hire and fire them.

Evaluating Teachers' Competence. Unfortunately (or perhaps fortunately), there is no easy way to assess a teacher's performance. But there have been many attempts to assess teachers' basic competence (see Millman & Darling-Hammond, 1990). For example, in 1986 some 210,000 teachers in Texas were administered a specially developed test of basic communication skills (Texas Examination of Current Administrators and

Teachers, or TECAT). The test was designed to identify teachers whose basic literacy was so poor that they could not justifiably be classed as anything but incompetent. Shepard and Kreitzer (1987) report that following a massive preparatory program involving workshops, review courses, and study books, almost 97 percent of the teachers passed the test on the first administration and 99 percent had passed after a second examination. But 1,950 educators who were unable to pass the test lost their jobs; this number represents fewer than 1 percent of all teachers who took the test. (Interestingly, some 8,000 teachers and administrators did not take the test but still retained their positions.) Of the 1,950 individuals who failed the test, 887 had held academic positions (principals, superintendents, and teachers of academic subjects) and 1,063 had held nonacademic positions (including teachers of physical education, industrial arts, music, art, English as a second language, and health, as well as school counselors).

Shepard and Kreitzer (1987) estimate the total cost of test development, teachers' preparation, and test administration and scoring at more than $35 million. Among the unexpected effects of this testing program was significant demoralization of teachers, many of whom objected to the implicit questioning of their competence and the largely negative portrayal of teachers' competence widely disseminated by the media. Furthermore, the questionable validity of the test and the fact that considerable effort and expense were devoted to remediation before teachers took the test detract considerably from its usefulness. It is perhaps revealing that such massive screenings of teachers' competence are extremely rare. Part of the problem, notes Reynolds (1992) is that we don't know very clearly what competent teaching is or what the differences are between highly competent and less competent teachers.

Although it is easy to understand the administration's and the public's wish to monitor teachers' behavior and its effects more closely, it is also easy to understand why a large number of teachers are reluctant to conform to increasing demands for manifested competence. Some subjects are more difficult than others to teach and to learn; some students learn more slowly or more rapidly; some teachers are better than other teachers at their profession.

One way to increase and monitor teachers' responsiveness to parental and administrative expectations is through the widespread requirement that teachers specify instructional objectives for their courses. But this is not the most important reason for using instructional objectives; their contribution to good teaching and learning is even more important.

Mager's Instructional Objectives

To be useful, says Mager (1962), instructional objectives must specify clearly what the learner must be able to do following instruction. A useful instructional objective is a statement of the instructor's goals *in behavioral terms*—that is, worded in terms of the actual, observable performance of the student. This type of instructional objective serves as a description of course goals and as a guide for instructional strategy. Furthermore, it serves as a guide for assessing students' and teachers' performance.

Consider the following statements of instructional objectives:

1. The student should understand evolutionary theory.
2. The student should be able to state the two Darwinian laws of evolution and give examples of each.

Mager argues that the second objective is more useful than the first for several reasons. The second objective specifies exactly what students must do to demonstrate that they have reached the course goal, it provides the teacher with specific guidelines for determining whether course goals have been reached, and it suggests what must be taught if course goals are to be reached.

The first statement, because of its use of the ambiguous term *understand* and the global phrase "evolutionary theory," does none of these things. It is clearly open to misinterpretation. Similarly, terms such as *know, appreciate,* and *master* are rarely found in the kind of objectives Mager recommends unless the nature of knowing, appreciating, or mastering is also clearly spelled out. For example, the president's phrase "use the mind well," needs to be made more specific if it is to be useful. We need to know what is involved in "using the mind well."

A second quality of meaningful instructional objectives is that they often establish specific criteria of acceptable performance. Consider the following statements:

1. The learner will be able to translate a simple passage from French to English.
2. The learner will be able to translate a simple passage from French to English without use of a dictionary. The passage will be taken from the prescribed text, and the translation will be considered correct if there are no more than 5 errors for each 100 words of text and acceptable if the translation is completed in no more than 20 minutes for each 100 words.

The second statement is more precise than the first, and again it is more useful for both the instructor and the learner. It specifies the nature of the expected behavior and the constraints under which it is to be performed to be considered acceptable.

Writing good instructional objectives is a time-consuming task. However, carefully prepared objectives can be of tremendous assistance to teachers in planning instructional strategies and in evaluating both their own performance and that of their students. In addition, if statements of behavioral objectives are given to each student at the beginning of courses, units, or lessons, they can be of tremendous value to the learner. In Mager's words, "If you give each learner a copy of your objectives, you may not have to do much else" (1962, p. 53).

Other Views on Instructional Objectives

Not all educators agree that Mager's approach to instructional objectives is the best. A number argue that the use of behavioral objectives presents several definite disadvantages.

Eisner's Expressive Objectives. For example, Eisner (1967) suggests that strict adherence to behavioral objectives restricts the development of curriculum, discourages other important learning outcomes, and fails to recognize that attitudes are among the most important outcomes of instruction. Accordingly, he argues that a teacher's instructional objectives should include not only performance objectives of the kind described by Mager but also **expressive objectives**. Expressive objectives involve a conscious recognition by the teacher that the visible and measurable outcomes of a learning experience are not the only outcomes of that experience (and, in many cases, not always the most important). For example, a reading teacher should intend to teach reading (an outcome that can easily be expressed in terms of Mager's instructional objectives) and should try to instill positive attitudes toward reading (an outcome less easily expressed in Mager's terms).

Gronlund's General and Specific Objectives. Another viewpoint on instructional objectives, advanced by Gronlund (1972, 1975), is particularly relevant here. To begin with, Gronlund agrees that Mager's emphasis on precise, performance-oriented objectives is both appropriate and effective for simple skills and for content areas that can be described in terms of specific items of information. Such emphasis is considerably less appropriate, however, for more complex subjects and more advanced cognitive behaviors. For these, Gronlund (1972) suggests that teachers express primary objectives in general rather than specific terms. Each primary objective should then be elaborated in terms of more specific learning outcomes or, in many cases, in terms of examples of behaviors that would reflect the primary objective.

The president's admonition that schools should "ensure that all students learn to use their minds" is a highly general objective. However, the extent to which it has been accomplished (or is being accomplished) can be ascertained far more easily if we can describe specific examples of performances or products that illustrate "using the mind." There is an important difference between these examples of behaviors and Mager's instructional objectives. Mager's objectives specify actual behaviors that constitute instructional objectives in and of themselves. What Gronlund recommends, however, are not objectives per se but are instead examples of the type of evidence that a teacher can look for to determine whether the primary objective has been attained. This approach, as is shown in the examples that follow, may be used to describe expressive objectives as well. For instance, the primary objective might be the development of a certain attitude; specific behaviors would serve as evidence of attainment of that attitude. (Figure 13.2 summarizes the differences among these three viewpoints.)

Examples. To illustrate and clarify the preceding passage, consider the following objectives for a poetry unit. Objectives based on Mager's approach might include such statements as

1. The student should be able to name the titles and authors of five poems in the unit.
2. The student should be able to recite, with no more than three errors, ten consecutive lines from a single poem in the unit.

Eisner's expressive objectives might center on the desirability of having a student develop positive feelings for poetry and/or for specific poems and poets:

1. The student should develop an appreciation for the Romantic poets.

Finally, Gronlund's objectives might begin with an expressive objective such as the preceding one and then elaborate further with one or more of the following behavioral examples:

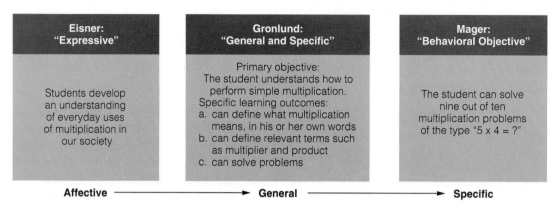

Eisner: "Expressive"	Gronlund: "General and Specific"	Mager: "Behavioral Objective"
Students develop an understanding of everyday uses of multiplication in our society	Primary objective: The student understands how to perform simple multiplication. Specific learning outcomes: a. can define what multiplication means, in his or her own words b. can define relevant terms such as multiplier and product c. can solve problems	The student can solve nine out of ten multiplication problems of the type "5 × 4 = ?"

Affective ⟶ General ⟶ Specific

FIGURE 13.2 Different types of instructional objectives.

2. The student chooses to read (or write) poetry during a free reading period.

3. The student attempts to evaluate poetry as being good or bad (or to compare different poems).

In summary, each of these three approaches to the formulation of instructional objectives has its advantages and disadvantages. Mager's approach emphasizes specificity and objective behaviors and is particularly useful for simple skills and factual content areas. Eisner's approach recognizes the importance of affective outcomes of instructional procedures. Gronlund's suggestions are useful for more complex subject areas and for higher-level intellectual processes and can also be used to formulate expressive objectives. There is clearly room for each in the conscientious teacher's repertoire.

Objectives and Teacher-Made Tests

Objectives are desired outcomes. School-related goals include both the specific instructional objectives of teachers and the wider objectives of curricula, programs, principals, and communities—things like "using the mind" and "being responsible citizens." Questions relating to the wider objectives of education have traditionally been in the domains of philosophy, politics, and economics rather than psychology, and such objectives are seldom evaluated directly in schools—although perhaps they should be. Most classroom evaluation has to do with a teacher's more specific objectives.

Bloom's Taxonomy. Bloom, Engelhart, Furst, Hill, and Krathwohl (1956) and Krathwohl, Bloom, and Masia (1964) have provided an exhaustive and useful list of cognitive and affective educational objectives. The usefulness of lists such as these (referred to as *taxonomies*) is that they can serve as guides in determining the goals for a lesson or course. The taxonomy of objectives for the cognitive domain, for example, describes a class of objectives, a list of educational objectives that correspond to this class, and test questions that illustrate it (see Table 13.2). The six hierarchical classes of objectives in that domain are, from the lowest to the highest level: **knowledge**, **comprehension**, **application**, **analysis**, **synthesis**, and **evaluation**. Each of these is broken down into subdivisions. You are referred to the handbook of objectives (Bloom, Engelhart, Furst, Hill, & Krathwohl, 1956) for a detailed consideration of Bloom's taxonomy of educational objectives.

In an earlier section we noted the importance of what teachers test—how what they test determines what and how students learn. We noted also that schools tend to evaluate students

TABLE 13.2 Bloom's Cognitive Domain, Defined and Illustrated

CLASS OF OBJECTIVES	EXAMPLE
1. Knowledge (items of factual information)	Who wrote *A Midsummer Night's Dream*?
2. Comprehension (understanding; obtaining meaning from communication)	What was the author trying to say?
3. Application (using information, principles, and the like to solve problems)	Given what you know about the authenticity of the first quarto and about weather conditions in England in the summer of 1594, when do you think the play was written?
4. Analysis (arriving at an understanding by looking at individual parts)	Find the most basic metaphors in Act 1 and explain their meaning.
5. Synthesis (arriving at an understanding by looking at the larger structure or by combining individual elements)	Identify the four themes in *A Midsummer Night's Dream*, and discuss how they contribute to the central action.
6. Evaluation (arriving at value judgments)	Do you agree with the statement that *A Midsummer Night's Dream* is Shakespeare's first undisputed masterpiece? Explain your answer.

on the basis of how many textbook- and teacher-presented facts they remember rather than on the basis of how much they understand, how cleverly they generalize and extrapolate, or how elegantly they formulate hypotheses and generate new concepts. Research on Bloom's taxonomy corroborates this unhappy finding. Fleming and Chambers (1983) analyzed more than 8,800 questions used primarily in high school tests. Nearly 80 percent dealt only with knowledge of facts and specifics—the lowest level in Bloom's taxonomy (see the box entitled "Remembering and Thinking").

Blueprints for Teacher-Made Tests

We should emphasize at the outset that a test—whether it is a teacher-made test or a standardized test—is not like other common measuring instruments, such as rulers, scales, and thermometers. Rulers measure whatever they measure directly; our psychological and educational instruments

measure indirectly. In effect, a student's test performance consists of a sample of behaviors (selected from a large number of potential behaviors) that (we assume) represents some knowledge, ability, or attitude that we use as the basis for making inferences. The inferences we make about knowledge, ability, or other student characteristics are never based on direct measurement; they are simply inferences—educated bits of speculation based on nothing more than a sample of behavior. Hence, the question of precisely which behaviors to sample is important.

As you probably know, the business of preparing tests, exams, and quizzes is frequently a pretty haphazard process. Teachers, who have a general idea of the sorts of things they want their students to learn, sit down near the end of the unit or term and fashion a compilation of questions that they hope will measure reasonably accurately some of the things they intended to teach. Some teachers are better than others at putting together appropriate questions. Many,

however, might be helped considerably by learning more clearly the characteristics of good and bad test items (discussed later in this chapter) and by systematically attempting to blueprint their tests even before they begin to teach the relevant series of lessons.

A **test blueprint** is, in effect, a table of specifications for a test. It specifies the topics to be tested, the nature of the questions to be used, how many questions will relate to each topic, and the sorts of cognitive processes to be sampled. Test blueprints need not be developed only by the teacher; they can also involve the collaboration of students. Constructing the blueprint can do a great deal to clarify instructional goals, both for the teacher and for students. It can also contribute in important ways to the teacher's selection of instructional strategies and to the students' monitoring of their own learning processes.

Detailed test blueprints that take into consideration differences among possible learning outcomes can be based on systems such as Bloom's taxonomy. A typical test blueprint based on portions of this taxonomy takes the form of a table that lists all relevant topics down the side and all relevant domains across the top and that specifies the number of items for each topic relating to each domain (see Table 13.3). However, most teachers and students might find it considerably easier and more useful to use a classification that differentiates among learning outcomes that students can define and understand more easily. Popham (1981) suggests, for example, that items be divided simply in terms of whether they involve recall or go beyond recall.

There are a number of other ways to devise test blueprints, some of which are easier and more useful in certain subjects. In physical education classes, for example, in which Bloom's taxonomy and other similar classifications are not highly relevant, teachers might simply make a list of the skills that students are expected to acquire. This

TABLE 13.3 A Simple Test Blueprint, Based on Bloom's Taxonomy, Cognitive Domain, for Chapter 6 of This Text

CHAPTER 6 TOPICS	NUMBER OF ITEMS BY DOMAIN						
	KNOWLEDGE	COMPREHENSION	APPLICATION	ANALYSIS	SYNTHESIS	EVALUATION	
Cognition	4	3	3	2	3	1	
Bruner's theory	3	4	3	2	2	1	
Ausubel's theory	3	3	2	2	2	1	
Instruction	4	3	3	2	2	3	
Totals	14	13	11	8	9	6	61

list of skills, together with an indication of the criteria that will be used as evidence of skill mastery, serves as a test blueprint. Unfortunately, this kind of test blueprint in physical education classes is rare. Most often, teachers rely on informal, intuitive evaluation. And although there is clearly a need for such evaluation, it is seldom as impartial as more formal evaluation. Nor does it serve nearly as well as a guide to instruction.

CHARACTERISTICS OF A GOOD MEASURING INSTRUMENT

Probably the most important characteristic of a good test from the students' point of view is that it be *fair*. Essentially, this means that the test should reflect instructional objectives *as they are understood by students*—that is, it should reflect what was to be learned (and, presumably, taught).

From a measurement point of view, good measuring instruments have two important qualities: *validity* and *reliability*.

Validity

A test is valid if it measures what it is intended to measure; many tests don't, or they measure many other things as well and are consequently not very dependable. **Validity** is the most important characteristic of a measuring instrument. If a test does not measure what it purports to, the scores derived from it are of no value whatsoever.

Face Validity. There are several different ways to measure or estimate validity—several indexes of validity (see Figure 13.3). The first, **face validity**, is the extent to which the test *appears* to measure what it is supposed to measure. This is probably the easiest type of validity to determine; if a test *looks* valid, it at least has face validity. Face validity is especially important for teacher-made tests; students should know just by looking at a test that they are being tested on the appropriate things. A mathematics test that has face validity will consist of items that look like mathematics items.

In some circumstances, however, test makers carefully avoid any semblance of face validity. Tests designed to measure personality characteristics such as honesty or openness, for example, are likely to be highly invalid if they appear to measure what they are actually intended to measure. Because we know that dishonest people might well lie to us, we are not likely to obtain an accurate measure of their honesty if we let them know that that is what we are interested in. Better to deceive them, lie to them, to determine what liars and scoundrels they really are.

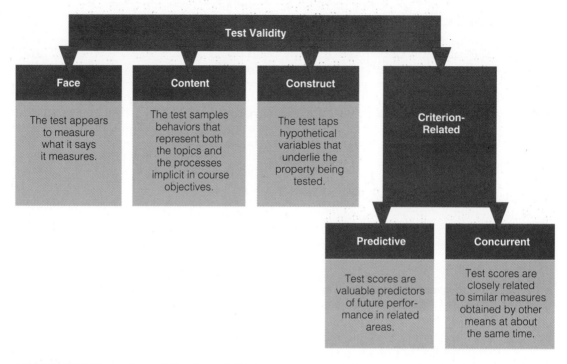

FIGURE 13.3 Types of test validity: determining that a test measures what it purports to measure.

Content Validity. A second important index of the extent to which a test measures what it purports to measure, **content validity**, is assessed by analyzing the content of test items in relation to the objectives of the course, unit, or lesson. Content validity is perhaps the most crucial kind of validity for measurements of school achievement. A test with high content validity includes items that sample all important course objectives (both content [product] and process objectives) in proportion to their importance. Thus if some of the objectives of an instructional sequence are the development of cognitive processes, a relevant test will have content validity to the extent that it samples these processes. And if 40 percent of the course content (and, consequently, of the course objectives) deals with knowledge (rather than with comprehension, analysis, and so on), 40 percent of the test items should assess knowledge.

Determining the content validity of a test is largely a matter of careful, logical analysis. One main advantage of preparing a test blueprint of the kind described earlier is that it ensures content validity.

Note that tests and test items do not possess validity as a sort of intrinsic quality; that is, a test is not generally valid or generally invalid. Rather, it is valid for certain purposes and with certain individuals and invalid for others. For example, if the following item is intended to measure comprehension, it does not have content validity:

How many different kinds of validity are discussed in this chapter?

a. 1

b. 2

c. 3

d. 5

e. 10

remembering and thinking

The six classes of objectives described by Bloom and associates (1956) fall into two broad classes: those that involve remembering and those that require thinking. Only the knowledge objectives fall into the first category (knowledge of specifics, knowledge of ways and means of dealing with specifics, and knowledge of the universals and abstractions in a field). All these objectives emphasize *remembering*.

Most teachers want to teach for understanding (comprehension, application, and so on) as well as for recall. Yet few know clearly the precise skills involved in intellectual activities such as comprehension, application, synthesis, analysis, or evaluation. The two most frequently confused skills are comprehension and application.

Comprehension is the lowest level of understanding, implying no more than the ability to apprehend the substance of what is being communicated without necessarily relating it to other material. It can be tested through items that require the students to translate (change from one form of communication to another, express in their own words), interpret (explain or summarize), or extrapolate (predict consequences or arrive at conclusions).

Application, on the other hand, requires that learners be able to use what they comprehend—that they abstract from one situation to another. Application cannot be tested simply by asking that students interpret or translate; they must also be required to abstract the material to see its implications.

Two final points should be made. The first is a simple appeal: Familiarize yourself with this taxonomy because of its implications both for teaching and for testing. The second is a reiteration of an obvious point: Your instructional objectives (what you want of your students) are communicated directly and effectively to your students through your measurement devices. Even if you emphasize repeatedly that you want to teach for comprehension and other high-level skills, you will probably not be successful unless you construct achievement tests that reflect these objectives. In the final analysis, your students will study what you test.

If, on the other hand, the item were intended to measure knowledge of specifics, it would have content validity. And an item such as the following might have content validity with respect to measuring comprehension:

Explain why face validity is important for teacher-constructed tests.

Note, however, that this last item measures comprehension only if students have not been explicitly taught an appropriate answer; that is, it is possible to teach principles, applications, analyses, and so on as *specifics*, so that questions of this sort require no more than recall of knowledge. What an item measures is not inherent in the item itself so much as in the relationship between the material as it has been taught to the student and what the item requires.

Construct Validity. A third type, **construct validity**, is conceptually more difficult than either face or content validity. It is somewhat less relevant for teacher-constructed tests but highly relevant for many other psychological measures (personality and intelligence tests, for example). In essence, a construct is a hypothetical variable—an unobservable characteristic or quality, often inferred from theory. For example, a theory might specify that individuals who are highly intelligent should be reflective rather than impulsive. One way to determine the construct validity of a test designed to measure intelligence would then be to look at how well it correlates with measures of reflection and impulsivity. (See Chapter 7 for a discussion of correlation.)

Criterion-Related Validity. One principal use of tests is to predict future performance. Thus, we assume that all students who do well on year-end fifth-grade achievement tests will do reasonably well in sixth grade. We also predict that those who perform poorly on these tests will not do well in sixth grade, and we might use this prediction as justification for having them fail fifth grade. The extent to which our predictions are accurate reflects **criterion-related validity**. One component of this form of validity, just described, is labeled **predictive validity** and is easily measured by looking at the relationship between performance on a test and subsequent performance. Thus, a college entrance examination designed to identify students whose chances of college success are high has predictive validity to the extent that its predictions are borne out.

Concurrent validity, a second aspect of criterion-related validity, is the relationship between a test and other measures of the same behaviors. For example, the most accurate way to measure intelligence is to administer a time-consuming and expensive individual test; a second way is to administer a quick, inexpensive group test; a third, far less consistent approach, is to have teachers informally assess intelligence on the basis of what they know of their students' achievement and effort. Teachers' assessments are said to have concurrent validity to the extent that they correlate with the more formal measures. In the same way, the group test is said to have concurrent validity if it agrees well with measures obtained in other ways.

A Changing Conception of Validity. Tests have a profound influence not only on those who take them but on the entire educational system. Maguire (1992) shows how departmental exams that are common to an entire school system influence how teachers teach. And Wolf, Bixby, Glenn, and Gardner make the point that current testing practices in schools are "exercises in detection and selection rather than generation" (1991, p. 32). As such, they foster a narrow, predictable, memory-based approach to teaching and learning. These authors argue that teachers need new forms of assessment that "permit the assessment of thinking rather than simply the possession of information" (p. 33).

Recognition of the influence of assessment on learning and teaching suggests a new way of looking at validity, says Moss (1992). This view of the validity of assessment takes into consideration the effects of tests on learning. For example, if one of the purposes of testing is to foster thinking, we have to look at the extent to which our tests succeed in promoting thinking in order to determine their validity.

The development of some approaches to assessment that emphasize students' performance (portfolios, for example) is one manifestation of this new view of validity. Some of these approaches are described later in this chapter.

Reliability

A good measuring instrument must not only be valid; it must also be *reliable*. This means that the test should measure whatever it measures consistently. An intelligence test that yields a score of 170 for a student one week and a score of 80 the next week is probably somewhat unreliable (unless something has happened to the student during the week).

Types of Reliability. An instrument that is highly unreliable cannot be valid. Put another way, if a test measures what it purports to, and if what it measures does not fluctuate unpredictably, the test will yield similar scores on different occasions. Hence, one way to assess **reliability** is to correlate results obtained by giving the test twice or by giving two different forms of the same test. This is called **repeated-measures reliability** or **parallel-forms reliability**.

Another way to determine reliability, called **split-half reliability** or **equivalence reliability**, is to divide the test into halves and correlate the scores obtained on each half (Wiersma & Jurs, 1985). If all items are intended to measure the same things, the scores on the halves should be similar.

Factors That Affect Reliability. One factor that contributes to the reliability of a test is the stability of what is being measured. Clearly, if a characteristic fluctuates dramatically over time, measurements of the characteristic will also fluctuate. However, most of what we measure in psychology and education is not expected to fluctuate unpredictably; that is, although we expect change in many characteristics, we can often predict the nature of the change. Students are expected to read better, understand more clearly, solve more problems, and generally improve cognitively throughout the course of their schooling. Tests that are valid and reliable should reflect these changes.

A second important factor, particularly with respect to teacher-constructed, multiple-choice, or true-false tests, is chance. As an example, consider a test consisting of twenty true-false items. The chance of getting any single item correct, if the student knows next to absolutely nothing, is one out of two. Hence, unless Lady Luck is looking pointedly in the other direction, the average score of a large class of hypothetical know-nothings should be about 50 percent. And some of the luckier individuals in this class may have astoundingly high scores. But a subsequent administration of this or of a parallel examination might lead to startlingly different results.

One way to increase test reliability is obvious: Make tests longer. Of course, this does not mean that all short objective tests must be avoided. In the long run, the effects of chance tend to even out; one hundred short tests, taken all together, make up one long, sometimes highly reliable test. The most important admonition is simply that the teacher should not place undue confidence in the results of only a handful of short tests in which the effects of chance cannot easily be controlled.

Although a test cannot be valid without also being reliable, it can be highly reliable without being valid. Consider the following intelligence test:

Lefrançois' Dumb Scale of Intelligence

Instructions
Join the dot to the square with four separate, parallel, but orthogonal lines.*

Scoring
Minimum score: 100

Add 50 for half a correct answer (i.e., two lines) _____

Add 25 for another half _____

Total (maximum 175) _____

Interpretation
If you scored:

100—you are very bright

150—you are a genius

175—you are God

This intelligence test has been demonstrated to be extremely reliable (as well as extremely democratic). In other words, it is extremely consistent: Testees obtain the same scores repeatedly. Bright people usually score 100; geniuses, 150; and God, 175. Unfortunately, however, it is desperately invalid.

*PPC: I don't think that's possible.
Author: You score 100. Bravo!

STANDARDIZED TESTS

A test is a collection of tasks (items or questions) assumed to be a representative sample of the behaviors that the tester wishes to assess. Given that human beings vary in countless ways, there are countless types of tests and countless examples of each type. A few examples of some psychological tests (creativity and intelligence) were given in Chapter 7. These tests are referred to as **standardized tests**. They are so called because they provide standards (also called "norms") by which to judge the performance of individual students. Thus, intelligence tests are typically standardized in such a way that average performance is reflected in a score close to 100. In addition, the norms for intelligence tests tell us what distribution of scores we might expect for a large group.

A large collection of tests that are particularly important for classroom teachers is standardized achievement tests. These professionally developed tests are available for virtually every school subject and are designed to provide teachers, school administrators, and parents with information about the relative performance of individual students, classes, or schools. The indication of relative performance typically is derived by comparing the students' test results to the norms provided with the test. Hence, almost all standardized tests include the testing material itself and a manual that specifies the objectives of the test (what it is designed to measure), the age and grade levels for which it is appropriate, the samples on which it was standardized, and tables for converting the students' raw scores to scores that can be compared directly with the test norms.

Many school jurisdictions make routine use of achievement tests. One study reports that students between first and fifth grades can expect to take an average of one and one-half standardized achievement tests a year (Levin, 1983). Unfortunately, teachers don't often use the results of these tests to modify their instructional procedures, although they might use them to make decisions about students' placement.

Minimum Competency Testing

An ongoing controversy concerns the use of standardized tests in schools. On the one hand, many educators feel that the tests are unfair, biased, unreliable, and often invalid—that they are excellent examples of "science and technology run amok" (Wigdor & Garner, 1982). On the other hand, many argue that in spite of their weaknesses, tests are more likely to be valid, reliable, objective, and fair than are other forms of evidence upon which teachers and educators base their judgments.

During the middle decades of this century, it seemed that the antitesting movement might become dominant. Increasing numbers of school jurisdictions began to abandon the use of standardized tests; their use seemed incompatible with the cry for equity (R. L. Linn, 1986). But the pendulum now seems to have swung in the opposite direction once more. One important reason for this most recent swing was the publication of the report *A Nation at Risk* (National Commission on Excellence in Education, 1983). Among other things, the report put forth a cry for excellence rather than simply for equity and raised the frightening possibility that American schoolchildren might be seriously deficient in basic reading, writing, and arithmetic skills. The report lent support to the concept of **minimum competency testing**, a general term for batteries of tests, often administered statewide, to determine whether students have achieved some minimum standard of competency.

Some Objections. Minimum competency tests have been legally challenged on the grounds that they are unfair and discriminatory; however, challenges have typically been unsuccessful (Perkins, 1982).

Some object to the wide-scale use of standardized tests for other reasons. First, as Haladyna, Nolen, and Haas (1991) point out, raising educational achievement is equated too often with raising test scores. M. L. Smith's interviews of teachers indicate that when the results of standardized tests are made public, teachers often experience "feelings of shame, embarrassment, guilt, and anger" (1991, p. 9). As a result, it is not uncommon for teachers to prepare their students specifically to write a given test—a practice that can seriously change the validity of the test. Furthermore, note Nolen, Haladyna, and Haas (1992), while teaching to a test might improve students' marks, it does not actually raise achievement. In fact, it typically encourages memorization of specifics rather than the growth of understanding and thinking.

Sternberg (1992) suggests that standardized tests have changed little since their appearance early in this century—except that they are a little easier to administer, a little more reliable, perhaps more attractively packaged. But they still measure pretty much the same things they've always measured: basic memory and some analytical abilities. We need alternatives, he claims, that also measure the more creative and pragmatic facets of intelligence and that begin to tap how people think and learn.

One other objection to standardized competency testing, claim Paris, Lawton, Turner, and Roth (1991), is that it may have a progressively more negative effect on students. In their surveys of large numbers of students, they found that many of them, especially the lower achievers, became increasingly more anxious about tests. As a result, some cheated, and some simply stopped trying.

Uses of Standardized Tests

There are, nevertheless, at least five distinct and important uses for standardized tests in schools (R. L. Linn, 1986). The first is placement in special education programs. As we saw in Chapter 7, intelligence tests are widely used for this purpose. However, legal challenges of their fairness have often been successful, especially when it could be shown that a test was biased toward a certain group. These legal challenges have resulted in the modification of some tests to reduce their biases, the translation of tests into different languages, and the use of a variety of assessment procedures in addition to intelligence tests. Recall that Public Law 94-142 mandates each of these changes.

A second use of standardized tests is to certify students' achievement. Minimum competency tests are a clear example of this use, as are the variety of standardized entrance examinations used to decide whether to accept an applicant for a course of studies and final examinations used to determine success or failure after a course of studies.

In addition to these two principal uses, standardized tests are being used in some jurisdictions to determine the competency of teachers, to evaluate schools (through the performance of students), and for instructional diagnosis.

Test Norms

To use and interpret standardized tests, it is important to know about the types of scores and norms that are used with them.

Grade-Equivalent Norms. Among the various norms that are sometimes provided with standardized tests, **grade-equivalent scores** are the most common. Such norms allow teachers to convert a raw score on a test to a grade equivalent. For example, students who take a standardized reading test will typically have their scores expressed as a grade level: 3, 3.5, 5, and so on.

Several cautions are in order when interpreting grade-equivalent scores. First—and this applies to all standardized tests—it is extremely important to make sure that the test is suitable for the children and that the norms are appropriate. In the same way that intelligence tests are often biased against groups on whom they were not normed, so too achievement tests are often biased against students whose school curriculum is different from that of the norming population or whose social, language, and ethnic backgrounds are different.

Once you have determined that an achievement test is suitable and that grade-equivalent scores are therefore meaningful, it is important to know precisely what their meaning is. A grade-equivalent reading score of 5 obtained by a fourth-grade student does not mean that the student should be in fifth grade. In fact, the raw test score (*raw* means the actual, untransformed score on the test) that corresponds to this grade-equivalent score is simply the average score of a large number of fifth-grade students. A few fifth-grade students will have scored much higher or much lower. Similarly, many fourth-grade students in the norming group will have raw scores as high as some of the fifth-grade pupils. Hence, an achievement test does not separate cleanly among different grade levels—it does not give us an absolutely accurate index of what grade level a student should be. Furthermore, achievement tests given at different times of the year can produce markedly different results. H. W. Bernard (1966) reports, for example, that those administered immediately after summer vacation often average a full half-grade lower than scores obtained the previous June.

Age-Equivalent Norms. Although most achievement tests designed for use in schools provide grade-equivalent scores, many also provide one or more of a variety of other types of norms, including age equivalents (and others, such as Z-scores, T-scores, percentiles, and stanines, explained in the box entitled "Norms and the Normal Distribution"). **Age-equivalent scores**, as the label implies, are norms expressed in terms of ages rather than grades. Such norms make provisions for converting raw scores to age equivalents that can be interpreted as meaning that a student is functioning at a level comparable to the average for a specific age group. Age-equivalent scores are more common for intelligence tests and other measures of ability or aptitude than they are for achievement tests. This is largely because it is more meaningful to say that a person is intellectually at the level of a four-year-old or a nine-year-old than to say that someone reads at a four-year-old or a nine-year-old level. When interpreting age-equivalent scores, observe the same cautions as when interpreting grade-equivalent scores. The most important caution is that these scores represent averages; hence, there is a wide range of scores within most groups. In addition, because standardized tests are far from completely valid or completely reliable, we should be careful not to rely on them too heavily.

TEACHER-MADE TESTS

A majority of the tests used in the classroom are made by classroom teachers, and some of these tests are highly representative of course objectives, are at an appropriate level of difficulty, and are used in reasonable and wise ways. Other tests are less well made.

Teacher-made tests can be used for a variety of purposes, only one of which is the assigning of grades. Other than this, a test can be used to determine whether students are ready to begin a unit of instruction, to indicate to the teacher how effective instructional procedures are, to identify learning difficulties, to determine what students know and what they don't know, to predict their probability of success on future learning tasks, to motivate students to learn, and as a learning experience.

Teacher-made tests are usually of the paper-and-pencil variety, although sometimes a sample of nonverbal behavior might be used for assessment. For example, in physical education, in art, in drama, and in some workshop courses, students are sometimes asked either to produce something or to perform. Increasingly, performance-based assessment may also be required in other subjects such as mathematics, where teachers are interested in examining the processes by which students arrive at answers rather than simply the products. That is, examiners may pay increasing attention to what have been labeled "educational quality indicators" (more about this approach later in this chapter).

At present, the dominant form of classroom assessment continues to be teacher-made, written tests that are typically objective, essay, or both. An essay test requires a written response of some length for each question. Objective tests, however, normally require little writing, and the scoring procedure is highly uniform (hence, objective).

Objective Tests

The four major types of objective test items are completion, matching, true-false, and multiple choice. Examples of each are given in Figure 13.4.

Essay Versus Objective Tests

Objective tests of the kind just described and the more subjective essay tests can be used to measure almost any significant aspect of students' behavior. However, some course objectives are more easily assessed with one type of test than with the other. Several of the major differences between essay and objective tests are given here. These differences can serve as a guide in deciding which to use in a given situation. Often, a mixture of both can be used to advantage (See box entitled, "To Be Objective or Subjective"):

- It is easier to tap higher-level processes (analysis, synthesis, and evaluation) with an essay examination, although it is possible to do the same thing with objective items. Essay examinations can be constructed to allow students to organize knowledge, to make inferences from it, to illustrate it, to apply it, and to extrapolate from it.

- The content of essay examinations is often more limited than the content of the more objective tests. Because essay exams usually consist of fewer items, the range of abilities or of information sampled may be reduced. The objective question format, in contrast, permits coverage of more content per unit of testing time.

- Essay examinations allow for more divergence. Students who do not like to be restricted in their answers often prefer essays over more objective tests.

1. *Completion*
   Test blueprints are often based on _____ taxonomy. Predictive and concurrent validity are two types of _____ validity

2. *Matching*
   _____ Z-scores 1. mean = 50; standard deviation = 10
   _____ T-scores 2. mean = 0; standard deviation = 1
   _____ stanine   3. mean = 5; standard deviation = 2

3. *True-False*
   a. A good achievement test should result in a grade-equivalent score of between 4 and 5 for an average fourth-grade class.
   b. Content validity can be determined by making a careful, logical analysis of the relationship of test items to course objectives.

4. *Multiple choice*
   The extent to which a test appears to measure what it is intended to measure defines:
   a. content validity
   b. face validity
   c. construct validity
   d. test reliability
   e. criterion-related validity

FIGURE 13.4 The four major types of objective test items.

- Constructing an essay test is considerably easier and less time consuming than making up an objective examination. In fact, an entire test with an essay format can often be written in the same time it would take to write no more than two or three good multiple-choice items.

- Scoring essay examinations usually requires much more time than scoring objective tests.

The question is purely rhetorical. Not only does it have no answer, but it deserves none. Very few teachers will ever find themselves in situations in which they must always use either one form of test or the other. Some class situations, particularly those in which size is a factor, may lend themselves more readily to objective test formats; in other situations, essay formats may be better; sometimes a combination of both may be desirable. The important point is that each has advantages and disadvantages. A good teacher should endeavor to develop the skills necessary for constructing the best items possible in a variety of formats without becoming a passionate advocate of one over the other.

The good teacher also needs to keep in mind that there are alternatives to assessment other than the usual objective or essay tests, or standardized tests. Many of these are assessments of students' performances rather than simply products. They might involve keeping portfolios of students' work, writing anecdotal records, or looking for other evidence of the *quality* of students' learning and thinking.

This is especially true when tests can be scored electronically (as objective tests are in most universities and in an increasing number of schools). The total time involved in making and scoring a test is less for essay examinations than for objective tests if classes are small (twenty students or fewer, perhaps) but is considerably less for objective tests than for essay tests as the number of students increases (see Figure 13.5).

- The reliability of essay examinations is much lower than that of objective tests, primarily because of the subjectivity involved in their scoring. In one study, 300 essays were rated by 53 judges on a 9-point scale (Educational Testing Service, 1961). Slightly more than one-third of the papers received all grades possible; that is, each of these papers received the highest possible grade from at least one judge, the lowest possible grade from at least one other, and every other possible grade from at least one judge. Another 37 percent of the papers each received 8 of the 9 different grades; 23 percent received 7 of the 9.

Other studies have found that a relatively poor paper that is read after an even poorer one will tend to be given a higher grade than if it is read after a good paper, that some graders consistently give moderate marks whereas others give extremely high and low marks, although the average grades given by each might be similar; that knowledge of who wrote the paper tends to affect scores, sometimes beneficially and sometimes to the student's detriment; and that if the first few answers on an essay examination are particularly good, overall marks tend to be higher than if the first answers are poor.

There are a number of methods for increasing the scorer's reliability for essay examinations, not the least of which is simply being aware of possible sources of unreliability. Some of the suggestions given in the box entitled "Norms and the Normal Distribution" may be of value in this regard.

Suggestions for Constructing Tests

The advantages of a particular type of test can often be increased if its items are constructed carefully. By the same token, the disadvantages can also be made more severe through faulty item construction. Essay examinations, for example, are said to be better for measuring "higher" processes. Consider the following item:

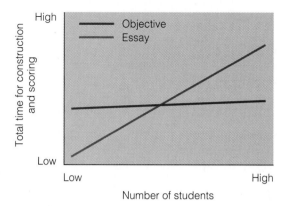

High

Total time for construction and scoring

Low

Low — Number of students — High

Objective
Essay

FIGURE 13.5 The relationship between class size and total time required for test construction and scoring for two types of test.

List the kinds of validity discussed in this chapter.

If the tester's intention is to sample analysis, synthesis, or evaluation, this item has no advantage over many objective items. However, an item such as the following might have an advantage:

Discuss similarities and differences among three of the different types of validity discussed in this chapter.

Several specific suggestions follow for the construction of essay tests and of multiple-choice tests, the most preferred among objective-item forms.

Essay Tests. The following suggestions are based in part on Gronlund (1968):

1. Essay questions should be geared toward sampling processes not easily assessed by objective items (for example, analysis, synthesis, or evaluation).

2. As for all tests, essay questions should relate directly to the desired outcomes of the learning procedure. This should be clearly understood by the students as well.

3. Questions should be specific if they are to be scored easily. If the intention is to give marks

for illustrations, the item should specify that an illustration is required.

4. A judicious sampling of desired behavior should make up the substance of the items.

5. If the examiner's intention is to sample high-level processes, sufficient time should be allowed for students to complete the questions.

6. The weighting of various questions, as well as the time that should be allotted to each, should be specified for the student.

7. The questions should be worded so that the teacher's expectations are clear to both the student and the teacher.

There are ways to make the scoring more objective as well. One is to outline model answers before scoring the test (that is, write out an answer that would receive full points). Another is to score all answers for one item before going on to the next. The purpose of this is to increase uniformity of scoring. A third suggestion is simply that the scorer should intend to be objective. For example, if poor grammar in a language-arts test results in the loss of five points on one paper, grammar that is half as bad on another paper should result in the loss of two and a half points.

Multiple-Choice Items. A multiple-choice item consists of a statement or series of statements (called the "stem") and three to five alternatives, only one of which is the correct or best solution. The other alternatives are referred to as *distractors*. Each of the distractors is a response that should appear plausible if students do not know the answer. If students do know the correct answer, distractors should, of course, appear less plausible. Listed here are a number of suggestions for writing multiple-choice items. Most are common sense (which makes them no less valid):

• Both stems and alternatives should be clearly worded, unambiguous, grammatically correct, specific, and at the appropriate level of difficulty. In addition, stems should be clearly meaningful by themselves.

norms and the normal distribution

If you were to throw 100 coins onto a table 1,000 times and record the number of heads and tails that came up each of the 1,000 times, a figure representing your tallies would probably look very much like the one in this box (in which the "0" represents 50 heads and 50 tails and the scale on either side represents an increasing proportion of heads or tails).

The figure shows a **normal curve**—a mathematical

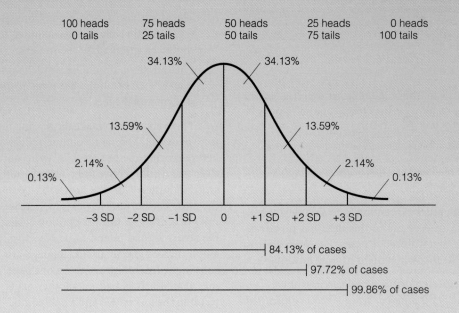

| 100 heads | 75 heads | 50 heads | 25 heads | 0 heads |
| 0 tails | 25 tails | 50 tails | 75 tails | 100 tails |

34.13%   34.13%

13.59%   13.59%

2.14%   2.14%

0.13%   0.13%

−3 SD −2 SD −1 SD 0 +1 SD +2 SD +3 SD

84.13% of cases

97.72% of cases

99.86% of cases

abstraction to which the majority of the observations that concern us in the social sciences and in education conform. When we know that a set of observations, such as test scores, is distributed normally, we also know what a graphic representation of these scores would look like if we had enough of them. We know that most of the scores would cluster around the **mean** (arithmetic average) and that there would be fewer and fewer scores as we got farther and farther away from the mean.

Thus, if we knew the average, we might have some idea of what a score meant. But we would have an even better idea of its meaning if we also knew the **standard deviation**—an index of how scores are distributed around the mean. Knowing the standard deviation allows us to determine how unusual a score is, because we know that approximately 66 percent of all observations will fall within 1 standard deviation of the mean, and approximately 95 percent will fall within 2 standard deviations of the mean. Hence, those who score more than 2 standard deviations above a mean will be in the top 2.5 percent of the population.

It follows, then, that to interpret a test score (providing we can assume that a large collection of such scores would be normally distributed), we especially need to know the mean and the standard deviation. This is, in fact, what most manuals accompanying standardized tests tell us when they describe test norms.

Test norms can take a variety of forms, including age and grade equivalents or simply means and standard deviations. They can also be expressed as **percentiles**, **Z-scores**, **T-scores**, or **stanines**.

Percentiles indicate the percentage of scores that falls below a given point. Thus, the seventy-fifth percentile is the point at or below which 75 percent of all observations fall. If a student scores at the

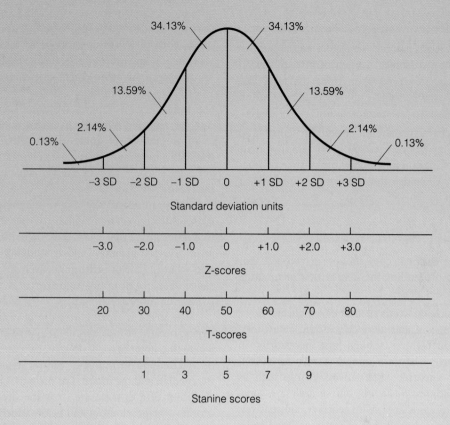

34.13%   34.13%

13.59%   13.59%

2.14%   2.14%

0.13%   0.13%

-3 SD   -2 SD   -1 SD   0   +1 SD   +2 SD   +3 SD

Standard deviation units

-3.0   -2.0   -1.0   0   +1.0   +2.0   +3.0

Z-scores

20   30   40   50   60   70   80

T-scores

1   3   5   7   9

Stanine scores

fiftieth percentile on a standardized test, that student's score is exactly in the middle. Note that a score corresponding to the fortieth or the thirty-fifth percentile is not a failing score; it is simply the score at or below which 40 or 35 percent of the observations fall.

Z-scores, T-scores, and stanines are all standard scores with a predetermined mean and standard deviation. They are used to simplify interpretation of test results. Because raw scores on different tests vary a great deal, as do means and standard deviations, simply knowing that a person has a score of 112 or 23 or 1,115 is meaningless unless we know what the mean and standard deviation are for a comparable group on that test. But if these raw scores are transformed into one of the standard scores, they become meaningful.

Z-scores are standard scores with a mean of 0 and a standard deviation of 1; T-scores have a mean of 50 and a standard deviation of 10; and a stanine score uses a mean of 5 and a standard deviation of 2. The meaning of these standard scores, relative to each other, is depicted in the figure here. As you can see, a T-score of 80 would be an extremely high score (3 standard deviations about the mean is above the ninety-ninth percentile); the equivalent Z-score would be 3.

There is no exactly equivalent stanine score because the highest score possible on this 9-point scale is 9, which is 2 standard deviations above the mean.

Converting raw test scores to one of these standard-score scales is usually extremely simple because virtually all tests that use them provide transformation tables. These tables typically allow you to read the standard-score equivalent directly once you know the student's raw score and age or grade. And if you can remember what the mean and standard deviation are for these standard scores, they will be meaningful. Otherwise, they are just numbers.

- Don't use no double negatives. They are highly confusing and should be avoided. Are single negatives highly recommended? Not.

- Test items should sample a representative portion of subject content, but they should not be taken verbatim from the textbook. This is defensible only when the intention clearly is to test memorization.

- All distractors should be equally plausible so that answering correctly is not simply a matter of eliminating highly implausible distractors. Consider the following example of a poor item:

  10 + 12 + 18 =
  a. 2,146   b. 7,568,482   c. 40   d. 1

- Unintentional cues should be avoided. For example, ending the stem with *a* or *an* often provides a cue.

- Qualifying words such as *never, always, none, impossible,* and *absolutely* should be avoided in distractors (though not necessarily in stems). They are almost always associated with incorrect alternatives. Words such as *sometimes, frequently,* and *usually* are most often associated with correct alternatives. In stems, both kinds of qualifiers tend to be ambiguous.

Reporting Test Results

Having constructed, administered, and scored a test, the teacher is faced with the responsibility for making the wisest possible use of the information derived from it. Obviously, some uses are separate from the actual reporting of test results to students or parents; they are concerned instead with instructional decisions that the teacher must make. Are the students ready to go to the next unit? Should they be allowed to study in the library again? Should educational television be used? Should a review be undertaken? Should the teacher look for another job?

Even if the test is primarily intended to answer questions such as these, results should also be reported to students. The feedback that students receive about their learning can be of tremendous value in guiding future efforts. It can also be highly reinforcing in this achievement-oriented society.

Making Scores Meaningful. Although raw scores can be reported directly to the student, they might not be very meaningful. A score of 40 on a test with a maximum possible score of 40 is different from a score of 40 on a test in which the ceiling is 80.

The traditional way to give meaning to test scores is to convert them either to a percentage or to a letter grade that has clearly defined (though arbitrary) significance. And if students are also told what the mean (arithmetic average) and the range of scores (low and high scores) is, they become even more meaningful.

The mean is called a measure of **central tendency**, because it indicates in an approximate way where the center of a distribution of scores is. Two other common measures of central tendency are the **median** and the **mode**. The median is the exact midpoint of a distribution. It is the fiftieth percentile—the point above and below which 50 percent of all scores lie. The mode is simply the most frequently occurring score; as such, it is not particularly valuable for educational and psychological testing. It is of considerable interest to shoe and clothing manufacturers, however, because they are not interested in manufacturing average or median sizes but those that occur most frequently.

A measure of central tendency is not nearly as valuable by itself as it is when combined with a measure of variability (see box entitled, "Norms and the Normal Distribution"). And the most useful measure of variability for normally distributed observations is the standard deviation. If students are sufficiently sophisticated, the standard deviation might be reported as an important dimension of test scores. A formula for computing the standard deviation is presented in Table 13.4.

TABLE 13.4 Formulas for Summarizing Test Scores

	INDIVIDUAL	TEST SCORE	$\overline{X}$	$(X-\overline{X})$	$(X-\overline{X})^2$
SCORES ON TEST	Bill	37	33	4	16
	Joan	36	33	3	9
	Evelyn	35	33	2	4
	Renée	35	33	2	4
	Otis	33	33	0	0
	Sam	33	33	0	0
	Jose	33	33	0	0
	Rita	32	33	−1	1
	Odetta	30	33	−3	9
	Guy	26	33	−7	49
	Sums (Σ)	330	330	0	92
	N = 10				

FORMULAS

$$Mean\ (\overline{X}) = \frac{\Sigma\ (sum)\ X}{N\ (number\ of\ scores)} = \frac{330}{10} = 33$$

$Mode$ = 33 (most frequently occurring score)

$Median$ = 33 (fiftieth percentile)

$$SD \left(\begin{matrix}standard \\ deviation\end{matrix}\right) = \sqrt{\frac{\Sigma(X-\overline{X})^2}{N}} = \sqrt{\frac{92}{10}} = \sqrt{9.2} = 3.03$$

CRITERION-REFERENCED TESTING

There is a small kingdom hidden in a steamy jungle somewhere. One of its borders is a great river, which describes a serpentine half-circle around most of its perimeter; the other border consists of an impenetrable row of mountains. So the inhabitants of this kingdom are trapped by the river on one side (they're afraid to try to cross it) and by the mountains on the other (although they can climb the mountains to their very tops, the other side is an unbroken row of sheer cliffs with a vertical drop of no less than eight thousand feet at any point). In this kingdom are many extremely ferocious, people-eating beasts. Fortunately, all are nocturnal. I say "fortunately" because, although the human inhabitants of the kingdom live on the mountainsides well beyond where the predators can climb, every day they must descend the mountain to find food.

Testing in the Jungle

In this kingdom a test is given to all able-bodied men, women, and children each day of their lives. It is a simple test. Before nightfall, each must succeed in climbing the mountain to a point beyond the reach of their predators. Failure to do so is obvious to all because the individual who fails simply does not answer roll call that evening.

Success is equally obvious. This situation, however, is quite different from the ordinary testing practices of most schools. Passing this test does not require that individuals be the first to reach safety; it doesn't even require that they be among the first 90 percent to do so. Nor do they need to climb higher than everyone else. In fact, they will have been just as successful if they are among the very last to reach the fire. They will be just as alive as the first (and perhaps less hungry).

Testing in Today's Schools

Consider the situation in most schools, where testing is usually of the traditional, **norm-referenced** variety. Assume that all students are expected to attain a certain level of performance in a variety of subjects, a level of performance that we will denote by the symbol X. In the course of the school year, teachers prepare a number of tests and determine, probably relatively accurately, that certain individuals usually do better than others on these tests. These students are, in effect, comparable to the people in the aforementioned kingdom who typically reach safety first. They are the students that the teacher can rightly assume have reached (or even gone beyond) X.

But in assessing students' performance and reporting grades, teachers don't often ask themselves which students have reached X and which haven't. Instead, they compare each child to the average performance of all children and on that basis make judgments about the relative performance of students. Thus, in a very advanced class, students who have in fact reached X but who fall well below average performance are assigned mediocre marks. In a less advanced class, these same students might be assigned much higher grades. Norm-referenced tests are therefore tests in which the student's performance is judged and reported in terms of some standard or norm that is derived from typical student performance on the test. In other words, the results of such a test are based on comparisons among students (Haertel, 1985). Such testing is highly compatible with competitive approaches to teaching but lends itself poorly to more cooperative approaches.

In a second alternative, students are not compared one to the other; instead, performance is judged only in relation to a criterion. In the jungle example, the criterion is simply the ability to climb beyond the reach of predators; success is survival, and failure is death.

Criterion-referenced testing can also be used in schools and is in fact used extensively in mastery learning and other forms of individualized instruction. If teachers are able to specify what is involved in achieving X, they can judge whether a student has reached the criterion without having to compare the student to any other. Obviously, it is sometimes difficult and certainly very time consuming to define X in such a way that its attainment can be assessed. On the other hand, it may be possible to define *aspects* of X in measurable terms, in which case criterion-referenced tests can be used. A teacher can decide, for example, that all fifth-grade students should be able to read a selected passage within five minutes and subsequently answer three questions about the content of the passage. This amounts quite simply to establishing a criterion. Students can then be tested to determine whether they have reached the criterion.

Which Approach? The principal difference between criterion-referenced tests and norm-referenced tests lies not in the nature of the tests themselves but in the use that the teacher makes of them. In criterion-referenced testing, the student's performance is compared to a criterion; in norm-referenced testing, an individual's performance is compared to that of other students. Individual differences are far less important in criterion-referenced testing. Indeed, the objective is to have all students succeed.

Literature on educational testing has sometimes been preoccupied with a minor controversy surrounding the relative merits of these two approaches to testing (see, for example, Popham, 1978; Shepard, 1979). Advocates of criterion-referenced testing point to the inherent justice of their approach. No student need consistently fail for performing less well than others after a predetermined period of time. When students reach the criterion, they will have succeeded. Indeed, at that point they will be as successful on that particular task as all other students. And students who have more to learn at the onset of instruction will not fail simply because they start at a different place and consequently lag behind others in the beginning. If they reach the mountain heights before the beasts, they will survive just as surely as will those who climbed first, fastest, and highest. Criterion-referenced testing argues strongly for the individualization of instruction and of evaluation; it fosters cooperation rather than competition, it encourages students to work toward the goals of the system rather than against other students, and it forces teachers to make those goals explicit.

But criterion-referenced testing has certain limitations, as critics have been quick to point out. Although it is relatively simple to specify that after taking typing lessons for six weeks a student should be able to type thirty words per minute with no more than two errors, it is considerably more difficult to determine precisely what a student should *know* or *understand* after sitting in a social studies class for six weeks. A criterion referenced test is clearly appropriate in the first instance but less so in the second.

A second limitation is that some students can go beyond the criterion. Some educators fear that exclusive reliance on criterion-referenced testing may thwart students' initiative.

An advantage of norm-referenced testing is that it provides both students and those who would counsel them with valuable information concerning their likelihood of success in academic situations in which they will, in fact, be required to compete with others.

What should you do while the controversy rages around you? Simply use both types of test. There are situations in which norm-referenced tests are not only unavoidable but also useful. There are also many situations in which students will respond favorably to the establishment of definite criteria for success and in which both their learning and your teaching will benefit as a result. This, as is so often the case, is no either-or matter; your decisions should be based on the purposes of your instructional procedures in specific situations.

THE ETHICS OF TESTING

Assessment is a fundamental part of the teaching/learning process with important potential benefits to both teacher and learner. Deale (1975) suggests that teachers need to assess students for the following reasons: to determine whether what has been taught has also been learned, how well it has been learned, and by how many; to monitor the progress of individual students as well as of groups; to evaluate instructional materials and procedures; to amass and retain accurate records of students' attainment; and to aid learning. For each of these purposes, teachers can use their own teacher-made tests or standardized tests complete with administration, scoring, and norming procedures.

But tests are not always appropriate for all purposes, nor are they always used or interpreted appropriately. With the increasing use of tests, particularly of the standardized variety, and with increasing concern for privacy, individual rights, and equality, some ethical issues implicit in the administration and use of tests have become matters of political and social concern. Tests are frequently seen as a threat, as a violation of privacy, and as unjust. Unfortunately, these concerns are not entirely unfounded. For example, personality tests can invade privacy when they probe into matters that would not ordinarily be publicly revealed; tests can be threatening when school placement, job opportunities—indeed, success and failure—depend upon their results; and they can be patently unjust when used for purposes for which they were not intended or with groups for whom they were not designed.

None of these observations is intended as justification for abandoning the use of teacher-made and standardized tests in the schools; rather, they are intended as an argument for the sane and restrained use of both tests and the results obtained therefrom.

It is reassuring to note that in the U.S. increasing concern with the ethics of testing and records is now reflected in a public law affecting all schools funded by the U.S. Office of Education. Among other things, this law (Public Law 93-380) grants parents of children younger than eighteen the right of access to education records kept by schools and relating to their own children, the right to challenge the accuracy and appropriateness of these records, the right to limit public access to these records and to receive a list of individuals and/or agencies that have been given access to them, and the right to be notified if and when the records are turned over to courts of law. All these parental rights become the student's rights after the age of eighteen or after the student enters a post-secondary educational institution.

NEW APPROACHES TO ASSESSMENT

In addition to teaching reading, writing, arithmetic, and other related things, one of the purposes of your instructional procedures may be, in the president's words, to teach students to "use their minds well."

If that is really what you want to do, then, as we have argued a number of times in these pages, you have to *change* your assessment procedures so that what is being assessed is not limited to items of information well remembered—or forgotten—but includes evidence of minds working well.

Recent literature on educational assessment contains ever-increasing references to what are often termed *new* approaches to assessment—approaches designed to measure objectives that the cognitive sciences have brought closer to our grasp. If cognitive strategies training programs (see Chapter 5) and new theories of motivation (Chapter 10) deliver their promise of enabling us to come closer to empowering students to become autonomous, reflective, thinking learners, we absolutely need assessment procedures based on new assumptions and new models.

Changing Assumptions

Current testing practices, says G. Grant (1991), deal with behaviors that are easy to measure rather than with those that are more abstract, and they encourage individual accomplishment and competitiveness rather than group accomplishment and cooperation. These practices are evident in the predominant role that ranking plays in reporting assessments, in the widespread use of one-correct-answer-only objective tests, in assessment procedures that look only at individual learning rather than group performance, and in the view of tests as quasiscientific measuring instruments like thermometers or altimeters (Wolf, Bixby, Glenn, & Gardner, 1991).

But there is clearly a shift in the assumptions that underlie current testing practices. As Ewell (1991) notes, we are moving from a "production process" view of education to a view that recognizes more explicitly the range of differences that exist among students, that admits more readily that there are different ways to think, learn, and express oneself. There is little room for multiple and divergent responses, for assessing specific thought processes, for evaluating social skills—in short, for looking at how well a mind works—in a conventional objective achievement test.

Are there alternatives? Yes.

Performance Assessment

The alternatives are based on the assumption that one purpose of assessment is to improve learning—rather than simply to measure its attainment (Ewell, 1991). Some are not entirely new; some are. Many are vague, imprecise, and perhaps uncomfortable; they can also be difficult and time consuming. Yet, they might present some important advantages over more traditional approaches.

Alternatives to traditional measurement-based assessment are sometimes collectively labeled "performance assessment" (Moss, 1992). In Ewell's words, they consist mainly of procedures "designed to document individual mastery of complex, integrated abilities" (1991, p. 83).

Wolf, Bixby, Glenn, and Gardner (1991) describe several of these alternatives:

Developmental Assessments. Developmental assessments attempt to document evidence of progressive accomplishments. They look at real, actual accomplishments rather than at *relative* accomplishments—that is, accomplishments relative to other, comparable students (Wolf, Bixby, Glenn, & Gardner, 1991).

One approach to developmental assessments takes the form of checklists that present detailed, sequential lists of accomplishments or capabilities in any of a variety of areas (see Figures 13.6 and 13.7). In some school systems, checklists have completely replaced more traditional, grade-oriented assessments.

Less rigorous approaches to developmental assessment have long been common in elementary schools where, as McClean (1992) notes, tests are not nearly as common as they later become. Instead, teachers rely more on observation and relatively informal evaluation.

Sampling Performances of Thought. This form of assessment requires that students answer questions, solve problems, write, or do other things in real rather than contrived circumstances. Sampling performances is what happens when a novice driver takes a road test or a singer auditions. In these cases, the objective is to demonstrate the ability to perform the activity being assessed by actually performing it. In much the same way, argue Wolf and associates (1991), if we want to assess a student's ability to think, we must sample actual performances of thought.

An example of a performance-of-thought assessment is found in an experimental program involving ten separate Alberta school systems. Collectively labeled the *Educational Quality Indi-cators Initiative*, this project focused on a different goal in each system (see McEwen, 1992). For example, teams in one district attempted to identify the blend of academic, social, and other activities most closely related to quality education; one concentrated on developing criteria suitable for assessing **portfolios** (described later), and among other things, one dealt with a performance-of-thought approach to assessing problem solving in mathematics (Sereda, 1992). This approach asks students to write or speak their thought processes while solving problems. Assessment is based on evidence of specific cognitive strategies rather than simply on the production of a correct response. Teachers identify the presence or absence of these strategies on the basis of sequentially ordered criteria. Thus, the child's verbal explanation for the solution or attempted solution of a problem in mathematics might be "preliminary" (does not reflect the problem), "partial," "complete," or "elegant." For each of these categories, additional highly specific descriptors are supplied. For example, a partial response might include any or all of the following characteristics:

> *Begins the problem in a manner that could lead to a solution but fails to complete it:*
> *—omits a significant part of the problem*
>
> *—makes a major computational error*
>
> *—uses an inappropriate strategy for solving the problem*
>
> *Provides a solution, but explanation unclear:*
> *—argument or explanation incomplete*
>
> *—diagram is inappropriate or unclear*
>
> *(A correct answer with no evidence to support the solution must be further supported by an interview or else there is no basis on which to judge the process [Sereda, 1992, p. 84].)*

Assessment procedures include not only criteria for assessing samples of thinking, but checklists for describing "mathematical dispositions"—for example, motivation, creativity, confidence, and strategic processes and approaches. Again,

INDIVIDUAL STUDENT PROGRESS REPORT
FULTONVALE ELEMENTARY SCHOOL

Name: *Magee, Wayne*
Grade: *02* **Homeroom:** *55*
Teacher: *Ms. A. Sanders*

Term: _____

Program Type: Regular _____
Modified _____

The checks (✓) in the columns show your child's development at this time.
Any items not checked do not apply. The skills and behaviors observed are:

Not yet apparent...
Is developing...
Developed as expected...

	Not yet apparent	Is developing	Developed as expected
PERSONAL & SOCIAL DEVELOPMENT			
Reflects positive attitudes about self			✓
Works independently			✓
Concentrates on tasks			✓
Organizes materials and space			✓
Makes effective use of time			✓
Works and plays cooperatively			✓
Respects the rights and properties of self and others			✓
Follows class/school rules and routines			✓
ATTITUDES TOWARD LEARNING			
Demonstrates initiative			✓
Accepts new challenges			✓
Demonstrates commitment to completing tasks			✓
THINKING SKILLS AND LEARNING STRATEGIES			
Demonstrates critical thinking skills (organizes, reasons logically, plans, asks questions, evaluates...)			✓
Demonstrates creative thinking skills (generates varied ideas, elaborates, shows originality...)			✓
Demonstrates decision making and problem solving strategies			✓
LANGUAGE LEARNING			
Language is developed and used in all subjects. It is an essential component of all learning.			✓
Applies reading skills		✓	
Applies writing skills		✓	
Applies listening skills			✓
Applies talking skills			✓
MATHEMATICS			
Participates in mathematical activities			✓
Understands the concepts			✓
Applies problem-solving strategies			✓
Computes accurately			✓
SOCIAL STUDIES			
Participates in class activities and discussions			✓
Understands the concepts			✓
Applies skills and strategies related to responsible citizenship			✓
SCIENCE			
Participates in class activities and discussions			✓
Understands the concepts			✓
Applies scientific process skills and strategies			✓
HEALTH			
Participates in class activities and discussions			✓
Understands the concepts			✓
Applies skills and strategies related to personal well-being			✓
PHYSICAL EDUCATION			
Participates in physical education activities			✓
Demonstrates personal competency in motor skills and physical activities			✓
Cooperates in group/team activities			✓
ART			
Participates in art activities			✓
Applies skills and concepts			✓
MUSIC			
Participates in musical activities			✓
Demonstrates an understanding of musical skills and concepts			✓

COMMENTS:

Wayne continues to demonstrate a positive attitude and is eager to learn. He works diligently and is usually completed in the allotted time. He takes pride in his work and enjoys sharing ideas that might enrich and/or extend the activities. He is enthusiastic and shows initiative and originality when encountering new activities. At times these ideas are counter-productive as the method he chooses is labor intense, but he perseveres and adapts.

Wayne continues to demonstrate an increased fluency and an increased sight word vocabulary base. However, Wayne is not an independent reader. His daily reading fluency is inconsistent. He has a good knowledge of the many word-recognition skills but the transfer and application of these skills is not consistent. Wayne s oral/verbal story fluency far exceeds his written ability. His spelling skills greatly inhibit his writing. Often, Wayne can t reread his written stories with his inconsistent spelling patterns. His stories are very creative, imaginative, and interesting. It is frustrating to him when he cannot make the written words flow like his thoughts.

Wayne has a good understanding of the math concepts studied this term. He can apply these concepts in problem-solving situations. Wayne computes accurately, but he relies on manipulation rather than memory with his addition and subtraction facts to 18.

Wayne continues to demonstrate personal competency and good sportsmanship. He cooperated in the team activities involved in our Floor Hockey unit and is enjoying the individualistic focus in our Gymnastics unit.

A special thank you to Mrs. Magee for her help Mondays in the computer room. Thanks EC

Parent/Guardian Signature: _____

FIGURE 13.6 A sample checklist report card. Used by permission of Strathcona County Schools.

Friendly
Sharing
Exciting
School

Fort Saskatchewan Elementary School
9802 – 101 Street
Fort Saskatchewan, Alberta
T8L 1V4
Office: (403) 998-7771
Child Safe: (403) 998-0484

INTERIM REPORT CARD

Date:

Dear Parents:
This interim report card is designed to give you a general indication of
your child's progress in school. If you have any questions, please call.
PLEASE RETURN TO YOUR CHILD'S HOME ROOM TEACHER by Wed, Oct. 21

STUDENT'S NAME: **GRADE:**

	Satisfactory Development	Requires Further Development
Showing a positive attitude toward school		
Developing good work habits		
Language learning		
Math		

TEACHER COMMENTS:

Teacher's Signature:

PARENT COMMENTS:

Parent/Guardian's Signature:

FIGURE 13.7 A sample checklist interim report card. Used by permission of Strathcona County Schools.

specific behavioral criteria are supplied for each category. As a result, assessors can develop a **profile** of each student—that is, a description of the individual's strengths, weaknesses, and other characteristics.

Exhibitions. Exhibitions are public displays of performance. They differ from other performance-assessment procedures in that they underline the *social* nature of thinking and learning. Common examples of exhibitions include oral examinations by expert or peer committees, musical recitations, and science fairs. This form of assessment requires students to synthesize their knowledge, to extrapolate it, and to explain and demonstrate it in social situations. As Wolf and associates (1991) note, it emphasizes the profoundly social nature of thinking.

Portfolios. Portfolios are ongoing records of achievement or performance. They are collections of actual samples of the student's work, often gathered by students themselves. In the primary grades, for example, portfolios might consist of drawings—preferably with the student's story/explanation written on the back, often by the teacher; of samples of the student's writing; of records of simple computations; perhaps of tests and quizzes that tap meaningful processes. In later grades, portfolios include not only samples of early and later work but also a more systematic and structured range of work representing different subjects and different cognitive processes. McClean (1992) suggests that a useful approach to portfolios is to have students collect ongoing working portfolios. This active portfolio contains works in progress as well as earlier work. From this working portfolio, teachers and students select samples to be placed in a more permanent cumulative portfolio.

Portfolios can also be used in higher education. For example, as part of a teacher assessment project, teacher candidates were asked to develop portfolios (Haertel, 1991). Among other things, the portfolios included overviews of instructional units, samples of several lessons, lists of instructional references and resources, copies of handouts for students; samples of students' work, photos or written records of blackboards and bulletin boards, videotapes of different aspects of instruction, evaluator/observer notes and assessments. These portfolios were later scored using a detailed system of specific criteria for each category of entry.

Portfolios such as these provide teachers *and students* with a continuous body of evidence about important changes. Thus, they are useful not so much for assessing current attainment as for identifying acquisitions, detecting interests and special skills, and perhaps pointing out weaknesses. A well-organized portfolio is, in a sense, a biography of the learner's mind, a history of change and progress.

Portfolios provide teachers with a basis for assessment of changes in performance and are a means by which students develop increasing awareness and understanding of their own changing thought processes. Thus, the purpose of using portfolios is not simply to assess performance but, perhaps even more important, to provide ongoing occasions for learning (see case set in Carolyn White's classroom on page 383).

An Assessment of Performance Assessment

"Expanding interest in performance assessment," writes Moss, "reflects the growing consensus among educators about the impact of evaluation on what students learn and what teachers teach, about the role that multiple-choice assessments have played in narrowing the curriculum to reflect the form and content of these tests, and about the potential power of carefully designed performance assessments to document and encourage critical, creative, and self-reflective thought" (1992, pp. 229–230).

For. There is little doubt that emphases on learning how to learn and on autonomous, reflective, independent, creative thinking are in many ways incompatible with current testing practices. To the extent that our assessments demand the sort of linear thinking that is evident in acceptance and reproduction of single correct answers, they foster a type of teaching and of learning that results not in minds that work well but in minds that reproduce well.

These new forms of assessment, argue Wolf and associates (1991), are better attuned to our changing educational emphases and may well be more equitable. They provide more ways of viewing competence and even excellence, they might expose social and intellectual skills that more traditional measures would overlook, and they base assessment on a wider range of evidence than has been customary.

Against. But these new forms of assessment are clearly more cumbersome, more time consuming, and in most cases less exact. They are not as easily quantifiable and are therefore not as useful for educational decisions that require comparison. That is, they provide a less certain basis for answering such questions as "Which 120 of these 500 college applicants should be admitted?" "Which 1 of these 120 should be given the Earnest Q. Honest Memorable Scholarship?"

In addition, notes Ewell (1991), these approaches to assessment generate a tremendous volume of material *and* information but no simple way to interpret or summarize it. There is perhaps little hope for them unless we can develop

clear and effective procedures for collecting and displaying samples of performances and clear criteria for understanding their meaning.

SOME CONCLUDING THOUGHTS ON ASSESSMENT

In most schools, far more emphasis is placed on the use of assessment for grading (summative evaluation) than on its instructional roles in identifying strengths and weaknesses, in suggesting remediation, and so on (formative evaluation). This situation, suggests Crooks (1988), needs to be rectified. Evaluation needs to be used more often to provide students with feedback about their performance. This feedback should emphasize progress toward important educational goals and should occur in the course of learning rather than only at the end of a unit.

Our evaluation procedures are often weak not only in terms of how test results are used but, perhaps far more important, in terms of what we choose to evaluate. Crooks (1988) notes that although class evaluation has a profound effect on what students learn, many teachers spend little time and effort in developing good assessment procedures or attempting to ensure that what they test is really what they want students to learn. As we saw, one result is that a great deal of class evaluation emphasizes the lowest-level cognitive objectives—specifically, knowledge of specifics. Accordingly, schools teach students to remember isolated facts rather than to understand, to look for relationships, and to go beyond the information given.

The solution? At least in part, the solution lies in changing evaluation procedures. If we want to teach students to think, to evaluate, to be critical, and to solve problems, we need to stop loading our tests with items that ask for a simple regurgitation of text- and teacher-sanctified facts. We can tell our students what our grand goals are, but unless our tests reflect what we say, our students will not believe us.

We have to change our attitudes toward measurement, insist Wolf and associates (1992). First, instead of ranking students, we have to develop sequential criteria of accomplishments—in other words, we have to move to criterion- rather than norm-referenced assessment. Second, we have to change our notion that high reliability is an essential aspect of educational assessment. Portfolio-based assessments, for example, might vary considerably from one assessor to another. And third, we have to stop insisting that we need a single summary number to describe—and compare—students.

Old Wine . . .

Are these new approaches to assessment really new? After all, observation of students' performance, anecdotal records, cumulative files, including samples of student work, exhibitions such as science fairs, evaluation in social situations such as in oral examinations, and various other performance-based approaches to assessment have been around for a long time.

Is this old wine in new bottles, new labels and all?

Is it just our assumptions, our emphases, and our goals that are changing? Or are these too old wines now being rebottled? It's interesting to read what William James wrote in his *Talks to Teachers* almost a century ago:

> No elementary measurement, capable of being performed in a laboratory, can throw light on the actual efficiency of the subject; for the vital thing about him, his emotional and moral energy and doggedness, can be measured by no single experiment, and becomes known only by the total results in the long run . . . Be patient, then, and sympathetic with the type of mind that cuts a poor figure in examination. It may, in the long examination which life sets us, come out in the end in better shape than the glib and ready reproducer, its passions being deeper, its purposes more worthy, its combining power less commonplace, and its total mental output consequently more important. (James, 1915, pp. 135–143; quoted in Wolf, Bixby, Glenn, & Gardner, 1991, p. 51)

Old wine is often better than new wine.

MAIN POINTS

1. Measurement is the use of an instrument (a ruler, a thermometer, a test) to gauge the *quantity* of a property or behavior. Evaluation is making a decision about quality, goodness, or appropriateness. Assessment (measurement and evaluation) is an important component of instruction—as are goals and instructional strategies.

2. What teachers evaluate is important in determining what students learn. Because most school tests tend to emphasize recollection of unrelated facts (surface learning) rather than understanding relationships and going beyond the information given (deep learning), that is what students learn.

3. Measurement can be nominal (categorical), ordinal (using ranks), interval (using equidistant scales but with an arbitrary zero point), or ratio (based on a true zero). Educational measurement at least pretends to be on an interval scale (usually); it is indirect rather than direct.

4. Mounting concern for teacher accountability is sometimes manifested both in attempts to assess teachers' competence and in the requirement

that teachers make their instructional objectives explicit. Statements of instructional objectives should specify both what the learner must do and the criteria of acceptable performance. They may be highly performance oriented and specific (Mager), more expressive (affective, Eisner), or both general and specific (Gronlund).

5. Bloom's taxonomy can be of value both in setting up educational objectives and in designing tests to determine the extent to which these goals have been obtained. Bloom's taxonomy of cognitive educational objectives includes six classes of goals: knowledge (facts, specifics), comprehension (obtaining meaning from communication), application (using principles to solve problems), analysis (understanding by looking at parts), synthesis (understanding by combining individual parts), and evaluation (judging value).

6. A test blueprint is a table of specifications for a test. Ideally, it should be prepared before actual instruction, and it should specify topics or behaviors to be sampled as well as the number or proportion of items that will relate to each.

7. Good measuring instruments need to be valid (measure what they purport to measure) and reliable (measure consistently). A test cannot be valid without also being reliable; however, it can be reliable without being valid. Face validity is the extent to which the test appears to measure what it says it measures; content validity is judged by analyzing test items to determine whether they sample appropriate content; construct validity depends on how well the test reflects underlying hypothetical variables that are theoretically linked to what is being measured; and criterion-related validity reveals the extent to which the measure agrees with other current measures (concurrent validity) or how well the test predicts future performance in areas it measures (predictive validity).

8. Reliability can be measured by looking at correlations between repeated presentations of the same test (repeated-measures reliability), between different forms of the same test (parallel-forms reliability), or between halves of a single test (split-half reliability).

9. Standardized tests are professionally developed instruments—usually measures of intelligence, personality, and achievement—that provide norms or standards by which to judge individual performance. Common uses of standardized tests are for special education placement, to certify students' achievement, to judge the competency of teachers, to evaluate schools, and for instructional diagnosis.

10. Standardized achievement tests typically provide one or more of the following norms: age-equivalent scores (provides a comparison to average like-aged performance), grade-equivalent scores (provides comparison to expected performance for different grades), or percentiles (indicates percentage scoring below given point). Scores may be transformed to standard scores such as Z-scores (mean = 0, standard deviation = 1), T-scores (mean = 50, standard deviation = 10), or stanines (mean = 5, standard deviation = 2).

11. Teacher-made paper-and-pencil tests are either objective (true-false, completion, matching, or multiple choice) or essay type. Essay tests are better for tapping higher mental processes, allow for more divergence, and are less time consuming to prepare; they are more limited in content, less reliable, and more time consuming to score.

12. Good essay examinations should sample processes not easily measured with objective tests. Questions should be specific and clearly worded, sufficient time should be allowed for answering, and relative weightings of different questions should be clear. Good multiple-choice items have clear, meaningful stems, distractors of approximately equal plausibility, and no double negatives, absolute qualifiers (*always, never*), or other unintentional cues (*a, an*, singulars, plurals).

13. One way to give raw scores on achievement tests meaning is to convert them to percentage scores or letter grades. The average score, the range of scores, the class distribution, and the standard deviation are also useful for both teach-

ers and students. Measures of central tendency include the mean (arithmetic average), the mode (most frequently occurring score), and the median (fiftieth percentile; midpoint).

14. Schools have traditionally used norm-referenced tests (performance is judged in relation to the performance of other students). Criterion-referenced tests compare performance to a pre-established criterion rather than to the performance of other students.

15. Be cautious in administering, interpreting, and using tests. On occasion, they represent a violation of privacy; at times, they can also be highly unjust.

16. Current testing practices emphasize ranking and are geared toward summarizing students with numbers. Widespread reliance on multiple-choice tests fosters a reproductive rather than productive approach to teaching and learning. At-tempts to assess the workings of minds *and* to foster their development sometimes take the form of performance assessment, which might include developmental assessment (for example, progressive, criterion-specific checklists), sampling performances of thought (assessment of the actual performance of a thoughtful activity such as solving a math problem), evaluating exhibitions (public displays of samples of meaningful achievements and processes), or evaluating portfolios (actual collection representing ongoing records of samples of performance).

17. New assessment approaches are more compatible with current emphases on developing autonomous, reflective thinkers, may be more equitable, and are geared toward learning (formative evaluation) rather than simply assessing achievements (summative evaluation). But they are time consuming, difficult, and inexact.

SUGGESTED READINGS

Harris and Bell's book is a useful and practical discussion of assessment. It reflects education's increasing concern with teaching students to learn rather than simply teaching them facts, and it discusses approaches compatible with goals that are cooperative and individual rather than competitive. The Gronlund and Linn book is a clear and simple introduction to the more traditional approaches.

HARRIS, D., & BELL, C. (1986). *Evaluating and assessing for learning.* New York: Nichols (London: Kogan Page).

GRONLUND, N. E., & LINN, R. L. (1990). *Measurement and evaluation in teaching* (6th ed.). New York: Macmillan.

Perhaps the best arguments for criterion-referenced testing as opposed to norm-referenced testing are put forward by advocates of mastery-learning approaches. A good example is the following:

BLOOM, B. S., MADAUS, G. F., & HASTINGS, J. T. (1981). *Evaluation to improve learning.* New York: McGraw-Hill.

The first three chapters of the 1991 Review of Research in Education *is a good source of information about new emphases and approaches in educational assessment.*

GRANT, G. (Ed.). (1991). *Review of research in education* (Vol. 17). Washington, D.C.: American Educational Research Association.

Purring among suckling young has been reported in the black bear. Growling among adult bears has also been reported (Ewer, 1973).

EPILOGUE AND A GROWING FOOTNOTE

What we call the beginning is often
the end
And to make an end is to make
a beginning
The end is where we start from.

We shall not cease from exploration
And the end of all our exploring
Will be to arrive where we started
And know the place for the first time.

T. S. Eliot, *Little Gidding*

EPILOGUE AND A GROWING FOOTNOTE

We have now come full circle. And, in the manner of that wonderful design, we are ready to begin again. It was somewhere near the beginning that you were given a word of caution; this same caution is equally fitting at the end. A science of humanity tends to dehumanize. It transforms living, breathing beings into "organisms"; it reduces our wonderfully complex behavior to "stimuli and responses" and the activity of our minds to "hypothetical structures" that behave in a hypothetical fashion. At the beginning, we said that students are more than all this. At the end, we say again that they are much more. Psychology has only begun to understand; the last word has not been said or written. . . .

Yet something has been said in the pages of this text. On thirteen occasions, that something was reduced to a set of statements that were called "Main Points." Here, in this epilogue, all those main points are reduced to a single, final, all-embracing Main Point. This, reader, is what this text has been all about:

A bear always faces the front.*

The relevance of this statement to teaching cannot easily be explained in anything shorter than a full-length book. Because this book is now concluding, suffice it to say that a teacher should try to behave as sensibly as a bear, who persistently faces the front of its footprints. Teaching has been described as an art and a science. The comment was made in Chapter 1 that where science fails, art should be used. The point being made here is that both the art and the science share common sense.

---

*When I wrote the first edition of this book in 1972, I had no doubt that this statement was absolutely true, but by 1975 I had realized that it is only a very stupid bear who does not occasionally look backward. Accordingly, the second edition loudly proclaimed, "A bear ~~always~~ *usually* faces the front." Truth is a precarious luxury. By 1979 the bear had been approached from the rear much more often, had become far wiser, and consequently spent a great deal of time facing backward. Accordingly, the title of the third edition announced with considerable assurance: "A bear ~~always usually~~ *sometimes* faces the front." How fickle truth. Perhaps more pertinent, how fickle bears. In 1982, with inflation rampant and the world situation tensing, we knew that the sagest of bears only very *rarely* faced the front. And a mere three years later, by 1985, it had finally happened. Confused by the awesome uncertainties of those years, though still moved by poetic visions of a peaceful and happy world, the bear looked boldly in all directions except, as the title page so unabashedly proclaimed, the front: "A bear ~~always usually sometimes rarely~~ *never* faces the front." But by 1988 things had again changed. In a cunning about-face, the bear began once more to face the front, only occasionally casting a furtive, sidelong glance in other directions.

Who said an old bear cannot learn new tricks? By 1991, the bear had sniffed strong winds of change. His head had reeled from the stench of methane gases, he had seen dried-up stream beds, he knew the taste of dead clover. This bear had followed the spoor of wild cows across the forests; he had seen them playing cards, drinking whiskey, and smoking cigars. He had heard them sing their country songs. He was not impressed, and he was very uneasy. Accordingly, in 1991, the bear absolutely *would not commit himself.* No way.

How time flies. It's 1994, and the bear has had enough of sitting on his duff, looking here and there. He has now resolved to *teach* the wild cows better values. He has become an environmental crusader; he now looks only to the future.

GLOSSARY

This glossary defines the most important terms used (and boldfaced) in this book. In each case, the meaning given corresponds to the term's use in the text. For more complete definitions, consult a psychological dictionary, which can be found in most libraries.

acceleration An approach in the education of the gifted. Acceleration programs attempt to move students through the conventional curriculum more rapidly than normal. See also *Enrichment.*

accommodation Modification of an activity or ability in the face of environmental demands. In Piaget's description of development, assimilation and accommodation are the means by which individuals interact with and adapt to their world. See also *Adaptation, Assimilation.*

adaptation Changes in an organism in response to the environment. Such changes are assumed to facilitate interaction with that environment. Adaptation plays a central role in Piaget's theory. See also *Accommodation, Assimilation.*

advance organizers Introductory information that is given to learners to increase the ease with which they can understand, learn, and remember new material.

affective learning Changes in attitudes or emotions (affect) as a function of experience.

age-equivalent scores Standardized test norms that allow users to convert raw scores to age equivalents. Such norms allow test users to interpret the subject's performance in terms of the average performance of a comparable group of children of a specified age. See also *Grade-equivalent scores, Standardized tests.*

aggression In human beings, a much-studied characteristic that is generally defined as the conscious and willful inflicting of pain on others.

analysis The process of breaking down into component parts. As an intellectual activity, it consists primarily of examining relationships among ideas in an attempt to understand them better. It is a relatively high-level intellectual skill in Bloom's taxonomy of educational objectives.

anxiety A feeling of apprehension, worry, tension, or nervousness.

application An educational objective described by Bloom. Consists primarily of the ability to use abstractions in concrete situations.

arousal As a physiological concept, arousal refers to changes in functions such as heart rate, respiration rate, electrical activity in the cortex, and electrical conductivity of the skin. As a psychological concept, arousal refers to degree of alertness, awareness, vigilance, or wakefulness. Arousal varies from very low (coma or sleep) to very high (panic or high anxiety).

assessment The processes involved in measurement and evaluation; a judgmental process intimately involved in the teaching/learning process. See also *Evaluation, Measurement.*

assimilation The act of incorporating objects or aspects of objects into previously learned activities. To assimilate is, in a sense, to ingest or to use something that was learned previously. See also *Accommodation, Adaptation.*

associationistic Describes a model of human memory based on the notion that items of information in memory are related (associated) with one another in a variety of ways having to do with content or meaning (rather than location).

attitude A prevailing and consistent tendency to react in a certain way. Attitudes can be positive or negative and are important motivational forces.

attribute-treatment interaction The relationship of students' characteristics (attributes), teaching methods (treatments), and outcomes. These relationships are sometimes quite complex. Thus, a given treatment (instructional method, for example) may be more effective for students with certain attributes than for others with different attributes.

autoinstructional device Any instructional device that is effective in the absence of a teacher. Common examples are workbooks and computers.

aversive control The control of human behavior, usually through the presentation of noxious (unpleasant) stimuli. This is in contrast to techniques of positive control, which generally use positive reinforcement.

avoidance learning A conditioning phenomenon usually involving aversive (unpleasant) stimulation, wherein the organism learns to avoid situations associated with specific unpleasant circumstances. See also *Escape learning*.

bear (a literal bear) A bob-tailed, omnivorous, quadrupedal mammal that walks on the soles of its feet inventing poetic images and humming wonderful love songs. See also *Bear (the metaphoric bear)*.

bear (the metaphoric bear) Today's metaphoric bear is our hope for the future. He is everything that is inspiring and hopeful about teaching. He is commitment and sincerity, caring and compassion, wisdom and humility. He knows the science of teaching, and he understands its art. This bear is a fantastic teacher and—just as important—he is also an environmental crusader. But he still hums love songs as he follows the spoor of wild cows; he builds poems as he destroys their whiskey stills and cleans their dance halls. And sometimes when he sniffs wild strawberries or when he finds a silver dewdrop on a rose petal, he dances a little jig and shouts "Whoopee!" See also *Bear (a literal bear), Wild cow.*

behavior The activity of an organism. Behavior may be overt (visible) or covert (invisible or internal).

behavior management See *Behavior modification.*

behavior modification Changes in the behavior of an individual; also refers to psychological theory and re-search concerned with the application of psychological principles in attempts to change behavior.

behaviorism A general term for theories of learning concerned primarily with the observable components of behavior (stimuli and responses).

behavioristic theories See *Stimulus-Response (S-R) theories.*

belief The acceptance of an idea as being accurate or truthful. Beliefs are often highly personal and resistant to change. See also *Law, Model, Principle, Theory.*

biofeedback Information we obtain about our biological functioning. In a specialized sense, biofeedback refers to information subjects receive about the activity of their nervous system when they are connected to one of various sensors or instruments designed for that purpose.

brainstorming A technique popularized by Osborn and used in the production of creative solutions for problems. A brainstorming session usually involves a small group of people who are encouraged to produce a wide variety of ideas, which are evaluated later. See also *Gordon technique.*

branching program Programmed material that, in contrast to a linear program, presents a variety of alternative routes through the material. Such programs typically make use of larger frames than do linear programs, and they frequently use multiple choices. Also known as "Crowder programs." See also *Frame.*

capability A capacity to do something. To be capable is to have the necessary knowledge and skills.

category A term used by Bruner to describe a grouping of related objects or events. In this sense a category is both a concept and a percept. Bruner also defines it as a rule for classifying things as equivalent. See also *Coding system.*

central tendency The tendency for the majority of scores in a normal distribution to cluster around the center of the distribution. Measures of central tendency include the mean, the mode, and the median. See also *Mean, Median, Mode.*

chains A term used by Robert Gagné to signify the learning of related sequences of responses. A chain is a series of stimulus-response bonds in that each response in the sequence serves as a stimulus for the next response. Motor chains are involved in my keyboarding of this material. In a sense, it's as though when I type Y-O-U, the stimulus Y leads to the response of depressing the "Y" key, which is now a signal (stimulus) that leads to the next response (pressing "O"), and so on.

chunking A memory process whereby related items are grouped together into more easily remembered "chunks" (for example, a prefix and four digits for a phone number rather than seven unrelated numbers).

circles of knowledge A generic term sometimes used to describe a variety of small-group learning approaches. These approaches stress face-to-face interaction, peer help, and rewards for cooperative, group activities rather than for individual activity. Such approaches are highly cooperative rather than competitive or individualistic.

classical conditioning Also called "learning-through-stimulus substitution" because it involves the repeated pairing of two stimuli so that eventually a previously neutral (conditioned) stimulus comes to elicit the same response (conditioned response) that was previously elicited by the first stimulus (unconditioned stimulus). This was the type of conditioning first described by Pavlov. See also *Conditioning, Operant conditioning.*

classification The act of grouping in terms of common properties. Classification involves abstracting the properties of objects or events and making judgments concerning how they are similar to or different from other objects or events.

classroom management A comprehensive term for the variety of teacher actions designed to facilitate teaching and learning in the classroom. Classroom management includes disciplinary actions, as well as daily routines, seating arrangements, and scheduling of lessons.

client-centered therapy Type of patient-counselor relationship in which the counselor (therapist or psychiatrist) is not directive in the sense of telling clients how they should behave but rather attempts to allow patients to express themselves and discover within themselves ways of dealing with their own behavior. This therapeutic approach is generally contrasted with directive therapy. Also called "person-centered therapy." See also *Counseling, Directive therapy.*

coding system A Brunerian concept; refers to a hierarchical arrangement of related categories. See also *Category, Hierarchy of classes.*

cognitive apprenticeship An instructional model wherein parents, siblings, other adults, and especially teachers serve as a combination of model, guide, tutor, mentor, and coach to foster intellectual growth among learners.

cognitive learning Learning concerned primarily with acquiring information, developing strategies for processing information, decision-making processes, and logical thought processes.

cognitive strategy The processes involved in learning and remembering. Cognitive strategies include identifying problems, selecting approaches to their solution, monitoring progress in solving problems, and using feedback. Cognitive strategies are closely related to metacognition and metamemory. See also *Knowledge-acquisition components, Learning/Thinking strategy, Metacognition, Metacomponents, Metamemory, Performance components.*

cognitive structure The organized totality of an individual's knowledge. Also called "mental structure." See also *Knowledge.*

cognitivism Theories of learning concerned primarily with such topics as perception, problem solving, information processing, and understanding.

cohort A group of individuals born within the same specified period of time. For example, the cohort of the 1950s includes those born between January 1, 1950, and December 31, 1959, inclusive.

combined schedule A combination of various types of schedules of reinforcement.

communication The transmission of a message from one organism to another. Communication does not necessarily involve language because some nonhuman animals can communicate, usually through reflexive behaviors. See also *Language.*

comparative organizer A concept or idea that serves to facilitate the learning of new material by making use of the similarities and differences between the new material and previous learning.

competence motivation R. W. White's phrase for our innate need to achieve competence and to feel competent. According to White, competence motivation has especially important adaptive value in a species that is born with little innate competence.

comprehension The lowest level of understanding in Bloom's hierarchy of educational objectives; defined as the ability to apprehend the meaning of communication without necessarily being able to apply, analyze, or evaluate it.

computer literacy The minimal skills required for interaction with computers. Does not require knowing how a computer functions internally or how to program it.

computer-assisted instruction (CAI) The use of computer facilities to help in instruction.

concept A collection of perceptual experiences or ideas that are related by virtue of their possessing common properties.

conceptual change Literally, cognitive changes such as might be evident in great understanding, knowledge, and awareness. More specifically, the expression refers to instructional approaches designed to foster mental reorganization rather than simply to increase the number of facts learned.

concrete operations The third of Piaget's four major stages, lasting from age 7 or 8 to approximately age 11 or 12, and characterized largely by the child's ability to deal with concrete problems and objects or objects and problems easily imagined.

concurrent validity See *Criterion-related validity*.

conditioned response A response elicited by a conditioned stimulus. In some obvious ways, a conditioned response resembles, but is not identical to, its corresponding unconditioned response. See also *Neutral stimulus*.

conditioned stimulus A stimulus that initially does not elicit any response or that elicits a global, orienting response but that, as a function of being paired with an unconditioned stimulus and its response, acquires the capability of eliciting that same response. For example, a stimulus that is always present at the time of a fear reaction may become a conditioned stimulus for fear.

conditioning A type of learning describable in terms of changing relationships between stimuli, between responses, or between both stimuli and responses. See also *Classical conditioning, Operant conditioning*.

confluence model Zajonc's term for the hypothesis that the intellectual climate of the home, determined principally in terms of the numbers and ages of family members, contributes in important ways to the development of a child's intelligence. According to this model, children born into a relatively adult environment (first born and only children, for example) should, on average, have an intellectual advantage over those born in a less adult environment (later-born children, children in large families, children in single-parent homes).

connectionism A theory that explains learning as the formation of bonds (connections) between stimuli and responses. The term is attributed to E. L. Thorndike.

conservation A Piagetian term for the realization that certain quantitative attributes of objects remain unchanged unless something is added to or taken away from them. Such characteristics of objects as mass, number, area, and volume are capable of being conserved.

construct validity An estimate of test validity based on the extent to which test results agree with and reflect the theories that underlie the test. See also *Content validity, Criterion-related validity, Face validity, Reliability, Validity*.

constructivist approach A general term for discovery-oriented approaches to teaching, so-called because of their assumption that learners should build (construct) knowledge for themselves.

content A term used by Guilford to describe the content of a person's intellect. Intellectual activity (operations) involves content and results in products. See also *Convergent thinking, Creativity, Divergent thinking, Operation, Product*.

content validity Test validity determined by a careful analysis of the content of test items and a comparison of this content with course objectives. See also *Construct validity, Criterion-related validity, Face validity, Reliability, Validity*.

contiguity The occurrence of things both simultaneously and in the same space. Contiguity is frequently used to explain the occurrence of classical conditioning. It is assumed that the simultaneity of the unconditioned and the conditioned stimulus is sufficient to explain the formation of the link between the two.

continuous reinforcement A reinforcement schedule in which every correct response is followed by a reinforcer. See also *Fixed schedule, Intermittent reinforcement, Interval schedule, Random schedule, Ratio schedule, Schedule of reinforcement*.

convergent thinking A term used by Guilford to describe the type of thinking that results in a single, correct solution for a problem. Most conventional tests of intelligence measure convergent rather than divergent thinking. See also *Content, Creativity, Divergent thinking, Operation, Product*.

correlation A statistical relationship between variables. See also *Variable*.

correlative subsumption The type of learning that takes place when new information requires an extension of what was previously known and could not, therefore, have been derived directly from it. See also *Derivative subsumption, Subsumption*.

counseling The act of giving advice. See also *Client-centered therapy, Directive therapy*.

creativity Generally refers to the capacity of individuals to produce novel or original answers or products.

The term *creative* is an adjective that may be used to describe people, products, or processes. See also *Convergent thinking, Divergent thinking.*

criterion-referenced test Test in which the student is judged relative to a criterion rather than relative to the performance of other students. The teacher decides beforehand the specific performance expected and tests to see whether the student has reached this criterion. See also *Norm-referenced test.*

criterion-related validity A measure of the extent to which predictions based on test results are accurate (predictive validity) and the extent to which the test agrees with other related measures (concurrent validity). Also called "predictive validity." See also *Construct validity, Content validity, Face validity, Reliability, Validity.*

critical period A period in development during which exposure to appropriate experiences or stimuli will bring about specific learning much more easily than is the case at other times. See also *Imprinting.*

crystallized abilities Cattell's term for intellectual abilities that are highly dependent on experience (verbal and numerical abilities, for example). These abilities do not appear to decline significantly with advancing age. See also *Fluid abilities.*

culture The pattern of socially acceptable behaviors that characterizes a people or a social group. It includes all the attitudes and beliefs that the group has about the things it considers important.

declarative knowledge All the facts, information, and experiences that are part of what we know. See also *Procedural knowledge.*

deferred imitation The ability to imitate people or events in their absence. Deferred imitation is assumed to be crucial in the development of language abilities.

derivative subsumption The type of subsumption (or learning) that takes place when new material can be derived directly from what is already known. See also *Correlative subsumption, Subsumption.*

desist To stop, to refrain from. In education, "desists" are teacher behaviors intended to make a student stop (desist from) some ongoing or impending misbehavior. Desists may take the form of threats, simple requests, orders, pleas, and so on. See also *With-it-ness.*

development The growth, maturational, and learning processes from birth to maturity. See also *Growth, Maturation.*

differential reinforcement of successive approximations The procedure of reinforcing only some responses and not others. Differential reinforcement is used in the *shaping* of complex behaviors. See also *Shaping.*

direct reinforcement The type of reinforcement that affects the individual in question directly rather than vicariously. See also *Vicarious reinforcement.*

directive therapy Type of counselor-client relationship in which the counselor takes the major responsibility for directing the client's behavior. See also *Counseling.*

discipline The control aspects of teaching.

discovery learning The acquisition of new information or knowledge largely as a result of the learner's own efforts. Discovery learning is contrasted with expository or reception learning and is generally associated with Bruner, among others. See also *Reception learning.*

discriminated stimulus A stimulus that is perceived by the organism. In operant conditioning, the discriminated stimulus elicits the response.

discrimination Processes involved in learning that certain responses are appropriate in specific situations but inappropriate in other similar situations. Generalization is an opposite process. See also *Generalization.*

disinhibition The appearance of a suppressed behavior. See also *Inhibitory-disinhibitory effect.*

disposition An inclination or a tendency to do (or not to do) something; an aspect of motivation. See also *Motivation.*

dissociability A term used by Ausubel to indicate the ease with which material that is to be recalled can be separated (dissociated) from other related material that is also in memory.

distance receptors The senses that receive stimulation from a distance (for example, hearing and vision).

divergent thinking An expression used by Guilford to describe the type of thinking that results in the production of several different solutions for one problem. Divergent thinking is assumed to be closely related to creative behavior, and the term is used interchangeably with the term *creativity.* See also *Convergent thinking, Creativity.*

diversity of training Bruner's expression relating to his belief that exposure to information under a wide range of circumstances is conducive to discovering relationships among concepts.

drive The tendency to behave that is brought about by an unsatisfied need—for example, the hunger drive is related to the need for food. See also *Need, Need-drive theory.*

educational psychology A science concerned primarily with the study of human behavior in educational settings. Applies existing psychological knowledge to instructional problems and develops new knowledge and procedures.

egocentrism A way of functioning characterized by an inability to assume the point of view of others. A child's early thinking is largely egocentric.

eidetic imagery A particularly vivid type of visual image in memory. In many ways, it is almost as though the individual were actually able to look at what is being remembered—hence the synonym "photographic memory."

elicited response A response brought about by a stimulus. The expression is synonymous with the term *respondent*. See also *Operant, Respondent, Unconditioned response*.

eliciting effect Imitative behavior in which the observer does not copy the model's responses but simply behaves in a related manner. See also *Imitation, Inhibitory-disinhibitory effect, Modeling effect*.

emitted response A response not elicited by a stimulus but simply emitted by the organism. An emitted response is, in fact, an operant.

empower To enable; to give power to. One of the most important goals of education is to empower students by providing them with both specific information and learning/thinking strategies and by developing within them the feelings of personal power that come with the realization that one is competent and worthwhile.

enactive A term used by Bruner to describe young children's representation of their world. It refers specifically to the belief that children represent the world in terms of their personal actions. See also *Iconic, Symbolic*.

encoding A process whereby we derive meaning from the environment. To encode is to represent in another form. At a mental level, encoding involves the process of abstracting—representing as a concept or a meaning.

enrichment An approach in the education of gifted children. Enrichment involves providing students with additional and different school experiences rather than simply moving them more rapidly through the conventional curriculum. Also called the "revolving door" model. See also *Acceleration*.

environmentalism The belief that whatever a child becomes is determined by experience (the environment) rather than by genetic makeup.

equilibration A Piagetian term for the process by which we maintain a balance between assimilation (using old learning) and accommodation (changing behavior, learning new things). Equilibration is essential for adaptation and cognitive growth.

equivalence reliability An estimate of the consistency of a test based on the extent to which different forms of the test yield similar results. Common measures of equivalence reliability are provided by split-halves or parallel-forms approaches. See also *Parallel-forms reliability, Split-half reliability*.

escape learning A conditioning phenomenon whereby the organism learns means of escaping from a situation, usually following the presentation of aversive (unpleasant) stimulation. See also *Avoidance learning*.

evaluation In contrast to measurement, involves making a value judgment—deciding on the goodness or badness of performance; also denotes the highest-level intellectual skill in Bloom's taxonomy of educational objectives, in which it is defined as the ability to render judgments about the value of methods or materials for specific purposes, making use of external or internal criteria. See also *Assessment, Measurement*.

exclusion A time-out punishment procedure whereby a child is not removed from the situation but is excluded from ongoing activities, often by being made to sit behind a screen, in a corner, or facing away from the class. See also *Isolation, Nonexclusion, Time-out*.

exemplary model A good example. A teacher, for example.

expectations Anticipated behavior. Teachers' expectations are particularly important because they may affect the behavior of some students.

expository organizer An idea or concept that serves as a description (exposition) of concepts that are relevant to new learning.

expressive objectives Instructional objectives that are concerned with the affective (emotional) components of learning rather than simply with content or performance.

extinction The cessation of a response as a function of the withdrawal of reinforcement. See also *Forgetting*.

extinction rate Time lapse between the cessation of a response and the withdrawal of reinforcement.

extrinsic reinforcement Reinforcement that comes from outside rather than from within—for example, high grades, praise, or money. See also *Intrinsic reinforcement*.

face validity The extent to which a test appears to be measuring what it is intended to measure. See also *Construct validity, Content validity, Criterion-related validity, Reliability, Validity.*

fact Something that observation leads us to believe is true or real. Ideally, the observations that determine our facts are sufficiently objective and repeatable that they provide us with some assurance that they accurately reflect the way things actually are.

fixed schedule A type of intermittent schedule of reinforcement in which the reinforcement occurs at fixed intervals of time (an interval schedule) or after a specified number of trials (a ratio schedule). See also *Continuous reinforcement, Intermittent reinforcement, Interval schedule, Random schedule, Ratio schedule, Schedule of reinforcement.*

fluid abilities Cattell's term for intellectual abilities that seem to underlie much of our intelligent behavior and that are not highly affected by experience (for example, general reasoning, attention span, and memory for numbers). Fluid abilities are more likely to decline in old age. See also *Crystallized abilities.*

forgetting The cessation of a response as a function of the passage of time; not to be confused with extinction. See also *Extinction.*

formal operations The last of Piaget's four major stages. It begins around age 11 or 12 and lasts until age 14 or 15. It is characterized by the child's increasing ability to use logical thought processes.

formative evaluation Evaluation undertaken before and during instruction, designed primarily to assist the learner in identifying strengths and weaknesses. Formative evaluation is a fundamental part of the process of instruction. See also *Summative evaluation.*

frames Units of information presented in programmed instruction. A frame not only presents information but also usually requires the student to make a response.

fraternal twins Twins whose genetic origins are two different eggs. Such twins are as genetically dissimilar as nontwin siblings. See also *Identical twins.*

g Abbreviation for *general intelligence*—a basic intellectual capability sometimes assumed to underlie all manifestations of intelligence.

gender roles Attitudes, personality characteristics, behavior, and other qualities associated with being male or female. Gender roles define masculinity and femininity. Also called "sex roles." See also *Sex typing.*

generalization The transference of a response from one stimulus to a similar stimulus (stimulus generalization) or the transference of a similar response for another response in the face of a single stimulus (response generalization). A child who responds with fear in a new situation that resembles an old, fear-producing situation is showing evidence of stimulus generalization. Also called "transfer." See also *Discrimination.*

generalized reinforcer A stimulus that is not reinforcing before being paired with a primary reinforcer. Generalized reinforcers are stimuli that are present so often at the time of reinforcement that they come to be reinforcing for a wide variety of unrelated activities. Stimuli such as social prestige, praise, and money are generalized reinforcers for human behavior. See also *Primary reinforcer.*

Gordon technique A creativity-enhancing technique very similar to brainstorming except that an abstraction of a problem rather than a specific problem is presented. See also *Brainstorming.*

grade-equivalent scores Standardized test norms that allow users to convert raw scores to grade equivalents—that is, that allow the user to conclude that the testee has performed at a level comparable to that of average children at a specified grade level. See also *Age-equivalent scores, Standardized tests.*

grammar Characteristic system of word forms and syntax of a language. See also *Syntax.*

group test A type of test, usually used to measure intelligence, that may be given to large groups of subjects at one time. It is typically of the pencil-and-paper variety. See also *Individual test.*

growth The quantitative, physical aspects of development. See also *Development, Maturation.*

hardware The physical components of a computer, including monitors, controllers, keyboards, chips, cards, circuits, drives, printers, and so on. See also *Software.*

hierarchy of classes An arrangement of concepts or classes in terms of their inclusiveness. At the top of the hierarchy is the concept (class) that is most inclusive (for example, writing instruments); below this highly inclusive concept are those that are included in it (for example, pens, typewriters, pencils, and so on). See also *Coding system.*

holistic education A comprehensive term for educational approaches that attempt to remedy what is seen as traditional education's failure to educate the whole brain. Advocates of holistic education believe that the right hemisphere, which speculation links with art, music, and emotion, is neglected by curricula that stress reason, logic, language, science, and mathematics.

holophrase A sentencelike word uttered by young children early in the course of learning a language. A holophrase is a single word into which the child packs as much meaning as an adult would convey by using a much longer phrase.

humanism A philosophical and psychological orientation that is primarily concerned with our humanity— that is, with our worth as individuals and with those processes that are considered to make us more human.

iconic A term that refers to a stage in the development of the child's representation of his or her world. The term is used by Bruner to describe an intermediate stage of development characterized by a representation of the world in terms of relatively concrete mental images. See also *Enactive, Symbolic.*

identical twins Twins whose genetic origin is one egg. Such twins are genetically identical. See also *Fraternal twins.*

identity A logical rule that specifies that certain activities leave objects or situations unchanged. See also *Reversibility.*

imitation Copying behavior. To imitate a person's behavior is simply to use that person's behavior as a pattern. Bandura and Walters describe three different effects of imitation. See also *Eliciting effect, Inhibitory-disinhibitory effect, Modeling effect, Observational learning.*

imprinting Unlearned, instinctlike behaviors that are not present at birth but that become part of an animal's repertoire after exposure to a suitable stimulus during a critical period. The "following" behavior of young ducks, geese, and chickens is an example. See also *Critical period.*

individual education plan (IEP) An individualized instructional program tailored to a child's specific pattern of needs and abilities. IEPs may be used for gifted, learning-disabled, retarded, or average children. Also called "individualized program plan."

individual test A test, usually used to measure intelligence, that can be given to only one individual at a time. See also *Group test.*

individually guided education (IGE) An individual approach to instruction based on the principle of un-graded schools. It makes use of teams of teachers, extensive in-service teacher training, individual programming for each student, home involvement, and the continual development of new curriculum material. Like IPI (see next entry), it is also based on mastery learning. See also *Individual education plan.*

individually prescribed instruction (IPI) A complex instructional system that involves reorganizing the entire curriculum for each subject (and over a wide range of grades) into a series of sequential units with clearly defined objectives and tests for each unit. Students progress at their own rate as they master each unit. See also *Individual education plan, Individually guided instruction.*

inhibition In imitative learning, the suppression of a previously acquired behavior. This sometimes occurs when a learner observes a model being punished for the behavior. See also *Inhibitory-disinhibitory effect.*

inhibitory-disinhibitory effect The type of imitative behavior that results either in the suppression (inhibition) or appearance (disinhibition) of previously acquired deviant behavior. See also *Disinhibition, Eliciting effect, Imitation, Modeling effect, Observational learning.*

instinct A complex, species-specific, relatively unmodifiable pattern of behaviors such as migration or nesting in some birds and animals. Less complex inherited behaviors are usually referred to as "reflexes."

instruction The arrangement of external events in a learning situation in order to facilitate learning, retention, and transfer.

instructional objective The goal or intended result of instruction. Objectives may be short-range or long-range. Also referred to as "behavioral objectives."

intellectual skills Robert Gagné's term for the outcomes of the learning process. He describes seven such skills ranging from simple conditioned responses to abstract problem solving.

intelligence A property measured by intelligence tests; seems to refer primarily to the capacity of individuals to adjust to their environments.

intelligence quotient (IQ) A simple way to describe intelligence by assigning it a number that represents the ratio of mental to chronological age, multiplied by 100. Average IQ is therefore 100 and is based on a comparison between an individual's performance and that of comparable others.

intermittent reinforcement A schedule of reinforcement that does not present a reinforcer for all correct responses. Also called "partial reinforcement." See also *Continuous reinforcement, Fixed schedule, Interval schedule, Random schedule, Ratio schedule, Schedule of reinforcement.*

interval scale A measurement scale that has no true zero but on which numerical indicators are arbitrarily set. Intervals between numbers are assumed to be equal in such a scale (a thermometer, for example).

interval schedule An intermittent schedule of reinforcement that is based on the passage of time. See also *Continuous reinforcement, Fixed schedule, Intermittent reinforcement, Random schedule, Ratio schedule, Schedule of reinforcement.*

intrinsic reinforcement Reinforcement that comes from within the individual rather than from the outside (satisfaction, for example). Also called "internal reinforcement." See also *Extrinsic reinforcement.*

intuitive thinking One of the substages of Piaget's preoperational thought, beginning around age 4 and lasting until age 7 or 8, marked by the child's ability to solve many problems intuitively and by the inability to respond correctly in the face of misleading perceptual features of problems. See also *Preconceptual thinking, Preoperational thinking.*

isolation A time-out procedure in which a child is removed from an area of reinforcement (typically the classroom, although sometimes the playground or other areas) and isolated in a different place. See also *Exclusion, Nonexclusion, Time-out.*

jargon The unique, technical vocabulary of a discipline—sometimes useful but not always essential.

jargon shock My tongue was in my cheek in Chapter 3, but I'm glad you checked here. See *Jargon.*

knowledge A generic term for the information, the ways of dealing with information, the ways of acquiring information, and so on that an individual possesses; also the lowest-level objective in Bloom's taxonomy of educational objectives. See also *Cognitive structure.*

knowledge base The storehouse of concepts, information, associations, and procedures that we accumulate over time.

knowledge of results Knowledge about the correctness or incorrectness of a response. Knowledge of results is usually immediate in programmed instruction.

knowledge-acquisition components One of Sternberg's three facets of human intelligence, related to procedures used for learning new information (sepa-

rating the important from the unimportant, associating items of information, comparing the new with the old). See also *Cognitive strategy, Learning/Thinking strategy, Metacognition, Metacomponents, Metamemory, Performance components.*

language The use of arbitrary sounds in the transmission of messages from one individual or organism to another. Language should not be confused with communication. See also *Communication.*

language immersion An approach to teaching a second language that involves placing the learner in an environment in which only the second language is used.

lateral thinking de Bono's term for a way of thinking that leads to creative solutions. See also *Vertical thinking.*

lateralization A term that refers to the division of functions and capabilities between the two hemispheres of the brain.

law A statement that is accurate beyond reasonable doubt. See also *Belief, Model, Principle, Theory.*

law of effect A Thorndikean law of learning that states that it is the effect of a response that leads to its being learned (stamped in) or not learned (stamped out).

law of multiple responses One of Thorndike's laws based on his observation that learning involves the emission of a variety of responses (multiple responses) until one (presumably an appropriate one) is reinforced. It is because of this law that Thorndike's theory is often referred to as a "theory of trial-and-error learning."

law of prepotency of elements A Thorndikean law of learning that states that people tend to respond to the most striking of the various elements that make up a stimulus situation.

law of readiness A Thorndikean law of learning that takes into account the fact that certain types of learning are impossible or difficult unless the learner is ready. In this context, "readiness" refers to maturational level, previous learning, motivational factors, and other characteristics of the individual that relate to learning.

law of response by analogy An analogy is typically an explanation, comparison, or illustration based on similarity. In Thorndike's system, response by analogy refers to responses that occur because of similarities between two situations.

law of set or attitude A Thorndikean law of learning that recognizes the fact that we are often predisposed to respond in certain ways as a result of our experiences and previously learned attitudes.

learning Changes in behavior due to experience; does not include changes due to motivation, fatigue, or drugs.

learning disability A depression in the ability to learn specific things (for example, reading or arithmetic), in which the learning difficulties are not related to mental retardation or emotional disturbance.

learning style A unique and important learner variable manifested in differences in biological rhythms (morning versus evening people), perceptual strengths (visual versus auditory learners), sociological preference (large- versus small-group instruction), attention span (long or short), and a wealth of personality variables (dependence/independence, for example).

learning theory Psychological theories concerned primarily with questions about how people learn, how they acquire information, and how they behave.

learning/thinking strategy Processes involved in learning and thinking; another expression for "cognitive strategy," introduced to emphasize that the strategies involved in cognition (knowing) are also involved in learning and thinking. See also *Cognitive strategy, Knowledge-acquisition components, Metacomponents, Metamemory, Performance components.*

levels of processing An information-processing theory, attributed to Craik and Lockhart, maintaining that memory is a function of the level to which information is processed. At the lowest level, a stimulus is simply recognized as a physical event (and is available momentarily in short-term sensory memory); at a much deeper level, a stimulus is interpreted in terms of its meaning (and is available in long-term memory).

linear program The presentation of programmed material in such a manner that all learners progress through the same material in the same order. Linear programs typically make no provision for individual differences in learning; the material, however, is broken up into very small steps (frames). See also *Branching program, Frame.*

link system A memory system whereby items to be remembered are associated one with the other by means of a series of related visual images. See also *Loci system, Phonetic system.*

loci system A mnemonic system whereby items to be remembered are associated with visual images of specific places. See also *Link system, Phonetic system.*

Logo Seymour Papert's computer language, designed to be easily enough understood by young children to allow them to learn programming skills easily and painlessly as they might learn an exciting new game. The program uses a "turtle"—a small creature that can be instructed (that is, programmed) to move in different ways, tracing various geometric designs as it moves.

long-term memory A type of memory whereby, with continued rehearsal and recoding of sensory information (processing in terms of meaning, for example), material will be available for recall over a long period of time.

mainstreaming The practice of placing students in need of special services in regular classrooms rather than segregating them.

mastery learning An instructional approach described by Bloom in which a learning sequence is analyzed into specific objectives and progress requires that each learner master sequential objectives.

mastery of specifics A Brunerian term for the learning of details. Mastery of relevant specifics is necessary for acquiring concepts and discovering relationships among them.

maturation The process of normal physical and psychological development. Maturation is defined as occurring independently of particular experiences. See also *Development, Growth.*

mean The arithmetic average of a set of scores. In distributions that are skewed (top- and bottom-heavy), the mean is not the best index of central tendency; that is, it is not necessarily at the middle of the distribution. See also *Central tendency, Median, Mode.*

measurement The application of an instrument to gauge the quantity of something, as opposed to its quality. Assessing quality involves evaluation, not measurement. See also *Assessment, Evaluation.*

median The midpoint or fiftieth percentile of a distribution; the point at or below which 50 percent of all scores fall. See also *Central tendency, Mean, Mode.*

memory The effects that experiences are assumed to have on the human mind. Refers to the storage of these effects. See also *Retention, Retrieval.*

mental retardation A significant general depression in the ability to learn, usually accompanied by deficits in adaptive behavior.

mental structure See *Cognitive structure.*

mentor Individual engaged in a one-to-one teaching/learning relationship in which the teacher (mentor) serves as a fundamentally important model with respect to values, beliefs, philosophies, and attitudes, as well as a source of more specific information. See also *Tutor*.

metacognition Knowledge about knowing. As we grow and learn, we develop notions of ourselves as learners. Accordingly, we develop strategies that recognize our limitations and that allow us to monitor our progress and to take advantage of our efforts. See also *Cognitive strategy, Learning/Thinking strategy, Metamemory*.

metacomponents One of Sternberg's three components of human intelligence. Metacomponents include the skills involved in planning, monitoring, and evaluating cognitive performance—in other words, the skills of metacognition. See also *Knowledge-acquisition components, Metacognition, Metamemory, Performance components*.

metamemory The knowledge we develop about our own memory processes—our knowledge about how to remember, rather than simply our memories. See also *Cognitive strategy, Metacognition*.

metaneeds Maslow's term for "higher" needs, also called "growth needs." Concerned with psychological, self-related, functions rather than with biology. Include "need" to know truth, beauty, justice, and to self-actualize.

méthode clinique Piaget's experimental method. It involves an interview technique in which questions are determined largely by the subject's responses. Its flexibility distinguishes it from ordinary interview techniques.

microcomputers Most modern home and business computers. They are termed *micro* because chip technology has resulted in a dramatic reduction in their size.

minimum competency testing A global term for the administration of batteries of tests designed to determine whether students, or teachers, have reached some minimum level of competency in basic areas such as language and mathematics.

mode The most frequently occurring score(s) in a distribution.

model A representation, usually abstract, of some phenomenon or system. Alternatively, a pattern for behavior that can be copied by someone. See also *Belief, Law, Principle, Theory*.

modeling effect The type of imitative behavior that involves learning a novel response. See also *Eliciting effect, Imitation, Inhibitory-disinhibitory effect, Observational learning*.

morphological analysis A creativity-enhancing technique, advanced by Arnold, involving the analysis of problems into their component parts and subsequent attempts to brainstorm each of these component parts.

motivation The causes of behavior. Our motives are the reasons why we engage in some behaviors and not in others. They are what initiate behavior and what direct it. See also *Disposition*.

motor learning Learning that involves muscular coordination and physical skills. Such common activities as walking and driving a car involve motor learning.

need Ordinarily refers to a lack or deficit in the human organism. Needs may be either unlearned (for example, the need for food or water) or learned (the need for money). See also *Drive, Need-drive theory*.

need state Bruner's expression describing the arousal level of an organism.

need-drive theory A motivation theory that attempts to explain human behavior on the basis of the motivating properties of needs. Such theories typically assume that humans have certain learned and unlearned needs, which give rise to drives, which in turn are responsible for the occurrence of behavior. See also *Drive, Need*.

negative correlation The type of relationship that exists between two variables when high values in one are associated with correspondingly low values in the other.

negative reinforcer A stimulus that has the effect of increasing the probability of occurrence of the response that precedes it. Negative reinforcement ordinarily takes the form of an unpleasant or noxious stimulus that is removed as a result of a specific response. See also *Positive reinforcer, Reinforcement, Reinforcer, Reward*.

neonate A newborn infant. The neonatal period terminates when the infant regains birth weight (about two weeks after birth).

neuron (nerve cell) An elongated cell that forms part of the nervous system. The main part of the neuron is the cell body; the elongated part is the axon.

neutral stimulus A stimulus that does not initially lead reliably to a predictable response. For example, neutral stimuli are not associated with emotional responses until learning has occurred, at which point they are referred to as conditioned (rather than neutral) stimuli. See also *Conditioned response*.

nominal scale A crude measurement scale that does no more than provide descriptive labels.

nonexclusion The mildest form of time-out procedure; the child is not allowed to participate in ongoing activity but is required to observe. See also *Exclusion, Isolation, Time-out.*

normal curve A mathematical function that can be represented in the form of a bell-shaped curve. A large number of naturally occurring events are normally distributed (the vast majority of the events [or scores] cluster around the middle of the distribution [around the mean or median], with progressively fewer scores being farther and farther away from the average).

norm-referenced test A test in which the student is competing against the performance of other students rather than in relation to some preestablished criterion of acceptable performance. See also *Criterion-referenced test.*

object concept Piaget's expression for the child's understanding that the world is composed of objects that continue to exist apart from his or her perception of them.

obliterative subsumption The incorporation of new material into preexisting cognitive structure so that the new material eventually becomes indistinguishable—in other words, becomes obliterated (reaches *zero dissociability*, in Ausubel's terms). In effect, obliterative subsumption is forgetting. See also *Correlative subsumption, Derivative subsumption, Subsumption.*

observational learning A term used synonymously with the expression "learning through imitation." See also *Imitation.*

operant Skinner's term for a response not elicited by any known or obvious stimulus. Most significant human behaviors appear to be operants (for example, writing a letter or going for a walk). See also *Elicited response, Respondent, Unconditioned response.*

operant conditioning A type of learning that involves an increase in the probability that a response will occur as a function of reinforcement. Most of Skinner's experimental work investigates the principles of operant conditioning. See also *Classical conditioning, Conditioning.*

operation (1) A Piagetian term that remains relatively nebulous but refers essentially to a thought process. An operation is an action that has been internalized in the sense that it can be "thought" and is reversible in the sense that it can be "unthought." (2) A term used by Guilford to describe major kinds of intellectual activity, such as remembering, evaluating, and divergent and convergent thinking. See also *Content, Convergent thinking, Creativity, Divergent thinking, Product.*

ordinal scale A scale of measurement that permits no more than simple ranking. An ordinal scale does not have a true zero, nor are the intervals between units on the scale necessarily equal. Using an ordinal scale, it is possible to say that A is greater than B and that B is greater than C but never by how much.

overlapping Kounin's term for the simultaneous occurrence of two or more events in the classroom, each requiring the teacher's attention. Good class managers can handle overlapping events without disrupting the flow of classroom activities.

parallel-forms reliability A measure of test consistency (reliability) obtained by looking at the correlation between scores obtained by the same individual on two different but equivalent (parallel) forms of one test. See also *Equivalence reliability, Repeated-forms reliability, Split-half reliability.*

penalty The type of punishment that involves losing or giving up something pleasant.

percentile The point at or below which a specified percentage of scores fall. For example, the fiftieth percentile is the point at or below which 50 percent of all scores fall. A score of 50 percent is not necessarily at the fiftieth percentile.

perception The translation of physical energies into neurological impulses—that is, stimuli into sensations—that can be interpreted by the individual.

performance Actual behavior. The inference that learning has occurred is typically based on observed changes in performance.

performance components One of Sternberg's three components of human intelligence. Performance components are the skills and processes actually used in carrying out intellectual tasks (reasoning, encoding, analyzing, remembering, and so on). See also *Knowledge-acquisition components, Metacomponents.*

personalized system of instruction (PSI) An instructional approach developed by Keller, based in part on Bloom's mastery learning, in which course material is broken down into small units, study is largely individual, a variety of study material is available, and progress depends on performance on unit tests. Sometimes called "the Keller plan." See also *Individual education plan, Individually guided education, Individually prescribed instruction.*

person-centered therapy See *Client-centered therapy.*

phenomenal field The feelings, perceptions, and awareness that an individual has at any given moment. See also *Phenomenology.*

phenomenology An approach concerned primarily with how individuals view their own world. Its basic assumption is that each individual perceives and reacts to the world in a unique manner and that it is this phenomenological world view that is important in understanding the individual's behavior. See also *Phenomenal field.*

phonetic system A particularly powerful mnemonic system that makes use of associations between numbers and letters combined to form words; visual images associated with these words are then linked with items to be remembered. Professional memorizers often use some variation of a phonetic system. See also *Link system, Loci system.*

phonology The structure of speech sounds of a language.

physiological needs Basic biological needs, such as the need for food and water.

portfolio In educational assessment, a collection of actual samples of students' performances and achievements.

positive control The control of human behavior, usually through the presentation of pleasant stimuli. This is in contrast to techniques of aversive control, which generally use negative reinforcement.

positive correlation The type of relationship that exists between two variables so that high or low scores on one are associated with correspondingly high or low scores on the other.

positive reinforcer A stimulus that increases the probability that a response will recur as a result of being added to a situation after the response has occurred once. Usually takes the form of a pleasant stimulus (reward) that results from a specific response. See also *Negative reinforcer, Reinforcement, Reinforcer, Reward.*

pragmatics The implicit language rules that govern practical things such as when to speak and how to take turns in conversation.

preconceptual thinking The first substage in the period of preoperational thought, beginning around age two and lasting until age four. It is so called because the child has not yet developed the ability to classify. See also *Intuitive thinking, Preoperational thinking.*

predictive validity See *Criterion-related validity.*

Premack principle The recognition that behaviors that are chosen frequently by an individual (and that are therefore favored) may be used to reinforce other, less frequently chosen behaviors. (For example: "You can watch television when you have finished your homework.")

preoperational thinking The second of Piaget's four major stages, lasting from around age 2 to age 7 or 8. It consists of two substages: intuitive thinking and preconceptual thinking. See also *Intuitive thinking, Preconceptual thinking.*

primary reinforcer A stimulus that is reinforcing in the absence of any learning. Such stimuli as food and drink are primary reinforcers because, presumably, an organism does not have to learn that they are pleasant. See also *Generalized reinforcer.*

principle A statement relating to some uniformity or predictability. Principles are far more open to doubt than are laws but are more reliable than beliefs. See also *Belief, Law, Model, Theory.*

principle of opposite control Describes the tendency for sensations and movements on either side of the body to be controlled by the opposite cerebral hemisphere.

proactive inhibition The interference of earlier learning with the retention of subsequent learning. See also *Retroactive inhibition.*

procedural knowledge Knowing how to do something; knowing procedures as well as facts (declarative knowledge). See also *Declarative knowledge.*

processing The intellectual or cognitive activities that occur as stimulus information is reacted to, analyzed, sorted, organized, and stored in memory or forgotten.

product A term used by Guilford to describe the result of applying an operation to content. A product may take the form of a response. See also *Content, Convergent thinking, Creativity, Divergent thinking, Operation.*

profile A description of individual patterns of strengths, weaknesses, or abilities.

programmed instruction An instructional procedure that makes use of the systematic presentation of information in small steps (frames), in the form of a workbook or some other device. Programs typically require learners to make responses and provide immediate knowledge of results.

prompts Devices used in programmed instruction to ensure that the student will probably answer correctly. They may take a variety of forms.

psychological hedonism The belief that humans act primarily to avoid pain and to obtain pleasure.

psychological needs Human needs other than those dealing with basic physical requirements such as food, sex, water, and temperature regulation (physiological needs). Psychological needs described by Maslow include the need to belong, to feel safe, to love and be loved, to maintain a high opinion of oneself, and to self-actualize. See also *Self-actualization.*

psychology The science that examines human behavior (and that of other animals as well).

puberty Sexual maturity.

pubescence Changes of adolescence leading to sexual maturity.

punishment Involves either the presentation of an unpleasant stimulus or the withdrawal of a pleasant stimulus as a consequence of behavior. Punishment should not be confused with *negative reinforcement.*

random schedule A type of intermittent schedule of reinforcement. It may be of either the interval or the ratio variety and is characterized by the presentation of rewards at random intervals or on random trials. Although both fixed and random schedules may be based on the same intervals or on the same ratios, one can predict when reward will occur under a fixed schedule, whereas it is impossible to do so under a random schedule. Also called "variable schedule." See also *Continuous reinforcement, Fixed schedule, Intermittent reinforcement, Interval schedule, Ratio schedule, Schedule of reinforcement.*

rate of learning A measure of the amount of time required to learn a correct response, or, alternatively, a measure of the number of trials required before the correct response occurs.

ratio scale A measurement scale in which there is a true zero and in which differences between units on the scale are equal. Educational and psychological measurements do not involve ratio scales, although we sometimes act as though they do—as, for example, when we assume that the difference between a percentage score of 78 and 79 is the same as that between 84 and 85. Weight is measured on a ratio scale.

ratio schedule An intermittent schedule of reinforcement that is based on a proportion of correct responses. See also *Continuous reinforcement, Fixed schedule, Intermittent reinforcement, Interval schedule, Random schedule, Schedule of reinforcement.*

reception learning The type of learning that involves primarily instruction or tuition rather than the learner's own efforts. Teaching for reception learning, often associated with Ausubel, usually takes the form of expository or didactic methods; that is, the teacher structures the material and presents it to learners in relatively final form rather than asking them to discover that form. See also *Discovery learning.*

reciprocal determinism Bandura's label for the recognition that even though environments affect individuals in important ways, individuals also affect environments by selecting and shaping them. Thus, the influence (determinism) is two-way (reciprocal).

reinforcement The effect of a reinforcer; specifically, to increase the probability that a response will occur. See also *Negative reinforcer, Positive reinforcer, Reinforcer, Reward.*

reinforcement menu A list of activities, objects, or other consequences from which students can select reinforcers.

reinforcer A stimulus that causes reinforcement. See also *Negative reinforcer, Positive reinforcer, Reinforcement, Reward.*

reliability The consistency with which a test measures whatever it measures. A perfectly reliable test should yield the same scores on different occasions (for the same individual), providing what it measures has not changed. Most educational and psychological tests are severely limited in terms of reliability. See also *Construct validity, Content validity, Criterion-related validity, Face validity, Validity.*

relief A common expression for negative reinforcement—the type of reinforcement that results when an unpleasant stimulus is removed as a consequence of behavior. See also *Negative reinforcement.*

remedial frame A frame in a branching program to which students are referred when they make an incorrect response. The purpose of the remedial frame is to provide information required for a subsequent correct response.

repeated-measures reliability An estimate of the consistency (reliability) of a test based on the degree of agreement among scores obtained from different presentations of the same test. See also *Parallel-forms reliability.*

reprimand A common form of mild punishment that takes the form of an expression of disapproval. Reprimands are often verbal ("You shouldn't do that") but can also be nonverbal (a head shake). See also *Response cost, Time-out.*

respondent A term used by Skinner in contrast to the term *operant.* A respondent is a response that is elicited by a known, specific stimulus. Unconditioned responses are examples of respondents. See also *Elicited response, Operant, Unconditioned response.*

response Any organic, muscular, glandular, or psychic process that results from stimulation.

response cost A mild form of punishment whereby tangible reinforcers that have been given for good behavior are taken away for misbehaviors. Response-cost systems are often used in systematic behavior-management programs. See also *Reprimand, Time-out*.

response rate The number of responses emitted by an organism in a given period of time. Response rates for operant behaviors appear to be largely a function of the schedules of reinforcement used.

retention A term often used as a synonym for memory. See also *Memory, Retention*.

retrieval A term for the ability to bring items of information or impressions out of memory. It is often assumed that to forget is not to lose from memory but simply to lose the ability to retrieve from memory. See also *Memory, Retention*.

retroactive inhibition The interference of subsequently learned material with the retention of previously learned material. See also *Proactive inhibition*.

reversibility A logical property manifested in the ability to reverse or undo activity in either an empirical or a conceptual sense. An idea is said to be reversible when a child realizes the logical consequences of an opposite action. See also *Identity*.

reward An object, stimulus, event, or outcome that is perceived as being pleasant and that may therefore be reinforcing. See *Negative reinforcer, Positive reinforcer, Reinforcement, Reinforcer*.

schedule of reinforcement The time and frequency of presentation of reinforcement to organisms. See also *Continuous reinforcement, Fixed schedule, Intermittent reinforcement, Interval schedule, Random schedule, Ratio schedule*.

schemata (singular: *schema*) The label used by Piaget to describe a unit in cognitive structure. A schema is, in one sense, an activity together with whatever structural connotations that activity has. In another sense, a schema may be thought of as an idea or a concept.

science An approach and an attitude toward knowledge that emphasize objectivity, precision, and replicability.

script Term describing our knowledge of what goes with what and in what sequence. Scripts are a part of cognitive structure that deals with the routine and the predictable.

self-actualization The process or act of becoming oneself, of developing one's potentialities, of achieving an awareness of one's identity, of self-fulfillment. The

term is central in humanistic psychology. See also *Psychological needs*.

self-efficacy A term that refers to judgments we make about how efficacious (effective) we are in given situations. Judgments of self-efficacy are important in determining an individual's choice of activities and in influencing the amount of interest and effort expended.

semantics The meanings of the words of a language.

sensorimotor intelligence The first stage of development in Piaget's classification. It lasts from birth to approximately age two and is so called because children understand their world during that period primarily in terms of their activities in it and sensations of it.

sensory memory See *Short-term sensory storage*.

seriation The ordering of objects in terms of one or more properties. To seriate is to place in order.

set A predisposition to react to stimulation in a given manner.

sex typing The learning of behaviors according to the gender of an individual in a given society; the acquisition of masculine and feminine gender roles. See also *Gender roles*.

shaping A technique whereby animals and people are taught to perform complex behaviors that were not previously in their repertoires. The technique involves reinforcing responses that become increasingly closer approximations of the desired behavior. Also called the "method of successive approximations" or "the method of differential reinforcement of successive approximations." See also *Differential reinforcement of successive approximations*.

short-term memory A type of memory in which material is available for recall for a matter of seconds. Short-term memory involves primarily rehearsal rather than more in-depth processing. It defines our immediate consciousness. Also called "primary memory" or "working memory."

short-term sensory storage The phrase refers to the simple sensory recognition of such stimuli as a sound, a taste, or a sight. Also called "sensory memory."

Skinner box Various experimental environments used by Skinner in his investigations of operant conditioning. The typical Skinner box is a cagelike structure equipped with a lever and a food tray attached to a food mechanism. It allows the investigator to study operants (for example, bar pressing) and the relationship between an operant and reinforcement.

social learning The acquisition of patterns of behavior that conform to social expectations; learning what is acceptable and what is not acceptable in a given culture.

socialization The complex process of learning both those behaviors that are appropriate within a given culture and those that are less appropriate. The primary agents of socialization are home, school, and peer groups.

software Computer instructions; programs. Also called "courseware." See also *Hardware*.

SOMPA See *System of Multicultural Pluralistic Assessment*.

split-half reliability An index of test reliability (consistency) derived by arbitrarily dividing a test into parallel halves (odd- and even-numbered items, for example) and looking at the agreement between scores obtained by each individual on the two halves. See also *Equivalence reliability, Parallel-forms reliability*.

standard deviation A mathematical measure of the distribution of scores around their mean. In a normal distribution, approximately two-thirds of all scores fall within one standard deviation on either side of the mean, and almost 95 percent fall within two standard deviations of the mean.

standard language The socially prestigious form of a society's dominant language; the form that is taught in schools and against which other dialects are judged for correctness.

standardized tests Professionally developed—rather than teacher-made—tests that provide the user with norms (standards) and that typically indicate the average or expected performance of groups of subjects of certain grades and/or ages. See also *Age-equivalent scores, Grade-equivalent scores*.

stanines Standard scores that make use of a nine-point scale with a mean of 5 and a standard deviation of 2.

stimulus (plural: *stimuli*) Any change in the physical environment capable of exciting a sense organ.

stimulus-response (S-R) theories Learning theories with primary emphasis on stimuli and responses and the relationships between them. These theories are also called "behavioristic theories."

student-centered teaching Rogers's expression for an approach to teaching based on a philosophy of self-discovered learning. The approach requires that the teacher genuinely care for students as individuals and that students be allowed to determine for themselves what is important in their lives.

subsumer The term used by Ausubel to describe a concept, an idea, or a combination of concepts or ideas

that can serve to organize new information. Cognitive structure is therefore composed of subsumers.

subsumption Ausubel's term for the integration of new material or information with existing information. The term implies a process in which a new stimulus becomes part of what is already in cognitive structure. See also *Correlative subsumption, Derivative subsumption, Obliterative subsumption*.

summative evaluation The type of evaluation that occurs at the end of an instructional sequence and that is designed primarily to provide a grade. See also *Formative evaluation*.

superstitious schedule A fixed-interval schedule of reinforcement in which the reward is not given after every correct response but rather after the passage of a specified period of time. It is so called because it leads to the learning of behaviors that are only accidentally related to the reinforcement.

symbolic The final stage in the development of a child's representation of his or her world. The term is used by Bruner and describes the representation of the world in terms of arbitrary symbols. Symbolic representation includes representation in terms of language as well as in terms of theoretical or hypothetical systems. See also *Enactive, Iconic*.

symbolic model A model other than a real-life person. Any pattern for behavior may be termed a symbolic model if it is not a person. For example, books, television, and written instructions can provide symbolic models.

syntax The arrangement of words to form sentences. See also *Grammar*.

synthesis Putting together of parts in order to form a whole; complementary to analysis; a high-level intellectual ability in Bloom's taxonomy of educational objectives.

System of Multicultural Pluralistic Assessment (SOMPA) Mercer's battery of ten separate individual measures of medical status (hearing, vision, health), social functioning (school achievement), and ability, taking into account social and ethnic background. The SOMPA is designed to overcome the limitations of more conventional approaches to assessing ability among cultural and social minorities.

task analysis The process of analyzing what is to be learned in terms of a sequential series of related tasks. Essentially, task analysis provides the teacher with knowledge of important skills and knowledge that might be prerequisite for what is to be taught.

technology of teaching A Skinnerian phrase for the systematic application of the principles of behaviorism (especially of operant conditioning) to classroom practice.

test anxiety A characteristic evident in a fear of taking tests and an expectation of poor performance. Evidence suggests that test anxiety can impair performance on tests.

test blueprint A table of specifications for a teacher-made test. A good test blueprint provides information about the topics to be tested, the nature of the questions to be used, and the objectives (outcomes) to be assessed.

theory A body of information pertaining to a specific topic, a method of acquiring and/or dealing with information, or a set of explanations for related phenomena. See also *Belief, Law, Model, Principle.*

theory of trial-and-error learning See *Law of multiple responses.*

third-force psychology A general expression for humanistic approaches to psychology such as those exemplified by the work of Carl Rogers and Abraham Maslow. The first two "forces" are psychoanalysis and behaviorism (S-R psychology).

time-out A procedure in which students are removed from situations in which they might ordinarily be rewarded. Time-out procedures are widely used in classroom management. See also *Exclusion, Isolation, Nonexclusion, Reprimand, Response cost.*

tracking An instructional procedure that involves dividing the members of a class into groups according to their ability.

transductive reasoning The type of reasoning that proceeds from particular to particular rather than from particular to general or from general to particular. One example of transductive reasoning is the following:
Cows give milk.
Goats give milk.
Therefore, goats are cows.

transfer See *Generalization.*

trial-and-error learning Thorndikean explanation for learning based on the idea that when placed in a problem situation, an individual will emit a number of responses but will eventually learn the correct one as a result of reinforcement. Trial-and-error explanations for learning are sometimes contrasted with insight explanations.

T-score A standardized score with a preset mean of 50 and a standard deviation of 10. A T-score of 70 is therefore quite high because 70 is two standard deviations above the mean and only approximately 2.5 percent of all scores ordinarily fall beyond that point.

tutor Teacher involved in a one-on-one teaching situation. Tutors are frequently other students, or may be other teachers or experts. See also *Mentor.*

unconditioned response A response that is elicited by an unconditioned stimulus. See also *Elicited response, Operant, Respondent.*

unconditioned stimulus A stimulus that elicits a response before learning. All stimuli that are capable of eliciting reflexive behaviors are examples of unconditioned stimuli. For example, food is an unconditioned stimulus for the response of salivation.

validity The extent to which a test measures what it says it measures. For example, an intelligence test is valid to the extent that it measures intelligence and nothing else. Educational and psychological tests are limited by their frequently low validity. See also *Construct validity, Content validity, Criterion-related validity, Face validity, Reliability.*

variable A property, measurement, or characteristic that is susceptible to variation. In psychological experimentation, qualities of human beings such as intelligence and creativity are considered variables. See also *Correlation.*

variable schedule See *Random schedule.*

vertical thinking de Bono's term for thought processes that lead to correct, appropriate, and accepted solutions. This term is in contrast to lateral thinking, which leads to creative solutions. See also *Lateral thinking.*

vicarious reinforcement Reinforcement that results from observing someone else being reinforced. In imitative behavior, observers frequently act as though they are being reinforced when in fact they are not being reinforced; rather, they are aware, or simply assume, that the model is being reinforced. See also *Direct reinforcement.*

wild cow (almost literal) A bovine creature found in both forested and nonforested regions of the world. Wild cows are particularly unrestrained creatures, given to a great variety of social and solitary diversions, including playing cards, smoking cigars, and drinking whiskey. They also like to dance and to ice skate, and some are quite wonderful surfers. Sadly, they do not fly nearly as well as pigs. See also *Bear, Wild cow (metaphoric).*

wild cow (metaphoric) Wild cows are a lot of the things that are wrong with this planet: starvation, pollution, illiteracy, preventable infant mortality, famine, terrorism, resource depletion, AIDS, murder, puny teacher salaries, and on and on. See also *Bear, Wild cow (almost literal)*.

with-it-ness Kounin's expression for a quality of teacher behavior manifested in the teacher's awareness of all the important things happening in a classroom. Teachers who are high in with-it-ness make more effective use of desists. See also *Desists*.

working memory See *Short-term memory*.

zero dissociability See *Obliterative subsumption*.

zone of proximal growth Vygotsky's phrase for the individual's current potential for further intellectual development. Conventional measures of intelligence assess current intellectual development rather than potential for future development. Vygotsky believed that the zone of proximal growth (future potential) might be assessed by further questioning and the use of hints and prompts while administering a conventional intelligence test.

Z-score A standardized score with a mean of 0 and a standard deviation of 1. Hence, a Z-score of +3 is very high; a score of −3 is very low.

BIBLIOGRAPHY

Adams, J. C., Jr. (1968). The relative effects of various testing atmospheres on spontaneous flexibility, a factor of divergent thinking. *Journal of Creative Behavior, 2,* 187–194.

Adamson, G. (1983, January). The coin with more than two sides. *ATA Magazine,* pp. 28–30.

Addison, R. M., & Homme, L. E. (1966). The reinforcing event (RE) menu. *Journal of the National Society for Programed Instruction,* 8–9.

Ahsen, A. (1977a). *Psych eye: Self-analytic consciousness.* New York: Brandon House.

———. (1977b). Eidetics: An overview. *Journal of Mental Imagery, 1,* 5–38.

Alexander, P. A., & Judy, J. E. (1988). The interaction of domain-specific and strategic knowledge in academic performance. *Review of Educational Research, 58,* 375–404.

Alschuler, A. S. (1972). *Motivating achievement in high-school students: Education for human growth.* Englewood Cliffs, N.J.: Educational Technology Publications.

Altus, W. D. (1967). Birth order and its sequelae. *International Journal of Psychiatry, 3,* 23–42.

American Psychiatric Association. (1980, March). *Diagnostic and statistical manual of mental disorders* (3rd ed.). Washington, D.C.: American Psychiatric Association.

———. (1987). *Diagnostic and statistical manual of mental disorders* (3rd ed. rev.). Washington, D.C.: American Psychiatric Association.

Ames, C. (1992). Classrooms: Goals, structures, and student motivation. *Journal of Educational Psychology, 84,* 261–271.

Ames, R., & Ames, C. (Eds.). (1984). *Research on motivation in education (Vol. I): Student motivation.* New York: Academic Press.

Anastasi, A. (1958). Heredity, environment, and the question ``how?'' *Psychological Review, 65,* 197–208.

Anderson, C. W., & Smith, E. L. (1984). Children's preconceptions and content-area textbooks. In G. G. Duffy, L. R. Roehler, & J. Mason (Eds.), *Comprehension instruction: Perspectives and suggestions.* New York: Longman.

Anderson, J. R. (1983). *The architecture of cognition.* Cambridge, Mass.: Harvard University Press.

Anderson, L. W., & Block, J. H. (1977). Mastery learning. In D. J. Treffinger, J. K. Davis, & R. E. Ripple (Eds.), *Handbook on teaching educational psychology.* New York: Academic Press.

Andrews, G. R., & Debus, R. L. (1978). Persistence and causal perception of failure: Modifying cognitive attributions. *Journal of Educational Psychology, 70,* 154–166.

Arlin, M. (1984). Time, equality, and mastery learning. *Review of Educational Research, 54,* 65–86.

Arlin, P. K. (1975). Cognitive development in adulthood: A fifth stage? *Developmental Psychology, 11,* 602–606.

Arnold, J. E. (1962). Useful creative techniques. In S. J. Parnes & H. F. Harding (Eds.), *A sourcebook for creative thinking.* New York: Scribner.

Aronfreed, J. (1968). Aversive control of socialization. In D. Levine (Ed.), *Nebraska Symposium on Motivation.* Lincoln, Neb.: University of Nebraska Press.

Atkinson, J. W., & Raynor, J. O. (1978). *Personality, motivation, and achievement.* New York: Wiley.

Atkinson, R. C., & Shiffrin, R. M. (1968). Human memory: A proposed system and its control processes. In K. W. Spence & J. T. Spence (Eds.), *The psychology of learning and motivation* (Vol. 2). New York: Academic Press.

Ausubel, D. P. (1958). *Theory and problems of child development.* New York: Grune & Stratton.

———. (1963). *The psychology of meaningful verbal learning.* New York: Grune & Stratton.

———. (1968). *Educational psychology: A cognitive view.* New York: Holt, Rinehart & Winston.

———. (1977). The facilitation of meaningful verbal learning in the classroom. *Educational Psychologist, 12,* 162–178.

Ausubel, D. P., & Robinson, F. G. (1969). *School learning: An introduction to educational psychology.* New York: Holt, Rinehart & Winston.

Axelrod, S., & Apsche, J. (Eds.). (1983). *The effects of punishment on human behavior.* New York: Academic Press.

Babad, E. Y. (1985). Some correlates of teachers' expectancy bias. *American Educational Research Journal, 22,* 175–183.

Baer, R. A., Tishelman, A. C., Degler, J. D., Osnes, P. G., & Stokes, T. F. (1992). Effects of self- vs. experimenter-selection of rewards on classroom behavior in young children. *Education and Treatment of Children, 15,* 1–14.

Bandura, A. (1962). Social learning through imitation. In N. R. Jones (Ed.), *Nebraska Symposium on Motivation.* Lincoln, Neb.: University of Nebraska Press.

———. (1969). *Principles of behavior modification.* New York: Holt, Rinehart & Winston.

———. (1977). *Social learning theory.* Morristown, N.J.: General Learning Press.

———. (1981). Self-referent thought: A developmental analysis of self-efficacy. In J. H. Flavell & L. Ross (Eds.), *Social cognitive development: Frontiers and possible futures.* Cambridge, England: Cambridge University Press.

———. (1986). *Social foundations of thought and action: A social cognitive theory.* Englewood Cliffs, N.J.: Prentice-Hall.

———. (1991). Social cognitive theory of self-regulation. *Organizational Behavior and Human Performance, 50,* 248–287.

Bandura, A., Ross, D., & Ross, S. (1963). Imitation of film mediated aggressive models. *Journal of Abnormal and Social Psychology, 66,* 3–11.

Bandura, A., & Walters, R. (1963). *Social learning and personality development.* New York: Holt, Rinehart & Winston.

Bangert, R. L., Kulik, J. A., & Kulik, C. C. (1983). Individualized systems of instruction in secondary schools. *Review of Educational Research, 53,* 143–158.

Baratz, J. D. (1969). A bi-dialectical task for determining language proficiency in economically disadvantaged Negro children. *Child Development, 40,* 889–901.

Bardwell, R. (1984). The development and motivational function of expectations. *American Educational Research Journal, 21,* 461–472.

Barell, J. (1991). *Teaching for thoughtfulness: Classroom strategies to enhance intellectual development.* New York: Longman.

Barnett, W. S., & Escobar, C. M. (1987). The economics of early educational intervention: A review. *Review of Educational Research, 57,* 387–414.

Barth, R. (1979). Home-based reinforcement of school behavior: A review and analysis. *Review of Educational Research, 49,* 436–458.

Basseches, M. (1984). *Dialectical thinking and adult development.* Norwood, N.J.: Ablex Publishing.

Bell-Gredler, M. E. (1986). *Learning and instruction: Theory into practice.* New York: Macmillan.

Belmont, J. M. (1989). Cognitive strategies and strategic learning: The socio-instructional approach. *American Psychologist, 44,* 142–148.

Bennett, N. (1976). *Teaching styles and pupil progress.* Cambridge, Mass.: Harvard University Press.

Berliner, D. C. (1983). Developing conceptions of classroom environments: Some light on the T in classroom studies of ATI. *Educational Psychologist, 18,* 1–13.

Berlyne, D. E. (1960). *Conflict, arousal and curiosity.* New York: McGraw-Hill.

Bernard, H. W. (1966). *Human development in western culture* (2nd ed.). Boston: Allyn & Bacon.

Bernard, L. L. (1924). *Instinct: A study in social psychology.* New York: Holt, Rinehart & Winston.

Bernhard, J. K. (1992). Gender-related attitudes and the development of computer skills: A preschool intervention. *The Alberta Journal of Educational Research, 38*, 177–188.

Bialystok, E. (1988). Levels of bilingualism and levels of linguistic awareness. *Developmental Psychology, 24*, 560–567.

Biggs, J. B. (1991). *Teaching for learning: The view from cognitive psychology.* Hawthorn, Australia: The Australian Council for Educational Research.

Bijou, S. W., & Sturges, P. S. (1959). Positive reinforcers for experimental studies with children—Consumables and manipulatables. *Child Development, 30,* 151–170.

Blase, J. J., & Pajak, E. F. (1985). How discipline creates stress for teachers. *Canadian School Executive, 4,* 8–11.

Bloom, B. S. (1964). *Stability and change in human characteristics.* New York: Wiley.

———. (1976). *Human characteristics and school learning.* New York: McGraw-Hill.

———. (1981). *All our children learning: A primer for parents, teachers, and other educators.* New York: McGraw-Hill.

———. (1984). The 2 Sigma problem: The search for methods of group instruction as effective as one-to-one tutoring. *Educational Researcher, 13,* 4–15.

———. (1987). A response to Slavin's mastery learning reconsidered. *Review of Educational Research, 57,* 507–508.

Bloom, B. S., Engelhart, M. B., Furst, E. J., Hill, W. H., & Krathwohl, D. R. (1956). *Taxonomy of educational objectives: Handbook I: Cognitive domain.* New York: Longman, Green.

Bloom, B. S., Madaus, G. F., & Hastings, J. T. (1981). *Evaluation to improve learning.* New York: McGraw-Hill.

Blumenfeld, P. C. (1992). Classroom learning and motivation: Clarifying and expanding goal theory. *Journal of Educational Psychology, 84,* 272–281.

Bolles, R. C. (1974). Cognition and motivation: Some historical trends. In B. Weiner (Ed.), *Cognitive views of human motivation.* New York: Academic Press.

Borg, W. R. (Project Director). (1973). *Protocol materials.* Salt Lake City, Utah: University of Utah Protocol Project.

Boring, E. G. (1923). Intelligence as the tests test it. *New Republic, 35,* 35–37.

Borkowski, J. G., Milstead, M., & Hale, C. (1988). Components of children's metamemory: Implications for strategy generalization. In F. E. Weinert & M. Perl-

mutter (Eds.), *Memory development: Universal changes and individual differences.* Hillsdale, N.J.: Erlbaum.

Borton, T. (1970). *Reach, touch, and teach: Student concerns and process education.* New York: McGraw-Hill.

Bossert, S. T. (1988). Cooperative activities in the classroom. In E. Z. Rothkopf (Ed.), *Review of research in education* (Vol. 15). Washington, D.C.: American Educational Research Association.

Bower, G. H. (1981). Mood and memory. *American Psychologist, 36,* 129–148.

Bowlby, J. (1982). *Attachment and loss (Vol. 1): Attachment* (2nd ed.). London: Hogarth Press.

Bradshaw, G. L., & Anderson, J. R. (1982). Elaborative encoding as an explanation of levels of processing. *Journal of Verbal Learning and Verbal Behavior, 21,* 165–174.

Bradshaw, J. L. (1989). *Hemispheric specialization and psychological function.* New York: Wiley.

Brandon, P. R., Newton, B. J., & Hammond, O. W. (1987). Children's mathematics achievement in Hawaii: Sex differences favoring girls. *American Educational Research Journal, 24,* 437–461.

Bransford, J. D. (1979). *Human cognition: Learning, understanding and remembering.* Belmont, Calif.: Wadsworth.

Bransford, J. D., & Johnson, M. K. (1973). Consideration of some problems in comprehension. In W. G. Chase (Ed.), *Visual information processing* (pp. 383–438). New York: Academic Press.

Bransford, J., Sherwood, R., Vye, N., & Rieser, J. (1986). Teaching thinking and problem solving. *American Psychologist, 41,* 1078–1089.

Brantner, J. P., & Doherty, M. A. (1983). A review of timeout: A conceptual and methodological analysis. In S. Axelrod & J. Apsche (Eds.), *The effects of punishment on human behavior.* New York: Academic Press.

Braun, C. (1976). Teacher expectations: Sociopsychological dynamics. *Review of Educational Research, 46,* 185–213.

Brisk, M. E. (1991). Toward multilingual and multicultural mainstream education. *Journal of Education, 173,* 114–129.

Bronfenbrenner, U. (1977). Is early intervention effective? In S. Cohen & T. J. Comiskey (Eds.), *Child development: Contemporary perspectives.* Itasca, Ill.: F. E. Peacock.

———. (1989). Ecological systems theory. In R. Vasta (Ed.), *Annals of child development* (Vol. 6). Greenwich, Conn.: JAI Press.

Brophy, J. E. (1981). Teacher praise: A functional analysis. *Review of Educational Research, 51* (1), 5–32.

———. (1983). If only it were true: A response to Greer. *Educational Researcher, 12,* 10–12.

Brophy, J. E., & Evertson, C. M. (1974). *Process-product correlations in the Texas teacher effectiveness study: Final report.* Research Report No. 74–4. Austin, Texas: Research and Development Center for Teacher Education, University of Texas.

———. (1976). *Learning from teaching: A developmental perspective.* Boston: Allyn & Bacon.

Brophy, J. E., & Good, T. L. (1974). *Teacher-student relationships: Causes and consequences.* New York: Holt, Rinehart & Winston.

Brown, J. S., Collins, A., & Duguid, P. (1989). Situated cognition and the culture of learning. *Educational Researcher, 18,* 32–42.

Bruner, J. S. (1957a). On going beyond the information given. In *Contemporary approaches to cognition.* Cambridge, Mass.: Harvard University Press.

———. (1957b). On perceptual readiness. *Psychological Review, 64,* 123–152.

———. (1961a). The act of discovery. *Harvard Educational Review, 31,* 21–32.

———. (1961b). *The process of education.* Cambridge, Mass.: Harvard University Press.

———. (1966). *Toward a theory of instruction.* Cambridge, Mass.: Harvard University Press.

———. (1973). Organization of early skilled action. *Child Development, 44,* 1–11.

———. (1983). *Child's talk.* New York: Norton.

———. (1985). Models of the learner. *Educational Researcher, 14,* 5–8.

———. (1986). *Actual minds, possible worlds.* Cambridge, Mass.: Harvard University Press.

———. (1990). *Acts of meaning.* Cambridge, Mass.: Harvard University Press.

Bruner, J. S., Goodnow, J. J., & Austin, G. A. (1956). *A study of thinking.* New York: Wiley.

Budoff, M., & Gottlieb, J. (1976). Special-class EMR children mainstreamed: A study of an aptitude (learning potential) treatment interaction. *American Journal of Mental Deficiency, 81,* 1–11.

Burns, R. B. (1984). How time is used in elementary schools: The activity structure of classrooms. In L. W. Anderson (Ed.), *Time and school learning: Theory, research and practice.* London: Croom Helm.

Burns, R. B., & Anderson, L. W. (1987). The activity structure of lesson segments. *Curriculum Inquiry, 17,* 31–53.

Burt, C. L. (1958). The inheritance of mental ability. *American Psychologist, 13,* 1–15.

Calfee, R. (1981). Cognitive psychology and educational practice. In D. C. Berliner (Ed.), *Review of research in education* (Vol. 9). Washington, D.C.: American Educational Research Association.

———. (1985). Computer literacy and book literacy: Parallels and contrasts. *Educational Researcher, 14,* 8–13.

Calfee, R., & Drum, P. (1986). Research on teaching reading. In M. C. Wittrock (Ed.), *Handbook of research on teaching* (3rd ed.). New York: Macmillan.

Cameron, A. W. (1956). *A guide to Eastern Canadian mammals.* Ottawa: Department of Northern Affairs and National Resources.

Carey, S. T. (1987). Reading comprehension in first and second languages of immersion and Francophone students. *Canadian Journal for Exceptional Children, 3,* 103–108.

Carroll, J. B. (1963). A model of school learning. *Teachers College Record, 64,* 723–733.

———. (1989). The Carroll model: A 25-year retrospective and prospective view. *Educational Researcher, 18* (1), 26–31.

Case, R. (1975). Gearing the demands of instruction to the developmental capacities of the learner. *Review of Educational Research, 45,* 59–87.

———. (1985). *Intellectual development: A systematic reinterpretation.* New York: Academic Press.

Case, R., Haward, S., Lewis, M., & Hurst, P. (1988). Toward a neo-Piagetian theory of cognitive and emotional development. *Developmental Review, 8,* 1–51.

Cattell, R. B. (1971). *Abilities: Their structure, growth and action.* Boston: Houghton Mifflin.

Cermak, L. S., & Craik, F. I. (Eds.). (1979). *Levels of processing in human memory.* Hillsdale, N.J.: Erlbaum.

Chapman, J. W. (1988). Learning disabled children's self-concepts. *Review of Educational Research, 58,* 347–371.

Chester, R. D. (1992). Views from the mainstream: Learning disabled students as perceived by regular education classroom teachers and by non-learning disabled secondary students. *Canadian Journal of School Psychology, 8,* 93–102.

Chi, M. T. H., & Glaser, R. (1980). The measurement of expertise: Analysis of the development of knowledge and skill as a basis for assessing achievement. In E. L. Baker & E. S. Quellmalz (Eds.), *Educational testing and evaluation: Design, analysis and policy.* Beverly Hills, Calif.: Sage.

Chomsky, N. (1957). *Syntactic structures.* The Hague: Mouton.

———. (1965). *Aspects of the theory of syntax.* Cambridge, Mass.: MIT Press.

Clarizio, H. F. (1992). Teachers as detectors of learning disability. *Psychology in the Schools, 29,* 28–34.

Clarizio, H. F., & Yelon, S. L. (1974). Learning theory approaches to classroom management: Rationale and intervention techniques. In A. R. Brown & C. Avery (Eds.), *Modifying children's behavior: A book of readings.* Springfield, Ill.: Thomas.

Clark, B. (1983). *Growing up gifted: Developing the potential of children at home and at school* (2nd ed.). Columbus, Ohio: Merrill.

Clark, R. E. (1982). Antagonism between achievement and enjoyment in ATI studies. *Educational Psychology, 13,* 92–101.

Clawson, E. U., & Barnes, B. R. (1973). The effects of organizers on the learning of structured anthropology materials in the elementary grades. *Journal of Experimental Education, 42,* 11–15.

Clements, D. H. (1991). Enhancement of creativity in computer environments. *American Educational Research Journal, 28,* 173–187.

Coburn, P., Kelman, P., Roberts, N., Snyder, T. F. F., Watt, D. H., & Weiner, C. (1982). *Practical guide to computers in education.* Reading, Mass.: Addison-Wesley.

Cohen, D. K. (1972). Does IQ matter? *Current, 141,* 19–30.

Coladarci, A. P. (1956). The relevancy of educational psychology. *Educational Leadership, 13,* 489–492.

Colby, A., & Kohlberg, L. (1984). Invariant sequence and internal consistency in moral judgment stages. In W. M. Kurtines & J. L. Gewirtz (Eds.), *Morality, moral behavior, and moral development* (pp. 41–51). New York: Wiley.

Collett, J., & Serrano, B. (1992). Stirring it up: The inclusive classroom. *New Directions for Teaching and Learning, 49,* 35–48.

Collins, A., Brown, J. S., & Newman, S. E. (1989). Cognitive apprenticeship: Teaching the craft of reading, writing, and mathematics. In L. B. Resnick (Ed.), *Knowing, learning, and instruction: Essays in honor of Robert Glaser.* Hillsdale, N.J.: Erlbaum.

Collins, W. A. (1983). Interpretation and inference in children's television viewing. In J. Bryant & D. R. Anderson (Eds.), *Children's understanding of television: Research on attention and comprehension.* New York: Academic Press.

Combs, A. W. (1982). *A personal approach to teaching: Beliefs that make a difference.* Boston: Allyn & Bacon.

Cook, T. D., Appleton, H., Conner, R. F., Shaffer, A., Tamkin, G., & Weber, S. J. (1975). *"Sesame Street" revisited.* New York: Russell Sage Foundation.

Coon, C. L. (1915). *North Carolina schools and academies.* Raleigh, N.C.: Edwards and Broughton.

Coopersmith, S. (1967). *The antecedents of self-esteem.* San Francisco: Freeman.

Copeland, W. D. (1987). Classroom management and student teachers' cognitive abilities: A relationship. *American Educational Research Journal, 24,* 219–236.

Corno, L., & Snow, R. E. (1986). Adapting teaching to individual differences among learners. In M. C. Wittrock (Ed.), *Handbook of research on teaching* (3rd ed.) (pp. 605–629). New York: Macmillan.

Côté, A. D. J. (1968). *Flexibility and conservation acceleration.* Unpublished Ph.D. dissertation, University of Alberta, Edmonton, Alberta, Canada.

Cowed by cows. *Edmonton Journal,* June 11, 1992, p. B2.

Craik, F. M., & Lockhart, R. S. (1972). Levels of processing: A framework for memory research. *Journal of Verbal Learning and Verbal Behavior, 11,* 671–684.

Crockett, L. J., & Petersen, A. C. (1987). Findings from the Early Adolescence Study. In R. M. Lerner & T. T. Foch (Eds.), *Biological-psychosocial interactions in early adolescence: A life-span perspective.* Hillsdale, N.J.: Erlbaum.

Cronbach, L. J., & Snow, R. E. (1977). *Aptitudes and Instructional Methods.* New York: Irvington.

Crooks, T. J. (1988). The impact of classroom evaluation practices on students. *Review of Educational Research, 58,* 438–481.

Cropley, A. J. (1992). *More ways than one: Fostering creativity.* Norwood, N.J.: Ablex.

Cross, T. L., Coleman, L. J., & Terhaar-Yonkers, M. (1991). The social cognition of gifted adolescents in schools: Managing the stigma of giftedness. *Journal for the Education of the Gifted, 15,* 44–55.

Crowder, N. A. (1961). Characteristics of branching programs. In D. P. Scannell (Ed.), *Conference on programed learning*. Lawrence, Kansas: University of Kansas, Studies in Education.

———. (1963). On the differences between linear and intrinsic programming. *Phi Delta Kappan, 44,* 250–254.

Cummins, J. (1986). Empowering minority students: A framework for intervention. *Harvard Educational Review, 56,* 18–36.

Cummins, J., & Swain, M. (1986). *Bilingualism in education: Aspects of theory, research and practice.* London: Taylor & Fry.

Cziko, G. A. (1992). The evaluation of bilingual education. *Educational Researcher, 21,* 10–15.

Dansereau, D. F. (1985). Learning strategy research. In J. W. Segal, S. F. Chipman, & R. Glaser (Eds.), *Thinking and learning skills* (pp. 1, 209–240). Hillsdale, N.J.: Erlbaum.

Darley, J. M., & Shultz, T. R. (1990). Moral rules: Their content and acquisition. *Annual Review of Psychology, 41,* 525–556.

Das, J. P. (1992). Beyond a unidimensional scale of merit. *Intelligence, 16,* 137–149.

Dasen, P. R. (Ed.). (1977). *Piagetian psychology: Cross-cultural contributions.* New York: Gardner Press.

de Bono, E. (1970). *Lateral thinking: A textbook of creativity.* London: Ward Lock Educational.

———. (1976). *Teaching thinking.* London: Temple Smith.

de Charms, R. (1972). Personal causation training in the schools. *Journal of Applied Psychology, 2,* 95–113.

Deale, R. N. (1975). *Examinations bulletin 32: Assessment and testing in the secondary school.* London: Evans/Methuen.

Deaux, K. (1985). Sex and gender. *Annual Review of Psychology, 36,* 49–81.

Dennison, G. (1969). *The lives of children: The story of the First Street School.* New York: Random House (Vintage Books).

Derry, S. J., & Murphy, D. A. (1986). Designing systems that train learning ability: From theory to practice. *Review of Educational Research, 56,* 1–39.

Diaz, R. M. (1983). Thought and two languages: The impact of bilingualism on cognitive development. In E. W. Gordon (Ed.), *Review of research in education* (Vol. 10). Washington, D.C.: American Educational Research Association.

Dickens, C. (1843/1986). *A Christmas carol.* London: Octopus Books.

Downes, T. (1991). The changing nature of teaching: The increasing complexity of tasks and tools. *Education and Computing, 7,* 239–244.

Doyle, W. (1979). Making managerial decisions in classrooms. In D. Duke (Ed.), *78th yearbook of the National Society for the Study of Education: Part 2. Classroom management.* Chicago: University of Chicago Press.

———. (1986). Classroom organization and management. In M. C. Wittrock (Ed.), *Handbook of research on teaching* (3rd ed.) (pp. 392–431). New York: Macmillan.

Dunn, L. M. (1968). Special education for the mildly retarded—Is much of it justifiable? *Exceptional Children, 35,* 5–22.

Dunn, R., & Griggs, S. A. (1988). *Learning styles: Quiet revolution in American secondary schools.* Reston, Va.: National Association of Secondary School Principals.

Dweck, C. S. (1986). Motivational processes affecting learning. *American Psychologist, 41,* 1040–1048.

Edgerton, R. B. (1979). *Mental retardation.* Cambridge, Mass.: Harvard University Press.

Educational Testing Service. (1961). Judges disagree on qualities that characterize good writing. *ETS Development, 9,* 2.

Eilers, R. E., & Oller, D. K. (1988). Precursors to speech. In R. Vasta (Ed.), *Annals of child development* (Vol. 5). Greenwich, Conn.: JAI Press.

Eisenberg-Berg, N. (1979). Development of children's prosocial moral judgment. *Developmental Psychology, 15,* 38–44.

Eisner, E. W. (1967). Educational objectives: Help or hindrance? *School Review, 75,* 250–260.

———. (1982). An artistic approach to supervision. In T. J. Sergiovanni (Ed.), *Supervision of teaching (ASCD 1982 Yearbook).* Alexandria, Va.: Association for Supervision and Curriculum Development.

Elton, L. R. B., & Laurillard, D. M. (1979). Trends in research on student learning. *Studies in Higher Education, 4,* 87–102.

Engel, M. (1976). *Bear.* Toronto: McClelland and Stewart.

Ennis, R. H. (1976). An alternative to Piaget's conceptualization of logical competence. *Child Development, 47,* 903–919.

————. (1978). Conceptualization of children's logical competence: Piaget's propositional logic and an alternative proposal. In L. S. Siegel & C. J. Brainerd (Eds.), *Alternatives to Piaget: Critical essays on the theory.* New York: Academic Press.

Epstein, H. T. (1978). Growth spurts during brain development: Implications for educational policy. In J. S. Chall & A. F. Minsky (Eds.), *Education and the brain.* Chicago: University of Chicago Press.

Erickson, F., & Mohatt, G. (1982). Cultural organization of participation structures in two classrooms of Indian students. In G. Spindler (Ed.), *Doing the ethnography of schooling.* New York: Holt, Rinehart & Winston.

Erlenmeyer-Kimling, L., & Jarvik, L. F. (1963). Genetics and intelligence: A review. *Science, 142,* 1477–1478.

Evertson, C. M., Anderson, L. M., & Brophy, J. E. (1978). *Texas junior high school study: Final report of process-outcome relationships.* Research Report No. 4061 (Vol. 1). Austin, Texas: Research and Development Center for Teacher Education, University of Texas.

Ewell, P. T. (1991). To capture the ineffable: New forms of assessment in higher education. In G. Grant (Ed.), *Review of research in education* (Vol. 17). Washington, D.C.: American Educational Research Association.

Ewer, R. F. (1973). *The carnivores.* Ithaca, N.Y.: Cornell University Press.

Fahrmeler, L. C. (1991). The child within: Enhancing our creativity. *The Creative Child and Adult Quarterly, 16,* 30–37.

Fair, E. M. III, & Silvestri, L. (1992). Effects of rewards, competition and outcome on intrinsic motivation. *Journal of Instructional Psychology, 19,* 3–8.

Farnham-Diggory, S. (1990). *Schooling.* Cambridge, Mass.: Harvard University Press.

————. (1992). *Cognitive processes in education* (2nd ed.). New York: HarperCollins.

Feingold, A. (1992). Sex differences in variability in intellectual abilities: A new look at an old controversy. *Review of Educational Research, 62,* 61–84.

Fenstermacher, G. D., & Soltis, J. F. (1992). *Approaches to teaching.* New York: Teachers College Press.

Ferrington, G., & Loge, K. (1992). Virtual reality: A new learning environment. *The Computing Teacher, 20,* 16–19.

Feuerstein, R. (1979). *The dynamic assessment of retarded performers.* Baltimore: University Park Press.

————. (1980). *Instrumental enrichment: An intervention program for cognitive modifiability.* Baltimore: University Park Press.

Fischer, K. W., & Silvern, L. (1985). Stages and individual differences in cognitive development. *Annual Review of Psychology, 36,* 613–648.

Flanders, N. A. (1970). *Analyzing teacher behavior.* Reading, Mass.: Addison-Wesley.

Flavell, J. H. (1985). *Cognitive development* (2nd ed.). Englewood Cliffs, N.J.: Prentice-Hall.

Fleming, M., & Chambers, B. (1983). Teacher-made tests: Windows on the classroom. In W. E. Hathaway (Ed.), *New directions for testing and measurement: Vol. 19, Testing in the schools.* San Francisco: Jossey-Bass.

Fodor, E. N. (1972). Delinquency and susceptibility to social influence among adolescents as a function of level of moral development. *Journal of Social Psychology, 86,* 257–260.

Follman, J. (1991). Teachers' estimates of pupils' IQs and Pupils' tested IQs. *Psychological Reports, 69,* 350.

Freeman, D. (1983). *Margaret Mead and Samoa.* Cambridge, Mass.: Harvard University Press.

French, C., & French, F. (1991). Evaluating programs that claim to teach thinking skills: Critical issues and options. In R. M. Mulcahy, R. H. Short, & J. Andrews (Eds.), *Enhancing learning and thinking.* New York: Praeger.

Frisch, R. E., & Revelle, R. (1970). Height and weight at menarche and a hypothesis of critical body weights and adolescent events. *Science, 169,* 397–398.

Fuller, B., & Heyneman, S. P. (1989). Third world school quality: Current collapse, future potential. *Educational Researcher, 18,* 12–19.

Gabel, D. L., Kogan, M. H., & Sherwood, R. D. (1980). A summary of research in science education—1978. *Science Education, 64,* 429–568.

Gage, N. L. (1964). Theories of teaching. In E. R. Hilgard (Ed.), *Theories of learning and instruction: The sixty-third yearbook of the National Society for the Study of Education.* Chicago: University of Chicago Press.

Gagné, E. D. (1985). *The cognitive psychology of school learning.* Boston: Little, Brown.

Gagné, R. M. (1974). *Essentials of learning for instruction.* Hinsdale, Ill.: Dryden Press.

————. (1977a). *The conditions of learning* (3rd ed.). New York: Holt, Rinehart & Winston.

————. (1977b). Instructional programs. In M. H. Marx & M. E. Bunch (Eds.), *Fundamentals and applications of learning*. New York: Macmillan.

————. (1985). *The conditions of learning* (4th ed.). New York: Holt, Rinehart & Winston.

Gagné, R. M., & Briggs, L. J. (1983). *Principles of instructional design* (3rd ed.). New York: Holt, Rinehart & Winston.

Gagné, R. M., & Dick, W. (1983). Instructional psychology. *Annual Review of Psychology, 34*, 261–295.

Gallagher, J. J. (1960). *Analysis of research on the education of gifted children*. State of Illinois: Office of the Superintendent of Public Instruction.

Galton, F. (1869). *Hereditary genius: An inquiry into its laws and consequences*. London: Macmillan.

Gardner, H. (1983). *Frames of mind: The theory of multiple intelligences*. New York: Basic Books.

Gardner, H., & Hatch, T. (1989). Multiple intelligences go to school: Educational implications of the theory of multiple intelligences. *Educational Researcher, 18*, 4–10.

Gelman, R. (1982). Basic numerical abilities. In R. J. Sternberg (Ed.), *Advances in the psychology of human intelligence* (Vol. 1). Hillsdale, N.J.: Erlbaum.

Gelman, R., Meck, E., & Merkin, S. (1986). Young children's numerical competence. *Cognitive Development, 1*, 1–29.

Genesee, F. (1983). Bilingual education of majority language children: The immersion experiments in review. *Applied Psycholinguistics, 4*, 1–46.

————. (1985). Second language learning through immersion: A review of U.S. programs. *Review of Educational Research, 55*, 541–561.

Getzels, J. W., & Jackson, P. W. (1962). *Creativity and intelligence*. New York: Wiley.

Gilligan, C. (1982). *In a different voice: Psychological theory and women's development*. Cambridge, Mass.: Harvard University Press.

Gilligan, C., Kohlberg, L., Lerner, J., & Belenky, M. (1971). *Moral reasoning about sexual dilemmas: The development of an interview and scoring system*. Technical Report of the President's Commission on Obscenity and Pornography (Vol. 1). Washington, D.C.: U.S. Government Printing Office.

Glaser, R., & Bassok, M. (1989). Learning theory and the study of instruction. In M. R. Rosenzweig & L. W. Porter (Eds.), *Annual review of psychology, 40*, 631–666.

Glass, A. L., Holyoak, K. J., & Santa, J. L. (1979). *Cognition*. Reading, Mass.: Addison-Wesley.

Glasser, W. (1969). *Schools without failure*. New York: Harper & Row.

Goldenberg, C. (1992). The limits of expectations: A case for case knowledge about teacher expectancy effects. *American Educational Research Journal, 29*, 517–544.

Goldschmid, M. L., & Bentler, P. M. (1968). *Conservation concept diagnostic kit: Manual and keys*. San Diego, Calif.: Educational and Industrial Testing Service.

Goodenough, F. (1926). *Measurement of intelligence by drawings*. New York: Harcourt, Brace & World.

Gordon, M., Thomason, D., Cooper, S., & Ivers, C. L. (1991). *Journal of School Psychology, 29*, 151–159.

Gordon, T. (1974). *T.E.T.: Teacher effectiveness training*. New York: Peter H. Wyden.

Gordon, W. J. J. (1961). *Synectics: The development of creative capacity*. New York: Harper & Row.

Gould, S. J. (1981). *The mismeasure of man*. New York: Norton.

Grant, G. (1991). Introduction. In G. Grant (Ed.), *Review of research in education* (Vol. 17). Washington, D.C.: American Educational Research Association.

Grant, J. P. [Executive Director of the United Nations' Children's Fund (UNICEF)]. (1986). *The state of the world's children: 1986*. New York: Oxford University Press.

Greene, J. C. (1985). Relationships among learning and attribution theory motivational variables. *American Educational Research Journal, 22*, 65–78.

Greer, R. D. (1983). Contingencies of the science and technology of teaching and prebehavioristic research practices in education. *Educational Researcher, 12*, 3–9.

Gregorc, A. F. (1982). *Gregorc style delineator: Development, technical and administrative manual*. Maynard, Mass.: Gabriel Systems.

Grimmett, P. P., & Mackinnon, A. M. (1992). Craft knowledge and the education of teachers. In G. Grant (Ed.), *Review of research in education* (Vol. 18). Washington, D.C.: American Educational Research Association.

Grippin, P. C., & Peters, S. C. (1984). *Learning theories and learning outcomes: The connection*. Lanham, Md.: University Press of America.

Gronlund, N. E. (1968). *Constructing achievement tests*. Englewood Cliffs, N.J.: Prentice-Hall.

————. (1972). *Stating behavioral objectives for class-room instruction*. New York: Macmillan.

————. (1975). *Determining accountability for class-room instruction*. Itasca, Ill.: F. E. Peacock.

Gronlund, N. E., & Linn, R. L. (1990). *Measurement and evaluation in teaching* (6th ed.). New York: Macmillan.

Grossman, J. J. (Ed.). (1983). *Manual on terminology and classification in mental retardation, 1983 revision*. Washington, D.C.: American Association on Mental Deficiency.

Grossnickle, D. R., & Sesko, F. P. (1990). *Preventive discipline for effective teaching and learning*. Reston, Va.: National Association of Secondary School Principals.

Grotevant, H. D., Scarr, S., & Weinberg, R. A. (1977). Intellectual development in family constellations with adopted and natural children: A test of the Zajonc and Markus model. *Child Development, 48*, 1699–1703.

Guffey, D. G. (1991). Ritalin: What educators and parents should know. *Journal of Instructional Psychology, 19*, 167–169.

Guilford, J. P. (1950). Creativity. *American Psychologist, 5*, 444–454.

————. (1959). Three faces of intellect. *American Psychologist, 14*, 469–479.

————. (1962). Factors that aid and hinder creativity. *Teachers College Record, 63*, 380–392.

————. (1967). *The nature of human intelligence*. New York: McGraw-Hill.

Gullickson, A. R. (1985). Student evaluation techniques and their relationship to grade and curriculum. *Journal of Educational Research, 79*, 96–100.

Gump, P. V. (1969). Intra-setting analysis: The third grade classroom as a special but instructive case. In E. Williams & H. Rausch (Eds.), *Naturalistic viewpoints in psychological research*. New York: Holt, Rinehart & Winston.

Gustafsson, J. E., & Undheim, J. O. (1992). Stability and change in broad and narrow factors of intelligence from ages 12 to 15. *Journal of Educational Psychology, 84*, 141–149.

Gutiérrez, R., & Slavin, R. E. (1992). Achievement effects of the nongraded elementary school: A best evidence synthesis. *Review of Educational Research, 62*, 333–376.

Haddon, F. A., & Lytton, H. (1968). Teaching approach and the development of divergent thinking abilities in primary schools. *British Journal of Educational Psychology, 38*, 171–180.

Haertel, E. H. (1985). Construct validity and criterion-referenced testing. *Review of Educational Research, 55*, 23–46.

————. (1991). New forms of teacher assessment. In G. Grant (Ed.), *Review of research in education* (Vol. 17). Washington, D.C.: American Educational Research Association.

Haladyna, T. M., Nolen, S. B., & Haas, N. S. (1991). Raising standardized achievement test scores and the origins of test score pollution. *Educational Researcher, 20*, 2–7.

Hall, F. R., & Kelson, K. R. (1959). *The mammals of North America* (Vol. 2). New York: Ronald Press.

Hallahan, D. P., & Kauffman, J. M. (1991). *Exceptional children: Introduction to special education* (5th ed.). Boston: Allyn & Bacon.

Hallman, R. J. (1967). Techniques of creative teaching. *Journal of Creative Behavior, 1*, 325–330.

Halpern, D. F., & Coren, S. (1990). Laterality and longevity: Is left-handedness associated with younger age at death? In S. Coren (Ed.), *Left-handedness: Behavioral implications and anomalies*. Amsterdam, The Netherlands: Elsevier.

Haney, R. E., & Sorenson, J. S. (1977). *Individually guided science*. Reading, Mass.: Addison-Wesley.

Hanko, G. (1990). *Special needs in ordinary classrooms: Supporting Teachers* (2nd ed.). Oxford, England: Blackwell.

Harel, I. (Ed.). (1990). *Constructionist Learning*. Cambridge, Mass.: MIT Media Laboratory.

Hargreaves, D. H., Hester, S. K., & Mellor, F. J. (1975). *Deviance in classrooms*. Boston: Routledge & Kegan Paul.

Haring, N. G., & McCormick (Eds.). (1990). *Exceptional children and youth* (5th ed.). Columbus, Ohio: Merrill.

Harrington, J., Harrington, C., & Karns, E. (1991). The Marland report: Twenty years later. *Journal for the Education of the Gifted, 15*, 31–43.

Harris, B. D. (1963). *Children's drawings as measures of intellectual maturity*. New York: Harcourt, Brace & World.

Harris, D., & Bell, C. (1986). *Evaluating and assessing for learning*. New York: Nichols (London: Kogan Page).

Hartshorne, H., & May, M. A. (1928–1930). *Studies in the nature of character: Studies in deceit* (Vol. 1), *Studies in self–control* (Vol. 2), *Studies in the organization of character* (Vol. 3). New York: Macmillan.

Hauser, R. M., & Sewell, W. H. (1985). Birth order and educational attainment in full sibships. *American Educational Research Journal, 22,* 1–23.

Hebb, D. O. (1947). The effects of early experience on problem solving maturity. *American Psychologist, 2,* 306–307.

———. (1955). Drive and the CNS (conceptual nervous system). *Psychological Review, 62,* 243–354.

———. (1966). *A textbook of psychology* (2nd ed.). Philadelphia: Saunders.

Heckhausen, H., Schmalt, H., & Schneider, K. (1985). *Achievement motivation in perspective* (M. Woodruff & R. Wicklund, Trans.). New York: Academic Press.

Hembree, R. (1988). Correlates, causes, effects and treatment of test anxiety. *Review of Educational Research, 58,* 47–77.

Hess, R. D., & Azuma, H. (1991). Cultural support for schooling: Contrasts between Japan and the United States. *Educational Researcher, 20,* 2–8.

Hewett, S. (1968). *The emotionally disturbed child in the classroom.* Boston: Allyn & Bacon.

Heyns, O. S. (1967, February 4). Treatment of the unborn. *Woman's Own,* p. 18.

Higbee, K. L. (1977). *Your memory: How it works and how to improve it.* Englewood Cliffs, N.J.: Prentice-Hall.

Hill, K. T., & Wigfield, A. (1984). Test anxiety: A major educational problem and what can be done about it. *Elementary School Journal, 85,* 105–126.

Hintzman, D. L., & Ludham, G. (1980). Differential forgetting of prototypes and old instances: Simulation by an exemplar-based classification model. *Memory and Cognition, 8,* 378–382.

Hoffman, M. L. (1970). Conscience, personality, and socialization techniques. *Human Development, 13,* 90–126.

———. (1976). Empathy, role-taking, guilt, and development of altruistic motives. In T. Lick (Ed.), *Moral development and behavior.* New York: Holt, Rinehart & Winston.

Hoge, R. D. (1988). Issues in the definition and measurement of the giftedness construct. *Educational Researcher, 17,* 12–66.

Holland, J. L., Magoon, T. M., & Spokane, A. R. (1981). Counseling psychology: Career interventions, research, and theory. In M. R. Rosenzweig & L. W. Porter (Eds.), *Annual review of psychology* (Vol. 32). Palo Alto, Calif.: Annual Reviews.

Holstein, C. B. (1976). Irreversible, stepwise sequence in the development of moral judgment: A longitudinal study of males and females. *Child Development, 47,* 51–61.

Horn, J. L. (1976). Human abilities: A review of research and theory in the early 1970s. In M. R. Rosenzweig & L. W. Porter (Eds.), *Annual review of psychology* (Vol. 27). Palo Alto, Calif.: Annual Reviews.

Horn, J. L., & Donaldson, G. (1980). Cognitive development in adulthood. In O. G. Brim, Jr., & J. Kagan (Eds.), *Constancy and change in human development.* Cambridge, Mass.: Harvard University Press.

Horowitz, F. D., & O'Brien, M. (1986). Gifted and talented children: State of knowledge and directions for research. *American Psychologist, 41,* 1147–1152.

Horton, D. L., & Mills, C. B. (1984). Human learning and memory. *Annual Review of Psychology, 35,* 361–394.

Horwitz, R. A. (1979). Psychological effects of the open classroom. *Review of Educational Research, 49,* 71–86.

Huber, G. L., Sorrentino, R. M., Davidson, M. A., Epplier, R., & Roth, J. W. H. (1992). Uncertainty orientation and cooperative learning: Individual differences within and across cultures. *Learning and Individual Differences, 4,* 1–24.

Hughes, J. N. (1988). *Cognitive behavior therapy with children in schools.* New York: Pergamon.

Humphreys, L. G. (1985). A conceptualization of intellectual giftedness. In F. D. Horowitz & M. O'Brien (Eds.), *The gifted and talented: Developmental perspectives* (pp. 331–360). Washington, D.C.: American Psychological Association.

Hunt, E. (1989). Cognitive science: Definition, status, and questions. *Annual Review of Psychology, 40,* 603–629.

Hunt, J. M. (1961). *Intelligence and experience.* New York: Ronald Press.

Husén, T., & Tuijnman, A. (1991). The contribution of formal schooling to the increase in intellectual capital. *Educational Researcher, 20,* 17–25.

Inhelder, B., & Piaget, J. (1958). *The growth of logical thinking from childhood to adolescence.* New York: Basic Books.

Intons-Peterson, M. J. (1988). *Gender concepts of Swedish and American youth.* Hillsdale, N.J.: Erlbaum.

Jacklin, C. N. (1989). Female and male: Issues of gender. *American Psychologist, 44,* 127–133.

Jacobi, M. (1991). Mentoring and undergraduate academic success: A literature review. *Review of Educational Research, 61,* 505–532.

James, W. (1890). *The principles of psychology.* New York: Holt, Rinehart & Winston.

Janos, P. M., & Robinson, N. M. (1985). Psychosocial development in intellectually gifted children. In F. D. Horowitz & M. O'Brien (Eds.), *The gifted and talented: Developmental perspectives* (pp. 149–195). Washington, D.C.: American Psychological Association.

Jensen, A. (1980). *Bias in mental testing.* London: Methuen.

Jensen, A. R. (1968). Social class, race and genetics: Implications for education. *American Educational Research Journal, 5,* 1–42.

————. (1977). Cumulative deficit in IQ of blacks in the rural South. *Developmental Psychology, 13,* 184–191.

Jimenez, M. (1992). Surviving high school in the '90s. *Edmonton Journal,* Oct. 30, A1, A4.

Johnson, D., & Johnson, R. (1975). *Learning together and alone.* Englewood Cliffs, N.J.: Prentice-Hall.

Johnson, D. W., Johnson, R. T., Holubec, E. J., & Roy, P. (1984). *Circles of learning: Cooperation in the classroom.* Alexandria, Va.: Association for Supervision and Curriculum Development.

Johnson, D. W., Maruyama, G., Johnson, R., Nelson, D., & Skon, L. (1981). Effects of cooperative, competitive and individualistic goal structures on achievement: A meta-analysis. *Psychological Bulletin, 89,* 47–62.

Jones, E. H., & Montenegro, X. P. (1988). *Women and minorities in school administration: Facts and figures, 1987–1988.* Arlington, Va.: American Association of School Administrators.

Justice, E. (1985). Categorization as a preferred memory strategy: Developmental changes during elementary school. *Developmental Psychology, 21,* 1105–1110.

Juvonen, J., & Bear, G. (1992). Social adjustment of children with and without learning disabilities in integrated classrooms. *Journal of Educational Psychology, 84,* 322–330.

Kaess, W., & Zeaman, D. (1960). Positive and negative knowledge of results on a Pressey-type punchboard. *Journal of Experimental Psychology, 60,* 12–17.

Kagan, D. M. (1988). Teaching as clinical problem solving: A critical examination of the analogy and its implications. *Review of Educational Research, 58,* 482–505.

Kalish, H. I. (1981). *From behavioral science to behavior modification.* New York: McGraw-Hill.

Kamphaus, R. W. (1993). *Clinical assessment of children's intelligence.* Boston: Allyn & Bacon.

Kanchier, C. (1988). Maximizing potential of gifted and talented students through career education. *Agate, 2,* 6–13.

Kass, N., & Wilson, H. P. (1966). Resistance to extinction as a function of percentage of reinforcement, number of training trials, and conditioned reinforcement. *Journal of Experimental Psychology, 71,* 355–357.

Kaufman, K. F., & O'Leary, K. D. (1972). Reward, cost, and self-evaluation procedures with schizophrenic children. Unpublished manuscript, State University of New York. Cited in K. D. O'Leary & S. G. O'Leary, *Classroom management: The successful use of behavior modification.* New York: Pergamon Press.

Kavale, K., & Forness, S. (1985). *The science of learning disabilities.* San Diego, Calif.: College-Hill Press.

Kazdin, A. E., & Bootzin, R. R. (1972). The token economy: An evaluative review. *Journal of Applied Behavior Analysis, 5,* 343–372.

Kegan, R. (1982). *The evolving self: Problem and process in human development.* Cambridge, Mass.: Harvard University Press.

Keith, T. Z., & Cool, V. A. (1992). Testing models of school learning: Effects of quality of instruction, motivation, academic coursework, and homework on academic achievement. *School Psychology Quarterly, 7,* 207–226.

Keller, F. S. (1968). Good-bye teacher. . . . *Journal of Applied Behavior Analysis, 1,* 79–89.

Kelly, T. J., Bullock, L. M., & Dykes, M. K. (1977). Behavior disorders: Teachers' perceptions. *Exceptional Children, 43,* 316–318.

Kennedy, M. M. (1978). Findings from the follow-through planned variation study. *Educational Researcher, 7,* 3–11.

Kitano, M. K. (1991). A multicultural educational perspective on serving the culturally diverse student. *Journal for the Education of the Gifted, 15,* 4–19.

Klausmeier, H. J., Rossmiller, R. A., & Saily, M. (1977). *Individually guided elementary education: Concepts and practices.* New York: Academic Press.

Koch, H. L. (1955). Some personality correlates of sex, sibling position, and sex of sibling among five- and six-year-old children. *Genetic Psychology Monographs, 52,* 3–50.

Koffka, K. (1935). *Principles of Gestalt psychology.* New York: Harcourt, Brace, & World.

Kohl, H. R. (1969). *The open classroom: A practical guide to a new way of teaching.* New York: Random House (Vintage Books).

Kohlberg, L. (1964). Development of moral character and moral ideology. In M. L. Hoffman & L. W. Hoffman (Eds.), *Review of child development research* (Vol. 1). New York: Russell Sage Foundation.

———. (1971). Stages of moral development as a basis for moral education. In C. Beck, E. V. Sullivan, & B. Crittendon (Eds.), *Moral education: Interdisciplinary approaches.* Toronto: University of Toronto Press.

Kohlberg, L., & Candee, D. (1984). The relationship of moral judgment to moral action. In W. M. Kurtines & J. L. Gewirtz (Eds.), *Morality, moral behavior, and moral development* (pp. 52–73). New York: Wiley.

Kounin, J. S. (1970). *Discipline and classroom management.* New York: Holt, Rinehart & Winston.

Kozma, R. B. (1991). Learning with media. *Review of Educational Research, 61,* 2, 179–211.

Kozulin, A. (1990). *Vygotsky's psychology: A biography of ideas.* New York: Harvester Wheatsheaf.

Krathwohl, D. R., Bloom, B. S., & Masia, B. B. (1964). *Taxonomy of educational objectives, the classification of educational goals. Handbook II: Affective domain.* New York: McKay.

Krech, D., Rosenzweig, M., & Bennett, E. L. (1960). Effects of environmental complexity and training on brain chemistry. *Journal of Comparative and Physiological Psychology, 53,* 509–519.

———. (1962). Relations between brain chemistry and problem solving among rats raised in enriched and impoverished environments. *Journal of Comparative and Physiological Psychology, 55,* 801–807.

———. (1966). Environmental impoverishment, social isolation, and changes in brain chemistry and anatomy. *Physiology and Behavior, 1,* 99–104.

Kristiansen, R. (1992). Evolution or revolution? Changes in teacher attitudes toward computers in education, 1970–1990. *Education and Computing, 8,* 71–78.

Kuhmerker, L. (Ed.). (1991). *The Kohlberg legacy for the helping professions.* Birmingham, Ala.: Religious Education Press.

Kulik, C. C., Kulik, J. A., & Bangert-Drowns, R. L. (1990). Effectiveness of mastery learning programs: A meta-analysis. *Review of Educational Research, 60,* 265–299.

Kulik, J. A., Kulik, C. C., & Cohen, P. A. (1979). A meta-analysis of outcome studies of Keller's Personalized System of Instruction. *American Psychologist, 34,* 307–318.

———. (1980). Effectiveness of computer-based college teaching: A meta-analysis of findings. *Review of Educational Research, 50,* 525–544.

Labouvie-Vief, G. (1980). Beyond formal operations: Uses and limits of pure logic in life-span development. *Human Development, 23,* 141–161.

———. (1986). Modes of knowledge and the organization of development. In M. L. Commons, L. Kohlberg, F. A. Richards, & J. Sinnott (Eds.), *Beyond formal operations. 3: Models and methods in the study of adult and adolescent thought.* New York: Praeger.

Lam, T. C. L. (1992). Review of practices and problems in the evaluation of bilingual education. *Review of Educational Research, 62,* 181–203.

Lambert, W. E. (1975). Culture and language as factors in learning and education. In A. Wolfgang (Ed.), *Education of immigrant students.* Toronto: Ontario Institute for Studies in Education.

Landry, R. (1987). Additive bilingualism, schooling, and special education: A minority group perspective. *Canadian Journal for Exceptional Children, 3,* 109–114.

Lapsley, D. K. (1990). Continuity and discontinuity in adolescent social cognitive development. In Montemayor, R., Adams, G. R., & Gullotta, T. P. (Eds.), *From childhood to adolescence: A transitional period?* (Advances in Adolescent Development, Vol. 2). Newbury Park, Calif.: Sage Publications.

Laurillard, D. (1988). Computers and the emancipation of students: Giving control to the learner. In P. Ramsden (Ed.), *Improving learning: New perspectives.* London: Kogan Page.

Lee, E. S. (1951). Negro intelligence and selective migration: A Philadelphia test of the Klineberg hypothesis. *American Sociological Review, 16,* 227–233.

Lefrançois, G. R. (1966). *The acquisition of concepts of conservation.* Unpublished doctoral dissertation, University of Alberta, Edmonton, Alberta, Canada.

———. (1968). A treatment hierarchy for the acceleration of conservation of substance. *Canadian Journal of Psychology, 22,* 277–284.

———. (1982). *Psychological theories and human learning* (2nd ed.). Monterey, Calif.: Brooks/Cole.

———. (1992). *Of children: An introduction to child development* (7th ed.). Belmont, Calif.: Wadsworth.

———. (1993). *The lifespan* (4th ed.). Belmont, Calif.: Wadsworth.

Leinhardt, B., & Greeno, J. G. (1986). The cognitive skill of teaching. *Journal of Educational Psychology, 78,* 75–95.

Leinhardt, G. (1990). Capturing craft knowledge in teaching. *Educational Researcher, 19,* 18–25.

Lepper, M. R. (1981). Intrinsic and extrinsic motivation in children: Detrimental effects of superfluous social controls. In W. A. Collins (Ed.), *Aspects of the development of competence: The Minnesota Symposium on Child Psychology* (Vol. 14). Hillsdale, N.J.: Erlbaum.

Lepper, M. R., & Greene, D. (1975). Turning play into work: Effects of adult surveillance and extrinsic rewards on children's intrinsic motivation. *Journal of Personality and Social Psychology, 31,* 479–486.

Levin, B. (1983, March). Teachers and standardized achievement tests. *Canadian School Executive,* p. 11.

Levine, R. A. (1987). Women's schooling, patterns of fertility, and child survival. *Educational Researcher, 16,* 21–27.

Lewin, R. (1975, September). Starved brains. *Psychology Today,* pp. 29–33.

Lindholm, K. J., & Aclan, Z. (1991). Bilingual proficiency as a bridge to academic achievement: Results from bilingual/immersion programs. *Journal of Education, 173,* 99–113.

Linn, M. C. (1985). The cognitive consequences of programming instruction in classrooms. *Educational Researcher, 14,* 14–29.

Linn, R. L. (1986). Educational testing and assessment: Research needs and policy issues. *American Psychologist, 41,* 1153–1160.

———. (Ed.). (1992). *Intelligence: Measurement, theory, and public policy.* Champaign, Ill.: University of Illinois Press.

Little, J. W. (1990). The mentor phenomenon and the social organization of teaching. In C. B. Cazden (Ed.), *Review of research in education* (Vol. 16). Washington, D.C.: American Educational Research Association.

Lockhead, J. (1985). New horizons in educational development. In E. W. Gordon (Ed.), *Review of research in education* (Vol. 12). Washington, D.C.: American Educational Research Association.

Loftus, E. F. (1979). *Eyewitness testimony.* Cambridge, Mass.: Harvard University Press.

Lorenz, K. (1952). *King Solomon's ring.* London: Methuen.

Lovell, K. (1968). *An introduction to human development.* London: Macmillan.

Lowe, L. L. (1983, January). Creative learning through fine arts. *ATA Magazine, 63,* 20–23.

Lubar, J. F. (1991). Discourse on the development of EEG diagnostics and biofeedback for attention-deficit/hyperactivity disorders. *Biofeedback and Self-regulation, 16,* 201–225.

Luria, A. R. (1968). *The mind of a mnemonist: A Little Book About a Vast Memory.* New York: Avon Books.

Lynch, E. W., Simms, B. H., von Hippel, C. S., & Shuchat, J. (1978). *Mainstreaming preschoolers: Children with mental retardation.* Washington, D.C.: Head Start Bureau: U.S. Government Printing Office.

Lynn, D. B. (1974). *The father: His role in child development.* Monterey, Calif.: Brooks/Cole.

Maccoby, E. E., & Jacklin, C. N. (1974). *The psychology of sex differences.* Palo Alto, Calif.: Stanford University Press.

MacKay, A. (1982). *Project Quest: Teaching strategies and pupil achievement.* Occasional Paper Series, Centre for Research in Teaching, Faculty of Education, University of Alberta, Edmonton, Alberta, Canada.

Macmillan, D. L., Keogh, B. K., & Jones, R. L. (1986). Special educational research on mildly handicapped learners. In M. C. Wittrock (Ed.), *Handbook of research on teaching* (3rd ed.) (pp. 686–724). New York: Macmillan.

Macmillan, D. L., & Meyers, C. E. (1979). Educational labeling of handicapped learners. In D. C. Berliner (Ed.), *Review of research in education* (Vol. 7). Washington, D.C.: American Educational Research Association.

Mager, R. F. (1962). *Preparing instructional objectives.* Palo Alto, Calif.: Fearon.

Maguire, T. O. (1992). Grounded authentic assessment and teacher evaluation. In D. J. Bateson (Ed.), *Classroom testing in Canada: Proceedings of the Second Canadian Conference on Classroom Testing, June 1 and 2, 1990.* Vancouver: The University of British Columbia, The Centre for Applied Studies in Evaluation.

Marfo, K., Mulcahy, R. F., Peat, D., Andrews, J., & Cho, S. (1991). Teaching cognitive strategies in the classroom: A content-based instructional model. In R. M. Mulcahy, R. H. Short, & J. Andrews (Eds.), *Enhancing learning and thinking.* New York: Praeger.

Markle, S. M. (1964). *Good frames and bad: A grammar of frame writing.* New York: Wiley.

———. (1978). *Designs for instructional designers.* Champaign, Ill.: Stipes.

Markle, S. M., & Tiemann, P. W. (1974). Some principles of instructional design at higher cognitive levels. In R. Ulrich, T. Stachnik, & T. Mabry (Eds.), *Control of human behavior*. Glenview, Ill.: Scott, Foresman.

Marland, M. (1975). *The craft of the classroom: A survival guide to classroom management at the secondary school*. London: Heinemann Educational Books.

Marland, S. P. (1972). *Education of the gifted and talented*. Washington, D.C.: U.S. Government Printing Office.

Marquis, D. P. (1941). Learning in the neonate: The modification of behavior under three feeding schedules. *Journal of Experimental Psychology, 29*, 263–282.

Marshall, H., & Weinstein, R. (1984). Classroom factors affecting students' self-evaluations: An interactional model. *Review of Educational Research, 54*, 301–325.

Marton, F., & Saljo, R. (1984). Approaches to learning. In F. Marton (and others) (Eds.), *The experience of learning*. Edinburgh: Scottish Academic Press.

Maslow, A. H. (1970). *Motivation and personality* (2nd ed.). New York: Harper & Row.

Matthew, J. L., Golin, A. K., Moore, M. W., & Baker, C. (1992). Use of SOMPA in identification of gifted African-American children. *Journal for the Education of the Gifted, 15*, 344–356.

Matthews, D. B. (1991). The effects of school environment on intrinsic motivation of middle-school children. *Journal of Humanistic Education and Development, 30*, 30–36.

Matthews, L. H. (1969). *The life of mammals* (Vol. 1). New York: Universe Books.

Mayer, R. E. (1979). Can advance organizers influence meaningful learning? *Review of Educational Research, 49*, 371–383.

———. (1989). Models for understanding. *Review of Educational Research, 59*, 43–64.

McCain, G., & Segal, E. M. (1982). *The game of science* (4th ed.). Monterey, Calif.: Brooks/Cole.

McCaslin, M., & Good, T. L. (1992). Compliant cognition: The misalliance of management and instructional goals in current school reform. *Educational Researcher, 21*, 4–17.

McClean, L. (1992). Student evaluation in the ungraded primary school: The SCRP principle. In D. J. Bateson (Ed.), *Classroom testing in Canada: Proceedings of the Second Canadian Conference on Classroom Testing, June 1 and 2, 1990*. Vancouver: The University of British Columbia, The Centre for Applied Studies in Evaluation.

McClelland, D. C. (1958). Risk taking in children with high and low need for achievement. In J. W. Atkinson (Ed.), *Motives in fantasy, action, and society*. Princeton, N.J.: Van Nostrand.

———. (1973). Testing for competence rather than for "intelligence." *American Psychologist, 28*, 1–14.

McClelland, D. C., Atkinson, J. W., Clark, R. A., & Lowell, E. L. (1953). *The achievement motive*. New York: Appleton-Century-Crofts.

McClelland, D. C., & Winter, D. G. (1969). *Motivating economic achievement*. New York: Free Press.

McCleod, J., & Cropley, A. J. (1989). *Fostering academic excellence*. Oxford: Pergamon.

McCombs, B. L. (1982). Transitioning learning strategies research into practice: Focus on the student in technical training. *Journal of Instructional Development, 5*, 10–17.

McCullough, N. T. (1992). Teaching and learning with computers: A school-wide approach. *Computing Teacher, 20*, 8–9.

McDonald, L. (1993). *Task force on integration: Draft discussion paper*. Unpublished paper, Edmonton, Alberta: University of Alberta.

McEwen, N. (Chair). (1992). *The Educational Quality Indicators Initiative: A success story*. Symposium at the annual meeting of the Canadian Educational Researchers' Association and the Canadian Association for the Study of Educational Administration, Charlottetown, Prince Edward Island, June 6, 1992. Edmonton, Alberta: Alberta Education.

McFadden, A. C., Marsh, G. E. II, Price, B. J., & Hwang, Y. (1992). A study of race and gender bias in the punishment of school children. *Education and Treatment of Children, 15*, 140–146.

McGroarty, M. (1992). The societal context of bilingual education. *Educational Researcher, 21*, 7–9, 24.

McKeachie, W. J. (1984). Does anxiety disrupt information processing or does poor information processing lead to anxiety? *International Review of Applied Psychology, 33*, 187–203.

McKeachie, W. J., Pintrich, P. R., & Lin, Y. G. (1985). Learning to learn. In F. d'Ydwelle (Ed.), *Cognition, information processing and motivation* (pp. 601–618). Amsterdam: Elsevier.

McMann, N., & Oliver, R. (1988). Problems in families with gifted children: Implications for counselors. *Journal of Counseling and Development, 66,* 275–278.

McPhail, P., Ungoed-Thomas, J. R., & Chapman, H. (1972). *Moral education in the secondary school.* London: Longmans.

Meacham, M. L., & Wiesen, A. E. (1969). *Changing classroom behavior: A manual for precision teaching.* Scranton, Penn.: International Textbook.

Mead, M. (1935). *Sex and temperament in three primitive societies.* New York: New American Library.

Means, V., Moore, J. W., Gagné, E., & Hauck, W. E. (1979). The interactive effects of consonant and dissonant teacher expectancy and feedback communication on student performance in a natural school setting. *American Educational Research Journal, 16,* 367–373.

Mednick, S. A. (1962). The associative basis of the creative process. *Psychological Review, 69,* 220–232.

Meichenbaum, D. (1977). *Cognitive-behavior modification: An integrative approach.* New York: Plenum.

Meichenbaum, D. H., & Goodman, J. (1971). Training impulsive children to talk to themselves: A means of developing self-control. *Journal of Abnormal Psychology, 77,* 115–126.

Mercer, J. R. (1973). *Labeling the mentally retarded.* Berkeley, Calif.: University of California Press.

———. (1979). *System of Multicultural Pluralistic Assessment technical manual.* New York: Psychological Corporation.

Mercer, J. R., & Lewis, J. F. (1978). *System of Multicultural Pluralistic Assessment.* New York: Psychological Corporation.

———. (1979). *System of Multicultural Pluralistic Assessment student assessment manual.* New York: Psychological Corporation.

Merrill, P. F., Hammons, K., Tolman, M. N., Christensen, L., Vincent, B. R., & Reynolds, P. L. (1992). *Computers in education* (2nd ed.). Boston: Allyn & Bacon.

Michael, J. (1967). *Management of behavioral consequences in education.* Inglewood, Calif.: Southwest Regional Laboratory for Educational Research and Development.

Milgram, S. (1963). Behavioral study of obedience. *Journal of Abnormal and Social Psychology, 67,* 371–378.

Miller, G. A. (1956). The magical number seven, plus or minus two: Some limits on our capacity for processing information. *Psychological Review, 63,* 81–97.

Millman, J., & Darling-Hammond, L. (Eds.). (1990). *The new handbook of teacher evaluation: Assessing elementary and secondary school teachers.* Newbury Park, Calif.: Sage.

Mischel, W., & Baker, N. (1975). Cognitive appraisals and transformations in delay behavior. *Journal of Personality and Social Psychology, 31,* 254–261.

Mitchell, J. V., Jr. (Ed.). (1983). *Tests in print III: An index to tests, test reviews, and the literature on specific tests.* Lincoln, Neb.: Buros Institute of Mental Measurements, University of Nebraska Press.

Money, J., & Erhardt, A. A. (1972). *Man and woman, boy and girl: Differentiation and dimorphism of gender identity.* Baltimore: The Johns Hopkins University Press.

Moore, K. D., & Hanley, P. E. (1982). An identification of elementary teacher needs. *American Educational Research Journal, 19,* 137–144.

Morsink, C. V. (1985). Learning disabilities. In W. H. Berdine & A. E. Blackhurst (Eds.), *An introduction to special education* (2nd ed.). Boston: Little, Brown.

Moss, P. A. (1992). Shifting conceptions of validity in educational measurement: Implications for performance assessment. *Review of Educational Research, 62,* 229–258.

Mosston, M., & Ashworth, S. (1990). *The spectrum of teaching styles: From command to discovery.* New York: Longman.

Moynahan, E. O. (1973). The development of knowledge concerning the effects of categorization upon free recall. *Child Development, 44,* 238–245.

Mueller, J. H. (1992a). Anxiety and performance. In A. P. Smith and D. M. Jones (Eds.), *Handbook of human performance* (Vol. 3). London: Academic Press.

———. (1992b). *Test anxiety, study behaviors, and achievement.* Paper presented at the annual meeting of the Western Psychological Association, Portland, Oregon, April 30, 1992.

Mueller, S. L. (1992). The effect of a cooperative education work experience on autonomy, sense of purpose, and mature interpersonal relationships. *Journal of Cooperative Education, 27,* 27–35.

Mulcahy, B. F. (1991). Developing autonomous learners. *Alberta Journal of Educational Research, 37,* 385–397.

Mulcahy, R., Marfo, K., Peat, D., Andrews, J., & Clifford, L. (1986). Applying cognitive psychology in the classroom: A learning/thinking strategies instructional program. *Alberta Psychology, 15,* 9–12.

Mulcahy, R. F., Peat, D., Andrews, J., Darko-Yeboah, J., & Marfo, K. (1990). Cognitive-based strategy instruction. In J. Biggs (Ed.), *Learning processes and teaching contexts*. Melbourne: Australian Council for Educational Research.

Murnane, R. J., Singer, J. D., & Willett, J. B. (1988). The career paths of teachers: Implications for teacher supply and methodological lessons for research. *Educational Researcher, 17*, 22–30.

Myers, P. I., & Hammill, D. D. (1990). *Learning disabilities: Basic concepts, assessment practices, and instructional strategies* (4th ed.). Austin, Texas: pro-ed.

Naglieri, J. A. (1988). *DAP; draw a person: A quantitative scoring system*. New York: Harcourt Brace Jovanovich.

Nagy, P., & Griffiths, A. K. (1982). Limitations of recent research relating Piaget's theory to adolescent thought. *Review of Educational Research, 52*, 513–556.

National Center for Education Statistics. (1989). *Digest of education statistics. 1989* (25th ed.). Washington, D.C.: U.S. Department of Education.

National Commission on Excellence in Education. (1983). *A nation at risk: The imperative for educational reform*. Washington, D.C.: U.S. Government Printing Office.

Nay, W. R., Schulman, J. A., Bailey, K. G., & Huntsinger, G. M. (1976). Territory and classroom management: An exploratory case study. *Behavior Therapy, 7*, 240–246.

Neisser, U. (1976). *Cognition and reality*. San Francisco: Freeman.

Nelson, K. E. (1989). Strategies for first language teaching. In M. L. Rice & R. L. Schiefelbusch (Eds.), *Teachability of language*. Baltimore: Brookes.

Newell, A., & Simon, H. A. (1972). *Human problem solving*. Englewood Cliffs, N.J.: Prentice-Hall.

Newman, H. H., Freeman, F. N., Holzinger, K. J. (1937). *Twins: A study of heredity and environment*. Chicago: The University of Chicago Press.

Nicholls, J. G. (1978). The development of the concepts of effort and ability, perception of academic attainment, and the understanding that difficult tasks require more ability. *Developmental Psychology, 49*, 800–814.

Nickerson, R. S. (1986). Why teach thinking? In J. B. Baron & R. J. Sternberg (Eds.), *Teaching thinking skills: Theory and practice*. New York: Freeman.

———. (1988). On improving thinking through instruction. In E. Z. Rothkopf (Ed.), *Review of research in education* (Vol. 15). Washington, D.C.: American Educational Research Association.

Nolen, S. B., Haladyna, T. M., & Haas, N. S. (1992). Uses and abuses of achievement test scores. *Educational Measurement: Issues and Practices, 11*, 9–15.

Nussbaum, J. (1979). Children's conception of the earth as a cosmic body: A cross age study. *Science Education, 63*, 83–93.

O'Banion, D. R., & Whaley, D. L. (1981). *Behavior contracting: Arranging contingencies of reinforcement*. New York: Springer.

O'Leary, K. D., & Becker, W. C. (1967). Behavior modification of an adjustment class: A token reinforcement program. *Exceptional Children, 33*, 637–642.

———. (1968). The effects of a teacher's reprimands on children's behavior. *Journal of School Psychology, 7*, 8–11.

O'Leary, K. D., Kaufman, K. F., Kass, R. E., & Drabman, R. S. (1974). The effects of loud and soft reprimands on the behavior of disruptive students. In A. R. Brown & C. Avery (Eds.), *Modifying children's behavior: A book of readings*. Springfield, Ill.: Thomas.

Olson, D. R. (1985). Computers as tools of the intellect. *Educational Researcher, 14*, 5–7.

Osborn, A. (1957). *Applied imagination*. New York: Charles Scribner's.

Oser, F. K. (1986). Moral education and values education: The discourse perspective. In M. C. Wittrock (Ed.), *Handbook of research on teaching* (3rd ed.) (pp. 917–941). New York: Macmillan.

Padilla, A. M. (1991). English only vs. bilingual education: Ensuring a language-competent society. *Journal of Education, 173*, 38–51.

Padilla, A. M., Fairchild, H. H., & Valadez, C. (Eds.). (1990). *Bilingual Education: Issues and Strategies*. Beverly Hills, Calif.: Sage.

Page, E. B., & Grandon, G. M. (1979). Family configuration and mental ability: Two theories contrasted with U.S. data. *American Educational Research Journal, 16*, 257–272.

Pajares, M. F. (1992). Teachers' beliefs and educational research: Cleaning up a messy construct. *Review of Educational Research, 62*, 307–332.

Palardy, J. M. (1991). Behavior modification: It does work, but . . . *Journal of Instructional Psychology, 19*, 127–131.

Palincsar, M. S., & Brown, A. L. (1984). Reciprocal teaching of comprehension—fostering and monitoring activities. *Cognitive Instruction, 1*, 117–175.

Pallas, A. M., Natriello, G., & McDill, E. L. (1989). The changing nature of the disadvantaged population: Current dimensions and future trends. *Educational Researcher, 18,* 16–22.

Palmares, U., & Logan, B. (1975). *A curriculum on conflict management.* Palo Alto, Calif.: Human Development Training Institute.

Papalia, D. F. (1972). The status of several conservative abilities across the life-span. *Human Development, 15,* 229–243.

Papert, S. (1980). *Mindstorms: Children, computers, and powerful ideas.* New York: Basic Books.

———. (1987). Computer criticism vs. technocentric thinking. *Educational Researcher, 16* (1), 22–30.

Paris, S. G., Lawton, T. A., Turner, J. C., & Roth, J. L. (1991). A developmental perspective on standardized achievement testing. *Educational Researcher, 20,* 12–20.

Parke, R. D. (1974). Rules, roles, and resistance to deviation: Recent advances in punishment, discipline, and self-control. In A. Pick (Ed.), *Minnesota Symposia on Child Psychology* (Vol. 8). Minneapolis: University of Minnesota Press.

Parloff, M. B., London, P., & Wolfe, B. (1986). Individual psychotherapy and behavior change. *Annual Review of Psychology, 37,* 321–349.

Parmelee, A. H., Jr., & Sigman, M. D. (1983). Perinatal brain development and behavior. In P. H. Mussen (Ed.), *Handbook of child psychology* (4th ed.)., Vol. 2, *Infancy and developmental psychobiology,* edited by M. M. Haith & J. J. Campos. New York: Wiley.

Parnes, S. J. (1962). Do you really understand brainstorming? In S. J. Parnes & H. F. Harding (Eds.), *A sourcebook for creative thinking.* New York: Scribner.

———. (1967). *Creative behavior workbook.* New York: Scribner.

Parnes, S. J., & Harding, H. F. (Eds.). (1962). *A sourcebook for creative thinking.* New York: Scribner.

Parsons, J. B. (1983). The seductive computer: Can it be resisted? *ATA Magazine, 63,* 12–14.

Pazulinec, R., Meyerrose, M., & Sajwaj, T. (1983). Punishment via response cost. In S. Axelrod & J. Apsche (Eds.), *The effects of punishment on human behavior.* New York: Academic Press.

Pearce, J. C. (1971). *The crack in the cosmic egg.* New York: Fawcett Books.

———. (1977). *Magical child.* New York: Bantam Books.

Peat, D., Mulcahy, R. F., & Darko-Yeboah, J. (1989). SPELT (Strategies Program for Effective Learning/ Thinking): A description and analysis of instructional procedures. *Instructional Science, 18,* 95–118.

Perkins, M. R. (1982). Minimum competency testing: What? Why? Why not? *Educational Measurement Issues and Practice, 1,* 5–9.

Perry, R. (1966). *The world of the polar bear.* Seattle: University of Washington Press.

Peters, R. (1977). *The place of Kohlberg's theory in moral education.* Paper presented at the First International Conference on Moral Development and Moral Education, August 19–26, Leicester, England.

Petersen, A. C. (1988). Adolescent development. *Annual Review of Psychology, 39,* 583–607.

Piaget, J. (1932). *The moral judgment of the child.* London: Kegan Paul.

———. (1954). *The construction of reality in the child.* New York: Basic Books.

———. (1961). The genetic approach to the psychology of thought. *Journal of Educational Psychology, 52,* 275–281.

———. (1972). Intellectual development from adolescence to adulthood. *Human Development, 15,* 1–12.

Pinard, A., & Laurendeau, M. (1964). A scale of mental development based on the theory of Piaget: Description of a project (A. B. Givens, Trans.). *Journal of Research and Science Teaching, 2,* 253–260.

Pintrich, P. R., Cross, D. R., Kozma, R. B., & McKeachie, W. J. (1986). Instructional psychology. *Annual Review of Psychology, 37,* 611–651.

Platzman, K. A., Stoy, M. R., Brown, R. T., Coles, C. D., Smith, I. E., & Falek, A. (1992). Review of observational methods in attention deficit hyperactivity disorder (ADHD): Implications for diagnosis. *School Psychology Quarterly, 7,* 155–177.

Popham, W. J. (1978). The case for criterion-referenced measurement. *Educational Research, 7,* 6–10.

———. (1981). *Modern educational measurement.* Englewood Cliffs, N.J.: Prentice-Hall.

Postman, N., & Weingartner, C. (1971). *The soft revolution.* New York: Delacorte Press.

Prawat, R. S. (1991). The value of ideas: The immersion approach to the development of thinking. *Educational Researcher, 20,* 3–10.

Premack, D. (1965). Reinforcement theory. In D. Levine (Ed.), *Nebraska Symposium on Motivation.* Lincoln, Neb.: University of Nebraska Press.

Presland, J. (1989). Behavioural approaches. In T. Charlton & K. David (Eds.), *Managing misbehaviour: Strategies for effective managment of behaviour in schools.* London: Macmillan Education.

Pressley, M., Forrest-Pressley, D., & Elliott-Faust, D. J. (1988). What is strategy instructional enrichment and how to study it: Illustrations from research on children's prose memory and comprehension. In F. E. Weinert, & M. Perlmutter (Eds.), *Memory development: Universal changes and individual differences.* Hillsdale, N.J.: Erlbaum.

Purkey, W. W. (1984). *Inviting school success: A self-concept approach to teaching and learning* (2nd ed.). Belmont, Calif.: Wadsworth.

Ramsden, P. (1988a). Studying learning: Improving teaching. In P. Ramsden (Ed.), *Improving learning: New perspectives.* London: Kogan Page.

———. **(Ed.).** (1988b). *Improving learning: New perspectives.* London: Kogan Page.

Raphael, B. (1976). *The thinking computer: Mind inside matter.* San Francisco: Freeman.

Reese, H. W., & Overton, W. F. (1970). Models and theories of development. In L. R. Goulet & P. B. Baltes (Eds.), *Lifespan developmental psychology: Research and theory.* New York: Academic Press.

Renzulli, J. S. (1977). *The enrichment triad model: A guide for developing defensible programs for the gifted and talented.* Mansfield Center, Conn.: Creative Learning Press.

———. (1986). The three-ring conception of giftedness: A developmental model for creative productivity. In R. J. Sternberg & J. E. Davidson (Eds.), *Conceptions of giftedness.* Cambridge, England: Cambridge University Press.

Renzulli, J. S., Reis, S. M., & Smith, L. H. (1981). *The revolving door identification model.* Mansfield Center, Conn.: Creative Learning Press.

Renzulli, J. S., & Smith, L. H. (1978). *The learning styles inventory: A measure of student preference for instructional techniques.* Mansfield Center, Conn.: Creative Learning Press.

Resnick, L. B. (1981). Instructional psychology. *Annual Review of Psychology, 32,* 659–704.

Reynolds, A. (1992). What is competent beginning teaching? A review of the literature. *Review of Educational Research, 62,* 1–35.

Rhoades, J., & McCabe, M. E. (1985). *Simple cooperation in the classroom.* Willits, Calif.: ITA Publications.

Rice, M. L. (1989). Children's language acquisition. *American Psychologist, 44,* 149–156.

Richardson, V. (1990). Significant and worthwhile change in teaching practice. *Educational Researcher, 19,* 10–18.

Riegel, K. F. (1973). Dialectic operations: The final period of cognitive development. *Human Development, 16,* 346–370.

Robin, A. L. (1976). Behavioral instruction in the college classroom. *Review of Educational Research, 46,* 313–354.

Rogers, C. R. (1951). *Client-centered therapy: Its current practice, implications and theory.* Boston: Houghton Mifflin.

———. (1969). *Freedom to learn.* Columbus, Ohio: Merrill.

Rogers, C. R., & Skinner, B. F. (1956). Some issues concerning the control of human behavior: A symposium. *Science, 124,* 1057–1066.

Rolison, M. A., & Medway, F. J. (1985). Teachers' expectations and attributions for student achievement: Effects of label, performance pattern, and special education intervention. *American Educational Research Journal, 22,* 561–573.

Rosenshine, B., & Stevens, R. (1986). Teaching functions. In M. C. Wittrock (Ed.), *Handbook of research on teaching* (3rd ed.). New York: Macmillan.

Rosenthal, R. (1987). Pygmalion effects: Existence, magnitude, and social importance. A reply to Wineburg. *Educational Researcher, 16,* 37–41.

Rosenthal, R., & Jacobson, L. (1968a). *Pygmalion in the classroom: Teacher expectations and pupils' intellectual development.* New York: Holt, Rinehart & Winston.

———. (1968b, April). Teacher expectations for the disadvantaged. *Scientific American, 218,* 19–23.

Rosenzweig, M. R., & Leiman, A. L. (1982). *Physiological psychology.* Lexington, Mass.: Heath.

Ross, A. O. (1976). *Psychological aspects of learning disabilities and reading disorders.* New York: McGraw-Hill.

Ross, R. P. (1984). Classroom segments: The structuring of school time. In L. W. Anderson (Ed.), *Time and school learning: Theory, research and practice.* London: Croom Helm.

Ross, S. M., Rakow, E. A., & Bush, A. J. (1980). Instructional adaptation for self-managed learning systems. *Journal of Educational Psychology, 72,* 312–320.

Rubin, K. H., Attewell, P. W., Tierney, M. C., & Tumolo, P. (1973). Development of spatial egocentrism and conservation across the life-span. *Developmental Psychology, 9,* 432–437.

Rushton, J. (1988). Race differences in behaviour: A review and evolutionary analysis. *Journal of Personality and Individual Differences, 9,* 1009–1024.

Russell, J. A., & Ward, L. M. (1982). Environmental psychology. In M. R. Rosenzweig & L. W. Porter (Eds.), *Annual review of psychology* (Vol. 33). Palo Alto, Calif.: Annual Reviews.

Ryan, K., & Cooper, J. M. (1988). *Those who can, teach* (5th ed.). Boston: Houghton Mifflin.

Sadker, M., & Sadker, D. (1986). Sexism in the classroom: From grade school to graduate school. *Phi Delta Kappan, 68,* 512.

Sadker, M., Sadker, D., & Klein, S. (1991). In G. Grant (Ed.), *Review of research in education* (Vol. 17). Washington, D.C.: American Educational Research Association.

Salomon, G., & Gardner, H. (1986). The computer as educator: Lessons from television research. *Educational Researcher, 15,* 13–19.

Salomon, G., Perkins, D. N., & Globerson, T. (1991). Partners in cognition: Extending human intelligence with intelligent technologies. *Educational Researcher, 20,* 2–9.

Sarason, I. G. (1959). Intellectual and personality correlates of test anxiety. *Journal of Abnormal and Social Psychology, 59,* 272–275.

———. (1961). Test anxiety and intellectual performance. *Journal of Educational Psychology, 52,* 201–206.

———. (1972). Experimental approaches to test anxiety: Attention and the uses of information. In C. D. Spielberger (Ed.), *Anxiety: Current trends in theory and research* (Vol. 2). New York: Academic Press.

———. (1980). Introduction to the study of test anxiety. In I. G. Sarason (Ed.), *Test anxiety: Theory, research, and applications.* Hillsdale, N.J.: Erlbaum.

Satir, V. (1972). *Peoplemaking.* Palo Alto, Calif.: Science and Behavior Books.

Sattler, J. M. (1982). *Assessment of children's intelligence and special abilities* (2nd ed.). Boston: Allyn & Bacon.

Savell, J. M., Twohig, P. T., & Rachford, D. L. (1986). Empirical status of Feuerstein's "Instrumental Enrichment" (FIE) technique as a method of teaching thinking skills. *Review of Educational Research, 56,* 381–409.

Scanlon, R., Weinberger, J. A., & Weiler, J. (1970). IPI as a functioning model for the individualization of in-struction. In C. M. Lindvall & R. C. Cox (Eds.), *Evaluation as a tool in curriculum development: The IPI evaluation program.* AERA Monograph Series No. 5. Chicago: Rand McNally.

Schank, R. C., & Abelson, R. P. (1977). *Scripts, plans, goals and understanding.* Hillsdale, N.J.: Erlbaum.

Schniedewind, N., & Davidson, E. (1988). *Cooperative learning, cooperative lives: A sourcebook of learning activities for building a peaceful world.* Dubuque, Iowa: Wm. C. Brown.

Schultz, D. P. (1964). *Panic behavior.* New York: Random House.

Schunk, D. H. (1984). Self-efficacy perspective on achievement behavior. *Educational Psychologist, 19,* 48–58.

Scott, M. E. (1991). Parental encouragement of gifted–talented–creative (GTC) development in young children by providing freedom to become independent. *The Creative Child and Adult Quarterly, 16,* 26–29.

Scott, T., Cole, M., & Engel, M. (1992). Computers and education: A cultural constructivist perspective. In G. Grant (Ed.), *Review of research in education* (Vol. 18). Washington, D.C.: American Educational Research Association.

Sears, R. R., Maccoby, E. P., & Lewin, H. (1957). *Patterns of child rearing.* Evanston, Ill.: Row, Peterson.

Semmel, M. I., Gottlieb, J., & Robinson, N. M. (1979). Mainstreaming: Perspectives on educating handicapped children in public school. In D. C. Berliner (Ed.), *Review of research in education* (Vol. 7) (pp. 223–281). Washington, D.C.: American Educational Research Association.

Serafini, S. (1991). Multiculturalism in the schools of Canada: Presentation to the fourth conference of CCMIE. *Multiculturalism, 14,* 12–14.

Sereda, J. (1992). Educational quality indicators in art and mathematics. In N. McEwan (Chair) (1992), *The Educational Quality Indicators Initiative: A success story* (pp. 61–66) Symposium at the annual meeting of the Canadian Educational Researchers' Association and the Canadian Association for the Study of Educational Administration, Charlottetown, Prince Edward Island, June 6, 1992. Edmonton, Alberta: Alberta Education.

Seymour, D. (1971, November). Black children, black speech. *Commonwealth,* p. 19.

Shaklee, B. D. (1992). Identification of young gifted students. *Journal for the Education of the Gifted, 15,* 134–144.

Sharan, S., & Shachar, H. (1988). *Language and learning in the cooperative classroom.* New York: Springer-Verlag.

Sharan, Y., & Sharan, S. (1992). *Expanding cooperative learning through group investigation.* New York: Columbia University, Teachers College Press.

Shepard, L. A. (1979). Norm-referenced vs. criterion-referenced tests. *Educational Horizons, 58,* 26–32.

Shepard, L. A., & Kreitzer, A. E. (1987). The Texas teacher test. *Educational Researcher, 16,* 22–31.

Shepard, L. A., Smith, M. L., & Vojir, C. P. (1983). Characteristics of pupils identified as learning disabled. *American Educational Research Journal, 20,* 309–331.

Shepherd-Look, D. L. (1982). Sex differentiation and the development of sex roles. In B. B. Wolman and others (Eds.), *Handbook of developmental psychology.* Englewood Cliffs, N.J.: Prentice-Hall.

Shirley, M. (1933). *The first two years: A study of twenty-five babies. Vol. 2 of Intellectual Development.* Institute of Child Welfare Monographs (Series No. 7). Minneapolis, Minn.: University of Minnesota Press.

Shuell, T. J. (1986). Cognitive conceptions of learning. *Review of Educational Research, 56,* 411–436.

Shulman, L. S. (1986). Paradigms and research programs in the study of teaching. In M. C. Wittrock (Ed.), *Handbook of research on teaching* (3rd ed.). New York: Macmillan.

Siegler, R. S. (1989). Mechanisms of cognitive development. *Annual Review of Psychology, 40,* 353–379.

Silvernail, D. L. (1979). *Teaching styles as related to student achievement.* Washington, D.C.: National Education Association.

Simon, H. A. (1980). Cognitive science: The newest science of the artificial. *Cognitive Science, 4,* 33–46.

Simon, S. B., Howe, L. W., & Kirschenbaum, H. (1972). *Values clarification: A handbook of practical strategies for teachers and students.* New York: Hart.

Simpson, E. L., & Gray, M. A. (1976). *Humanistic education: An interpretation.* Cambridge, Mass.: Ballinger.

Skinner, B. F. (1948). *Walden II.* New York: Macmillan.

———. (1953). *Science and human behavior.* New York: Macmillan.

———. (1954). The science of learning and the art of teaching. *Harvard Educational Review, 24,* 86–97.

———. (1955). *Transcripts of New York Academy of Science, 17,* 546–587.

———. (1961). *Cumulative record* (rev. ed.). New York: Appleton-Century-Crofts.

———. (1965, October 16). Why teachers fail. *Saturday Review,* pp. 80–81, 98–102.

———. (1968). *The technology of teaching.* New York: Appleton-Century-Crofts.

———. (1971). *Beyond freedom and dignity.* New York: Knopf.

Slavin, R. E. (1980). Cooperative learning. *Review of Educational Research, 50,* 315–342.

———. (1983). *Student Team Learning: An overview and practical guide.* Washington, D.C.: National Education Association.

———. (1987). Mastery learning reconsidered. *Review of Educational Research, 57,* 175–213.

———. (1990a). Achievement effects of ability grouping in secondary schools: A best-evidence synthesis. *Review of Educational Research, 60,* 470–499.

———. (1990b). *Cooperative learning: Theory, research, and practice.* Englewood Cliffs, N.J.: Prentice-Hall.

Smedslund, J. (1961a). The acquisition of conservation of substance and weight in children. I. Introduction. *Scandinavian Journal of Psychology, 2,* 11–20.

———. (1961b). The acquisition of conservation of substance and weight in children. II. External reinforcement of conservation of weight and of operations of addition and subtraction. *Scandinavian Journal of Psychology, 2,* 71–84.

———. (1961c). The acquisition of conservation of substance and weight in children. III. Extension of conservation of weight acquired normally and by means of empirical controls on a balance scale. *Scandinavian Journal of Psychology, 2,* 85–87.

———. (1961d). The acquisition of conservation of substance and weight in children. IV. An attempt at extension of visual components of the weight concept. *Scandinavian Journal of Psychology, 2,* 153–155.

———. (1961e). The acquisition of conservation of substance and weight in children. V. Practice in conflict situations without external reinforcement. *Scandinavian Journal of Psychology, 2,* 156–160.

Smith, E. L. (1983). Teaching for conceptual change: Some ways of going wrong. In H. Helm & J. Novak (Eds.), *Proceedings of the International Seminar on Misconceptions in Science and Mathematics.* Ithaca, N.Y.: Cornell University Press.

Smith, M. L. (1991). Put to the test: The effects of external testing on teachers. *Educational Researcher, 20*, 8–11.

Snow, R. E., & Lohman, D. F. (1984). Toward a theory of cognitive aptitude for learning from instruction. *Journal of Educational Psychology, 76*, 347–376.

Snow, R. E., & Swanson, J. (1992). Instructional psychology: Aptitude, adaptation, and assessment. *Annual Review of Psychology, 43*, 583–626.

Soloman, G. (1992). Technology and the balance of power. *The Computing Teacher, 19*, 10–11.

Solomon, D., Watson, M. S., Delucchi, K. L., Schaps, E., & Battistich, V. (1988). Enhancing children's prosocial behavior in the classroom. *American Educational Research Journal, 25*, 527–544.

Sonnier, I. L. (Ed.). (1985). *Methods and techniques of holistic education.* Springfield, Ill.: Thomas.

Soper, J. D. (1964). *The mammals of Alberta.* Edmonton, Alberta: Hamly Press.

Southern, H. N. (1964). *The handbook of British mammals.* Oxford: Blackwell Scientific Publications.

Spearman, C. E. (1927). *The abilities of man.* New York: Macmillan.

Springer, S. P., & Deutsch, G. (1989). *Left brain right brain* (3rd ed.). New York: W. H. Freeman.

Stallings, J. A., & Stipek, D. (1986). Research on early childhood and elementary school teaching programs. In M. C. Wittrock (Ed.), *Handbook of research on teaching* (3rd ed.) (pp. 727–753). New York: Macmillan.

Stanley, J. C. (1976). The case for extreme educational acceleration of intellectually brilliant youths. *Gifted Child Quarterly, 20*, 66–75.

Statistics Canada (1992). *Earnings of men and women: 1990.* Ottawa: Minister of Industry, Science and Technology.

Sternberg, R. J. (1984a). A contextualist view of the nature of intelligence. *International Journal of Psychology, 19*, 307–334.

———. (1984b). Mechanisms of cognitive development: A componential approach. In R. J. Sternberg (Ed.), *Mechanisms of cognitive development.* San Francisco: Freeman.

———. (1984c). What should intelligence tests test? Implications of a triarchic theory of intelligence for intelligence testing. *Educational Researcher, 13*, 5–15.

———. (1985). *Beyond IQ: A triarchic theory of human intelligence.* New York: Cambridge University Press.

———. (1986). *Intelligence applied: Understanding and increasing your intellectual skills.* New York: Harcourt Brace Jovanovich.

———. (1992). Ability tests, measurements, and markets. *Journal of Educational Psychology, 84*, 134–140.

———. (Ed.). (1988). *The nature of creativity: Contemporary psychological perspectives.* Cambridge, Mass.: Cambridge University Press.

Steward, A. J. (Ed.). (1982). *Motivation and society.* San Francisco: Jossey-Bass.

Stipek, D. J. (1988). *Motivation to learn: From theory to practice.* Englewood Cliffs, N.J.: Prentice-Hall.

Stodolsky, S. S. (1984). Frameworks for studying instructional processes in peer work-groups. In P. L. Peterson, L. C. Wilkinson, & M. Hallinan (Eds.), *The social context of instruction.* New York: Academic Press.

Sullivan, E. V. (1977). *A study of Kohlberg's structural theory of moral development: A critique of liberal social science ideology.* Unpublished manuscript, Ontario Institute for Studies in Education, Toronto, Ontario.

Sullivan, E. V., & Quarter, J. (1972). Psychological correlates of certain postconventional moral types: A perspective on hybrid types. *Journal of Personality, 40* (2), 149–161.

Suls, J., & Kalle, R. J. (1979). Children's moral judgments as a function of intention, damage, and an actor's physical harm. *Developmental Psychology, 15*, 93–94.

Sutton, R. E. (1991). Equity and computers in the schools: A decade of research. *Review of Educational Research, 61*, 474–503.

Swing, S. R., & Peterson, P. L. (1982). The relationship of student ability and small-group interaction to student achievement. *American Educational Research Journal, 19*, 259–274.

Sykes, G., & Bird, T. (1992). Teacher education and the case idea. In G. Grant (Ed.), *Review of research in education* (Vol. 18). Washington, D.C.: American Educational Research Association.

Tavris, C., & Baumgartner, A. I. (1983, February). How would your life be different if you'd been born a boy? *Redbook*, 99.

Terman, L. M. (1925). *Genetic studies of genius. The mental and physical traits of a thousand gifted children* (Vol. 1). Stanford, Calif.: Stanford University Press.

Thomas, J. W. (1980). Agency and achievement: Self-management and self-regard. *Review of Educational Research, 50*, 213–240.

Thomas, R. M. (1992). *Comparing theories of child development* (3rd ed.). Belmont, Calif.: Wadsworth.

Thorndike, E. L. (1911). *Animal intelligence.* New York: Macmillan.

———. (1913). *The psychology of learning.* New York: Teachers College.

———. (1931). *Human learning.* New York: Appleton-Century-Crofts.

———. (1932). Reward and punishment in animal learning. *Comparative Psychology Monographs, 8* (39).

———. (1933). A proof of the law of effect. *Science, 77,* 173–175.

———. (1935). *The psychology of wants, interests, and attitudes.* New York: Appleton-Century-Crofts.

Thorndike, R. L., & Hagen, E. (1977). *Measurement and evaluation in psychology and education* (4th ed.). New York: Wiley.

Thorndike, R. L., Hagen, E., & Sattler, J. M. (1985). *Revised Stanford-Binet intelligence scale* (4th ed.). Boston, Mass.: Houghton Mifflin.

Thurstone, L. L. (1938). *Primary mental abilities. Psychometric Monographs.* Chicago: University of Chicago Press (No. 1).

Tobias, S. (1982, January). Sexist equation. *Psychology Today,* pp. 14–17.

Todman, J., & Lawrenson, H. (1992). Computer anxiety in primary schoolchildren and university students. *British Educational Research Journal, 18,* 63–72.

Toffler, A. (1970). *Future shock.* New York: Random House.

———. (1980). *The third wave.* New York: Morrow.

Torrance, E. P. (1962). *Guiding creative talent.* Englewood Cliffs, N.J.: Prentice-Hall.

———. (1966). *Torrance tests of creative thinking (Norms technical manual).* Princeton, N.J.: Personnel Press.

———. (1974). *Torrance tests of creative thinking.* Lexington, Mass.: Ginn.

———. (1984). *Mentor relationships: How they aid creative achievement, endure, change, and die.* Buffalo, N.Y.: Bearly Limited.

———. (1986). Teaching creative and gifted learners. In M. C. Wittrock (Ed.), *Handbook of research on teaching* (3rd ed.) (pp. 630–647). New York: Macmillan.

Tryon, G. S. (1980). The measurement and treatment of text anxiety. *Review of Educational Research, 50,* 343–372.

Tryon, R. C. (1940). Genetic differences in maze learning in rats. *Yearbook of the National Society for Studies in Education, 39,* 111–119.

Tsang, M. C. (1988). Cost analysis for educational policymaking: A review of cost studies in education in developing countries. *Review of Educational Research, 58,* 181–230.

Turiel, F. (1974). Conflict in transition in adolescent moral development. *Child Development, 45,* 14–29.

Turner, R. L., & Denny, D. A. (1969, February). Teacher characteristics, teacher behavior, and changes in pupil creativity. *Elementary School Journal,* pp. 265–270.

U.S. Bureau of the Census. (1991). *Statistical Abstracts of the United States, 1991) (*111th ed.). Washington, D.C.: U.S. Government Printing Office.

U.S. Department of Education. (1986). *What works: Research about teaching and learning.* Pueblo, Colo.: Consumer Information Center.

U.S. Office of Education. (1977, August 23). Implementation of part B of the Education of the Handicapped Act. *Federal Register, 42,* 42474–42518.

U.S. Office of Education. Office of Gifted and Talented. Council for Exceptional Children. (1978). *The nation's commitment to the education of gifted and talented children and youth: Summary of findings from a 1977 survey of states and territories.* Reston, Va.: Council for Exceptional Children.

Uguroglu, M. E., & Walberg, H. J. (1979). Motivation and achievement: A quantitative synthesis. *American Educational Research Journal, 6,* 191–206.

Ukrainian famine survivors recall season in hell. (1983). *Edmonton Journal,* October 20, p. A1.

Ulrich, R. E., & Azrin, N. H. (1962). Reflexive fighting in response to aversive stimulation. *Journal of Experimental Analysis of Behavior, 5,* 511–521.

Urban, K. K. (1991). Giftedness and behavioural disorders. *International Journal of Special Education, 6,* 12–27.

Urban, K. K., & Jellen, H. (1986). Assessing creative potential via drawing production: The Test for Creative Thinking-Drawing Production (TCT-DP). In A. J. Cropley, K. K. Urban, H. Wagner, & W. H. Wieczerkowski (Eds.), *Giftedness: A continuing worldwide challenge,* New York: Trillium.

Uzgiris, I. C., & Hunt, J. (1975). *Assessment in infancy: Ordinal scales of psychological development.* Urbana, Ill.: University of Illinois Press.

Valli, L. (1992). Beginning teacher problems: Areas for teacher education improvement. *Action in Teacher Education, 14,* 18–25.

Valsiner, J. (1987). *Culture and the development of children's action: A cultural-historical theory of developmental psychology.* New York: John Wiley.

Van Houten, R., & Doleys, D. M. (1983). Are social reprimands effective? In S. Axelrod & J. Apsche (Eds.), *The effects of punishment on human behavior.* New York: Academic Press.

Van Houten, R., Nau, P. A., MacKenzie-Keating, S., Sameoto, D., & Colavecchia, B. (1982). An analysis of some variables influencing the effectiveness of reprimands. *Journal of Applied Behavior Analysis, 15,* 65–83.

Velandia, W., Grandon, G. M., & Page, E. B. (1978). Family size, birth order, and intelligence in a large South American sample. *American Educational Research Journal, 15,* 399–416.

Vernon, P. E. (1969). *Intelligence and cultural environment.* London: Methuen.

Vygotsky, L. S. (1962). *Thought and language* (E. Hamsman and G. Vankan, Eds. and Trans.). Cambridge, Mass.: MIT Press.

———. (1978). *Mind in society.* Cambridge, Mass.: Harvard University Press.

———. (1986). *Thought and language* (translated and revised by A. Kozulin). Cambridge, Mass.: MIT Press.

Wadsworth, B. J. (1989). *Piaget's theory of cognitive and affective development* (4th ed.). New York: Longman.

Wagner, R. K., & Sternberg, R. J. (1984). Alternative conceptions of intelligence and their implications for education. *Review of Educational Research, 54,* 179–223.

Walberg, H. J. (1986). Syntheses of research on teaching. In M. C. Wittrock (Ed.), *Handbook of research on teaching* (3rd ed.). New York: Macmillan.

Walker, D. F., & Schaffarzick, J. (1974). Comparing curricula. *Review of Educational Research, 44,* 83–111.

Walker, H. (1979). *The acting-out child: Coping with classroom disruption.* Boston: Allyn & Bacon.

Walker, R. (1990, February 28). Governors set to adopt national education goals. *Education Week,* p. 16.

Wallach, M. A. (1985). Creativity testing and giftedness. In F. D. Horowitz & M. O'Brien (Eds.), *The gifted and talented: Developmental perspectives* (pp. 99–123). Washington, D.C.: American Psychological Association.

Wallach, M. A., & Kogan, N. (1965). *Modes of thinking in young children: A study of the creativity-intelligence distinction.* New York: Holt, Rinehart & Winston.

Walters, G. C., & Grusec, J. E. (1977). *Punishment.* San Francisco: Freeman.

Walters, R. H., & Llewellyn, T. E. (1963). Enhancement of punitiveness by visual and audiovisual displays. *Canadian Journal of Psychology, 17,* 244–255.

Walters, R. H., Llewellyn, T. E., & Acker, W. (1962). Enhancement of punitive behavior by audiovisual displays. *Science, 136,* 872–873.

Ward, W. D. (1991). *Applied behavior analysis in the classroom: The development of student competence.* Springfield, Ill: Charles C. Thomas.

Watson, J. B. (1913). Psychology as the behaviorist views it. *Psychological Review, 20,* 157–158.

———. (1916). The place of a conditioned reflex in psychology. *Psychological Review, 23,* 89–116.

———. (1930). *Behaviorism* (2nd ed.). Chicago: University of Chicago Press.

Webster, S. W. (1968). *Discipline in the classroom: Basic principles and problems.* New York: Chandler.

Wechsler, D. (1958). *The measurement and appraisal of adult intelligence* (4th ed.). Baltimore: Williams & Wilkins.

———. (1991). *Wechsler Intelligence Scale for Children—Third Edition: Manual.* New York: The Psychological Corporation.

Weinberg, R. (1989). Intelligence and IQ. *American Psychologist, 44,* 98–104.

Weiner, B. (1984). Principles for a theory of student motivation and their application within an attributional framework. In R. Ames & C. Ames (Eds.), *Research on motivation in education (Vol. 1): Student motivation.* New York: Academic Press.

———. (1986). *An attributional theory of motivation and emotion.* New York: Springer-Verlag.

Weinstein, C. F., & Mayer, R. F. (1986). The teaching of learning strategies. In M. C. Wittrock (Ed.), *Handbook of research on teaching* (3rd ed.) (pp. 315–327). New York: Macmillan.

Wellman, H. M., & Gelman, S. A. (1992). Cognitive development: Foundational theories of core domains. *Annual Review of Psychology, 43,* 337–375.

Wertsch, J. V. (1985). *Vygotsky and the social formation of mind.* Cambridge, Mass.: Harvard University Press.

West, L. (1988). Implications of recent research for improving secondary school science learning. In P. Ramsden (Ed.), *Improving learning: New perspectives.* London: Kogan Page.

West, L. W., & MacArthur, R. S. (1964). An evaluation of selected intelligence tests for two samples of Metis and Indian children. *Alberta Journal of Educational Research, 10,* 17–27.

Whelan, R. J. (1978). The emotionally disturbed. In E. L. Meyen (Ed.), *Exceptional children and youth: An introduction.* Denver: Love Publishing.

White, M. A. (1975). Natural rates of teacher approval and disapproval in the classroom. *Journal of Applied Behavior Analysis, 8,* 367–372.

White, R. T., & Tisher, R. P. (1986). Research on natural sciences. In M. C. Wittrock (Ed.), *Handbook of research on teaching* (3rd ed.). New York: Macmillan.

White, R. W. (1959). Motivation reconsidered: The concept of competence. *Psychological Review, 66,* 297–333.

Whitener, E. M. (1989). A meta-analytic review of the effect on learning of the interaction between prior achievement and instructional support. *Review of Educational Research, 59,* 65–86.

Wiersma, W., & Jurs, S. G. (1985). *Educational measurement and testing.* Boston: Allyn & Bacon.

Wigdor, A. K., & Garner, W. R. (Eds.). (1982). *Ability testing: Uses, consequences, and controversies, Part 1: Report of the Committee.* Washington, D.C.: National Academy Press.

Wilgosh, L. (1991). Underachievement and related issues for culturally different gifted children. *International Journal of Special Education, 6,* 82–93.

Williams, R. L., & Long, J. D. (1978). *Toward a self-managed lifestyle* (2nd ed.). Boston: Houghton Mifflin.

Wilson, K., & Tally, W. (1990). The "Palenque" project: Formative evaluation in the design and development of an optical disc prototype. In B. Flagg (Ed.), *Formative evaluation for educational technologies.* Hillsdale, N.J.: Lawrence Erlbaum.

Wilson, L. (1988). Phase change: Larry Wilson on selling in a brave new world. *Training, 11,* 14.

Wineburg, S. S. (1987). The self-fulfillment of the self-fulfilling prophecy: A critical appraisal. *Educational Researcher, 16,* 28–37.

Winick, M. (1976). *Malnutrition and brain development.* New York: Oxford University Press.

Winn, M. (1985). *The plug-in drug* (rev. ed.). New York: Viking.

Winsten, S. (1949). *Days with Bernard Shaw.* New York: Vanguard Press.

Wittrock, M. C. (1986). Students' thought processes. In M. C. Wittrock (Ed.), *Handbook of research on teaching* (3rd ed.) (pp. 297–314). New York: Macmillan.

———. (1992). An empowering conception of educational psychology. *Educational Psychologist, 27,* 129–141.

Wolf, D., Bixby, J., Glenn, J., & Gardner, H. (1991). To use their minds well: Investigating new forms of student assessment. In G. Grant (Ed.), *Review of research in education* (Vol. 17). Washington, D.C.: American Educational Research Association.

Wood, B. S. (1981). *Children and communication: Verbal and nonverbal language development* (2nd ed.). Englewood Cliffs, N.J.: Prentice-Hall.

Woodward, J., Carnine, D., & Gersten, R. (1988). Teaching problem solving through computer simulations. *American Educational Research Journal, 25,* 72–86.

Yoder, S. (1992). The turtle and the mouse . . . A tale. *The Computing Teacher, 20,* 41–43.

Zajonc, R. B. (1975, January). Birth order and intelligence: Dumber by the dozen. *Psychology Today,* pp. 37–43.

———. (1976). Family configuration and intelligence. *Science, 192,* 227–236.

———. (1986). The decline and rise of scholastic aptitude scores: A prediction derived from the confluence model. *American Psychologist, 41,* 862–867.

Zajonc, R., & Markus, G. B. (1975). Birth order and intellectual development. *Psychological Review, 82,* 74–88.

Zigler, E., & Hodapp, R. M. (1991). Behavioral functioning in individuals with mental retardation. *Annual Review of Psychology, 42,* 29–50.

Zimmerman, B. J., Bandura, A., & Martinez-Pons, M. (1992). Self-motivation for academic attainment: The role of self-efficacy beliefs and personal goal setting. *American Educational Research Journal, 29,* 663–676.

INDEX

Bandura, Albert, 101, 107, 110, 112, 113, 153, 278–281
Bangert, R. L., 342, 343
Bangert-Drowns, R. L., 341, 344
Barrett, W. S., 32, 187
Barth, R., 307
Basseches, M., 69
Bassok, M., 171, 354
Baumgartner, A. I., 53
Bear, G., 232
Becker, W. C., 304
Behavior
    explanation of, 391
    relationship between reinforcement and, 94–95
    socially accepted, 107
Behavior control, 242, 247
Behaviorism
    as approach to learning, 87
    cognitive perspective and, 132
    explanation of, 86, 120, 391
    humanism vs., 240
    motivation and, 274–275
    Watson's views of, 88, 259
Behavioristic theories. See also Stimulus-response (S-R) theories
    explanation of, 86, 104–105, 391
    problems with, 105
Behavior modification
    application of, 104
    cause of misbehavior and, 105
    cognitive, 314–317
    explanation of, 391
    process of, 303–304
Beliefs, 7, 10, 391
Bernard, H. W., 368
Bernard, L. L., 268
Bijou, S. W., 307
Bilingual education, 40
Bilingualism, 41–42
Biofeedback, 272, 391
Bird, T., 11
Birth order, 193–194, 196
Birthrate, 19–20, 39
Bixby, J., 364, 379
Blake, William, 176
Bloom, B. S., 28, 31, 170, 186, 211, 338, 341, 343, 363
Bloom's taxonomy, 358–361
Blumenfeld, P. C., 286
Bolles, R. C., 279
Borg, W. R., 296
Borkowski, J. G., 131
Borton, T., 248
Bossert, S. T., 254, 257
Bowlby, J., 269
Bradshaw, G. L., 129
Brain development, 28–31
Brainstorming, 213–215, 391
Branching programs

explanation of, 327, 391
illustration of, 329–330
Bransford, J. D., 128, 131–132
Brantner, J. P., 313, 314
Braun, C., 222
Bridie, James, 264
Briggs, L. J., 150
Brisk, M. E., 40
Bronfenbrenner, U., 74
Brophy, J. E., 105, 222, 275, 276
Brown, A. L., 256
Brown, J. S., 169
Browne, Sir Thomas, 238
Browning, Elizabeth Barrett, 176
Browning, Robert, 348
Bruner, J. S., 37, 108, 157–161, 168, 171, 352
Burgess, Gelett, 206
Burns, Robert, 290
Bush, George, 354

Calfee, R., 123, 127
Canada, 40, 53
Candee, D., 46
Capability, 85–86, 391
Carnine, D., 334
Carroll, John B., 339
Carroll, Lewis, 2
Case, R., 71, 126
Category, 157, 391
Cattell, R. B., 179, 182
Central tendency, 374, 391
Cerebral palsy, 233
Chains, 150, 391
Chambers, B., 359
Chapman, H., 46
Chi, M. T. H., 122
Chomsky, N., 38
Chunking, 124–125, 130, 392
Circles of knowledge, 253, 254, 392
Clarizio, H. F., 232, 311
Clark, R. E., 344–345
Classical conditioning
    behaviorism and, 88–89
    connectionism and, 90–92
    explanation of, 392
    instructional applications of, 89–90
    operant vs., 93
    Pavlov's, 87–88
Classification, 66, 392
Classroom environment
    ability to personalize, 300–301
    characteristics of, 293–294
    creativity and, 219
Classroom management
    as aspect of teaching process, 14
    context for preventive, 302–303
    control as element of, 294–295
    discipline and, 292
    explanation of, 292, 392

prosocial programs as aspect of, 317–318
Classroom management strategies
    behavior modification as, 303–304, 314–317. See also Behavior modification
    extinction as, 309–310
    Kounin's management model as, 295–299
    Marland's suggestions for, 299–301
    modeling as, 309
    overview of, 295
    punishment as, 310–312
    reprimand as, 312–313
    response cost as, 314
    systematic reinforcement programs as, 304–309
    time-out as, 313–314
    Webster's democratic procedures as, 301–303
Client-centered therapy, 241, 392
Clinical psychologists, 9
Coding systems, 157, 158, 392
Cognition, 56, 121, 134
Cognitive Abilities Test (CogAT), 191
Cognitive apprenticeship, 169, 392
Cognitive development
    acceleration of, 72
    educational implications of theories of, 71–74, 76
    explanation of, 56
    factors influencing, 31–32, 72–74, 76
    neo-Piagetian contributions to, 70–71
    Piagetian theories of, 56–70
    Vygotsky's theories of, 74–75
Cognitive learning, 86, 392
Cognitive strategies. See also Learning/thinking strategies
    ability to teach, 131–132, 134–135
    assumptions of, 156–157
    to behavior modification, 314–317
    discovery learning as, 158–160
    educational applications of, 132–133, 156–157
    explanation of, 122, 131, 134, 392
    humanism vs., 240
    meaningful learning through use of, 160–165
    monitoring and controlling one's own, 171
    to motivation, 279–287
    as outcomes of learning, 153, 154
    programs to teach, 135–138
    schemata and, 155–156
Cognitive structure
    explanation of, 59, 154–155, 392
    Piagetian, 59–70, 178
    schemata as metaphors for, 155–156
Cognitivism
    explanation of, 86, 87, 121, 392

Metastrategies program, 135, 138
Mèthode clinique, 57, 400
Meyerrose, M., 314
Meyers, C. E., 232
Michael, J., 307, 308
Microcomputers, 400
Milgram, S., 111
Miller, G. A., 123–125
Milne, A. A., 322
Milstead, M., 131
Minimum competency testing,
   366–367, 400
Minority groups
   IQ tests and, 186–187
   recognition of giftedness among, 210
Mnemonic devices, 141, 142
Mode, 373, 400
Modeling effect
   explanation of, 109, 400
   illustrations of, 110
Models
   confluence, 393
   effectiveness of, 311
   exemplary, 108–109, 395
   explanation of, 10–11, 400
   inhibitory-disinhibitory effect from
      use of, 309
   symbolic, 108, 405
Moore, K. D., 17
Moore, M. W., 190, 210
Moral development
   educational implications of, 46–47
   Kohlberg's stages of, 42–46
   male vs. female, 45–46
   overview of, 42
Morphological analysis, 215, 400
Moss, P. A., 364
Mosston, M., 256
Motivation
   achievement, 283, 284
   attribution theories and, 281–283
   behavioristic approach to, 274–275
   cognitive approach to, 279–281,
      284–287
   competence, 278, 392
   explanation of, 400
   historical approaches to, 267–270
   humanistic approach to, 275, 277–279
   intrinsic, 275
   observational learning and, 114
   relationship between arousal and,
      270–271
Motives, 266–267
Motor learning, 86, 400
Motor reproduction processes, 113–114
Motor skills, 153, 154
Moynahan, E. O., 130
Mueller, S. L., 256
Mulcahy, R., 13, 137, 169

Multiple-choice items, 371
Multiple responses law, 90, 91, 398
MURDER, 135

Naglieri, J. A., 191
Naïve theories, 9–10
National Research Center on the Gifted
   and Talented, 210
Nau, P. A., 313
Nay, W. R., 305
Need-drive theories, 269, 400
Needs
   awareness of, 269–270
   explanation of, 269, 400
   Maslow's theory of, 275, 277
Need state, 159, 400
Negative correlation, 184, 400
Negative reinforcement
   as method of aversive control, 98–99
   prevalence of, 98–99
   punishment vs., 98
   used in classrooms, 95–98, 104
Negative reinforcer, 400
Neisser, U., 121
Nelson, D., 256
Nelson, K. E., 38
Neonates, 57, 400. See also Infants
Neurons, 28, 400
Neutral stimulus, 88, 400
Newman, S. E., 169
Nicholls, J. G., 282
Nickerson, R. S., 13, 135, 170, 172
Nodes, 128
Nolen, S. B., 366, 367
Nominal scale, 353, 400
Nonexclusion, 314, 401
Nongraded schools, 258
Nonstandard language, 39–40
Normal curve, 401
Normal distribution, 372–373
Norm-referenced tests, 376–377, 401
Norms
   age-equivalent, 368
   grade-equivalent, 367–368
   normal distribution and, 372–373

Oak School experiment, 221–223
Object concept, 60, 401
Objective tests, 369, 370
Obliterative subsumption, 162, 401
O'Brien, M., 211
Observational learning, 112–114, 401.
   See also Imitation
O'Casey, Sean, 238
O'Leary, K. D., 304, 313, 314
Olson, D. R., 337
Open classrooms, 250, 251
Operant, 93, 401
Operant behavior, 92–93

Operant conditioning
   aversive control and, 98–99
   classical vs., 93
   classroom examples of, 96
   explanation of, 93–94, 401
   generalization and discrimination and,
      103–104
   instructional applications of, 104
   principles of, 94–95
   reinforcement and punishment and,
      95–98
   schedules of reinforcement and,
      99–102
   shaping as form of, 102–103
Operations
   as aspect of intellectual func-
      tioning, 201
   explanation of, 59, 401
Ordinal scale, 353, 401
Organization, 130, 135
Orwell, George, 348
Osborn, Alex, 213, 215
Oser, E. K., 46
Otis-Lennon School Ability Test, 191
Overlapping, 296, 401
Overton, W. F., 10

Pajares, M. F., 6
Palardy, J. M., 105
Palenque, 335
Palincsar, M. S., 256
Palmares, U., 317
Papert, S., 218, 336, 338
Parallel-forms reliability, 364, 401
Parents, as reinforcers, 307
Paris, S. G., 367
Parke, R. D., 316
Parnes, S. J., 214
Parsons, J. B., 332
Patterns, 141
Pavlov, I., 87
Pazulinec, R., 314
Peabody Picture Vocabulary Test-Revised
   (PPVT-R), 188–189
Peat, D., 13, 137
Peer approval, 103
Peer attention, 308
Penalty, 97, 401. See also Punishment
Percentiles, 372–373, 401
Perception
   distinction between conceptualization
      and, 61
   explanation of, 401
   reliance on, 63
Performance
   anxiety and test, 272
   assessment of, 378–379, 382–383
   attribution of, 282–283
   components of, 182, 183, 401